35,000
TENNESSEE MARRIAGE RECORDS
AND BONDS

1783 - 1870

Volume 1
A - F

Edited by:

The Rev. Silas Emmett Lucas, Jr.

and

Mrs. Ella Lee Sheffield

Please direct all correspondence and orders to:

www.southernhistoricalpress.com
or
SOUTHERN HISTORICAL PRESS, Inc.
PO BOX 1267
375 West Broad Street
Greenville, SC   29601
southernhistoricalpress@gmail.com

ISBN #0-89308-233-6

The Three Volume series: ISBN #0-89308-233-6

Printed in the United States of America

INTRODUCTION

In these three volumes we have tried to bring you the
marriage bonds and marriage records found in the index card
file at the Tennessee State Library and Archives in Nashville
between the period 1783 to about 1870. Many dedicated people
working long hours bring you this much needed information.
My thanks to Karan Moore Wilkins for many hours of typing the
three volumes, the indexers Nancy Clarke, Bertha Ellen Beall,
Leona Benice Mitchell, Marguerite Palmer Mitchell, and members
of the Southeast Historical and Genealogical Society, to the
index typist Karan Moore Wilkins, Roberta Holmes Carter and
Nancy Clark and then most of all my thanks to an understanding
and loving husband, Travis, through this past year in preparing
this information for you, the genealogist.

Ella Evadna Lee Sheffield

AARON, Henderson to Mary Rumfelt - issued July 5, 1842, m. by:
    Rev. James T. Morris, STEWART Co.

AARON, Martha M. to John Fox - BEDFORD Co.

ABANATHY, William to Cynthia Human - issued August 17, 1872, m. by:
    D. S. Long, J. P., August 18, 1872, FRANKLIN Co.

ABBEY, Richard to Mary Ann Compton - March 24, 1831, m. by: Wm. Hume,
    V. D. M., DAVIDSON Co.

ABBOTT, George to Frances Watson - issued July 25, 1827, m. by:
    P. C. Mills, J. P., July 25, 1827, SUMNER Co.

ABBOTT, George W. to Hariet Caroline Lane - issued March 12, 1846,
    Bondsman: Thomas Lyons, m. by: L. Priestley, J. P., March 14,
    1846, MONTGOMERY Co.

ABBOTT, James to Sarah Crimes - issued April 9, 1812, DAVIDSON Co.

ABBOTT, James to Mariah Stone - issued June 20, 1836, Bondsman:
    George Love, m. by: L. B. Laurence June 20, 1836, SUMNER Co.

ABBOTT, Martin to Mary Reynolds - issued October 3, 1844, m. by:
    Thomas Farmer, J. P., ROBERTSON Co.

ABBOTS, Sally to Asa Harris - issued October 7, 1815, DAVIDSON Co.

ABBUTT, George to Nancy Noble - issued March 21, 1811, Bondsman:
    James Abbutt, SUMNER Co.

ABBY, Anthony to Susan L. Compton - January 31, 1833, m. by: Wm. Hume,
    V. D. M., DAVIDSON Co.

ABEL, Francis to Barbara Harner - May 25, 1810, KNOX Co.

ABEL, John B. to Rhoda Johnston - issued August 29, 1818, m. by:
    West Walker, M. G., September 1, 1818, KNOX Co.

ABEL, Moses to Betsy McHenry - issued July 1, 1823, Bondsman:
    Geo. R. Cannon, KNOX Co.

ABEL, Peter to Amy Ward - issued February 16, 1815, KNOX Co.

ABERNATHA, C. H. to N. J. Hollis - issued January 13, 1849, m. by:
    B. Rawls, M. G., ROBERTSON Co.

ABERNATHY, Chas. H. to Nancy Crockett - issued December 24, 1845, m. by:
    David Abernathy, J. P., December 25, 1845, DAVIDSON Co.

ABERNATHY, Clayton D. to Augerona Cobb - issued October 24, 1826,
    Bondsman: Bary Abernathy, KNOX Co.

ABERNATHY, Freeman Jr. to Elizabeth Abernathy - issued December 26,
    1842, DAVIDSON Co.

ABERNATHY, Gilbert T. to Emily Tally - issued December 14, 1853,
    Bondsman: Jo Shackleford, m. by: H. Haddock, Elder, December 15,
    1853, MONTGOMERY Co.

ABERNATHY, Geo. W. to Mary Crockett - issued December 19, 1846, m. by:
    David Abernathy, J. P., December 29, 1846, DAVIDSON Co.

ABERNATHY, Harley D. to Sally Abernathy - October 22, 1810, Bondsman:
    John McTire, MAURY Co.

ABERNATHY, Henry M. C. to Alcy Caroline Graves - December 25, 1852,
    m. by: C. H. Lambeth, J. P., GILES Co.

1

ABERNATHY, Isaah to Mary Ann Birdsong - February 26, 1860, m. by:
Gilbert W. Bass, J. P., GILES Co.

ABERNATHY, James E. to Susanna Rebecca Denty - October 4, 1852, m. by:
W. T. Plummer, M. G., GILES Co.

ABERNATHY, James M. to Matilda Huffman - issued June 9, 1841, m. by:
William J. Drake, J. P., June 9, 1841, DAVIDSON Co.

ABERNATHY, Sally to Harley D. Abernathy - MAURY Co.

ABLE, Francis to Barbara Harner - issued May 25, 1816, KNOX Co.

ABNER, John W. to Kerziah Daugherty - issued March 4, 1844, m. by:
C. Woodall, J. P., ROBERTSON Co.

ABNEY, Harman to Adline Minerva Williams - issued November 30, 1847,
Bondsman: Wm. Gray, m. by: William Dinwiddie, M. G., December 2,
1847, MONTGOMERY Co.

ABSTON, Joel L. to Louisa Cage - issued December 30, 1825, Bondsman:
George Douglass, m. by: Chas. Watkins, J. P., December 30, 1825,
SUMNER Co.

ABSTON, Joshua to Winny Joiner - issued March 26, 1817, Bondsman:
Asa White, m. by: L. Hunt, J. P., March 26, 1817, SUMNER Co.

ABSTON, Merry C. to Mary Ann Douglas - issued April 3, 1832, Bondsman:
Edward Stratton, SUMNER Co.

ACHEY, Peter H. to Rebecca R. Moore - issued May 11, 1846, m. by:
Peter Owen, M. G., May 12, 1846, DAVIDSON Co.

ACKLEN, Christopher to Martha Kirby - issued August 27, 1810, Bondsman:
Henry Kirby, RUTHERFORD Co.

ACKLIN, Alexander S. to Jemima Oliver - issued January 11, 1849, m. by:
W. Denson, J. P., January 11, 1849, FRANKLIN Co.

ACKLIN, James V. to Sarah Rollins - issued September 9, 1839, m. by:
A. J. Steele, M. G., FRANKLIN Co.

ACKLIN, Syler to Creasy Parks - issued November 12, 1868, FRANKLIN Co.

ACKLIN, Wm. H. to E. P. Fletcher - issued December 6, 1847, m. by:
John Thomas Slatter, J. P., December 7, 1847, FRANKLIN Co.

ACOCK, Benjamin F. to Nancy R. Pendleton - issued September 3, 1850,
Bondsman: Jesse Sadler, m. by: Mark Senter, M. G., September 3,
1851, MONTGOMERY Co.

ACRE, John R. to Mary L. A. E. Ross - issued December 22, 1853,
Bondsman: Wm. B. Walington, m. by: John Gold, J. P., December 22,
1853, MONTGOMERY Co.

ACREE, Dandridge to Susan Bowman - issued May 13, 1817, Bondsman:
Thomas Yardley, RUTHERFORD Co.

ACREE, Geo. W. to Martha L. M. Pugh - issued November 18, 1844, m. by:
H. Fennell, J. P., November 19, 1844, STEWART Co.

ACREE, John S. to Anna Lambert - issued April 6, 1867, m. by:
Lewis Anderson, J. P., April 7, 1867, FRANKLIN Co.

ACREE, N. B. to Mary M. Rowlett - issued November 5, 1847, m. by:
C. Brandon, J. P., November 7, 1847, STEWART Co.

ACUFF, Alfred to Margaret Vitetoe - issued October 4, 1830, Bondsman:
Pleasant Watson, GRAINGER Co.

ACUFF, Alfred to Rebecca Dyer - issued August 2, 1832, Bondsman:
Richard Acuff, GRAINGER Co.

ACUFF, Benjamin to Viney Harman - issued April 4, 1805, Bondsman:
John Hall, Witnesses: Sam. D. Carrick, J. P., GRAINGER Co.

ACUFF, Benjamin to Eleanor Butler - issued August 22, 1835, Bondsman:
Kellar Mathis, m. by Nace Overall, M. G., August 23, 1835,
RUTHERFORD Co.

ACUFF, Charles to Elizabeth Long - issued November 14, 1829, Bondsman:
Andrew C. Eaton, GRAINGER Co.

ACUFF, Clabourn to Martha Hammers - issued March 27, 1830, Bondsman:
Richard Acuff, m. by: Jas. Kennon, M. G., GRAINGER Co.

ACUFF, David to Faney Malicoat - issued November 8, 1820, Bondsman:
John Acuff, m. by: James Kimon, M. G., GRAINGER Co.

ACUFF, Franky to Maser Garner - issued March 5, 1827, Bondsman:
James Mallicoat, m. by: Valentine Molder, J. P., March 5, 1827,
GRAINGER Co.

ACUFF, Henry to Mary Sandris - issued April 4, 1808, Bondsman:
William Acuff, GRAINGER Co.

ACUFF, James to Nancy Hutcherson - issued May 15, 1810, Bondsman:
Robert Watson, GRAINGER Co.

ACUFF, James to Sarah E. Harrell - issued December 21, 1830, Bondsman:
Thomas Acuff, GRAINGER Co.

ACUFF, Jeremiah to Rebeccah Caits - issued December 8, 1826, Bondsman:
Thos. Acuff, m. by J. Kennon, M. G., GRAINGER Co.

ACUFF, John to Nancy Harmon - issued December 17, 1817, Bondsman:
Nathan Kelly, m. by: John Hall, J. P., GRAINGER Co.

ACUFF, John to Sabra Malicoat - issued September 5, 1821, Bondsman:
Thomas Acuff, m. by: Jas. Hennon, M. G., GRAINGER Co.

ACUFF, John to Winney Kitts - issued October 6, 1831, Bondsman:
John Acuff, Jr., m. by: Joseph Clark, J. P., October 6, 1831,
GRAINGER Co.

ACUFF, Kain to Patsey Kitchen - issued July 29, 1797, Bondsman:
James Cocke, GRAINGER Co.

ACUFF, Richard to Patey Hailey - issued January 18, 1802, Bondsman:
Cain Acuff, GRAINGER Co.

ACUFF, Simon to Susan Strange - issued December 24, 1834, Bondsman:
William Acuff, m. by: Joseph Clark, J. P., December 25, 1834,
GRAINGER Co.

ACUFF, Thomas to Martha Sowders - issued December 11, 1810, Bondsman:
Richard Acuff, GRAINGER Co.

ACUFF, William to Magdaline Hall - issued January 28, 1804, Bondsman:
John Hall, Junior, GRAINGER Co.

ACUFF, William to Lucinda Vitetoe - issued February 12, 1835, Bondsman:
Thomas Acuff, m. by: Joseph Clark, J. P., GRAINGER Co.

ADAIR, Alexander to Barbara Foust - issued December 8, 1800, Bondsman:
David Adair, Witness: A. White, KNOX Co.

ADAIR, Alexander to Sarah A. M. C. Thompson - issued February 1, 1836,
Bondsman: Lewis Foust, m. by: G. S. White, M. G., February 4, 1836,
KNOX Co.

ADAIR, Isaac to Polly Granger - July 24, 1811, Bondsman: William McGhee, MAURY Co.

ADAIR, John J. to Margaret G. Holeman - issued October 25, 1843, m. by: W. L. Payne, J. P., ROBERTSON Co.

ADAMS, Aaron to Catherine Harris - issued February 11, 1817, Bondsman: Shadrick Rumley, m. by: Elijah Simpson, J. P., February 11, 1817, SUMNER Co.

ADAMS, Abraham to Nancy Adams - January 7, 1811, Bondsman: William Kennedy, WILSON Co.

ADAMS, Abednego to Mary E. Cannon - issued 1831, Bondsman: A. E. Cannon, KNOX Co.

ADAMS, Absolom to Mary C. Richardson - issued September, 1834, Bondsmen: Henry Ewing, Joseph W. Clay and John McGregor, RUTHERFORD Co.

ADAMS, Adam G. to Susan Porterfield - issued May 12, 1846, m. by: Robt. A. Lapsley, May 12, 1846, DAVIDSON Co.

ADAMS, Alexander G. to Mary Hollis - issued March 19, 1856, m. by: J. W. Smith, J. P., ROBERTSON Co.

ADAMS, Ann to William Taylor - MAURY Co.

ADAMS, Benjamin to Polly Lacy - m. by: Reuben Searcy, J. P., November 10, 1828, SUMNER Co.

ADAMS, Benjamin to Sarah P. Brown - m. by: Thos. Joyner, October 21, 1835, SUMNER Co.

ADAMS, Collin to Elizabeth W. Gunn - issued September 19, 1850, m. by: W. H. Adams, M. of Gos., ROBERTSON Co.

ADAMS, Daniel to Susanna Fielder - April 10, 1811, WILLIAMSON Co.

ADAMS, David to Betsey Fielder - September 10, 1816, WILLIAMSON Co.

ADAMS, Dudley to Sary Anne Townsend - issued September 1, 1825, Bondsman: H. Smith, m. by: Richard Johnson September 1, 1825, SUMNER Co.

ADAMS, Edward to Nancy Gilliam - issued May 8, 1827, Bondsman: William McKinney, RUTHERFORD Co.

ADAMS, Edwin to Lavina Ragsdale - issued December 4, 1837, m. by: Jacob Milton, M. G., December 5, 1837, WILSON Co.

ADAMS, Elijah to Elizabeth Miller - issued September 23, 1805, Bondsman: James Oglesby, SUMNER Co.

ADAMS, Elizabeth I. to James R. Wilson - BEDFORD Co.

ADAMS, George to Mary M. Clark - issued June 13, 1860, m. by: Wm. Draughon, J. P., June 14, 1860, ROBERTSON Co.

ADAMS, George W. to Ann Holland - issued May 19, 1855, m. by: T. H. Gardner, J. P., May 20, 1855, ROBERTSON Co.

ADAMS, Green B. to Metilda R. Jennings - issued October 17, 1835, Bondsman: John Reece, WILSON Co.

ADAMS, Greenberry to Sally Periman - issued June 23, 1825, Bondsman: Benjamin Periman, WILSON Co.

ADAMS, James to Catherine Casick - September 3, 1796, Security: William Adams, GREENE Co.

ADAMS, James to Jenny B. Thomas - -issued September 10, 1813, Bondsman: James Thomas, m. by: David Foster September 23, 1813, WILSON Co.

ADAMS, James to Elizabeth Tinsley - issued December 23, 1817, Bondsman: Richard Stone, m. by: Washington C. Bullard December 23, 1817, SUMNER Co.

ADAMS, James to Polly Harrison - m. by: S. H. Blythe, J. P., February 20, 1819, SUMNER Co.

ADAMS, James to Silva Houston - issued July 8, 1841, m. by: James Ross, Minister, July 8, 1841, STEWART Co.

ADAMS, James to Matilda H. McGee - issued June 27, 1852, Bondsman: H. S. T. Tate, m. by: R. P. Bowling, J. P., June 27, 1852, MONTGOMERY Co.

ADAMS, Jas. A. to Virginia A. Phillips - issued October 22, 1863, Bondsmen: Thos. A. Wilson, Jos. H. Thompson, Clk. per M. E. W. Dunaway, Dep. Clk., BEDFORD Co.

ADAMS, James H. to M. J. Walls - issued August 6, 1872, m. by: D. S. Long, J. P., August 8, 1872, FRANKLIN Co.

ADAMS, James L. to Louisa Gardner - issued October 23, 1834, m. by: M. Powell, J. P., ROBERTSON Co.

ADAMS, Jessee to Anna McCall - issued October 2, 1843, m. by: Madison Williams, J. P., October 2, 1843, FRANKLIN Co.

ADAMS, Jesse G. to Martha J. Adams - issued December 19, 1851, Bondsman: Winfield Roach, m. by: B..H. Williams, J. P., December 23, 1851, MONTGOMERY Co.

ADAMS, John to Nancy Jones - issued December 1, 1831, Bondsman: William Dunn, m. by: Wm. Neigh Jiowrs, M. G., WILSON Co.

ADAMS, John to Sarah A. Allen - issued July 15, 1846, m. by: B. Sharpe, J. P., July 15, 1846, DAVIDSON Co.

ADAMS, John to Lucretia Buckaloo - issued February 18, 1862, m. by: W. J. Calhoun, J. P., February 18, 1862, COFFEE Co.

ADAMS, John A. to Luina Runnels - issued February 16, 1856, m. by: Joseph Smith, M. G., February 17, 1856, FRANKLIN Co.

ADAMS, John C. to Mary Benson - issued June 9, 1850, m. by: D. G. Baird, J. P., ROBERTSON Co.

ADAMS, John F. to Mery Baggett - issued March 2, 1853, m. by: J. W. Sprouse, J. P., ROBERTSON Co.

ADAMS, John G. to Penine Rose - issued December 24, 1857, m. by: G. B. Mason, J. P., ROBERTSON Co.

ADAMS, John H. to Ellen Fletcher - issued September 17, 1849, Bondsman: B. Bayliss, m. by: John C. Mickle, J. P., September 19, 1849, MONTGOMERY Co.

ADAMS, John L. C. to Mary A. E. Binkley - issued August 3, 1855, m. by: A. Rose, M. G., August 6, 1855, ROBERTSON Co.

ADAMS, John M. to E. R. Bowden - issued August 4, 1857, m. by: L. D. Phillips, M. G., August 4, 1857, COFFEE Co.

ADAMS, John N. to Prince L. Norton - issued December 17, 1839, m. by: J. B. McFerrin, J. P., December 18, 1839, DAVIDSON Co.

ADAMS, John S. C. to Mary Cochran - issued July 6, 1850, m. by: A. Rose, M. G., July 9, 1850, ROBERTSON Co.

ADAMS, John W. to Sarah J. Durin - issued March 16, 1829, m. by:
John Wiseman, M. G., March 16, 1829, SUMNER Co.

ADAMS, John W. to E. Adams - issued December 30, 1845, m. by:
R. W. Bell, J. P., ROBERTSON Co.

ADAMS, John W. to Sarah J. Perry - issued April 10, 1852, m. by:
Thos. Finch, J. P., April 10, 1852, FRANKLIN Co.

ADAMS, John W. to Sarah C. Crawford - issued July 15, 1852, m. by:
J. M. Gunn, J. P., July 18, 1852, ROBERTSON Co.

ADAMS, Lewis V. to Mary A. Sand - issued October 10, 1839, m. by:
L. Ayre, J. P., ROBERTSON Co.

ADAMS, Luke P. to Sarah Uselton - issued December 22, 1830, m. by:
William Keele, M. G., December 23, 1830, RUTHERFORD Co.

ADAMS, Moses to Hasty Bass - issued July 23, 1800, Bondsman: James
Vinson, SUMNER Co.

ADAMS, Pinkney to America Jones - issued December 20, 1860, m. by:
W. H. Anthony, M. G., February 20, 1860, FRANKLIN Co.

ADAMS, R. L. to Martha A. Ogg - issued May 7, 1860, m. by: J. A. Bell,
J. P., May 15, 1860, ROBERTSON Co.

ADAMS, Richard M. to Amanda Morris - issued April 29, 1851, m. by:
James Sprouse, J. P., ROBERTSON Co.

ADAMS, Robert H. to Charlotte Montgomery - issued January 19, 1813,
Bondsman: Anderson Hutcheson, KNOX Co.

ADAMS, Robt. T. to Mary Hinson - issued June 24, 1847, m. by:
B. H. Sanders, J. P., June 24, 1847, STEWART Co.

ADAMS, Samuel to Mary Smith - February 3, 1797, Security: Barnet and
Larkin Brumley, GREENE Co.

ADAMS, Sam'l A. to Mary A. L. Ogburn - issued April 18, 1847, m. by:
Josiah Ferriss, J. P., April 18, 1847, DAVIDSON Co.

ADAMS, Thos to Angeline Linsey - issued February 1, 1847, Bondsman:
William Norris, m. by: J. C. Bryant, J. P., February 1, 1847,
MONTGOMERY Co.

ADAMS, Thos. A. to Martha Gardner - issued August 2, 1849, m. by:
J. Lawrence, J. P., ROBERTSON Co.

ADAMS, Thomas J. to Rhoda Jane Burtin - issued February 8, 1859, m. by:
M. A. Carden, J. P., February 8, 1859, COFFEE Co.

ADAMS, Thomas L. to Susan M. Rives - issued April 29, 1850,
MONTGOMERY Co.

ADAMS, Thomas S. to America Jane Haskins - issued September 24, 1843,
STEWART Co.

ADAMS, W. D. to Ann L. Rollow - issued April 2, 1852, Bondsman:
J. E. Broaddus, m. by: R. W. Nixon, M. G., April 4, 1852,
MONTGOMERY Co.

ADAMS, W. W. to Mary S. Woods - issued December 23, 1859, m. by:
John W. Smith, J. P., December 25, 1859, ROBERTSON Co.

ADAMS, William to Nancy Frazier - issued February 28, 1797, Bondsman:
William Thompson, Witness: Chas. McClung, Clk., KNOX Co.

ADAMS, William to Rebecca Craig - September 11, 1811, Bondsman:
George Agnew, MAURY Co.

ADAMS, William to Dorothy Richardson - issued July 7, 1818, Bondsman: Elisha Dismukes, m. by: B. Casilman, J. P., WILSON Co.

ADAMS, William to Elizabeth Goodloe - issued April 24, 1819, m. by: Jacob Wright, J. P., April 26, 1819, RUTHERFORD Co.

ADAMS, William to Mary Lewis - issued May 29, 1821, m. by: Geo. L. Smith, J. P., WILSON Co.

ADAMS, William to Jane Hall - issued December 27, 1836, Bondsman: Charles D. Morse, RUTHERFORD Co.

ADAMS, William to Jane Dickerson - issued March 3, 1851, ROBERTSON Co.

ADAMS, William to Martha A. Heathcoat - issued December 13, 1852, m. by: J. C. Montgomery, J. P., December 14, 1852, FRANKLIN Co.

ADAMS, Wm. to Eliza Massey - issued August 26, 1863, Bondsman: Joshua Pierce, BEDFORD Co.

ADAMS, William A. to Susan Chapman - issued April 26, 1849, m. by: G. B. Mason, J. P., ROBERTSON Co.

ADAMS, William H. to Sarah McMurry - issued September 18, 1839, m. by: J. Sprouse, J. P., September 20, 1839, ROBERTSON Co.

ADAMS, Wm. H. to Margaret Crafford - issued April 24, 1847, m. by: Wm. D. Baldwin, M. G., April 25, 1847, ROBERTSON Co.

ADAMS, Wm. L. to Mary E. Batts - issued January 30, 1844, m. by: Jas. L. Adams, J. P., February 1, 1844, ROBERTSON Co.

ADAMS, Wm. M. to Mary A. Seymore - issued November 2, 1843, m. by: U. Young, J. P., ROBERTSON Co.

ADAMS, William to Henrietta Payne - issued January 20, 1840, m. by: W. B. Burdess, J. P., January 21, 1840, ROBERTSON Co.

ADAMSON, David to Mary Anne Roberts - issued November 2, 1813, Bondsman: Abel L. Williams, Witness: A. Hutcheson, KNOX Co.

ADAMSON, Elijah to Susanah Hathaway - issued April 24, 1822, Bondsman: Jesse Pugh, WILSON Co.

ADAMSON, Isaac to Jane Underwood - July 28, 1821, KNOX Co.

ADAMSON, John to Polly David - issued October 3, 1825, Bondsman: Jesse Pugh, WILSON Co.

ADAMSON, John to Rebecca Neighbours - issued December 23, 1829, Bondsman: Thomas Belcher, WILSON Co.

ADAMSON, Simon to Susanah Hopkins - issued February 22, 1809, Bondsman: Stephen Hopkins, WILSON Co.

ADAMSON, Simon to Avaona Anna Jane Measles - issued November 5, 1840, Bondsman: Eli A. Pugh, m. by: James Turner, WILSON Co.

ADAMSON, Wells to Mary George - issued December 29, 1812, Bondsman: Charles Blakeley, Witness: A. Hutcheson, KNOX Co.

ADAMSON, William to Demorris Bledsoe - issued June 7, 1808, Bondsman: George Pue, WILSON Co.

ADAMSON, William to Sarah Hatheway - issued June 20, 1834, m. by: Wm. Laurence, J. P., June 22, 1834, WILSON Co.

ADCOCK, Anderson to Carlina Smiley - issued June 9, 1849, m. by: John Warren, J. P., June 14, 1849, ROBERTSON Co.

ADCOCK, Andrew to Terry Wilson - issued November 16, 1843, m. by:
Wm. D. Baldwin, M. G., November 20, 1842, ROBERTSON Co.

ADCOCK, Barney to Martha Higgins - issued December 24, 1814, Bondsman:
Adam Struder, RUTHERFORD Co.

ADCOCK, Carter to Dolly Railey - issued October 9, 1817, Bondsman:
Isaac Pearis, SUMNER Co.

ADCOCK, David W. to Martha Ann Crow - issued February 2, 1841, m. by:
J. Pendergrass, J. P., February 3, 1841, DICKSON Co.

ADCOCK, H. M. to Mildred W. Williams - issued January 14, 1853,
Bondsman: Joseph T. Johnson, m. by: Robert Williams, M. G.,
January 18, 1853, MONTGOMERY Co.

ADCOCK, Harman to Priscilla White - issued February 29, 1820, m. by:
Wm. Vinson, J. P., March 2, 1820, RUTHERFORD Co.

ADCOCK, Henderson to Mary Foster - issued June 17, 1834, Bondsman:
Wm. Adcock, m. by: J. F. Shapard, J. P. June 17, 1834, RUTHERFORD Co.

ADCOCK, Jesse to Sally M. Adcock - issued November 18, 1844, m. by:
David Gray, M. G., DICKSON Co.

ADCOCK, Joel to Fanny Shoecraft - issued October 9, 1853, m. by:
James Anderson, J. P., ROBERTSON, Co.

ADCOCK, John to Bersheba Green - issued November 9, 1822, m. by:
G. W. Oliver, J. P., November 9, 1822, RUTHERFORD Co.

ADCOCK, Mark M. to Mary Ashley - issued February 5, 1853, m. by:
N. Jernigan, J. P., February 13, 1853, COFFEE Co.

ADCOCK, Stephen to Polly Fox - issued June 12, 1824, Bondsman:
Lewis Dyal, m. by: Wm. Vinson, J. P., June 12, 1834, RUTHERFORD Co.

ADCOCK, Susan M. to G. W. Jernigan - BEDFORD Co.

ADCOCK, William to Sarah Joiner - issued February 6, 1844, m. by:
Banja. Rawls, M. Gospel, ROBERTSON Co.

ADCOCK, William to Sarah Thedford - issued January, 1845, m. by:
Sam'l. Tate, J. P., January 8, 1845, DICKSON Co.

ADCOCK, William to Eliza Crowden - issued January 30, 1850, m. by:
Madison Williams, J. P., January 31, 1850, FRANKLIN Co.

ADCOCK, William H. to Clary E. Stem - issued August 23, 1862, Bondsmen:
R. W. Turner, Jos. H. Thompson, Clk. per M. E. W. Dunaway, D. Clk.,
m. by: D. R. Hooker August 26, 1862, BEDFORD Co.

ADCOCK, Wiseman to Hannah Dial - issued April 8, 1844, m. by:
Madison Williams, J. P., April 8, 1844, FRANKLIN Co.

ADCOX, J. W. to M. J. Crabtree - issued December 14, 1867, FRANKLIN Co.

ADDINGTON, David to Malinda J. Cox - issued June 1, 1842, m. by:
C. A. Hunt, J. P., June 2, 1842, FRANKLIN Co.

ADDINGTON, Jason to Elizabeth Taylor - issued November 13, 1842, m. by:
H. Larkin, November 13, 1842, FRANKLIN Co.

ADDISON, Jonathan to Nancy Emeline Harbeson - issued December 27, 1839,
m. by: Jas. Woodard, J. P., ROBERTSON Co.

ADIER, Hiram to Marth Davis - issued January 21, 1853, VAN BUREN Co.

ADIER, John C. to Mary Smith - issued February 21, 1850, m. by:
James A. Haston, J. P., February 21, 1850, VAN BUREN Co.

ADKINS, Barnabas to Sarah Routh - issued September 28, 1831, Bondsman: John Chandler, m. by: Eli Clark, J. P., October 5, 1831, GRAINGER Co.

ADKINS, Calvin to Elenor Mitchell - issued September 29, 1834, m. by: Isaac Long, M. G., October 6, 1834, KNOX Co.

ADKINS, Emmanuel to Polena McNely - issued November 1, 1835, Bondsman: Joel Mallicoat, GRAINGER Co.

ADKINS, G. W. to N. M. Smith - issued February 10, 1840, FRANKLIN Co.

ADKINS, George to Catherine Kitts - issued February 3, 1829, Bondsman: Alexander Mcelhaney, m. by: Eli Clark, J. P., February 3, 1829, GRAINGER Co.

ADKINS, H. Madison to Lucy Ann Ray - m. by: John F. Hughes November, 1840, STEWART Co.

ADKINS, Harvey to Julia Heath - issued October 7, 1847, m. by: Benj. Sharpe, J. P., October 7, 1847, DAVIDSON Co.

ADKINS, James to Susan Nesbitt - issued November 11, 1850, Bondsman: Thos, Ramey, Esq., MONTGOMERY Co.

ADKINS, Lewis to Elizabeth Monroe - issued January 24, 1804, Bondsman: John Calvin, GRAINGER Co.

ADKINS, Lewis to Elizabeth George - July 8, 1813, KNOX Co.

ADKINS, Payton to Mary Lipford - issued March 2, 1825, Bondsman: Francis McNamsey, m. by: John Bayless, J. P., March 3, 1825, Witness: Wm. Swan, KNOX Co.

ADKINS, Richard to Polley Monroe - issued November 15, 1805, Bondsman: Davis Ray, Witness: Samuel Yancey, J. P., GRAINGER Co.

ADKINS, Richard to Nancy Wirick - issued December 17, 1819, Bondsman: Martin Thornburg, m. December 17, 1819, GRAINGER Co.

ADKINS, Stephen to Rebecca Vandagriff - issued January 6, 1835, Bondsman: James Brock, m. by: Joseph Clark, J. P., GRAINGER Co.

ADKINS, W. P. to Rebecca M. Morrison - issued April 21, 1854, m. by: W. R. Saddler, J. P., April 23, 1854, ROBERTSON Co.

ADKINS, William to Mahala Stublefield - issued October 13, 1825, Bondsman: Benjamin Spring, WILSON Co.

ADKINS, Wm. P. to Mary J. Reynolds - issued December 20, 1851, Bondsman: V. Q. Jarrell, m. by: R. W. Morrison, J. P., December 25, 1851, MONTGOMERY Co.

ADKINSON, Peter to Hariott Sharpe - issued September 11, 1821, Bondsman: John Williams, m. by: R. Houston, J. P., September 11, 1821, KNOX Co.

ADKINSON, Sarah to Z. A. Lentz - BEDFORD Co.

ADKINSON, Thomas to Elizabeth Lambert - issued October 9, 1819, Bondsman: Allen Smith, m. by: Jeremiah Hendrick, J. P., October 11, 1819, WILSON Co.

ADKINSON, William to Aramiata Reed - issued December 27, 1818, m. by: Jas. Johnson December 28, 1818, WILSON Co.

ADKINSON, William to Malinda Parker - issued November 27, 1828, Bondsman: M. Short, m. by: John F. Carr November 27, 1828, SUMNER Co.

ADKINSON, Wm. to Mary Ann Jane Mills - issued February 2, 1839, DICKSON Co.

AFFLACK, James to Nancy Warren - issued January 2, 1834, Bondsman:
George W. Anderson, m. by: B. T. Mottley, J. P., WILSON Co.

AFFLACK, Thomas B. to Martha D. Warren - issued December 28, 1827,
Bondsman: Lewis H. Dwyer, WILSON Co.

AFFLETT, John to Nancy Taylor - issued August 27, 1806, Bondsman:
David McMurry, WILSON Co.

AGEE, William to Syntha Wynn - issued September 29, 1841, m. by:
Charles Crafford, J. P., October 30, 1841, ROBERTSON Co.

AGEN, Joseph to Delilah Parks - issued February 25, 1847, DAVIDSON Co.

AGY, Isaac to Hannah Bounds - issued October 7, 1829, Bondsman:
John Archer, m. by: Wm. Lane, J. P., October 7, 1829, GRAINGER Co.

AIKIN, Armstead to Nancy Hardy - issued September 2, 1850, m. by:
James Woodard, J. P., September 5, 1850, ROBERTSON Co.

AIKIN, Michiel to Polly Reed - issued August 23, 1849, m. by:
J. C. Montgomery, J. P. August 28, 1849, FRANKLIN Co.

AIKIN, Patsey to William Roach - MAURY Co.

AIKMAN, Alexander to Prudence Stockton - issued December 18, 1797,
Bondsman: Samuel Stockton, Witness: Chas. McClung, Clk., KNOX Co.

AIKMAN, James to Patience Gallihorn - issued June 27, 1816, Bondsman:
James Boyd, Witness: A. Hutcheson, KNOX Co.

AILER, Luke to Edy Wood - September 24, 1828, m. by: Daniel Graves,
J. P., September 25, 1828, KNOX Co.

AILOR, John to Levena Harrell - issued September 30, 1833, Bondsman:
Hugh Jones, m. by: John Chesney, J. P., October 1, 1833,
GRAINGER Co.

AILOR, Samuel to Sally Warwick - issued March 14, 1827, m. by:
Geo. Graves, J. P., March 15, 1827, KNOX Co.

AINGELL, E. L. to L. J. May - issued May 25, 1860, m. by: E. Burr,
J. P., May 26, 1860, ROBERTSON Co.

AINSWORTH, Joseph to Mary A. Clinard - issued July 15, 1848, Bondsman:
Frederick Grimes, m. by: Stephen Cocke, J. P., July 16, 1848,
MONTGOMERY Co.

AIRES, Abner to Naomi Casteel - December 30, 1797, Security: John Melone,
GREENE Co.

AIRHART, Peter to Nancy Murphy - issued November 18, 1824, Bondsman:
Alexander McBath, m. by: Robert McBath November 18, 1824, Witness:
Wm. Swan, KNOX Co.

AKE, John M. to Nicy Rose - issued October 12, 1844, m. by: M. Catchings,
J. P., October 12, 1844, FRANKLIN Co.

AKE, John M. to Bethany Stephens - issued June 30, 1847, m. by:
M. Catchings, J. P., June 30, 1847, FRANKLIN Co.

AKEMAN, William to Jenny Montgomery - issued July 31, 1807, m. by:
John Love, Esq., August 5, 1807, KNOX Co.

AKEN, Allison to Mary P. M. Taylor - issued December 9, 1846, m. by:
Andrew J. G. Foster, M. G., STEWART Co.

AKERS, Richard to Anne Nickings - issued February 27, 1823, m. by:
Abner Hill, M. G., WILSON Co.

AKERS, Wm. R. to Mary E. McKnight - issued January 2, 1836, Bondsman: George McElroy, m. by: Jesse Alexander, V. D. M., January 7, 1836, RUTHERFORD Co.

AKIN, A. J. to Martha J. Bagby - issued December 21, 1855, m. by: G. B. Mason, J. P., December 23, 1855, ROBERTSON Co.

AKIN, Christian to Mary Brady - issued May 26, 1810, Bondsman: Henry Kirby, RUTHERFORD Co.

AKIN, Harrison W. to Mary A. Sanders - issued March 20, 1847, m. by: James Woodard March 23, 1847, ROBERTSON Co.

AKIN, James to Martha Jackson - issued July 17, 1847, STEWART Co.

AKIN, John to Fatama Colly - issued February 2, 1840, m. by: P. B. Morris, J. P., February 9, 1840, DAVIDSON Co.

AKIN, Joseph L. to Emaline Smelser - issued September 4, 1852, m. by: James Woodard, ROBERTSON Co.

AKIN, N. I. to A. M. Shackleford - issued July 21, 1858, m. by: James Woodard July 22, 1858, ROBERTSON Co.

AKIN, William to Mary Wright - issued August 7, 1822, RUTHERFORD Co.

AKINS, Henry to Sally Stell - issued February 23, 1815, Bondsman: Geo. W. Stell, WILSON Co.

AKINS, Willis to Polly B. Floyd - issued January 7, 1817, Bondsman: Reas Williams, GRAINGER Co.

ALBERT, John M. to Eliza M. Galloway - issued September 4, 1845, m. by: D. L. Godsey, Min., September 4, 1845, MEIGS Co.

ALBERT, Martin to Elizabeth Chamberlian - issued August 7, 1810, Bondsman: William Keith, GRAINGER Co.

ALBRIGHT, James M. to Margaret I. Halliburton - issued September 29, 1839, m. by: Thos. Jarragin, J. P., September 29, 1839, DICKSON Co.

ALBRIGHT, Thos. H. to Sarah H. Marshall - issued August 18, 1852, Bondsman: Thos. E. Wilcox, m. by: Mark Senter, M. G., August 1, 1852, MONTGOMERY Co.

ALBRIGHT, William to Asneth Stalcup - issued August 23, 1826, Bondsman: John Stalcup, m. by: Frances Johnson, M. G., August 23, 1826, SUMNER Co.

ALCLEY, Metes to Elizabeth Mitchell - issued July 21, 1845, m. by: T. B. McElwee, J. P., July 21, 1845, MEIGS Co.

ALDERSON, Armstead to Elizabeth Orr - m. by: John Gilbert, J. P., September 14, 1818, SUMNER Co.

ALDERSON, Armstead to Eliza Bradley - issued August 19, 1838, Bondsman: John Jackson, m. August 19, 1838, SUMNER Co.

ALDERSON, James to Palsey Morgan - issued May 24, 1834, m. by: J. Hobday, J. P., May 24, 1834, SUMNER Co.

ALDERSON, Jeremiah to C. (Crisia) Nolin - issued February 24, 1817, Bondsman: James Alderson, SUMNER Co.

ALDERSON, John to Polly Hodges - issued September 26, 1827, Bondsman: Creed Hodges, m. September 26, 1827, SUMNER Co.

ALDERSON, Reuben to Sally Stephens - m. by: Freeman Senter April 28, 1835, SUMNER Co.

11

ALDERSON, Richard D. to Mary Millins - issued February 2, 1831, m. by:
Henry Ridley, J. P., February 3, 1831, RUTHERFORD Co.

ALDERSON, Robert to Elizabeth Clark - issued May 24, 1830, Bondsman:
Wm. Alderson, m. by: Robert Norvell May 24, 1830, SUMNER Co.

ALDERSON, William to Tabitha Dinning - issued February 17, 1826,
Bondsman: John Dinning, m. by: Robert Norvell February 17, 1826,
SUMNER Co.

ALDRIDGE, Joel to Mary Jarnagin - issued March 2, 1824, Bondsmen:
Saml. Lowe, Robert-Triston, J. P., m. by: Robt. Triston, J. P.,
March 2, 1824, GRAINGER Co.

ALESS(?), Rachel to James Jones - GREENE Co.

ALEXANDER, Aaron to Susan Bradley - issued March 5, 1829, Bondsman:
Anderson Walker, WILSON Co.

ALEXANDER Abigail to John Taylor - GREENE Co.

ALEXANDER, Adlai to Sarah W. Sims - issued October 3, 1833, Bondsman:
Elisha Cox, RUTHERFORD Co.

ALEXANDER, Archibald to Agnes McGaughey - August 22, 1786, Security:
Jos. Posey and David Robinson, GREENE Co.

ALEXANDER, Benjamin to Ruth Wallace - September 16, 1799, Surety:
Robert Hook, BLOUNT Co.

ALEXANDER, Benjamin to Sarah Cloyd - issued July 21, 1802, Bondsman:
Sam'l Hogg, WILSON Co.

ALEXANDER, Daniel to Rachel Scott - issued June 9, 1822, Bondsman:
James Martin, WILSON Co.

ALEXANDER, David to Rebeccah McElwrath - issued October 16, 1811,
Bondsman: Thos. Brookshires, SUMNER Co.

ALEXANDER, Doran L. to Nancy Powell - issued June 21, 1824, RUTHERFORD Co.

ALEXANDER, Ebenezer to Margaret Ann White - issued October 15, 1829,
m. by: Charles Coffin, V. D. M., October 15, 1829, KNOX Co.

ALEXANDER, Ebenezer to Margaret Ann White - issued October 15, 1829,
Bondsman: Hu L. McClung, m. October 15, 1829, KNOX Co.

ALEXANDER, Ebenezer to Margaret A. M. McClung - issued January 31, 1833,
m. by: Thos. H. Nelson, M. G., January 31, 1833, KNOX Co.

ALEXANDER, Elijah to Lyda Frost - issued August 18, 1859, m. by:
Wm. Prince, J. P., August 19, 1859, FRANKLIN Co.

ALEXANDER, Ephraim to Lucy Parry - issued February 10, 1818, Bondsman:
William Bowen, KNOX Co.

ALEXANDER, Esther to Alexander Crawford - December 20, 1808, Bondsman:
Wilson Henderson(?), MAURY Co.

ALEXANDER, Ezekiel to Polly Cooper - issued October 8, 1810, Bondsman:
Abraham Cooper, WILSON Co.

ALEXANDER, George B. to Eliza Merchant - issued October 19, 1839,
Bondsman: Thos. Burke, m. by: Thos. Davis, J. P., October 20,
1839, WILSON Co.

ALEXANDER, George E. to Margaret W. Tate - issued March 6, 1834,
Bondsman: Richard Tate, m. by: John Beard, M. G., March 21, 1834,
WILSON Co.

ALEXANDER, Gidian to Elizabeth Borum - issued December 14, 1816,
Bondsman: David Barton, m. by: Wm. Steele, J. P., December 15,
1816, WILSON Co.

ALEXANDER, H. A. to Elizabeth Kennedy - issued February 10, 1866,
Bondsman: George H. Nixon, m. by: W. C. Davis, J. P., February 16,
1866, LAWRENCE Co.

ALEXANDER, Henry J. to Rebecca Hopkins - February 8, 1855, m. by:
L. A. Parsons, J. P., GILES Co.

ALEXANDER, Houston to Abby Connata - issued February 22, 1816, Bondsman:
Elijah Parsons, m. by: Abner W. Bone, J. P., February 23, 1816,
WILSON Co.

ALEXANDER, Hugh to Adaline Orr - issued December 18, 1827, Bondsman:
Samuel Brown, SUMNER Co.

ALEXANDER, Isaac to Nancy Parsons - issued June 20, 1814, Bondsman:
George Michie, WILSON Co.

ALEXANDER, James to Metilda Kirpatrick - February 3, 1808, MAURY Co.

ALEXANDER, James to Edith Akins - December 23, 1815, WILLIAMSON Co.

ALEXANDER, James to Elizabeth Doss - issued May 27, 1829, Bondsman:
James Pybass, m. by: Sam'l Jones, J. P., May 27, 1829,
RUTHERFORD Co.

ALEXANDER, James to Jane C. Stewart - m. by: H. B. Hill April 13, 1837,
SUMNER Co.

ALEXANDER, James to Mary P. Ford - issued June 24, 1842, m. by:
R. Wilson, J. P., June 26, 1842, STEWART Co.

ALEXANDER, James F. to Mary J. Lunn - issued September 1, 1864,
Bondsman: W. C. Davis, m. by: W. C. Davis, J. P., September 1,
1864, LAWRENCE Co.

ALEXANDER, John to Frances Roy - issued October 23, 1810, Bondsman:
Philip Letzinger, KNOX Co.

ALEXANDER, John to Kissey Carter - issued June 25, 1811, RUTHERFORD Co.

ALEXANDER, John to Sarah O'Neal - issued November 29, 1833, m. by:
Jesse Alexander, V. D. M., December 5, 1833, WILSON Co.

ALEXANDER, John D. to Mary R. Baird - issued November 11, 1837,
Bondsman: E. Sanders, m. by: William Eagleton, V. D. M.,
November 16, 1837, RUTHERFORD Co.

ALEXANDER, John H. to Barbara Smith - issued April 30, 1833, Bondsman:
Rob't. Smith, KNOX Co.

ALEXANDER, John M. to Sarah Strawbridge - issued June 25, 1841, m. by:
E. W. Smith June 27, 1841, STEWART Co.

ALEXANDER, Jonah to Elizabeth King - March 4, 1811, Bondsman: Samuel
King, MAURY Co.

ALEXANDER, Jonathan to Thursey Bridges - March 16, 1792, Security:
William Dewoody, GREENE Co.

ALEXANDER, Jonathan to Tressy Williams - issued April 27, 1838, Bondsman:
J. W. Hunt, RUTHERFORD Co.

ALEXANDER, Jordan to Margret Guinn - issued April 10, 1854, m. by:
M. Catchings, J. P., April 10, 1854, FRANKLIN Co.

ALEXANDER, Josephus to Cynthia Roberts - issued April 6, 1835,
    Bondsman: Joseph Plumlee, m. by: B. McNutt, J. P., April 12, 1835,
    KNOX Co.

ALEXANDER, Josiah A. to Susanna Gourley - issued May 4th, 1831, m.
    May 4, 1831, SUMNER Co.

ALEXANDER, Levi to Elizabeth Alford - issued February 20, 1830,
    Bondsman: John D. Fletcher, RUTHERFORD Co.

ALEXANDER, Marlin to Margaret Wygal - issued December 30, 1812, Bondsman:
    Matthew Alexander, SUMNER Co.

ALEXANDER, Michael to Eliza Powell - issued December 11, 1828, Bondsman:
    Wilie Powell, WILSON Co.

ALEXANDER, Nelson G. to Mary Patterson - issued May 13, 1828, Bondsman:
    James Carruth, m. by: Amzi Bradshaw May 13, 1828, WILSON Co.

ALEXANDER, Nicholas to Anne Smith - issued December 21, 1793, Bondsman:
    Richard Goodin, Witness: Chas. McClung, C. K. C., KNOX Co.

ALEXANDER, Nicholas to Annie Smith - December 31, 1796, KNOX Co.

ALEXANDER, Pritchard to Nancy Norman - issued July 2, 1804, Bondsman:
    Furney G. Norman, RUTHERFORD Co.

ALEXANDER, Samuel to Jane Clarke - issued October 11, 1830, Bondsman:
    Jno. Clark, m. by: Wm. Morris, J. P., October 12, 1830, KNOX Co.

ALEXANDER, Silas to Nancy Anderson - issued April 29, 1813, Bondsman:
    Raven C. Follis, SUMNER Co.

ALEXANDER, Stephen K. to Sarah Kennedy - August 23, 1803, GREENE Co.

ALEXANDER, Susanna to Jesse Overton - MAURY Co.

ALEXANDER, Thomas to Mary Russell - September 10, 1795, Security:
    James Russell, GREENE Co.

ALEXANDER, Thomas to Martha McCall - March 15, 1800, GREENE Co.

ALEXANDER, Thomas, Sen. to Nancy Wear - November 18, 1819, GREENE Co.

ALEXANDER, Thomas to Nancy Jennings - issued January 10, 1825, Bondsman:
    William S. Alexander, m. by: James Foster, J. P., January 18,
    1825, WILSON Co.

ALEXANDER, W. S. to Mary Ann Rickman - issued May 4, 1838, Bondsman:
    William H. Hall, m. by: H. B. Hall May 4, 1838, SUMNER Co.

ALEXANDER, William to Martha Haslet - issued October 20, 1796, Bondsman:
    William Haslet, Witness: And. White, KNOX Co.

ALEXANDER, William to Ana Bigham - September 5, 1800, Surety: Joseph
    Alexander, BLOUNT Co.

ALEXANDER, William to Betsy Norman - August 5, 1811, WILLIAMSON Co.

ALEXANDER, William to Elizabeth - October 17, 1817, KNOX Co.

ALEXANDER, William to Mariah Henshaw - February 17, 1820, GREENE Co.

ALEXANDER, William to Levisy Smith - issued March 28, 1834, Bondsman:
    John Smith, GRAINGER Co.

ALEXANDER, William to Matilda Allen - issued August 26, 1834, Bondsman:
    Lafayette Epps, RUTHERFORD Co.

ALEXANDER, Wm. H. to Nancy Laughlin - issued November 5, 1834, Bondsman: James H. Alexander, RUTHERFORD Co.

ALEXANDER, William K. to Mary Davis - July 8, 1802, GREENE Co.

ALEXANDER, Zebulum to Mary Ann Whaly - January 31, 1816, WILLIAMSON Co.

ALFORD, Brittain D. to Martha Graves - issued August 6, 1831, Bondsman: Solomon D. Wright, m. by: B. Graves, J. P., WILSON Co.

ALFORD, Burtis to Mary Bryant - issued February 21, 1807, Bondsman: Achilus Bryant, WILSON Co.

ALFORD, John to Jeney McElhatten - issued January 13, 1811, Bondsman: Thomas Turley, GRAINGER Co.

ALFORD, Julus to Ann Hays - issued February 18, 1806, Bondsman: Harman Hays, WILSON Co.

ALFORD, Lothwick B. to Lindy R. Hall - issued January 12, 1819, Bondsman: Dan'l. McAulay, m. by: S. Hunt, J. P., January 12, 1819, SUMNER Co.

ALFORD, R. N. to M. A. Edmiston - issued July 23, 1862, Bondsman: J. H. Keeton, m. by: Wm. B. Gillham, M. G., July 24, 1862, LAWRENCE Co.

ALFRED, W. D. to G. Menees - issued September 23, 1848, m. by: Jeremiah Batts, J. P., September 24, 1848, ROBERTSON Co.

ALISON, John to Nancy Brooks - issued June 25, 1859, m. by: Clinton Tucker, Mins., June 25, 1859, COFFEE Co.

ALLBRIGHT, Christian to Patsey Walker - issued January 6, 1812, KNOX Co.

ALLBRIGHT, Jacob P. to Elizabeth Hutchinson - issued March 27, 1848, Bondsman: William Allbright, m. by: R. W. Morrison, J. P., March 27, 1848, MONTGOMERY Co.

ALLBRIGHT, Wm. H. to Lydia Bowling - issued March 30, 1831, Bondsman: Jno. Garner, Witness: Wm. Swan, KNOX Co.

ALLBROOK, David to Sarah Ann Green - issued November 26, 1849, m. by: John P. Walker, J. P., November 26, 1849, FRANKLIN Co.

ALLDREDGE, William to Pasty McClain - issued November 12, 1821, Bondsman: William Olinger, KNOX Co.

ALLEN, A. J. to Elizabeth S. Orgain - issued May 24, 1852, Bondsman: Robert H. Pickering, m. by: W. Mooney, M. G., May 24, 1852, MONTGOMERY Co.

ALLEN, Absolum to Abby Dill - issued March 12, 1829, Bondsman: Sam'l Johnson, m. by: Dn'l Moser, J. P., March 13, 1829, WILSON Co.

ALLEN, Alex to Eliza Bean - issued March 2, 1869, FRANKLIN Co.

ALLEN, Alfred to Franky Benthall - issued December 31, 1825, Bondsman: David Allen, m. by: Elijah Boddie, J. P., December 31, 1825, SUMNER Co.

ALLEN, Archibald to Matilda Lambert - issued August 29, 1818, Bondsman: Wm. Hartsfield, m. by: John W. Payton, J. P., August 30, 1818, WILSON Co.

ALLEN, B. T. to Martha Pennell - issued February 1, 1846, Bondsman: Martin M. Pennell, m. by: W. B. Carney, J. P., February 1, 1846, MONTGOMERY Co.

ALLEN, Bailey F. to Mary Jane Osburn - issued December 24, 1845,
Bondsman: B. F. Bradley, m. by: R. W. Nixon, G. M., December 25,
1845, MONTGOMERY Co.

ALLEN, Benjamin to Sally Voorhies - August 10, 1811, Bondsman:
John Voorhies, MAURY Co.

ALLEN, Benjamin to Jane Johnson - issued August 8, 1834, Bondsman:
Edmund C. Lovern, m. by: Wm. Vinson, J. P., August 9, 1834,
RUTHERFORD Co.

ALLEN, Charles to Elizabeth Gill - June 6, 1808, MAURY Co.

ALLEN, David to Susanah Emory - issued December 22, 1828, m. by:
Elijah Boddie, M. P., December 22, 1828, SUMNER Co.

ALLEN, David D. to Miss Mary A. Ramey - issued January 18, 1850,
Bondsman: Jno. W. Daly, MONTGOMERY Co.

ALLEN, David L. to Julia Read - issued September 1, 1830, Bondsman:
William Barksdale, m. by: Peyton Smith September 7, 1830,
RUTHERFORD Co.

ALLEN, David M. to Frances A. Pope - issued June 5, 1841, DAVIDSON Co.

ALLEN, Donal B. to Mary J. Right - issued March 12, 1849, Bondsman:
J. R. Waller, MONTGOMERY Co.

ALLEN, Eli to Elizabeth Lasater - issued February 25, 1814, Bondsman:
Thomas Sypert, WILSON Co.

ALLEN, Eli to Elizabeth Lasater - issued February 25, 1814, m. by:
J. Winston, J. P., March 4, 1814, WILSON Co.

ALLEN, Elijah to Nancy Whitsides - issued November 16, 1830, Bondsman:
Luke P. Allen, m. by: John Parker November 16, 1830, SUMNER Co.

ALLEN, Felix A. to Betsey Ann Levy - m. November 23, 1838, DAVIDSON Co.

ALLEN, Frances to Henry Farnsworth - GREENE Co.

ALLEN, George C. to Martha Overton - issued October 27, 1842, m. by:
A. H. Kerr, M. G., October 27, 1842, DAVIDSON Co.

ALLEN, George W. to Louisa F. Douglas - m. by: Geo. Donnell, V. D. M.,
June 26, 1834, SUMNER Co.

ALLEN, George W. to Martha Elen Lee - issued July 15, 1847, m. by:
John T. Slatter, J. P., July 16, 1847, FRANKLIN Co.

ALLEN, Hannah to Alexander Williams - GREENE Co.

ALLEN, J. H. to Rebecca Lawson - issued February 13, 1866, m. by:
A. J. Simpson, J. P., February 15, 1866, FRANKLIN Co.

ALLEN, James to Rebecca Hall - December 19, 1799, Security: Samuel Craig,
GREENE Co.

ALLEN, James to Peggy Franklin - issued March 3, 1806, Bondsman:
Jas. Franklin, SUMNER Co.

ALLEN, James to Mary H. Wyllis - m. by: Henry K. Winbourn January 14,
1835, SUMNER Co.

ALLEN, James to Matilda Morgan - January 31, 1835, JEFFERSON Co.

ALLEN, Hartwell to Eliza Payne - issued April 29, 1854, m. by:
J. H. Gammon, ROBERTSON Co.

ALLEN, Henry to Polly Barns - issued December 18, 1804, Bondsman: Solomon Sholders, SUMNER Co.

ALLEN, Henry to Wenny Standly - September 28, 1813, WILLIAMSON Co.

ALLEN, Henry to Catharine A. Dycus - issued September 27, 1847, Bondsman: N. F. Trice, MONTGOMERY Co.

ALLEN, Isaac to Ruth Corder - July 2, 1790, Security: John Corder, GREENE Co.

ALLEN, James to Nancy Neil - issued November 15, 1838, Bondsman: Robert Givan, m. by: Sion Bass, M. G., WILSON Co.

ALLEN, James C. to Louisa A. Lyle - issued June 1, 1852, Bondsman: Lethridge Crockett, m. by: W. Mooney, M. G., June 1, 1852, MONTGOMERY Co.

ALLEN, James R. to Lusinda Smart - issued March 13, 1827, Bondsman: Abraham Wright, m. by: Wm. M. Swain, J. P., WILSON Co.

ALLEN, Jeremiah H. to Mary Holman - issued June 16, 1836, m. by: John Seay, M. G., June 18, 1836, WILSON Co.

ALLEN, Jessee to Cathrine Long - issued August 29, 1842, m. by: Wm. Lyons, J. P., August 31, 1842, FRANKLIN Co.

ALLEN, John to Laetitia Sanders - issued December 21, 1800, Bondsman: John F. Gillespie, SUMNER Co.

ALLEN, John to Elizabeth Martin - issued March 12, 1806, m. by: R. Houston, J. P. K. C., March 12, 1806, KNOX Co.

ALLEN, John to Nancy Wells - issued July 14, 1809, Bondsman: John D. Hodge, SUMNER Co.

ALLEN, John to Martha Freeman - October 20, 1810, WILLIAMSON Co.

ALLEN, John to Nancy C. Morton - issued August 18, 1823, Bondsman: John Still, RUTHERFORD Co.

ALLEN, John to Frany Adams - issued August 19, 1825, Bondsman: Zechariah Sommers, m. by: Joseph Fite, J. P., August 20, 1825, WILSON Co.

ALLEN, Jno. to Sophia Alexander - issued February 14, 1826, m. by: W. A. McCampbell, M. G., February 15, 1826, KNOX Co.

ALLEN, John to Sophia Alexander - issued February 14, 1828, Bondsman: Wm. Wall, KNOX Co.

ALLEN, John to Sarah G. Williamson - issued June 20, 1846, Bondsman: William Allen, m. by: John Mallory June 21, 1846, MONTGOMERY Co.

ALLEN, John G. to Nancy Holmes - issued March 24, 1825, Bondsman: James Holmes, m. by: Wm. Smith, J. P., March 24, 1825, SUMNER Co.

ALLEN, John H. to Martha Neal - issued October 16, 1840, Bondsman: George Neal, WILSON Co.

ALLEN, John H. to Mary L. Whitfield - issued November 23, 1846, m. by: James C. Anderson, M. G., November 25, 1846, DAVIDSON Co.

ALLEN, John M. to Emanthe P. Sparkman - February 20, 1859, m. by: J. P. Richardson, M. G., GILES Co.

ALLEN, John W. to Sarah P. Cartwright - issued December 11, 1839, DAVIDSON Co.

ALLEN, John W. to Eliza B. Corley - issued July 20, 1843, DAVIDSON Co.

ALLEN, La Fayett W. to Louisa Jane James - issued June 22, 1847, m. by:
John Hogan, J. P., June 27, 1847, DAVIDSON Co.

ALLEN, Larkin to Jemima Chapman - issued January 2, 1834, Bondsman:
Isaac J. Dodson, WILSON Co.

ALLEN, Leroy to Polly S. Midget - issued July 10, 1840, Bondsman:
Nathan Midget, WILSON Co.

ALLEN, Levi to Elizabeth Allen - issued November 3, 1821, Bondsman:
Webb Bloodworth, m. by: S. Hunt, J. P., November 3, 1821, SUMNER Co.

ALLEN, Luke P. to Margaret Parker - issued August 15, 1825, Bondsman:
John Parker, m. by: J. Parker August 15, 1825, SUMNER Co.

ALLEN, Lytle to Eliza Smith - issued December 16, 1818, Bondsman:
John Bell, SUMNER Co.

ALLEN, Mathew to Tennessee Walker - issued January 28, 1839, m. by:
J. T. Edgar January 28, 1839, DAVIDSON Co.

ALLEN, Memucan to Martha Edward - issued November 28, 1839, m. by:
Robert Grenn, J. P., ROBERTSON Co.

ALLEN, Orman to Betsey Beard - issued April 20, 1795, Bondsman:
Adam Beard, SUMNER Co.

ALLEN, Pinkney to Susan Bryant - issued December 18, 1873, m. by:
Jas. A. Hudgins, M. G., December 19, 1873, FRANKLIN Co.

ALLEN, R. A. to Mary Merrit - issued July 5, 1851, Bondsman: T. G. Smith,
m. by: J. G. Ward, M. G., June 24, 1851, MONTGOMERY Co.

ALLEN, R. A. to Hannah C. Luker - issued February 4, 1861, Bondsman:
Wade H. McCrory, m. by: W. H. McCrory, J. P., February 9, 1861,
LAWRENCE Co.

ALLEN, R. B. to Malinda Vawter - issued July 27, 1833, Bondsman:
H. Tennison, RUTHERFORD Co.

ALLEN, R. C. to Mary Smith - Bondsman: Wm. Smith, m. by: T. Ramey,
J. P., September 22, 1851, MONTGOMERY Co.

ALLEN, Rebecca J. to W. T. Kindrick - BEDFORD Co.

ALLENSWORTH, A. J. to Ellen E. Hughes - issued June 24, 1857, m. by:
J. W. Cullum, M. G., June 25, 1857, ROBERTSON Co.

ALLEN, Willis to Elizabeth Joyner - issued Aug. 12, 1824, Bondsman:
Yancey Masey, m. by: John Bond, WILSON Co.

ALLEN, Wm. T. to Lizzie Backwell - issued April 11, 1866, FRANKLIN Co.

ALLEN, Wm. to Virginia Shelton - issued January 22, 1861, m. by:
Jonn W. Smith, J. P., ROBERTSON Co.

ALLEN, Wm. to Mary Travis - issued November 9, 1846, STEWART Co.

ALLEN, William to Delpha Blankenship - issued July 13, 1841, Bondsman:
Saml. W. Woods, m. by: D. L. Godsey, Min., July 13, 1841, MEIGS Co.

ALLEN, William to Elenor Willis - issued February 15, 1836, Bondsman:
Robert Williams, SUMNER Co.

ALLEN, William to Sarah Read - issued April 7, 1828, m. by: Peyton
Smith April 22, 1828, RUTHERFORD Co.

ALLEN, William to Eliza Marshall - issued July 19, 1819, Bondsman:
Obadiah Finly, WILSON Co.

ALLEN, William to Susannah Chitwood - October 15, 1816, WILLIAMSON Co.

ALLEN, William to Margaret Ault - February 16, 1815, KNOX Co.

ALLEN, William to Nancy Duvall - issued January 23, 1812, Bondsman:
Thomas Howel, SUMNER Co.

ALLEN, William to Elon Harmon - issued August 31, 1790, Bondsman:
James Hays, SUMNER Co.

ALLEN, Wiley to Susan Whitehead - issued September 16, 1830, Bondsman:
Joseph Ligon, WILSON Co.

ALLEN, W. W. to Mary A. E. Sadler - issued December 19, 1840, m. by:
Jno. W. Hannah December 22, 1840, DAVIDSON Co.

ALLEN, W. H. to Mary C. Wright - issued September 3, 1846, Bondsman:
George P. Allen, m. by: Joseph E. Douglass, M. G., September 3,
1846, MONTGOMERY Co.

ALLEN, W. P. to Nannie V. Hackner - issued November 23, 1872, returned
January 10, 1873 not executed Clem Arledge, Clk, FRANKLIN Co.

ALLEN, Thomas J. to Martha Ann Dickson - issued December 23, 1843,
m. by: Charles Brook, M. G., December 24, 1843, STEWART Co.

ALLEN, Thomas H. to Eliner T. Angel - issued March 6, 1858, m. by:
H. W. Carroll, J. P., March 7, 1858, COFFEE Co.

ALLEN, Thomas to Elizabeth Morgan - April 27, 1839, JEFFERSON Co.

ALLEN, Susan A. to S. B. Foster - BEDFORD Co.

ALLEN, Stephen to Sarah Jett - issued February 14, 1851, FRANKLIN Co.

ALLEN, Sophia to J. H. Womack - BEDFORD Co.

ALLEN, Shadrack to Pauline Epps - issued July 9, 1840, m. by: Jesse Cox,
M. G., June 9, 1840, DAVIDSON Co.

ALLEN, Samuel to Sally Gillespie - issued May 18, 1825, m. by:
J. A. Mabry, J. P., May 19, 1825, KNOX Co.

ALLEN, Sampson to Polly Somers - issued July 10, 1811, Bondsman:
William Makwell, WILSON Co.

ALLEN, Robert C. to Susan F. Jarratt - issued December 13, 1837,
Bondsman: Claibourn Jarratt, m. by: G. H. Bransford, M. B.,
WILSON Co.

ALLEN, Robert to Martha Kerr - March 19, 1791, GREENE Co.

ALLEN, Richard W. to Sally Brown - issued March 22, 1830, Bondsman:
Levin Bradley, m. by: Frances Johnston, M. G., March 22, 1830,
SUMNER Co.

ALLEN, Reuben to Darky Cobb - issued November 18, 1834, Bondsman:
William Underwood, m. by: J. P. Shapard November 25, 1834,
RUTHERFORD Co.

ALLENSWORTH, D. J. to Elizabeth P. Jones - issued August 17, 1849,
Bondsman: Calvin Anderson, m. by: J. C. Bryan, J. P., August 17,
1848, MONTGOMERY Co.

ALLENSWORTH, Jackson to Joanna B. Fauntleroy - issued March 2, 1854,
Bondsman: Jospeh M. Fauntleroy, m. by: J. M. Bennett, M. G.,
March 2, 1854, MONTGOMERY Co.

ALLEY, Alfred to Nancy Forehand - issued January 19, 1839, m. by:
E. Crosswell, J. P., January 20, 1839, STEWART Co.

ALLEY, Benjamin to Susan Mitchell - issued May 5, 1841, m. by:
E. M. Patterson, J. P., May 6, 1841, DAVIDSON Co.

ALLEY, Ezekiel T. to Rebecca Webb - issued August 28, 1834, Bondsman:
Phineas Parker, m. by: J. Higgins, J. P., September 9, 1824,
RUTHERFORD Co.

ALLEY, Fielding to Susanna Bradley - issued January 23, 1825, m. by:
Samuel Cothran, J. P., January 23, 1825, SUMNER Co.

ALLEY, Henry to Frances Stevens - issued September 28, 1863, Bondsmen:
H. R. Brown, Jos, H. Thompson, Clk. per M. E. W. Dunaway, D. Clk.,
BEDFORD Co.

ALLEY, Isom P. to Mary C. Grills - issued March 14, 1826, Bondsman:
Harrison Smith, m. by: James Y. Crawford, M. G., March 14, 1826,
Witness: Wm. Swan, KNOX Co.

ALLEY, Jackson to Louisa Perkins - m. by: John Hobdy, J. P., May 30,
1835, SUMNER Co.

ALLEY, James to Nancy A. Brown - issued May 4, 1838, m. by: John Nugent,
J. P., May 4, 1838, FRANKLIN Co.

ALLEY, James A. to Elizabeth A. Hooper - issued August 23, 1841, m. by:
William L. Perry, J. P. R. C., ROBERTSON Co.

ALLEY, John to Margaret Johnson - February 13, 1786, Security:
David Hickey, GREENE Co.

ALLEY, John to Phebe Haley - issued January 3, 1838, m. by: P. M. Mazey,
Esq., January 4, 1838, DAVIDSON Co.

ALLEY, Jno. W. to Lucinda Smith - issued January 10, 1826, m. by:
Jno. Bayless, J. P., January 11, 1826, KNOX Co.

ALLEY, R. H. to M. E. Ogg - issued October 13, 1857, m. by:
Robert Williams, M. G., October 15, 1857, ROBERTSON Co.

ALLEY, R. H. to Sarah J. Keller - issued November 14, 1859, m. by:
Jerome B. Anderson, M. G., November 15, 1859, ROBERTSON Co.

ALLEY, R. H. to Aamanda L. Watkins - issued January 25, 1844, Bondsman:
Thomas S. Trigg, MONTGOMERY Co.

ALLEY, Vardeman to Martha Thomas - issued December 12. 1838, m. by:
N. B. Butler, J. P., December 13, 1838, DAVIDSON Co.

ALLEY, William to Judah Street - issued December 24, 1812, Bondsman:
Robert Cato, SUMNER Co.

ALLEY, William to Amanda Norton - July 15, 1858, m. by: Wm. Peaton,
J. P., GILES Co.

ALLIN, Edwin to Sarah Allin - December 22, 1801, Surety: Wm. Gaut,
BLOUNT Co.

ALLIN, George to Sally Johnson - issued August 28, 1806, Bondsman:
Solomon Harpole, WILSON Co.

ALLIN, Rewben to Jemima Lewis - issued January 21, 1811, Bondsman:
William Lewis, WILSON Co.

ALLISON, Agnes to William Henry - GREENE Co.

ALLISON, Alexander to Madaline T. Allcorn - issued June 5, 1832,
Bondsman: Wm. Martin, m. by: George Donnell, WILSON Co.

ALLISON, David to Isabella McConnell - issued September 12, 1822, m. by:
Peter Nance, J. P., September 12, 1822, KNOX Co.

ALLISON, David to Isabella McConnell - issued September 12, 1822,
Bondsman: Andrew Willoughby, KNOX Co.

ALLISON, Elizabeth to Hugh Blake - GREENE Co.

ALLISON, Fountain S. to Maris L. Emmit - issued May 12, 1839, m. by:
Uriah Young, J. P., ROBERTSON Co.

ALLISON, John to Vise Reeves - October 2, 1797, Security: Henry
Farnsworth, GREENE Co.

ALLISON, John to Meome (Naomi) Gellaspie - October 6, 1815, WILLIAMSON Co.

ALLISON, John to Margaret Bond - issued March 16, 1827, Bondsman:
John Bone, WILSON Co.

ALLISON, Joseph to Eliza Thompson - issued September 5, 1854, m. by:
W. C. Handley, J. P., September 10, 1854, FRANKLIN Co.

ALLISON, Matthias H. to Mary Ann Howland - issued August 31, 1829,
Bondsman: John F. Howland, RUTHERFORD Co.

ALLISON, Robert to Jenny Thompason - March 22, 1802, Surety:
Wm. Armstrong, BLOUNT Co.

ALLISON, Sam'l to Malinda Florida - issued November 20, 1827, Bondsman:
John Bond, m. by: Jeremiah McMinn November 27, 1827, WILSON Co.

ALLISON, Thomas to Nancy Ogelvie - October 26, 1811, WILLIAMSON Co.

ALLISON, Thomas to Nancy Jane Adams - issued January 18, 1855, m. by:
James Stevens, M. G., January 18, 1855, COFFEE Co.

ALLISON, Timothy M. to Sarah M. Ewing - issued January 21, 1840,
Bondsman: Thos. Baird, m. by: Joshua Lester, M. G., January 23,
1840, WILSON Co.

ALLISON, Wm. to Charity Upshaw - December 3, 1808, WILLIAMSON Co.

ALLISON, William to Sally McKinny - issued August 20, 1821, m. by:
John Haynie, M. G., August 20, 1821, KNOX Co.

ALLMAN, Nathan T. to Martha Mann - issued August 31, 1841, STEWART Co.

ALLMAN, Richard to Florida Lowry - issued June 19, 1836, Bondsman:
Isaac Miller, m. by: Geo. A. Sublett, J. P., June 19, 1836,
RUTHERFORD Co.

ALLMAN, Solomon to Elizabeth Puckett - issued July 28, 1824, Bondsman:
Thomas Allman, WILSON Co.

ALLMAN, William to Susanah R. Mitchell - issued December 8, 1817,
Bondsman: John H. Paskel, WILSON Co.

ALLRED, H. to Missouri Little - issued January 15, 1867, m. by:
W. W. Hawkins, M. G., January 16, 1867, FRANKLIN Co.

ALLRED, Reubin J. to Margaret Wilson - issued December 15, 1855, m. by:
Samuel Umbarger, J. P., December 16, 1855, COFFEE Co.

ALLS, Benjamin to Harah Shockley - issued December 18, 1856, VAN BUREN Co.

ALLSBROOKS, G. W. to Mary J. Hunt - issued September 25, 1848, m. by:
Jo M. Dye, J. P., September 26, 1848, MONTGOMERY Co.

ALLSBROOK, John to Polly Booker - issued January 8, 1851, m. by:
M. C. Banks, J. P., ROBERTSON Co.

ALLSOP, Randolph to Elizabeth O. Danniel - issued July 17, 1802,
    Bondsman: Robert Allsop, Witness: Luke Lea. Junr., GRAINGER Co.

ALLSTALL, Robert to Sally Long - issued February 19, 1814, Bondsman:
    Nicholas Beans, GRAINGER Co.

ALLSUP, James to Abigal Carmichal - issued August 17, 1797, Bondsman:
    Martin Ashburn, GRAINGER Co.

ALLSUP, James R. to Parthena Harris - issued September 10, 1831,
    Bondsman: William S. Dyer, GRAINGER Co.

ALLSUP, Thomas to Margaret Moore - issued November 9, 1810, Bondsman:
    John McBroom, GRAINGER Co.

ALLSUPT, John to Prudence Henderson - issued October 6, 1813, Bondsman:
    David Allsupt, SUMNER Co.

ALLY, Alexander to Rachel Binkley - issued August 6, 1842, m. by:
    S. Brewer August 7, 1842, ROBERTSON Co.

ALLY, Henderson to Elizabeth Perdue - m. by: Jos. McGlothlin, J. P.,
    January 14, 1835, SUMNER Co.

ALLY, James to Mary Brake - issued May 18, 1848, m. by:
    Allen McCaskill, J. P., May 18, 1848, STEWART Co.

ALMAN, John W. to Martha Allen - issued January 11, 1855, m. by:
    D. B. Muse, J. P., January 11, 1855, FRANKLIN Co.

ALMON, John L. to Nancy Appleton - issued January 26, 1857, m. by:
    John H. Gammon, M. G., ROBERTSON Co.

ALMON, Robert J. to Delila T. Dilling - issued December 29, 1853,
    Bondsman: May P. Almon, m. by: Uriah Smith, M. G., December 29,
    1853, MONTGOMERY Co.

ALMOND, Thaddeus S. to Mary Ann Gordon - issued March 21, 1839, m. by:
    D. Judd, L. E., March 21, 1839, DAVIDSON Co.

ALMOND, Thomas to Margaret Ellison - issued September 28, 1824,
    Bondsman: Thomas Almond, m. by: Nan. Overall, M. G., September 30,
    1824, WILSON Co.

ALONZO, Byan to N. I. Boyd - issued December 24, 1861, m. by: E. Burr,
    J. P., ROBERTSON Co.

ALCON, Noah to Mary J. Francisco - issued September 1, 1845, Bondsman:
    R. W. Hamilton, m. by: D. L. Godsey, Min., September 1, 1845,
    MEIGS Co.

ALSBROOK, Thomas to Lucina Daubs - issued July 17, 1841, m. by:
    H. Forey, J. P., ROBERTSON Co.

ALSBROOK, Thomas to Tennessee Owens - issued April 13, 1848, m. by:
    C. Grymes, J. P., April 13, 1848, DICKSON Co.

ALSBROOK, Thomas to J. A. Huddleston - issued April 12, 1859, m. by:
    A. Rose, J. P., ROBERTSON Co.

ALSBROOK, Wm. R. to Lucinda Webb - issued November 27, 1844, m. by:
    P. Martin, M. G., November 28, 1844, ROBERTSON Co.

ALSBROOK, Willie B. to Francis W. Connell - issued September 2, 1845,
    m. by: Thomas Martin September 3, ROBERTSON Co.

ALSBROOKS, David L. to Adaline A. Green - issued May 9, 1840, m. by:
    Banjamin Rawls, G. M., May 10, 1840, ROBERTSON Co.

ALSOP, William to Elizabeth Eades - issued April 10, 1823, m. by:
H. Robinson, J. P., April 10, 1823, RUTHERFORD Co.

ALSPAUGH, Henry P. S. to Nancy R. Reeves - issued September 3, 1853,
m. by: R. C. Smith, J. P., September 4, 1853, FRANKLIN Co.

ALSTON, James to Nancy Swansey - November 18, 1816, WILLIAMSON Co.

ALSUP, Adolph H. to Martha S. Manson - issued November 4, 1864,
Bondsman: Thos. W. McCulloch, m. by: J. T. Hughes November 8,
1854, MONTGOMERY Co.

ALSUP, Daniel N. to Susan Alsup - issued July 12, 1837, Bondsman:
James D. Gollady, WILSON Co.

ALSUP, Drury to Tabitha Brown - January 27, 1806, WILLIAMSON Co.

ALSUP, Gideon M. to Sarah A. C. Bryan - issued February 24, 1840,
Bondsman: Thos J. Baird, m. by: Joshua Lester, M. B., February 27,
1840, WILSON Co.

ALSUP, Henry to Mary Harris - issued December 14, 1817, Bondsman:
John Brown, m. by: James Moore, J. P., December 24, 1817,
GRAINGER Co.

ALSUP, Hiram to Mourning Alsup - issued April 6, 1835, Bondsman:
Nathan A. Alsup, WILSON Co.

ALSUP, Jeremiah to Lucy Brown - issued November 20, 1823, m. by:
Daniel Webb, M. G., November 20, 1823, SUMNER Co.

ALSUP, Robt. R. to Louis Smith - February 3, 1808, WILLIAMSON Co.

ALSUP, Samuel to Elizabeth Jennings - issued December 26, 1810,
Bondsman: Author Harris, WILSON Co.

ALSUP, Thomas H. to Emily White - issued January 13, 1863, Bondsman:
R. A. Hamsby, m. by: Wm. McMasters, J. P., January 14, 1863,
LAWRENCE Co.

ALSUP, William to Polly Lane - issued October 25, 1820, Bondsman:
Alsup, m. by: Joshua Lester, V. D. M., December 22, 1820, WILSON Co.

ALSUP, William to Morning Hill - issued November 29, 1826, Bondsman:
Solomon Bond, m. by: Jacob Martin, J. P., November 26, 1826,
WILSON Co.

ALSUP, William T. to Frances Byrns - issued March 8, 1840, m. by:
H. W. Pickett, M. G., March 12, 1840, WILSON Co.

ALVIS, William C. to Lucinda Simmons - issued October 11, 1836,
Bondsman: Abraham Muce, m. by: Taylor G. Gilliam December 11,
1836, SUMNER Co.

ALY (?), Solomon to Maria W. Luttrell - issued December 29, 1829,
Bondsman: Geo. J. Jones, m. by: J. Lewis January 5, 1830,
Witness: Wm. Swan, KNOX Co.

AMASON, John G. to Francis Nowlin - issued February 6, 1863, Bondsman:
Wm. Nowlin, Jos. H. Thompson, Clk. per James H. Neil, Dep. Clk.,
BEDFORD Co.

AMBROSE, Isreal to Gilly Wright - issued February 11, 1806, Bondsman:
John Wright, SUMNER Co.

AMES, Hardy to Polly Ridgeway - issued June 19, 1816, Bondsman:
Stephen Sypert, m. by: Abner Hill, M. G., June 20, 1816, WILSON Co.

AMES, Thomas to Elizabeth Aust - issued January 27, 1817, Bondsman:
Elijah Ruttledge, m. by: Abner Hill, M. G., January 29, 1817,
WILSON Co.

AMES, Thomas to Sally Ray - issued March 18, 1825, Bondsman: Harch
Ames, WILSON Co.

AMES, Thomas to Salley Ray - issued March 18, 1826, m. by:
Edward Willis, M. G., March 19, 1826, WILSON Co.

AMES, William to Ann Eagan - issued September 24, 1825, Bondsman:
Hardy Sypert, WILSON Co.

AMICK, A. J. to Jane Call - issued November 27, 1860, m. by:
Wm. W. Conn, M. G., December 6, 1860, COFFEE Co.

AMIX, Mary Ann to Thomas E. Manning - BEDFORD Co.

AMIX, Virginia to James Lawson - BEDFORD Co.

AMOND (?), George to Margaret Shalley - January 8, 1785, Security:
Luke Shalley, GREENE Co.

AMOND, James H. to Susan Vaughan - issued December 27, 1856, m. by:
James Seargent, J. P., December 28, 1856, FRANKLIN Co.

AMOS, Jackson to Elizabeth Musick - issued August 31, 1841, m. by:
W. L. Payne, J. P., ROBERTSON Co.

AMOS, Jesse to Mary Hunt - issued December 24, 1859, m. by:
H. W. Carroll, J. P., December 25, 1859, COFFEE Co.

ANDERSON, A. J. to Mary Westmer (Westner) - issued July 20, 1867,
m. by: W. M. Green July 21, 1867, FRANKLIN Co.

ANDERSON, A. J. S. to Martha J. Tarwaters - issued November 31, 1858,
m. by: L. N. Simpson November 31, 1858, FRANKLIN Co.

ANDERSON, Abram to Betsy Merchant - March 5, 1813, WILLIAMSON Co.

ANDERSON (?), Alexander to Mary Kelsay - January 5, 1797, Security:
Samuel Kelsay, GREENE Co.

ANDERSON, Alfred H. to Margret Finney - issued November 5, 1855, m. by:
Thos. Morris, J. P., November 11, 1855, FRANKLIN Co.

ANDERSON, Allen to Letty McCammon - issued December 21, 1835, Bondsman:
Andrew J. Brown, m. by: Richard Keyhill, J. P., December 22, 1835,
KNOX Co.

ANDERSON, Andrew to Margaret Roberts - issued December 11, 1797,
Bondsman: Henry Roberts, Witness: Joseph Greer, KNOX Co.

ANDERSON, Andrew to Dorkass Clark - issued October 15, 1812, Bondsman:
Wm. Griggs, SUMNER Co.

ANDERSON, Andrew B. to Adaline Dickenson - issued April 17, 1841, m. by:
I. T. Hines, J. P., April 18, 1841, FRANKLIN Co.

ANDERSON, B. F. to Elizabeth Neville - issued August 21, 1867, m. by:
W. W. Elliott, M. G., August 22, 1867, FRANKLIN Co.

ANDERSON, Banister to Betsey Anderson - issued July 10, 1816, Bondsman:
Patrick Anderson, m. by: Joseph T. Williams, J. P., July 11, 1816,
WILSON Co.

ANDERSON, Benjamin H. to Sarah J. Porter - issued July 28, 1853, m. by:
Benjamin Rawls, M. G., July 30, 1853, ROBERTSON Co.

ANDERSON, Charles to Mary Gilliland - issued June 4, 1817, RUTHERFORD Co.

ANDERSON, Charles to Polly Jetton - issued June 4, 1817, m. by:
Jas. S. Jetton, J. P., June 5, 1817, RUTHERFORD Co.

ANDERSON, Charles M. to Mary C. King - issued June 27, 1832, m. by:
V. D. Cowan, J. P., June 28, 1832, RUTHERFORD Co.

ANDERSON, Charles Madison to Elizabeth Vaughn - issued January 27,
1852, Bondsman: Alfred T. Howerton, m. by: J. C. Bryan, J. P.,
January 27, 1852, MONTGOMERY Co.

ANDERSON, D. P. to Mary Cooper - July 17, 1808, WILLIAMSON Co.

ANDERSON, Daniel to Ruth Rew - issued April 10, 1797, Bondsman:
Richard Keyhill, Witness: Hu. Law. White, KNOX Co.

ANDERSON, Daniel to Polly Humphry - issued August 27, 1828, m. by:
Elijah Johnson, J. P., August 28, 1828, KNOX Co.

ANDERSON, Daniel W. to Lucy A. Tiley - issued November 20, 1846,
DICKSON Co.

ANDERSON, David to Dicey Dial - issued August 1, 1867, m. by:
John Nugent, J. P., August 4, 1867, FRANKLIN Co.

ANDERSON, David L. to Nancy E. Woods - issued September 16, 1867,
m. by: Jas. Seargent, J. P., September 16, 1867, FRANKLIN Co.

ANDERSON, E. D. to Laura L. Miller - issued January 13, 1872, FRANKLIN Co.

ANDERSON, Edmund to Sarah Gleaves - issued June 18, 1831, Bondsman:
William P. McClain, WILSON Co.

ANDERSON, Edmund R. to Martha T. Henderson - issued November 20, 1820,
m. by: R. Henderson, V. D. M., November 20, 1820, RUTHERFORD Co.

ANDERSON, Eli H. to Martha Messick - issued February 3, 1857, m. by:
L. Burnum, J. P., February 4, 1857, COFFEE Co.

ANDERSON, Elijah to Harriet Burton - issued September 4, 1848, Bondsman:
Richard Dunlap, MONTGOMERY Co.

ANDERSON, Elizabeth Ann to John Perryman - GREENE Co.

ANDERSON, Emeline to James B. Muse - BEDFORD Co.

ANDERSON, Fancis (Francis) to Emalisa Lowery - issued February 22,
1856, m. by: F. G. Hamleton, J. P., February 22, 1856, VAN BUREN Co.

ANDERSON, Francis S. to Peggy Robinson - issued December 21, 1831,
Bondsman: Joel West, WILSON Co.

ANDERSON, Gabriel to Polly Truot - issued May 23, 1809, Bondsman:
Joshua Anderson, WILSON Co.

ANDERSON, Gabriel to Martha Walker - issued August 9, 1833, Bondsman:
John Burnett, RUTHERFORD Co.

ANDERSON, George to Samantha Smith - issued July 15, 1853, m. by:
Rev. James Watson, M. G., July 18, 1853, FRANKLIN Co.

ANDERSON, George W. to Martha Carter - issued November 30, 1820,
m. by: Cary James, D. M. E. C., November 30, 1820, RUTHERFORD Co.

ANDERSON, George W. to Mary Jane Baggett - issued January 6, 1866,
FRANKLIN Co.

ANDERSON, Henry to Tebitha Angeline Thacker - issued September 13,
1855, m. by: R. W. Casey, J. P., September 13, 1855, COFFEE Co.

ANDERSON, Henry G. to Drucilla C. McCampbell - issued March 6, 1837,
m. by: G. S. White, M. G., March 7, 1837, KNOX Co.

ANDERSON, Hiram to Sarah Hill - issued May 13, 1850, m. by:
J. C. Montgomery, J. P., May 13, 1850, FRANKLIN Co.

ANDERSON, Issac to Polly Rogers - issued October 25, 1816, Bondsman:
William Cantrell, m. by: S. Hunt, J. P., October 25, 1816,
SUMNER Co.

ANDERSON, Isaac to Martha Glass - issued October 7, 1847, DICKSON Co.

ANDERSON, J. R. to E. F. Batts - issued October 23, 1860, m. by:
J. T. W. Davis Minister Gospel, ROBERTSON Co.

ANDERSON, J. R. to Sarah A. Bruce - issued December 14, 1870,
FRANKLIN Co.

ANDERSON, J. W. to M. E. Barnes - issued May 19, 1869, m. by:
Wm. Prince, J. P., May 20, 1869, FRANKLIN Co.

ANDERSON, Jackson to Patsey Pace - issued December 19, 1825, m. by:
Wm. Stanfield December 22, 1825, RUTHERFORD Co.

ANDERSON, Jacob to Agnes Bryan - November 11, 1794, Security:
John Bryan, GREENE Co.

ANDERSON, Jacob M. to Nancy E. Bratton - issued September 11, 1855,
m. by: John G. Biddle, M. G., September 11, 1855, FRANKLIN Co.

ANDERSON, James to Elizabeth Chapman - issued August 13, 1807, Bondsman:
John Crawford, WILSON Co.

ANDERSON, James to Polly Biggs - issued September 13, 1817, Bondsman:
Adam Biggs, SUMNER Co.

ANDERSON, James to Anne Ford - issued November 3, 1818, m. by:
Peter Nance, J. P. K. C., November 5, 1818, KNOX Co.

ANDERSON, James to Rhoda Chumlea - issued January 25, 1827, m. by:
Wm. A. McCampbell January 25, 1827, KNOX Co.

ANDERSON, James to Mary Simpson - issued December 20, 1831, Bondsman:
Wm. Brown, m. by: Michael Davis, J. P., December 22, 1831, Witness:
Wm. Swan, KNOX Co.

ANDERSON, James M. to Sarah A. Kirby - issued October 6, 1832, m. by:
V. D. Cowan, J. P., October 11, 1832, RUTHERFORD Co.

ANDERSON, James to Charlotte E. Old - m. by: S. H. Turner, J. P.,
July 4, 1835, SUMNER Co.

ANDERSON, James to Sarah J. Wagoner - issued August 7, 1858, m. by:
James W. Williams, M. G., August 8, 1858, COFFEE Co.

ANDERSON, James to Susan Clanton - issued April 25, 1862, Bondsmen:
J. F. Taylor, Jos. H. Thompson, Clk. per James H. Neil, Dep. Clk.,
BEDFORD Co.

ANDERSON, James to Malinda Green - issued December 31, 1866, FRANKLIN Co.

ANDERSON, James H. to Cathrine Hammonds - issued May 31, 1869, FRANKLIN
Co.

ANDERSON, James W. to O. Powell - issued June 21, 1861, Bondsmen:
John McManos, Jos. H. Thompson, Clk. per N. F. Thompson, Dep. Clk.,
BEDFORD Co.

ANDERSON, Jo to Sarah A. Dickerson - issued October 1, 1859, m. by:
W. W. Wynn, M. G., October 2, 1859, ROBERTSON Co.

ANDERSON, John to Rachel Roberts - issued December 28, 1792, Bondsman:
Dan'l McDonald, Witness: Chas. McClung, C. K. C., KNOX Co.

ANDERSON, John to Usley Campbell - issued July 12, 1804, Bondsman: Alexander Campbell, GRAINGER Co.

ANDERSON, John to Elizabeth McNair - issued November 11, 1805, m. by: R. Houston, J. P. K. C., KNOX Co.

ANDERSON, John to Charity McPeters - August 26, 1808, MAURY Co.

ANDERSON, John to Ruth Blackley - issued August 16, 1813, Bondsman: James Husk, GRAINGER Co.

ANDERSON, John to Sarah Buckhanan - issued April 2, 1817, Bondsman: Isaac Anderson, m. by: McClarey April 2, 1817, SUMNER Co.

ANDERSON, John to Sally Durham - issued May 1, 1823, Bondsman: Sevier Massey, Witness: Wm. Swan, KNOX Co.

ANDERSON, John to Jane Roane - issued October 23, 1823, Bondsman: Andrew Roane, m. by: John Provine, M. G., WILSON Co.

ANDERSON, John to Nancy Grooms - issued December 24, 1824, Bondsman: William F. Sadler, m. by: Richard Johnson December 24, 1824, SUMNER Co.

ANDERSON, John to Mary Cothern - issued April 16, 1829, Bondsman: Balser Sherley, m. by: J. H. Alsup, J. P., GRAINGER Co.

ANDERSON, John to Nancy Pollard - issued March 26, 1835, Bondsman: James M. Blanton, RUTHERFORD Co.

ANDERSON, John to E. F. Reagen - issued January 7, 1840, m. by: M. Catchings, M. G., FRANKLIN Co.

ANDERSON, John to Polly Hagwood - issued May 18, 1841, m. by: Wm. Garrett, J. P., May 18, 1841, DICKSON Co.

ANDERSON, John to Sarah Ann Bonds - issued February 26, 1848, Bondsman: James Anderson, m. by: Jo Pollard, J. P., February 29, 1848, MONTGOMERY Co.

ANDERSON, John to Mary M. Blackburn - issued December 19, 1855, m. by: James Taylor, M. G., December 20, 1855, COFFEE Co.

ANDERSON, John to Mary Ann Gilliam - issued December 29, 1859, m. by: W. D. Coffey, J. P., December 28, 1859, COFFEE Co.

ANDERSON, John to Elizabeth Winford - issued January 7, 1869, FRANKLIN Co.

ANDERSON, John B. to Nancy Stamps - issued September 19, 1816, Bondsman: William Cantrell, SUMNER Co.

ANDERSON, John F. to Mary Stephens - issued August 27, 1854, m. by: Wm. Prince, J. P., August 27, 1854, FRANKLIN Co.

ANDERSON, John W. to Mary Ann Bass - issued September 21, 1836, m. by: Wilbon R. Winter, J. P., WILSON Co.

ANDERSON, Jonathan to Elizabeth Condon - issued April 14, 1813, Bondsman: David White, SUMNER Co.

ANDERSON, Joseph to Martha Crafford - issued March 13, 1839, m. by: Isaiah Warren March 14, 1839, ROBERTSON Co.

ANDERSON, Joseph to Sina Anderson - issued February 12, 1859, m. by: J. F. McCutchan, Mins., February 15, 1859, COFFEE Co.

ANDERSON, Joseph M. to Mary D. Sypert - issued September 24, 1835, Bondsman: W. M. Hall, m. by: F. G. Ferguson, WILSON Co.

ANDERSON, Joshua to Peggy Thomas - issued February 1, 1809, Bondsman: Henry Thomas, WILSON Co.

ANDERSON, Joshua to Polly Patton - issued April 4, 1807, Bondsman: Thomas Poteat, WILSON Co.

ANDERSON, Levi to Mariah Earp - issued September 12, 1833, Bondsman: Woodfin Nailor, m. by: A. S. Edwards, J. P., September 12, 1833, RUTHERFORD Co.

ANDERSON, Levi to Elizabeth Brown - issued June 25, 1859, m. by: J. A. Brantley, J. P., June 27, 1859, COFFEE Co.

ANDERSON, Lewis to Charlotte Moore - issued December 15, 1840, m. by: John McCutcheon December 17, 1840, FRANKLIN Co.

ANDERSON, M. A. to Julia Calloway - issued December 31, 1843, FRANKLIN Co.

ANDERSON, Mabin to Maria McCall - issued December 4, 1834, m. by: Geo. Donnell, V. D. M., December 4, 1834, SUMNER Co.

ANDERSON, Mansen to Elizabeth A. Taylor - issued February 27, 1861, m. by: J. F. L. Faris, J. P., February 28, 1861, COFFEE Co.

ANDERSON, Marcey to Frances Turner - issued March 29, 1830, Bondsman: Enoch Martin, m. by: Sam'l Lewis, J. P., March 29, 1830, SUMNER Co.

ANDERSON, Marion to Sarah J. Sutton - issued April 12, 1860, m. by: James Taylor, M. G., April 12, 1860, COFFEE Co.

ANDERSON, Martha to John B. Garrett - BEDFORD Co.

ANDERSON, Mary C. to George Englehardt - BEDFORD Co.

ANDERSON, Meeds P. to Martha Bass - issued February 4, 1832, Bondsman: W. P. McClain, m. by: B. Bridges, J. P., February 6, 1832, WILSON Co.

ANDERSON, Milton to Lizzie Miller - issued May 28, 1866, m. by: W. G. Watterson, M. G., May 29, 1866, FRANKLIN Co.

ANDERSON, Minor to Keziah Hopper - issued September 14, 1839, m. by: A. J. Steele September 15, 1839, FRANKLIN Co.

ANDERSON, N. F. to Marinda E. George - issued September 14, 1865, FRANKLIN Co.

ANDERSON, P. L. to Mary Carter - m. by: Rich. Johnson May 8, 1837, SUMNER Co.

ANDERSON, Patrick to Fanny Chandler - issued May 13, 1812, Bondsman: Richard Anderson, WILSON Co.

ANDERSON, Philip to Polly Macnatt - issued February 24, 1806, Bondsman: Levin Macnatt, WILSON Co.

ANDERSON, Pleasant H. to Catherine Cheek - issued __ 13, 1829, m. by: Ed Edwards October 14, 1829, ROBERTSON Co.

ANDERSON, Pling to Mary May - issued July 30, 1827, Bondsman: William Parker, m. by: Stephen R. Roberts, J. P., July 30, 1827, SUMNER Co.

ANDERSON, R. C. to Josaphine Holland - issued November 21, 1857, m. by: H. H. Orndorff, J. P., ROBERTSON Co.

ANDERSON, Robt. to Rebecca Wilkins - July 14, 1809, WILLIAMSON Co.

ANDERSON, Robert to Nancy Sands - issued December 1, 1810, Bondsman: John Roberts, WILSON Co.

ANDERSON, Robert to Permelia Winham - issued February 27, 1817, Bondsman:
Thos. Scurry, m. by: James Douglass, J. P., February 27, 1817,
SUMNER Co.

ANDERSON, Robert to Malisy Jones - issued June 1, 1829, Bondsman:
William Young, WILSON Co.

ANDERSON, Robert to Mary Smith - issued November 30, 1830, Bondsman:
William Pate, m. by: Peyton Smith December 2, 1830, RUTHERFORD Co.

ANDERSON, Robert M. to Catharine McCampbell - issued March 31, 1825,
m. by: Isaac Anderson, V. D. M., March 31, 1825, KNOX Co.

ANDERSON, Sampson to Elizabeth Hinton - issued July 23, 1827, Bondsman:
Albert G. Holmes, m. July 23, 1827, SUMNER Co.

ANDERSON, Samuel to Jennet Kelsy - February 25, 1800, Security:
James Anderson, GREENE Co.

ANDERSON, Samuel to Benthing Lowe - April 3, 1800, KNOX Co.

ANDERSON, Sam'l to Barthiny Lowe - issued April 3, 1811, Bondsman:
Henry Porter, KNOX Co.

ANDERSON, Samuel to Jan Bellmay - issued October 31, 1811, Bondsman:
Albert Holmes, SUMNER Co.

ANDERSON, Samuel to Ann Clark - issued August 25, 1812, Bondsman:
Andrew Anderson, SUMNER Co.

ANDERSON, Samuel to Elizabeth Burrus - issued January 21, 1819, Bondsman:
Henry D. Jamison, m. by: Robert Henderson January 21, 1819,
RUTHERFORD Co.

ANDERSON, Sam'l R. to Fanny Parish - issued February 20, 1811, Bondsman:
George Still, WILSON Co.

ANDERSON, Samuel Y. to Peggy McCurdy - August 14, 1811, Bondsman:
Andrew Boyd, MAURY Co.

ANDERSON, Sandridge T. to Mary E. Norton - issued September 7, 1858,
m. by: W. G. Pirtle, Esq., September 9, 1858, COFFEE Co.

ANDERSON, T. D. W. to Sarah F. Little - issued October 7, 1866, m. by:
J. P. Anderson, J. P., October 7, 1866, FRANKLIN Co.

ANDERSON, Thomas to Elizabeth McKorkle - issued March 13, 1809, Bondsman:
John H. Bowen, SUMNER Co.

ANDERSON, Thomas to Elizabeth Harris - issued July 24, 1814, Bondsman:
Richard Harris, GRAINGER Co.

ANDERSON, Thomas to Nancy Hartley - September 10, 1816, WILLIAMSON Co.

ANDERSON, Thomas to Elizabeth Duncan - issued May 6, 1852, m. by:
J. C. Montgomery, J. P., May 7, 1852, FRANKLIN Co.

ANDERSON, Thomas C. to Aseneth McMurry - issued June 18, 1834, Bondsman:
Hugh B. Hill, WILSON Co.

ANDERSON, Thomas D. W. to Elender Ferrell - issued April 21, 1858,
FRANKLIN Co.

ANDERSON, Thompson to Mary S. Johnson - issued July 31, 1834, ·Bondsman:
Geo. W. Smith, WILSON Co.

ANDERSON, Thornsberry to Fredonia Gates - issued January 29, 1848,
Bondsman: John H. Anderson, m. by: Jo. Pollard, J. P., January 30,
1848, MONTGOMERY Co.

ANDERSON, Uriah to Milly Jones - issued March 9, 1790, Bondsman: Robert Jones, SUMNER Co.

ANDERSON, W. G. S. to Queenie Gordon - issued November 23, 1863, Bondsman: E. E. McClain, LAWRENCE Co.

ANDERSON, W. J. to Ginory Grise - issued January 7, 1860, m. by: John W. Smith, J. P., January 8, 1860, ROBERTSON Co.

ANDERSON, W. M. to M. A. Shavers - issued July 23, 1874, FRANKLIN Co.

ANDERSON, W. S. to E. P. Blackburn - issued October 17, 1863, Bondsmen: C. B. Davis, Jos. H. Thompson, Clk. per M. E. W. Dunaway, D. Clk., BEDFORD Co.

ANDERSON, William to Betsey Jones - issued November 23, 1791, Bondsman: Stephen Anderson, SUMNER Co.

ANDERSON, William to Elizabeth Greenwood - issued March 4, 1807, Bondsman: Urica Anderson, WILSON Co.

ANDERSON, William to Annie Smith - issued May 3, 1814, Bondsman: William Stansberry, GRAINGER Co.

ANDERSON, William to Sophia Davis - issued January 6, 1815, Bondsman: Mathew Nelson, KNOX Co.

ANDERSON, William to Elizabeth Thompson - March 24, 1817, WILLIAMSON Co.

ANDERSON, William to Carolin Cathey - issued December 10, 1838, m. by: William Ellis, J. P., December 11, 1838, STEWART Co.

ANDERSON, William to Elizabeth Smallman - issued January 30, 1849, m. by: O. Denton, M. G., January 31, 1849, VAN BUREN Co.

ANDERSON, William to Lutilda Chesser - issued December 13, 1852, m. by: J. S. Hollis, J. P., December 14, 1852, ROBERTSON Co.

ANDERSON, William A. to Martha Ann Stevens - issued May 24, 1854, m. by: W. P. Harris, J. P., May 24, 1854, COFFEE Co.

ANDERSON, William B. to Elizabeth Collins - August 28, 1850, m. by: N. Hays, J. P., GILES Co.

ANDERSON, Wm. J. to Mary B. Childress - issued December 24, 1835, Bondsman: Anderson Burnett, m. by: H. Lindsay, M. G., December 26, 1835, KNOX Co.

ANDERSON, William J. to Sarah Sexton - issued March 16, 1847, m. by: John Randle, J. P., STEWART Co.

ANDERSON, William R. to Dicy Adaline Lewis - issued June 11, 1853, Bondsman: Wm. J. Lewis, m. by: T. H. Batson, J. P., June 12, 1853, MONTGOMERY Co.

ANDERSON, William T. to M. A. Rawls - issued August 26, 1860, m. by: J. B. Anderson, M. G., August 27, 1860, ROBERTSON Co.

ANDERSON, Willis to Elizabeth Kerly - issued April 7, 1830, Bondsman: Sam'l Anderson, m. by: Elijah Johnson, J. P., April 8, 1830, Witness: Wm. Swan, KNOX Co.

ANDERTON, John W. to Mary T. Heath - issued January 19, 1861, Bondsman: G. W. Heath, Jos. H. Thompson, Clk, m. by: John H. Holt, M. G., BEDFORD Co.

ANDERTON, William T. to Amanda Spears - issued May 3, 1873, FRANKLIN Co.

ANDES, Regina to George Trobough - GREENE Co.

ANDRES, John to Selain B. Bailiss - May 27, 1799, Surety:
    Washw. Snider, BLOUNT Co.

ANDREW, Alex to Mary Ann Conoway - issued December 25, 1840, DAVIDSON Co.

ANDREW, Peterson to Elizabeth Edwards - issued June 25, 1838, m. by:
    William Stringfellow, J. P., March 26, 1838, DAVIDSON Co.

ANDREWS, A. J. to Martha J. Tarwaters - issued November 3, 1858,
    FRANKLIN Co.

ANDREWS, Ananias to Sally McCrady - April 3, 1808, WILLIAMSON Co.

ANDREWS, Andrew S. to Elizabeth H. Andrews - December 18, 1816,
    WILLIAMSON Co.

ANDREWS, Benjamin to Polly Parker - issued May 22, 1827, Bondsman:
    James Naylor, WILSON Co.

ANDREWS, Ebenezer to Syntha C. Clifton - issued Dec. 20, 1830, Bondsman:
    Simpson Organ, m. December 22, 1830, WILSON Co.

ANDREWS, Goodrich to Aley B. Tarver - issued July 20, 1824, Bondsman:
    G. B. Andrews, WILSON Co.

ANDREWS, James to Elizabeth McDaniel - issued January 29, 1819, Bondsman:
    Robert Sims, WILSON Co.

ANDREWS, James to Elizabeth McDaniel - issued January 29, 1819, Bondsman:
    John Allen, m. by: Wm. L. Alexander, J. P., January 29, 1819,
    SUMNER Co.

ANDREWS, James M. to Elizabeth Stanfill - issued July 21, 1841,
    STEWART Co.

ANDREWS, John to Mary Harris - issued April 12, 1838, m. by: James
    Wilson, J. P., April 12, 1838, STEWART Co.

ANDREWS, Jones to Lucy Lanier - September 17, 1816, WILLIAMSON Co.

ANDREWS, Pernal H. to Susan Spears - issued March 16, 1830, Bondsman:
    G. A. Wilson, m. by: John Seay, M. G., March 17, 1830, WILSON Co.

ANDREWS, Purnal H. to Emiline Donnell - issued December 4, 1835,
    Bondsman: R. J. Andrews, m. by: B. Pyland, M. G., December 9,
    1835, WILSON Co.

ANDREWS, R. C. to Levina Baker - issued February 12, 1842, m. by:
    Wm. S. Smith, M. G., FRANKLIN Co.

ANDREWS, Rowland G. to Polly M. Sullivan - issued August 11, 1829,
    Bondsman: Stephen L. Hearn, m. by: Wilson Hearn, M. G., WILSON Co.

ANDREWS, Sam'l to Kitty Dunnagan - May 23, 1812, WILLIAMSON Co.

ANDREWS, Samuel W. to Susanna Brookman - issued January 15, 1842,
    DAVIDSON Co.

ANDREWS, Tapley to Nancy Ragsdale - February 13, 1809, WILLIAMSON Co.

ANDREWS, Walkers G. to Margaret ___ - issued November 4, 1835, Bondsman:
    E. R. Stewart, m. by: M. T. Cartwright, J. P., November 5, 1835,
    WILSON Co.

ANDREWS, Wilbon to Martha Shanks - issued October 17, 1837, Bondsman:
    R. G. Andrews, m. by: B. T. Mabry, L. E. C., October 18, 1837,
    WILSON Co.

ANDREWS, William to Nancy Grimes - February 22, 1813, WILLIAMSON Co.

ANDREWS, William to Elizabeth Stephens - November 18, 1816,
    WILLIAMSON Co.

ANDREWS, William M. to Elizabeth Silliman - issued March 19, 1828,
    Bondsman: George D. Moore, m. by: Wilson Hearn, M. G., March 20,
    1828, WILSON Co.

ANDREWS, William W. to Emily E. Summerhill - issued August 24, 1833,
    m. by: Jacob S. Hearn, M. G., August 26, 1833, WILSON Co.

ANGEL, James L. to Catherine Campbell - issued October 25, 1857,
    m. by: H. W. Carroll, J. P., October 25, 1857, COFFEE Co.

ANGEL, John to Polly Shaver - issued December 13, 1819, Bondsman:
    Enos Harper, SUMNER Co.

ANGEL, John J. to Azubah M. Taft - issued September 20, 1847, m. by:
    Wm. Reeves, J. P., September 21, 1847, FRANKLIN Co.

ANGEL, W. W. to Delany Love - m. by: L. B. Canard April 19, 1838,
    SUMNER Co.

ANGEL, Walthett to Polly Robertson - issued February 15, 1819, Bondsman:
    Thos. Murrey, SUMNER Co.

ANGLEA, James to Susannah Briley - issued July 3, 1824, Bondsman:
    Thomas Jourden, SUMNER Co.

ANGLIN, Aaron to Hannah McGee - issued January 26, 1819, Bondsman:
    Zachariah Hutchings, WILSON Co.

ANGLIN, John to Elizabeth Carver - issued September 1, 1809, Bondsman:
    Aaron Anglin, WILSON Co.

ANGLIN, Peyton to Malinda Couch - issued March 26, 1835, Bondsman:
    Anderson Anglin, RUTHERFORD Co.

ANGLIN, Thomas to Edith Culver - issued December 21, 1824, Bondsman:
    David W. Anglin, m. by: James Sandford December 21, 1824,
    RUTHERFORD Co.

ANGLIN, Thompson W. to Nancy J. Smith - issued June 11, 1846, Bondsman:
    Wm. M. Shelton, m. by: T. Ramey, J. P., June 11, 1836, MONTGOMERY Co.

ANGLIN, W. W. to Nancy Edwards - issued May 16, 1845, m. by:
    Rev. Sam'l White May 8, 1845, STEWART Co.

ANGLIN, William to Elizabeth Sheppard - issued December 21, 1814,
    Bondsman: Aaron Anglin, WILSON Co.

ANGLIN, William to Susannah Hay - issued August 6, 1842, DICKSON Co.

ANTHONY, Danuel to Sarah Thacker - issued November 20, 1856, m. by:
    M. A. Carden, J. P., November 20, 1856, COFFEE Co.

ANTHONY, Elizabeth to George Smith - GREENE Co.

ANTHONY, George to Nancy Borrin - issued July 25, 1827, Bondsman:
    Francis Borrin, m. by: Wm. Hobdy, J. P., July 25, 1827, SUMNER Co.

ANTHONY, Henry to Amelia Shy - issued January 21, 1825, Bondsman:
    Levi Shy, SUMNER Co.

ANTHONY, Jacob to Evaline A. Graham - issued April 11, 1825, Bondsman:
    Wm. McCullock, m. April 11, 1825, SUMNER Co.

ANTHONY, John D. to Mary Ann Dinty - issued March 27, 1830, Bondsman:
    David Bell, m. by: I. Lewis March 28, 1830, KNOX Co.

ANTHONY, John G. to Mahala D. German - March 2, 1830, WILLIAMSON Co.

ANTHONY, N. S. to Nannie C. Osborn - issued March 10, 1874, m. by:
R. A. Overby, J. P., March 12, 1874, FRANKLIN Co.

ANTHONY, Philip Jr. to Athalana Waggoner - issued February 7, 1838,
m. by: C. G. McPherson February 8, 1838, DAVIDSON Co.

ANTHONY, R. E. to B. W. Holder - issued December 23, 1863, Bondsman:
J. M. Buckaloo, Jos. H. Thompson, Clk., m. December 23, 1863,
BEDFORD Co.

ANTHONY, Stanford to Sarah Holder - issued September 12, 1843, m. by:
J. Byrom, J. P., September 12, 1843, FRANKLIN Co.

ANTHONY, William to Jane B. Warshall - issued June 11, 1817, m. by:
John Wiseman, M. G., June 11, 1817, SUMNER Co.

APPERSON, Edward to Sara M. Lane - issued December 2, 1852, Bondsman:
Wm. Whitlow, m. by: N. F. Trice, J. P., December 2, 1852,
MONTGOMERY Co.

APPERSON, George to Elisa Cole - issued May 9, 1826, Bondsman:
Edward White, m. by: Dnl. Moser, J. P., May 10, 1826, WILSON Co.

APPERSON, John B. to Susan A. Pollard - Bondsman: Jno. L. Wills,
MONTGOMERY Co.

APPLETON, James to Priscilla Miles - issued May 29, 1843, DAVIDSON Co.

APPLETON, James to Sarah J. Traughber - issued December 24, 1859,
m. by: Benjamin Gambill, J. P., December 27, 1859, ROBERTSON Co.

APPLING, Wm. to Mary Ann G. Nemo - issued December 19, 1829, Bondsman:
James Anderson, m. by: Seaton H. Turner, J. P., December 19, 1829,
SUMNER Co.

ARBUCKLE, Joseph to Lewhanna Clarke - issued September 21, 1822, m. by:
David Gordon September 22, 1822, RUTHERFORD Co.

ARBUCKLE, Ralston to Elizabeth Johns - issued June 17, 1837, Bondsman:
Jackson Wallace, m. by: Jordan Williford, J. P., June 18, 1837,
RUTHERFORD Co.

ARBUCKLE, William to Mary E. Harris - issued August 6, 1831, Bondsman:
D. N. Berry, WILSON Co.

ARCHER, Hezikiah to Patsey Mitchell - issued September 19, 1818,
Bondsman: James Nickens, WILSON Co.

ARCHER, Ichabed to Ann Eliza White - issued May 3, 1836, m. by:
M. Woollen, J. P., WILSON Co.

ARCHER, James B. T. to Isabella Speer - December 2, 1853, m. by:
Robert Caldwell, V. D. M., GILES Co.

ARCHER, Josiah to Gracy Burgess - issued March 7, 1831, Bondsman:
James N. King, m. by: W. Smith, J. P., March 7, 1831, SUMNER Co.

ARCHER, Samuel (a free man of color) to Elizabeth Parker (a free woman
of color) - issued January 12, 1838, Bondsman: William Sypert,
WILSON Co.

ARCHER, Samuel to Elizabeth Parker - issued January 13, 1838, Bondsman:
Joel Richardson, m. by: A. B. Duval January 13, 1838, SUMNER Co.

ARCHEY, D. A. to Louisa S. Allen - issued October 10, 1854, m. by:
Robert Williams, G. M., October 16, 1854, ROBERTSON Co.

ARCHEY, John to Sarah Claxton - issued January 16, 1806, Bondsman:
Josiah Kidwell, m. by: Henry Boatman, J. P., GRAINGER Co.

ARKINS, Reuben to Nancy Wilson - issued September 22, 1846, STEWART Co.

ARLEDGE, Clement to Eliza M. Roseborough - issued January 20, 1853,
m. by: W. Denson, J. P., January 20, 1853, FRANKLIN Co.

ARLEDGE, Coleman to Ann Campbell - issued November 3, 1851, m. by:
Wiley Denson, J. P., November 4, 1831, FRANKLIN Co.

ARLEDGE, Thomas to Mary Lefeber - issued December 9, 1869, m. by:
M. B. Clements, M. G., December 9, 1869, FRANKLIN Co.

ARLEDGE, Tillman to Martha Green - issued October 29, 1842, m. by:
A. J. Steel, M. G., October 30, 1842, FRANKLIN Co.

ARLEDGE, Tillman to Ellen Mason - issued July 10, 1855, m. by:
Wiley Denson, J. P., July 10, 1855, FRANKLIN Co.

ARLINGTON, George to Mary Ann Booton - issued January 10, 1840,
DAVIDSON Co.

ARMFIELD, R. G. to Betsey McDaniel - m. by: W. P. Rowles May 23, 1837,
SUMNER Co.

ARMINETT, Wm. to Elmira Wind - issued February 5, 1851, Bondsman:
D. Potter, MONTGOMERY Co.

ARMSTEAD, Wm. B. to Robena Woods - issued February 22, 1843, m. by:
J. T. Edgar February 22, 1843, DAVIDSON Co.

ARMSTRONG, Aaron to Elizabeth Bounds - issued February 3, 1819, Bondsman:
Moses Armstrong, m. by: Alexander McMillan February 4, 1819, KNOX Co.

ARMSTRONG, Abner to Sally Young - issued April 27, 1813, m. by:
Thomas Calhoon, V. D. M., April 28, 1813, WILSON Co.

ARMSTRONG, Addison W. to Nancy McMillan - March 21, KNOX Co.

ARMSTRONG, Addison W. to Nancy McMillan - issued March 26, 1825, m. by:
R. Houston March 22, 1825, KNOX Co.

ARMSTRONG, Alexander to Margaret McCollum - December 11, 1795, Security:
John Kennedy, GREENE Co.

ARMSTRONG, Alexander to Martha Merryman - issued July 17, 1834, m. by:
Wm. Craighead, J. P., July, 1834, KNOX Co.

ARMSTRONG, Alfred W. to Margaret Faulkner - issued November 15, 1836,
Bondsman: Wm. E. Cocke, m. by: J. E. Monson, J. P., GRAINGER Co.

ARMSTRONG, Archibald C. to Sally Reddict - issued January 23, 1819,
Bondsmen: Jas. Harrison and Nathaniel Prince, SUMNER Co.

ARMSTRONG, Benjamin to Nancy Mitchell - issued October 8, 1821, Bondsman:
Benjamin Mitchell, m. by: Jas. Moore, J. P., October 8, 1821,
GRAINGER Co.

ARMSTRONG, Benjamin to Nancy Bratwell - issued December 18, 1824,
Bondsman: Henry Johns, GRAINGER Co.

ARMSTRONG, Daniel B. to Mary Cook - issued October 15, 1846, m. by:
D. B. Kelley, J. P., October 15, 1846, FRANKLIN Co.

ARMSTRONG, David to Mary J. Miles - issued September 25, 1854,
FRANKLIN Co.

ARMSTRONG, David H. to Angaline C. Haynes - issued July 9, 1853,
Bondsman: A. Smith, m. by: Wilie Smith, J. P., July 10, 1853,
MONTGOMERY Co.

ARMSTRONG, Drury P. to Amelia Houston - issued February 17, 1823, m. by: James McMillan, J. P., February 18, 1823, KNOX Co.

ARMSTRONG, Eli to Louisa Harrison - issued February 1, 1845, m. by: W. R. Elliston, J. P., February 1, 1845, DAVIDSON Co.

ARMSTRONG, Elijah to Peggy Higgins - issued January 18, 1812, Bondsman: Joel Willard, WILSON Co.

ARMSTRONG, Elias James to Elizabeth M. Frierson - October 26, 1809, Bondsman: William M. Berryhill, MAURY Co.

ARMSTRONG, Ezekiel to Sally Hall - issued July 4, 1818, Bondsman: George McCrackin, RUTHERFORD Co.

ARMSTRONG, Frances to Maranda Stolts - issued December 2, 1844, m. by: James Sprouse, J. P., October 19, 1844, ROBERTSON Co.

ARMSTRONG, Hester A. to Walter W. Summers - issued June 19, 1861, Bondsmen: B. M. Tillman, Jos. H. Thompson, Clk. per N. F. Thompson, Dep. Clk., BEDFORD Co.

ARMSTRONG, Hugh C. to Mrs. Sarah Wilson - issued March 18, 1838, m. by: Robt. Boyd, C. Howell March 18, 1838, DAVIDSON Co.

ARMSTRONG, J. E. to Martha Armstrong - issued September 4, 1868, FRANKLIN Co.

ARMSTRONG, J. W. N. to Malinda Easterly - issued January 14, 1860, m. by: F. M. Jackson, Mins., January 17, 1860, COFFEE Co.

ARMSTRONG, James to Tennessee Thrower - issued July 4, 1859, m. by: C. C. Chapman, J. P., July 4, 1859, COFFEE Co.

ARMSTRONG, Jas. G. to Sarah Moore - issued April 28, 1847, m. by: T. S. Elliott, J. P., April 29, 1847, STEWART Co.

ARMSTRONG, Jas. J. to Elizabeth F. Thornton - September 5, 1861, m. by: H. P. Stanley, J. P., GILES Co.

ARMSTRONG, James L. to Sophia W. Smith - issued September 27, 1804, SUMNER Co.

ARMSTRONG, James M. to Polley Payne - issued September 12, 1817, Bondsman: Joseph Patton, WILSON Co.

ARMSTRONG, Jno. to Nancy Benthal - July 28, 1807, WILLIAMSON Co.

ARMSTRONG, John to Patsy McClain - issued November 3, 1818, Bondsman: James C. Luttrell, KNOX Co.

ARMSTRONG, Jno. M. to Elizabeth Briant - July 29, 1813, WILLIAMSON Co.

ARMSTRONG, John W. to Polina Scarborough - issued July 14, 1842, m. by: Rev. Jas. T. Morris, STEWART Co.

ARMSTRONG, John W. to A. C. Baker - issued January 19, 1869, m. by: D. P. Armstrong, J. P., January 21, 1869, FRANKLIN Co.

ARMSTRONG, Josephus to Sarah Williams - issued September 15, 1845, m. by: Jas. Woodard, J. P., September 18, 1845, ROBERTSON Co.

ARMSTRONG, Knox to Nancy C. Greer - issued August 16, 1828, Bondsman: Samuel Armstrong, m. by: Thomas D. Lansden, J. P., August 19, 1828, WILSON Co.

ARMSTRONG, Knox to Pernissa S. Witherspoon - issued December 22, 1834, m. by: Jesse Alexander, V. D. M., December 24, 1834, RUTHERFORD Co.

ARMSTRONG, Martin W. to Mary M. Armstrong - issued September 24, 1834,
   Bondsman: John Alexander, m. by: Jesse Alexander, V. D. M.,
   September 24, 1834, RUTHERFORD Co.

ARMSTRONG, Mary Lenora to James Dobbin - MAURY Co.

ARMSTRONG, Mathew to Nancy Marquess - m. by: L. B. Edwards November 2,
   1837, SUMNER Co.

ARMSTRONG, Nancy to James Rutlege - MAURY Co.

ARMSTRONG, Nathaniel to Caty Derreberry - September 5, 1807,
   WILLIAMSON, Co.

ARMSTRONG, Rachel to Jacob Braselton - GREENE Co.

ARMSTRONG, Richard to Mary Lester - October 24, 1797, Security:
   James Penny, GREENE Co.

ARMSTRONG, Robert to Polly Crane - 1797, KNOX Co.

ARMSTRONG, Robert to Caty Hogg - issued December 28, 1821, Bondsman:
   John Hogg, m. by: S. K. Blythe, J. P., December 28, 1821, SUMNER Co.

ARMSTRONG, Robert to Malinda Strother - m. February 1, 1837, SUMNER Co.

ARMSTRONG, Robert to Dorothy H. Inman - issued September 9, 1844,
   ROBERTSON Co.

ARMSTRONG, Sam'l M. to Charlotte Armstrong - issued March 15, 1824,
   m. by: R. Houston, J. P., March 16, 1824, KNOX Co.

ARMSTRONG, Sarah W. to George Dickey - MAURY Co.

ARMSTRONG, Syrus to Jane Maxwell - issued December 20, 1827, Bondsman:
   Joseph P. Wharton, WILSON Co.

ARMSTRONG, Thomas to Sinai Roney - issued October 27, 1825, Bondsman:
   Stephen H. Turner, m. by: E. Edwards October 27, 1825, SUMNER Co.

ARMSTRONG, William to Susannah Willis - issued March 18, 1842, m. by:
   John Nugent, J. P., March 16, 1842, FRANKLIN Co.

ARMSTRONG, William to Rebecca Chapman - issued April 3, 1855, m. by:
   Benjamin Cambell, J. P., April 6, 1855, ROBERTSON Co.

ARMSTRONG, Wm. C. to Hannah Denton Lucas - issued December 28, 1825,
   Bondsman: Josiah G. Armstrong, m. by: Wm. Morris, J. P., December 29,
   1825, KNOX Co.

ARMSTRONG, Wm. T. to Sarah Bell - issued March 29, 1842, Bondsman:
   H. Whitmore, m. by: John Taff, J. P., March 29, 1842, MEIGS Co.

ARMSTRONG, Zenas to Magdalen Knox - issued December 23, 1825, m. by:
   Jesse Alexander, V. D. M., December 27, 1825, RUTHERFORD Co.

ARNET, Jacob to Ann Coffy - issued November 3, 1819, Bondsman: John
   Coffy, m. by: Robert Goins, J. P., December 11, 1819, GRAINGER Co.

ARNETT, J. D. to Mattie Moore - issued January 1, 1872, m. by:
   M. H. Bone, M. G., January 3, 1872, FRANKLIN Co.

ARNETT, Wm. R. to Elizabeth Hatchett - issued January 3, 1853, m. by:
   Henry Larkin January 4, 1853, FRANKLIN Co.

ARNOLD, Asa to Tenacy Rucker - issued January 30, 1832, m. by:
   O. W. Crockett, J. P., RUTHERFORD Co.

ARNOLD, Booker to Sophia Smith - issued September 18, 1830, Bondsman:
   James W. Glass, RUTHERFORD Co.

ARNOLD, Butler to Rachael Hudson - issued November 7, 1816, Bondsman: George Ross, m. by: William Gray, J. P., WILSON Co.

ARNOLD, Daniel to Dicey Draper - issued September 24, 1828, Bondsman: George W. Lance, m. by: V. Swaney September 24, 1828, SUMNER Co.

ARNOLD, Davis to Martha Puckett - issued August 27, 1829, Bondsman: Stith Harrison, m. by: Williamson Williams, J. P., August. 28, 1829, WILSON Co.

ARNOLD, Davis to Susanah Bryson - issued May 14, 1816, Bondsman: Wilson L. Parmer, m. by: John McMinn, J. P., May 16, 1816, WILSON Co.

ARNOLD, Ebenezar to Evelina Dodson - issued February 9, 1822, Bondsman: A. W. Reese, SUMNER Co.

ARNOLD, Enoch to Sally Sullings - issued December 23, 1809, Bondsman: Presley Edwards, RUTHERFORD Co.

ARNOLD, Ezekiel to Mary Gilliland - issued January 2, 1816, m. by: L. Davis, J. P., January 4, 1816, RUTHERFORD Co.

ARNOLD, Green to Eleanor Gossett - issued December 10, 1832, Bondsman: Richard Arnold, m. by: J. L. Moore, J. P., December 11, 1832, WILSON Co.

ARNOLD, Henry G. to Mary Whitlock - issued July 7, 1835, Bondsman: Alfred H. Foster, m. by: B. W. Smith, J. P., July 9, 1835, WILSON Co.

ARNOLD, Henry S. to Clarissa Underwood - issued December 28, 1835, Bondsman: John Drennon, m. by: Joshua Woolen, M. G., December 29, 1835, WILSON Co.

ARNOLD, Hubert to Temperance Weaver - issued March 26, 1834, Bondsman: Daniel Weaver, m. by: A. S. Edwards, J. P., October 28, 1834, RUTHERFORD Co.

ARNOLD, J. L. to Sallie Davis - issued October 6, 1874, FRANKLIN Co.

ARNOLD, J. T. to Elizabeth Yarborough - issued September 22, 1866, FRANKLIN Co.

ARNOLD, James to Milly Gilliland - issued December 2, 1815, Bondsman: Winfield Pope, RUTHERFORD Co.

ARNOLD, James to Sarah T. Mitchell - issued December 22, 1824, Bondsman: John Gay, m. by: Hardy Hunt, J. P., December 23, 1824, WILSON Co.

ARNOLD, James to Polly McCall - issued February 11, 1829, Bondsman: Angus McCall, KNOX Co.

ARNOLD, James to Nancy Glass - issued January 18, 1830, m. by: John McMillan, J. P., January 19, 1830, KNOX Co.

ARNOLD, James G. to Mary S. Lannom - issued February 7, 1835, Bondsman: Tilman W. Lannom, RUTHERFORD Co.

ARNOLD, James W. to Lucinda Ladd - issued June 17, 1872, m. by: E. H. Bennett, M. G., June 17, 1872, FRANKLIN Co.

ARNOLD, Jeremiah to Elizabeth Stubblefield - issued January 1, 1839, m. by: A. B. Darrell February 4, 1839, FRANKLIN Co.

ARNOLD, John to Judy Brown - issued August 15, 1816, Bondsman: David Arnold, m. by: John McMinn, J. P., August 20, 1816, WILSON Co.

ARNOLD, John to Cara Warren - issued January 15, 1821, m. by: Cary James January 17, 1821, RUTHERFORD Co.

ARNOLD, John to Nancy Bond - issued January 12, 1829, m. by:
John McMinn, J. P., January 14, 1829, WILSON Co.

ARNOLD, John to Milethia Wells - issued September, 1855, m. by:
J. B. Rogers, J. P., September, 1855, FRANKLIN Co.

ARNOLD, John to Milly Jacobs - issued February 7, 1859, m. by:
W. G. Pirtle, J. P., February 8, 1859, COFFEE Co.

ARNOLD, John B. to Frances Young - issued July 29, 1828, Bondsman:
William Young, m. by: Thomas D. Lansden, J. P., July 31, 1821,
WILSON Co.

ARNOLD, John B. to Mary E. Anderson - issued September 30, 1854, m. by:
J. H. Lawrence, J. P., October 1, 1854, COFFEE Co.

ARNOLD, Joseph M. to Sarah Fergerson - m. by: Simpson West, J. P.,
October 7, 1855, FRANKLIN Co.

ARNOLD, Joshua to Mary F. Berry - issued July 28, 1861, m. by:
G. W. Featherston, M. G., ROBERTSON Co.

ARNOLD, Lucy H. to W. H. Morton - BEDFORD Co.

ARNOLD, Oliver to Hannah Melton - issued September 28, 1830, Bondsmen:
Jas. Wright and John Dearmond, m. by: Isaac Lewis September 28,
1830, Witness: Wm. Swan, KNOX Co.

ARNOLD, Oliver to Hannah Melton - September 28, 1833, KNOX Co.

ARNOLD, Peter to Nancy Harp - issued May 16, 1835, Bondsman:
Andrew S. Edwards, m. by: A. S. Edwards, J. P., May 17, 1825,
RUTHERFORD Co.

ARNOLD, Pleasant to Sythea Barns - issued May 6, 1822, Bondsman:
Thos. Arnold, m. by: James McDonnal, V. D. M., May 7, 1822,
WILSON Co.

ARNOLD, Ralph to Mourning Knuckles - issued July 27, 1847, m. by:
C. L. Blanton, J. P., August 3, 1847, FRANKLIN Co.

ARNOLD, Robert to Polly Gordon - December 6, 1810, Bondsman:
Moses Arnold, MAURY Co.

ARNOLD, T. W. to E. J. Wheeler - issued July 4, 1849, m. by:
Jas. Woodard, J. P., ROBERTSON Co.

ARNOLD, William to Eleanor Robinson - issued October 2, 1829, Bondsman:
John Drennon, m. by: Henry Ridley, J. P., October 2, 1829,
RUTHERFORD Co.

ARNOLD, William to Sindi Franklin - issued December 4, 1832, Bondsman:
Isham Franklin, m. by: E. Stephens, J. P., December 5, 1832,
WILSON Co.

ARNOLD, William to Cassandra Acklin - issued November 12, 1833,
Bondsman: Robt. B. Warren, RUTHERFORD Co.

ARNOLD, Wm. to Rebecka McNutt - issued March 27, 1834, m. by:
Rob't. H. Snoddy, M. G., March 27, 1834, KNOX Co.

ARNWIN, John to Clary Rector - issued December 24, 1802, Bondsman:
Bartin McFerron, GRAINGER Co.

ARNWINE, Daniel to Polley Rector - issued October 1, 1810, Bondsman:
Albartis Arnwine, GRAINGER Co.

ARWINE, James to Nancy Lively - issued September 15, 1821, Bondsman:
Alburtis Arwine, m. by: John Arwine, J. P., September 16, 1821,
GRAINGER Co.

ARRENTS, William to Artemizer Cross - issued February 13, 1844,
Bondsman: M. Shaver, m. by: Drury L. Godsey, M. G., MEIGS Co.

ARROWSMITH, Wm. to Mary E. Wilkerson - January 31, 1858, m. by:
J. C. Puman, M. G., GILES Co.

ARTHUR, Henry D. to Geney Riggs - October 28, 1841, m. by:
Warren W. Calhoun, J. P., Security: John Huggs, GILES Co.

ARTHUR, James to Hannah Howser - issued September 20, 1820, Bondsman:
Andrew McBath, m. by: Peter Nance, J. P. K. C., September 21,
1820, KNOX Co.

ARTHUR, Wm. to Lydia Howser - issued November 2, 1829, Bondsman:
John Wright, Witness: Wm. Swan, KNOX Co.

ARTHUR, Wm. A. to Nancy A. Yates - issued August 6, 1840, m. by:
E. S. Hall, J. P., August 6, 1840, DAVIDSON Co.

ASCUE, Sam'l. to Betsy Armstrong - August 21, 1806, WILLIAMSON Co.

ASHABRANAH, D. to E. R. Williams - issued October 27, 1853, m. by:
Jas. Woodard, J. P., October 28, 1853, ROBERTSON Co.

ASHBRAND, W. H. to Amanda Traughber - issued December 18, 1853, m. by:
Jas. Woodard, J. P., ROBERTSON Co.

ASHABRANER, Jno. W. to Maryett Willis - issued December 11, 1839,
m. by: Geo. Childress, J. P., ROBERTSON Co.

ASHABRANNAH, Abraham to Margarett Pitts - issued December 9, 1846,
m. by: D. G. Baird, J. P., December 17, 1846, ROBERTSON Co.

ASHBURN, John to Elizabeth Harris - issued October 24, 1844, Bondsman:
Franklin Pierce, m. by: B. F. McKenzie, J. P., October 24, 1844,
MEIGS Co.

ASHBY, Enoch to Rebecca Brockett - issued November 10, 1849, Bondsman:
Wm. Rideout, m. by: Mark Senter, M. G., September 11, 1849,
MONTGOMERY Co.

ASHER, Walter W. to Lydia Blackburn - issued October 29, 1822, m. by:
Edward Willis, WILSON Co.

ASHFORD, John to Jensey King - issued August 26, 1807, Bondsman:
Alston Elkins, WILSON Co.

ASHFORD, John to Jane Pippin - issued October 12, 1830, Bondsman:
John W. Blakemore, m. by: Sam'l Davis, J. P., October 12, 1830,
SUMNER Co.

ASHFORD, Josiah P. to E. Anthony - m. by: Robert Norvell January 11,
1837, SUMNER Co.

ASHFORD, Michael to Harriett Lockhard - issued October 26, 1827,
Bondsman: Hugh Tomlinson, m. by: Wm. H. Davis, J. P., October 30,
1827, RUTHERFORD Co.

ASHLEY, Daniel to Polly Suthard - issued April 16, 1844, m. by:
C. A. Hunt, J. P., April 25, 1844, FRANKLIN Co.

ASHLEY, Edward to Mary A. Williams - issued August 1, 1842, m. by:
Thomas Meadows, J. P., August 1, 1842, FRANKLIN Co.

ASHLEY, Elias to Rebecca H. Bradford - issued April 7, 1848, m. by:
C. A. Hunt, J. P., FRANKLIN Co.

ASHLEY, James to Lucy McCrary - issued September 3, 1823, Bondsman:
George McCrary, m. by: B. L. McFerrin, J. P., September 4, 1823,
RUTHERFORD Co.

ASHLEY, James M. to Lucinda Steel - issued September 9, 1871, FRANKLIN Co.

ASHLEY, John H. to Eliza Gilliam - issued September 1, 1843, FRANKLIN Co.

ASHLEY, Jourdan to Sophia Bradford - issued July 19, 1841, m. by:
C. A. Hunt, J. P., July 23, 1841, FRANKLIN Co.

ASHLEY, Michael to Lucinda Winkler - issued December 7, 1852, m. by:
G. W. Bowling, J. P., December 8, 1852, FRANKLIN Co.

ASHLEY, Moore to Elizabeth Sparkman - issued February 16, 1860, m. by:
P. Moore, M. G., February 16, 1860, VAN BUREN Co.

ASHLEY, Thos. M. to Elizabeth Shelton - issued November 2, 1809,
Bondsman: Thos. Brown, Witness: Jno. N. Gamble, KNOX Co.

ASHLEY, William to Susan Pruwitt - issued September 14, 1857, m. by:
J. H. Lawrence, J. P., September 15, 1857, COFFEE Co.

ASHLOCK, Benjamin to Elizabeth Cooper - issued June 5, 1812, Bondsman:
Thomas Knight, SUMNER Co.

ASHLOCK, Philip to Marian Melton - issued January 15, 1816, Bondsman:
David West, SUMNER Co.

ASHMORE, L. H. to Rebecca A. Massey - issued November 25, 1865, Bondsman:
M. J. McNeill, m. by: L. M. Sanford, J. P., November 26, 1865,
LAWRENCE Co.

ASHMORE, Elizabeth to Samuel Perry - GREENE Co.

ASHMORE, Hezekiah to Elizabeth Kerr - December 3, 1786, Security:
Nathaniel McMicken, GREENE Co.

ASHMORE, William to Mary Hadan - February 2, 1791, Security: John Wilson,
GREENE Co.

ASHWORTH, Eli to Cyrena Hickerson - issued August 31, 1841, m. by:
John Eubank, J. P., August 31, 1841, DICKSON Co.

ASHWORTH, Jasper R. to Casandra Berry - issued August 8, 1818, m. by:
Jas. Johnson, J. P., August 10, 1818, WILSON Co.

ASHWORTH, John to Rhoda Benton - issued September 5, 1847, m. by:
Thos. B. Matthews, J. P., ROBERTSON Co.

ASHWORTH, John C. to Nancy Cornett - issued August 17, 1841, m. by:
John Eubank, J. P., August 17, 1841, DICKSON Co.

ASINE, John to Nancy Morgan - December 17, 1808, WILLIAMSON Co.

ASINE, Sam'l. to Betsy Armstrong - August 21, 1806, WILLIAMSON Co.

ASKEW, Alford to Urania Lane - issued February 14, 1832, Bondsman:
Andrew Askew, WILSON Co.

ASKEW, Allen to Betsey Phipps - issued March 6, 1810, Bondsman:
D. Dement, SUMNER Co.

ASKEW, Elisha to Patsey Eubanks - issued January 20, 1821, Bondsman:
Richard Garrison, m. by: John McMurtry, M. G., January 20, 1821,
SUMNER Co.

ASKEW, Issac to Mabala Allen - issued September 10, 1813, Bondsman:
Webb Bloodworth, SUMNER Co.

ASKEW, John to Penelope Edwards - issued November 21, 1848, m. by:
Allen McCaskill, J. P., November 22, 1848, STEWART Co.

ASKEW, Wenbourn to Mary Ann Downs - issued June 23, 1842, m. by:
    W. C. Jones, J. P., June 23, 1842, STEWART Co.

ASKIN, Lexington to Martha Seargent - issued January 15, 1853, m. by:
    J. C. Montgomery, J. P., January 18, 1853, FRANKLIN Co.

ASPEY, George to Lucrecy Brown - issued June 12, 1817, Bondsman:
    David Brown, WILSON Co.

ASPLEY, John to Milly Senter - issued July 12, 1816, Bondsman:
    William Aspley, SUMNER Co.

ASPLEY, Lemuel to Nancy Hannah - issued December 24, 1823, m. by:
    Richard Johnson December 24, 1823, SUMNER Co.

ASQUE, Elizabeth to Jacob Rook - MAURY Co.

ASTAN, Daniel to Jane D. Bell - issued August 5, 1817, Bondsman:
    James Slate, m. by: Thos. Calhoon, M. G., August 6, 1817, WILSON Co.

ASTIN, Zachariah to Patsey Thomson - issued August 26, 1807, Bondsman:
    John Moore, Witness: John Moore, J. P., GRAINGER Co.

ASTON, Joseph to Clarissa B. Reed - issued July 30, 1836, Bondsman:
    Daniel Safferan, SUMNER Co.

ATCHISON, Adam to Maryan Jones - issued August 13, 1804, Bondsman:
    John Barnett, SUMNER Co.

ATCHISON, John G. to Nancy Mabry - issued December 11, 1821, SUMNER Co.

ATCHISON, Nathan to Nelly Bearnard - issued May 24, 1804, Bondsman:
    Jacob Bearnard, SUMNER Co.

ATCHISON, Nathan to Lucusia Barnard - issued January 2, 1809, Bondsman:
    John Chapman, SUMNER Co.

ATCHISON, William to Darcus Barnard - issued January 2, 1809, Bondsman:
    John Chapman, SUMNER Co.

ATCHLEY, Seth to E. M. Francisco - issued February 18, 1840, Bondsman:
    Jas. H. Vernon, m. by: Richad Simpson, M. G., March 5, 1840,
    MEIGS Co.

ATHEAN, Edmon to Relay Longwith - issued August 16, 1827, Bondsman:
    Wm. Packett, KNOX Co.

ATHERLY, John to Nancy Joiner - issued November 6, 1809, Bondsman:
    Leaborn Pruett, SUMNER Co.

ATHERLY, John to Polly Williams - issued February 22, 1819, Bondsman:
    James Atherly, m. by: Jos. T. Williams February 25, 1819, WILSON Co.

ATHONY, Phillip to Polly Hill - issued September 15, 1860, m. by:
    G. W. Martin, M. G., September 18, 1860, ROBERTSON Co.

ATKIN, Charles W. to Harriet Gill - issued August 24, 1826, Bondsman:
    James Hare, m. by: Geo. Atkin, M. G., August 24, 1826, KNOX Co.

ATKIN, George to Emily Thatcher - issued June 29, 1819, Bondsman:
    John Sutherland, KNOX Co.

ATKIN, Stephen to Milly Rectar - issued January 2, 1832, Bondsman:
    James H. Starnes, GRAINGER Co.

ATKINS, Addison L. to Nancy Coffman - issued October 29, 1838,
    DAVIDSON Co.

ATKINS, Charles to Elizabeth Miller - June 15, 1784, Security: John
    Miller, GREENE Co.

ATKINS, Charles W. to Mary Henry - issued July 8, 1837, Bondsman:
P. A. Waters, m. by: T. Sullins July 9, 1837, KNOX Co.

ATKINS, George S. to Charles Ann Rhodes King - issued September 10,
1842, m. by: Allen Elliott September 12, 1842, STEWART Co.

ATKINS, H. Milton to Elizabeth B. Williams - issued November 11, 1840,
m. by: Rev. Allen Elliott November 11, 1840, STEWART Co.

ATKINS, J. S. to Lucy Stout - issued November 16, 1856, m. by:
T. H. Gardner, J. P., December 17, 1856, ROBERTSON Co.

ATKINS, James J. to Dolly An Vickers - STEWART Co.

ATKINS, John to Nelly McElhaney - issued May 28, 1823, Bondsman:
Joel Philips, m. by: Jas. Kennon, M. G., May 28, 1823, GRAINGER Co.

ATKINS, John H. to Prussia Denny - issued August 17, 1852, Bondsman:
Joseph B. Carrington, MONTGOMERY Co.

ATKINS, Joseph to Dice Holbert - issued October 13, 1825, Bondsman:
Stephen Halbert, m. by: E. Nelson, J. P., October 20, 1825,
Witness: Wm. Swan, KNOX Co.

ATKINS, Lewis G. to Avey Heflen - issued August 15, 1846, m. by:
Robt. Wilson, J. P., August 16, 1846, STEWART Co.

ATKINS, Moses to Polly Phipps - issued April 27, 1829, Bondsman:
Hugh Jones, m. by: Alexander Hamilton, J. P., April 27, 1829,
GRAINGER Co.

ATKINS, Nathan to Anna Needham - issued August 7, 1830, Bondsman:
James F. Hooper, GRAINGER Co.

ATKINS, Philip to Salley Bradshaw - issued October 24, 1812, Bondsman:
James Lauderdale, SUMNER Co.

ATKINS, R. S. to Bettie Ray - issued January 12, 1870, m. by: Rev.
J. C. Miles January 12, 1870, FRANKLIN Co.

ATKINS, William to Polly B. Floyd - issued January 9, 1827, m. by:
J. C. Bunch, J. P., GRAINGER Co.

ATKINS, William to Eliza Kerksey - issued July 24, 1848, m. by:
James Chambers, J. P., July 26, 1848, STEWART Co.

ATKINS, Winright to Sally Claunch - issued November 11, 1828, Bondsman:
John Mallicoat, m. by: Isaiah C. Bunch, J. P., November 13, 1828,
GRAINGER Co.

ATKINSON, Henry to Matilda Anderson - issued February 1, 1842,
STEWART Co.

ATKINSON, Henry to Gabnilla Boyd - issued December 15, 1848, m. by:
R. T. Adams, J. P., December 17, 1848, STEWART Co.

ATKINSON, James H. to Susan Ellis - issued February 20, 1832, m. by:
Peyton Smith March 1, 1832, RUTHERFORD Co.

ATKINSON, John to Sally Short - November 2, 1815, WILLIAMSON Co.

ATKINSON, John H. to Mary P. Hall - February 20, 1823, WILLIAMSON Co.

ATKINSON, Joseph S. to Mary Guthrie - issued July 25, 1827, m. by:
John Powell, J. P., July 26, 1826, WILSON Co.

ATKINSON, Royal to Rebecca Doak - issued December 20, 1821, Bondsman:
James Johnson, m. by: Wm. Seawell, WILSON Co.

ATKINSON, T. W. Jr. to Henrietta A. Tanner - issued January 25, 1847,
    Bondsman: Thos. H. Jackson, m. by: James R. Plummer, Jr.,
    January 25, 1847, MONTGOMERY Co.

ATKINSON, Thomas to Elizabeth Johnson - issued November 4, 1848, m. by:
    Allen McCaskill, J. P., November 4, 1848, STEWART Co.

ATKINSON, William L. to Eliza Cobb - issued September 19, 1821,
    Bondsman: William J. Anderson, m. by: Jas. Hinnon, M. G.,
    GRAINGER Co.

ATKINSON, Willis to Nancy Barnard - issued December 18, 1810, Bondsman:
    James Jones, SUMNER Co.

ATKISEN, Anny to William Hogan - MAURY Co.

ATKISON, Jesse to Patsy Goodrum - issued January 25, 1817, Bondsman:
    Absalom Atkison, m. by: James White January 25, 1817, KNOX Co.

ATKISSON, Arthur to Cassa Breese - August 16, 1813, WILLIAMSON Co.

ATOLTZ, B. F. to Amanda Winn - issued January 13, 1849, m. by:
    Jeremiah Batts, J. P., ROBERTSON Co.

ATWELL, Don D. to Julia Gears - issued January 9, 1838, Bondsman:
    Tilmon J. Wilkerson, m. by: Geo. Donnell, V. D. M., January 10,
    1838, WILSON Co.

ATWELL, Jacob H. to Nancy A. Looney - issued October 31, 1865, Bondsman:
    Thos. D. Choate, m. by: Wm. Pullen, J. P., October 31, 1865,
    LAWRENCE Co.

ATWOOD, Thompson to Frances Lawrence - issued December 19, 1831,
    Bondsman: William G. Berks, WILSON Co.

AULL, R. P. to Sarah E. Atkinson - issued September 15, 1854,
    ROBERTSON Co.

AULT, Andrew J. to Mary Rutherford - issued September 21, 1837,
    Bondsman: Josiah Roady, m. by: James McNutt, J. P., September 21,
    1837, KNOX Co.

AULT, Jacob to Sally Griffin - February 3, 1811, KNOX Co.

AULT, Jacob to Sarah Hannah - issued March 15, 1815, Bondsman:
    James Breese, Witness: A. Hutcheson, KNOX Co.

AULT, Jacob to Sally Griffy - issued February 3, 1830, Bondsman:
    John Ault, Witness: Wm. Swan, KNOX Co.

AULT, John to Peggy Hastings - November 22, 1809, KNOX Co.

AULT, John to Amanda Hainey - issued September 19, 1818, m. by:
    John Haynie, M. G., September 20, 1818, KNOX Co.

AULT, Thomas to Peggy Baker - July 9, 1810, KNOX Co.

AUST, Frederick to Matilda Allen - issued April 6, 1825, Bondsman:
    John Conger, WILSON Co.

AUST, Joseph to Rebecca Williams - issued May 8, 1828, Bondsman:
    Frederick Aust, m. by: Archd D. Duval May 8, 1828, SUMNER Co.

AUSTELL, C. B. to Ellen Seargent - issued December 11, 1858, m. by:
    Rev. A. J. Baird January 1, 1859, FRANKLIN Co.

AUSTELL, Joseph to Susan Williams - issued March 20, 1873, m. by:
    J. F. Smithson, M. G., March 20, 1873, FRANKLIN Co.

AUSTIN, Ashley L. to Susan G. Booker - issued March 13, 1831, Bondsman:
A. F. Young, SUMNER Co.

AUSTIN, Dickinson to Sally Hall - issued December 24, 1827, Bondsman:
Thomas Potts, Jr., m. by: Reuben Searcy, J. P., December 24,
1827, SUMNER Co.

AUSTIN, Dickson to Emily Anderson - issued March 23, 1835, Bondsman:
James H. Busby, m. by: Henry K. Winbourn March 23, 1835, SUMNER Co.

AUSTIN, Edwin to Lucinda J. Johnson - issued August 13, 1839, m. by:
Wm. H. Hagens, J. P., August 15, 1839, DAVIDSON Co.

AUSTIN, Egleston to Amanda Stealy - issued October 12, 1829, Bondsman:
V. D. Austin, m. by: Lewis M. Woodson October 12, 1829, SUMNER Co.

AUSTIN, Emily F. to John Rowe - BEDFORD Co.

AUSTIN, James to Nancy Bandy - issued September 27, 1830, Bondsman:
John Austin, SUMNER Co.

AUSTIN, James to Heneretta Rogers - issued February 3, 1872, m. by:
James Brazier, J. P., February 6, 1872, FRANKLIN Co.

AUSTIN, John to Penalope Creach - issued June 25, 1838, m. by:
M. B. Stuart, J. P., June 27, 1838, DICKSON Co.

AUSTIN, John B. to Fredonia Walker - issued January 12, 1847, DICKSON Co.

AUSTIN, Jordon to Lucy Patton - issued October 1, 1834, m. by:
William Barr, J. P., October 1, 1834, SUMNER Co.

AUSTIN, Newton C. to Elizabeth L. Peay - issued December 17, 1842,
DAVIDSON Co.

AUSTIN, Owen E. to Tabitha Jane Covington - issued November 23, 1829,
Bondsman: Jerry W. Kirby, RUTHERFORD Co.

AUSTIN, S. B. to Margrett Boman - issued March 3, 1867, m. by:
Thos. Mosley, J. P., March 3, 1867, FRANKLIN Co.

AUSTIN, Volentine to Maria (illegible) - issued July 6, 1822, Bondsman:
Isaac G. Coles, SUMNER Co.

AUSTIN, Washington to Mary Gipson - issued December 20, 1845, m. by:
Allen Gipson, J. P., December 20, 1845, FRANKLIN Co.

AUSTIN, Wilkenson D. to Amanda M. Booker - issued July 31, 1829,
Bondsman: David Padgett, m. by: John Wiseman, M. G., July 31,
1829, SUMNER Co.

AUSTIN, William to Rebecker Moses - issued March 28, 1798, Bondsman:
Steven Austin, Witness: Samuel Lusk, GRAINGER Co.

AUSTIN, William to Frances Mitchell - issued November 4, 1826, Bondsman:
Henry Vaughn, m. by: W. Smith, J. P., November 4, 1826, SUMNER Co.

AVANT, Benjamin W. to Nancy Lytle - issued September 9, 1835, Bondsman:
Wm. H. Sneed, m. by: G. Baker September 9, 1835, RUTHERFORD Co.

AVARITT, Luttleton to Sarah Head - issued April 19, 1821, m. April 19,
1821, RUTHERFORD Co.

AVENT, Harris to Dolly Trice - issued February 10, 1809, Bondsman:
Robt. Trousdale, SUMNER Co.

AVERST, Thomas H. to Rebecca Ann Lemay - issued September 11, 1845,
m. by: John Gold, J. P., September 11, 1845, MONTGOMERY Co.

AVERETT, Thomas to Narcessa Moreland - issured November 9, 1844,
   m. by: R. Wilson, J. P., November 11, 1845, STEWART Co.

AVERITT, Elijah to Charlott Edwards - issued March 19, 1852, Bondsman:
   William Edwards, MONTGOMERY Co.

AVRITT, John G. to Mary Dalton - m. by: John Wiseman February 7, 1837,
   SUMNER Co.

AVERITT, Peter J. to Eliza Ann Lay - issued August 27, 1853, Bondsman:
   J. S. Lay, MONTGOMERY Co.

AVERITT, Thomas H. to Rebecca Tyre - issued November 1, 1853, Bondsman:
   George W. Phillips, m. by: Wilie Smith, J. P., November 1, 1853,
   MONTGOMERY Co.

AVERY, Allen to Polly Wynne - issued December 29, 1817, Bondsman:
   John Smith, WILSON Co.

AVERY, George S. to Judy Chandler - issued March 9, 1822, Bondsman:
   Edings Chandler, WILSON Co.

AVERY, William to Permelia Sperry - issued December 16, 1817, Bondsman:
   Peter Sullivan, m. by: Jacob Brown, J. P., December 17, 1817,
   WILSON Co.

AVORY, John W. to Malinda Ann Tarver - issued January 23, 1824, Bondsman:
   Wm. Murray, WILSON Co.

AVORY, John W. to Malinda Ann Tarver - issued January 23, 1826, m. by:
   Jacob Sullivan, WILSON Co.

AWALT (Awatt), Jacob P. to Rebecca P. Morgan - issued January 2, 1839,
   FRANKLIN Co.

AWALT (Awatt), John to Mickey Brimage - issued July 18, 1846, m. by:
   D. O. McElroy, J. P., July 19, 1846, FRANKLIN Co.

AWALT (Awatt), Joshua F. to Susan Brown - issued October 4, 1858,
   FRANKLIN Co.

AWALT (Awatt), Wm. C. to Susan M. Bean - issued September 20, 1854,
   m. by: A. J. Wiseman, J. P., September 21, 1854, FRANKLIN Co.

AWATT (Awalt), Jacob P. to Rebecca P. Morgan - issued January 2, 1839,
   FRANKLIN Co.

AWATT (Awalt), John to Mickey Brimage - issued July 18, 1846, m. by:
   D. O. McElroy, J. P., July 19, 1846, FRANKLIN Co.

AWATT (Awalt), Joshua F. to Susan Brown - issued October 4, 1858,
   FRANKLIN Co.

AWATT (Awalt), Wm. C. to Susan M. Bean - issued September 20, 1854,
   m. by: A. J. Wiseman, J. P., September 21, 1854, FRANKLIN Co.

AXUM, William to Mary H. Williams - issued December 24, 1837, Bondsman:
   Newbern P. Stone, WILSON Co.

AXUM, William to Mary H. Williams - issued December 24, 1837, m. by:
   J. Irby, J. P., December 25, 1837, WILSON Co.

AYDELOTT, J. D. to Sarah E. Grizzard - issued July 3, 1843, m. by:
   A. L. P. Green, M. G., August 31, 1843, DAVIDSON Co.

AYERS, Alfred M. to Mary M. Knox - issued March 12, 1838, Bondsman:
   J. H. Fisher, m. by: John J. Sloan, M. G., March 13, 1838, WILSON
   Co.

AYERS, Levi Q. to Virginia Hutchins - issued December 29, 1851, m. by:
W. J. Fox, V. D. M., December 30, 1851, FRANKLIN Co.

AYERS, Richard S. to Laura Pope - issued September 5, 1874, m. by:
Rev. H. J. Byrom, M. G., September 6, 1874, FRANKLIN Co.

AYLER, Wm. Preston to Lucretia Chandler - issued December 17, 1828,
Bondsman: Sam'l R. Rodgers, m. by: Sam'l S. McCampbell December 18,
1828, KNOX Co.

AYLES, William Porter to Lucinda Chambers - December 17, KNOX Co.

AYMETTE, William to Louisa J. Hamilton - issued January 24, 1820,
m. by: Edm'nd Jones, D. M. E. C., RUTHERFORD Co.

AYRES, James E. to Sarah A. Crutcher - February 6, 1859, m. by:
B. M. Gallary, GILES Co.

AYRES, Jesse to Elizabeth Reed - issued November 3, 1819, m. by:
Wm. Morris, J. P. K. C., November 5, 1819, KNOX Co.

AYRES, Jesse to Elizabeth Reed - issued November 5, 1820, Bondsman:
Hugh Brown, KNOX Co.

AYRES, Jesse to Elizabeth Reed - issued November 3, 1820, m. by:
Wm. Morris, J. P., November 5, 1820, KNOX Co.

AYRES, John to M. R. Willis - issued December 10, 1851, m. by:
Tho. W. Felts, ROBERTSON Co.

AYRES, John to F. C. A. Fry - issued December 22, 1852, m. by:
F. R. Gooch, M. G., ROBERTSON Co.

AYRES, Joseph to Letty Shelton - issued August 23, 1836, m. by:
James C. England August 25, 1836, KNOX Co.

AYRES, Peggy to William Churchwell - MAURY Co.

AYRES, Samuel to Kesiah Roberts - issued November 30, 1822, m. by:
Sam'l Sample, J. P., December 12, 1822, KNOX Co.

AYRES, W. W. to Nancy Johnson - issued October 25, 1842, m. by:
Richd. W. Bell, J. P., 25, 1842, ROBERTSON Co.

AYRES, Wm. to Martha Ann Trice - issued December 2, 1844, m. by:
Charles Grafford, J. P., December 3, 1844, ROBERTSON Co.

AYRES, Wm. H. to Dulana Tate - issued August 28, 1852, m. by:
John Chitwood, J. P., September 10, 1852, FRANKLIN Co.

AYTES, Hiram to Rebecca Sparkman - issued November 25, 1834, Bondsman:
James Bise, GRAINGER Co.

AYTES, James to Jane Miller - issued September 26, 1818, Bondsman:
William Inglebarger, m. by: Robert Gaines, J. P., September 27,
1818, GRAINGER Co.

AYTES, John to Elizabeth Tally - issued September 16, 1819, Bondsman:
Wyatt Beckham, WILSON Co.

AYTES, John to Elizabeth Bunch - issued September 7, 1834, Bondsman:
James Boyd, J. P., m. by: H. Humbard, J. P., GRAINGER Co.

AZBELL, T. J. to Caldonia Davis - issued December 12, 1864, Bondsman:
Calvin Franklin, m. by: R. L. McLaren, J. P., December 13, 1864,
LAWRENCE Co.

BAALWRIGHT, Thos. to Clarissa Wade - July 13, 1812, WILLIAMSON Co.

BABB, Abel O. to Juliet Straughn - issued October 10, 1841, m. by:
Banja. Gambill, J. P., ROBERTSON Co.

BABB, Alsey to Susan McIntosh - issued March 31, 1853, m. by:
Isaac Steele, ROBERTSON Co.

BABB, Bennet to Abegal Guthrie - issued January 21, 1817, Bondsman:
Mathew Horn, m. by: John Jarratt January 22, 1817, WILSON Co.

BABB, Bennett to Rachael White - issued June 20, 1837, Bondsman:
B. W. Ireland, m. by: Joseph B. Wynn, M. G., WILSON Co.

BABB, Elizabeth to John Morrison - GREENE Co.

BABB, J. W. to M. J. Roney - issued January 3, 1859, m. August 7,
1859, ROBERTSON Co.

BABB, James to Annus Jones - issued November 9, 1842, m. by:
Greenberry Kelly November 10, 1842, ROBERTSON Co.

BABB, James B. to Caroline Wilson - issued December 19, 1853, m. by:
W. H. Rife, J. P., ROBERTSON Co.

BABB, John to Lucy A. Goulding - issued September 4, 1844, m. by:
D. G. Baird, J. P., September 5, 1844, ROBERTSON Co.

BABB, Joseph to F. Rose - issued April 13, 1842, m. by: Isaac Steel,
ROBERTSON Co.

BABB, Mary to Johnathan Humber - GREENE Co.

BABB, P. P. to G. Ann Hight - issued June 10, 1845, m. by:
D. G. Baird, J. P., ROBERTSON Co.

BABB, Philip to Elizabeth Hearnbard (?) - February 17, 1785, Security:
John Noniman, GREENE Co.

BABB, Sarah to Robert Greene - GREENE Co.

BABB, Stephen to Sarah Morrow - February 12, 1788, GREENE Co.

BABB, T. J. to Sarah E. Brewer - issued June 25, 1860, m. by:
G. W. Featherston, M. G., June 28, ROBERTSON Co.

BABB, Thomas to Polly Powel - issued April 27, 1819, Bondsman:
Thomas Guthrie, m. by: John Jarratt April 29, 1819, WILSON Co.

BABB, Thomas to Hicksey Hunt - issued April 2, 1821, Bondsman:
Henry B. Babb, m. by: John Jarratt April 3, 1821, WILSON Co.

BABB, Thomas to Elizabeth Bridges - issued March 31, 1835, Bondsman:
William T. Powell, m. by: E. P. Horn, J. P., WILSON Co.

BABB, William to Nancy Ross - issued March 6, 1819, Bondsman: William
Hartsfield, m. by: John Jarratt March 11, 1819, WILSON Co.

BABB, Young to Martha Freeman - issued August 22, 1848, m. by:
Greenberry Kelly, M. G., ROBERTSON Co.

BABER, Benjamin to Malinder R. - issued December 18, 1821, m. by:
S. Hunt, J. P., December 18, 1821, SUMNER Co.

BABER, Lewis to Lucinda Israel - issued January 7, 1829, m. by:
Wm. B. Garns, J. P., January 8, 1829, KNOX Co.

BABER, W. L. to Martha J. Price - issued October 14, 1845, m. by:
C. D. Elliott, M. G., October 15, 1845, DAVIDSON Co.

BABER, Woodson to Jane McCloud - issued November 17, 1824, Bondsman:
Michael Smith, m. by: William B. Garns, J. P., November 21, 1824,
KNOX Co.

BABRING, John to Betsy Smith - May 22, KNOX Co.

BACCHUS, John to Sary James - issued August 22, 1818, Bondsman:
    David Hayes, RUTHERFORD Co.

BACHELOR, Jno. to Nancy Clarkston - issued November 17, 1813, Bondsman:
    Asa Todd, WILSON Co.

BACHUS, James H. to Martha Echols - issued July 6, 1837, Bondsman:
    Thos. Sypert, m. by: John Hearn, J. P., WILSON Co.

BACHUS, William to Martha Sims - issued July 30, 1835, Bondsman:
    John Sims, m. by: W. R. D. Phipps, J. P., WILSON Co.

BACON, Charles P. to Margaret Ratliff - issued December 17, 1844,
    m. December 17, 1844, MONTGOMERY Co.

BACON, James H. to Sarah Luster - issued May 16, 1839, m. by:
    R. B. C. Howell, Pastor, May 16, 1839, DAVIDSON Co.

BADGER, Felix to Amanda Eleazer - issued December 20, 1843, m. by:
    E. Hanks, M. G., December 21, 1843, DICKSON Co.

BADGET, Thomas to Jane Badget - issued September 16, 1816, Bondsman:
    James Johnson, m. by: Jas. Douglass, J. P., September 16, SUMNER Co.

BAGGETT, Granberry to Mary J. Crawford - issued January 14, 1845,
    m. by: Charles Crafford, J. P., January 16, 1845, ROBERTSON Co.

BAGGETT, G. L. to Amanda M. Dozier - issued October 12, 1858, m. by:
    G. B. Mason, J. P., October 14, 1858, ROBERTSON Co.

BAGGETT, Henry to Mary Weaver - issued May 26, 1851, Bondsman:
    Thos. R. Clark, m. by: A. Baggett, J. P., May 21, 1851,
    MONTGOMERY Co.

BAGGETT, James to Nancy Davis - issued October 19, 1839, m. by:
    Benjamin Darrow, October 21, 1839, DICKSON Co.

BAGGETT, James to Elizabeth Powers - issued March 10, 1852, Bondsman:
    E. L. Miller, m. by: Mark Senter, M. G., March 10, 1852,
    MONTGOMERY Co.

BAGGETT, James B. to Nancy F. Harrison - issued October 1, 1849,
    FRANKLIN Co.

BAGGETT, Josiah to Harriette A. Suggs - issued December 30, 1847,
    m. by: R. J. Halliburton, J. P., December 30, 1847, DICKSON Co.

BAGGETT, Moses A. to Missouri C. Majors - issued November 27, 1848,
    m. by: W. M. Watson, J. P., November 29, 1848, FRANKLIN Co.

BAGGETT, Samuel W. G. to Catherine Lovett - issued March 3, 1863,
    Bondsmen: J. H. Harrison, Jos. H. Thompson, Clk. per M. E. W.
    Dunaway, Dep. Clk, BEDFORD Co.

BAGGETT, Thomas H. to Margret J. Smith - issued October 6, 1856, m. by:
    L. N. Simpson, J. P., October 10, 1856, FRANKLIN Co.

BAGGETT, W. G. to L. A. Clark - issued November 8, 1850, m. by:
    E. Baggett, J. P., November 10, 1850, ROBERTSON Co.

BAGGETT, W. R. to Martha S. Frame - issued October 13, 1859, m. by:
    Thos. Finch, J. P., October 13, 1859, FRANKLIN Co.

BAGGETT, William to Sarah Underwood - issued April 9, 1850, Bondsman:
    James Baggett, MONTGOMERY Co.

BAGGOTT, John S. to Elizabeth Camden - issued August 9, 1853, m. by:
    E. A. Rutledge, J. P., August 9, 1853, COFFEE Co.

BAGWELL, Allen to Sarah Lancaster - October 14, 1815, KNOX Co.

BAGWELL, Lumford to Rispa Truett - issued April 14, 1820, Bondsman: William Tervell, m. by: John Bond, V. D. M., March 19, 1821, WILSON Co.

BAGWELL, William M. to Mary Ann Brown - issued September 28, 1852, Bondsman: Edward Hewett, MONTGOMERY Co.

BAILE, Ishmael H. to Jane M. Adams - m. by: L. M. Woodson October 29, 1836, SUMNER Co.

BAILES, Daniel to Elizabeth Hawkins - issued February 16, 1801, Bondsman: Henry Hawkins, GRAINGER Co.

BAILES, John to Sarah Hawkins - issued October 12, 1802, Bondsman: Henry Hawkins, GRAINGER Co.

BAILEY, Alex to Elizabeth David - October 30, 1805, WILLIAMSON Co.

BAILEY, Campain to Jane Hall - issued February 18, 1833, Bondsman: Edward Johnson, RUTHERFORD Co.

BAILEY, Charlott to W. M. Jones - issued August 24, 1863, Bondsman: R. W. Cates, BEDFORD Co.

BAILEY, Cornelius to Amanda M. Duren - issued January 1, 1842, m. by: Martin Usery, J. P., January 4, 1842, DAVIDSON Co.

BAILEY, Cornelius W. to Rebeccah Patterson - issued January 9, 1827, Bondsman: Peter Patterson, m. by: Joshua Lester, V. D. M., WILSON Co.

BAILEY, Ephraim to Margaret Johnson - June 28, 1790, Security: Jacob Johnson, GREENE Co.

BAILEY, Geo. W. to Sarah W. Bell - issued June 26, 1848, m. by: James Gunn, E. M. C., June 29, 1848, ROBERTSON Co.

BAILEY, James S. to Lucy Puckett - issued December 4, 1826, Bondsman: Stanlope Sharpe, m. by: Joshua Lester, V. D. M., WILSON Co.

BAILEY, Jamison to Mary Smothers - issued August 16, 1835, Bondsman: Archibald Stinson, RUTHERFORD Co.

BAILEY, John to Nancy Tunnell - September 24, 1799, Security: Stephen Tunnell, GREENE Co.

BAILEY, Richard to Nancy Hunt - issued October 7, 1839, m. by: P. B. Morris October 7, 1839, DAVIDSON Co.

BAILEY, Sally to William Pullen - MAURY Co.

BAILEY, Thomas B. to Sarah M. Ewing - issued July 21, 1846, Bondsman: W. C. Adams, m. by: J. C. Bryan, J. P., July 20, 1846, MONTGOMERY Co.

BAILEY, Thomas M. to Martha Jane Coleman - issued August 19, 1848, m. by: B. Herndon, J. P., August 19, 1848, STEWART Co.

BAILEY, William to Sally Tally - issued November 14, 1818, m. by: Jas. Cross, J. P., November 19, 1818, WILSON Co.

BAILEY, William to Charlotte Taylor - issued November 13, 1847, m. by: Wm. Bell, J. P., November 14, 1847, STEWART Co.

BAILEY, William to Laura Poteete - issued January 1, 1862, Bondsman: Wm. T. Jackson, m. by: Wm. T. Jackson, J. P., January 2, 1862, LAWRENCE Co.

BAILEY, Wm. A. to Martha A. M. Johnson - issued August 30, 1846,
m. by: J. P. Bellamy, L. E. of M. E. Church, August 22, 1846,
MONTGOMERY Co.

BAILEY, Willie A. to Sarah A. Jackson - issued August 19, 1861, Bondsman:
James Griffin, m. by: W. H. Lumpkins, J. P., August 19, 1861,
LAWRENCE Co.

BAILISS, C. W. to Virginia Carney - issued November 26, 1850, Bondsman:
W. E. Dortch, MONTGOMERY Co.

BAILS, Asher to Sally King - issued July 22, 1824, m. by: B. McNutt,
J. P., July 22, 1824, KNOX Co.

BAILS, H. D. to Mary A. Grymes - issued July 17, 1845, m. by:
John Eubank, J. P., DICKSON Co.

BAILY, Claibourn to Francis Philips - issued December 27, 1827,
Bondsman: Robert Wilson, WILSON Co.

BAILY, George B. to Eliza Scott - issued November 27, Bondsman:
Alfred E. Donnell, m. by: James Foster, J. P., November 27, 1834,
WILSON Co.

BAILY, George C. to Polly Ann Baily - issued August 19, 1848, m. by:
B. Herndon, J. P., August 19, 1848, STEWART Co.

BAILY, William to Peyton Tally - issued November 14, 1819, Bondsman:
Peyton Tally, WILSON Co.

BAILY, William to Elizabeth Puckett - issued June 1, 1831, Bondsman:
James S. Baily, m. by: Joshua Lester, V. D. M., WILSON Co.

BAINBRIDGE, John E. to E. C. Hill - issued September 6, 1861, m. by:
G. W. Martin, M. G., September 10, 1861, ROBERTSON Co.

BAINS, John T. to Susan Hope - issued August 3, 1859, ROBERTSON Co.

BAINS, Joshua to Nancy Ruiff - issued January 10, 1807, Bondsman:
Henry Rieff, WILSON Co.

BADGETT, James to Susan Harris - November 23, KNOX Co.

BADGETT, James to Mary Ann Moore - September 8, KNOX Co.

BADGETT, James to Susan Harris - issued November 23, 1821, Bondsman:
Joshua Freeman, m. by: Peter Nance, J. P., November 23, 1821,
KNOX Co.

BADGETT, James to Fanny Williams - issued October 5, 1822, m. by:
P. Nance, J. P., October 7, 1822, KNOX Co.

BADGETT, Jesse to Sarah Routon - issued August 4, 1829, Bondsman:
H. R. Cox, WILSON Co.

BADGETT, John to Elizabeth Green - issued January 31, 1829, Bondsman:
William Cox, WILSON Co.

BADGETT, Ransom to Somyra Hunter - issued June 8, 1830, Bondsman:
Jno. Garner, m. by: J. Johnson, J. P., June 8, 1830, Witness:
Wm. Swan, KNOX Co.

BADGETT, Robert D. to Mary Ferguson - issued March 23, 1829, m. by:
W. Lyon, J. P., March 27, 1829, KNOX Co.

BAGBY, Aaron T. to Mary E. Connell - issued October 19, 1852, m. by:
J. M. Stemmons October 20, 1852, ROBERTSON Co.

BAGBY, Benjamin to Martha Woodson - issued July 12, 1855, m. by:
W. R. Sadler, J. P., July 15, 1855, ROBERTSON Co.

BAGBY, James to D. A. Morris - issued June 17, 1867, FRANKLIN Co.

BAGBY, Robert to Mary E. Mimms - issued October 9, 1855, m. by:
John H. Gammon, M. G., ROBERTSON Co.

BAGGET, Benjamin F. to Susan Porter - issued December 15, 1845, m. by:
Tho. Cook, J. P., ROBERTSON Co.

BAGGETT, A. C. to Mary J. Bradberry - issued September 14, 1852, m. by:
John T. Slatter, J. P., September 15, 1852, FRANKLIN Co.

BAGGETT, Abel G. to Nancy Beckum - issued January 19, 1847, m. by:
John Thos. Slatter, J. P., January 19, 1847, FRANKLIN Co.

BAGGETT, Abram to Nancy Runnels - issued July 19, 1838, m. by:
Joseph Smith, M. G., July 19, 1838, FRANKLIN Co.

BAGGETT, Abram to Elizabeth Guess - issued October 26, 1844, m. by:
Arledge Brown, M. G., October 27, 1844, FRANKLIN Co.

BAGGETT, Benjamin to Elizabeth Bone - issued February 4, 1849, Bondsman:
H. Yarbrough, MONTGOMERY Co.

BAGGETT, Burrell W. to Martha S. Shannon - issued January 27, 1857,
m. by: James Cook, J. P., January 28, 1857, ROBERTSON Co.

BAGGETT, E. to A. L. Shannon - issued September 4, 1850, m. by:
Eli Baggett, J. P., ROBERTSON Co.

BAIRD, Rev. A. J. to Miss M. M. Britton - issued May 8, 1850,
MONTGOMERY Co.

BAIRD, Alexander to Margaret Smith - issued October 10, 1838, Bondsman:
C. L. Crawford, WILSON Co.

BAIRD, Andrew to Patsey Hunt - issued January 8, 1814, Bondsman:
David Baird, m. by: Ransom Gwyn, J. P., January 13, 1814, WILSON Co.

BAIRD, Batt to Elizabeth Askew - issued September 27, 1824, Bondsman:
James Baird, m. by: John Bond, V. D. M., October 15, 1824,
WILSON Co.

BAIRD, Clinton to Patsey Harris - issued August 7, 1822, m. by:
Edward Harris, J. P., August 8, 1822, WILSON Co.

BAIRD, David to Polly Avery - issued February 14, 1824, Bondsman:
William Wynne, m. by: J. Gray, J. P., February 19, 1824, WILSON Co.

BAIRD, G. W. to M. E. Traughber - issued October 7, 1847, m. by:
Thomas Farmer, J. P., ROBERTSON Co.

BAIRD, Hardy H. to Nancy Baird - issued September 30, 1825, Bondsman:
Bartholomew Baird, m. by: Jas. Sullivan, WILSON Co.

BAIRD, Isham to Clarissa Bushrod - issued October 21, 1795, Bondsman:
Griswold Latimer, SUMNER Co.

BAIRD, James to Elizabeth Richmond - issued April 20, 1819, Bondsman:
Thomas Richmond, m. by: Edward Harris, J. P., April 22, 1819,
WILSON Co.

BAIRD, James H. to Julia Jennings - issued February 20, 1837, Bondsman:
Rutherford R. Barton, m. by: J. T. Stevenson, J. P., March 1,
1837, WILSON Co.

BAIRD, James P. to Eleanor W. Kirk - issued August 8, 1833, m. by:
William Eagleton, V. D. M., August 8, 1833, RUTHERFORD Co.

BAIRD, James W. to Sara Jane McLean - issued September 23, 1835,
    Bondsman: J. M. Baird, m. by: H. B. Warren, M. G., September 30,
    1835, RUTHERFORD Co.

BAIRD, John to Elener Bell - issued October 19, 1824, Bondsman:
    David Baird, WILSON Co.

BAIRD, Lemuel M. to Violet L. Henderson - issued July 25, 1827, Bondsman:
    Thomas C. Nelson, m. by: J. W. Hall, RUTHERFORD Co.

BAIRD, Levi to Dicy Fox - issued September 6, 1833, m. by:
    G. A. Huddleston, J. P., WILSON Co.

BAIRD, Lindley to Lewarken Medley - issued November 3, 1827, Bondsman:
    Henry Codey, m. by: Wm. Willis, J. P., November 7, 1827, WILSON Co.

BAIRD, Martin to Elizabeth A. Henderson - issued October 29, 1835,
    Bondsman: C. R. Johns, m. by: William Eagleton, V. D. M.,
    October 29, 1835, RUTHERFORD Co.

BAIRD, Thomas to Mary Martin - issued September 5, 1836, m. by:
    James Bond, V. D. M., September 8, 1836, WILSON Co.

BAIRD, Tho. to E. T. Cole - issued August 22, 1842, m. by: Isaac Steel
    August 24, 1850, ROBERTSON Co.

BAIRD, William to Lucinda Baird - issued August 22, 1825, Bondsman:
    Seldon Baird, m. by: John Bond, V. D. M., September 8, 1825,
    WILSON Co.

BAIRD, William to Emeline C. Baird - issued August 22, 1838, Bondsman:
    C. L. Crawford, m. by: Jas. Baird, J. P., August 23, 1838,
    WILSON Co.

BAIRD, Wm. H. to Mary Jane Gordon - January 4, 1858, m. by:
    L. M. Harwell, GILES Co.

BAIRD, Wilson to Eliza Baird - issued August 19, 1839, Bondsman:
    Batt Baird, WILSON Co.

BAIRD, Zeb to Sally Willis - issued July 13, 1838, m. by: W. C. Jones,
    J. P., July 15, 1838, STEWART Co.

BAIRD, Zebulon to Cloey Hunt - issued November 14, 1807, Bondsman:
    John Searcy, WILSON Co.

BAKER, Abraham to Rebecca Phillips - April 30, 1812, WILLIAMSON Co.

BAKER, Alijah to Rachael Wiles - issued December 17, 1842, m. by:
    R. W. January December 17, 1842, DAVIDSON Co.

BAKER, B. F. to Lucy Ann Wright - issued May 2, 1840, m. by:
    Jas. H. Cook, Esq., May 21, 1840, DAVIDSON Co.

BAKER, Charles to Margaret Lowe - December 18, KNOX Co.

BAKER, Christian to Elizabeth Hendrixon - issued May 5, 1830, Bondsman:
    Thomas Jones, m. by: Michael Davis, J. P., May 6, 1830, KNOX Co.

BAKER, Christopher to Rebecka Bolton - issued October 6, 1830,
    Bondsman: James H. Cowan, m. by: E. Nelson, J. P., October 10,
    1830, KNOX Co.

BAKER, Daniel to Sally Woodward - issued May 4, 1810, Bondsman:
    Benja. Baker, WILSON Co.

BAKER, David to Rose Ann Awatt (Awalt) - issued March 2, 1854, m. by:
    L. Brandon March 2, 1854, FRANKLIN Co.

BAKER, Edward P. to Elizabeth G. Crowley - issued October 27, 1831,
    Bondsman: Caleb C. Cummings, WILSON Co.

BAKER, Elijah to Ann E. Smith - issued February 10, 1844, FRANKLIN Co.

BAKER, Francis to Tennessee C. Thorn - issued January 5, 1840,
    DAVIDSON Co.

BAKER, G. L. to Mary Durham - issued November 26, 1874, m. by:
    C. E. Gillespie, M. G., November 29, 1874, FRANKLIN Co.

BAKER, George T. to Elizabeth Swann - issued July 1, 1848, m. by:
    Nathaniel Wilder, J. P., July 2, 1848, FRANKLIN Co.

BAKER, Giles W. to Mary J. Farris - issued September 7, 1863, Bondsman:
    J. R. Sheperson, Jos. H. Thompson, Clk. per M. E. W. Dunaway,
    Dep. Clk, BEDFORD Co.

BAKER, Hampton A. to Menervi E. Harris - issued October 21, 1837, m. by:
    Wm. H. Murray, J. P., November 7, 1837, RUTHERFORD Co.

BAKER, Henry to Jarida Ald - issued February 13, 1797, Bondsman:
    Jacob Schrider, KNOX Co.

BAKER, Henry to Rhoda Havin - issued January 24, 1823, Bondsman:
    Richard Havin, m. by: John Gass, J. P., February 6, 1823, Witness:
    Wm. Swan, KNOX Co.

BAKER, Hiram to Lucinda Monroe - issued August 17, 1833, Bondsman:
    Wm. Hollingsworth, m. by: James Lacey, M. G., August 17, 1833,
    GRAINGER Co.

BAKER, Hugh to Caty Eaken - issued May 21, 1840, Bondsman: Robt. Pence,
    m. by: Richard Simpson, M. G., June 18, 1840, MEIGS Co.

BAKER, Isaac Jun. to Sarah Jones - February 22, 1800, Security:
    Isaac Baker, Sen., GREENE Co.

BAKER, Isaac to Sarah Hickey - issued October 16, 1832, Bondsman:
    Hugh McCall, Witness: Wm. Swan, KNOX Co.

BAKER, Isham to Sally Caldwell - issued March 2, 1822, Bondsman:
    Isaac Lawrence, WILSON Co.

BAKER, Isham M. to Clarissa Ferguson - issued July 1, 1853, Bondsman:
    George M. Bell, m. by: Moses Steels, J. P., July 3, 1853,
    MONTGOMERY Co.

BAKER, J. H. W. to Mary March - issued February 27, 1841, m. by:
    J. W. Ferguson, J. P., ROBERTSON Co.

BAKER, J. J. to Mary J. F. Buckner - issued December 11, 1871, m. by:
    D. S. Long, J. P., December 14, 1871, FRANKLIN Co.

BAKER, Jabas G. to Stacy Simmons - issued January 20, 1847, m. by:
    Micagh Simons, J. P., January 21, 1847, VAN BUREN Co.

BAKER, Jacob to Elizabeth Finger - issued March 7, 1818, Bondsman:
    Vincent Taylor, m. by: H. Robinson, J. P., March 12, 1818,
    RUTHERFORD Co.

BAKER, James to Levina Donnell - issued October 4, 1824, Bondsman:
    James B. Murry, WILSON Co.

BAKER, James to Choischana Watson - issued February 11, 1840, m. by:
    W. S. Perry, J. P., ROBERTSON Co.

BAKER, James H. to Mariah Jones - issued March 7, 1840, m. by:
    E. H. East, J. P., March 7, 1840, DAVIDSON Co.

BAKER, James M. to Polly Harrel - issued July 26, 1836, Bondsman: Joseph W. Harrel, m. by: Freeman Senter July 26, 1836, SUMNER Co.

BAKER, James M. to Caroline Goodrich - issued January 11, 1840, m. by: Thomas Jarragin, J. P., February 14, 1840, DICKSON Co.

BAKER, James M. to Parantte True - issued October 12, 1842, DAVIDSON Co.

BAKER, Jane to Joseph Hanes - September 4, 1810, Bondsman: John Baker, MAURY Co.

BAKER, John to Susanna Lamkin - November 18, 1793, Security: Sam. Baker and George Kesters, GREENE Co.

BAKER, John to Nancy Davis - October 2, 1798, Security: Nathan Davis, GREENE Co.

BAKER, John to Jenney Bearding - issued February 13, 1809, Bondsman: John Powel, WILSON Co.

BAKER, John to Julia Strong - issued August 14, 1811, Bondsman: Abram Trigg, SUMNER Co.

BAKER, John to Elizabeth Derriberry - November 26, 1811, WILLIAMSON Co.

BAKER, John to Mary Young - issued December 4, 1812, Bondsman: K. S. Blythe, SUMNER Co.

BAKER, John to Ellen Graves - issued July 28, 1830, Bondsman: Jesse Lewis, m. by: E. Nelson, J. P., August 5, 1830, Witness: Wm. Swan, KNOX Co.

BAKER, John to Emaline Howerton - issued November 28, 1837, Bondsman: William Hollingsworth, m. by: Joseph Clark, J. P., November 28, 1837, GRAINGER Co.

BAKER, John to Cynthia Frame - issued March 11, 1844, m. by: Loyd Richardson, M. G., March 14, 1844, FRANKLIN Co.

BAKER, John A. to Eliza Walker - issued February 17, 1842, m. by: John Eubank, J. P., February, 1842, DICKSON Co.

BAKER, John G. to Mary Jane Warmack - issued January 10, 1843, DAVIDSON Co.

BAKER, John P. to Lucenda South - issued February 16, 1861, m. by: H. W. Carrell, J. P., February 18, 1861, COFFEE Co.

BAKER, John W. to Polley Boleman - issued September 16, 1802, Bondsman: Benjamin Baker, WILSON Co.

BAKER, Jonathan to Sally Eagan - issued May 26, 1821, Bondsman: Jesse Shaw, m. by: Wilson Hearn, J. P., WILSON Co.

BAKER, Jonathan to Lucy Ann Foster - issued November 24, 1824, Bondsman: James Allcorn, m. by: Burchell Douglas, J. P., December 2, 1824, WILSON Co.

BAKER, Jonathan S. to Martha H. Browder - issued April 11, 1853, Bondsman: George M. Moore, m. by: G. R. Browder, M. G., April, 1853, MONTGOMERY Co.

BAKER, Joseph C. to Samamtha J. Whitmore - issued August 1, 1857, m. by: A. Rose, J. P., August 2, 1857, ROBERTSON Co.

BAKER, Jourdan to Elizabeth Early - issued July 17, 1824, Bondsman: Merry S. Bottom, SUMNER Co.

BAKER, Julious J. to Elisabeth Howard - issued March 30, 1852, m. by:
F. E. Plumlee, J. P., March 30, 1852, VAN BUREN Co.

BAKER, Leonard D. to Sarah A. Johnson - issued July 15, 1837, Bondsman:
Owen T. Barbee, m. by: John Seay, M. G., August 18, 1837, WILSON Co.

BAKER, Leonard D. to Lamiza D. Gamer - issued January 18, 1842, m. by:
A. L. P. Green, M. G., January 18, 1842, DAVIDSON Co.

BAKER, Leonidas W.(?) to Susan M. Park - issued April 9, 1829, m. by:
Tho. H. Nelson April 9, 1829, KNOX Co.

BAKER, Leonidas W. to Susan Wells Park - issued April 9, 1829, Bondsman:
W. B. A. Ramsey, KNOX Co.

BAKER, Levi A. to Kitty Walton - issued December 10, 1825, Bondsman:
William Walton, m. by: Hugh Kirkpatrick, M. G., December 10, 1825,
SUMNER Co.

BAKER, Martin to Polly Ellis - issued May 31, 1809, Bondsman: Simeon
Ellis, SUMNER Co.

BAKER, Mary to John Bird, GREENE Co.

BAKER, Michael to Catharine Dolon - issued July 24, 1854, Bondsman:
Francis Holt, m. by: F. Alaysing George Orenge (Catholic Priest)
July 26, 1854, MONTGOMERY Co.

BAKER, Morgan W. to Elizabeth Hurt - m. by: S. H. Turner November 6,
1834, SUMNER Co.

BAKER, Porter to Martha H. Looney - issued February 16, 1830,
Bondsman: Jas. B. Garrison, m. by: Josiah Walton, J. P.,
February 16, 1830, SUMNER Co.

BAKER, Richard to Elizabeth Scott - issued June 17, 1854, Bondsman:
Marcus Boyer, m. by: H. F. Beaumont, M. G., June 23, 1854,
MONTGOMERY Co.

BAKER, Robert I. to Frances A. Boyers - issued August 31, 1843, m. by:
U. Young, J. P., ROBERTSON Co.

BAKER, Robt. A. to Virginia Kirksey - issued October 7, 1848, m. by:
R. T. Adams, J. P., October 9, 1848, STEWART Co.

BAKER, Rufus to Emma J. Thompson - issued November 23, 1867, m. by:
John Nugent, J. P., November 25, 1867, FRANKLIN Co.

BAKER, Samuel to Nancy Prather - April 20, 1793, Security: Nathan Davis,
GREENE Co.

BAKER, Samuel to Elizabeth Partin - issued February 12, 1852, m. by:
E. H. Ikard, J. P., February 12, 1852, FRANKLIN Co.

BAKER, Samuel to Lanesa Panyne (Payn) - issued April 23, 1859, m. by:
P. Moore, M. G., April 25, 1859, VAN BUREN Co.

BAKER, Solomon to Susannah Bayless - issued November 25, 1822, Bondsman:
Ro. Kirkpatrick, m. by: Wm. B. Carns, J. P., November 28, 1822,
Witness: Wm. Swan, KNOX Co.

BAKER, Thomas W. to Esther McMillan - October 3, 1814, KNOX Co.

BAKER, William to Mary Sturdivent Jones - issued April 22, 1805,
Bondsman: John Moore, GRAINGER Co.

BAKER, William to Jane Miller - issued December 20, 1814, Bondsman:
James Henderson, RUTHERFORD Co.

BALARD, William to Rinand Cathar - issued January 1, 1817, m. by:
David Tate, J. P., January 2, 1817, GRAINGER Co.

BAKER, Wm. L. to Mary E. Webb - issued October 7, 1873, FRANKLIN Co.

BAKER, William L. to Lucinda J. Johnson - issued May 12, 1845, m. by:
Wm. Hand, J. P., May 15, 1845, DICKSON Co.

BAKER, Wm. J. to Mary Ann Case - issued December 13, 1827, m. by:
Tho. H. Nelson December 13, 1827, KNOX Co.

BAKER, Wm. H. to Feliciana Degrove - issued March 10, 1845, m. by:
J. T. Wheat, Rr. of Ct. Ch., March 10, 1845, DAVIDSON Co.

BAKER, Wm. H. to Elvira Luster - issued August 8, 1839, m. by:
P. B. Morris, J. P., August 8, 1839, DAVIDSON Co.

BAKER, William D. to Marilla Martin - issued November 4, 1823, Bondsman:
Joseph D. Baker, RUTHERFORD Co.

BAKER, William to Fereby E. Swann - issued November 7, 1857, FRANKLIN Co.

BAKER, William to Sarah Jones - issued March 10, 1848, Bondsman:
Jas. Haddock, m. by: N. F. Trice, J. P., March 10, 1848,
MONTGOMERY Co.

BAKER, William to Mary Jane Wilson - issued December 7, 1842, m. by:
John Beard, M. G., December 8, 1842, DAVIDSON Co.

BAKER, William to Betsey Treadwell - issued June 21, 1817, Bondsman:
James Douglas, m. by: S. Hunt, J. P., June 21, 1817, SUMNER Co.

BAKER, William to Sarah Howser - issued December 16, 1822, Bondsman:
Jacob Howser, m. by: Robert McBath, Esq., December 17, 1822,
Witness, W. Swan, KNOX Co.

BALCH, Anne Wilkes to William Gamble - GREENE Co.

BALCH, Anne Wilkes to William White - GREENE Co.

BALCH, Dorcas to Robert Wily - GREENE Co.

BALCH, Elizabeth to Robert Henderson - GREEME Co.

BALCH, John to Sophia Stone - m. by: Wm. Walton January 17, 1833,
SUMNER Co.

BALCH, Rachel to John Houston - GREENE Co.

BALDRICH, James to Lyddia Pickins - September 11, 1809, Bondsman:
John Craig, MAURY Co.

BALDRIDGE, Alvin to Margaret Barr - issued August 18, 1832, Bondsman:
Richard J. Thompson, SUMNER Co.

BALDRIDGE, David C. to Sarah Howell - issued February 21, 1834, Bondsman:
John L. Dickey, RUTHERFORD Co.

BALDRIDGE, Francis to Frances Dickey - issued November 18, 1811,
RUTHERFORD Co.

BALDRIDGE, Josiah W. to Sarah Hodges - issued February 27, 1823, m. by:
Hugh Kirkpatrick February 27, 1823, SUMNER Co.

BALDRIDGE, Matthew to Elizabeth Howell - issued January 16, 1836,
m. by: W. P. Booker, J. P., January 21, 1836, RUTHERFORD Co.

BALDRIDGE, Nelson to Elizabeth Hartman - issued February 29, 1840,
DAVIDSON Co.

BALDRIDGE, Thompson to Susan Armstrong - m. by: Charles Watkins, J. P.,
July 13, 1833, SUMNER Co.

BALDRY, R. L. A. to Mary Ann Fuqua - issued August 27, 1857, m. by:
W. S. Baldry, M. G., ROBERTSON Co.

BALDTHRISS, E. S. to Eveline W. Dowdy - issued March 12, 1839, STEWART Co.

BALDWIN, Aaron to Henrietta Tally - March 2, 1811, WILLIAMSON Co.

BALDWIN, Abram to Martha Ann McMurry - issued November 28, 1839, m. by:
Tho. Cook, J. P., ROBERTSON Co.

BALDWIN, Henry to Charlotte Armstrong - issued February 9, 1829,
Bondsman: Joseph A. Brooks, m. by: R. Houston, J. P., February 10,
1829, KNOX Co.

BALDWIN, John to Nancy A. Cannon - issued March 5, 1857, m. by:
Jesse B. White, J. P., ROBERTSON Co.

BALDWIN, Merchant to Martha C. Buckley - issued December 29, 1835,
Bondsman: Richard Barber, m. by: Williamson Williams, M. G.,
December 31, 1835, WILSON Co.

BALDWIN, Moses to Eliza Killingsworth - issued February 6, 1817, m. by:
Wm. Alldredge, J. P. K. C., February 12, 1817, KNOX Co.

BALDWIN, Moses to Margaret Cahoe - issued June 2, 1817, m. by:
Tho. H. Nelson June 3, 1817, KNOX Co.

BALDWIN, Samuel P. to Nancy Catherine Borren - issued January 5, 1860,
m. by: Jesse B. White, J. P., ROBERTSON Co.

BALDWIN, William to Betsey Luttrell - issued March 25, 1809, Bondsman:
Abijah Harris, m. by: R. Houston, J. P. K. C., March 25, 1809,
KNOX Co.

BALE, James to Evalina Barry - issued February 22, 1811, SUMNER Co.

BALES, Aaron to Else Manifold - issued December 3, 1811, KNOX Co.

BALES, Aaron to Else Manifold - issued December 3, 1811, m. by:
John Love, Esq., December 3, 1811, KNOX Co.

BALES, David to Rebecca Tracy - issued July 13, 1825, Bondsman:
Elijah Butler, m. by: Samuel Dorris July 13, 1825, SUMNER Co.

BALES, John M. to Sarah Ann Jane Clardy - April 29, 1953, Security:
Nathaniel (x) Clardy, Jr., GILES Co.

BALES, Kaleb to Anne Smith - March 19, 1800, KNOX Co.

BALES, Nathan to Sarah Moore - issued January 9, 1832, m. by:
Isaac Lewis January 10, 1832, KNOX Co.

BALES, Ruben W. to Mary A. Frame - issued February 16, 1843, m. by:
Wm. T. Wells, M. G., February 16, 1843, FRANKLIN Co.

BALES, Solomon to Barbary Stewart - issued January 27, 1835, Bondsman:
Wm. Horner, m. by: Jacob Nutty, M. G., January 27, 1835, KNOX Co.

BALEW, Micajah B. to Polly Brooks - issued August 3, 1831, m. by:
Michael Davis, J. P., August 5, 1831, KNOX Co.

BALEY, Samuel to Mariah Adcock - issued November 28, 1838, m. by:
B. Rawls, M. G., ROBERTSON Co.

BALL, Betsy to Jesse Profitt - GREENE Co.

BALL, Harrison to Mary E. Alley - issued December 15, 1843, m. by:
John Corbitt, J. P., December 24, 1843, DAVIDSON Co.

BALL, James to Biddy Brezeal - issued September 4, 1800, Bondsman:
James Orr, SUMNER Co.

BALL, James to Clarine Rice - issued February 6, 1821, Bondsman:
John Ball, m. by: William Lane, J. P., February 8, 1821,
GRAINGER Co.

BALL, James to Anna Carr - issued January 12, 1822, Bondsman: James Carr,
m. by: James Car, J. P., January 12, 1822, SUMNER Co.

BALL, John to Catherine Headrick - issued September 8, 1819, Bondsman:
Daniel Underhill, m. by: William Lane, J. P., September 9, 1819,
GRAINGER Co.

BALL, Osbourne to Patsey Thomason - issued September 26, 1803, Bondsman:
Thomas Bunch, GRAINGER Co.

BALL, Thomas to Betsy Ferguson - issued September 24, 1828, m. by:
Wm. Sawyers, J. P., October 1, 1828, KNOX Co.

BALL, Thomas O. to Nancy Robinson - issued January 14, 1860, m. by:
G. D. Emerson, J. P., January 13, 1860, COFFEE Co.

BALL, William to Margaret Widner - issued May 1, 1813, Bondsman:
Isaac Dyer, GRAINGER Co.

BALL, Young to Mary Dalton - m. by: Z. G. Goodall August 31, 1838,
SUMNER Co.

BALLAH, John to Rachel Rice - November 21, 1796, Security: Spencer Rice,
GREENE Co.

BALLANCE, Joshua to Marjory Roberts - December 29, 1808, WILLIAMSON Co.

BALLANCE, William to Barberry Highs - September 12, 1799, Security:
James Rankin, GREENE Co.

BALLARD, Andrew J. to Nancy Franklin - issued April 22, 1837, m. by:
James Rodgers, J. P., April 25, 1837, KNOX Co.

BALLARD, Avery to Anne Wallis - issued August 4, 1825, m. by:
Jas. S. Jetton, J. P., August 11, 1825, RUTHERFORD Co.

BALLARD, Elizabeth to John Maworth - GREENE Co.

BALLARD, Henry M. to Jermima Burgess - issued May 5, 1838, m. by:
John Nugent, J. P., May 6, 1838, FRANKLIN Co.

BALLARD, James to Catherine Russell - issued January 26, 1843, STEWART Co.

BALLARD, Lewis to Ruth Pace - issued July 19, 1824, Bondsman:
Willie Ballard, RUTHERFORD Co.

BALLARD, Richard to Nancy Grayson - issued September 16, 1812, Bondsman:
John Simmons, GRAINGER Co.

BALLARD, S. Y. to Martha Gillentine - issued September 22, 1855, m. by:
Peter Carter, J. P., September 23, 1855, VAN BUREN Co.

BALLARD, Sarah to John Fitzgerald - GREENE Co.

BALLARD, Spencer to Rebecca Fraizer - December 7, 1796, Security:
(Newhope Quaker Meeting), GREENE Co.

BALLARD, William to Lucy B. Graham - issued November 18, 1835, Bondsman:
Robert Anderson, RUTHERFORD Co.

BALLARD, William to Hannah Brown - issued May 13, 1842, m. by:
    John Crobitt, J. P., May 13, 1842, DAVIDSON Co.

BALLARD, William to Cynthia A. Tipps - issued August 29, 1860, m. by:
    M. R. Mann, J. P., August 30, 1860, FRANKLIN Co.

BALLARD, Wm. E. to Martha Campbell - issued September 6, 1847, m. by:
    Josiah Ferris, J. P., September 6, 1847, DAVIDSON Co.

BELLENGER, Mary to Samuel Mills - GREENE Co.

BALLENTINE, Caster F. to Nancy Taylor - issued November 28, 1828,
    Bondsman: Caleb Taylor, m. by: Wm. W. Elis, J. P., December 1,
    1828, WILSON Co.

BALLENTINE, George W. to Mary G. Childress - April 25, 1851, m. by:
    C. P. Reece, M. G., GILES Co.

BALLENTINE, Jesse to Lydia Ballentine - issued December 26, 1827,
    Bondsman: James C. Fathera, RUTHERFORD Co.

BALLENTINE, William to Sarah Baker - issued June 27, 1840, DAVIDSON Co.

BALLEW, Aaron to Martha Nichols - issued August 26, 1823, Bondsman:
    Daniel Nichols, RUTHERFORD Co.

BALLINGER, Aron to Sarah Dobbin - issued August 18, 1830, Bondsman:
    Cames Coffee, m. by: Henry Alsup, J. P., GRAINGER Co.

BALLINGER, David to Sarah Willson - issued March 6, 1837, Bondsman:
    James Wilson, m. by: William Hickle, M. G., March 6, 1837,
    GRAINGER Co.

BALLINGER, James to Anne Dow - October 25, 1826, KNOX Co.

BALLINGER, James to Anne Dove - issued October 25, 1827, Bondsman:
    Absalom Rutherford, m. by: Wm. Sawyers, J. P., October 25, 1827,
    Witness: Wm. Swan, KNOX Co.

BALTHROP, James C. to Marry Russell - issued December 9, 1839, m. by:
    Jas. Daniel, J. P., December 7, 1839, DICKSON Co.

BALTHROP, W. H. to M. J. Harris - issued December 28, 1855, m. by:
    Robert Williams, J. P., January 1, 1856, ROBERTSON Co.

BALTHROP, Wm. D. to Dilly A. E. Sladen - issued February 22, 1847,
    DICKSON Co.

BALTHROP, Willie to Mary Dodson - issued January 12, 1819, Bondsman:
    William Glover, SUMNER Co.

BALTIMORE, William P. to Mary Magdline Burks - issued September 28,
    1853, m. by: N. Jernigan, M. G., September 28, 1853, COFFEE Co.

BANDY, Apperson to Elizabeth Walker - issued December 22, 1834, Bondsman:
    Answorth Harrison, m. by: Silas Tarver December 25, 1834, WILSON Co.

BANDY, Edward to Evalina Harper - issued September 11, 1827, Bondsman:
    James Cain, m. September 11, 1827, SUMNER Co.

BANDY, Epson to Harriett Pearce - issued June 2, 1822, Bondsman:
    Allen Smith, SUMNER Co.

BANDY, Jesse to Martha Daub - issued April 1, 1846, m. by:
    J. L. Adams, J. P., ROBERTSON Co.

BANDY, Jimason to Elizabeth Wright - issued May 10, 1822, m. by:
    Isaac Lindsey, M. G., May 10, 1822, SUMNER Co.

BANDY, Jimerson to Elizabeth Taylor - issued July 8, 1815, Bondsman:
Silas Freeman, WILSON Co.

BANDY, John to Elizabeth Martin - issued December 31, 1823,
m. December 31, 1823, SUMNER Co.

BANDY, Parran to Lytia Rice - issued December 25, 1809, Bondsman:
Ransom Gwyn, WILSON Co.

BANDY, Reuben E. to Mary Williams - issued February 15, 1840, Bondsman:
Briant Bandy, m. by: B. F. McKenzie, J. P., February 16, 1840,
MEIGS Co.

BANDY, Richard to Kesiah Pearis - issued December 30, 1817, Bondsman:
Jamison Bandy, SUMNER Co.

BANDY, Richard C. to Eliza Grizzard - issued May 17, 1841, m. by:
J. B. McFerrin, M. G., May 17, 1841, DAVIDSON Co.

BANDY, Thomas to Elizabeth Yarnell - issued August 17, 1829, Bondsmen:
David Hooks and James Harris, m. by: Wm. Morris, J. P., August 17,
1829, Witness: Wm. Swan, KNOX Co.

BANDY, Willsher to Nancy Johnson - issued January 6, 1808, Bondsman:
Jesse Cage, WILSON Co.

BANDY, Woodford to Nancy Austin - issued January 12, 1830, Bondsman:
James Austin, SUMNER Co.

BANDY, Woodford to Martha Busby - issued July 2, 1832, Bondsman:
James H. Busby, m. by: Seaton H. Turner, J. P., July 2, 1832,
SUMNER Co.

BANE, Edwin to City Rackley - m. by: John L. Swaney, J. P., December 10,
1823, SUMNER Co.

BANFIELD, Asa to Amand Linch - issued September 22, 1842, m. by:
William L. Perry, J. P., ROBERTSON Co.

BANISTER, H. to Hester Ann Workman - issued May 1, 1851, MONTGOMERY Co.

BANK, Isaac to Elizabeth Forkner - issued October 30, 1816, KNOX Co.

BANKETON, Grimes to Polly Ann Falls - issued February 17, 1844,
Bondsman: John Starnes, m. by: Wm. Johns, J. P., February 17,
1844, MEIGS Co.

BANKS, Alexander to Ann Daniel - issued March 11, 1830, Bondsman:
Hill Cryer, SUMNER Co.

BANKS, David to Elizabeth Lawrence - issued November 28, 1823, m. by:
Lent Brown, D. M. E. C., December 9, 1823, RUTHERFORD Co.

BANKS, David to Sarah A. Lasater - issued January 23, 1852, m. by:
A. B. Cummings, M. G., January 25, 1852, FRANKLIN Co.

BANKS, Elisha A. to Mary Coulson - issued November 16, 1860, m. by:
J. B. Williams, Mins., November 17, 1860, COFFEE Co.

BANKS, G. E. to Mattie Johnston - issued January 10, 1870, m. by:
Andrews, M. G., December 10, 1870, FRANKLIN Co.

BANKS, G. G. to Elizabeth Philips - issued February 24, 1859, m. by:
Wm. H. Phillips, J. P., February 24, 1859, FRANKLIN Co.

BANKS, George F. to Maria W. Sims - issued December 29, 1832, m. by:
Thos. Sanders, J. P., January 1, 1833, RUTHERFORD Co.

BANKS, J. J. to Joicy Banks - issued January 7, 1869, m. by: John
Armstrong, J. P., January 7, 1869, FRANKLIN Co.

BANKS, James A. to Louisa J. Mitchell - issued October 14, 1854,
m. by: Rev. J. Watson, M. G., October 15, 1854, FRANKLIN Co.

BANKS, James R. to Emeline Collins - issued November 4, 1856, m. by:
A. B. Cunningham, M. G., November 4, 1856, FRANKLIN Co.

BANKS, John to Margret Gipson - issued February 9, 1846, m. by:
Allen Gipson, J. P., February 9, 1846, FRANKLIN Co.

BANKS, John F. L. to Nancy C. Banks - issued December 2, 1850, m. by:
Wm. H. Byrom, J. P., December 2, 1850, FRANKLIN Co.

BANKS, John O. to Lucinda Harpole - issued January 11, 1858, m. by:
Samuel Umbarger, J. P., January 11, 1858, COFFEE Co.

BANKS, John W. to Luraney Nixon - issued December 23, 1874, m. by:
Rev. H. J. Byrom December 23, 1874, FRANKLIN Co.

BANKS, Jordan to Sarah Long - issued August 24, 1843, m. by:
John Weaver, M. G., August 24, 1843, FRANKLIN Co.

BANKS, Joseph to Mary Stamps - issued June 24, 1858, FRANKLIN Co.

BANKS, Jourdan to Rachiel Barnes - issued December 31, 1838, m. by:
William Simmons December 31, 1838, FRANKLIN Co.

BANKS, M. L. to Jane Stroud - issued November 16, 1854, m. by:
Samuel Umbarger, J. P., November 16, 1854, COFFEE Co.

BANKS, Samuel M. to Ann R. McCarty - m. by: S. R. Roberts, J. P.,
November 29, 1828, SUMNER Co.

BANKS, Solomon to Matilda Runnels - issued July 31, 1850, m. by:
A. B. Cummins, M. G., August 4, 1850, FRANKLIN Co.

BANKS, Solomon to Catherine Duncan - issued December 27, 1853, m. by:
E. A. Rutledge, J. P., December 27, 1853, COFFEE Co.

BANKS, Thomas to Nancy McGee - issued September 12, 1843, m. by:
Wm. Ellis, J. P., September 13, 1843, STEWART Co.

BANKS, William to Sarah Texanna Roughton - issued July 20, 1858, m. by:
Samuel Umbarger, J. P., July 23, 1858, COFFEE Co.

BANKS, William R. to Carolina Mitchell - issued December 12, 1845,
m. by: John Nugent, J. P., December 12, 1845, FRANKLIN Co.

BANNING, Alexander to Elizabeth Smith - issued November 5, 1822, m. by:
John Clark, J. P., November 7, 1822, RUTHERFORD Co.

BANTON, John to Polly Bruce - issued April 21, 1810, Bondsman:
Robt. Bruce, SUMNER Co.

BANTON, Lewis to Mary Abston - issued November 24, 1818, Bondsman:
Asal White, SUMNER Co.

BANZER, George to Louisa Kuhlmann - issued May 16, 1842, m. by:
Benjamin Sharpe, J. P., May 16, 1842, DAVIDSON Co.

BARBEE, A. W. to Rachel Cole - issued May 17, 1849, m. by: J. J. Travis,
J. P., May 18, 1849, FRANKLIN Co.

BARBEE, Abner Cain to Mary Ann M. Trice - issued December 22, 1846,
Bondsman: S. G. Barbee, m. by: L. M. Cherry, J. P., December 24,
1846, MONTGOMERY Co.

BARBEE, Angustus to Sarah Wynn - issued October 21, 1844, Bondsman:
Richard Duncan, m. by: John T. Duncan, J. P., October 24, 1844,
MONTGOMERY Co.

BARBEE, George B. to Nancy C. Chapman - issued December 8, 1840, m. by:
William L. Baldry, G. M., ROBERTSON Co.

BARBEE, James to Malinda Smart - issued April 20, 1838, Bondsman:
C. W. Cummings, m. by: Sion Bass, M. G., April 30, 1838; WILSON Co.

BARBEE, John to Hester Ann Wilson - issued May 9, 1853, Bondsman:
Bartley Barbee, m. by: Wilie Smith, J. P., May 10, 1853,
MONTGOMERY Co.

BARBEE, Joseph to Rachel Compton - issued August 7, 1820, Bondsman:
Archamal Bass, WILSON Co.

BARBEE, Joseph to Hesther Taylor - issued March 21, 1833, m. by:
Wilson Hearn March 25, 1833, WILSON Co.

BARBEE, Joseph C. to Elizabeth Scoggin - issued March 15, 1839, m. by:
Geo. Childress, J. P., March 15, 1839, ROBERTSON Co.

BARBEE, Joseph S. to Delpha Walker - issued August 14, 1837, Bondsman:
Owen T. Barbee, m. by: Wilson Hearn, M. G., August 15, 1837,
WILSON Co.

BARBEE, Robt. to Ellen F. Toler - issued February 24, 1851, Bondsman:
Bartly Barbee, MONTGOMERY Co.

BARBEE, W. J. to Melard Trice - issued January 2, 1849, Bondsman:
Jo. Pollard, MONTGOMERY Co.

BARBER, Elisha to Ann Patrick - issued January 9, 1839, m. by:
N. B. Butler, J. P., January 9, 1839, DAVIDSON Co.

BARBER, Ira to Nancy Leith - issued December 10, 1819, Bondsman:
John Barber, m. by: J. A. Browning, M. G., December 17, 1819,
WILSON Co.

BARBER, Jacob to Hester Barber - issued October 22, 1835, Bondsman:
M. T. Cartwright, m. by: M. T. Cartwright, J. P., WILSON Co.

BARBER, James to Nancy Lovin - issued February 17, 1827, Bondsman:
William Barber, RUTHERFORD Co.

BARBER, John to Nancy Ware - issued January 7, 1839, Bondsman:
E. Brantly, m. by: J. Provine, M. G., January 8, 1839, WILSON Co.

BARBER, John G. to Sarah E. Williams - issued January 9, 1856, m. by:
Wm. Hill, M. G., January 10, 1856, FRANKLIN Co.

BARBER, Joel to Elizabeth Tucker - issued June 4, 1827, Bondsman:
John Sanders, RUTHERFORD Co.

BARBER, Joseph to Martha M. Ligon - issued July 15, 1835, Bondsman:
Henry Barber, WILSON Co.

BARBER, Thos. to Margaret Barber - issued April 10, 1834, Bondsman:
Wade Jarrett, m. by: H. G. Warren, M. G., April 10, 1834,
RUTHERFORD Co.

BARBER, Sherod to Martha Tatum - issued July 25, 1846, m. by:
Benj. Sharpe, J. P., July 25, 1846, DAVIDSON Co.

BARBER, William to Eunice Wilson - issued September 29, 1824, m. by:
Sam'l Sample, J. P., September 30, 1824, KNOX Co.

BARBER, William to Sarah Williams - issued March 4, 1833, Bondsman:
Nelson P. Modrall, m. by: H. B. Warren, M. G., March 4, 1833,
RUTHERFORD Co.

BARBOUR, Daniel to Sally Wyatt - m. by: Freeman Senter August 15, 1835,
SUMNER Co.

BARBOUR, John to Jonah L. Barbour - issued January 2, 1830, Bondsman: Overton B. Morris, RUTHERFORD Co.

BARBY, Elza to Polly Maples - issued May 23, 1820, Bondsman: John Perrin, m. by: William Hankins, J. P., May 23, 1820, GRAINGER Co.

BARCLAY, Felix to Price Brock - issued January 17, 1799, Bondsman: F. A. Ramsey, Witness: Chas. McClung, Clk., KNOX Co.

BARE, Henry to Malinda Frie - issued April 2, 1838, MEIGS Co.

BAREFOOT, Noah to Patsey Cook - issued April 1, 1826, Bondsman: Benja. Goodwin, WILSON Co.

BAREN, Francis to Edy Wimberly - issued March 30, 1805, Bondsman: John Baren, SUMNER Co.

BAREN, Stephen to Susan Wimbelly - issued April 19, 1821, Bondsman: Francis Baren, m. by: John Gilbert, J. P., April 19, 1821, SUMNER Co.

BARFOOT, Jonathan to Nanny White - January 2, 1812, WILLIAMSON Co.

BARFORD, Kinchen to Nancy Maddox - issued November 5, 1838, m. by: William L. Perry, J. P. R. C., ROBERTSON Co.

BARGER, Jacob to Eveline Smith - issued May 22, 1833, m. by: Wm. Lyons, J. P., May 23, 1833, KNOX Co.

BARGER, John to Susanna Symons - January 29, 1799, Security: Leonard Symons and John Wilson, GREENE Co.

BARGER, Nicholas to Polly Sterling - issued January 6, 1825, Bondsman: James Watt, m. by: Tho. H. Nelson January 6, 1825, KNOX Co.

BARHAM, Henry to Lucy Ann Rust - issued September 8, 1852, m. by: Thos. W. Ruffin, J. P., September 14, 1852, ROBERTSON Co.

BARHAM, J. G. to M. F. Rust - issued July 20, 1851, m. by: T. W. Ruffin, J. P. C., ROBERTSON Co.

BARHAM, John to Fanny Markham - issued January 7, 1817, Bondsman: Eli Giles, SUMNER Co.

BARHAM, Joseph W. to Harriet N. Gatewood - issued May 24, 1856, m. by: W. R. Sadler, J. P., May 25, 1856, ROBERTSON Co.

BARHAM, Thomas to Elizabeth Perry - issued July 23, 1821, Bondsman: John Barham, m. by: V. Landers, J. P., July 23, 1821, SUMNER Co.

BARHAM, W. R. to N. C. Watts - issued October 22, 1858, m. by: W. R. Sadler, J. P., October 24, 1858, ROBERTSON Co.

BARLINGER, Jonathan to Kitty Goodall - issued January 10, 1812, Bondsman: William Cartwright, SUMNER Co.

BARKER, A. D. to L. Simmons - issued July 29, 1847, m. by: Jas. Woodard, J. P., ROBERTSON Co.

BARKER, Benjamin to Rosanna Reagor - issued January 24, 1864, Bondsman: Calvin N. Pearson, Jos. H. Thompson, Clk., m. by: John E. Frost January 27, 1864, BEDFORD Co.

BARKER, D. B. to M. L. Branch - issued December 6, 1865, m. by: Thos. J. Shaw, M. G., December 7, 1865, FRANKLIN Co.

BARKER, David to Betsey Spencer - January 6, 1807, WILLIAMSON Co.

BARKER, Hardin to Annice Wilson - issued November 20, 1823, m. by:
James McMillan, J. P., November 20, 1823, KNOX Co.

BARKER, Isreal to Polly Brackin - issued March 14, 1809, SUMNER Co.

BARKER, Joshua to Anne Smith - issued September 17, 1816, Bondsman:
James Kirkpatrick, m. by: Hugh Kirkpatrick, M. G., September 17,
1816, SUMNER Co.

BARKER, Nathan to Priscilla Meallias - issued May 27, 1829, Bondsman:
Thomas Jorden, SUMNER Co.

BARKER, Richard to Susanna Williams - issued March 15, 1836, Bondsman:
Robert Whittier, WILSON Co.

BARKFIELD, George to Tennessee Mansker - issued September 8, 1859,
m. by: J. B. Anderson, M. G., September 8, 1859, ROBERTSON Co.

BARKLEY, Benjamin to Lydia Reader - issued December 23, 1819, Bondsman:
William Morgan, m. by: John W. Payton, J. P., WILSON Co.

BARKLEY, Benjamin G. to Ann Eliza Wynn - issued November 6, 1837,
Bondsman: Berry Young, WILSON Co.

BARKLEY, Harris to Martha Jones - issued December 17, 1840, Bondsman:
L. B. Green, m. by: Thos. Davis, WILSON Co.

BARKSDALE, Hickerson to Harriet Lowe - issued June 23, 1830, Bondsman:
Asa B. Douglas, WILSON Co.

BARKSDALE, Randolph to Susan Williams - issued November 16, 1824,
Bondsman: Thos. H. Read, RUTHERFORD Co.

BARKSDALE, W. O. to Josephine Talley - issued October 17, 1853,
Bondsman: Jesse Sadler, m. by: Mark Senter, M. G., October 20,
1853, MONTGOMERY Co.

BARKSDALE, Wm. to Nancy Lester - October 14, 1813, WILLIAMSON Co.

BARKSDALE, William to Ann Eliza Calhoun - issued May 14, 1829, Bondsman:
Ransford McGrigor, RUTHERFORD Co.

BARKSDALE, William C. to Amanda D. Martin - issued September 7, 1852,
Bondsman: James H. Robb, m. by: Thos. Watts, M. G., September 7,
1852, MONTGOMERY Co.

BARLETT, Franklin to Polly Micks - issued April 13, 1822, Bondsman:
George L. Smith, WILSON Co.

BARLEY, Joseph W. to Margrett R. Parker - issued November 31, 1860,
m. by: Thos. R. Woodward December 21, 1860, FRANKLIN Co.

BARLOW, Alfred to Elizabeth Gibson - issued June 23, 1834, m. by:
Wm. R. Matthews, J. P., June 24, 1834, RUTHERFORD Co.

BARLOW, Benjamin D. to Fanny Molloy - issued October 15, 1832, m. by:
G. Baker October 18, 1832, RUTHERFORD Co.

BARLOW, Benjamin D. to Mary Jane Kirby - issued December 22, 1834,
Bondsman: Wm. Spence, RUTHERFORD Co.

BARLOW, Franklin to Elenor Johnson - issued December 17, 1863, Bondsman:
Louis Moore, LAWRENCE Co.

BARLOW, John S. to Elenor Johnson - issued September 6, 1865, Bondsman:
Thomas D. Choate, m. by: A. P. Freeman, J. P., September 6, 1865,
LAWRENCE Co.

BARLOW, William to Elizabeth C. Hall - issued December 6, 1837, m. by:
Isaiah Robinson, J. P., December 6, 1837, RUTHERFORD Co.

BARNARD, Elisha to Polly Bradley - m. by: H. House April 25, 1837, SUMNER Co.

BARNARD, James to Jessia Short - issued August 25, 1813, Bondsman: Zadoch Barnard, SUMNER Co.

BARNARD, James to Betsey Hunter - issued September 6, 1822, Bondsman: John Hinton, SUMNER Co.

BARNARD, James to Peggy Ball - issued January 1, 1826, Bondsman: John Mills, m. by: D. McAnally, J. P., January 1, 1826, GRAINGER Co.

BARNARD, Sanford to Sarah Bradley - issued May 25, 1838, Bondsman: Randolph Maberry, SUMNER Co.

BARNARD, Thos. to Sally Williams - issued August 9, 1836, Bondsman: Benjamin Gribble, m. by: J. H. House August 1, 1836, SUMNER Co.

BARNER, Sterling M. to Sarah Jane West - issued August 8, 1838, m. by: J. T. Edgar August 8, 1838, DAVIDSON Co.

BARNES, Ansalam to Miram Leak - June 26, 1816, WILLIAMSON Co.

BARNES, Benjamin to Catahrine Zachary - issued April 20, 1842, m. by: E. M. Patterson, J. P., April 20, 1842, DAVIDSON Co.

BARNES, Berry to Harriett Hooser - issued December 15, 1839, m. by: M. Catchings, J. P., December 15, 1839, FRANKLIN Co.

BARNES, Bird to Mary Jane Moody - issued September 26, 1866, m. by: W. G. Guinn September 21, 1866, FRANKLIN Co.

BARNES, Charley to Mary Pace - issued September 1, 1858, m. by: James Seargent September 1, 1858, FRANKLIN Co.

BARNES, Clinton M. to Lucretia Mantello - issued October 28, 1858, m. by: A. Rose, J. P., ROBERTSON Co.

BARNES, Cyris to Piety Swann - issued February 28, 1843, m. by: John Nugent, J. P., February 28, 1843, FRANKLIN Co.

BARNES, Daniel T. to Susan L. Sims - issued October 31, 1816, m. by: Edm'd Jones October 31, 1816, RUTHERFORD Co.

BARNES, Danl. W. to Virginia Little - issued September 12, 1862, Bondsman: W. M. Puckett, Jos. H. Thompson, Clk., BEDFORD Co.

BARNES, Dennis to Delely King - issued December 22, 1841, m. by: W. Taylor, J. P., December 22, 1841, FRANKLIN Co.

BARNES, Dennis to Nancy A. Pellam - issued November 27, 1865, FRANKLIN Co.

BARNES, Edmund to Elizabeth Wynns - issued March 17, 1842, m. by: Allen McCaskill, J. P., STEWART Co.

BARNES, George to Caroline C. McNeil - issued November 21, 1843, ROBERTSON Co.

BARNES, George to Margret Pelham - issued May 23, 1859, m. by: Wm. Prince, J. P., May 23, 1859, FRANKLIN Co.

BARNES, George to Symantha Short - issued May 21, 1867, m. by: James Seargent, J. P., May 22, 1867, FRANKLIN Co.

BARNES, George to Nancy Brewer (MB) - issued November 22, 1869, FRANKLIN Co.

BARNES, George W. to Ella Jane Luker - August 31, 1841, m. by: Jesse Luker, J. P., GILES Co.

BARNES, George W. to Malinda J. Newman - issued August 31, 1855, m. by: S. P. Whitten--, M. G., September 3, 1855, FRANKLIN Co.

BARNES, H. B. to M. E. Chance - issued October 12, 1850, m. by: F. R. Gooch, L. O., October 13, 1850, ROBERTSON Co.

BARNES, Hillard to Mary Lockheart - issued May 18, 1841, m. by: Allen McCaskill, J. P., STEWART Co.

BARNES, Jecheland to Betsey Walker - March 2, 1802, Security: John Leek, BLOUNT Co.

BARNES, Jeremiah to Mary Lagooch - August 6, 1816, WILLIAMSON Co.

BARNES, Jeremiah to Willy Combs - issued August 2, 1847, STEWART Co.

BARNES, Jessee to Ann Moody - issued July 17, 1867, m. by: James Seargent, J. P., July 17, 1867, FRANKLIN Co.

BARNES, John to L. J. Holiway - issued October 4, 1872, m. by: A. B. Darrell, M. G., October 25, 1872, FRANKLIN Co.

BARNES, John F. to Eliza Ann Ellis - issued January 12, 1846, DAVIDSON Co.

BARNES, Jonas to Caroline Hays - issued May 18, 1849, m. by: J. C. Montgomery, J. P., May 20, 1849, FRANKLIN Co.

BARNES, Jonas to Mary Overton - issued May 19, 1860, m. by: John D. Lynch, J. P., May 20, 1860, FRANKLIN Co.

BARNES, Jonas to Nancy C. Sansom - issued October 4, 1865, m. by: M. Catchings, J. P., October 6, 1865, FRANKLIN Co.

BARNES, Joseph to Malinda Hill - issued February 3, 1849, m. by: Madison Williams, J. P., February 4, 1849, FRANKLIN Co.

BARNES, Kinchen to Elizabeth Braswell - issued July 22, 1806, Bondsman: Ruffin Deloach, SUMNER Co.

BARNES, Larry S. to Beady M. Batts - issued February 20, 1840, m. by: Robert Green, J. P., February 21, 1840, ROBERTSON Co.

BARNES, Luther M. to Nancy Anderson - issued October 17, 1845, m. by: Allen Knight, J. P., November 5, 1845.

BARNES, Marcus H. to Mary Ann Rowe - issued January 16, 1838, m. by: T. Fuquay January 16, 1838, DAVIDSON Co.

BARNES, Nathan to Eliazbeth Holliman - issued January 2, 1826, Bondsman: Ashley Stanfield, SUMNER Co.

BARNES, Peter to Nancy Jane Garner - issued July 2, 1849, m. by: M. Catchings, J. P., July 2, 1849, FRANKLIN Co.

BARNES, Richard to Elizabeth Thompson - issued December 28, 1847, m. by: James Bledsoe, J. P., December 28, 1847, FRANKLIN Co.

BARNES, Thomas to Alice Buchanan - issued June 21, 1798, Bondsman: Tabitha Buchanan, Witness: H. L. White, KNOX Co.

BARNES, Turner to Betsey Anderson - issued March 26, 1817, Bondsman: John Bell, SUMNER Co.

BARNES, Uriah E. to Elizabeth Tacker - January 25, 1842, m. by: M. V. Luna, J. P., Security: James C. Shores, GILES Co.

BARNES, W. J. to Lucinda Draughon - issued August 1, 1844, m. by: R. W. Bell, J. P., ROBERTSON Co.

BARNES, William to Jennie Walker - October 21, 1800, Security:
William Walker, BLOUNT Co.

BARNES, William to Christian Bowerman - December 16, 1801, Bondsman:
Peter Bowerman, BLOUNT Co.

BARNES, William to Mary Jones - issued May 6, 1859, m. by:
L. F. Dilliard, J. P., May 6, 1859, COFFEE Co.

BARNES, William H. to Maggie Horne - issued August 21, 1872, FRANKLIN Co.

BARNES, Wm. R. to Elizabeth Ann Wells - issued October 19, 1843, m. by:
David Abernathy, J. P., October 19, 1843, DAVIDSON Co.

BARNES, Wm. T. to Fanny Ann Weaks - issued March 13, 1845, m. by:
C. Travis, J. P., March 16, 1845, STEWART Co.

BARNES, Wright to Kitty Stone - issued September 30, 1812, Bondsman:
Orran Faulk, SUMNER Co.

BARNES, Wright to Nancy Doughtry - issued November 5, 1825, Bondsman:
Solomon Sholders, m. by: Elijah Boddie, J. P., November 5, 1825,
SUMNER Co.

BARNET, John to Polly McAdow - issued September 23, 1807, Bondsman:
James McAdow, WILSON Co.

BARNET, Joseph to Elizabeth Sand - issued December 14, 1839, m. by:
L. Ayres, J. P., ROBERTSON Co.

BARNET, Margaret to Anthony Pate - GREENE Co.

BARNET, Moses to Rebecca Fisher - issued May 8, 1816, Bondsman:
Jeremiah Fisher, m. by: Ranson Gwyn, J. P., May 9, 1816, WILSON Co.

BARNET, Thomas to Penelope Ogelvie - June 14, 1815, WILLIAMSON Co.

BARNET, William to Casander Barnet - issued September 25, 1806,
Bondsman: Nathan Atcheson, SUMNER Co.

BARNETT, Ambrose to Sarah Sanders - issued February 15, 1832, m. by:
Thos. Sanders, J. P., February 16, 1832, RUTHERFORD Co.

BARNETT, B. J. to Amanda Rutledge - issued October 31, 1862, Bondsman:
W. J. Roan, m. by: W. C. Davis, J. P., October 31, 1862, LAWRENCE Co.

BARNETT, Benjamin to Eveline Moor - issued October 26, 1849, m. by:
John Gold October 23, 1848, MONTGOMERY Co.

BARNETT, E. E. to J. E. Campbell - issued October 27, 1863, Bondsman:
J. G. Russell, Jos. H. Thompson, Clk. per M. E. W. Dunaway,
D. Clk., BEDFORD Co.

BARNETT, H. to S. A. Hendly - issued August 2, 1867, m. by: J. Crawford
August 2, 1867, FRANKLIN Co.

BARNETT, Isaac to Nancy Long - issued May 13, 1826, Bondsman:
James H. Long, m. by: John Bond, V. D. M., May 14, 1826, WILSON Co.

BARNETT, James to Peggy Abbott - issued October 25, 1811, Bondsman:
George Abbott, SUMNER Co.

BARNETT, James to Mary E. Lenton - issued March 6, 1865, m. by:
J. Walworth, Chap. 43 Reg. Wis. Vols., March 7, 1865, FRANKLIN Co.

BARNETT, James M. to Elizabeth Coker - issued August 16, 1825, Bondsman:
Chas. Coker, Witness: Wm. Swan, KNOX Co.

BARNETT, James P. to Peggy Gibson - September 10, 1810, WILLIAMSON Co.

BARNETT, James W. to Sarah Spray - issued October 25, 1856, m. by:
A. B. Cunningham, M. G., October 26, 1856, FRANKLIN Co.

BARNETT, Jaramiah to Sarah York - issued April 27, 1822, Bondsman:
Andrew Philips, m. by: Valentine Molder, J. P., April 27, 1822,
GRAINGER Co.

BARNETT, John to Betsey Hunter - issued December 26, 1819, Bondsman:
Dempsey Hunter, SUMNER Co.

BARNETT, John W. to Mary Coker - issued February 26, 1817, m. by:
S. Montgomery February 27, 1817, KNOX Co.

BARNETT, Levi to Elizabeth Williams - issued October 9, 1835, Bondsman:
William Holt, m. by: B. B. Dickins, J. P., October 11, 1835,
RUTHERFORD Co.

BARNETT, Robert to Elizabeth Porter - April 16, 1811, KNOX Co.

BARNETT, Thomas to Henny Noble - issued January 27, 1806, Bondsman:
Jeremiah Claxton, SUMNER Co.

BARNETT, William to Rosannah Kirkum - November 3, 1806, KNOX Co.

BARNETT, William to Cynthia Clay - issued June 29, 1818, Bondsman:
Epaphroditus Hightower, Junr., m. by: John Hall, J. P., GRAINGER Co.

BARNETT, William to Peggy Gunn - issued January 9, 1827, Bondsman:
Robert Raymay, m. by: Thomas D. Lansden, J. P., WILSON Co.

BARNETT, Wm. to Elizabeth Morson - issued March 21, 1838, STEWART Co.

BARNHART, Adam to Elizabeth Broyles - October 28, 1806, Security:
James Oliphant and Jacob Earnest, GREENE Co.

BARNHART, Felix to Manervy J. McKeon - issued December 18, 1845,
Bondsman: Wm. C. Lillard, m. by: Drury L. Godsey, M. G., December 18,
1845, MEIGS Co.

BARNHILL, James M. to Delilah Stephens - issued February 4, 1818,
Bondsman: Bachel Barnhill, RUTHERFORD Co.

BARNS, John to Mary Turney - issued December 27, 1796, Bondsman:
Elisha Clary, SUMNER Co.

BARNS, Robert to Joanna Leffler - issued July 23, 1830, Bondsman:
Albert Westbrooks, SUMNER Co.

BARNS, Samuel to Sally Jewel - issued September 28, 1796, Bondsman:
William Snoddfeald, SUMNER Co.

BARNS, Thomas to Polly Nickins - issued January 15, 1831, Bondsman:
James Nickins, WILSON Co.

BARNS, William to Christiana Bowerman - December 16, 1801, Security:
Peter Bowerman, BLOUNT Co.

BARNS, William C. to Nancy Curry - issued July 7, 1829, Bondsman:
Alfred M. Beard, m. by: W. Walton July 7, 1829, SUMNER Co.

BARNS, Zachariah to Elizabeth Jops (or Tops) - issued June 14, 1828,
Bondsman: Nicholas Drumhelln, SUMNER Co.

BARNSFIELD, Williams to Mary Merchant - issued December 22, 1838,
Bondsman: Allgood Woollard, m. by: Jas. C. Willeford December 23,
1838, WILSON Co.

BARNWELL, Robt. H. to Jane Barnwell - issued October 7, 1819, Bondsman:
George Shetterly, m. by: John Haynie October 7, 1819, KNOX Co.

BARNWELL, Rob't. H. to Eliza Jane White - issued September 25, 1834, m. by: J. Anderson, J. P., September 25, 1834, KNOX Co.

BARNWELL, Wm. L. to Sarah Turbeville - issued October 21, 1830, m. by: Isaac Lewis October 21, 1830, KNOX Co.

BARR, Alexander to Martha Webb - issued June 9, 1845, STEWART Co.

BARR, Caleb to Priscilla Miers - issued July 4, 1826, Bondsman: Solomon Sholders, m. by: Wm. Walton, J. P., July 4, 1826, SUMNER Co.

BARR, Delamere to Jane Jetton - issued August 29, 1833, Bondsman: H. Graham, m. by: Geo. A. Sublett, J. P., August 29, 1833, RUTHERFORD Co.

BARR, Erastus to Eliza J. Collins - issued March 25, 1853, m. by: G. Orgain, J. P., March 27, 1853, MONTGOMERY Co.

BARR, G. W. to Jane Cannon - issued January 30, 1850, m. by: W. H. Bugg, J. P., ROBERTSON Co.

BARR, Henry P. to Kiziah Collins - issued August 13, 1847, m. August 13, 1847, STEWART Co.

BARR, Hugh to Katy Hodge - issued November 23, 1813, Bondsman: Robt. Hodge, SUMNER Co.

BARR, Isaac to Elvina Cook - issued December 27, 1853, m. by: O. H. Morrow, M. G., December 29, 1853, ROBERTSON Co.

BARR, James H. to Eliza Miller - issued September 22, 1825, Bondsman: Samuel W. Barr, m. by: David Foster, M. G., WILSON Co.

BARR, James W. to Martha Miers - issued October 14, 1830, Bondsman: Wm. McElurath, m. by: Barton Brown October 14, 1830, SUMNER Co.

BARR, John to Elizabeth Cronk - January 11, 1810, KNOX Co.

BARR, John to Jenny Dunlap - issued September 22, 1798, Bondsman: Henry Hipshur, m. by: Samuel Yancey, J. P., GRAINGER Co.

BARR, John W. to Agnes McCord - May 22, 1811, Bondsman: William McCord, MAURY Co.

BARR, Joseph to Mary Taylor - issued June 1, 1836, Bondsman: Solomon Shoulders, m. by: Elijah Boddie June 1, 1836, SUMNER Co.

BARR, Robert to Cynthia Jones - issued December 27, 1823, m. by: Richard Johnson December 27, 1823, SUMNER Co.

BARR, Silas to Hannah White - issued February 2, 1809, Bondsman: John Barr, SUMNER Co.

BARR, William G. to Chany Lane - issued February 6, 1823, m. by: R. Gwyn, J. P., February 11, 1823, WILSON Co.

BARRENS, James to Malinda Wilson - issued May 8, 1860, m. by: W. G. Pirtle, J. P., May 13, 1860, COFFEE Co.

BARRET, David to Jemima Allin - issued November 11, 1809, Bondsman: Johnson Bandy, WILSON Co.

BARRET, Thomas to Charlotte Reason - issued July 18, 1803, Bondsman: John Reason, SUMNER Co.

BARRETT, Charles to Eliza Butcher - issued February 13, 1839, m. by: Daniel Judd, L. E., February 14, 1839, DAVIDSON Co.

BARRETT, David to Patsey Ingmay - issued December 11, 1813, Bondsman: George Barrett, SUMNER Co.

BARRETT, James to Nancy Langford - issued September 19, 1818, Bondsman: William L. Bledsoe, m. September 19, 1818, SUMNER Co.

BARRETT, Josiah to Louisa Teysdale - issued December 17, 1821, Bondsman: Nicholas Latimer, SUMNER Co.

BARRETT, Levi to Minerva Rainey - issued November 12, 1829, Bondsman: William Stokes, RUTHERFORD Co.

BARRETT, Randle C. to Rhoda Reynolds - issued March 9, 1840, m. by: Joshua Lester, J. P., March 11, 1840, WILSON Co.

BARRINGTON, Washington to Susan Easters - issued December 13, 1821, m. by: H. Robinson, J. P., December 13, 1821, RUTHERFORD Co.

BARRON, John to Sarah Millar - issued November 23, 1836, Bondsman: Jesse Williams, GRAINGER Co.

BARROTT, David to Nancy Hales - issued February 9, 1811, Bondsman: Solomon Barnes, SUMNER Co.

BARROW, James C. to Susan Boon - issued February 10, 1830, Bondsman: Barrel Tisdale, SUMNER Co.

BARROW, James C. to Susan E. Boon - issued February 10, 1831, m. by: F. E. Pitts February 10, 1831, SUMNER Co.

BARROW, Jno. E. to Catharine S. Gingrey - issued October 5, 1843, m. by: W. H. Wharton October 5, 1843, DAVIDSON Co.

BARROW, Reason to Caroline White - issued August 4, 1831, Bondsman: John Bell, m. by: Isaac Lindsey, E. M. C. C., August 4, 1831, SUMNER Co.

BARROW, Robt. J. to Mary E. Crabb - issued July 11, 1839, m. by: J. Thos. Wheat, M. G., July 11, 1839, DAVIDSON Co.

BARROW, William to Mariam Cartmell - issued July 3, 1832, Bondsman: Elijah Boddie, m. by: Burrell Tisdale July 3, 1832, SUMNER Co.

BARRY, A. F. to Mary E. Jones - issued September 5, 1855, m. by: G. W. Featherstone, V. D. M., September 6, 1855, ROBERTSON Co.

BARRY, Francis to Sarah Frost - issued July 4, 1813, Bondsman: Jonathan Hady, SUMNER Co.

BARRY, Isaac to Susan Allen - issued January 28, 1856, m. by: R. H. Harrison, J. P., March 24, 1856, ROBERTSON Co.

BARRY, J. C. to M. Byran - issued August 22, 1861, m. by: T. O. Tarpley, J. P., August 22, 1861, ROBERTSON Co.

BARRY, James to Polly Sanders - issued December 6, 1809, Bondsman: William H. Douglass, SUMNER Co.

BARRY, Richard H. to Elizabeth J. Haynes - issued October 26, 1841, m. by: R. B. C. Howell, M. G., October 26, 1841, DAVIDSON Co.

BARRY, Thomas to Sarah Peyton - issued November 16, 1830, Bondsman: A. F. Young, SUMNER Co.

BARRY, Thomas to Harriet Allen - issued August 8, 1856, m. by: Thomas West, M. G., August 10, 1856, ROBERTSON Co.

BARRY, William to Ann B. Councell - issued January 22, 1829, Bondsman: Lloyd Rutherford, m. by: T. H. Nelson January 22, 1829, KNOX Co.

BARRY, William L. to Malinda Jernigan - issued September 22, 1841,
m. by: W. L. Payne, J. P., September 23, 1841, ROBERTSON Co.

BARRY, William P. to Eleanor Wright - issued October 3, 1837, m. by:
W. P. Payne, J. P., November 2, 1837, ROBERTSON Co.

BARSKIN, Robert to Rachel Rickett - issued November 3, 1813, Bondsman:
James McKnight, WILSON Co.

BARSLEY, Shelby to John Ellen Pence - issued September 29, 1860, m. by:
Isaac Steel, ROBERTSON Co.

BARTEE, A. J. to Louisa Elliott - issued April 3, 1854, Bondsman:
J. R. Broedon, m. by: A. Outlaw, J. P., April 4, 1854, MONTGOMERY Co.

BARTEE, G. W. to Susan A. Moore - issued August 4, 1852, Bondsman:
Wm. O'Neal, MONTGOMERY Co.

BARTEE, Jessie M. to Lucy Ann Bullock - issued February 7, 1852,
Bondsman: J. H. Ogburn, MONTGOMERY Co.

BARTELL, Bartley to Emily E. Darnell - issued January 21, 1850, Bondsman:
John Bartell, MONTGOMERY Co.

BARTEN, William to Rebecca Marshall - issued February 8, 1816, Bondsman:
Smith Hansbrough, WILSON Co.

BARTHOLMEW, Joseph to Nancy Willis - issued October 31, 1833, Bondsman:
Joel Read, m. by: Michael Davis, J. P., October 31, 1833, KNOX Co.

BARTHOLOMEW, Thomas to Margaret Horton - issued February 16, 1836,
m. by: J. Kirkpatrick, J. P., February 19, 1836, WILSON Co.

BARTHOLOMU, A. J. to Amanda Gainus - issued August 6, 1859, m. by:
A. Rose, J. P., August 7, 1859, ROBERTSON Co.

BARTLER, Francis A. to Sarah Jane Dravit (Dranit) - issued August 17,
1865, m. by: R. A. Barthonert (Barthovert) August 17, 1865,
FRANKLIN Co.

BARTLET, Joseph to Patience McCoy - issued April 3, 1798, Witness:
Chas. McClung and H. L. White, KNOX Co.

BARTLETT, G. L. to Mary A. Glover - issued August 12, 1857, m. by:
H. H. Orndorff, J. P., August 14, 1857, ROBERTSON Co.

BARTLETT, J. M. to Nancy Baker - issued September 5, 1853, m. by:
J. M. P. Hickerson, M. G., September 6, 1853, COFFEE Co.

BARTLETT, John M. to Martha Foust - issued November 8, 1831, Bondsman:
M. H. Biles, WILSON Co.

BARTLETT, Joseph to Patience McCoy - issued 1825, Bondsman:
Is. Bradley, Witness: H. L. White, KNOX Co.

BARTLETT, Joshua C. to Nancy Sweate - issued December 2, 1835, Bondsman:
M. Johnson, WILSON Co.

BARTLETT, Robert to Jane M. Gunn - issued April 15, 1843, m. by:
J. M. Gunn, J. P. R. C., April 16, 1843, ROBERTSON Co.

BARTLETT, Thomas to Nancy Brooks - April 30, 1811, Bondsman:
Andrew Forgey, MAURY Co.

BARTON(?), A. I. to Martha Evans - issued May 22, 1861, Bondsmen:
Emsmas Winford, Jos. H. Thompson, Clk., m. by: H. F. Holt, J. P.,
BEDFORD Co.

BARTON, David to Sarah Borum - issued October 7, 1811, Bondsman:
Richard Borum, WILSON Co.

BARTON, Elisha to Cyntha Bowman - issued May 24, 1831, Bondsman:
Edwin Folks, SUMNER Co.

BARTON, Francis A. to Ervin J. McAdams - issued July 23, 1861, Bondsman:
J. M. Brown, Jos. H. Thompson, Clk., James H. Neil, Dep. Clk.,
m. by: H. C. Blessing, J. P., BEDFORD Co.

BARTON, Gabriel to Jane Johnson - issued December 28, 1819, Bondsman:
Samuel Calhoon, m. by: Thos. Calhoon, V. D. M., December 29,
1819, WILSON Co.

BARTON, Hale to Lucinda E. Rucker - issued January 12, 1829, Bondsman:
Wm. T. Christy, RUTHERFORD Co.

BARTON, Henry to Sarah J. Durham - issued September 13, 1865, Bondsman:
John F. Kilpatrick, m. by: Stephanus Busby, J. P., September 14,
1865, LAWRENCE Co.

BARTON, Isaac to Charity Baker - issued April 10, 1821, Bondsman:
John Mason, KNOX Co.

BARTON, Isaac to Charity Baker - issued April 10, 1821, m. by:
James Dixon April 10, 1821, KNOX Co.

BARTON, James to Betsey Childress - issued August 30, 1821, Bondsman:
Larkin Carman, SUMNER Co.

BARTON, James to Betsey Childress - issued January 29, 1822, Bondsman:
Stephen Brundige, SUMNER Co.

BARTON, James to Nancy Flora - issued February 25, 1832, Bondsman:
Pleasant M. Senter, m. by: Elihu Mallikan, M. G., GRAINGER Co.

BARTON, John to Elizabeth Coon - issued November 17, 1847, Bondsman:
Robert Frazier, MONTGOMERY Co.

BARTON, John P. to Martha Johnson - issued December 14, 1831, Bondsman:
Joshua Pemberton, WILSON Co.

BARTON, Joshua to Elizabeth A. Barton - issued March 1, 1834, Bondsman:
John Smith, m. by: Jordan Willeford, J. P., March 5, 1834,
RUTHERFORD Co.

BARTON, Kendell C. to Lockey Jarman - issued January 7, 1838, Bondsman:
J. C. Word, WILSON Co.

BARTON, Robert to Polly Bankhead - issued January 7, 1817, m. by:
Jordan Willeford, J. P., January 9, 1817, RUTHERFORD Co.

BARTON, Robert D. to Ruthey Barton - issued August 15, 1836, Bondsman:
Wm. H. Ivie, m. by: C. Jones, J. P., August 16, 1836, RUTHERFORD Co.

BARTON, Rutherford R. to Avey Tilda McLarin - issued August 21, 1838,
Bondsman: Zebulon Baird, m. by: Wm. Barton, M. G., WILSON Co.

BARTON, Stephen to Ellennor Baird - issued February 14, 1807, Bondsman:
Zebulon Baird, WILSON Co.

BARTON, Thomas to Tabitha Hodges - issued October 6, 1811, Bondsman:
Jesse Hodges, WILSON Co.

BARTON, Thomas to Judah Knight - issued February 16, 1819, Bondsman:
Ezekiel Carothers, m. by: S. H. Blythe, J. P., February 16, 1819,
SUMNER Co.

BARTON, Thomas H. to Nancy Austin - issued June 16, 1832, Bondsman:
John H. Turner, SUMNER Co.

BARTON, William to Margaret Lain - issued December 19, 1835, Bondsman:
James H. Baird, m. by: B. Graves, J. P., WILSON Co.

BARUFIELD, George to Polly Williams - issued February 24, 1827, Bondsman:
William M. Justic, WILSON Co.

BARUS, Adams to Polly Leonard - issued February 1, 1807, Bondsman:
Joshua Barus, WILSON Co.

BASFORD, Jacob B. to Ann Eliza Bethune - issued October 14, 1854,
Bondsman: Franklin Weakley, m. by: J. B. Walton, M. G.,
October 19, 1854, MONTGOMERY Co.

BASFORD, James to Mary Bradshaw - issued October 7, 1815, Bondsman:
Robert McCerary, WILSON Co.

BASFORD, James to Charity Isboll - issued July 16, 1846, Bondsman:
G. W. Warfield, m. by: M. Ramey July 23, 1846, MONTGOMERY Co.

BASFORD, Jospeh J. to Mary Ann Alley - issued March 13, 1854, Bondsman:
Franklin Weakley, m. by: Isaac Watters, M. G., March, 1854,
MONTGOMERY Co.

BASFORD, Thos. to Eliza Wright - issued December 19, 1853, Bondsman:
Jacob Stack, m. by: J. B. Walton, M. G., December 22, 1853,
MONTGOMERY Co.

BASHER, Bazil to Peggy Horton - issued July 31, 1800, KNOX Co.

BASKETT, Newman to Phebe Ann Franklin - issued January 16, 1837,
m. by: J. D. Bennett, J. P., January 17, 1837, KNOX Co.

BASKIN, John to Mary Middleton - December 7, 1790, Security:
Wm. Bigham and Jacob McConnell, GREENE Co.

BASKIN, William to Rebecca Belt - issued February 22, 1817, Bondsman:
Aaron Gibson, m. by: Presley Lester, V. D. M., February 23, 1817,
WILSON Co.

BASKINS, Hugh F. to Sally Ann Lacefield - issued December 16, 1840,
Bondsman: Jacob M. Casilman, m. by: Joshua Woollen December 22,
1840, WILSON Co.

BASKINS, Thomas to Susan Arnold - issued April 16, 1828, Bondsman:
Tilman Patterson, m. by: Thomas D. Lansden, J. P., April 19,
1828, WILSON Co.

BASON, Abner to Mary Hinshaw - issued October 14, 1809, Bondsman:
Robert Fields, Witness: Robert F. Jack, J. P., GRAINGER Co.

BASS, Alex. (a free man of color) to Eleanor Scott (a free woman of
color) - issued June 7, 1832, Bondsman: Izzecier Scott, m. by:
G. H. Bussard, J. P., WILSON Co.

BASS, Alfred to Lucinda Mitchell - issued March 6, 1832, Bondsman:
John Gray, WILSON Co.

BASS, Archamack to Rachael Phillips - issued June 18, 1822, Bondsman:
Sion Bass, WILSON Co.

BASS, Augustus to Susan Hamilton - issued May 12, 1847, DAVIDSON Co.

BASS, Benjamin F. to Mrs. Rebecca Thompson - issued November 18, 1834,
Bondsman: J. M. Barry, RUTHERFORD Co.

BASS, Cader to Lucy York - issued August 22, 1833, Bondsman: Moses Odum,
WILSON Co.

BASS, David to Harriet Harris - issued August 27, 1826, Bondsman:
Thomas Cox, WILSON Co.

BASS, Dolphan to Frances Gaddy - issued October 23, 1818, Bondsman:
Thomas Phillips, WILSON Co.

BASS, Dread to Nancy Brian - issued August 7, 1807, Bondsman: Jacob McDermet, WILSON Co.

BASS, Etheldred to Nancy Barton - issued November 29, 1822, Bondsman: John Bass, WILSON Co.

BASS, Ezekiel to Maria Barbee - issued August 17, 1830, Bondsman: Elias Bass, WILSON Co.

BASS, Giles W. to Susan Keith - issued October 12, 1839, FRANKLIN Co.

BASS, Gilford to Polly Proctor - issued August 18, 1820, Bondsman: John Beardin, Jr., SUMNER Co.

BASS, H. C. to Mahala Smith - issued February 18, 1840, FRANKLIN Co.

BASS, Harmon T. to Nancy W. Estes - issued December 25, 1840, Bondsman: William J. Pride, m. by: E. J. Allen December 27, 1840, WILSON Co.

BASS, Henry to Sinah Phillips - issued October 29, 1830, Bondsman: Archinack Bass, WILSON Co.

BASS, J. to Elizabeth Griffin - issued June 22, 1846, m. by: W. C. Jones, J. P., July 1, 1846, STEWART Co.

BASS, James Jr. to Eliza House - issued September 22, 1819, m. by: Peyton Smith September 23, 1819, RUTHERFORD Co.

BASS, John to Jenney Dunlop (Dunlap) - issued September 22, 1798, Bondsman: Henry Hipshur, m. by: Samuel Yancey, J. P., September 22, 1798, GRAINGER Co.

BASS, John to Elizabeth G. McDermont - issued February 1, 1825, Bondsman: William Baird, m. by: Geo. Clark, J. P., February 10, 1825, WILSON Co.

BASS, John to Susan Barbee - issued September 14, 1836, m. by: Sion Bass, M. G., WILSON Co.

BASS, John H. to M. E. Darwin - issued October 21, 1867, m. by: W. G. Guinn, M. G., October 24, 1867, FRANKLIN Co.

BASS, John M. to Matilda Hammer - issued December 19, 1867, FRANKLIN Co.

BASS, Jones to Kissiah Rowland - issued September 10, 1811, Bondsman: Green Williams, WILSON Co.

BASS, Jones to Delila Ellis - issued June 15, 1835, Bondsman: John H. Dew, WILSON Co.

BASS, Kenedy to Fanny Barnett - issued October 9, 1806, Bondsman: John Gray, WILSON Co.

BASS, Richard to Emily Duke - issued December 28, 1824, Bondsman: Isaac Jenkins, WILSON Co.

BASS, Sion to Polly Perry - issued February 25, 1809, Bondsman: Richardson Perry, WILSON Co.

BASS, Sion to Sally Phillips - issued August 2, 1823, Bondsman: John Bass, WILSON Co.

BASS, Solomon to Mahala Crisp - issued February 5, 1829, m. by: Thom. B. Bridges, J. P., February 6, 1829, WILSON Co.

BASS, Solomon to Elizabeth Parten - issued December 27, 1830, Bondsman: Cader Bass, WILSON Co.

BASS, Thomas S. to Anne Marun E. Shine - November 8, 1817, WILLIAMSON Co.

BASS, Warren to Mary Barbee - issued December 27, 1832, Bondsman: John Bass, m. by: Levi A. Durham, M. G., __ 17, 1833, WILSON Co.

BASS, William to Nancy Phillips - issued October 30, 1832, Bondsman: Benjamin Phillips, WILSON Co.

BASS, William to Lucinda Farnbrough - issued October 10, 1838, Bondsman: Isaac L. Howse, m. by: G. Baker October 11, 1836, RUTHERFORD Co.

BASS, William F. to Althenia Russell - issued October 27, 1870, m. October 27, 1870, FRANKLIN Co.

BASS, William R. to Mary Smith - issued June 20, 1849, m. by: J. C. Montgomery, J. P., June 20, 1849, FRANKLIN Co.

BASSETT, Spencer to Febly Lebow - issued September 20, 1814, Bondsman: Benjamin Mumpower, GRAINGER Co.

BASSFORD, Kenchen to Minerva Lancaster - issued September 30, 1845, m. by: R. Pennington, J. P., October 2, 1845, ROBERTSON Co.

BASSHAM, James M. to Susan F. Legg - issued May 17, 1864, Bondsman: James M. Turner, m. by: J. P. Richardson, M. G., May 18, 1864, LAWRENCE Co.

BASSHAM, Wm. D. to Kessiah R. Palmer - issued March 20, 1865, Bondsman: J. S. Jones, m. by: J. P. Richardson, M. G., March 21, 1865, LAWRENCE Co.

BASQUIT, Abraham to Miss Martha Ann Warden - issued August 20, 1850, Bondsman: Oliver P. Futherson, m. August 20, 1850, MONTGOMERY Co.

BATCHELDOR, John to Hannah McGloughlin - issued May 25, 1811, Bondsman: Moses Morris, SUMNER Co.

BATEMAN, Asail to Milly Johnston - issued April 30, 1818, Bondsman: Richard Moore, SUMNER Co.

BATEMAN, August to Ellen Sutton - issued May 29, 1854, Bondsman: R. T. Harris, m. by: H. Watts, J. P., March 29, 1854, MONTGOMERY Co.

BATEMAN, H. S. to Martha A. White - issued November 1, 1847, m. by: C. D. Elliott, M. G., November 1, 1847, DAVIDSON Co.

BATEMAN, Jeremiah to Nancy Morris - issued April 13, 1841, m. by: J. Hill, J. P., April 13, 1841, DICKSON Co.

BATEMAN, John to Elizabeth King - issued February 4, 1840, m. by: E. S. Hall, J. P., February 4, 1840, DAVIDSON Co.

BATEMAN, John to Martha McGee - issued June 26, 1862, Bondsman: James Hatchett, Jos. H. Thompson, Clk. per James H. Neil, D. Clk., BEDFORD Co.

BATEMAN, John L. to Lydia Ann Read - issued December 21, 1843, m. by: T. Ball, M. G., December 21, 1843, DAVIDSON Co.

BATEMAN, Simon to Penny Brady - November 4, 1807, WILLIAMSON Co.

BATEMAN, Stephen to Malinda Knight - issued December 26, 1833, Bondsman: Cullen Sanders, m. by: Joshua Woollen, M. G., WILSON Co.

BATEMAN, William to Elizabeth Pearre - December 11, 1817, WILLIAMSON Co.

BATEMAN, William D. to Parthenia H. Blount - issued December 15, 1842, m. by: James Daniel, J. P., December 15, 1842, DICKSON Co.

BATES, Allen to Mary Helton - issued June 12, 1826, Bondsman: Alexander Bates, GRAINGER Co.

BATES, Daniel M. to Mary Hays - issued February 13, 1849, m. by:
John F. Farris, J. P., February 13, 1849, FRANKLIN Co.

BATES, David to Elizabeth Akridge - February 23, 1812, WILLIAMSON Co.

BATES, James to Sally Stephenson - issued March 14, 1814, Bondsman:
James Bradberry, WILSON Co.

BATES, John to Didamy Bohannon - December 20, 1796, KNOX Co.

BATES, John to Polly Hill - issued April 2, 1832, Bondsman:
William S. Hill, m. by: B. Bridges, J. P., April 6, 1832, WILSON Co.

BATES, John to Ann Brown - issued December 1, 1837, Bondsman:
William Bates, WILSON Co.

BATES, John B. to Aramanda (?) S. Jordan - November 25, 1862, Security:
William Tinsley, GILES Co.

BATES, Joseph B. to Clerinda Cherry - issued March 3, 1838, m. by:
P. Presley, J. P., March 6, 1836, STEWART Co.

BATES, M. W. to Margaret I. Karr - issued October 16, 1863, Bondsman:
Jos. H. Thompson and Clerk, BEDFORD Co.

BATES, R. T. to Nancy Shoo - issued January 13, 1868, m. by:
James Seargent, J. P., January 19, 1868, FRANKLIN Co.

BATES, Ulysess to M. O. Hunt - issued August 10, 1868, m. by:
A. T. Crawford, M. G., August 11, 1868, FRANKLIN Co.

BATES, William to Susan Wright - m. by: Samuel Cochran, J. P.,
November 3, 1834, SUMNER Co.

BATES, William to Margaret Wright - issued May 28, 1838, Bondsman:
William Hester, m. by: Gedeon H. Bransford, M. G., May 29, 1838,
WILSON Co.

BATES, Willis H. to Elizabeth Hawkins - m. by: J. B. Brizendine
December 9, 1837, SUMNER Co.

BATEY, Benjamin to Evaline A. Morton - issued December 6, 1824,
m. by: Peyton Smith December 7, 1824, RUTHERFORD Co.

BATEY, Christopher to Mahaley Puckett - issued January 16, 1822, m. by:
Peyton Smith, M. G., January 17, 1822, RUTHERFORD Co.

BATEY, Eleazer to Winney Roberts - issued August 16, 1835, Bondsman:
John Cooper, m. by: B. B. Dickins, J. P., August 17, 1835,
RUTHERFORD Co.

BATEY, George Washington to Mary Jane Crockett - issued December 20,
1836, Bondsman: George W. House, m. by: Martin Clark, E. M. E. C.,
December 22, 1836, RUTHERFORD Co.

BATEY, Isaac to Susan Gwin - issued August 3, 1824, Bondsman:
John Calvert, m. by: David Batton, J. P., August 5, 1824,
RUTHERFORD Co.

BATEY, Joseph to Anne B. Webber - issued September 27, 1827, Bondsman:
Moses G. Reeves, m. by: Jordan Willeford, J. P., September 28,
1827, RUTHERFORD Co.

BATEY, William to Sarah Grissum - issued September 3, 1827, Bondsman:
Henry Partin, m. by: Thomas S. Green, J. P., September 4, 1827,
WILSON Co.

BATEY, William to America S. Crockett - issued December 5, 1836,
Bondsman: Geo. W. Batey, m. by: Martin Clark, E. M. E. C.,
December 6, 1826, RUTHERFORD Co.

BATEY, William D. to Matilda McKee - issued March 1, 1827, Bondsman: John Sullivan, RUTHERFORD Co.

BATEY, William F. to Elizabeth Sills - issued November 15, 1815, Bondsman: Thos. G. Watkins, m. by: Edm'd Jones, RUTHERFORD Co.

BATMAN, Beurriah to Sally Magness - issued June 7, 1810, Bondsman: Drury Reeves, WILSON Co.

BATSON, Calvin S. to Eveline I. Ellis - issued December 4, 1841, m. by: Rev. William Guthrie December 9, 1841, DICKSON Co.

BATSON, Tachanah to Arabella Turner - issued October 18, 1845, DICKSON Co.

BATSON, W. B. to Virginia Morris - issued September 20, 1854, m. by: Samuel A. Nesbitt, J. P., September 21, 1854, MONTGOMERY Co.

BATTE, William to Amanda Pryor - issued February 28, 1827, Bondsman: Overton W. Crockett, RUTHERFORD Co.

BATTLE, J. A. to Fannie Womack - issued April 21, 1871, FRANKLIN Co.

BATTLE, Joel A. to Adaline Mosely - issued July 21, 1837, Bondsman: Geo. S. Golladay, m. by: F. E. Pitts, M. G., July 22, 1837, WILSON Co.

BATTLE, Joel Allen to Sarah M. Searcy - issued December 12, 1831, m. by: Peyton Smith December 15, 1831, RUTHERFORD Co.

BATTLE, William M. to Sarah Jane Smith - issued July 23, 1828, m. by: Peyton Smith July 24, 1828, RUTHERFORD Co.

BATTON, Money to Nancy Featherston - issued October 14, 1817, Bondsman: Henry M. Hutson, RUTHERFORD Co.

BATTS, Benj. to Sarah Gupton - m. by: J. H. Majors, J. P., January 3, 1851, MONTGOMERY Co.

BATTS, John to Nancy Nanny - issued May 16, 1846, Bondsman: Morgan Murrah, m. by: J. C. Wheatley, J. P., May 17, 1846, MONTGOMERY Co.

BATTS, John T. to Mary Price - issued December 31, 1840, m. by: Williamson Burgess, J. P., ROBERTSON Co.

BATTS, Johnathan to Mary M. Bandy - issued February 4, 1843, m. by: J. L. Adams, J. P., February 5, 1843, ROBERTSON Co.

BATTS, M. D. W. to Arrena Dunn - issued July 7, 1855, m. by: W. S. Adams, J. P., July 15, 1855, ROBERTSON Co.

BATTS, Thomas to Viola A. Bowman - issued November 17, 1825, m. by: Silas H. Morrison November 17, 1825, RUTHERFORD Co.

BAUGH, G. N. to M. V. Booker - issued October 21, 1853, m. by: James Woodard, J. P., ROBERTSON Co.

BAUGH, John A. to Mary Anne Marable - issued August 13, 1829, Bondsman: Harison Patillo, RUTHERFORD Co.

BAUGH, V. A. to Mernerva Cabler - issued February 15, 1845, m. by: W. D. F. Sawrie, M. G., February 16, 1845, DAVIDSON Co.

BAUMGARNER, Peter to Nancy Gregory - issued September 29, 1817, RUTHERFORD Co.

BATTS, Thomas to Viola A. Bowman - issued November 17, 1825, m. by: Silas H. Morrison November 17, 1825, RUTHERFORD Co.

BAUGH, G. N. to M. V. Booker - issued October 21, 1853, m. by:
James Woodard, J. P., ROBERTSON Co.

BAUGH, John A. to Mary Anne Marable - issued August 13, 1829, Bondsman:
Harison Patillo, RUTHERFORD Co.

BAUGH, V. A. to Mernerva Cabler - issued February 15, 1845, m. by:
W. D. F. Sawrie, M. G., February 16, 1845, DAVIDSON Co.

BAUMGARNER, Peter to Nancy Gregory - issued September 29, 1817,
RUTHERFORD Co.

BAXTER, David to Cynthia H. Dickson - issued November 28, 1822, m. by:
Jas. S. Jetton, J. P., November 28, 1822, RUTHERFORD Co.

BAXTER, George W. to Rebecca Ann Hooker - issued July 15, 1833,
Bondsman: Wm. Doncho, WILSON Co.

BAXTER, J. K. P. to Millie Stephens - issued January 19, 1859, m. by:
James B. Foster, J. P., January 19, 1859, FRANKLIN Co.

BAXTER, James M. to Sarah R. Grant - issued January 3, 1840, Bondsman:
Jas. C. Word, m. by: S. Tarver, J. P., January 5, 1840, WILSON Co.

BAXTER, Jefferson to Rebecca Wynn - issued September 27, 1830, Bondsman:
Robert Gary, WILSON Co.

BAXTER, John to Susan A. Railey - issued December 14, 1841, DAVIDSON Co.

BAXTER, John H. to Cathrine Sewell - issued May 10, 1854, m. by:
J. B. Foster, J. P., May 12, 1854, FRANKLIN Co.

BAXTER, Robt. to Sarah J. Connell - issued July 8, 1846, m. by:
Robt. Williams, M. G., ROBERTSON Co.

BAXTER, Samuel to Sarah M. Dickson - issued March 24, 1825, m. by:
William Bumpass, M. G., March 24, 1825, RUTHERFORD Co.

BAXTER, Samuel to Frances Irby - issued August 27, 1825, Bondsman:
Jacob Wilhelms, m. by: John W. Peyton, J. P., September 1, 1825,
WILSON Co.

BAXTER, Squire B. to Elender Sewell - issued June 15, 1850, m. by:
Allen Gilliam, M. G., June 15, 1850, FRANKLIN Co.

BAXTER, Wm. P. to Sarah A. Atchley - issued October 11, 1851, m. by:
L. P. Sims, J. P., October 11, 1851, FRANKLIN Co.

BAY, Thomas to Polly Eddings - issued January 2, 1833, Bondsman:
Robert Davis, WILSON Co.

BEYLES, Samuel to Susanah Hawkins - issued December 24, 1810, Bondsman:
Henry Hawkins, GRAINGER Co.

BAYLESS, Arthur M. to Martha E. Bradley - issued August 11, 1864,
Bondsman: Thomas Alexander, m. by: Wm. C. Davis, J. P., August 12,
1864, LAWRENCE Co.

BAYLESS, Isaac to Susannah Sumpter - issued July 18, 1820, m. by:
William B. Carns, J. P. K. C., July 27, 1820, KNOX Co.

BAYLESS, Isaac to Betsy Sumpter - November 23, 1821, m. by: Wm. B. Carns
November 28, 1821, KNOX Co.

BAYLESS, John to Lucinda Whitecotton - issued March 2, 1822, Bondsman:
Robert Smith, m. by: Wm. B. Carns, J. P., March 5, 1822, Witness:
Wm. Swan, KNOX Co.

BAYLESS, Reese to Francis Draper - issued October 29, 1830, Bondsman:
    Wm. Crippen, m. by: E. Nelson, J. P., November 4, 1830, Witness:
    Wm. Swan, KNOX Co.

BAYLESS, Samuel to Nanny Lister - March 9, KNOX Co.

BAYLESS, Samuel to Nancy Lister - issued March 9, 1827, Bondsman:
    Isaac Bayless, m. by: Samuel Love, M. G., March 15, 1827, KNOX Co.

BAYLISS, B. to N. J. Hogan - issued August 12, 1848, Bondsman:
    R. D. Newton, MONTGOMERY Co.

BAYLISS, Joel to Susan Neblett - issued November 20, 1847, Bondsman:
    E. Wynn, m. by: N. F. Trice, J. P., November 20, 1847, MONTGOMERY Co.

BAYLISS, Samuel to Mary E. Brickle - issued November 11, 1847,
    Bondsman: E. B. Halsel, m. by: J. C. Bryan, J. P., November 11,
    1847, MONTGOMERY Co.

BAYNE, John to S. J. Dodd - m. by: H. A. Belote October 6, 1838,
    SUMNER Co.

BAYNE, Mathew to Phebe Carman - issued January 19, 1820, Bondsman:
    Thomas Pritchett, SUMNER Co.

BAYNES, Elsworth to Peggy White - issued August 28, 1806, Bondsman:
    Jacob Seavea, SUMNER Co.

BAYS, Caty to Ezekial Broyles - GREENE Co.

BAYTES, D. M. to Sarah Holder - issued March 18, 1841, FRANKLIN Co.

BEACH, Andrew S. to Martha C. Thompson - issued July 21, 1839, m. by:
    Wm. Hasell Hunt, J. P., July 22, 1839, DAVIDSON Co.

BEACH, Hyram to F. B. Smith - issued July 29, 1848, m. by: Robert Green,
    J. P., July 30, 1848, ROBERTSON Co.

BEACH, W. B. to J. A. McNeil - issued December 19, 1859, m. by:
    F. C. Plasters, M. G., December 22, 1859, ROBERTSON Co.

BEACON, Thomas L. to Eliza Mildred Madison - issued May 20, 1845,
    Bondsman: Joseph A. Yates, m. by: James Reasons, J. P., May 20,
    1845, MONTGOMERY Co.

BEADLE, Joseph to Patience Ann Wommack - issued September 4, 1832,
    Bondsman: Benjamin Phillips, WILSON Co.

BEADLE, Joseph to Susan Lester - issued September 9, 1840, Bondsman:
    S. M. Alexander, m. by: Archamack Bass September 10, 1840, WILSON Co.

BEADLES, Henry to Mary Ann Alexander - issued September 22, 1835,
    Bondsman: Joseph Beadles, WILSON Co.

BEADLES, John to Mary Sublett - issued August 2, 1821, m. by:
    G. W. Oliver, J. P., August 2, 1821, RUTHERFORD Co.

BEADWELL, Jesse to Sarah Callume - issued December 21, 1805, Bondsman:
    William Patton, GRAINGER Co.

BEAL, Dodson to Mary Spradlin - issued February 3, 1858, m. by:
    Samuel Umbarger, J. P., February 3, 1858, COFFEE Co.

BEALES, William to Rachel Pierce - March 12, 1797, KNOX Co.

BEALL, Sam'l to Hanna Luttrell - issued October 28, 1816, Bondsman:
    Francis A. Ramsey, Witness: Andw. Hutcheson, KNOX Co.

BEALS, Abram to Sarah Hammer - February 25, 1837, JEFFERSON Co.

BEALS, Abram to Abigail Morgan - July 29, 1855, JEFFERSON Co.

BEALS, Charity to Marmaduke McNees - GREENE Co.

BEALS, Hannah to William Ellis - GREENE Co.

BEALS, Hannah to Samuel Brown - GREENE Co.

BEALS, Hannah to John Marshall - GREENE Co.

BEALS, Jacob to Ruth Morgan - April 28, 1838, JEFFERSON Co.

BEALS, James E. to Susanna Morgan - July 29, 1857, JEFFERSON Co.

BEALS, John to Abigail Morgan - September 1821, JEFFERSON Co.

BEALS, Thomas to Margaret Brown - March 18, 1820, Security:
    Newhope Quaker Meeting, GREENE Co.

BEALSEY, James H. to Polly B. Proctor - issued September 19, 1841,
    m. by: Benjamin Gambill, J. P., ROBERTSON Co.

BEAN, Aaron to Mary Barbara Nigh - October 13, 1800, Security:
    William Moore, GREENE Co.

BEAN, Aaron to Catherine Carwiles - issued February 22, 1829, Bondsman:
    Robt. Mitchell, GRAINGER Co.

BEAN, Andrew to Cynthia Pedigo - issued November 25, 1835, m. by:
    R. H. Snoddy, M. G., November 12, 1835, KNOX Co.

BEAN, Andrew to Cynthia Pedigo - issued November 25, 1835, Bondsman:
    Jno. Dawson, KNOX Co.

BEAN, C. C. to Martha Sanders - issued June 7, 1857, m. by:
    Simpson West, J. P., June 7, 1857, FRANKLIN Co.

BEAN, C. H. to Mary J. Travis - issued October 18, 1856, m. by:
    A. J. Wiseman, J. P., October 19, 1856, FRANKLIN Co.

BEAN, E. R. to C. Johnson (MB) - issued November 24, 1869, FRANKLIN Co.

BEAN, Ezekael M. to Eliza E. Marshall - issued August 19, 1854, m. by:
    A. J. Wiseman, J. P., August 22, 1854, FRANKLIN Co.

BEAN, George to Peggy Ashart - issued July 10, 1798, Bondsman:
    George Bean, Witness: Sm'l Yancey, GRAINGER Co.

BEAN, George to Prudence Cope - issued February 11, 1800, Bondsman:
    James Ore, Witness: Sm'l Yancey, GRAINGER Co.

BEAN, Hazard to Nancy Howard - issued November 25, 1805, Bondsman:
    Abraham Howard, GRAINGER Co.

BEAN, Jacob M. to Nancy Bowling - issued May 11, 1840, m. by:
    George Hudspeth, J. P., FRANKLIN Co.

BEAN, James to Mary Dorse - issued September 11, 1834, m. by:
    Zac. Boothe, J. P., September 11, 1834, KNOX Co.

BEAN, James M. to Rebecca Ann Arnold - m. by: Simpson West, J. P.,
    June 7, 1857, FRANKLIN Co.

BEAN, Jesse to Polly Kirkendol - issued December 21, 1805, Bondsman:
    Robert Bean, RUTHERFORD Co.

BEAN, John to Sarah Jordan - May 12, 1788, Security: William Richey,
    GREENE Co.

BEAN, John to Matilda Strain - issued December 13, 1825, m. by:
Joel Smith, J. P., December 15, 1825, RUTHERFORD Co.

BEAN, John to Sarah Carroll - July 26, 1837, KNOX Co.

BEAN, Obediah to Margaret Gipson - m. by: M. Catchings, J. P.,
March 24, 1853, FRANKLIN Co.

BEAN, Obediah to Nancy A. Miller - issued August 22, 1857, m. by:
John Hendly, J. P., August 22, 1857, FRANKLIN Co.

BEAN, Rebecca to William Wagoner - GREENE Co.

BEAN, Robert to Cristina Miller - issued October 7, 1817, Bondsman:
William B. Bowen, GRAINGER Co.

BEAN, Sarah to Samuel Wear - GREENE Co.

BEAN, William to Polley McElheny - issued July 23, 1808, Bondsman:
John McElheny, GRAINGER Co.

BEAN, William C. to Elizabeth Burchett - issued December 23, 1841,
m. by: P. B. Morris, J. P., December 23, 1841, DAVIDSON Co.

BEAR (?), Jane to James Millikin - GREENE Co.

BEAR, John W. to Frances E. Miller - issued December 16, 1846, Bondsman:
John R. Gaster, m. by: W. B. Carney, J. P., December 16, 1846,
MONTGOMERY Co.

BEARD, Adam to Caty Barkley - issued March 10, 1795, Bondsman:
Orman Allen, SUMNER Co.

BEARD, Adam to Elizabeth Smith - issued May 12, 1812, Bondsman:
Andrew Smith, SUMNER Co.

BEARD, Alfred M. to Louisianna Vinson - issued July 29, 1824, Bondsman:
Alfred M. Beard, m. by: Thos. Anderson, J. P., July 29, 1824,
SUMNER Co.

BEARD, David to Jenny Wallace - issued March 24, 1800, Bondsman:
James Wallace, SUMNER Co.

BEARD, Francis to Peggy Brown - April 12, 1811, Bondsman: Andrew Brown,
MAURY Co.

BEARD, George to Matilda Noel - June 8, 1806, WILLIAMSON Co.

BEARD, Henry to Tabitha Malone - issued January 20, 1829, Bondsman:
Carson Dobbins, m. January 20, 1829, SUMNER Co.

BEARD, Henry N. to Elizabeth B. Stalcup - issued November 7, 1825,
Bondsman: William Neal, SUMNER Co.

BEARD, Isham to Ruthy Linsey - issued September 20, 1846, m. by:
J. J. Travis, J. P., September 21, 1846, FRANKLIN Co.

BEARD, John to Margaret Cloid - issued August 27, 1827, Bondsman:
David Cloid, m. by: David Foster, M. G., August 30, 1827, WILSON Co.

BEARD, Jno. J. to Jane McCarrol - issued July 26, 1837, Bondsman:
Jno. R. Davis, m. by: John Nester, Esq., July 27, 1837, Witness:
M. M. Swan, KNOX Co.

BEARD, Joseph W. to Lurenna Neal - issued November 14, 1825, Bondsman:
David Beard, m. by: Francis Johnston, M. G., November 14, 1825,
SUMNER Co.

BEARD, Polly to David Erwin - MAURY Co.

BEARD, Thos. C. to Nancy Hall - issued March 21, 1816, m. by:
David Foster, M. G., March 21, 1816, RUTHERFORD Co.

BEARD, William to Molly Neamour - issued May 25, 1812, KNOX Co.

BEARD, Wm. to Paralee Clark - issued May 1, 1849, m. by: C. Grymes,
J. P., May 1, 1849, DICKSON Co.

BEARD, William E. to Eoline Vinson - issued August 20, 1829, Bondsman:
A. F. Young, m. by: Thos. Anderson, J. P., August 20, 1829,
SUMNER Co.

BEARDEN, Benjamin B. to Nancy Maxey - issued August 24, 1853, Bondsman:
Peter S. Rhinehart, m. by: John S. Major, J. P., August 23, 1853,
MONTGOMERY Co.

BEARDEN, Edwin B. to Mary F. Meek - April 16, 1850, m. by:
W. T. Plummer, M. G., GILES Co.

BEARDEN, Haywood to Elizabeth Weakley - issued June 6, 1851, Bondsman:
Jas. Field, m. by: R. H. Weakley, J. P., June 7, 1850, MONTGOMERY Co.

BEARDEN, Jno. to Caroline O'Dell - issued September 14, 1829, Bondsman:
B. M. Wallace, m. by: Wm. S. McCampbell, J. P., September 15,
1829, KNOX Co.

BEARDEN, Marcus D. to Anny E. Cocke - issued July 25, 1820, Bondsman:
W. H. Stockton, m. by: George Atkin, M. Preacher, GRAINGER Co.

BEARDEN, Orang D. to Margaret Woodvill - issued April 30, 1824,
Bondsman: Henry Woodvill, m. by: John Bonner, J. P., WILSON Co.

BEARDEN, Richard to Catharine Scott - issued January 16, 1832, Bondsman:
Seth Lea, m. by: G. Birdwell, M. G., January 19, 1832, Witness:
Wm. Swan, KNOX Co.

BEARDON, Solomon to Nancy Morris - issued September 30, 1818, Bondsman:
John Riggs, m. September 30, 1818, SUMNER Co.

BEARDEN, Solomon to Rebecca Woodrum - issued June 12, 1819, Bondsman:
John Riggs, m. by: John Bonner, J. P., June 17, 1819, WILSON Co.

BEARDUNE, Isaac to Elizabeth Sutton - issued September 2, 1849,
Bondsman: Thos. Beardune, m. by: R. H. Weakley, J. P., September 2,
1849, MONTGOMERY Co.

BEARFOOT, Noah to Elizabeth Cook - issued January 7, 1819, m. by:
G. W. Banton, J. P., January 12, 1819, RUTHERFORD Co.

BEASLEY, Abraham to Barbara Damewood - issued August 5, 1817, m. by:
John Thompson, J. P. K. C., August 7, 1817, KNOX Co.

BEASLEY, Benny to Mary Jackson - issued September 13, 1819, Bondsman:
Edmond Jackson, m. by: Jos. T. Bell, J. P., September 16, 1819,
WILSON Co.

BEASLEY, Charles to Delilah Owen - March 5, 1810, WILLIAMSON Co.

BEASLEY, Dillard to Sally Harris - issued October 26, 1813, Bondsman:
Thomas Lock, WILSON Co.

BEASLEY, Fanning J. to Joannah Williams - issued November 9, 1843,
m. by: W. L. Baldry, Gospel Minister, ROBERTSON Co.

BEASLEY, John W. to Nancy Coatney - December 22, 1805, WILLIAMSON Co.

BEASLEY, John W. to Nancy Sutton - issued August 6, 1846, m. by:
Daniel Judd, L. E. of M. E. C., August 6, 1846, DAVIDSON Co.

BEASLEY, Josiah to Elizabeth Tarpley - issued December 7, 1819,
    Bondsman: Stith T. Tarpley, WILSON Co.

BEASLEY, Robert to Sarah Cunningham - issued July 2, 1829, Bondsman:
    Ira Lynch, m. by: Stephen McDonald - WILSON Co.

BEASLY, John to Rebecca Smothers - issued December 28, 1862, Bondsman:
    J. M. Rippy, Jos. H. Thompson, Clk., BEDFORD Co.

BEASLY, John C. to Mary Allen - issued January 4, 1836, Bondsman:
    Joseph Barbor, m. by: J. Hobday January 4, 1836, SUMNER Co.

BEASON, Henry to Sally Ross - issued September 8, 1828, Bondsman:
    David Beson, SUMNER Co.

BEATIE, John to Sally Rider - July 15, 1800, Security: John Bradley,
    BLOUNT Co.

BEATY, James to Fanny Priest - November 4, 1813, WILLIAMSON Co.

BEATY, James to Judith Scott - issued September 7, 1815, Bondsman:
    Alexander Pool, RUTHERFORD Co.

BEATY, John to Johanar Moore - May 27, 1807, WILLIAMSON Co.

BEATY, Nathaniel to Margaret Smith - issued May 2, 1829, Bondsman:
    Nicholas Harris, RUTHERFORD Co.

BEAUCHAMP, John W. to Mary Wilson - issued September 12, 1826, Bondsman:
    James Cloyd, m. by: Wm. Steele, J. P., WILSON Co.

BEAUMONT, Charles W. to Nancy Bradley - issued September 2, 1841,
    m. by: Call. A. Slater, ROBERTSON Co.

BEAUMONT, Franklin S. to Louisa E. Conrad - issued November 21, 1864,
    Bondsman: John Almon, m. by: A. R. Ervin, M. G., November 21,
    1854, MONTGOMERY Co.

BEAUMONT, Sterling F. to Mattie L. Conrad - issued May 24, 1853,
    Bondsman: Joseph T. Johnson, m. by: A. L. P. Green, M. G., May 24,
    1853, MONTGOMERY Co.

BEAVER, James R. to N. J. Brown - issued September 11, 1871, m. by:
    R. R. Tucker, M. G., September 11, 1871, FRANKLIN Co.

BEAVER, Jesse to Sarah B. Wems - issued June 18, 1821, m. by:
    Jas. Carr, J. P., June 18, 1821, SUMNER Co.

BEAVER, Jessee to Betsy Carr - issued November 1, 1838, m. by:
    W. M. Smith, M. G., FRANKLIN Co.

BEAVER, Lemuel to Belinda Moore - March 20, 1837, m. by: Robert Neal,
    J. P., GILES Co.

BEAVER, Willis to Anny Rushing - issued May 2, 1838, m. by: James Wilson,
    J. P., May 3, 1838, STEWART Co.

BEAVERS, Abraham to Dilly Crutchfield - issued November 21, 1823,
    Bondsman: Gilbert B. Clark, RUTHERFORD Co.

BEAVERS, Susan to John Gibson - BEDFORD Co.

BEAZLEY, Charles to Caroline Conley - issued January 1, 1839, m. by:
    John Hogan, J. P., January 4, 1839, DAVIDSON Co.

BEAZLEY, Chas. G. to Elizabeth Ozment - issued May 26, 1846, m. by:
    L. C. Bryan, P. G., July 19, 1846, DAVIDSON Co.

BEAZLEY, Thos. H. to Lorenda Cunningham - issued March 13, 1847,
m. by: Wm. D. Baldwin, M. G., March 16, 1847, DAVIDSON Co.

BEAZLEY, William B. to Mary B. Champ - issued December 14, 1842,
m. by: C. D. Elliott, M. G., December 14, 1842, DAVIDSON Co.

BEBB, Thos. to Mirah Fielson - November 28, 1815, WILLIAMSON Co.

BECK, William D. to Sarah Williams - issued September 7, 1855, m. by:
Uriah Sherrill, M. G., September 9, 1855, FRANKLIN Co.

BECKHAM, Peter to Sarah A. Davidson - issued July 26, 1865, Bondsman:
C. B. Davis, m. by: H. B. Wester, M. G., July 30, 1865, LAWRENCE Co.

BECKHAM, W. T. to Cornelia J. Hubble - issued November 13, 1865,
Bondsman: James Lowry, m. by: W. P. Warren, M. G., November 15,
1865, LAWRENCE Co.

BECKHAM, William J. to Therra Booth - October 2, 1849, Security:
Thomas W. Peterson, GILES Co.

BECKNELL, Stephen to Mollie Gilbert - issued December 5, 1873,
FRANKLIN Co.

BECTON, Frederick E. to Cathrine Harris - issued August 9, 1823, m. by:
Peyton Smith, M. G., August 9, 1823, RUTHERFORD Co.

BECTON, Frederick E. to Eliza P. Yandell - issued January 13, 1824,
m. by: R. MacGowan January 18, 1824, RUTHERFORD Co.

BECTON, George W. to Martha L. Henderson - issued April 30, 1833,
Bondsman: B. W. Avent, m. by: John Lane, RUTHERFORD Co.

BECTON, John M. to Eleanor E. Sharpe - issued January 16, 1827, Bondsman:
Pleasant H. Mitchell, RUTHERFORD Co.

BECTON, William J. to Mary Y. Robb - issued May 26, 1827, Bondsman:
William S. Butler, RUTHERFORD Co.

BEDFORD, John R. to Matilda Smith - issued December 6, 1809, Bondsman:
Joseph Herndon, RUTHERFORD Co.

BEDFORD, R. H. to Lucinda Kesee - issued March 16, 1847, m. by:
A. B. C. Howell, M. G., March 16, 1847, DAVIDSON Co.

BEDFORD, Robert to Mary Coleman Bedford - issued February 10, 1804,
Bondsman: Peter Legrand, RUTHERFORD Co.

BEDFORD, Thomas to Nancy Wade - issued February 12, 1828, m. by:
Peyton Smith February 13, 1828, RUTHERFORD Co.

BEDSAUL, George to Dicey Howell - issued August 1, 1818, Bondsman:
Welcom Howel, m. by: John Kidwell, M. G., GRAINGER Co.

BEDSOLT, Daniel to Polly Martin - issued April 16, 1818, m. by:
James A. Hain, J. P. K. C., April 19, 1818, KNOX Co.

BEECH, Alden C. to Virginia H. Vaughn - issued April 9, 1846, m. by:
C. D. Elliott, M. G., April 9, 1846, DAVIDSON Co.

BEELER, Abraham to Mary Jack - issued September 26, 1816, Bondsman:
Joseph Beeler, GRAINGER Co.

BEELER, Daniel to Wyney Wolfenbarger - issued November 25, 1825, m. by:
J. C. Bunch, J. P., GRAINGER Co.

BEELER, David to Mary Dyer - issued October 18, 1831, Bondsman:
James McCubbin, m. by: Joseph Clark, J. P., GRAINGER Co.

BEELER, George Junr. to Polley Hammock - issued January 30, 1810,
    Bondsman: George Beeler, Senr., GRAINGER Co.

BEELER, Isaac to Polly Wolfenbarger - issued December 28, 1826,
    Bondsman: Jacob Beeler, GRAINGER Co.

BEELER, Jacob to Nancy Cleveland - issued January 10, 1831, Bondsman:
    Isaac Beeler, m. by: Eli Clark, J. P., GRAINGER Co.

BEELER, Jacob to Lucinda Hollingsworth - issued February 1, 1836,
    Bondsman: Joseph Beeler, GRAINGER Co.

BEELER, John to Hannah Vandergriff - issued April 19, 1802, Bondsman:
    Thomas Dunn, GRAINGER Co.

BEELER, John to Anna Mefford - issued February 24, 1823, Bondsman:
    Daniel Cardwell, GRAINGER Co.

BEELER, John to Anna Shelton - issued June 23, 1830, Bondsman:
    Joseph Petre, m. by: Joseph Clark, J. P., June 23, 1830, GRAINGER Co.

BEELER, John C. to Elizabeth Parker - issued September 26, 1811,
    Bondsman: John Barham, SUMNER Co.

BEELER, Joseph to Anna Parker - issued October 21, 1834, Bondsman:
    Benjm. McFarland, m. by: Joseph Clark, J. P., GRAINGER Co.

BEELER, Peter to Anna Vance - issued December 21, 1831, Bondsman:
    Joseph Bunch, GRAINGER Co.

BEESLEY, Christopher to Susan J. Rideout - issued December 16, 1835,
    Bondsman: Isaac L. House, m. by: Martin Clark, E. M. E. C.,
    December 17, 1835, RUTHERFORD Co.

BEESLEY, Durant to Harriet Blackman - issued December 6, 1823, Bondsman:
    Jesse Covington, m. by: Peyton Smith December 11, 1823,
    RUTHERFORD Co.

BEESLEY, John P. to Evelina T. Avent - issued September 16, 1834,
    Bondsman: John P. Graham, m. by: Martin Clark, E. M. E. C.,
    September 16, 1834, RUTHERFORD Co.

BEESLEY, Major P. to Emeline Simmons - issued April 5, 1834, Bondsman:
    Benjamin Marable, RUTHERFORD Co.

BEESON, Abner to Susannah Dimmut - issued July 19, 1806, m. by:
    R. Houston, J. P. K. C., July 19, 1806, KNOX Co.

BEIELY, Jacob to Sally Brown - issued November 2, 1825, m. by:
    Jno. A. Swan, J. P., November 3, 1825, KNOX Co.

BELBRO, William to Margaret McFarlin - issued September 3, 1817,
    Bondsman: Jno. McFarlin, m. by: James Whitsite September 11, 1817,
    WILSON Co.

BELCHER, David to Elizabeth Whitehead - issued February 12, 1836,
    Bondsman: Field Tanner, m. by: Robert H. Ellis, M. G., February 14,
    1834, WILSON Co.

BELCHER, James to Rebeckey Tally - issued July 20, 1826, Bondsman:
    David Phillips, WILSON Co.

BELCHER, James B. to Katherine George - issued December 3, 1832,
    Bondsman: Zedie Mullin, WILSON Co.

BELCHER, John to Matha Coleman - January 12, 1812, WILLIAMSON Co.

BELCHER, John R. to Amerilla Swinney - issued January 25, 1832,
    Bondsman: Robt. M. Ellis, m. by: B. S. Mabry, WILSON Co.

BELCHER, Madison to Mary D. Young - issued June 20, 1840, Bondsman:
James S. Young, m. by: H. W. Pickett, M. G., June 25, 1840,
WILSON Co.

BELCHER, Pleasant G. to Sally Belcher - issued March 19, 1828,
Bondsman: James Powell, WILSON Co.

BELCHER, Sutton to Abegale Ellis - issued September 16, 1817, Bondsman:
James Ellis, WILSON Co.

BELCHER, Thomas to Delily Adamson - issued April 27, 1827, Bondsman:
Zeddock Mullinall, WILSON Co.

BELCHER, William to Louisa C. P. Aston - issued November 5, 1840,
Bondsman: M. Goldston, m. by: R. D. Bell, M. G., November 7,
1840, WILSON Co.

BELCHER, William O. to Frances C. Chandler - issued November 28, 1837,
Bondsman: Benjamin Gill, m. by: Robert H. Ellis, J. P., November 30,
1837, WILSON Co.

BELCHER, Woodford to Lucy Chandler - issued December 26, 1835,
Bondsman: John Reece, WILSON Co.

BELEW, Dennis to Nancy S. Ezell - issued October 26, 1862, Bondsman:
Hosea Miles, m. by: J. W. Powell, J. P., October 27, 1862,
LAWRENCE Co.

BELEW, Jonathan to A. L. Kelton - issued October 15, 1863, Bondsman:
Jno. Gaither, m. by: J. P. Richardson, M. G., October 15, 1863,
LAWRENCE Co.

BELEW, Renny to Ann E. Lumpkin - issued November 22, 1865, Bondsman:
Wm. H. Newton, m. by: Wm. C. Newton, J. P., November 23, 1865,
LAWRENCE Co.

BELEW, W. J. to Jolina I. Springer - issued November 30, 1865,
Bondsman: Wm. H. Newton, LAWRENCE Co.

BELFORD, John B. to Ruth Brown - issued July 7, 1806, Bondsman:
John Pursley, WILSON Co.

BELISLE, West to Fanny Acree - issued February 2, 1848, m. by:
P. Herndon, J. P., February 3, 1848, STEWART Co.

BELL, A. J. to Ellen J. A. Foster - issued September 27, 1847,
DAVIDSON Co.

BELL, A. L. to Rebecca Patton - issued July 26, 1830, Bondsman:
John Priesley, m. July 26, 1830, SUMNER Co.

BELL, Alfred to Jane Hainey - issued July 5, 1821, Bondsman:
Mabene Anderson, m. by: S. K. Blythe, J. P., July 5, 1821,
SUMNER Co.

BELL, Allen to Eliza Marks - issued July 28, 1835, Bondsman:
William Swan, m. by: Sion Bass, WILSON Co.

BELL, Amzi L. to Rhoda McCall - issued November 28, 1832, Bondsman:
Franklin Potts, m. by: J. W. Hall November 28, 1832, SUMNER Co.

BELL, Andrew to Mary Frey - issued January 2, 1843, ROBERTSON Co.

BELL, Bailie H. to Eleanor Carter - issued November 7, 1838, Bondsman:
John J. Carter, m. by: A. M. Stone, M. G., WILSON Co.

BELL, Benjamin to Polly Spring - issued November 22, 1825, Bondsman:
Benjamin Spring, WILSON Co.

BELL, Benjamin T. to Charlotte Goodall - issued January 30, 1819,
Bondsman: Thomas Cartwright, m. by: Joseph T. Bell, J. P.,
February 4, 1819, WILSON Co.

BELL, Burrel to Sophia Yancey - January 17, 1797, Surety: Austin
Yancey, BLOUNT Co.

BELL, Catherine to Thomas Ratson - GREENE Co.

BELL, Charles C. to Minerva Henry - issued November 1, 1858, m. by:
W. W. Pepper, Judge and C, November 4, 1858, ROBERTSON Co.

BELL, Edmund G. to Martha Gomer - issued April 3, 1834, m. by:
Tandy Monday, J. P., April 3, 1834, KNOX Co.

BELL, Elisha to Sarah E. Collier - issued October 27, 1842, m. by:
Rev: Uriah Smith October 27, 1842, DICKSON Co.

BELL, Ewin to Elizabeth G. Swan - issued December 20, 1830, Bondsman:
John Swan, m. by: Wilson Hearn, M. G., December 23, 1830, WILSON Co.

BELL, Henry to Elizabeth Brunson - issued December 7, 1846, m. by:
T. S. Elliott, J. P., December 11, 1846, STEWART Co.

BELL, Henry J. to Sarah J. Mayes - issued November 11, 1852, m. by:
John Crafford, J. P., November 12, 1852, ROBERTSON Co.

BELL, Hezekiah to Susan Fisher - issued December 23, 1837, Bondsman:
Wm. M. Caplinger, m. by: Jonathan Bailey, J. P., January 2, 1837,
WILSON Co.

BELL, Hiram to Julia Crafford - issued July 11, 1853, m. by:
W. D. Baldwin, V. D. M., ROBERTSON Co.

BELL, Houston to Sarah Bonds - issued April 25, 1838. Bondsman:
Cary Morris, m. by: Thos. Davis, J. P., WILSON Co.

BELL, Hugh H. to Prudence L. Bradford - issued December 23, 1841,
m. by: R. B. C. Howell, M. G., December 23, 1841, DAVIDSON Co.

BELL, Isaac to Sally Stubblefield - issued May 31, 1820, Bondsman:
John Brown, m. by: Jas. Carr May 31, 1820, SUMNER Co.

BELL, J. C. to Mary Milekin - issued February 11, 1858, m. by:
W. C. Haislip, M. G., ROBERTSON Co.

BELL, James to Sarah Newton - November 17, 1797, Security: J. Hamilton,
GREENE Co.

BELL, James to Betsey Easbery - issued June 9, 1808, Bondsman:
Frederick Brown, SUMNER Co.

BELL, James to Nancy Stephenson - issued January 13, 1820, m. by:
T. H. Nelson, M. G., January 13, 1820, KNOX Co.

BELL, James to Nancy Stephenson - issued January 13, 1820, Bondsman:
James Stephenson, KNOX Co.

BELL, James to Martha Marcum - issued December 18, 1837, Bondsman:
Mathew Hutchinson, SUMNER Co.

BELL, James B. to Virginia Thomas - issued May 12, 1851, m. by:
Joseph Willis, M. G., May 13, 1851, ROBERTSON Co.

BELL, James F. to Nancy Wall - December 21, 1830, WILLIAMSON Co.

BELL, Jas. F. to Sarah H. Pone - issued December 17, 1867, FRANKLIN Co.

BELL, James G. to Phebe Lacey - issued November 16, 1831, m. by:
Lindsay Childress, J. P., November 20, 1831, KNOX Co.

BELL, James M. to Elizabeth Oneal - issued November 14, 1838, Bondsman:
Harris Fuller, m. by: Solomon Caplinger, J. P., WILSON Co.

BELL, James S. to Jenny Bell - issued November 21, 1809, Bondsman:
William Bell, KNOX Co.

BELL, James S. to Nancy Conner - issued April 28, 1823, m. by:
J. B. Wynn, M. G., April 29, 1823, KNOX Co.

BELL, Jefferson to Leathy Johnson - issued October 11, 1824, Bondsman:
James Johnson, m. by: Wilson Hearn October 24, 1824, WILSON Co.

BELL, Jobe to Celia Braidges - October 27, 1816, WILLIAMSON Co.

BELL, Joel to Pernecia F. Woodard - issued August 25, 1859, m. by:
John W. Smith, J. P., September 1, 1859, ROBERTSON Co.

BELL, Joel E. to Rebecca Williams - issued September 15, 1847, m. by:
James Woodard, Esq., ROBERTSON Co.

BELL, John to Jane Craig - April 17, 1796, Surety: James Bell, BLOUNT Co.

BELL, John to Sally Dickinson - issued December 10, 1815, Bondsman:
Jonathan Currin, RUTHERFORD Co.

BELL, John to Mary Sullivant - issued August 29, 1818, Bondsman:
Zachariah P. Bell, RUTHERFORD Co.

BELL, John to Sarah Grogen - issued April 16, 1839, Bondsman:
Bailey Bell, m. by: Solomon Caplinger, J. P., WILSON Co.

BELL, John to Frances Johnson - issued March 21, 1846, m. by:
Benj. Sharpe, J. P., March 21, 1846, DAVIDSON Co.

BELL, John to Ann P. Coleman - December 26, 1855, m. by: C. H. Lambeth,
GILES Co.

BELL, Jr., Jno. to Julia Woodard - issued April 20, 1861, m. by:
A. B. Coke, M. G., April 24, 1861, ROBERTSON Co.

BELL, John C. to Susannah J. McCord - issued June 21, 1845, m. by:
H. Larkins, M. G., May 20, 1846, FRANKLIN Co.

BELL, Jonathan C. to Mary Barmore - August 13, 1860, m. by:
Robert Caldwell, V. D. M., GILES Co.

BELL, Joseph to Betsy Widener - November 21, 1818, KNOX Co.

BELL, Joseph to Jane Donnell - issued August 24, 1826, Bondsman:
Jesse M. Wade, m. by: Wm. M. Swain, J. P., WILSON Co.

BELL, Joseph to Mary Lain - issued December 1, 1840, Bondsman:
Henry Edward, m. by: James Bond December 10, 1840, WILSON Co.

BELL, Josph H. to Sally Shumate - May 19, 1808, WILLIAMSON Co.

BELL, Joseph M. to Elisabeth C. Essex - issued August 27, 1818, Bondsman:
James McBride, m. August 27, 1818, SUMNER Co.

BELL, Joseph W. to Nancy Mosley - issued December 28, 1835, Bondsman:
Benjamin H. Bell, m. by: Andrew M. McKee, J. P., January 7, 1836,
RUTHERFORD Co.

BELL, L. J. to Laura V. Henry - issued May 16, 1859, m. by: A. B. Coke,
M. G., May 19, 1959, ROBERTSON Co.

BELL, Lemuel A. to Arelda Jane Rushing - issued February 10, 1845, m. by:
Allen McCaskill, J. P., February 10, 1845, STEWART Co.

BELL, Loyd to Betsy Keys - issued April 12, 1826, Bondsman:
Barkley Walker, Witness: Wm. Swan, KNOX Co.

BELL, Micajah to Peggy Lee - issued April 9, 1818, Bondsman:
James Johnson, SUMNER Co.

BELL, Middleton to Rebecca Gibson - issued August 11, 1807, Bondsman:
William Gibson, WILSON Co.

BELL, Nathaniel to Lucinda Smith - issued February 4, 1826, Bondsman:
E. Sherrill, m. by: Jacob Sullivan February 5, 1826, WILSON Co.

BELL, Nebuchadnezar S. to Emelin Futhy - issued June 5, 1832, m. by:
W. A. McCampbell, M. V. D., June 7, 1832, KNOX Co.

BELL, O. G. to Emily Horn - issued July 1, 1847, DAVIDSON Co.

BELL, Orville to Rebecca Oliver - issued December 21, 1853, m. by:
R. M. Haggard, M. G., December 22, 1853, FRANKLIN Co.

BELL, Patton to Jane Gilbert - issued April 28, 1827, Bondsman:
Jacob Brown, m. by: Wm. Hobdy, J. P., April 28, 1827, SUMNER Co.

BELL, Philip D. to Harriet Jane Murphy - issued August 21, 1827,
Bondsman: Hugh M. Murphy, KNOX Co.

BELL, Pleasant to Lucinda Gaines - issued June 26, 1832, Bondsman:
Sam'l Escue, SUMNER Co.

BELL, R. G. to E. M. Gunn - issued February 7, 1854, m. by: F. R. Gooch,
M. G., February 8, 1854, ROBERTSON Co.

BELL, R. W. to Susan Gunn - issued April 9, 1840, m. by: L. Adams,
M. C. M. E. Church, ROBERTSON Co.

BELL, Ro. to Malinda Scott - issued February 20, 1823, m. by:
Jno. Bayless, J. P., February 21, 1823, KNOX Co.

BELL, Robert to Margarett F. McGundy - issued June 4, 1816, Bondsman:
Robert Desha, Jr., SUMNER Co.

BELL, Robert to Polly Hooker - issued January 14, 1830, Bondsman:
Alexander Simmons, WILSON Co.

BELL, Robert to Mary Wood - issued January 12, 1836, Bondsman:
Alfred Wood, m. by: Tandy Munday, J. P., January 20, 1836, KNOX Co.

BELL, Robert D. to Elizabeth Roane - issued December 13, 1826, Bondsman:
James Astoce, m. by: Thos. Calhoon, V. D. M., December 14, 1826,
WILSON Co.

BELL, Ruthy to Thomas Bell - issued September 22, 1862, Bondsman:
R. A. Clark, Jos. H. Thompson, Clk. per M. E. W. Dunaway, D. Clk.,
BEDFORD Co.

BELL, Sampson to Polly M. Bradley - issued May 14, 1836, m. by:
John Borum May 16, 1836, WILSON Co.

BELL, Samuel to Eliza McCleary Beard - issued October 10, 1821, Bondsman:
James Mitchell, m. by: Wilson Hearn, M. G., October 11, 1821,
WILSON Co.

BELL, Samuel to Rebecca M. Peayn - issued March 19, 1827, Bondsman:
Joseph Hollis, RUTHERFORD Co.

BELL, Samuel to Milly Moor - issued May 9, 1829, Bondsman: A. Brogan,
WILSON Co.

BELL, Samuel N. to Charlott Hammer - issued April 13, 1835, m. by:
J. M. Kelley, M. G., KNOX Co.

BELL, Samuel P. to Mary A. Sanford - issued August 28, 1837, m. by:
B. B. Hall September 31, 1837, RUTHERFORD Co.

BELL, Sterling to Polly Spencer - October 10, 1808, MAURY Co.

BELL, Thomas to Elener Tillery - January 22, 1805, KNOX Co.

BELL, Thomas to C ty Dolly - November 6, 1805, WILLIAMSON Co.

BELL, Thomas to Sarah M. Knox - issued June 4, 1846, Bondsman:
Wm. S. Knox, m. by: J. C. Weakley, J. P., June 10, 1846,
MONTGOMERY Co.

BELL, Thomas to Rosa Ann Harris - issued January 10, 1850, Bondsman:
Abner Hunter, m. by: Lewis Lowe, M. G., January 17, 1850,
MONTGOMERY Co.

BELL, Thomas to Ruthy Bell - issued September 22, 1862, Bondsman:
R. A. Clark, Jos. H. Thompson, Clk. per M. E. W. Dunaway, D. Clk.,
BEDFORD Co.

BELL, Uriah to Elmina M. Warren - November 16, 1859, m. by:
McHenry Sumner, M. G., GILES Co.

BELL, Wiley W. to Susan J. Crags - issued May 9, 1829, Bondsman:
Jesse L. Moore, m. by: Wm. M. Swain, J. P., May 10, 1829, WILSON Co.

BELL, William to Elizabeth Fairless - issued October 25, 1830, Bondsman:
Wm. Bell, Sr., m. by: J. P., Hogan, J. P., October 25, 1830,
SUMNER Co.

BELL, William to Sarah B. Bell - issued January 5, 1845, m. by:
Jesse Edwards, Minister, January 5, 1845, DICKSON Co.

BELL, Wm. H. to Nancy Tate - issued February 6, 1845, m. by:
David Jones, J. P., February 9, 1845, ROBERTSON Co.

BELL, William L. to Elizabeth Grymes - issued August 25, 1840, m. by:
R. Chadoin August 25, 1840, DICKSON Co.

BELL, Wm. M. to Susan Lows - issued February 13, 1825, m. by:
R. H. King, M. G., February 13, 1825, KNOX Co.

BELL, Wm. W. to Susan Low - issued February 13, 1824, m. by:
R. H. King February 13, 1824, KNOX Co.

BELL, William W. to Sarah Ann Golladay - issued May 10, 1838, Bondsman:
Saml. Yerger, m. by: George Donnell, V. D. M., WILSON Co.

BELL, Zack H. to Eliza J. Powell - issued November 11, 1851, m. by:
J. M. Gunn, J. P., ROBERTSON Co.

BELL, Zadoch to Katherine Lowrance - issued July 26, 1821, m. by:
Nace Overall, M. G., July 26, 1821, RUTHERFORD Co.

BELLAH, John to Sarah Davidson - issued April 30, 1816, m. by:
Jas. S. Jetton, J. P., May 2, 1816, RUTHERFORD Co.

BELLEMY, Benoni to Caroline Trudy - issued July 11, 1843, STEWART Co.

BELLEN, Reuben to Catherine Vaughan - issued January, 1825, RUTHERFORD Co.

BELLEW, Peter to Mary Casselberry - issued July 22, 1800, Bondsman:
George Cummings, SUMNER Co.

BELLIEW, William to Temperence Wolf - issued November 27, 1839, m. by:
E. M. Patterson, J. P., November 28, 1839, DAVIDSON Co.

BELOTE, Henry to Harriett Boon - issued April, 1821, Bondsman:
John Swaney, m. by: W. Smith, J. P., April, 1821, SUMNER Co.

BELOTE, Henry H. to Martha M. Goodall - issued May 4, 1829, Bondsman:
Nathaniel Herndon, m. by: S. R. Roberts, J. P., May 4, 1829,
SUMNER Co.

BELOTE, Jeremiah to Nancy M. Wilson - issued December 22, 1829,
Bondsman: R. T. Warner, SUMNER Co.

BELOTE, Smitle to Nancy Gill - issued November 2, 1812, Bondsman:
William Gill, WILSON Co.

BELT, Arthur to Peggy Todd - issued August 26, 1835, Bondsman:
Arthur H. Belt, RUTHERFORD Co.

BELT, Benjamin to Louisa Todd - issued August 1, 1834, RUTHERFORD Co.

BELT, Benjamin to Polly Reed - issued August 20, 1827, Bondsman:
Edward Campbell, m. by: Walter Carruth, J. P., August 30, 1827,
WILSON Co.

BELT, Hyram to Aberilla Medford - issued June 26, 1818, Bondsman:
Thomas Keele, m. by: William Mankin, J. P., July 8, 1818,
RUTHERFORD Co.

BELT, Jeremiah to Mary Reed - issued September 17, 1840, Bondsman:
Benjamin Belt, m. by: Williamson Williams, M. G., WILSON Co.

BELT, John to Mary Bonfield - issued June 2, 1832, Bondsman:
Thos. Campbell, m. by: Williamson Williams, J. P., June 3, 1832,
WILSON Co.

BELT, Reason to Elizabeth Williams - issued November 24, 1832,
Bondsman: John Thompson, WILSON Co.

BELT, Thomas to Mary Belt - issued November 20, 1839, Bondsman:
Benj. Belt, m. by: Wm. Barton, M. G., November 29, 1839, WILSON Co.

BELT, William to Matilda Campbell - issued December 3, 1832, Bondsman:
Benjamin Belt, m. by: Thomas Smith, M. C., WILSON Co.

BELTON, Dudley to Janey Rolan - issued February 29, 1824, Bondsman:
David Counts, m. February 29, 1824, GRAINGER Co.

BEMISS, Sam'l M. to M. F. Lockert - issued October 16, 1849, Bondsman:
Joshua Grant, m. by: J. T. Hendrick, M. G., October 16, 1849,
MONTGOMERY Co.

BENBROOK, Daniel to Margaret Boyer - issued December 18, 1827, Bondsman:
A. F. Young, m. December 18, 1827, SUMNER Co.

BENBROOK, Elbert to Polly Chapman - issued April 22, 1828, Bondsman:
James Alderson, m. by: Robert Norvell April 22, 1828, SUMNER Co.

BENBROOK, Nathan to Sally McGuire - issued November 9, 1816, Bondsman:
Elijah Sneed, m. by: John Benbrook November 9, 1816, SUMNER Co.

BENDER, Bernice to Elizabeth Ann Smith - issued February 24, 1834,
Bondsman: William D. Smith, m. by: Barton Brown, M. G., February 25,
1834, WILSON Co.

BENDER, Burrell to Elizabeth Smith - issued August 10, 1832, Bondsman:
Turner Vaughn, m. by: J. H. Davis, J. P., August 17, 1832,
WILSON Co.

BENEIT, Ernest to Fanny Gains - issued October 30, 1817, Bondsman:
Walter Keeble, RUTHERFORD Co.

BENETT, William to Ely Tippet - issued January 31, 1814, Bondsman:
John C. Johnson, WILSON Co.

BENFIELD, Agnes to Alexander Suit - GREENE Co.

BENGIE, James S. to May Harris - issued January 28, 1849, Bondsman:
Joseph Bengie, m. by: T. Ramey, J. P., May 3, 1849, MONTGOMERY Co.

BENNET, Jacob to Ceta Bonds - issued September 7, 1815, Bondsman:
James Bennet, WILSON Co.

BENNET, James to Nancy Stoks - issued February 9, 1841, m. by:
H. Ferrel, J. P., February 9, 1841, STEWART Co.

BENNET, Thomas to Elizabeth Bond - issued December 21, 1815, Bondsman:
Truman Modglin, WILSON Co.

BENNET, Thomas to Bridget Toole - May 10, 1859, m. by: John Scollard,
GILES Co.

BENNET, Winney to John Massey - August 23, 1817, GREENE Co.

BENNETT, A. C. to Virginia Wilson - issued March 2, 1868, m. by:
D. S. Long, J. P., March 3, 1868, FRANKLIN Co.

BENNETT, Alexander to Rebedah Yarborough - October 1, 1808, WILLIAMSON Co.

BENNETT, Baxter to Elizabeth Chandler - issued June 3, 1828, Bondsman:
Eli Gladstone, WILSON Co.

BENNETT, Cooper to Anne Miller - March 18, 1815, WILLIAMSON Co.

BENNETT, Drury to Elizabeth Manier - December 10, 1811, WILLIAMSON Co.

BENNETT, Francis M. to Francis McKelvey - issued November 24, 1857,
m. by: Lewis Anderson, J. P., November 26, 1857, FRANKLIN Co.

BENNETT, George to Polly Rounsavall - October 6, 1813, WILLIAMSON Co.

BENNETT, George to Mary Womack - m. by: M. Catchings, J. P., May 3,
1851, FRANKLIN Co.

BENNETT, Giles A. to Elizabeth C. Lynch - issued January 4, 1846,
m. by: John Nugent, J. P., January 4, 1846, FRANKLIN Co.

BENNETT, H. R. to Clarisa Keaton - issued September 20, 1838, m. by:
John P. Walker September, 1838, FRANKLIN Co.

BENNETT, Harman to Mary A. Rose - issued September 12, 1865, FRANKLIN Co.

BENNETT, Isaac to Elizabeth Hutcherson - issued March 27, 1852, m. by:
R. C. Smith, J. P., March 28, 1852, FRANKLIN Co.

BENNETT, Jacob. to Agnes Richey - March 12, 1786, Security: William
Richey, GREENE Co.

BENNETT, James to Hannah Parkes - issued May 12, 1845, m. by:
G. D. Fullmer, J. P., May 12, 1845, DAVIDSON Co.

BENNETT, James to Mary Swann - issued January 8, 1852, m. by:
John Nugent, J. P., January 8, 1852, FRANKLIN Co.

BENNETT, James to Dosha Decherd - issued December 8, 1852, m. by:
John Nugent, J. P., December 8, 1852, FRANKLIN Co.

BENNETT, James D. to Dorcas Irwin - issued January 1, 1831, m. by:
Sam'l. Fleming, J. P., January 1, 1831, KNOX Co.

BENNETT, James S. to Polly Edwards - issued December 1, 1839, Bondsman: Jarratt W. Edwards, m. by: James Bond, M. G., December 10, 1839, WILSON Co.

BENNETT, Joel to Jane Geivin - issued February 17, 1842, m. by: H. Ferrel, J. P., February 17, 1842, STEWART Co.

BENNETT, John to Martha A. Adams - issued October 6, 1853, m. by: Joseph Smith October 7, 1853, FRANKLIN Co.

BENNETT, John to Martha S. Leathers - issued May 3, 1862, Bondsman: J. C. Coleman, Jos. H. Thompson, Clk. per M. E. Dunaway, Dep. Clk., BEDFORD Co.

BENNETT, John C. to Martha A. Moore - issued November 16, 1837, Bondsman: Thomas J. Stratton, m. by: John Kelley, M. G., WILSON Co.

BENNETT, John K. to Lavenia Parks - issued September 24, 1873, m. by: J. M. F. Smithson, M. G., September 25, 1873, FRANKLIN Co.

BENNETT, John M. to Maria Boren - issued February 15, 1844, m. by: John Nugent, J. P., February 15, 1844, FRANKLIN Co.

BENNETT, Joseph to Orina Harlow - issued August 3, 1829, Bondsman: Robert Simpson, m. by: Joshua Lester, V. D. M., WILSON Co.

BENNETT, Joseph to Nancy Merrett - issued October 21, 1839, Bondsman: Isham S. Green, m. by: Thos. Davis, J. P., October 22, 1839, WILSON Co.

BENNETT, L. G. to Ibby Dial - issued July 27, 1847, m. by: Jno. P. Miller, J. P., July 30, 1847, FRANKLIN Co.

BENNETT, Pernell to Arnis Williams - issued October 9, 1820, Bondsman: Ang. Lane, m. by: John Bond, V. D. M., October 11, 1820, WILSON Co.

BENNETT, Presley to Nancy Crews - issued July 3, 1823, Bondsman: Walter Childress, m. by: Rob't. McBath July 3, 1823, Witness: Wm. Swan, KNOX Co.

BENNETT, Richard to Polly Bell - issued February 25, 1811, Bondsman: John Shepperd, SUMNER Co.

BENNETT, Samuel to Sarah Hill - issued August 20, 1856, m. by: James Seargent, J. P., August 20, 1856, FRANKLIN Co.

BENNETT, Samuel H. to Catharine C. Johnson - October 14, 1850, m. by: G. D. Taylor, GILES Co.

BENNETT, Simon W. to Elizabeth Finney - issued January 18, 1854, m. by: John Nugent, J. P., January 18, 1854, FRANKLIN Co.

BENNETT, Simpson to Nancy Jackson - issued August 26, 1826, Bondsman: Randal McDonald, m. by: Stephen McDonald, J. P., December 14, 1826, WILSON Co.

BENNETT, Simpson to May Ann Jackson - issued November 12, 1831, Bondsman: Robert Jackson, m. by: Stephen McDonald, J. P., December 1, 1831, WILSON Co.

BENNETT, Solomon to Melvina Russell - issued July 19, 1845, m. by: P. Lynch, J. P., July 20, 1845, STEWART Co.

BENNETT, Thomas to Matilda Crockett - issued July 20, 1842, DAVIDSON Co.

BENNETT, Thomas to Elizabeth Harper - issued February 26, 1846, m. by: W. Crockett, J. P., February 26, 1846, DAVIDSON Co.

BENNETT, Thomas to Manerva Bryant - issued January 14, 1874, m. by: W. G. Miller, M. G., January 15, 1874, FRANKLIN Co.

BENNETT, W. A. to M. A. Ireland - issued April 2, 1860, m. by:
H. Warren, J. P., April 3, 1860, ROBERTSON Co.

BENNETT, Walter to Jincy Reynolds - August 22, 1808, WILLIAMSON Co.

BENNETT, William to Susannah Tucker - issued January 10, 1816, m. by:
John Fulton, J. P., January 23, 1816, RUTHERFORD Co.

BENNETT, Wm. to Mary A. Williams - issued August 9, 1852, m. by:
John Byrom, M. G., August 11, 1852, FRANKLIN Co.

BENNETT, William M. to Mary J. Thompson - issued December 22, 1847,
m. by: Isaac Steel December 23, 1847, ROBERTSON Co.

BENNINGFIELD, James W. to Elizabeth Jones - issued December 24, 1840,
m. by: John Wright, J. P., December 24, 1840, DAVIDSON Co.

BENSEY, Payton to Nancy Champion - issued October 9, 1844, m. by:
B. Herndon, J. P., October 13, 1844, STEWART Co.

BENSON, Benjamin F. to Sarah F. Gourley - issued July 16, 1844,
Bondsman: G. W. Sims, m. by: J. P. Fryar, M. G., July 16, 1844,
MEIGS Co.

BENSON, Calvin to Miss. Polly Harris - issued May 24, 1840, m. by:
Robt. Green, J. P., ROBERTSON Co.

BENSON, Edward to Miram Harrison - issued May 10, 1838, Bondsman:
Alexander Benson, m. May 10, 1838, SUMNER Co.

BENSON, Elijah to G. L. A. L. Baldry - issued August 20, 1846, m. by:
Wm. L. Bardry, Gos. Minister, ROBERTSON Co.

BENSON, Elvis to Sarah Bigbee - issued December 25, 1852, m. by:
J. C. Barbee, J. P., December 26, 1852, ROBERTSON Co.

BENSON, James to Lency Winsett - April 5, 1816, WILLIAMSON Co.

BENSON, John to Mary Anne Higginbotham - issued November 7, 1829,
Bondsman: Allen Gowen, RUTHERFORD Co.

BENSON, John C. to Sally Traughber - issued May 19, 1841, m. by:
Benja. Gambill, J. P., ROBERTSON Co.

BENSON, Martin G. to Nancy Williamson - issued August 16, 1856, m. by:
J. W. Cullum, M. G., August 19, 1856, ROBERTSON Co.

BENSON, Matthias to Hannah Smith - issued August 1, 1826, m. by:
Geo. Atkin, M. G., August 1, 1826, KNOX Co.

BENSON, Perry P. to Nancy M. Hill - issued December 21, 1839, Bondsman:
Wm. J. Pride, WILSON Co.

BENSON, Washington to Margaret Dunn - issued September 16, 1833,
Bondsman: Hardy Travis, RUTHERFORD Co.

BENSON, William to Catherine Higenbotham - issued December 28, 1830,
m. by: Joseph Gowen, J. P., December 29, 1830, RUTHERFORD Co.

BENTHAL, Willis to Darcas Potcet - m. October 23, 1823, SUMNER Co.

BENTHALL, Daniel to Frankey Patton - issued January 28, 1822, Bondsman:
William McCall, m. by: Thos. Anderson, J. P., January 28, 1822,
SUMNER Co.

BENTHALL, George to Sally Brown - issued March 8, 1825, Bondsman:
Littleton Burchat, WILSON Co.

BENTHALL, Laben to Levina Lannum - issued April 1, 1824, Bondsman:
Alexander Carter, RUTHERFORD Co.

BENTHALL, Littleton to Susannah Stanley - issued April 9, 1818,
    Bondsman: Benjamin Stanley, m. by: John W. Payton, WILSON Co.

BENTLEY, James M. to Nancy Rutledge - issued September 26, 1833,
    Bondsman: James R. Youree, WILSON Co.

BENTLEY, Jeremiah to Nancy Patton - m. by: H. B. Hill January 12, 1836,
    SUMNER Co.

BENTLEY, John to Rachel Brown - issued February 5, 1806, Bondsman:
    John L. Swaney, SUMNER Co.

BENTLEY, Jr., John to Martha Ann Bunton - m. by: James Charlton
    July 29, 1833, SUMNER Co.

BENTLEY, William to Nancy Youree - issued January 3, 1825, Bondsman:
    Reuben Blackemore, m. by: Jno. Swaney, J. P., January 3, 1825,
    SUMNER Co.

BENTON, Daniel W. to Susan A. Fryar - issued October 27, 1857, m. by:
    J. T. Craig, J. P., November 1, 1857, ROBERTSON Co.

BENTON, Daniel W. to Amanda E. Fryor - issued January 19, 1859, m. by:
    Jesse B. White, J. P., January 20, 1859, ROBERTSON Co.

BENTON, E. to E. Draughon - issued December 9, 1847, m. by: P. Martin,
    ROBERTSON Co.

BENTON, E. to Nancy Powell - issued August 31, 1851, m. by:
    D. Hering, J. P. R. C., ROBERTSON Co.

BENTON, E. P. to Lucy Ann Porter - issued April 7, 1856, m. by:
    J. W. Cullum, M. G., April 8, 1856, ROBERTSON Co.

BENTON, Ephriam to Scina Moore - issued January 18, 1851, m. by:
    Jas. Woodard, ROBERTSON Co.

BENTON, George B. to Ann Pope - issued December 4, 1856, m. by:
    J. W. Cullum, M. G., December 4, 1856, ROBERTSON Co.

BENTON, Green to Mary Morris - issued January 29, 1840, m. by:
    D. R. Harris, G. M., ROBERTSON Co.

BENTON, Green to Emily S. Bell - issued April 5, 1859, m. by:
    John A. Ellis, M. G., ROBERTSON Co.

BENTON, Grover M. to Mary Hudson - issued July 10, 1840, Bondsman:
    Richard Grisham, m. by: John Seabern, J. P., July 12, 1840,
    MEIGS Co.

BENTON, Isaac to Nancy Ingram - issued November 22, 1827, m. by:
    E. M. Eagleton, M. G., November 22, 1827, KNOX Co.

BENTON, James to Mary Dickerson - issued June 4, 1842, m. by:
    Jesse L. Ellis, J. P., June 5, 1842, ROBERTSON Co.

BENTON, Jesse to Polly Childress - January 4, 1817, WILLIAMSON Co.

BENTON, John to David Shelby, Esq.

    Dear Sir:
        The Bearer John Benton having given me Satisfactory Security
    for his true performance of his article of covenent with me.
        I have no objections to his commiting matrimony. I am Sir
    with respect & Esteem.

                            Yr. Mots. aft. Serv.
                                G. Winchester

BENTON, John to Jane Kendrick - issued March 18, 1793, SUMNER Co.

BENTON, John F. to Martha Ann Willson - issued August 2, 1853, m. by:
Peter Hinkle, Esq., August 4, 1853, ROBERTSON Co.

BENTON, John G. to Martha Murphy - issued December 18, 1853, m. by:
F. R. Gooch, M. G., ROBERTSON Co.

BENTON, Joseph W. to Nancy Rains - issued January 27, 1847, m. by:
Edward Slater, M. G., January 28, 1847, DAVIDSON Co.

BENTON, Malichi to Rozane Benton - issued October 4, 1860, m. by:
W. W. Pepper, Judge of Circuit Court, ROBERTSON Co.

BENTON, Rich. to Nancy Binkley - issued January 20, 1853, m. by:
Robert Draughon, J. P., ROBERTSON Co.

BENTON, Saml. to Mary Hunter - March 21, 1808, WILLIAMSON Co.

BENTON, Thos. H. to Mary Pepper - issued May 1, 1861, m. by:
H. Warren, J. P., ROBERTSON Co.

BENTON, Thomas H. to Mary E. Graham - issued August 1, 1861, m. by:
B. H. Adams, J. P., August 1, 1861, COFFEE Co.

BENTON, W. I. to Angeline Binkley - issued February 28, 1855, m. by:
G. Benton, J. P., ROBERTSON Co.

BENTON, William to Fanny Dodd - issued February 22, 1812, Bondsman:
Moses Pruett, WILSON Co.

BENTON, William F. to Nancy E. Willson - issued May 13, 1853, m. by:
W. D. Baldwin, V. D. M., May 15, 1853, ROBERTSON Co.

BERFORD, K. H. to Evey L. Awatt (Awalt) - issued October 28, 1843,
m. by: John W. Spearman, M. G., November 7, 1843, FRANKLIN Co.

BERKLEY, John to Polly Bradley - June 6, 1811, WILLIAMSON Co.

BERKLEY, Robert to Sarah Goalston - issued July 21, 1830, Bondsman:
Frances Anderson, WILSON Co.

BERKLEY, Seborn to Martin Fritzwell - issued September 22, m. by:
Thos. S. Elliott, M. G., September 23, 1841, STEWART Co.

BERNARD, David to Pheby Ferguson - issued February 22, 1823, Bondsman:
Patrick Rains and Thos. Edwards, SUMNER Co.

BERNARD, Horatio to Jane Atherly - issued April 11, 1825, Bondsman:
Evans Mabry, WILSON Co.

BERNARD, Horatio to Margaret M. Williamson - issued October 11, 1826,
Bondsman: Henry F. Smith, m. by: B. Graves, J. P., WILSON Co.

BERNARD, Jacob to Charlotte Bandy - issued September 28, 1824, Bondsman:
Elisha Bernard, SUMNER Co.

BERNARD, James to Martha Griffin - issued September 14, 1838, Bondsman:
Milton McGehe, m. by: Wm. Barton, M. G., September 16, 1838,
WILSON Co.

BERNARD, William to Catherine Barksdale - issued November 15, 1823,
Bondsman: William Dickinson, m. by: Richard Dobbs December 25,
1823, RUTHERFORD Co.

BERNARD, Wm. A. to E. I. McMillin - issued June 25, 1843, m. by:
John M. Nolen June 26, 1843, ROBERTSON Co.

BERNARD, Zadock to Hannah Kimbel - issued October 29, 1817, SUMNER Co.

BERRY, Alvin to Agness Haley - issued September 16, 1842, m. by:
David Jones, J. P., September 21, 1842, ROBERTSON Co.

BERRY, Augustus D. to Adeline Farnham - issued August 21, 1841,
DAVIDSON Co.

BERRY, Benjamin to Mary Oakley - issued November 4, 1839, Bondsman:
Dake Young, m. by: Archamab Bass, M. G., November 6, 1839,
WILSON Co.

BERRY, David N. to Martha C. Smith - issued March 20, 1832, Bondsman:
H. S. Barry, m. by: P. Y. Davis, M. G., March 27, 1832, WILSON Co.

BERRY, Ephriam to Minerva Martin - issued January 9, 18__, m. by:
R. G. Cole, J. P., January 11, 1846, ROBERTSON Co.

BERRY, Francis P. M. to Betsey Sellers - February 15, 1810, Bondsman:
Samuel Crawford, MAURY Co.

BERRY, Geo. C. to Mary Forguson - issued December 21, 1825, Bondsman:
Thomas Anderson, Witness: Wm. Swan, KNOX Co.

BERRY, Green to Martha Miles - issued August 18, 1855, m. by:
J. H. Jones, J. P., August 18, 1855, COFFEE Co.

BERRY, Hugh L. to Anne Parker - issued February 14, 1827, Bondsman:
Jno. Brown, m. by: Sam Flenniken, J. P., February 15, 1827, KNOX Co.

BERRY, James to Rebecca Rogers - August 20, 1798, BLOUNT Co.

BERRY, James to Mary Ann Taylor - issued February 2, 1819, Bondsman:
E. Burk, WILSON Co.

BERRY, James to Elizabeth Pitt - issued October 15, 1846, m. by:
G. D. Fullman, J. P., October 15, 1846, DAVIDSON Co.

BERRY, James to Melissa A. Webb - issued December 22, 1860, m. by:
J. W. Featherston, M. G., December 23, 1860, ROBERTSON Co.

BERRY, Jesse to Milly Shanks - issued February 18, 1820, Bondsman:
George Donnell, m. by: Joshua Lester, V. D. M., February 24, 1820,
WILSON Co.

BERRY, Jo. D. to Elizabeth Kinnamon - issued November 2, 1830, Bondsman:
Michael Davis, m. by: Michael Davis, J. P., November 2, 1830,
KNOX Co.

BERRY, John to Elizabeth Campbell - issued October 12, 1809, Bondsman:
John Givins, WILSON Co.

BERRY, John to Elvira Harris - issued August 13, 1813, Bondsman:
Sam'l Harris, WILSON Co.

BERRY, John to America Anderson - issued June 7, 1839, m. by:
Henry Larkin August 4, 1839, FRANKLIN Co.

BERRY, John to Mary Jane Bass - issued June 5, 1852, m. by: H. V. Brown,
Cath. Priest, June 5, 1852, FRANKLIN Co.

BERRY, John to Rachiel Garner - issued August 23, 1858, m. August 23,
1858, FRANKLIN Co.

BERRY, John C. to Nancy B. Ramsey - issued December 20, 1833, Bondsman:
Sam'l G. Thompson, RUTHERFORD Co.

BERRY, John S. to Susan Fleshart - issued January 3, 1829, Bondsman:
David Bell, m. by: Tho. H. Nelson January 3, 1829, KNOX Co.

BERRY, Michael to Nancy A. S. Nesbitt - issued January 7, 1846, m. by:
L. R. Dennis, M. G., DICKSON Co.

BERRY, Pleasant to M. W. Wrights - issued December 28, 1858, m. by:
Thos. West, M. G., ROBERTSON Co.

BERRY, Ross B. to Nancy Baxter - issued February 15, 1855, m. by:
James Seargent, J. P., February 15, 1855, FRANKLIN Co.

BERRY, Thos. S. to Eliza Ann Puckett - issued January 16, 1833,
Bondsman: James C. Taylor, RUTHERFORD Co.

BERRY, W. G. to Stacy Shelton - issued September 30, 1867, m. by:
J. W. Williams, J. P., September 30, 1867, FRANKLIN Co.

BERRY, W. K. to Sophia Payne - issued October 15, 1855, m. by:
G. W. Featherston, M. G., October 17, 1855, ROBERTSON Co.

BERRY, William to Sally Simpson - issued March 17, 1819, Bondsman:
Sanford Simpson, KNOX Co.

BERRY, Wm. to Ruthy White - issued September 27, 1819, Bondsman:
William Price, m. by: Wm. A. McCampbell, Esq., September 27,
1819, Witness: Wm. C. Mynatt, KNOX Co.

BERRY, Wm. W. to Jane Eliza White - issued March 10, 1840, m. by:
John W. Ogden, M. G., March 10, 1840, DAVIDSON Co.

BERRYHILL, Joe to Mary Delzell - issued December 17, 1874, m. by:
Asa D. Oakley, M. G., December 19, 1874, FRANKLIN Co.

BERRYHILL, Lewis to Sarah Mahaffee - issued February 27, 1863, m. by:
L. E. Jones, M. G., March 1, 1863, FRANKLIN Co.

BERRYHILL, Linsfield to Mary A. Wilks - issued January 17, 1854, m. by:
Jas. B. Foster, J. P., January 17, 1854, FRANKLIN Co.

BERRYHILL, Robert A. to Sarah A. Conn - issued August 2, 1852, m. by:
N. L. Power, M. G., August 2, 1852, FRANKLIN Co.

BERRYMAN, Benjamin V. to Elizabeth F. Bracken - m. by: Robert Norvell
January 21, 1833, SUMNER Co.

BERRYMAN, Talliaferro to Margaret E. Whitsett - issued March 1, 1837,
m. by: William D. Nelson, J. P., March 2, 1837, RUTHERFORD Co.

BERT, John A. L. to M. M. Griggs - issued May 12, 1847, m. by: Wm. Shaw,
M. G., May 13, 1847, DAVIDSON Co.

BERTHELL, John to Marthe Etheredge - DICKSON Co.

BESHIER, Lorenzo to Mary E. North - issued September 16, 1873, m. by:
F. A. Shoup, Priest, D. E. C., September 18, 1873, FRANKLIN Co-

BESON, David to Polly Short - issued October 16, 1828, Bondsman:
Wm. Clendenning, SUMNER Co.

BESS, Andrew J. to Harriett Mitchell - issued June 1, 1842, m. by:
E. M. Patterson, J. P., June 3, 1842, DAVIDSON Co.

BEST, George to Sarah A. Blankenship - issued July 1, 1829, Bondsman:
Allen Blankenship, RUTHERFORD Co.

BEST, Geo. C. to Lacky (or Locky) Howell - issued November 8, 1830,
Bondsman: Sylvanus Howell, KNOX Co.

BEST, S. to M. A. Vance - issued April 17, 1866, m. by: W. B. Watterson,
April 18, 1866, FRANKLIN Co.

BETHEL, W. D. to Elizabeth Hammons - issued May 19, 1959, m. by:
A. D. Trimble, M. G., May 19, 1859, FRANKLIN Co.

BETHOON, Kenneth to Delilah Ragsdale - issued June 4, 1811, Bondsman: Richard Ragsdale, WILSON Co.

BATHUM (?), Isaac to Elizabeth Biggs - Samuel Lewis, GRAINGER Co.

BETHSHARES, Thomas to Ersula Burlison - issued April 5, 1821, m. by: Peyton Smith, M. G., April 5, 1821, RUTHERFORD Co.

BETHSHEARS, Wm. S. to Martha L. Johnson - issued November 15, 1825, m. by: Peyton Smith, M. G., November 20, 1825, RUTHERFORD Co.

BETT, John to Aley Smith - issued September 7, 1835, Bondsman: Benjamin Bett, WILSON Co.

BETTES, Moses W. to Elizabeth B. Hope - issued April 17, 1845, m. by: John Beard, M. G., April 17, 1845, DAVIDSON Co.

BETTIS, Alford to Margaret Conger - issued March 3, 1822, Bondsman: William Bettis, m. by: Abner Hill, M. G., March 5, 1822, WILSON Co.

BETTIS, John to Sally Bradley - issued January 10, 1807, Bondsman: Hugh Bradley, WILSON Co.

BETTIS, John to Milly Jolly - issued July 13, 1824, Bondsman: William Bettis, WILSON Co.

BETTIS, Lucinda to Levi Cooley - BEDFORD Co.

BETTIS, Ozburn to Martha Wilkinson - issued August 19, 1840, Bondsman: Thomas Goldston, m. by: R. L. Mayson, J. P., August 30, 1840, WILSON Co.

BETTIS, Samuel to Achaza Chapman - issued October 12, 1811, Bondsman: William Bettis, WILSON Co.

BETTIS, Tillman to Sally ___ (?) - issued May 10, 1809, Bondsman: Richard Carr, WILSON Co.

BETTIS, William to Winney Lambath - issued March 17, 1812, Bondsman: Samuel Bettis, WILSON Co.

BETTIS, Wyett to Melly Powers - issued August 7, 1806, Bondsman: John Bettis, WILSON Co.

BEVARD, Lawrence to Betsey White - issued May 7, 1816, Bondsman: Thomas Scurry, SUMNER Co.

BEVEL, Wm. H. to Mary Manning - issued December 26, 1845, m. by: Benjamin Sharpe, J. P., December 26, 1845, DAVIDSON Co.

BEVER, James to Mariah Bunch - issued February 27, 1825, Bondsman: Joel Meador, m. February 27, SUMNER Co.

BEVIL, Henry O. to Mary F. Silvertooth - issued November 7, 1874, m. by: J. A. Hudgins, M. G., November 8, 1874, FRANKLIN Co.

BEVIL, John to Isabella M. Baggett - issued January 9, 1854, m. by: J. A. Silvertooth, J. P., January 9, 1854, FRANKLIN Co.

BIAN, Pryor to Elizabeth Smith - issued August 14, 1830, Bondsman: Claiborn Godwin, GRAINGER Co.

BIBB, Henry A. to Milberry Massie - issued September 29, 1842, m. by: John Eubanks, J. P., September 29, 1842, DICKSON Co.

BIBB, Henry G. to Sarah Adams - issued July 30, 1843, m. by: U. Young, J. P., ROBERTSON Co.

BIBB, John M. to Caroline Johnson - issued October 12, 1838, m. by: Empson, Bishop, October 11, 1838, DICKSON Co.

BIBB, Minor to Lydia Pryor - issued June 24, 1840, m. by: M. B. Stuart,
J. P., June 25, 1840, DICKSON Co.

BIBB, Samuel A. to Martha Carr - issued February 2, 1848, m. by:
John Brown, M. P., DICKSON Co.

BIBB, Vernon F. to Elizabeth Bibb - issued July 30, 1840, m. by:
Empson Bishop, July 30, 1840, DICKSON Co.

BIBB, Wm. to Jerusha Denkins - issued February 7, 1843, STEWART Co.

BIBB, William E. to Katherine Hightower - issued October 4, 1840,
m. by: James Woodard, J. P., ROBERTSON Co.

BIBBINS, Elijah to Franky Soloman - issued October 17, 1821, Bondsman:
John Soloman, m. by: James G. Harris, J. P., October 18, 1821,
GRAINGER Co.

BIBBONS, Joseph to Martha Pratt - issued February 19, 1853, m. by:
J. C. Montgomery, J. P., February 20, 1853, FRANKLIN Co.

BIBBS, John to Levico Manley - issued September 11, 1826, m. by:
John Bayless, J. P., September 12, 1826, KNOX Co.

BIBLE, John to Rebecca Coffett - July 12, 1797, Security: John Wilson,
GREENE Co.

BIBLE, Mary to Jacob Easterly - January 26, 1798, Security:
Christopher Bible, GREENE Co.

BICE, Elijah to Polly Ann Lee - issued August 16, 1847, m. by:
D. D. McElroy, J. P., August 17, 1847, FRANKLIN Co.

BICKERS, Samuel to Elizabeth Morris - issued August 22, 1821, Bondsman:
Levi Donnell, m. by: John W. Payton, J. P., August 23, 1821,
WILSON Co.

BICKERS, William to Mary Allen - issued July 18, 1836, m. by:
John Bell, J. P., July 19, 1836, WILSON Co.

BICKERSON, William to Lizzie McPherson - issued March 1, 1872, m. by:
Joseph D. Sherrill, M. G., March 1, 1872, FRANKLIN Co.

BICKERTON, James to Mary Thomas - issued September 3, 1822, m. by:
Nace Overall, M. G., September 3, 1822, RUTHERFORD Co.

BICKLEY, J. T. to Joe Wiseman - issued September 28, 1870, FRANKLIN Co.

BICKLEY, W. L. to Mary J. Turner - issued April 24, 1860, m. by:
W. W. Estill, M. G., April 24, 1860, FRANKLIN Co.

BICKNELL, Harriett E. to S. E. Jones - issued September 26, 1863,
Bondsman: W. T. Gowan, Jos. H. Thompson, Clk. per M. E. W.
Dunaway, D. Clk., BEDFORD Co.

BICKWELL, D. K. to Callie Brown - issued September 4, 1865, m. by:
E. P. Anderson, Minister, September 5, 1865, FRANKLIN Co.

BIDDLE, Daniel M. to Mary Pride - issued February 24, 1847, m. by:
J. B. McFerrin February 24, 1847, DAVIDSON Co.

BIGBEE, John C. to Harriet E. Clerk - issued August 13, 1842, m. by:
Greenberry Kelly, ROBERTSON Co.

BIGEE, Geo. W. to Lucinda Inman - issued July 30, 1840, m. by:
Ed Edwards August 2, 1840, ROBERTSON Co.

BIGGERS, Joseph to Polly Robinson - August 23, 1817, WILLIAMSON Co.

BIGGERS, Joshua to Polly Deans - issued March 6, 1822, Bondsman:
James Dickerson, m. by: J. L. Swaney, M. P., March 6, 1822,
SUMNER Co.

BIGGERS, Wm. to Elizabeth Johnson - issued January 2, 1845, m. by:
Wm. Greer, Jr., January 2, 1845, DAVIDSON Co.

BIGGS, Adam to Sally Miller - issued June 6, 1816, Bondsman:
Thos. Scurry, SUMNER Co.

BIGGS, Henry to Margaret Brylie - m. by: E. L. Martin November 3, 1835,
SUMNER Co.

BIGGS, James to Jane Carney - issued November 10, 1825, Bondsman:
Edmond Barrow, SUMNER Co.

BIGGS, James to Martha Cohorn - issued March 22, 1828, Bondsman:
William Franklin, SUMNER Co.

BIGGS, John to Nancy Barrow - m. by: Ed. Edwards June 14, 1823, SUMNER Co.

BIGGS, John to Adeline Rayl - issued March 11, 1834, Bondsman:
George W. Rayl, m. by: Pleasant Dewitt, M. G., March 13, GRAINGER Co.

BIGGS, Joseph to Patsy Kelly - issued January 29, 1803, Bondsman:
Elijah Biggs, SUMNER Co.

BIGGS, Josiah to Nancy Redfern - issued June 27, 1842, m. by:
W. L. Payne, J. P., ROBERTSON Co.

BIGGS, Leroy W. to Charlotte Gower - issued March 29, 1839, m. by:
Wm. Crockett, J. P., March 31, 1839, DAVIDSON Co.

BIGGS, Mathew to Pauline Shaddock - issued April 3, 1847, Bondsman:
John Step, m. by: T. H. Batson, J. P., April 18, 1847, MONTGOMERY Co.

BIGGS, Mathew to Pauline Shaddock - issued April 3, 1848, Bondsman:
M. P. Hagood, m. by: T. H. Batson, J. P., April 5, 1848,
MONTGOMERY Co.

BIGGS, Nathan to Elizabeth Curtis - issued December 6, 1839, m. by:
P. Priestly, J. P., December 6, 1839, STEWART Co.

BIGGS, Simpson to Sally Cochran - issued September 6, 1831, Bondsman:
Henry Pitt, m. by: Chas. W. __(?) September 6, 1830, SUMNER Co.

BIGGS, William to Rebecca Ann Crafton - issued April 22, 1856, m. by:
W. M. C. Barr, J. P., April 23, 1856, ROBERTSON Co.

BIGHAM, Elihu H. to Mary Sisenby - issued April 18, 1823, Bondsman:
Robert Bigham, RUTHERFORD Co.

BILDERBACH, Jacob to Polly Probst - March 26, 1810, KNOX Co.

BILES, Harbert to Martha Anne Rutledge - issued March 22, 1825, m. by:
Peyton Smith March 22, 1825, RUTHERFORD Co.

BILES, Jonathan to Polly Barnet - issued August 6, 1807, Bondsman:
John Barnet, WILSON Co.

BILL, John to Elisa L. Cook - m. by: Hugh C. Read, M. G., September 22,
1846, ROBERTSON Co.

BILLBRO, William to Elizabeth Johnson - issued September 3, 1827,
Bondsman: J. B. White, WILSON Co.

BILLINGS, James J. S. to Lucinda America Nance - issued November 4,
1845, m. by: R. B. C. Howell, M. G., November 4, 1845, DAVIDSON Co.

BILLINGS, James M. to Sarah Organ - issued September 5, 1835, Bondsman: James R. Ellis, WILSON Co.

BILLINGS, M. H. to Nancy Irby - issued September 15, 1835, Bondsman: A. W. Leatherwood, WILSON Co.

BILLINGSLEY, Cyrus to Elisabeth Plumlee - issued December 20, 1858, m. by: Joseph Cummings, J. P., December 22, 1858, VAN BUREN Co.

BILLINS, John to Rebecca Barns - issued February 2, 1804, Bondsman: Michael Robertson, SUMNER Co.

BINGHAM, Alvan to Jane Baldridge - issued December 25, 1810, Bondsman: John Turner, SUMNER Co.

BINGHAM, Arithuse to J. P. Glover - issued February 16, 1863, Bondsman: J. T. Taylor, Jos. H. Thompson, Clk. per M. E. W. Dunaway, Dep. Clk., BEDFORD Co.

BINGHAM, Francis G. to Elizabeth I. Dean - issued June 4, 1853, Bondsman: Jo P. Thomas, m. by: G. Maddin June 4, 1853, MONTGOMERY Co.

BINGHAM, H. A. to Sally Gossage - issued February 26, 1840, m. by: Wm. T. Wells, M. G., February 26, 1840, FRANKLIN Co.

BINGHAM, Isaac to Elizabeth Stone - issued August 29, 1863, Bondsman: J. B. Goodwin, BEDFORD Co.

BINGHAM, John A. to Margaret Sims - issued July 11, 1831, Bondsman: Benjamin L. Massey, m. by: Amzi Bradshaw, M. G., July 13, 1831, WILSON Co.

BINGHAM, John W. to Mary Elizabeth Osborn - issued November 19, 1857, m. by: E. B. Puckett, L. D. M. E. Ch. So., November 19, 1857, COFFEE Co.

BINGHAM, Robert D. to Isbel Sims - issued November 18, 1840, Bondsman: James G. Simms, m. by: B. Pyland, M. G., November 19, 1840, WILSON Co.

BINGHAM, William to Polley Bingham - issued May 21, 1810, Bondsman: James Fowler, GRAINGER Co.

BINGHAM, William to Mary Hoover - issued October 15, 1829, Bondsman: Christopher Hoover, m. by: William Keele, M. G., October 19, 1829, RUTHERFORD Co.

BINKLEY, A. T. to S. J. Reaves - issued January 5, 1849, m. by: Alex Lowe, Minister, ROBERTSON Co.

BINKLEY, Anthony L. to Mary Benton - issued January 27, 1848, m. by: Thos. Martin, L. E., ROBERTSON Co.

BINKLEY, Asa N. to Milly Durard - issued February 11, 1845, DAVIDSON Co.

BINKLEY, C. A. to M. E. Binkley - issued January 1, 1851, m. by: M. C. Banks, J. P., ROBERTSON Co.

BINKLEY, Charles to Lucinda Darrow - issued March 17, 1842, DAVIDSON Co.

BINKLEY, David to Huldy Durard - issued February 13, 1838, DAVIDSON Co.

BINKLEY, Elisha to Harriet J. McCormack - issued August 6, 1841, m. by: John Forbes, J. P., August 8, 1841, ROBERTSON Co.

BINKLEY, F. M. to Catharine Crocket - issued February 23, 1846, Bondsman: Joseph Carmao, m. by: T. H. Batson, J. P., February 26, 1846, MONTGOMERY Co.

BINKLEY, J. H. to Esther Ann Ferguson - issued January 27, 1847,
     m. by: Allen Knight, J. P., February 4, 1847, DAVIDSON Co.

BINKLEY, Jacob to Sarah Lee - issued April 12, 1839, m. by:
     B. F. Binkley April 28, 1839, DAVIDSON Co.

BINKLEY, John H. to Mary Walker - issued December 23, 1829, Bondsman:
     Henry McCulloch, m. by: John Lane, RUTHERFORD Co.

BINKLEY, John H. to Sarah A. Martin - issued August 17, 1857, m. by:
     C. T. Craig, J. P., ROBERTSON Co.

BINKLEY, Prestor to Eliza Ann Farmer - issued March 12, 1842, DAVIDSON Co.

BINKLEY, Tazwell M. to Matilda Boyd - issued October 6, 1842, DAVIDSON Co.

BINKLEY, William C. to Nancy Ann Pool - issued September 8, 1855,
     m. by: J. T. Craig, J. P., September 9, 1855, ROBERTSON Co.

BIRAM, Moses to Elizabeth Crawford - issued August 10, 1820, Bondsman:
     Joshua Smith, SUMNER Co.

BIRCH, John Jordon to Sally Caldwell - issued September 13, 1811,
     Bondsman: David Caldwell, WILSON Co.

BIRD, Abraham to Amey Adkins - issued December 24, 1805, Bondsman:
     Joel Martin, GRAINGER Co.

BIRD, Amos to Anne Gillespie - issued January 21, 1794, Bondsmen:
     Amos Bird, Junr. and Abraham Bird, Witness: Chas. McClung, KNOX Co.

BIRD, Betsy to Joel Long - January 20, 1808, Security: Nicholas Long
     and Jacob Bird, GREENE Co.

BIRD, David to Elizabeth Broyles - December 15, 1802, Security:
     Ephraim Broyles, GREENE Co.

BIRCH, John Jordon to Sally Caldwell - issued September 13, 1811,
     Bondsman: David Caldwell, WILSON Co.

BIRD, Abraham to Amey Adkins - issued December 24, 1805, Bondsman:
     Joel Martin, GRAINGER Co.

BIRD, Amos to Anne Gillespie - issued January 21, 1794, Bondsmen:
     Amos Bird, Junr. and Abraham Bird, Witness: Chas. McClung, KNOX Co.

BIRD, Betsy to Joel Long - January 20, 1808, Security: Nicholas Long
     and Jacob Bird, GREENE Co.

BIRD, David to Elizabeth Broyles - December 15, 1802, Security:
     Ephraim Broyles, GREENE Co.

BIRD, David to Mary Broyles - February 14, 1804, Security: Ephraim
     Broyles, GREENE Co.

BIRD, Drury Jr. to Sarah Wofford - issued March 11, 1847, m. by:
     Asa D. Scarborough, J. P., March 11, 1847, STEWART Co.

BIRD, George to Lydia A. C. Burns - issued August 18, 1865, Bondsman:
     Robert McClure, m. by: H. B. Wester, M. G., August 20, 1865,
     LAWRENCE Co.

BIRD, Helyard to Catherine Noe - issued February 5, 1835, Bondsman:
     John Easley, m. by: John Craig, M. G., GRAINGER Co.

BIRD, Jacob to Millie Dunn - February 8, 1800, Security: John Bird,
     GREENE Co.

BIRD, James to Catherine Cook - issued May 12, 1838, m. by:
B. Herndon, J. P., May 16, 1838, STEWART Co.

BIRD, John to Mary Baker - March 19, 1801, Security: Lewis Broyles,
GREENE Co.

BIRD, John to Mary Rimel - March 2, 1807, Security: Jacob Bird and
Seth Babb, GREENE Co.

BIRD, John to Tabby Taylor - April 14, 1812, WILLIAMSON Co.

BIRD, John to Rachael Hixon - issued June 7, 1832, Bondsman: John Hixon,
GRAINGER Co.

BIRD, John H. to Elizabeth White - issued October 13, 1865, Bondsman:
W. J. McAnally, m. by: H. B. Wester, M. G., October 15, 1865,
LAWRENCE Co.

BIRD, Joseph to Sally Newberry - April 18, 1808, Security: David Bird
and Jacob Seaton, GREENE Co.

BIRD, Moses to Peggy Potts - January 15, 1816, WILLIAMSON Co.

BIRD, Redman to Mary Daniel - issued January 20, 1834, Bondsman:
Hillard Bird, m. by: James Lacey, M. G., GRAINGER Co.

BIRD, Samuel to Rebecca McCollester - July 1, 1809, Bondsman: Joseph
Sewell, MAURY Co.

BIRD, Sarah to John Seaton - December 28, 1793, Security: John Byrd,
GREENE Co.

BIRD, Thomas to Malvina Goins - April 11, 1835, KNOX Co.

BIRD, Thomas G. to Catherine Couch - issued December 6, 1865, Bondsman:
John M. Robertson, m. by: R. L. McLaren, J. P., December 7, 1865,
LAWRENCE Co.

BIRDIN, William to Eleanor Hutson - issued January 27, 1794, Bondsman:
James Anderson, Witness: Chas. McClung, C. K. C., KNOX Co.

BIRDSONG, John H. to Martha E. Johnson - issued October 16, 1848,
m. by: A. J. Gilmore, M. G., October 16, 1848, FRANKLIN Co.

BIRDWELL, George to Elizabeth Russell - issued July 31, 1815, Bondsman:
Sam'l G. Ramsey, KNOX Co.

BIRDWELL, John W. to Elizabeth M. Harris - issued October 6, 1847,
m. by: F. Fanning October 6, 1847, DAVIDSON Co.

BIRLEY, John to Sarah Seals - issued February 21, 1847, Bondsman:
W. S. Humphries, MONTGOMERY Co.

BISHOP, Drury to Margret Watt - issued March 1, 1821, m. by:
William Bumpass, M. G., March 24, 1821, RUTHERFORD Co.

BISHOP, Edmond to Anna Russell - October 18, 1810, Bondsman:
Benjamin Lewis, MAURY Co.

BISHOP, Harris G. to Isabella Carmichael - issued July 11, 1825,
Bondsman: Andrew M. Brown, m. by: R. Houston, J. P., July 14,
1825, KNOX Co.

BISHOP, J. L. to Sarah E. Cooper - issued December 25, 1863, Bondsman:
W. H. A. Atkins, m. by: Wm. A. Harris, M. G., December 26, 1863,
LAWRENCE Co.

BISHOP, Jacob to Anne Gammon - 1797, KNOX Co.

BISHOP, John to Easter Ann Thompson - issued February 5, 1842, m. by:
John Corbitt, J. P., July 5, 1842, DAVIDSON Co.

BISHOP, John to Jane Morgan - issued August 10, 1846, DICKSON Co.

BISHOP, John to Amanda M. Reynolds - issued October 2, 1873, m. by:
G. W. Bowling, J. P., October 2, 1873, FRANKLIN Co.

BISHOP, John L. to Sarah Farmer - issued June 6, 1855, m. by: D. B. Muse,
J. P., June 6, 1855, FRANKLIN Co.

BISHOP, Joseph to Sally Norris - issued September 16, 1800, Bondsman:
James Norris, SUMNER Co.

BISHOP, Joseph to Elizabeth Childress - issued January 31, 1829,
Bondsman: Solomon Reed, RUTHERFORD Co.

BISHOP, Lewis to Susan Mynatt - issued September 23, 1830, Bondsman:
Moses Lindsay, m. by: Samuel Love, M. G., September 23, 1830,
KNOX Co.

BISHOP, Neal to Annis Davis - issued May 6, 1823, m. by: Henry Trott,
J. P., May 7, 1823, RUTHERFORD Co.

BISHOP, Prestly to Polly Weakly - issued September 26, 1848, Bondsman:
Zachariah Batson, MONTGOMERY Co.

BISHOP, Regen (Rizen?) L. to Rebecca Howell - March 1, 1811, Bondsman:
John Moorhead, MAURY Co.

BISHOP, Sterling to Mary Cochran - issued May 19, 1815, Bondsman:
Abner Howell, RUTHERFORD Co.

BISHOP, Sterling to Mary Tucker - issued July 20, 1816, m. by:
William Edwards, J. P., July 25, 1816, RUTHERFORD Co.

BISHOP, Sterling to Judith Davis - issued July 27, 1823, Bondsman:
John M. Davis, RUTHERFORD Co.

BISHOP, T. L. to M. E. Mills - issued June 27, 1852, Bondsman:
J. C. Shelton, m. by: Wilie Smith, J. P., June 27, 1852, MONTGOMERY
Co.

BISHOP, William to Mary Davis - issued March 2, 1829, Bondsman:
Pleasant Childress, m. by: H. Trott, J. P., RUTHERFORD Co.

BISHOP, William to Sarah Knuckles - issued January 22, 1845, m. by:
Sandridge Arnett, J. P., January 22, 1845, FRANKLIN Co.

BISHOP, Wm. to Elizabeth Payne - issued November 7, 1865, m. by:
D. S. Long, J. P., November 24, 1865, FRANKLIN Co.

BISHOP, Wm. to Sallie Hill - issued September 30, 1867, m. by:
J. P. Wedington, J. P., September 30, 1867, FRANKLIN Co.

BISHOP, Wm. to Ellen Finney - issued March 27, 1868, m. by: John Nugent,
J. P., March 29, 1868, FRANKLIN Co.

BISHOP, William to Sarah E. Crawford - issued October 10, 1871, m. by:
John Donaldson, J. P., October 10, 1871, FRANKLIN Co.

BISHOP, Wm. E. to N. E. Neal (MB) - issued January 12, 1871, m. by:
G. W. Bowling, J. P., January 11, 1871, FRANKLIN Co.

BISHOP, Wm. H. to Mary M. Swearingame - issued December 2, 1874,
m. by: M. Carter, M. G., December 6, 1874, FRANKLIN Co.

BISHOP, William J. to Mary E. Hardin - issued May 18, 1861, Bondsman:
S. A. Carrell, m. by: S. A. Carrell, J. P., May 19, 1861,
LAWRENCE Co.

BITER, John M. to Jennette March - issued March 14, 1840, m. by:
John Eubank, J. P., DICKSON Co.

BITNER, William to Delilah Prather - August 31, 1813, Security:
John Broyles, GREENE Co.

BIVENS, William to Rebecka Raigan - issued July 5, 1827, m. by:
Geo. Atkin, M. G., July 5, 1827, KNOX Co.

BIVINS, David to Elizabeth Hunt - issued February 24, 1834, Bondsman:
Benjamin Lillard, m. by: John L. Jetton, J. P., February 28,
1834, RUTHERFORD Co.

BIVINS, James to Leodocia Brashear - issued June 26, 1826, m. June 29,
1826, RUTHERFORD Co.

BIVINS, James P. to Martha D. Stewart - issued October 14, 1841,
m. by: A. Justin, J. P. for R. C., ROBERTSON Co.

BIVINS, Richard W. to Rebecca Banes - issued July 2, 1833, Bondsman:
Joshua Barton, m. by: Jordan Willeford, J. P., July 3, 1833,
RUTHERFORD Co.

BIZZEL, Isaac to Zilpa Musgrave - February 19, 1817, WILLIAMSON Co.

BLACK, Alexander to Tabitha Dodson - November 18, 1809, WILLIAMSON Co.

BLACK, Gabriel to Jenny McKain - issued March 15, 1796, Bondsman:
Pearce Wall, SUMNER Co.

BLACK, George to Eliza Anderson - issued December 8, 1829, Bondsman:
Jesse Rippy, m. by: Jonathan Davis, J. P., December 8, 1829,
SUMNER Co.

BLACK, J. F. to E. N. Poe - issued December 23, 1867, m. by:
J. B. Hudgins, M. G., December 26, 1867, FRANKLIN Co.

BLACK, James H. to Lucy Ann Lee - issued October 16, 1846, Bondsman:
S. P. Hodges, m. by: T. H. Batson, J. P., November 5, 1846,
MONTGOMERY Co.

BLACK, Jas. L. to Mary A. Eason - issued May 9, 1861, Bondsman:
Wm. H. Black, Jos. H. Thompson, Clk., BEDFORD Co.

BLACK, John to Orpeth Simpson - December 31, 1807, WILLIAMSON Co.

BLACK, John to Cena Blackamore - issued May 5, 1808, Bondsman:
Robert White, SUMNER Co.

BLACK, John F. to Mary Sarton - issued January 14, 1839, m. by:
Thos. Howard, J. P., January 17, 1839, FRANKLIN Co.

BLACK (Blake), Mark to Susan Bruce - October 8, 1807, WILLIAMSON Co.

BLACK, Mary to William Houston - November 26, 1789, Security:
Michael Harrison, GREENE Co.

BLACK, Michael to Isabella Fikes - issued January 7, 1822, Bondsman:
Jacob Graves, m. by: Addison Foster, J. P., January 7, 1822,
SUMNER Co.

BLACK, Michael to Prudence Stewart - issued May 23, 1846, Bondsman:
J. W. Wisdom, m. by: J. Williams, J. P., May 24, 1846, MONTGOMERY Co.

BLACK, Patton M. to Francis L. Denson - issued November 1, 1848,
m. by: W. Denson, J. P., November 2, 1848, FRANKLIN Co.

BLACK, Robert to Rebecca Miller - issued April 5, 1833, Bondsman:
Samuel H. Laughlin, m. by: W. R. Jarratt, M. G., April 9, 1833,
RUTHERFORD Co.

BLACK, Robert D. to Elizabeth Ann Baskins - issued March 2, 1835,
    Bondsman: Robt. M. Baskins, m. by: Joshua Woollen, M. G.,
    WILSON Co.

BLACK, Samuel to Sophia Decherd - issued June 28, 1853, m. by:
    W. J. Fox, V. D. M., June 28, 1853, FRANKLIN Co.

BLACK, Sam'l P. to Fanny Sanders - issued December 23, 1805, Bondsman:
    James Cage, SUMNER Co.

BLACK, Spotswood H. to Anne Acklin - issued October 6, 1829, Bondsman:
    Elijah Staton, RUTHERFORD Co.

BLACK, Thomas C. to Catherine W. Morton - issued May 5, 1835, Bondsman:
    Geo. D. Crosthwait, m. by: Martin Clark, E. M. E. C., May 6,
    1835, RUTHERFORD Co.

BLACK, W. G. to Nancy Billingsly - issued March 11, 1851, Bondsman:
    J. W. Smith, m. by: A. Baggett, J. P., March 11, 1851,
    MONTGOMERY Co.

BLACK, William to Nancy Clay - issued July 24, 1828, Bondsman: Jacob
    Nunaly, m. July 24, 1828, SUMNER Co.

BLACK, William C. to Caroline N. Hall - issued October 26, 1831,
    Bondsman: Stephen C. Chitwood, SUMNER Co.

BLACK, William P. to Susan Hendricks - issued January 7, 1868,
    FRANKLIN Co.

BLACKARD, Joshus to Louisa Dorris - issued March 7, 1840, m. by:
    Jas. Sprouse, J. P., March 8, 1840, ROBERTSON Co.

BLACKARD, Thomas to Elizabeth Lay - issued September 9, 1823, m. by:
    Wm. Montgomery September 9, 1823, SUMNER Co.

BLACKBURN, Alexander to Harriet Campbell - issued December 12, 1833,
    Bondsman: Andrew Scott, m. by: J. H. Gass, M. G., December 12,
    1833, KNOX Co.

BLACKBURN, Andrew to Margaret Samples - November 9, 1791, Security:
    John Blackburn, GREENE Co.

BLACKBURN, Arch. to Martha Jordan - issued May 17, 1854, m. by:
    Jas. Woodard, J. P., ROBERTSON Co.

BLACKBURN, Debulon to Polly Smith - issued January 29, 1833, m. by:
    B. Graves, J. P., WILSON Co.

BLACKBURN, E. P. to W. S. Anderson - issued October 17, 1863,
    Bondsman: C. B. Davis, Jos. H. Thompson, Clk. per M. E. W. Dunaway,
    D. Clk., BEDFORD Co.

BLACKBURN, Elijah to Margaret Rutledge - August 31, 1807, WILLIAMSON Co.

BLACKBURN, Ferninand to Mary Anne Marable - issued January 15, 1827,
    Bondsman: William C. Edwards, RUTHERFORD Co.

BLACKBURN, Henry to Thedocia A. Bandy - m. by: Henry K. Winbourn
    September 19, 1835, SUMNER Co.

BLACKBURN, James to Nancy Reynolds - issued December 2, 1829, Bondsman:
    Sam'l Hinds, m. by: E. Nelson, J. P., December 2, 1829, KNOX Co.

BLACKBURN, James H. to Catherine Swift - issued August 27, 1859, m. by:
    J. F. England, M. G., August 28, 1859, ROBERTSON Co.

BLACKBURN, James M. to Mary E. Maddox - issued July 4, 1851, m. by:
    Robert Draughon, J. P., ROBERTSON Co.

BLACKBURN, John to Jemima Boulter - issued December 18, 1805, Bondsman: Samuel Branson, GRAINGER Co.

BLACKBURN, John to Caty Carver - issued February 23, 1812, Bondsman: William Blackburn, WILSON Co.

BLACKBURN, John A. to Anna Colvin - issued October 12, 1832, Bondsman: Hugh Jones, m. by: Samuel Lovel, M. G., October 12, 1832, GRAINGER Co.

BLACKBURN, John H. to Eliza Tennessee Timmons - issued March 25, 1858, m. by: E. B. Puckett, L. D. or M. E. Church So., March 25, 1858, COFFEE Co.

BLACKBURN, Mary to James Moyer - November 3, 1789, Security: John Blackburn, GREENE Co.

BLACKBURN, Meredith to Amanda M. Binkley - issued August 16, 1839, m. by: A. Justice, J. P., August 17, 1839, ROBERTSON Co.

BLACKBURN, Salathial to Elizabeth Mitchell - issued January 3, 1829, m. by: E. Nelson January 6, 1829, KNOX Co.

BLACKBURN, Thomas to Polly Moulder - issued April 11, 1827, Bondsman: Jacob Capps, m. by: Velantine Molder, J. P., April 11, 1827, GRAINGER Co.

BLACKBURN, Washington to Lavina Sullivan - issued January 29, 1829, Bondsman: Thomas Ames, m. by: Edward Willis, M. G., WILSON Co.

BLACKBURN, William to Lucy Clark - issued August 14, 1821, Bondsman: Lewis Blackburn, m. by: E. Willis, M. G., August 16, 1821, WILSON Co.

BLACKBURN, William to Mary ___ (?) - issued April 6, 1859, m. by: James Taylor, M. G., April 7, 1859, COFFEE Co.

BLACKBURN, William H. to Sarah Fletcher - issued June 16, 1825, Bondsman: Bird Gwil, m. by: B. Graves, J. P., June 19, 1825, WILSON Co.

BLACKBURN, William H. to Carline W. Menees - issued June 7, 1839, m. by: Patrick Martin, M. G., June 10, 1849, ROBERTSON Co.

BLACKBURN, William H. to Elizabeth Menees - issued May 14, 1846, m. by: Thomas Martin, ROBERTSON Co.

BLACKEMORE, Reuben to Betsey Bently - issued March 28, 1821, Bondsman: John Belote, m. March 28, 1821, SUMNER Co.

BLACKFORD, William H. to Demaris Ann Parkell - issued December 17, 1838, Bondsman: Henry Carter, WILSON Co.

BLACKMAN, G. W. to Elizabeth G. Vibbet - issued January 12, 1861, m. by: Wm. T. Byrom, J. P., January 13, 1861, FRANKLIN Co.

BLACKMAN, Learner to Elizabeth Elliott - issued June 22, 1813, Bondsman: James Odom, SUMNER Co.

BLACKMAN, Ollie M. to Johanna F. Mayfield - issued December 15, 1835, Bondsman: E. A. C. Norman, m. by: Martin Clark, E. M. E. C., December 21, 1835, RUTHERFORD Co.

BLACKMORE, A. G. to Harriet Sanders - issued January 31, 1838, m. by: Rich'd Johnson January 31, 1838, SUMNER Co.

BLACKMORE, D. C. to Emily C. Jackson - issued August 31, 1853, m. by: F. C. Plaster, Pastor of Red River Church, ROBERTSON Co.

BLACKMORE, George to Sally Thompson - issued September 10, 1787, Bondsman: Geo. D. Blackmore, SUMNER Co.

BLACKMORE, George D. to Patsey Hannah - issued December 31, 1821, Bondsman: Ashley Stanfield, SUMNER Co.

BLACKMORE, Wm. M. to Rachel J. Barry - issued June 26, 1832, Bondsman: J. Y. Blythe, SUMNER Co.

BLACKSHER, Ezekiel to Izbel Dobson - May 17, 1814, WILLIAMSON Co.

BLACKWELL, A. P. to F. E. Moseley - issued March'13, 1872, FRANKLIN Co.

BLACKWELL, Blueford to Caroline Raymer - issued March 5, 1847, m. by: Allen Knight March 10, 1847, DAVIDSON Co.

BLACKWELL, G. W. to V. C. Marberry - issued April 30, 1867, m. by: Thos. Loney, M. G., April 30, 1867, FRANKLIN Co.

BLACKWELL, Henry to Patsy Brown - issued June 14, 1812, Bondsman: Moses Brown, WILSON Co.

BLACKWELL, Henry to Jane Stewart - issued February 9, 1839, m. by: Jas. H. Cook, J. P., February 11, 1839, DAVIDSON Co.

BLACKWELL, James to Lucy Wallace - m. by: William Adkins, M., March 28, 1843, DICKSON Co.

BLACKWELL, James to Cintha Bleadsoe - issued September 12, 1844, m. by: Benj. Darrow, M. G., September 12, 1844, DICKSON Co.

BLACKWELL, Joel to Sarah E. Graham - issued January 24, 1843, m. by: Wm. S. Smith, M. G., FRANKLIN Co.

BLACKWELL, John M. to S. E. A. Dugger - issued May 28, 1863, Bondsman: Wm. Eakin, m. by: N. Gower, M. G., May 28, 1863, LAWRENCE Co.

BLACKWELL, Josiah to Betsy Hunt - issued February 9, 1843, m. by: Daniel Judd, L. E., February 9, 1843, DAVIDSON Co.

BLACKWELL, Micah to Rebecca Crain - issued November 25, 1845, m. by: James G. Hinson __(?) 21, 1845, DICKSON Co.

BLACKWELL, R. W. to Mary Harris - issued January 17, 1851, Bondsman: Wm. Chadwick, m. by: G. Orgain January 22, 1851, MONTGOMERY Co.

BLACKWELL, Sarah A. to James H. Harrison - Bondsman: Jos. H. Thompson, Clk., m. by: Adam S. Riggs, M. G., BEDFORD Co.

BLACKWELL, Thos. S. to Catharine Dickins - issued November 29, 1838, m. by: E. H. East, J. P., November 29, 1838, DAVIDSON Co.

BLACKWELL, William to Eliza Dines - March 29, 1838, m. by: Isaac Baker, J. P., MEIGS Co.

BLACKWELL, William to Sarah Torian - issued February 4, 1852, Bondsman: William L. Stephens, m. by: John Gold, J. P., February 5, 1852, MONTGOMERY Co.

BLACKWOOD, Agnes to Thomas Simpson - GREENE Co.

BLACKWOOD, Elizabeth to Joseph Casey - GREENE Co.

BLACKWOOD, Hugh to Mary V. Farris - issued December 26, 1850, m. by: Thomas Finch, J. P., December 26, 1850, FRANKLIN Co.

BLACKWOOD, James to Anna Thomas - issued May 11, 1819, m. by: Nace Overall, M. G., May 20, 1819, RUTHERFORD Co.

BLACKWOOD, Johney to Margret F. Blackwood - issued April 29, 1839, m. by: G. Hudspeth, J. P., April 29, 1839, FRANKLIN Co.

BLACKWOOD, Spyway E. to Cathrine Garret - issued April 26, 1832,
Bondsman: Thos. W. McMurtry, m. by: Dan'l Latimer, J. P., April 26,
1832, SUMNER Co.

BLACKWOOD, William to Elizabeth Casey - January 26, 1793, Security:
John W. Bowers, GREENE Co.

BLACKWOOD, William to Elizabeth Banks - issued December 26, 1849,
m. by: A. B. Cunningham, M. G., December 27, 1849, FRANKLIN Co.

BLACKWOOD, Wm. J. to Mary Ann Knight - issued January 17, 1852, FRANKLIN
Co.

BLAIN, A. M. to Martha Dinning - issued July 23, 1840, m. by:
Ed Edwards, ROBERTSON Co.

BLAIN, Robert to Aelcey Willson - issued March 8, 1805, Bondsman:
James Willson, GRAINGER Co.

BLAINE, Alexander to Mary Childress - issued August 27, 1836, Bondsman:
Chas. P. Chapman, m. by: G. S. White, M. G., August 27, 1836,
KNOX Co.

BLAIR, Alexander F. to Emily J. Tally - issued March 1, 1836, m. by:
B. T. Mattley, J. P., March 2, 1836, WILSON Co.

BLAIR, Alexander M. to Matilda W. Henderson - issued September 14,
1829, Bondsman: Levi Reeves, m. by: J. W. Hall September 17,
1829, RUTHERFORD Co.

BLAIR, Benjamin T. to Jane G. Nevins - issued March 12, 1827, Bondsman:
William Nevins, RUTHERFORD Co.

BLAIR, C. F. to Mattie J. Duncan - issued December 19, 1866, m. by:
J. P. Payne, J. P., December 20, 1866, FRANKLIN Co.

BLAIR, Henry to Rachel McDougle - issued January 21, 1853, m. by:
G. W. Leigh, J. P., January 28, 1852, MONTGOMERY Co.

BLAIR, Ira L. to Mary A. Sadler - issued July 28, 1832, m. by:
B. B. Dickins, J. P., July 29, 1832, RUTHERFORD Co.

BLAIR, J. H. to Sarah Ann Elliott - Bondsman: W. M. Finley, m. by:
J. G. Ward, M. G., March 14, 1852, MONTGOMERY Co.

BLAIR, J. L. W. to Fanny W. Rowe - issued March 1, 1865, m. by:
W. G. Guin March 2, 1865, FRANKLIN Co.

BLAIR, James Junr. to Mary Kelso - issued May 25, 1814, Bondsman:
James Blair, Senr., GRAINGER Co.

BLAIR, James to Marilla May - m. by: James F. Ross, J. P., December,
1825, RUTHERFORD Co.

BLAIR, James to Anne S. McWhirter - issued October 11, 1830, Bondsman:
James W. Moses, m. by: Ambrose F. Mizkell, M. G., WILSON Co.

BLAIR, John to Mary E. Utley - issued September 11, 1845, m. by:
A. G. Goodlett, M., September 28, 1845, DAVIDSON Co.

BLAIR, John K. to Susan Smith - issued June 23, 1846, DAVIDSON Co.

BLAIR, Joseph to Celey Whittle - issued September 4, 1816, m. by:
Sam'l Sample, J. P. K. C., September 10, 1816, KNOX Co.

BLAIR, Joseph to Aly Hunter - issued November 30, 1825, Bondsman:
Henry Wyrick, m. by: Noah Jarnagin, J. P., November 30, 1825,
GRAINGER Co.

BLAIR, R. C. to Lydia A. Rawls - issued October 13, 1856, m. by:
    Benj. Rawls, M. G., October 14, 1858, ROBERTSON Co.

BLAIR, Robt. W. to Amanda Mynatt - issued July 14, 1834, m. by:
    Wm. Hickle, M. G., July 17, 1834, KNOX Co.

BLAIR, Samuel to Joanna Perrin - issued April 10, 1799, Bondsman:
    George Combs, Witness: Sml. Yancey, GRAINGER Co.

BLAIR, Samuel to Elizabeth King - November 11, 1799, Security:
    John King, GREENE Co.

BLAIR, William to Betsey McDowell - December 2, 1799, BLOUNT Co.

BLAIR, William to Sally Staggs - issued December 13, 1814, Bondsman:
    Hugh Blair, RUTHERFORD Co.

BLAIR, William to Lamiza Felts - issued December 22, 1842, DAVIDSON Co.

BLAIR, Wm. G. to Ann E. Allen - issued December 17, 1845, m. by:
    P. Ball, M. G., December 18, 1845, DAVIDSON Co.

BLAIR, Wm. L. J. to Margaret Williams - issued February 23, 1825,
    Bondsman: Jas. P. Thompson, m. by: Peyton Smith February 24,
    1825, RUTHERFORD Co.

BLAKARD, Job to Biddy Trusty - issued December 31, 1821, Bondsman:
    Andrew Clarey, m. December 31, 1821, SUMNER Co.

BLAKE, Adam B. to Jane I. Kennedy - issued February 19, 1824, Bondsman:
    John Craighead, KNOX Co.

BLAKE, Elizabeth to John Chestnut - April 19, 1794, Security:
    James Campbell, GREENE Co.

BLAKE, Henry to Joannah Ward - issued June 20, 1840, Bondsman:
    N. F. Drake, m. by: A. B. Richmond, J. P., July 2, 1840, WILSON Co.

BLAKE, Henry J. to Sarah C. Gasten - issued March 7, 1865, Bondsman:
    Newton Kelsey, m. by: L. M. Sanford, J. P., March 9, 1865,
    LAWRENCE Co.

BLAKE, Hugh to Elizabeth Allison - August 5, 1793, Security:
    James Russell, GREENE Co.

BLAKE, Joab to Debitha Lowe - issued December 4, 1824, Bondsman:
    Jno. Long, m. by: John Kidwell, M. G., December 4, 1824, GRAINGER Co.

BLAKE, John R. to Susan F. Hancock - issued October 22, 1851, Bondsman:
    R. F. Bridewater, m. by: James Allmon October 23, 1851,
    MONTGOMERY Co.

BLAKE, John W. to Margaret B. Kidwell - issued November 19, 1818,
    Bondsman: John Ramsey, m. by: John Kidwell, M. G., November 26,
    1818, GRAINGER Co.

BLAKE, Margaret to Jacob Chestnut - GREENE Co.

BLAKE, Thomas E. to Amanda Bridgewater - issued December 1, 1828,
    Bondsman: Wm. Turner, SUMNER Co.

BLAKE, Willby to Mary Midkiff - issued March 19, 1811, Bondsman:
    Isaiah Midkiff, GRAINGER Co.

BLAKELEY, Alexander to Sarah Lackey - issued November 18, 1799,
    Bondsman: William Dodd, Witness: A. W. White, KNOX Co.

BLAKELY, Ann to Thomas J. Frierson - November 6, 1810, Bondsman:
    Moses G. Frierson, MAURY Co.

BLAKELEY, John W. to Cathrine H. Pruet - issued April 17, 1872, FRANKLIN Co.

BLAKELY, Charles to Polly Ruth - issued November 27, 1815, KNOX Co.

BLAKELY, John to Levina Brown - issued June 6, 1817, Bondsman: Joshua Brown, KNOX Co.

BLAKELY, John S. to Jane Kenedy - issued July 11, 1846, STEWART Co.

BLAKELY, William to Nancy Dobson - November 5, 1806, WILLIAMSON Co.

BLAKELY, William to Elizabeth Sanders - issued August 1, 1818, Bondsman: Thomas Sanders, RUTHERFORD Co.

BLAKEMORE, Albert G. to Edna B. Sanders - issued July 10, 1831, Bondsman: J. J. Finley, WILSON Co.

BLAKEMORE, Edward to Sophia J. Murry - issued October 21, 1826, Bondsman: James Hail, SUMNER Co.

BLAKEMORE, Fieldon N. to Rebecka Johnston - issued February 2, 1820, Bondsman: Stephen R. Roberts, SUMNER Co.

BLAKEMORE, James B. to Margaret W. Fussell - issued September 25, 1828, m. by: Henry Ridley, J. P., September 25, 1828, RUTHERFORD Co.

BLAKEMORE, Jefferson to Lena Willis - issued December 3, 1824, Bondsman: Joseph Rice, SUMNER Co.

BLAKEMORE, John to Victory Rankin - issued November 7, 1811, Bondsman: Wm. Hall, SUMNER Co.

BLAKEMORE, John to Dolly L. Butterworth - issued November 12, 1826, Bondsman: Granville L. Pearce, m. by: Isaac Lindsey, E. M. C., November 12, 1826, SUMNER Co.

BLAKEMORE, John to Nancy Allen - issued July 12, 1860, m. by: John H. Holt, M. G., July 12, 1860, FRANKLIN Co.

BLAKEMORE, Lee C. to Charlotte Johnson - issued March 18, 1823, Bondsman: Lucilius Winchester, m. by: Rich'd Johnson March 18, 1823, SUMNER Co.

BLAKEMORE, T. F. to Susan P. Bailey - issued December 18, 1849, Bondsman: F. G. Irwin, m. by: A. B. Russell, M. G., December 19, 1848, MONTGOMERY Co.

BLAKEMORE, William to Jane Davis - issued January 30, 1822, m. by: Carey James, D. M. E. C., January 31, 1822, RUTHERFORD Co.

BLAKSEY, Robert J. to Zilpha Donaldson - issued June 13, 1850, Bondsman: Benj. D. Lee, m. by: J. Mallory, M. G., June 12, 1850, MONTGOMERY Co.

BLALOCK, Charles to Patsey Tucker - issued January 5, 1826, Bondsman: James Mays, m. by: John W. Payton, J. P., WILSON Co.

BLALOCK, Giles to Martha Beverly - issued August 3, 1837, m. by: J. D. Gilman, J. P., August 8, 1837, RUTHERFORD Co.

BLALOCK, Henry to Sarah Houk - issued April 11, 1825, Bondsman: Jno. Rogers, m. by: Geo. Atkin, M. G., April 11, 1825, KNOX Co.

BLALOCK, Jesse to Nancy Averitt - issued December 27, 1833, Bondsman: Asa Coulter, RUTHERFORD Co.

BLALOCK, Julius to Truce Bell - issued December 22, 1825, Bondsman: George W. Horn, m. by: Thos. S. Green, J. P., WILSON Co.

BLALOCK, Vachel to Patsey Chapple - issued January 19, 1806, Bondsman: Aley Elkins, WILSON Co.

BLALOCK, Zachariah to Frances Vanover - m. by: Freeman Senter, M. G., December 28, 1835, SUMNER Co.

BLAND, Charles to Nancy Cates - issued July 25, m. by: Joseph Gowen, J. P., August 4, 1825, RUTHERFORD Co.

BLAND, Isaac to Parlie Saunders - m. by: Robt. Patton February 16, 1837, SUMNER Co.

BLAND, William D. to Viney Beadles - issued December 26, 1839, Bondsman: John W. Bland, m. by: Saml. H. Porterfield, J. P., WILSON Co.

BLANE, Jacob to Nancy Loyd - issued September 8, 1840, m. by: Thos. Fuqua, M. G., September 11, 1840, DAVIDSON Co.

BLANG, George to Margaret Bell - November 4, 1818, KNOX Co.

BLANG, P. L. to Sarah Ann Bell - issued January 8, 1836, Bondsman: Adam Formwalt, m. by: J. Nutty, M. G., January 8, 1836, KNOX Co.

BLANK, William to Fanny Hill - December 30, 1806, WILLIAMSON Co.

BLANKENSHIP, Allen to Eliza J. Spinks - issued July 4, 1828, Bondsman: William Mitchell, WILSON Co.

BLANKENSHIP, Benjamin to Mary G. Butts - issued December 19, 1827, Bondsman: John Blankenship, RUTHERFORD Co.

BLANKENSHIP, Branch to Prudence Cogwell - issued July 16, 1840, Bondsman: Daniel Blankenship, WILSON Co.

BLANKENSHIP, John to Margaret McDaniel - issued October 30, 1835, Bondsman: H. G. Hosea Ward, m. by: Williamson Williams, WILSON Co.

BLANKENSHIP, John C. to Eliz. Murphy - issued November 30, 1841, m. by: Benjamin Rawls, G. M., ROBERTSON Co.

BLANKENSHIP, John C. to Mary Catharine Sensency - issued September 11, 1845, Bondsman: Jas. M. Love, m. by: Thomas B. Ripley, M. G., September 11, 1845, MONTGOMERY Co.

BLANKENSHIP, John M. to Lucy Via - issued August 12, 1836, Bondsman: Robert W. Searcy, m. by: G. B. Lannom August 14, 1836, RUTHERFORD Co.

BLANKENSHIP, L. F. to Virginia Ross - issued November 9, 1852, Bondsman: Addison Rust, MONTGOMERY Co.

BLANKENSHIP, Matthew to Naomi Owen - issued October 1, 1825, m. by: H. Trott, J. P., October 13, 1825, RUTHERFORD Co.

BLANKENSHIP, Reuben to Jane Couch - December 20, 1815, KNOX Co.

BLANKENSHIP, Sylvester to Hannah Witherspoon - issued October 13, 1830, Bondsman: David Witherspoon, RUTHERFORD Co.

BLANKENSHIP, Thomas to Mary McKelvey - issued October 10, 1824, Bondsman: Gilbert B. Clark, RUTHERFORD Co.

BLANKINSHIP, Elijah to Polly Anderson - issued February 15, 1841, m. by: Thos. S. Elliott, J. P., February 16, 1841, STEWART Co.

BLANKS, Wm. D. to Narcissa W. Horn - issued September 23, 1849, Bondsman: Jno. R. Finch, m. by: N. F. Trice, J. P., September 23, 1849, MONTGOMERY Co.

BLANSET, William to Patsy Lane - issued October 2, 1822, Bondsman: Hugh Jones, m. by: Thomas Brown, J. P., October 2, 1822, GRAINGER Co.

BLANTON, Charles L. to Jane S. Vanzant - issued November 25, 1842, m. by: W. G. Guinn, M. G., FRANKLIN Co.

BLANTON, Charles L. to Lucy J. Moseley - issued May 20, 1850, FRANKLIN Co.

BLANTON, Henson G. to Cornelius E. Vanzant - issued September 16, 1844, m. by: C. A. Hunt, J. P., September 17, 1844, FRANKLIN Co.

BLANTON, James J. to Clarinda Black - issued March 10, 1852, Bondsman: Joseph T. Steward, MONTGOMERY Co.

BLANTON, John S. to Lucy C. Wakefield - issued June 19, 1852, m. by: Rev. J. W. Spearman June 24, 1852, FRANKLIN Co.

BLANTON, John W. to Lucy B. Buck - issued December 4, 1851, Bondsman: W. F. Fall, m. by: J. T. Hendrick December 4, 1851, MONTGOMERY Co.

BLANTON, S. A. J. to J. S. Carney - issued June 11, 1862, Bondsman: James Green, Jos. H. Thompson, Clk. per James H. Neil, Dep. Clk., BEDFORD Co.

BLANTON, Sophia T. to James Albert Knott - issued September 8, 1863, Bondsman: Jos. H. Thompson, Clk. per James H. Neil, Dep. Clk., BEDFORD Co.

BLANTON, Thomas to Mahalia Homes - issued March 2, 1839, Bondsman: Charles Prater, m. by: Wm. Green, M. G., March 7, 1839, MEIGS Co.

BLASANGAM, William to Ann Collins - issued April 10, 1811, Bondsman: Wm. Hannah, SUMNER Co.

BLAZE, George to Elizabeth Loyd - issued January 17, 1822, Bondsman: Lamuel Loyd, m. by: Abner Hill, M. G., WILSON Co.

BLEDSOE, Miss to Rev. Joshua Bell - GIBSON Co.

BLEDSOE, A. S. to M. J. Anderson - issued June 6, 1867, m. by: J. M. Cowan, V. D. M., June 6, 1867, FRANKLIN Co.

BLEDSOE, Abraham to Melly Weathered - issued May 4, 1805, Bondsman: Jas. Rawlings, SUMNER Co.

BLEDSOE, David to Elizabeth Charlton - m. by: John Wiseman, M. G., June 19, 1828, SUMNER Co.

BLEDSOE, David L. to Elizabeth Moore - issued November 26, 1829, Bondsman: Solomon Shoulders, m. by: Wm. Walton, J. P., November 26, 1829, SUMNER Co.

BLEDSOE, Miss Dulciena M. to M. V. Harrison, Esq. - MONTGOMERY Co.

BLEDSOE, Miss Elizabeth to Dr. John L. Hadly, Jun. - SUMNER Co.

BLEDSOE, Miss Elizabeth T. to George W. Fry, Esq. - CARROLL Co.

BLEDSOE, Geo. W. to Martha Ann Lauderdale - issued August 29, 1834, m. by: J. W. Hall August 29, 1834, SUMNER Co.

BLEDSOE, Henry to Nancy Gillespie - issued May 22, 1805, Bondsman: Thos. Gillespie, SUMNER Co.

BLEDSOE, Mr. Horace G. to Miss Elizabeth H. Thomas - National Banner and Nashville Whig, June 1, 1831, MAURY Co.

BLEDSOE, Isaac to Sally W. Hanner - issued November 23, 1836, Bondsman: M. B. Turner, m. by: John Wiseman November 23, 1836, SUMNER Co.

BLEDSOE, Isaac N. to Nancy Lee - m. by: John Parker, M. G., August 3, 1835, SUMNER Co.

BLEDSOE, Isaac W. to Nancy Lockette - issued April 23, 1804, Bondsman:
James Blackmore, SUMNER Co.

BLEDSOE, James to Harriet Higgins - issued December 24, 1836, Bondsman:
Allin Carter, m. by: John Wiseman December 24, 1836, SUMNER Co.

BLEDSOE, James to Rebecca Call - issued September 12, 1851, m. by:
John Roleman, J. P., September 12, 1851, FRANKLIN Co.

BLEDSOE, James to Lizzie Hannah - issued March 16, 1865, m. by:
W. W. Estill, M. G., March 16, 1865, FRANKLIN Co.

BLEDSOE, Mr. Jesse to Miss Martha C. Williams - Nashville Republican
and State Gazette, January 28, 1834, DAVIDSON Co.

BLEDSOE, Miss Louisa to Mr. David Bailey - National Banner and Nashville
Whig, June 2, 1827, MADISON Co.

BLEDSOE, Oscar F. to Martha A. Wynne - issued January 28, 1835,
Bondsman: J. Y. Blythe, WILSON Co.

BLEDSOE, Philadelphia to Polly Howell - issued October 9, 1807, KNOX Co.

BLEDSOE, Philadelphia to Mildred Kendrick - issued February 24, 1818,
m. by: Thomas Hudiburgh February 24, 1818, KNOX Co.

BLEDSOE, Ptolemy to Margaret Allin - issued February 4, 1813, m. by:
James McAdow, J. P., WILSON Co.

BLEDSOE, Miss Sarah G. to H. I. Bodley, Esq. - married in Lexington, Ky.

BLEDSOE, Thomas J. to Mahala White - m. by: James Wallace September 28,
1833, SUMNER Co.

BLEDSOE, William J. to Miss Juliana Goode - National Banner and
Nashville Whig, February 25, 1837, m. by: Rev. Barnes.

BLEDSOE, Wm. J. to Amentha Allen - issued December 21, 1849, m. by:
Madison Williams, J. P., December 22, 1849, FRANKLIN Co.

BLEDSOE, William L. to Mary Sanford - issued October 12, 1812, Bondsman:
Jacob C. Cook, SUMNER Co.

BLESSING, Jacob to Lucretia Gallathan - issued March 9, 1817, Bondsman:
Nicholas Null, m. March 10, 1817, RUTHERFORD Co.

BLEVENS, Philip to Harriet Blakely - issued January 10, 1839, Bondsman:
B. F. Locke, m. by: D. F. Godsey, M. G., January 10, 1839, MEIGS Co.

BLEVENS, Richard to Mary Duyless - issued May 6, 1802, Bondsman:
William Barton, GRAINGER Co.

BLEVINS, Moses to Elizabeth Thomas - issued August 27, 1839, Bondsman:
R. J. Powers, m. by: D. L. Godsey, Minst., August 29, 1839,
MEIGS Co.

BLEVINS, Richard to Elizabeth Arenton - November 5, 1800, BLOUNT Co.

BLEVINS, Thos. to Levina P. Gorley - issued June 13, 1839, m. by:
Daniel Cate, J. P., July 1, 1839, MEIGS Co.

BLEWETT, Thomas G. to Laura Martin - December 5, 1850, m. by:
G. D. Taylor, GILES Co.

BLEWITT, George L. to Nancy L. Harris - issued September 23, 1841,
m. by: R. D. Harris, G. M., ROBERTSON Co.

BLICK, W. P. to Ann Camelay - issued January 4, 1842, m. by:
Jas Woodard, J. P., ROBERTSON Co.

BLIGE, Jonathan to Nancey Shelton - issued December 29, 1797, Bondsman: Wm. Kirkham, GRAINGER Co.

BLOODSWORTH, David to P. Harris - issued July 18, 1835, Bondsman: Delon Devaden, RUTHERFORD Co.

BLOODSWORTH, Jesse to Narcissa __(?) - issued December 11, 1809, Bondsman: William Bloodsworth, WILSON Co.

BLOODSWORTH, Jesse to Jane Tucker - issued June 28, 1826, Bondsman: Wm. Bloodworth, WILSON Co.

BLOODWORTH, Alfred to Lucinda Bloodworth - issued March 26, 1832, Bondsman: C. Vinsor, WILSON Co.

BLOODWORTH, Chapman to M. L. Forrester - m. by: B. S. Rutherford October 30, 1838, SUMNER Co.

BLOODWORTH, David to Matilda Tucker - issued December 28, 1833, m. by: Silas Tarver, J. P., December 29, 1833, WILSON Co.

BLOODWORTH, Edwin to Delila Griffin - April 8, 1811, WILLIAMSON Co.

BLOODWORTH, Henry to Dolly Griffin - issued May 28, 1806, Bondsman: Miles Anderson, SUMNER Co.

BLOODWORTH, Jesse to Celia Tucker - issued February 14, 1824, Bondsman: Benjamin Tucker, m. by: John W. Payton, J. P., February 17, 1824, WILSON Co.

BLOODWORTH, John to Mary Bloodworth - m. by: A. B. Duval December 23, 1835, SUMNER Co.

BLOODWORTH, Lemueal to Polly Camhorn - issued February 5, 1824, Bondsman: William Bloodworth, SUMNER Co.

BLOODWORTH, Thomas to Aly White - issued October 13, 1808, Bondsman: Serrel White, m. by: S. Hunt, J. P., October 13, 1808, SUMNER Co.

BLOODWORTH, Web to Mary Benthall - issued December 18, 1804, Bondsman: David Allen, SUMNER Co.

BLOODWORTH, William to Malvina Straton - m. by: P. Bradford December 9, 1838, SUMNER Co.

BLOODWORTH, Wilson to Alsy Eagan - issued February 14, 1836, m. by: Elisha Vaughn, M. G., February 16, 1836, WILSON Co.

BLOUNT, Jackson to Sarah Brewington - issued May 16, 1863, Bondsman: James Sheperson and W. H. McLane, Jos. H. Thompson, Clerk, BEDFORD Co.

BLOUNT, Willie Augustus to Delia Blakemore - issued December 22, 1823, m. by: Peyton Smith December 24, 1823, RUTHERFORD Co.

BLURTON, Brient to Nancy Ross - issued October 31, 1812, Bondsman: Hinton Blurton, WILSON Co.

BLURTON, Henry to Wealthy Williams - issued January 24, 1834, Bondsman: Paton Neel, WILSON Co.

BLURTON, Hinton to Susanah Howell - issued February 28, 1816, Bondsman: John Willis, m. by: James Foster, J. P., WILSON Co.

BLURTON, John to Sally McMinnaway - issued March 29, 1811, Bondsman: Ebenezar Donelson, WILSON Co.

BLYTHE, Alexander to Eliza Kiely - issued November 2, 1830, Bondsman: John S. Kennedy, WILSON Co.

BLYTHE, Richard to Mary Anderson - issued November 4, 1812, Bondsman:
S. K. Blythe, SUMNER Co.

BLYTHE, Samuel to Dotia Trigg - issued October 25, 1809, Bondsman:
P. W. Trigg, SUMNER Co.

BLYTHE, Thomas to M. E. Davis - issued August 18, 1863, Bondsman:
J. P. Tayes, m. by: R. L. McLaren, J. P., August 20, 1863,
LAWRENCE Co.

BOAKFIELD, Hiram to Martha Harris - issued March 5, 1855, m. by:
W. S. Baldry, M. G., March 6, 1855, ROBERTSON Co.

BOAS, William to Harriat Simpson - issued April 20, 1822, Bondsman:
Presley Simpson, m. by: William Flowers, Sr., May 4, 1822,
WILSON Co.

BOATMAN, Elijah to Elizabeth Flora - issued January 5, 1831, Bondsman:
Edward Wilson, GRAINGER Co.

BOATMAN, Ezechael to Mary Boatman - issued January 23, 1834, Bondsman:
John Cox, m. by: Elihu Millikan, M. G., GRAINGER Co.

BOATMAN, George to Sarah Cox - issued November 20, 1833, Bondsman:
John Evans, m. by: Elihu Milliken, M. G., GRAINGER Co.

BOATMAN, Henry to Edy Cox - issued May 20, 1833, Bondsman: James Riggs,
m. by: Elihu Millikan, M. G., GRAINGER Co.

BOATMAN, Richard to Sidney Darnold - issued November 24, 1827, Bondsman:
William Boatman, m. by: E. Millikan, M. G., November 24, 1827,
GRAINGER Co.

BOATMAN, William to Elizabeth Howell - issued February 19, 1807,
Bondsman: Benjamin Howell, GRAINGER Co.

BOATMAN, Wm. to A. M. Harris - issued September 26, 1865, m. by:
Wm. W. Conn, M. G., October 3, 1865, FRANKLIN Co.

BOATRIGHT, Chasley H. to Louisa Taylor - issued March 21, 1818, Bondsman:
John Harris, m. by: Caleb Witt, M. G., March 29, 1818, GRAINGER Co.

BOATRIGHT, James to Elizabeth Taylor - issued June 14, 1834, Bondsman:
Hugh McElhaney, GRAINGER Co.

BOATRIGHT, John to Sarah Morgan - issued January 16, 1832, Bondsman:
Ahab Bowen, m. by: Jas. Kennon, M. G., GRAINGER Co.

BOATRIGHT, Samuel to Jain Ruth - issued November 7, 1808, Bondsman:
James Boatright, Witness: Sterling Cocke, J. P., GRAINGER Co.

BOATRIGHT, William to Jemima Bowen - issued July 22, 1808, Bondsman:
John Moore, m. by: Sm'l. Yancey, J. P., July 22, 1808, GRAINGER Co.

BOATRIGHT, William to Nancy Morgan - issued April 28, 1821, Bondsman:
Edward Tate, m. by: J. C. Bunch, J. P., April 29, 1821, GRAINGER Co.

BOAZ, Daniel A. to Cynthia Rice - issued April 3, 1838, Bondsman:
William R. Dodson, WILSON Co.

BOAZ, Daniel A. to Cynthia Rice   - 4-3-1838
                  Nancy A. Rice   - 4-19-1843
                  Rebecca P. Rice - 5-19-1852

BOAZ, Edmond to Betsey Proctor - issued November 27, 1813, Bondsman:
Samuel K. Blythe, SUMNER Co.

BOAZ, Edmund to Nancy Nowlin - issued March 28, 1810, Bondsman:
John Reeves, SUMNER Co.

BOAZ, Obadiah to Eliza Prudence King - issued November 18, 1823,
    m. by: Isaac Anderson, M. G., November 25, 1823, KNOX Co.

BOBBELL, John to Lucy Jones - issued October 3, 1846, m. by: Joseph Pitt,
    ROBERTSON Co.

BOBBETT, James to Julia A. Whetter - issued December 3, 1849, m. by:
    B. W. Bradley, J. P., 1850, ROBERTSON Co.

BOBBS, Wm. to Frances Wyett - issued February 22, 1838, STEWART Co.

BOBO, Elisha to Mary A. Horton - issued November 21, 1842, m. by:
    A. R. David, J. P., November 29, 1842, FRANKLIN Co.

BOBO, James S. to Mary I. Philpot - issued January 12, 1863, Bondsman:
    John E. Bobo, Jos. H. Thompson, Clk., BEDFORD Co.

BOBO, John E. to Phoebe A. Jackson - issued November 27, 1855, m. by:
    L. Brandon December 27, 1855, FRANKLIN Co.

BODE, Andrew to Maria C. Gold Kamp - issued February 1, 1845, m. by:
    J. Schacht, Priest, February 4, 1845, DAVIDSON Co.

BODENHAMER, John L. to Harriett A. Howard - January 23, 1860, Security:
    James R. Horner, GILES Co.

BODINE, Jefferson to Peggy Furgason - issued December 22, 1823, Bondsman:
    Thomas L. Bonner, m. by: John Bonner, J. P., December 26, 1823,
    WILSON Co.

BODINE, Westin to Rebecca Moseley - issued February 4, 1840, Bondsman:
    S. B. Murray, m. by: Isaac Hunter, J. P., February 6, 1840,
    WILSON Co.

BODINE, Wiley to Nancy Rutchledge - issued August 20, 1820, Bondsman:
    John Stuart, WILSON Co.

BODINE, Wiley to Nancy Rutledge - issued August 20, 1825, m. by:
    John Bonner, p. P., WILSON Co.

BODKINS, John to Lucinda Riddell - issued September 3, 1863, Bondsman:
    W. F. Blanton, m. by: W. T. Jackson, J. P., September 6, 1863,
    LAWRENCE Co.

BODY, Elijah to Mariah Elliott - issued December 25, 1816, Bondsman:
    Ashley Stanfield, m. by: Hardy M. Cryer December 25, 1816, SUMNER Co.

BOEMAN, George to Mary Ann Stewart - issued February 15, 1846, m. by:
    Benj. Sells, J. P., February 5, 1846, FRANKLIN Co.

BOGARD, E. T. to Elmera Travis - issued June 15, 1848, m. by:
    S. S. Mallory, M. G., June 19, 1848, STEWART Co.

BOGARD, George to Zesphy Bogard - issued August 18, 1846, m. by:
    B. F. Fraser, J. P., August 18, 1847, STEWART Co.

BOGARD, Stephen to Nancy Jackson - STEWART Co.

BOGEL, Joseph H. to Mary Summers - issued September 14, 1829, m. by:
    H. W. Pickett, V. D. M., September 17, 1829, WILSON Co.

BOGGES, Henry to Harriet C. Goddard - issued April 29, 1833, m. by:
    J. Johnson, J. P., April 29, 1833, KNOX Co.

BOGGS, John D. to Elizabeth Darnell - issued January 8, 1855, m. by:
    John Hendley, J. P., January 8, 1855, FRANKLIN Co.

BOGGS, S. J. to Mahala A. Boren - issued October 30, 1867, m. by:
    W. W. Hawkins, M. G., October 30, 1867, FRANKLIN Co.

BOGLE, Andrew to Sally Gibson - issued September 18, 1832, Bondsman: Adam Tittle, WILSON Co.

BOGLE, Hugh to Hannah Caldwell - April 2, 1801, Security: Andrew Bogle, Sr., BLOUNT Co.

BOGLE, Hugh to Rachel Bogle - issued December 23, 1822, Bondsman: James Bogle, SUMNER Co.

BOGLE, James to Jane Milligan - issued December 18, 1832, Bondsman: William Milligan, m. by: John McMinn, J. P., December 20, 1832, WILSON Co.

BOGLE, Jas. B. to Emma E. Mann - issued December 22, 1874, m. by: G. E. Gillaspie, M. G., December 22, 1874, FRANKLIN Co.

BOGLE, John to John Bryson - issued September 11, 1835, Bondsman: John Bryson, WILSON Co.

BOGLE, Joseph to Margaret Houston - January 20, 1786, Security: William Houston, GREENE Co.

BOGLE, Joseph to Sarah Harris - issued February 10, 1832, Bondsman: William Matthews, WILSON Co.

BOGLE, Joseph H. to Rachel Turney - issued November 23, 1835, m. by: John Sneed, J. P., November 24, 1835, WILSON Co.

BOGLE, Robert to Sally Brison - issued June 2, 1808, Bondsman: Thomas Leech, WILSON Co.

BOGLE, Robert R. to Elizabeth H. Jennings - issued October 8, 1839, Bondsman: James Turner, m. by: James Turner, J. P., October 9, 1839, WILSON Co.

BOGLE, Samuel to Nelly Williams - September 14, 1797, Security: James Upton, BLOUNT Co.

BOGLE, Thomas to Rachel Brison - issued February 26, 1811, Bondsman: Joseph Brison, WILSON Co.

BOGLE, William R. to Julia Jones - issued May 26, 1832, Bondsman: Elihu Witherspoon, WILSON Co.

BOHANAN, Wm. E. to Nancy Ann Smith - issued February 25, 1867, m. by: J. B. Foster, J. P., March 4, 1867, FRANKLIN Co.

BOHANN, Hosea to Elizabeth Hill - issued February 21, 1866, FRANKLIN Co.

BOHANNAN, Charles H. to Amanda J. Wallace - issued August 28, 1874, m. by: James Seargent, J. P., August 29, 1874, FRANKLIN Co.

BOICE, John K. to Martha A. Bowen - issued November 24, 1845, DICKSON Co.

BOILES, Charles to Polly Old - May 17, 1808, WILLIAMSON Co.

BOLEN, C. L. to N. J. Patterson - issued August 26, 1868, m. by: A. J. Simpson, J. P., August 26, 1868, FRANKLIN Co.

BOLEN, Nathan to Nancy Lister - issued March 12, 1827, Bondsman: Robt. T. Lyles, Witness: Wm. Swan, KNOX Co.

BOLES, Robert to Patsey Barker - issued December 4, 1817, Bondsman: Amos Reynolds, RUTHERFORD Co.

BOLES, S. H. to Mary R. Parham - issued July 12, 1848, Bondsman: R. L. Smith, m. by: I. T. Hendricks, M. G., July 13, 1848, MONTGOMERY Co.

BOLIN, H. C. to Viney Smith - issued February 12, 1866, FRANKLIN Co.

BOLIN, James to Sarah Jane Lovin - issued August 15, 1862, Bondsman:
Adam Comer, Jos. H. Thompson, Clk. per N. F. Thompson, Dep. Clk.,
BEDFORD Co.

BOLIN, Joseph to Mary Smith - issued January 11, 1858, m. by:
L. N. Simpson, J. P., January 16, 1868, FRANKLIN Co.

BOLIN, Melton to Sarah A. Knight - issued May 1, 1865, FRANKLIN Co.

BOLIN, Wm. H. to Cathrine Shelton - issued May 10, 1858, m. by:
L. N. __(?) May 10, 1858, FRANKLIN Co.

BOLING, Alexander to Mary Gilmore - issued February 27, 1825, Bondsman:
David Coats, m. by: Joseph Dyer, J. P., February 27, 1825,
GRAINGER Co.

BOLING, Edmund to Sally Going - issued January 3, 1824, Bondsman:
Shadrach Going, m. by: Isaiah Midkiff, J. P., GRAINGER Co.

BOLING, Jas. to Charlotte Baxter (or Barton) - February 2, 1807,
WILLIAMSON Co.

BOLING, Noble to Elizabeth Grissom - issued November 15, 1844, m. by:
Harmon York, J. P., December 23, 1844, VAN BUREN Co.

BOLLES, Reuben to Catherine Vaughan - issued January 6, 1825, m. by:
B. F. Liddon January 6, 1825, RUTHERFORD Co.

BOLTON, Danial to Dicy Smiddy - issued April 2, 1820, Bondsman:
Daniel Woldridge, m. by: David Tate, J. P., April 6, 1820,
GRAINGER Co.

BOLTON, Thomas to Elizabeth James - issued September 16, 1809,
Bondsman: John Blackburn, GRAINGER Co.

BOMAN, John W. to Elisa A. Coffman - issued August 9, 1850, Bondsman:
M. E. Wilcox, m. by: James L. Garnet August 9, 1850, MONTGOMERY Co.

BOMAR, E. T. to Jennie Holt - issued August 16, 1861, Bondsman:
H. I. George, Jos. H. Thompson, Clk., m. by: Anderson Sharp,
M. G., August 18, 1861, BEDFORD Co.

BOMAR, Elijah to Frances McGee - issued September 7, 1863, Bondsman:
E. L. Bomar, BEDFORD Co.

BOMAR, Pearce Y. to Mahaly E. McGhie - issued January 30, 1862,
Bondsman: E. T. Bomar, Jos. H. Thompson, Clk. per N. F. Thompson,
Dep. Clk., m. by: A. Sharp, M. G., BEDFORD Co.

BOMAR, Robert to Sally Shelton - issued January 8, 1811, Bondsman:
Ralph Shelton, GRAINGER Co.

BOMER, William to Elizabeth Terry - August 14, 1816, WILLIAMSON Co.

BOMER, William to Zibiah Freeman - issued October 20, 1841, DAVIDSON Co.

BOMER, Wm. to Elmyra A. Beck - issued November 7, 1855, m. by:
Wm. Hill, M. G., November 7, 1855, FRANKLIN Co.

BOND, Allen to Elizabeth Donoho - issued March 26, 1817, Bondsman:
Jesse Dillon, m. March 26, 1817, SUMNER Co.

BOND, Asap M. to Levica Robertson - issued October 23, 1837, Bondsman:
Henderson Esther, m. by: William Alsup, J. P., October 23, 1837,
WILSON Co.

BOND, Benjamin to Barbara Dale - issued August 6, 1805, Bondsman:
William Harmon, GRAINGER Co.

BOND, David to Lydia Jones - issued March 26, 1819, Bondsman:
Claiborn H. Rhodes, m. by: John Fakes, J. P., WILSON Co.

BOND, Francis W. to Eliza Smith - issued June 17, 1852, Bondsman:
Joseph E. Bond, m. by: J. G. Ward, M. G., June 17, 1852,
MONTGOMERY Co.

BOND, George to Hannah Burns - March 5, 1799, Security: David Parhine
and John Reed, GREENE Co.

BOND, Green to Elizabeth Williams - issued December 22, 1834, Bondsman:
Thomas Williams, m. by: Wm.son Williams, M. G., December 23,
1834, WILSON Co.

BOND, James to Sarah Clemmons - issued December 28, 1824, Bondsman:
Joshua Lester, WILSON Co.

BOND, James to Sarah Clemmons - issued December 28, 1825, Bondsman:
William Bond, m. by: Joshua Lester, M. G., January, 1825, WILSON Co.

BOND, Jesse to Sarah Sypert - issued March 15, 1827, Bondsman:
Drury Dance, m. by: John Bond, V. D. M., WILSON Co.

BOND, John to Sarah Hunter - September 21, 1808, WILLIAMSON Co.

BOND, John to Sarah Cummings - issued October 15, 1808, Bondsman:
James Bond, WILSON Co.

BOND, John to Bidsey Calliss - issued February 15, 1826, m. by:
John Bond, V. D. M., WILSON Co.

BOND, John to Julian Kines - issued January 31, 1846, Bondsman:
Bartholemew Carver, m. by: J. Nolen, J. P., January 31, 1846,
MONTGOMERY Co.

BOND, John B. to Kitty Stone - issued December 20, 1819, Bondsman:
John Stamp, SUMNER Co.

BOND, Luallen to Nancy C. Wigington - issued June 12, 1863, Bondsman:
Percy Myers, m. by: J. M. Powell, J. P., June 13, 1863,
LAWRENCE Co.

BOND, Michael to Elizabeth King - issued February 8, 1828, Bondsman:
Thomas King, m. by: James Foster, J. P., February 21, 1828,
WILSON Co.

BOND, Robert to Elizabeth Climer - issued November 9, 1836, Bondsman:
Samuel B. Gibson, m. by: J. Hooker, M. G., WILSON Co.

BOND, Samuel to Elizabeth Melton - issued July 24, 1827, Bondsman:
Elisha Bond, WILSON Co.

BOND, Soloman to Francis Alsup - issued October 9, 1815, Bondsman:
Asop Alsup, WILSON Co.

BOND, William to Nancy Dabney - December 20, 1808, WILLIAMSON Co.

BOND, William to Elizabeth Kelle - 1809, KNOX Co.

BOND, William to Lovely Simmons - issued __(?) 16, 1826, m. by:
John Bond, V. D. M., WILSON Co.

BOND, William to Margaret M. Alexander - issued December 11, 1834,
Bondsman: Henry Edwards, m. by: John Beard, M. G., WILSON Co.

BONDS, Alfred S. to Mary Elizabeth Kincaid - June 27, 1852, m. by:
B. W. White, M. C. of C., GILES Co.

BONDS, Elisha to Elizabeth Truett - issued February 18, 1824, Bondsman: Hanny Truett, m. by: John Bond, V. D. M., February 19, 1824, WILSON Co.

BONDS, Elisha to Patsey Bennett - issued January 18, 1825, Bondsman: John Merritt, m. by: James Bonds, V. D. M., January 20, 1825, WILSON Co.

BONDS, John to Mary Damron - Bondsman: Leevi Cooper, m. by: Isaac J. Ellis June 1, 1851, MONTGOMERY Co.

BONDS, Robert to Polly Benton - issued March 31, 1812, Bondsman: Alexander Carter, WILSON Co.

BONDS, William to Elizabeth Stewart - issued May 13, 1834, Bondsman: Cullen Carter, m. by: J. Hooker, M. G., WILSON Co.

BONDURANT, Robert to Pemilia Moseley - issued November 10, 1824, Bondsman: E. A. White, WILSON Co.

BONE, Adney to Martha A. McMinn - issued February 6, 1830, Bondsman: Wm. B. Merritt, m. by: J. Provine, M. G., WILSON Co.

BONE, Andrew M. to Lucinda Moore - May 31, 1811, WILLIAMSON Co.

BONE, Azor to Hulda W. Sherrill - issued December 18, 1821, Bondsman: Geo. K. Smith, m. by: John Provine, M. G., WILSON Co.

BONE, Elihu to Nancy B. Warnick - issued March 1, 1815, m. by: David Foster, V. D. M., March 2, 1815, RUTHERFORD Co.

BONE, Enos to Lucy Hern - issued May 27, 1826, Bondsman: James P. Henry, m. by: James Foster, J. P., June 1, 1826, WILSON Co.

BONE, James to Thelia Shapard - issued October 29, 1829, Bondsman: Hugh S. Locke, RUTHERFORD Co.

BONE, James C. to Mary W. Smith - issued November 26, 1824, Bondsman: David K. Donnell, m. by: William Williams, J. P., December 1, 1824, WILSON Co.

BONE, James C. to Nancy Bone - issued January 28, 1829, Bondsman: James Scott, m. by: Williamson Williams, J. P., January 29, 1829, WILSON Co.

BONE, John to Lavina McMinn - issued September 7, 1822, m. by: Thos. Calhoon, V. D. M., WILSON Co.

BONE, John to Pamelia Darrow - issued February 19, 1838, m. by: Wm. McMurry, J. P., February 20, 1838, DICKSON Co.

BONE, John M. to Lucy Webb - issued April 4, 1835, Bondsman: Harrison Ward, m. by: Abner W. Tarver, V. D. M., WILSON Co.

BONE, John M. to Sarah Anne Rebecca Coleman - issued April 13, 1836, Bondsman: Benjamin C. James, RUTHERFORD Co.

BONE, Richard J. to Sarah Foutch - issued September 28, 1839, Bondsman: Herod Foutch, WILSON Co.

BONE, Robert to Polly S. Gun - issued November 24, 1819, Bondsman: Abner W. Lansden, WILSON Co.

BONE, William to Fanniy Mayo - issued February 1, 1845, m. by: S. B. Davidson, J. P., February 6, 1845, DAVIDSON Co.

BONE, William R. to Elizabeth Phelps - issued October 3, 1833, m. by: R. P. Donnell, J. P., WILSON Co.

BONE, Young Ewen to Dorchas Stepenson - June 31, 1815, WILLIAMSON Co.

BONER, James H. to Nancy Lay - issued November 28, 1843, DAVIDSON Co.

BONNER, Benjamin to Lucy Lock - issued August 10, 1812, Bondsman:
Thomas Locke, WILSON Co.

BONNER, Jackson to Nancy Elizabeth Bryan - issued January 10, 1857,
m. by: Thomas B. Springs, Mins., January 13, 1857, COFFEE Co.

BONNER, Thomas to Polly Granade - issued October 1, 1810, Bondsman:
James L. Rawlings, WILSON Co.

BONNER, Thomas to Mary Ferguson - m. by: Thos. Blakemore June 21, 1823,
SUMNER Co.

BONNER, Thomas E. to Manerva M. Bonner - issued September 11, 1834,
Bondsman: B. A. Latimer, m. by: John Seay, M.G., WILSON Co.

BONNER, Williamson to Marino Redditt - issued January 18, 1819, Bondsman:
Lewis Schluter, SUMNER Co.

BENHAM, Benjamin to Olive Saffell - April 3, 1797, Security:
Samuel Saffell, GREENE Co.

BOOKER, Alice M. to R. S. Brown - issued February 11, 1864, Bondsman:
Jos. H. Thompson and Clerk, BEDFORD Co.

BOOKER, Dalton to Rebecca Wooten - issued September 25, 1820, Bondsman:
Olive Dickason and John R. Dalton, m. by: John Wiseman September 25,
1820, SUMNER Co.

BOOKER, George to Sally Bond - issued January 2, 1822, Bondsman:
Thomas Devault, m. by: William Lane, J. P., January 2, 1822,
GRAINGER Co.

BOOKER, Henry T. to Dolly Lane - issued January 9, 1828, Bondsman:
James Jones, m. by: Wm. Lane, J. P., January 9, 1828, GRAINGER Co.

BOOKER, James to Betsy Zachary - issued March 4, 1833, m. by:
Wm. Sawyers, J. P., March 7, 1833, KNOX Co.

BOOKER, John to Lucretia Townsend - issued August 23, 1826, Bondsman:
Wm. A. Lauderdale, SUMNER Co.

BOOKER, John to Lusinda B. Griffis - issued February 18, 1828, Bondsman:
Green H. Hancock, m. by: Thomas S. Green, J. P., February 18,
1828, WILSON Co.

BOOKER, Noah to Lewesa Payne - issued November 21, 1846, m. by:
A. Justice, J. P., November 22, 1846, ROBERTSON Co.

BOOKER, P. R. to Susannah M. Gray - April 16, 1806, WILLIAMSON Co.

BOOKER, Samuel to Mary Taylor - issued August 13, 1839, Bondsman:
Elijah B. Drake, m. by: Silas Tarver, J. P., August 15, 1839,
WILSON Co.

BOOKER, William B. to Anne Smith - issued November 9, 1824, Bondsman:
William Ledbetter, m. by: Peyton Smith November 10, 1824,
RUTHERFORD Co.

BOOKER, Willie to Sally Joplin - issued April 15, 1824, Bondsman:
William Alexander, m. by: James Foster, J. P., WILSON Co.

BOOKERVILLE, Thomas B. to Eliza Ball - m. by: Rich'd Johnson October 27,
1834, SUMNER Co.

BOOKOUT, John to Stacy Brummett - issued February 16, 1831, Bondsman:
Elijah Nelson, m. by: Elijah Nelson, J. P., KNOX Co.

BOOKOUT, John M. to Peggy Guinn - issued June 12, 1820, m. by:
John Gass, J. P. K. C., June 16, 1820, KNOX Co.

BOOKOUT, Thomas to Nancy Lumpkin - issued January 30, 1829, Bondsman:
Jno. M. Bookout, m. by: E. Nelson February 4, 1829, KNOX Co.

BOOMER, Peter to Rebeccah Farmer - March 7, 1800, KNOX Co.

BOON, Azariah B. to Mary A. Johnson - issued October 12, 1840, m. by:
U. Young, J. P., ROBERTSON Co.

BOON, John to Sally Garrison - issued February 8, 1815, Bondsman:
William Oakley, WILSON Co.

BOON, John to Viny B. Williams - issued September 24, 1847, Bondsman:
Wm. Jackson, m. by: H. McFall, J. P., September 26, 1847,
MONTGOMERY Co.

BOON, John P. to Penelope E. Boon - issued April 5, 1847, m. by:
Jesse Edwards, M. G., STEWART Co.

BOON, Nathan to Betsey Thorn - issued December 29, 1808, Bondsman:
Robert Lytle, SUMNER Co.

BOONE, Benjamin H. to Eliza Jane Gossett - issued March 11, 1847,
Bondsman: William Gossett, m. by: P. Priestly (seal), J. P.,
March 11, 1847, MONTGOMERY Co.

BOONE, James to Sophia Smith - issued August 31, 1825, m. by:
Wm. Stanfield September 1, 1825, RUTHERFORD Co.

BOOTH, C. A. to Margret A. Pyland - issued November 12, 1870, m.
November 16, 1870, FRANKLIN Co.

BOOTH, John W. to Louisa J. Payne - issued February 24, 1872, m. by:
C. C. Rose, J. P., February 25, 1872, FRANKLIN Co.

BOOTH, Lewis to Winnie Richardson - issued July 23, 1804, Bondsman:
Robt Wildure, SUMNER Co.

BOOTH, Samuel to Mary P. Tilman - issued March 10, 1823, Bondsman:
Geo. C. Booth, m. by: G. W. Banton, J. P., March 12, 1823,
RUTHERFORD Co.

BOOTH, Samuel to Sarah Ealey - issued June 15, 1827, Bondsman:
David Bass, WILSON Co.

BOOTH, Zachariah to Mary C. Massengill - issued May 12, 1814, Bondsman:
Tho. H. Nelson, KNOX Co.

BOOTHE, Robert to Minerva Payne - issued November 2, 1818, m. by:
Edward Willis, M. G., November 5, 1818, WILSON Co.

BOOTHE, Robert to Minerva Payne - issued November 2, 1819, Bondsman:
William Payne, WILSON Co.

BOOTHE, Samuel to Louisa Graves - issued April 14, 1827, Bondsman:
Samuel Walker, m. by: B. Graves April 19, 1827, WILSON Co.

BOOTHMAN, E. to Mary Nichols - issued March 10, 1868, FRANKLIN Co.

BORDEN, Adam to Betsy Huchison - September 4, 1800, BLOUNT Co.

BORDEN, Daniel to Catherine Newton - January 9, 1798, Security:
John Jones, GREENE Co.

BORDEN, Esther to John Graham - January 2, 1789, Security: James Graham,
GREENE Co.

BORDER, L. R. to Mary Edwards - issued January 12, 1857, m. by:
F. C. Plaster January 20, 1857, ROBERTSON Co.

BORDERS, William to Polly Graves - m. by: Henry S. Anthony, Jr.,
December 10, 1835, SUMNER Co.

BOREN, Bailey to Polly Herals - issued April 5, 1840, m. by:
James Woodard, J. P., ROBERTSON Co.

BOREN, Bazel to Agness Huddleston - issued May 31, 1844, m. by:
A. Justice, J. P., June 2, 1844, ROBERTSON Co.

BOREN, Dan'l to Nancy McClure - issued July 10, 1872, m. by:
E. Hawkins July 11, 1872, FRANKLIN Co.

BOREN, Eli to L. A. Barker - issued June 1, 1848, m. by: Jas. Woodard,
ROBERTSON Co.

BOREN, Elijah F. to Sarah Nance - issued April 17, 1825, m. by:
Peyton Smith April 28, 1825, RUTHERFORD Co.

BOREN, John to Mary A. Wells - issued December 14, 1842, m. by:
U. Young, J. P., ROBERTSON Co.

BOREN, Richard to Miley Bush - issued September 20, 1824, Bondsman:
Stephen Boren, m. by: Wm. Hobdey, J. P., September 20, 1824,
SUMNER Co.

BOREN, Rhcid. A. to Leatha Newton - issued December 7, 1848, m. by:
F. R. Gooch, S. L., ROBERTSON Co.

BOREN, Varary to Kerziah Boren - issued December 17, 1840, m. by:
R. B. Mitchell, ROBERTSON Co.

BOREN, William to Julian Dye - issued December 2, 1812, Bondsman:
Hugh W. Latimer, SUMNER Co.

BORINE(?), Sarah to Evan Jones - GREENE Co.

BORING, Amos to Nancy Etter - issued January 11, 1817, Bondsman:
Eli Smith, m. by: James Whitsett, J. P., January 13, 1817,
RUTHERFORD Co.

BORING, Jacob to Ann Ross - issued January 4, 1807, Bondsman:
Samuel Ross, WILSON Co.

BORING, M. to Elizabeth McCullough - issued March 14, 1827, m. by:
J. A. Mabry, J. P., March 15, 1827, KNOX Co.

BORPO, Alexander to Mary McCormack - issued July 26, 1817, m. by:
A. McEwen, J. P., July 28, 1817, RUTHERFORD Co.

BORTHICK, John to Eleanor Pond - issued December 9, 1847, m. by:
Isaac Steel, ROBERTSON Co.

BORUM, Henry to Martha Cartwright - issued November 11, 1840, Bondsman:
T. T. Armstrong, m. by: Jonathan Bailey, J. P., November 12,
1840, WILSON Co.

BORUM, Hiram to Nancy Tucker - issued February 3, 1840, Bondsman:
George Jewell, WILSON Co.

BORUM, James to Martha Ann Borum - issued October 27, 1829, Bondsman:
Francis Eubanks, WILSON Co.

BORUM, William to Eliza White - issued February 16, 1833, m. by:
F. S. Harris, J. P., February 21, 1833, WILSON Co.

BOSLEY, Charles Jr. to Martha A. Carden - issued March 30, 1842, m. by:
J. T. Edgar March 30, 1842, DAVIDSON Co.

BOSLEY, Peyton R. to Catharine Mary Jane Sanders - issued October 3, 1831, Bondsman: Josiah R. Franklin, m. by: John M. Holland, M. G., October 3, 1831, SUMNER Co.

BOSTIC, Chesley B. to Francis Griffin - issued December 13, 1842, m. by: William Little, J. P., December 10, 1842, FRANKLIN Co.

BOSTICK, B. R. to M. M. Bennett - issued September 16, 1866, m. by: A. D. Oakley, M. G., September 18, 1866, FRANKLIN Co.

BOSTICK, Berry to S. A. Buckner - issued January 15, 1870, m. by: D. S. Long, J. P., January 16, 1870, FRANKLIN Co.

BOSTICK, Chesley B. to Susan S. Stovall - issued May 7, 1852, m. by: R. C. Smith, J. P., May 9, 1852, FRANKLIN Co.

BOSTICK, F. G. to Polly Partin - issued December 15, 1865, FRANKLIN Co.

BOSTICK, James A. to Maria Z. Smith - issued May 20, 1839, m. by: Jno. B. McFerrin, M. G., May 23, 1839, DAVIDSON Co.

BOSTICK, John to Polly Hyde - December 18, 1815, WILLIAMSON Co.

BOSTICK, John H. to Catharine L. Temple - issued December 18, 1838, m. by: W. D. F. Sawrie, M. G., December 20, 1838, DAVIDSON Co.

BOSTICK, Jno. H. R. to Jane E. Winford - issued September 25, 1848, m. by: W. G. Guinn, M. G., September 26, 1848, FRANKLIN Co.

BOSTICK, Nathan to Caroline Stovall - issued July 17, 1841, m. by: Clinton A. Hunt, J. P., July 18, 1841, FRANKLIN Co.

BOSTICK, Richard W. H. to Rebecca L. Cannon - issued January 19, 1841, m. by: C. D. Elliott, M. G., January 19, 1841, DAVIDSON Co.

BOSWELL, George G. to Elizabeth M. C. Buckingham - issued November 23, 1846, m. by: Jas. T. Morris, J. P., November 23, 1846, STEWART Co.

BOSWELL, John F. to Martha L. Clark - issued December 30, 1874, FRANKLIN Co.

BOSWORTH, James M. to Julia A. M. Dudley - issued July 27, 1830, m. by: Isaac Lewis July 27, 1830, KNOX Co.

BOTHICK, John to Nancy Carr - issued June 25, 1839, m. by: Isaac Steel, ROBERTSON Co.

BOTKIN, Hugh to Rachel Keener - March 17, 1801, KNOX Co.

BOTTOM, Geraldus to Emily M. Spinks - issued June 1, 1840, Bondsman: Mark Whitaker, m. by: Silas Tarver, J. P., June 4, 1840, WILSON Co.

BOTTOM, J. A. to E. F. Sandofer - issued April 5, 1849, m. by: Jas. Woodard, ROBERTSON Co.

BOUGH, John A. to M. I. Blanchard - issued April 2, 1854, m. by: James Woodard, J. P., ROBERTSON Co.

BOUGHTER, Samuel to Sarah M. West - m. by: Jess Edwards Mi, DICKSON Co.

BOULTON, John to Elizabeth Hamock - issued August 21, 1805, Bondsman: John Hammack, GRAINGER Co.

BOULTON, Peter to Salomy Coffman - issued February 1, 1819, Bondsman: Thomas Waggoner, m. by: Martin Cleveland, J. P., February 5, 1819, GRAINGER Co.

BOUND, John W. to Polly Carter - issued March 30, 1829, Bondsman: C. G. Bowen, m. by: Wm. A. McCampbell, J. P., March 31, 1829, KNOX Co.

BOUNDS, Francis to Amy White - issued January 18, 1799, Bondsman:
John Bounds, KNOX Co.

BOUNDS, Robt. T. to Clarissa I. Logan - issued December 12, 1863,
Bondsman: Danl. Clift, Jos. H. Thompson, Clk., BEDFORD Co.

BOUNDS, Washington Wm. to Rebecka Fisher - issued September 27, 1832,
m. by: B. McNutt, J. P., September 27, 1832, KNOX Co.

BOURFINDE, Theodore to Sarah C. Holt - issued June 10, 1856, m. by:
William Worthington, J. P., June 12, 1856, VAN BUREN Co.

BOURN, Alexander to Harriet Newman - issued January 8, 1848, m. by:
Thos. W. Felts January 13, 1848, ROBERTSON Co.

BOURNE, John to Mary Hitt - issued December 30, 1843, m. by:
Thomas W. Ruffin, J. P., January 1, 1844, ROBERTSON Co.

BOURNE, Thomas G. to Elizabeth J. Long - issued November 24, 1846,
m. by: R. B. C. Howell, M. G., November 25, 1846, DAVIDSON Co.

BOUSH, R. A. to Jeanie M. West - issued October 26, 1846, m. by:
Richard P. Miles, Bishop of Nashvulle, October 26, 1846, DAVIDSON Co.

BOWDEN, Bennett to Polly Naily - issued October 22, 1822, m. by:
G. Mirtle, J. P., October 24, 1822, WILSON Co.

BOWDON, James C. to Ann A. Green - issued December 24, 1847, m. by:
Rev. A. J. Steel, FRANKLIN Co.

BOWDOWN, Enoch to Delilah Hughs - issued September 24, 1824, Bondsman:
Daniel Cardwell, GRAINGER Co.

BOWEN, Abner to Jenny Thompson - November 27, 1805, KNOX Co.

BOWEN, Abner to Elizabeth Renshaw - issued August 22, 1824, Bondsman:
Arnot Jones, m. by: James Sandford, RUTHERFORD Co.

BOWEN, Ahab to Mary L. Easley - issued March 21, 1835, Bondsman:
William K. Latham, m. by: Jas. Kennon, M. G., GRAINGER Co.

BOWEN, Andrew to Catherine Hawith - issued August 26, 1816, Bondsman:
Eli Clark, m. by: John Hall, J. P., GRAINGER Co.

BOWEN, Benj. B. to Wineford Walker - issued January 11, 1838, m. by:
David Gray, M. G., DICKSON Co.

BOWEN, Charles to Salley Vasser - issued June 29, 1827, Bondsman:
Caswell Vasser, RUTHERFORD Co.

BOWEN, David to Elizabeth Dennis - issued October 8, 1825, Bondsman:
William Carder, m. by: Thos. Brown, J. P., October 8, 1825,
GRAINGER Co.

BOWEN, George to Telitha Meanally - issued November 15, 1824, Bondsman:
T. D. Knight, GRAINGER Co.

BOWEN, Henry to Rachel Mayse - issued May 6, 1823, Bondsman:
William F. Tate, m. by: Jas. Kenmore, M. G., May 6, 1823,
GRAINGER Co.

BOWEN, J. C. to M. A. Fountane - issued July 21, 1858, m. by:
Benj. Rawls, M. G., ROBERTSON Co.

BOWEN, James to Polly McGinnis - issued October 20, 1798, Bondsman:
John McElheny, GRAINGER Co.

BOWEN, James to Nancey Ledbetter - issued May 15, 1805, Bondsman:
Henry Bowen, Senr., GRAINGER Co.

BOWEN, James to Catherine Maclin - issued January 5, 1816, m. by:
William Bumpass, D. D., January 9, 1816, RUTHERFORD Co.

BOWEN, John to Jane Crawford - issued December 28, 1796, Bondsman:
David Maxwell, KNOX Co.

BOWEN, John to Jane Bridgeman - issued November 7, 1823, Bondsman:
Reese Bowen, m. by: Jas. Kennon, M. G., November 7, 1823,
GRAINGER Co.

BOWEN, Nicholas to Polly May - issued November 16, 1822, Bondsman:
Armsted Kirk, GRAINGER Co.

BOWEN, Nicholas to Polly May - issued November 16, 1823, m. by:
Jas. Kennon, M. G., GRAINGER Co.

BOWEN, Samuel D. to Mary A. Jackson - issued May 5, 1847, DICKSON Co.

BOWEN, Thomas to Lucy Drew - issued January 24, 1807, Bondsman:
William Drew, WILSON Co.

BOWEN, Thomas to Rebecca Walkup - issued October 15, 1821, m. by:
Cullin Curlee, RUTHERFORD Co.

BOWEN, William to Amelia Sloane - issued February 19, 1805, m. by:
R. Houston, J. P. K. C., February 19, 1805, KNOX Co.

BOWEN, William B. to Polly Brown - issued December 3, 1815, Bondsman:
Robert Alstot, GRAINGER Co.

BOWEN, Wm. R. to Matilda E. Sprenkles - issued December 27, 1837,
Bondsman: Wm. Dunlap, m. by: J. M. Kelley, M. G., December 28,
1837, KNOX Co.

BOWENS, L. C. to S. F. Bush - issued December 18, 1871, m. by:
J. M. Darwin, M. G., December 18, 1871, FRANKLIN Co.

BOWER, K. C. to Elizabeth C. Bowers - issued December 19, 1849,
Bondsman: Jas. S. Bowers, m. by: John Mallory, M. G., December 24,
1849, MONTGOMERY Co.

BOWER, William to Jenny McNight - issued March 28, 1812, KNOX Co.

BOWERMAN, Michael to Cathy Bowers - February 25, 1800, BLOUNT Co.

BOWERS, Bastley to Marge Mahafey - Bondsman: Jeremiah Bonner, WILSON Co.

BOWERS, Edward D. to Mary Frances Cardin - April 27, 1953, Security:
Jas. L. Baugh, GILES Co.

BOWERS, G. W. to Martha J. Williams - issued May 9, 1865, m. by:
W. W. Estill, M. G., May 11, 1865, FRANKLIN Co.

BOWERS, Green C. to Susan Forbis - issued February 6, 1835, Bondsman:
James M. Provine, m. by: Stephen McDonald February 12, 1835,
WILSON Co.

BOWERS, J. H. to Mary A. Cunningham - issued May 30, 1866, m. by:
W. W. Estill, M. G., May, 1866, FRANKLIN Co.

BOWERS, James to Lucretia Lewis - issued February 13, 1841, m. by:
James Wilson, J. P., February 20, 1841, STEWART Co.

BOWERS, James D. to Frances I. Mallory - issued September 9, 1850,
Bondsman: Jas. C. Wall, MONTGOMERY Co.

BOWERS, Jeremiah to Margaret Easten - issued September 4, 1809,
Bondsman: Nathan Parker Jr., SUMNER Co.

BOWERS, Jesse to Nancy Mann - issued November 8, 1810, Bondsman:
Thomas Bradley, WILSON Co.

BOWERS, John to Ann Frazier - April 25, 1797, Security: Abner Frazier,
GREENE Co.

BOWERS, John to Cloe Arwine - issued March 11, 1829, Bondsman:
Andrew Bowers, GRAINGER Co.

BOWERS, John to Jane Sypert - issued June 21, __(?), Bondsman:
Zechairah Wherry, m. by: George Donnell, V. D. M., June 22, 1837,
WILSON Co.

BOWERS, John to Sarah J. Gossett - issued May 27, 1845, m. by:
L. Brewer, M. G., May 28, 1845, ROBERTSON Co.

BOWERS, John C. to Cordelia H. Lewis - issued November 15, 1853,
Bondsman: Dawson T. Allen, m. by: B. Bayliss, J. P., November 20,
1853, MONTGOMERY Co.

BOWERS, John M. to Mary C. Horn - issued October 10, 1851, Bondsman:
J. A. Senseny, m. by: John Mallory, M. G., October 12, 1851,
MONTGOMERY Co.

BOWERS, John W. to Elizabeth Haslet - June 16, 1787, Security:
James Bowers, GREENE Co.

BOWERS, Joseph to Louisa Mann - issued September 7, 1846, Bondsman:
W. Horn, m. by: Judson Horn, J. P., September 8, 1846, MONTGOMERY Co.

BOWERS, Kinchen C. to Elizabeth C. Bowers - issued December 19, 1849,
m. December 24, 1849, MONTGOMERY Co.

BOWERS, L. D. to Julia Pepper - issued June 3, 1846, m. by:
Alex Lowe, Minister, ROBERTSON Co.

BOWERS, L. W. to H. M. Anderson - issued June 5, 1861, m. by:
W. H. Bugg, J. P., ROBERTSON Co.

BOWERS, Mary to James Davis - GREENE Co.

BOWERS, Reece to Mary Moody - issued April 4, 1825, Bondsman:
Warham Easley, m. by: James Kennon, M. G., April 4, 1825, GRAINGER Co.

BOWERS, Richard to Rebecca Galbraith - August 1, 1791, Security:
William Galbraith, GREENE Co.

BOWERS, Samuel to Julia A. Francis - issued July 22, 1851, m. by:
Madison Williams, J. P., July 22, 1851, FRANKLIN Co.

BOWERS, Sandford to Emily Collier - issued October 14, 1853, Bondsman:
Dickson P. Allen, m. by: Conrad Fredrick, J. P., October 18, 1853,
MONTGOMERY Co.

BOWERS, Solomon to Martha Ann Allen - issued December 17, 1846, m. by:
John T. Slatter, J. P., December 18, 1846, FRANKLIN Co.

BOWERS, Stephen C. to Nancy Lasiter - issued June 8, 1830, Bondsman:
Wm. Wormack, m. by: Patton, J. P., June 8, 1830, SUMNER Co.

BOWERS, W. J. to S. A. Glisson - issued July 8, 1859, m. by:
F. R. Gooch, M. G., July 9, 1859, ROBERTSON Co.

BOWERS(?), William to C. Wilson(?) - September 30, 1793, Security:
John W. Bowers, GREENE Co.

BOWERS, William P. to Martha S. McCaslin - issued May 26, 1842, m. by:
Jonas Shivers, J. P., May 16, 1842, DAVIDSON Co.

BOWIE, John to Susan Redfern - issued October 22, 1842, m. by:
Isaac Steel, G. M., ROBERTSON Co.

BOWIE, Langdon to Eliza Coffin - issued July 21, 1829, Bondsman:
W. B. A. Ramsey, KNOX Co.

BOWIE, Langdon to Eliza Coffin - issued July 21, 1829, m. by:
Charles Coffin, V. D. M., July 21, 1829, KNOX Co.

BOWLEN, Matthew C. to Martha Short - issued April 24, 1811, Bondsman:
Greenberry Howard, SUMNER Co.

BOWLES, John to Polly Anderson - issued February 17, 1812, Bondsman:
Wm. Ogles, SUMNER Co.

BOWLES, Zacharia to Minerva Harper - m. by: Henry K. Winbourn October 13,
1834, SUMNER Co.

BOWLINE, B. to E. Newman - issued April 7, 1850, m. by: John W. Hanner,
M. G., ROBERTSON Co.

BOWLING, Archibald Duval to Adaline M. Duval - issued June 28, 1819,
Bondsman: Sam'l Gwin, m. by: James Gwin, M. G., June 28, 1819,
SUMNER Co.

BOWLING, David to Rolly Rail - issued December 13, 1804, Bondsman:
William Rail, GRAINGER Co.

BOWLING, Ezekiel to Nancy Gowing - issued December 2, 1824, Bondsman:
Pleasant Weston, m. by: Isaiah Midkiff, J. P., December 2, 1824,
GRAINGER Co.

BOWLING, George to Nancy Kirby - issued January 23, 1823, Bondsman:
Meredith Hodges, m. by: M. Hodges, J. P., January 23, 1823,
SUMNER Co.

BOWLING, James H. to Jane S. Grant - issued March 17, 1852, Bondsman:
George Bell, m. by: Robert Williams March 17, 1852, MONTGOMERY Co.

BOWLING, James W. to Nancy L. Wakefield - issued January 17, 1859,
m. by: Wm. H. Anthony January 18, 1859, FRANKLIN Co.

BOWLING, John to Ruan Flemming - issued January 1, 1836, Bondsman:
James Pybass, RUTHERFORD Co.

BOWLING, Noble to Katty Clift - issued December 8, 1826, Bondsman:
James Farr, m. by: Eli King, J. P., December 14, 1826, KNOX Co.

BOWLING, O. H. to Elizabeth A. Shannon - issued September 21, 1860,
ROBERTSON Co.

BOWLING, R. P. to Mary A. Whillies - issued April 10, 1850, Bondsman:
Hel Thornton, MONTGOMERY Co.

BOWLING, Samuel P. to Laura V. Enochs - issued May 10, 1873, m. by:
J. C. Mails, M. G., May 14, 1873, FRANKLIN Co.

BOWLLAND, William to Susan Drake - issued July 4, 1857, m. by:
Rev'd Hugh S. Montgomery July 5, 1357, COFFEE Co.

BOWMAN, Carter to Francis Badgett - issued December 1, 1829, Bondsman:
Alexander Williams, m. by: Elijah Johnson, J. P., December 13,
1829, KNOX Co.

BOWMAN, Charity to Leonard Eddleman - GREENE Co.

BOWMAN, Edward S. to Letha Jane Alexander - issued April 3, 1841,
FRANKLIN Co.

BOWMAN, Elizabeth to William Johnson - September 8, 1800, Security:
    Joseph St. John, GREENE Co.

BOWMAN, Henry to Barbara Starns - January 15, 1800, Security:
    Leonard Dell, GREENE Co.

BOWMAN, Jacob to Catherine Starns - January 5, 1797, Security:
    Samuel Kelsay, GREENE Co.

BOWMAN, Jacob to Margaret Johnson - July 7, 1797, Security: James Magee,
    GREENE Co.

BOWMAN, James to Elizabeth Bowman - issued May 31, 1816, Bondsman:
    John T. Bowman, SUMNER Co.

BOWMAN, James to Elizabeth Taylor - issued February 14, 1818, Bondsman:
    Thomas Taylor, WILSON Co.

BOWMAN, James to Dovey Hamilton - issued February 20, 1819, m. by:
    Robt. Henderson February 21, 1819, RUTHERFORD Co.

BOWMAN, Jas. to Mary Hickerson - issued August 20, 1840, m. by:
    E. S. Hall, J. P., August 20, 1840, DAVIDSON Co.

BOWMAN, James A. to Sarah Stanfield - m. by: James Charlton, J. P.,
    February 4, 1823, SUMNER Co.

BOWMAN, James F. to Mary Brown - issued July 11, 1830, m. by:
    O. W. Crockett, J. P., RUTHERFORD Co.

BOWMAN, Joanna to Elijah McNew - GREENE Co.

BOWMAN, John to Peggy Jack - April 21, 1800, KNOX Co.

BOWMAN, John to Caroline Smith - issued October 4, 1837, m. by:
    John Lane, M. G., October, 1837, RUTHERFORD Co.

BOWMAN, Jonoah to Betsey Cavett - issued January 1, 1799, Bondsman:
    Thomas Dodson, Witness: H. L. White, KNOX Co.

BOWMAN, Joseph to Rhoda Chandler - January 5, 1792, Security:
    Absalom Haworth, GREENE Co.

BOWMAN, Joseph to Peggy Hamilton - issued May 14, 1806, Bondsman:
    J. W. Hamilton, SUMNER Co.

BOWMAN, Joseph A. to Lucy Caroline White - issued August 21, 1843,
    m. by: John W. Ogden, M. G., August 24, 1843, DAVIDSON Co.

BOWMAN, Nancy to Henry Kidway - GREENE Co.

BOWMAN, Samuel to Betsy Heppenstall - issued December 31, 1823, m. by:
    B. McNutt, J. P., January 1, 1824, KNOX Co.

BOWMAN, Samuel P. to Mary A. Trigg - issued April 19, 1837, m. by:
    Sam'l Cosby April 19, 1837, RUTHERFORD Co.

BOWMAN, William to Nancy McKahan - issued September 9, 1824, Bondsman:
    David Counts, m. by: Isaiah Midkiff, J. P., September 9, 1824,
    GRAINGER Co.

BOWMAN, William to Hannah Isbell - issued August 8, 1839, m. by:
    M. Catchings, J. P., September 15, 1839, FRANKLIN Co.

BOWMER, Peter to Mary Beman - June 10, 1801, KNOX Co.

BOWMON, William C. to Nancy Denton - issued July 9, 1841, VAN BUREN Co.

BOX, Jonathan to Jane McNiece - issued February 3, 1819, Bondsman: Robert Box, m. by: Jas. Moore, J. P., February 7, 1819, GRAINGER Co.

BOX, Samuel to Jimima Murphy - issued June 9, 1814, Bondsman: James Ezell, GRAINGER Co.

BOX, Samuel to Catherine Ricketts - issued October 25, 1818, Bondsman: Archibald Pugh, m. by: Robert Ganes, J. P., November 8, 1818, GRAINGER Co.

BASE(?), William to Elizabeth Green - issued August 4, 1837, Bondsman: Robert Cardwell, m. by: William Mays, J. P., August 4, 1837, GRAINGER Co.

BOYCE, Alfred K. to Martha A. Bowen - issued December 16, 1845, m. by: John W. Ogden, M. G., November 25, 1845, DICKSON Co.

BOYCE, J. B. to L. J. Duncan - issued January 12, 1869, FRANKLIN Co.

BOYD, Alexander to Rosanah Boyd - issued June 2, 1807, Bondsman: John Boyd, WILSON Co.

BOYD, Alexander to Catherine Starnes - August 21, 1820, KNOX Co.

BOYD, Armistead to Polly Cook - December 28, 1808, WILLIAMSON Co.

BOYD, Benj. to Cynthia Brooks - issued November 9, 1826, Bondsman: James Kennedy, KNOX Co.

BOYD, Benj. S. to Cynthia Brooks - issued November 9, 1826, m. by: Tho. H. Nelson, M. G., November 9, 1826, KNOX Co.

BOYD, Charles H. to Harriett Cage - issued December 7, 1831, Bondsman: David M. Fulton, m. by: James Charlton, J. P., February 14, 1831, SUMNER Co.

BOYD, Coleman to Eliza Ann Sayles - issued October 30, 1854, m. by: G. B. Mason, J. P., October 31, 1854, ROBERTSON Co.

BOYD, Frances to Margaret Atkins - issued September 13, 1852, m. by: Robert Williams, M. G., September 23, 1852, ROBERTSON Co.

BOYD, George to Martha A. Walker - February 20, 1821, WILLIAMSON Co.

BOYD, George E. to Mary Adaline Adkins - issued August 16, 1853, Bondsman: J. J. Hameltt, m. by: Joseph Willis, M. G., September 28, 1853, MONTGOMERY Co.

BOYD, J. R. to M. J. Garrett - issued November 30, 1847, FRANKLIN Co.

BOYD, James to Sarah Sloan - April 4, 1786, Security: William Sloan, GREENE Co.

BOYD, James to Ann Miller - February 15, 1797, Surety: James Sloss, BLOUNT Co.

BOYD, James to Hannah McMurray - September 3, 1799, Surety: Gideon Blackburn, BLOUNT Co.

BOYD, James to Mariah Dumumbrane - issued September 3, 1840, m. by: George Childress, J. P., ROBERTSON Co.

BOYD, James A. to Susan Brodie - issued January 23, 1849, Bondsman: Robert H. Crews, m. by: Allison Akin, M. G., January 25, 1849, MONTGOMERY Co.

BOYD, James B. to Julia Y. Yates - issued January 24, 1833, Bondsman: Wm. Moody, m. by: John Dotson, J. P., GRAINGER Co.

BOYD, James H. to Fanny Weatherspoon - issued December 30, 1822, Bondsman: William D. Jordan, m. by: Jesse Alexander, V. D. M., December 31, 1822, RUTHERFORD Co.

BOYD, James H. to Rosannah E. Boyd - issued January 12, 1836, Bondsman: David M. Henderson, m. by: Jesse Alexander, V. D. M., January 13, 1836, RUTHERFORD Co.

BOYD, James M. to Martha Thomas - issued September 11, 1830, Bondsman: David N. Berry, WILSON Co.

BOYD, Joel to Lucinda Boyte - issued February 12, 1845, m. by: P. Lynch, J. P., February 12, 1845, STEWART Co.

BOYD, John to Cathy Holoway - September 30, 1799, BLOUNT Co.

BOYD, John to Elizabeth E. Boyd - issued January 17, 1835, Bondsman: Wm. Boyd, m. by: Jesse Alexander, V. D. M., January 18, 1835, RUTHERFORD Co.

BOYD, John to Margaret Mitchell - issued January 17, 1850, VAN BUREN Co.

BOYD, John M. to Nancy Ann Clay - issued November 27, 1842, m. by: John McCaslin, J. P., November 29, 1842, DICKSON Co.

BOYD, John R. to Nancy Wood - December 17, 1816, WILLIAMSON Co.

BOYD, Joseph to Peggy Kilburn - February 22, 1822, KNOX Co.

BOYD, Joseph M. to Mary T. Pratt - issued August 14, 1851, m. by: Willie Smith, J. P., August 14, 1851, MONTGOMERY Co.

BOYD, Mack to Derinda Summers - issued November 30, 1830, m. by: John S. Lowe, J. P., December 3, 1830, RUTHERFORD Co.

BOYD, Marcus D. to Miss Sarah Ballentine - issued February 6, 1850, Bondsman: Q. H. Floyd, m. by: Wm. Shelton, J. P., February 10, 1850, MONTGOMERY Co.

BOYD, Mary to John Sloan - GREENE Co.

BOYD, Milton B. to Isabel M. Dabbs - issued January 9, 1840, DAVIDSON Co.

BOYD, Milton B. to Isabell M. Dabbs - issued January 9, 1841, DAVIDSON Co.

BOYD, Paul W. to Isabella Boyd - issued May 11, 1833, Bondsman: Robert Boyd, RUTHERFORD Co.

BOYD, Robert to Margaret Meek - April 3, 1793, KNOX Co.

BOYD, Robert to Elizabeth Gardner - issued August 11, 1806, Bondsman: John Boyd, WILSON Co.

BOYD, Robert to Margarett Watkins - m. by: Wm. Montgomery, J. P., April 5, 1820, SUMNER Co.

BOYD, Robert to Margarete Watkins - issued April 5, 1826, Bondsman: David Hutchison, SUMNER Co.

BOYD, Robert to Margaret T. Witherspoon - issued August 24, 1829, Bondsman: James H. Boyd, RUTHERFORD Co.

BOYD, Robert to Rebecca Jane Campbell - issued December 15, 1842, m. by: B. M. Barnes, J. P., December 15, 1842, DAVIDSON Co.

BOYD, Samuel to Dorcas E. McNutt - issued August 31, 1829, Bondsman: Edward R. Davis, m. by: Edward R. Davis, J. P., September 3, 1829, KNOX Co.

BOYD, Saml. B. to Susan H. Mason - issued December 4, 1828, m. by:
Tho. H. Nelson, M. G., December 4, 1828, KNOX Co.

BOYD, Samuel B. to Susan H. Mason - issued December 4, 1828, Bondsman:
Sam'l R. Rodgers and Wm. S. Kennedy, KNOX Co.

BOYD, Sarah to John Dagley - MAURY Co.

BOYD, Siras to Rosey Savely - issued April 19, 1825, Bondsman:
Thomas Duke, SUMNER Co.

BOYD, William to Faethy Lawrence - issued October 9, 1815, Bondsman:
Allen J. C. Dearing, WILSON Co.

BOYD, William to Eliza Reynolds - September 4, 1822, KNOX Co.

BOYD, William to Martha Berget - issued December 24, 1840, m. by:
Isaac Steel, G. M., ROBERTSON Co.

BOYD, William to Susan E. Noe - issued January 17, 1848, Bondsman:
W. S. McClure, m. by: P. Priestly, J. P., January 17, 1848,
MONTGOMERY Co.

BOYD, William to Eliza Hillis - issued December 28, 1850, VAN BUREN Co.

BOYD, William L. to Tennessee Coleman - issued May 7, 1845, m. by:
W. H. Wharton May 7, 1845, DAVIDSON Co.

BOYD, William M. to Isabella M. McKnight - issued March 24, 1834, m. by:
Jesse Alexander, V. D. M., March 27, 1834, RUTHERFORD Co.

BOYD, William P. to Catharine Waggoner - issued December 30, 1840,
m. by: E. H. East, J. P., December 30, 1840, DAVIDSON Co.

BOYDER, William H. to Louisa J. E. Hanson - issued October 24, 1843,
ROBERTSON Co.

BOYER, Henry to Mary Gambell - issued January 2, 1808, Bondsman:
John Gambell, SUMNER Co.

BOYER, Wm. D. to R. W. Wisdom - issued July 10, 1847, Bondsman:
T. W. Wisdom, m. by: Wm. Shelton, M. G., July 13, 1847, MONTGOMERY Co.

BOYERS, David to Charlotte Clark - issued January 22, 1812, Bondsman:
none, SUMNER Co.

BOYERS, Robert M. to Elizabeth Banks - issued December 28, 1817,
Bondsman: Joel Parrish, SUMNER Co.

BOYKIN, Mathew J. to Nancy Kean - issued July 19, 1834, m. by:
Jas. L. Marlin, J. P., July 19, 1834, SUMNER Co.

BOYKIN, Samuel to Deborrah Pike - m. by: Taylor G. Gilliam March 28,
1837, SUMNER Co.

BOYKIN, Wmson to Elisabeth Fry - July 16, 1805, WILLIAMSON Co.

BOYKIN, Williamson to Malinda Malone - September 10, 1815, WILLIAMSON Co.

BOYLE, Cornelius to Tabitha E. G. Allen - issued August 30, 1838,
m. by: John Wright, J. P., August 30, 1838, DAVIDSON Co.

BOYLE, Hugh to Eliza Spooner - issued March 10, 1821, Bondsman:
Abram Martin, SUMNER Co.

BOYLE, James to Nancy Campbell - issued August 25, 1817, Bondsman:
John Boyle, SUMNER Co.

BOYLES, Baley to Elizabeth Pentacost - issued September 30, 1832,
Bondsman: Thomas Meadow, m. by: Luke P. Allen September 30, 1832,
SUMNER Co.

BOYLES, J. H. to M. E. White - issued January 13, 1859, m. by:
H. L. Covington, J. P., January 16, 1859, ROBERTSON Co.

BOYLES, James to Malinda Williams - issued May 4, 1824, Bondsman:
Perrin Bandy, m. May 4, 1824, SUMNER Co.

BOYLES, Obadiah to Sally Espey - issued May 21, 1816, m. by:
H. Robinson, J. P., May 28, 1816, RUTHERFORD Co.

BOYLES, Richard to Any Center - issued May 27, 1827, Bondsman:
Michael Tracy, SUMNER Co.

BOYLES, Thomas H. to Delila England - issued October 1, 1844, m. by:
Thomas Farmer, J. P., October 6, 1844, ROBERTSON Co.

BOYTT, Jonathan to Eady Myres - issued August 7, 1842, m. by:
B. Herndon, J. P., August 8, 1842, STEWART Co.

BOZEL, Jonathan to Nancy Mills - August 19, 1796, Surety: Samuel
Huchison, BLOUNT Co.

BRABSON, John to Martha Smith - issued October 22, 1834, Bondsman:
Stephen Butler, m. by: James Lacey, M. G., GRAINGER Co.

BRABSON, Margaret to Larner Ingram - GREENE Co.

BRABSTON, Vincent B. to Sarah Smith - issued January 28, 1835, Bondsman:
Henry Counts, m. by: Levi Satterfield, M. G., GRAINGER Co.

BRACK, Go. to Rebecca Bobbett - issued May 28, 1851, m. by:
W. W. Williams, J. P., June 1, 1851, ROBERTSON Co.

BRACKEN, Edmond to Margaret Cline - issued March 12, 1831, Bondsman:
Michael Cline, m. by: J. Davis, J. P., March 12, 1831, SUMNER Co.

BRACKEN, James B. to Eliza Bracken - issued April 20, 1824, Bondsman:
Sam'l Tyree, m. by: Meredith Hodges, J. P., April 20, 1824,
SUMNER Co.

BRACKEN, Jesse to Rebecca Woodall - issued June 18, 1830, Bondsman:
Joseph Kelly, m. by: John T. Carr, J. P., June 18, 1830, SUMNER Co.

BRACKEN, John to Patsey Martin - issued February 8, 1812, Bondsman:
Edmund Browning, SUMNER Co.

BRACKEN, Jr., William to Rachel Morris - issued May 4, 1825, Bondsman:
John Morris, SUMNER Co.

BRACKEN, Jr., William to Rachel Morris - issued May 4, 1826, m. by:
W. Smith, J. P., May 4, 1826, SUMNER Co.

BRACKEN, Willie to Levesta Bell - issued February 22, 1819, Bondsman:
Jeremiah Spencer, m. by: Addison Foster, J. P., February 22,
1819, SUMNER Co.

BRACKET, Morgan to Elizabeth Mayfield - issued November 1, 1841,
Bondsman: John Fooshee, m. by: Absolem Fooshee, J. P., November 4,
1841, MEIGS Co.

BRACKET, William to (Miss) Eliza J. Gilbreath - issued October 21,
1845, Bondsman: Samuel O. Wood, m. by: John Seabourn, J. P.,
October 22, 1845, MEIGS Co.

BRACKIN, William to Penelope Searcy - issued November 20, 1805,
Bondsman: Howard Douglass, SUMNER Co.

BRACKINS, Alfred to Margaret McCoy - issued January 2, 1841, Bondsman: James Johnston, m. by: Wm. Green, M. G., January 3, 1841, MEIGS Co.

BRACKMAN, Herman K. to Mary Cathanne - issued July 29, 1847, m. by: J. Schacht July 30, 1847, DAVIDSON Co.

BRACKWELL, Nowell to Penelope A. C. Brown - issued March 8, 1842, m. by: William Herrin March 9, 1842, DAVIDSON Co.

BRACY, Benj. P. to N. A. Alsbrook - issued July 18, 1846, m. by: A. Justice, J. P., July 19, 1846, ROBERTSON Co.

BRACY, John W. to Nancy Wooton - m. by: Wm. C. Bransford, M. G., November 14, 1835, SUMNER Co.

BRACY, Saml. H. to Mary E. Marlon - issued August 21, 1846, m. by: N. H. Ryan, J. P., ROBERTSON Co.

BRACY, Thomas W. to Martha P. Alsbrook - issued February 25, 1842, m. by: A. Justin, J. P., February 27, 1842, ROBERTSON Co.

BRACY, W. L. to Elizabeth J. Felts - issued September 27, 1856, m. by: George W. Martin, M. G., ROBERTSON Co.

BRADBERRY, Charles to Nancy Fields - issued October 24, 1824, Bondsman: Henry Robertson, WILSON Co.

BRADBERRY, George to Sarah Oneal - issued January 17, 1846, Bondsman: Edwd, S. Walton, m. by: R. W. Nixon, G. M., January 18, 1846, MONTGOMERY Co.

BRADBERRY, James to Elizabeth Golston - issued August 14, 1816, Bondsman: Elisha Cole, m. by: Abner Hill August 16, 1816, WILSON Co.

BRADBERRY, James C. to Charlotte Organ - issued March 1, 1824, Bondsman: Ewing Wilson, WILSON Co.

BRADBERRY, John to Barshaba Golston - issued November 2, 1817, Bondsman: Thomas Arrington, m. by: Abner Hill, M. G., WILSON Co.

BRADBERRY, Joshua to Susan Brinson - issued April 26, 1821, Bondsman: Joseph Bradley, m. by: Thomas S. Green, J. P., April 10, 1821, WILSON Co.

BRADBERRY, M. A. to Sarah Graves - issued June 10, 1866, FRANKLIN Co.

BRADBERRY, Michael to Dice Merriman - issued March 23, 1822, m. by: Wm. Morris, J. P., March 26, 1822, KNOX Co.

BRADBURY, R. S. to Elizabeth Ford - issued December 23, 1846, Bondsman: Jorden Niblett, m. by: W. B. Carney, J. P., December 24, 1846, MONTGOMERY Co.

BRADDOCK, John to Nelly Leonard - issued February 9, 1807, Bondsman: Richardson Bery, WILSON Co.

BRADDOCK, Rolla Smith to Eliza Beard - issued March 14, 1838, m. by: Daniel Judd, L. E., March 15, 1838, DAVIDSON Co.

BRADDY, Benjamin to Charlotte Farriss - issued September 30, 1822, m. by: Jacob Payne, J. P., September 30, 1822, RUTHERFORD Co.

BRADEN, Catherine to Harvey Puckett - WILLIAMSON Co.

BRADEN, James to Betsey M. Merrett - issued April 12, 1817, Bondsman: Alexander Braden, m. by: James Foster, J. P., April 17, 1817, WILSON Co.

BRADEN, Jesse to Lila Vickers - issued August 28, 1818, m. by: T. A. Ramsey, J. P. K. C., August 31, 1818, KNOX Co.

BRADEN, Wm. to Julia Ann McHaffie - issued September 20, 1830, Bondsman:
David McHaffie, m. by: E. Nelson, J. P., September 23, 1830,
KNOX Co.

BRADFORD, A. W. to Celia M. Bradford - issued August 31, 1857,
FRANKLIN Co.

BRADFORD, A. W. to C. M. Bradford - issued August 31, 1859, FRANKLIN Co.

BRADFORD, Alexander B. to Darthula Q. Miller - issued September 10,
1824, m. by: Tho. H. Nelson September 16, 1824, KNOX Co.

BRADFORD, Alford to Cathrine Robertson - issued May 15, 1850, FRANKLIN Co.

BRADFORD, Anthony to Susan Guin - issued July 15, 1850, m. by:
M. Catchings, J. P., July 15, 1850, FRANKLIN Co-

BRADFORD, Arther to Martha Gifford - issued May 1, 1853, m. by:
F. B. Wade, J. P., May 1, 1853, FRANKLIN Co.

BRADFORD, Elijah to Sarah Robinson - issued September 12, 1844, m. by:
Benjamin Sells, J. P., September 15, 1844, FRANKLIN Co.

BRADFORD, Ephraim to Sarah Craig - issued December 4, 1860, m. by:
L. P. Myrick, J. P., December 4, 1860, FRANKLIN Co.

BRADFORD, J. R. to Nancy J. Clark - issued August 24, 1860, m. by:
L. P. Myrick, J. P., August 26, 1860, FRANKLIN Co.

BRADFORD, Jessee to Mariah Harington - issued May 6, 1858, FRANKLIN Co.

BRADFORD, John to Susannah Story - issued January 21, 1800, Bondsman:
John Russell, Witness: Sm'l Yancey, GRAINGER Co.

BRADFORD, John to Louisa M. Wilson - issued March 2, 1850, FRANKLIN Co.

BRADFORD, Larkin to Narcissa Foot - issued November 24, 1856, m. by:
G. R. Gunn, J. P., November 25, 1856, ROBERTSON Co.

BRADFORD, Obediah to Sarah Jane Arnold - issued July 11, 1873, m. by:
Meredith Carter July 13, 1873, FRANKLIN Co.

BRADFORD, Thomas to Isbel Miller - issued September 21, 1843, m. by:
Samuel Taylor, J. P., September 24, 1843, FRANKLIN Co.

BRADFORD, S. to E. V. Demoss - issued January 6, 1840, m. by:
J. T. Edgar January 7, 1840, DAVIDSON Co.

BRADFORD, William to Nancy Boyles - issued March 26, 1812, Bondsman:
Levi D. Ellis, SUMNER Co.

BRADFORD, William M. to Susan F. Henderson - issued February 16, 1848,
m. by: Rev. A. J. Steel, FRANKLIN Co.

BRADFORD, Z. J. to Mary Harris - issued August 17, 1854, m. by:
A. I. Brights, J. O., August 20, 1854, ROBERTSON Co.

BRADLEY, Abram to Zelpha Dorris - issued June 27, 1818, Bondsman:
David Bradley, m. by: John Gilbert, J. P., June 27, 1818, SUMNER Co.

BRADLEY, Achilles to Nancy Dowell - issued June 3, 1819, Bondsman:
John Bradley, m. by: John Bayless, J. P. K. C., June 3, 1819,
KNOX Co.

BRADLEY, Albert to Emily Devault - issued January 7, 1834, Bondsman:
Hamilton Snead, WILSON Co.

BRADLEY, B. H. to Nancy C. Coleman - issued November 20, 1861, m. by:
G. W. Martin, M. G., ROBERTSON Co.

BRADLEY, Benj. W. to Harriet Williams - issued January 31, 1840,
m. by: J. W. Hunt, J. P., February 14, 1840, ROBERTSON Co.

BRADLEY, Charles to Polly Bradley - issued November 28, 1825, Bondsman:
William Jenkins, WILSON Co.

BRADLEY, Charles to Agnis Calhoun - issued August 13, 1831, Bondsman:
Wm. Martin, WILSON Co.

BRADLEY, Charles to Rebecca Bobbitt - issued July 30, 1847, m. by:
J. W. Hunt, J. P., August 10, 1847, ROBERTSON Co.

BRADLEY, David to Nancy Taylor - issued August 29, 1803, Bondsman:
John Taylor, SUMNER Co.

BRADLEY, David to Rebecah Granger - issued October 18, 1806, Bondsman:
John Taylor, SUMNER Co.

BRADLEY, David to Lucy Kirkum - issued January 12, 1818, Bondsman:
Joshua Bradley, m. January 12, 1818, SUMNER Co.

BRADLEY, David to Jinny Allen - issued March 29, 1822, Bondsman:
Wm. H. Douglas, SUMNER Co.

BRADLEY, David C. to Abigail Calhoun - issued August 10, 1837, Bondsman:
Thomas G. Sanders, WILSON Co.

BRADLEY, Edmond S. to Mary B. Donoho - issued December 4, 1833,
Bondsman: Burson Harris, m. by: Jesse Alexander, V. D. M.,
December 11, 1833, RUTHERFORD Co.

BRADLEY, Elijah to Emily Munday - issued August 16, 1828, m. by:
Robt. Tindell, J. P., August 16, 1828, KNOX Co.

BRADLEY, Elijah to Mahala McCormack - issued April 30, 1834, m. by:
Jesse Gambling, J. P., April 30, 1834, SUMNER Co.

BRADLEY, Evret to Anna Bundy - issued May 17, 1834, Bondsman:
James Hankins, m. by: John Borum May 20, 1834, WILSON Co.

BRADLEY, George to Polly Oxford - May 28, 1807, WILLIAMSON Co.

BRADLEY, George W. to D. P. Wisdom - Bondsman: T. M. Wisdom, MONTGOMERY Co.

BRADLEY, Henry to Nancy Kerley - issued May 8, 1811, Bondsman: Wm. Hall,
SUMNER Co.

BRADLEY, Henry to Mary J. House - issued February 4, 1863, Bondsman:
W. W. Gillispie, m. by: J. B. Clayton, J. P., February 5, 1863,
LAWRENCE Co.

BRADLEY, Hezekiah to Mary Dejernatt - issued May 10, 1837, Bondsman:
William Holland, m. by: John Borum May 12, 1837, WILSON Co.

BRADLEY, Hugh to Patsey Hunter - issued August 10, 1812, Bondsman:
James Bradley, WILSON Co.

BRADLEY, Irvin to Caroline Jones - issued May 26, 1845, m. by:
S. Mizell, J. P., May 27, 1845, STEWART Co.

BRADLEY, Isom to Susannah Mattucks - May 13, 1798, BLOUNT Co.

BRADLEY, J. J. to E. Holmes - issued September 5, 1846, m. by:
J. W. Hunt, J. P., September 7, 1848, ROBERTSON Co.

BRADLEY, J. J. to E. F. Justice - issued February 5, 1849, m. by:
J. W. Hunt, J. P., February 6, 1849, ROBERTSON Co.

BRADLEY, J. W. to T. G. Cardwell - m. by: C. G. Browning May 22, 1837,
SUMNER Co.

BRADLEY, James to Susan H. Davis - issued October 8, 1829, Bondsman:
Solomon Davis, m. by: Wm. Smith, J. P., October 8, 1829, SUMNER Co.

BRADLEY, James to Jane Bradly - issued October 2, 1839, Bondsman:
Harrison Doughty, m. by: Jonathan Bailye, J. P., November 11,
1839, WILSON Co.

BRADLEY, James to Elizabeth White - issued November 6, 1839, Bondsman:
D. G. Hankins, m. by: Sion Bass, M. G., WILSON Co.

BRADLEY, James B. to Catharine McAden - issued February 5, 1828,
Bondsman: Henry Strange, SUMNER Co.

BRADLEY, James R. to Mary E. Liles - issued March 29, 1864, Bondsman:
John A. Bradley, m. by: C. B. Porter, G. M., March 31, 1864,
LAWRENCE Co.

BRADLEY, Jesse to Lucinda Trible - issued January 17, 1816, Bondsman:
Stephen Trible, m. by: James Gwin, M. G., January 17, 1816,
SUMNER Co.

BRADLEY, Jesse to Mary Kirby - m. by: William Woodall November 19,
1837, SUMNER Co.

BRADLEY, John to Elizabeth Goostree - issued January 17, 1816, Bondsman:
Stephen Trible, m. by: James Gwin, M. G., January 17, 1816,
SUMNER Co.

BRADLEY, Jno. to Polley Gray - issued November 6, 1816, Bondsman:
Willie Turner, m. by: William Gray, J. P., November 7, 1816,
WILSON Co.

BRADLEY, John to Melinda Dowel - issued February 17, 1818, Bondsman:
Elijah Dowel, m. by: John Bayless, J. P. K. C., February 24, 1818,
KNOX Co.

BRADLEY, John to May Humbard - issued June 16, 1827, Bondsman:
William Humbard, m. by: Robert Gaines, J. P., June 16, 1827,
GRAINGER Co.

BRADLEY, John to Hannah Churchman - issued September 9, 1829, Bondsman:
Pierce Bradshaw, m. by: G. B. Mitchell, J. P., GRAINGER Co.

BRADLEY, John D. to Patsey Trice - issued May 22, 1810, Bondsman:
Wm. H. Douglass, SUMNER Co.

BRADLEY(?), John G. to E. C. Felts - issued September 4, 1849, m. by:
A. B. Sayor September 6, 1849, ROBERTSON Co.

BRADLEY, Joseph to Nancy Haney - issued September 1, 1842, STEWART Co.

BRADLEY, Joshua to Jane Hall - issued May 26, 1812, Bondsman:
John Bradley, SUMNER Co.

BRADLEY, Joshua to Elizabeth Kirkham - issued August 4, 1830, Bondsman:
David Bradley, m. by: Sam'l Cochran, J. P., August 4, 1830,
SUMNER Co.

BRADLEY, Luke to Agatha Woodall - issued January 20, 1816, Bondsman:
Jonathan Woodall, m. by: Edward Gwin, J. P., January 20, 1816,
SUMNER Co.

BRADLEY, Luke to Sally Brigance - issued December 8, 1824, m. by:
Sm. C. Cochran, J. P., December 8, 1824, SUMNER Co.

BRADLEY, Moses to Nancy Brown - issued April 2, 1853, m. by:
G. W. Bowling, J. P., April 4, 1853, FRANKLIN Co.

BRADLEY, Moten to Martha Ann Tucker - November 3, 1860, m. by:
H. P. Stanley, J. P., GILES Co.

BRADLEY, Nathan to Ally Boren - m. by: J. Hobdy, J. P., March 11,
1835, SUMNER Co.

BRADLEY, Philander D. to Margaret E. Wright - issued March 22, 1856,
m. by: R. H. Harrison, J. P., March 24, 1856, ROBERTSON Co.

BRADLEY, Reuben to Susan Woodall - m. by: Henry K. Winbourn January 20,
1834, SUMNER Co.

BRADLEY, Richard to Sally Martin - issued March 31, 1812, Bondsman:
Jonathan Spooner, SUMNER Co.

BRADLEY, Robert to Nancy Bradley - issued January 5, 1818, Bondsman:
Sam'l Mading, SUMNER Co.

BRADLEY, Robert to Lurany Osbourn - issued January 7, 1826, Bondsman:
John Graves, SUMNER Co.

BRADLEY, Samuel to Nancy G. Cardwell - issued March 18, 1811, Bondsman:
Benjamin Clary, SUMNER Co.

BRADLEY, Thomas to Edith West - issued November 6, 1811, Bondsman:
John West, SUMNER Co.

BRADLEY, Thomas to Betsey Ritter - issued October 29, 1816, Bondsman:
Thos. Scurry, SUMNER Co.

BRADLEY, Thomas to Catharine Caplinger - issued March 10, 1821,
Bondsman: William Robinson, m. by: Wm. Steele March 11, 1821,
WILSON Co.

BRADLEY, Thomas to Susan Harpole - issued March 7, 1829, Bondsman:
James McDaniel, WILSON Co.

BRADLEY, Walter L. to Margarett E. Sanford - issued January 7, 1852,
Bondsman: Joseph Linebaugh, m. by: Mark Senter, M. G., January 7,
1852, MONTGOMERY Co.

BRADLEY, Wm. to Mary Murphy - June 24, 1799, Surety: Thos. Murphy,
BLOUNT Co.

BRADLEY, William to Polly Clampet - October 20, 1802, Security:
Elijah Clampet, BLOUNT Co.

BRADLEY, William to Sally Stalcup - issued June 19, 1812, Bondsman:
John Taylor, SUMNER Co.

BRADLEY, William to Sally Goff - issued January 24, 1825, Bondsman:
David Bradley, SUMNER Co.

BRADLEY, William to Sarah Perrin - issued August 18, 1830, Bondsman:
Archy Smith, m. by: G. B. Mitchell, J. P., GRAINGER Co.

BRADLEY, Willie to Betsy Dowell - issued December 6, 1825, Bondsman:
Achilles Bradley, m. by: Wm. B. Carns, J. P., December 8, 1825,
KNOX Co.

BRADLY, Augustian to Rachel Hazlewood - issued January 24, 1837, m. by:
T. G. Craighead, J. P., January 29, 1837, KNOX Co.

BRADLY, Daniel to Lydia Chasteen - issued December 23, 1839, Bondsman:
Joseph Jenkins, m. by: Solomon Caplinger, J. P., December 24,
1839, WILSON Co.

BRADLY, Isaac to Catherine Gough - issued August 20, 1825, Bondsman:
Robt. Bradley, SUMNER Co.

BRADLY, Jubilee to Nancy Gains (or Goin) - issued April 10, 1837, m. by:
Jas. D. Murray, J. P., April 13, 1837, KNOX Co.

BRADLY, Levy to Nancy Green - issued December 22, 1841, Bondsman:
J. L. Green, m. by: A. Fooshee, J. P., December 23, 1841, MEIGS Co.

BRADSHAW, A. C. to Elizabeth Harvey - issued May 16, 1863, Bondsman:
James A. Hodge, BEDFORD Co.

BRADSHAW, David to Terrissa Carson - issued December 23, 1816, Bondsman:
Alexander C. Caruth, m. by: Abner Caruth, J. P., December 29,
1816, WILSON Co.

BRADSHAW, Ishmel to Levicy McWhirter - issued July 20, 1819, Bondsman:
Thomas Mitchell, m. by: Jos. T. Williams, J. P., July 21, 1819,
WILSON Co.

BRADSHAW, Iva to Eliza E. Russell - issued December 31, 1860, m. by:
James Seargent, J. P., January 1, 1861, FRANKLIN Co.

BRADSHAW, James to Mary Ann Ford - issued December 20, 1847, Bondsman:
Henry Jones, m. by: John Gold, J. P., December 20, 1847,
MONTGOMERY Co.

BRADSHAW, James G. to Ann Slagle - issued September 12, 1862, Bondsman:
Edmund Winters, m. by: P. L. Simms September 14, 1862, LAWRENCE Co.

BRADSHAW, Jane to Thomas Rankin - February 21, 1789, Security:
William Rankin, GREENE Co.

BRADSHAW, Joel to Mary Coffee - issued September 24, 1833, Bondsman:
Thos. Clevenger, GRAINGER Co.

BRADSHAW, John to Oney Henry - issued September 4, 1804, Bondsman:
Hugh Henry, SUMNER Co.

BRADSHAW, John to Mary Jane Hickey - issued May 28, 1840, m. by:
J. Thos. Wheat, Rec. of Cr. Ch., DAVIDSON Co.

BRADSHAW, R. H. to Susan Barker - issued February 20, 1860, m. by:
M. W. Winters, J. P., ROBERTSON Co.

BRADSHAW, Samuel to Mary Jane Jeter - issued June 30, 1852, Bondsman:
Robert Jeter, m. by: J. C. Bryan, J. P., June 30, 1852, MONTGOMERY Co.

BRADSHAW, Thomas to Martha Thompkins - issued August 31, 1831, Bondsman:
William Pitner, WILSON Co.

BRADSHAW, William to Betsey Erspy - issued November 11, 1800, Bondsman:
John Hodge, SUMNER Co.

BRADSHAW, William to Betsey Stubblefield - issued August 19, 1803,
Bondsman: Daniel Trigg, SUMNER Co.

BRADSHAW, Wilson to Polly Spickard - issued March 2, 1824, Bondsman:
Sion Duke, WILSON Co.

BRADSHAW, Wilson to Nancy D. Mitchell - issued May 2, 1829, Bondsman:
Thomas Mitchell, m. by: E. P. Horn, J. P., WILSON Co.

BRADY (or Bradley), Absolum to Polly Mayberry - issued April 12, 1836,
Bondsman: Randal Mayberry, m. by: J. Hobday April 12, 1836,
SUMNER Co.

BRADY, Frederick to Betsey Hooker - issued March 10, 1818, m. by:
George Uselton, J. P., March 15, 1818, RUTHERFORD Co.

BRADY, John to Polly Chamberlin - March 14, 1805, WILLIAMSOM Co.

BRADY, John A. to Bedory F. Brittle - issued July 5, 1843, m. by:
R. Eskew July 6, 1843, DAVIDSON Co.

BRADY, William to Harriette Keeble - issued November 20, 1819, m. by:
Robert Henderson November 20, 1819, RUTHERFORD Co.

BRAGG, Benj. to Mary J. Langston - issued January 16, 1858, m. by:
J. W. Bell, J. P., January 17, 1858, FRANKLIN Co.

BRAGG, Calvin to Elizabeth J. McBride - issued August 31, 1857, m. by:
Samuel Umbarger, J. P., September 1, 1857, COFFEE Co.

BRAGG, J. C. to E. Spradlen - issued June 29, 1853, m. by: David
Simpson, J. P., July 3, 1853, COFFEE Co.

BRAGG, J. W. to Mollie J. West - issued November 30, 1871, FRANKLIN Co.

BRAGG, James to Cinda Clench - issued July 24, 1832, m. by:
John Latham, J. P., GRAINGER Co.

BRAGG, Nathan to Martha Marlow - issued May 22, 1841, STEWART Co.

BRAGG, Richard to Debby Jones - issued July 24, 1816, Bondsman:
William Morrison, m. by: James G. Harris, J. P., July 25, 1816,
GRAINGER Co.

BRAGG, Thomas to Catherine Cherry - issued February 10, 1818, m. by:
Gideon Rucker, M. B. C., February 12, 1818, RUTHERFORD Co.

BRAGG, Thos. to Martha Mann - issued January 28, 1844, m. by:
R. Cooley, J. P., January 28, 1844, STEWART Co.

BRAIN, Joseph to Ann Brown - issued May 26, 1846, m. by:
Thos. W. Ruffin, J. P., ROBERTSON Co.

BRAKE, Henry to Nancy Fowler - issued December 26, 1843, m. by:
William Ellis, J. P., December 28, 1843, STEWART Co.

BRAKE, James to Manda Doyal - issued December 5, 1840, m. by:
D. R. Harris, G. M., ROBERTSON Co.

BRAKE, Randle to Catherine Brake - issued December 30, 1845, m. by:
Wm. Ellis, J. P., January 1, 1845, STEWART Co.

BRAKEFIELD, B. to A. Aleom - issued February 25, 1850, m. by:
G. B. Mason, ROBERTSON Co.

BRAKEFIELD, Byram to Ann Benton - issued May 7, 1841, m. by:
Tho. E. T. McMurry, J. P., ROBERTSON Co.

BRAKEFIELD, J. N. to Darcus Russell - issued September 27, 1847, m. by:
Allen Gilliam, P. G., September 27, 1847, FRANKLIN Co.

BRAKEFIELD, James to Susan Harris - issued January 11, 1851, m. by:
G. B. Mason, J. P., ROBERTSON Co.

BRAKEFIELD, Jesse to Elizabeth Brakefield - issued June 7, 1845, m. by:
R. B. Rose, J. P., June 8, 1845, ROBERTSON Co.

BRAKEFIELD, W. to A. Alcorn - issued February 25, 1850, m. by:
G. B. Mason, J. P., ROBERTSON Co.

BRAKEFIELD, W. T. to Isabel Mattenbee - issued December 2, 1859,
FRANKLIN Co.

BRAKEFIELD, W. W. to R. E. West - issued July 13, 1872, m. by:
R. F. Oakley, J. P., July 14, 1872, FRANKLIN Co.

BRAKEFIELD, Wm. to Elizabeth Vance - issued February 27, 1840, m. by:
U. Young, J. P., ROBERTSON Co.

BRAKEFIELD, Willis S. to Sarah B. Adams - issued January 14, 1852,
m. by: Thos. Finch, J. P., January 14, 1852, FRANKLIN Co.

BRAKEFIELD, Joseph to Mary K. Chapman - issued December 31, 1855,
m. by: John W. Smith, J. P., January 1, 1856, ROBERTSON Co.

BRALEY, James to Martha Marten - issued November 12, 1353, m. by:
A. D. Parks, M., November 13, 1853, COFFEE Co.

BRALEY, Samuel to Peggy McSpadden - issued December 20, 1815, Bondsman:
Samuel McSpadden, m. by: Thos. Calhoon, M. G., December 21, 1815,
WILSON Co.

BRALEY, Walter to Lottie Ann Farris - issued April 3, 1851, m. by:
Wm. G. Guinn April 4, 1851, FRANKLIN Co.

BRAMLETT, Franklin M. to Penelope May - October 7, 1852, m. by:
G. D. Taylor, GILES Co.

BRAMLETT, H. A. to M. Pless - issued February 10, 1870, FRANKLIN Co.

BRAMLETT, Lonsford M. to Sarah Slater - June 29, 1815, WILLIAMSON Co.

BRAMLEY, James to Teressa Parnell - issued September 22, 1847, m. by:
C. L. Blanton, J. P., September 23, 1847, FRANKLIN Co.

BRANCH, Andrew J. to Abigail Payne - issued September 14, 1835,
Bondsman: R. C. Branch, WILSON Co.

BRANCH, Benjamin to Sarah Moore - issued January 25, 1823, Bondsman:
George Brison, m. by: Robert Williams, M. G., January 30, 1823,
WILSON Co.

BRANCH, D. G. to Leah Hardy - issued February 3, 1866, FRANKLIN Co.

BRANCH, James H. to Eleanor D. Neal - issued February 12, 1840, Bondsman:
George Neal, m. by: James Young, J. P., February 19, 1840, WILSON Co.

BRANCH, John P. to Josephine J. Woods - issued November 18, 1841,
m. by: Robt. A. Lapsley November 18, 1341, DAVIDSON Co.

BRANCH, K. to Margaret Casey - issued October 20, 1847, m. by:
Edm'd Slater, M. G., October 20, 1847, DAVIDSON Co.

BRANCH, Robert C. to Sarah Neal - issued September 4, 1835, Bondsman:
G. W. Clark, m. by: Wm. Lawrence, J. P., September 9, 1835,
WILSON Co.

BRANCH, Thomas to Jane Moon - issued October 13, 1827, Bondsman:
George Neal, WILSON Co.

BRANCH, Thos. to Mary Henderson - issued September 28, 1835, Bondsman:
Wm. D. Moore, Witness: Geo. M. White, KNOX Co.

BRANCH, W. A. to Louisa Jane Sisk - issued July 13, 1840, m. by:
John Baker, J. P., July, 1840, FRANKLIN Co.

BRANCH, W. A. to Anna J. Ivey - issued June 1, 1872, FRANKLIN Co.

BRAND, T. T. to Catherine Wolf - issued September 10, 1845, m. by:
Benj. Sharpe, J. P., September 11, 1845, DAVIDSON Co.

BRANDON, B. B. to Rachiel Ables - issued May 27, 1861, m. by:
E. P. Anderson, P. G., May 28, 1861, FRANKLIN Co.

BRANDON, Cornelius to ___(?) - issued January 25, 1805, Bondsman:
Joseph Tennison, RUTHERFORD Co.

BRANDON, George to Jane Gillespie - issued March 22, 1815, KNOX Co.

BRANDON, George to Jane Tilford - issued September 16, 1823, Bondsman: Thomas Smoot, RUTHERFORD Co.

BRANDON, George to Susan Broom - issued May 11, 1843, m. by: W. L. Gowen, M. G., May 16, 1843, STEWART Co.

BRANDON, James to Rebecca Craft - issued January 3, 1825, m. by: Cullin Curlee, J. P., January 13, 1825, RUTHERFORD Co.

BRANDON, James to Mary J. Franks - issued September 28, 1865, Bondsman: John S. Gaither, m. by: William Gilmore, M. G., September 28, 1865, LAWRENCE Co.

BRANDON, John L. to Elizabeth Bean - issued October 19, 1874, FRANKLIN Co.

BRANDON , John W. to Eliza Jane Rich - issued April 10, 1841, m. by: C. A. Hunt, J. P., April 11, 1841, FRANKLIN Co.

BRANDON, Mary to John Lea - GREENE Co.

BRANDON, Nathan to Sarah Ann Scarborough - issued October 15, 1842, m. by: Rev. Jas. T. Morris, STEWART Co.

BRANDON, William to Jane Cooper - m. by: John Wiseman December 14, 1837, SUMNER Co.

BRANDON, Wm. B. to Nancy C. Parks - issued September 25, 1855, m. by: B. M. Haggard, M. G., September 26, 1855, FRANKLIN Co.

BRANDSFORD, Wesley to Chrissie Thomas - issued December 5, 1860, m. by: A. P. McFerrin, Minister, December 6, 1860, ROBERTSON Co.

BRANHAM, Aaron to Betsy Franklin - issued January 22, 1824, Bondsman: James Murphy, KNOX Co.

BRANHAM, Albert G. to Elizabeth S. Furguson - issued March 1, 1848, Bondsman: John D. Furguson, m. by: R. F. Furguson March 2, 1848, MONTGOMERY Co.

BRANHAM, John to Marian Parker - issued May 10, 1820, Bondsman: Pascal Head and Wm. Hall, m. by: John Wiseman May 10, 1820, SUMNER Co.

BRANHAM, Lea to Durino Lingo - issued December 22, 1836, Bondsman: Yearly Thompson, KNOX Co.

BRANHAM, Randal to Susan Horsly - issued April 30, 1832, Bondsman: David Dickinson, m. by: Austin Johnson April 30, 1832, SUMNER Co.

BRANKLEY, Wilson to Elizabeth Walker - issued April 9, 1844, m. by: R. Pennington, J. P., April 11, 1844, ROBERTSON Co.

BRANNON, Albert to Martha Partin - issued March 19, 1846, m. by: Allen Gipson, J. P., March 19, 1846, FRANKLIN Co.

BRANNON, Geo. W. to Mary A. Lee - issued February 11, 1856, m. by: Lewis Anderson, J. P., February 15, 1856, FRANKLIN Co.

BRANNON, James C. to Martha Jane Nichols - issued August 8, 1846, m. by: J. M. Mitchell, M. G., August 14, 1846, FRANKLIN Co.

BRANNON, John M. to Mary A. Rogers - issued October 7, 1839, m. by: Joseph Smith October 8, 1839, FRANKLIN Co.

BRANNON, Joseph to Elizabeth Lomax - issued July 9, 1828, Bondsman: Thos. Jourdan, m. by: S. R. Robus, J. P., July 9, 1828, SUMNER Co.

BRANNON, Robert to Elizabeth Swann - issued August 11, 1852, m. by: John Nugent, J. P., August 12, 1852, FRANKLIN Co.

BRANNON, William to Susan Ring - issued July 25, 1832, Bondsman:
John Kindree, m. by: Thos. P. Holman, J. P., WILSON Co.

BRANNON, William B. to Mary Ann Chapman - issued May 29, 1846, m. by:
John J. Travis, J. P., May 29, 1846, FRANKLIN Co.

BRANNON, Williamson to C. Cherry - issued February 26, 1840, FRANKLIN Co.

BRANNUM, Beaverage to Sally Brannum - issued November 7, 1804, Witness:
Sm'l Yancey, J. P., GRAINGER Co.

BRANNUM, James to Sally Brannum - issued November 7, 1804, Bondsman:
Beverage Brannum, GRAINGER Co.

BRANON, John to Donah Scott - September 17, 1800, KNOX Co.

BRANSFORD, L. M. to Helen Anderson - issued January 1, 1847, m. by:
Jonah Ferriss, J. P., January 1, 1847, DAVIDSON Co.

BRANSON, Benjamin to Ann Acuff - issued January 11, 1836, Bondsman:
Simeon Acuff, m. by: Joseph Clark, J. P., GRAINGER Co.

BRANSON, David to Hannah Jackson - December 2, 1799, Security:
James Penny and Robert Branson, GREENE Co.

BRANSON, David to Susannah Bolton - issued September 22, 1806, Bondsman:
Abraham Prewitt, m. by: Sam. D. Carrick, J. P., GRAINGER Co.

BRANSON, James to Flora Watson - issued July 18, 1835, Bondsman:
Benjamin Branson, m. by: J. Kennon, M. G., GRAINGER Co.

BRANSON, John to Martha Watson - issued January 16, 1837, Bondsman:
Stokley Vititoe, m. by: John Robertson, J. P., January 16, 1837,
GRAINGER Co.

BRANSON, Johnathan to Elizabeth Hammack - issued May 10, 1807, Bondsman:
Thomas Bolton, GRAINGER Co.

BRANSON, Nathaniel to Mary Dalton - issued January 14, 1812, Bondsman:
Charlton Dyer, GRAINGER Co.

BRANSON, Semuel to June Watson - issued May 20, 1806, Bondsman:
Abraham Brunt, GRAINGER Co.

BRANSON, Withbaler to Jane Hardison - issued January 1, 1843, m. by:
D. G. Baird, J. P., ROBERTSON Co.

BRANTLEY, Charles to Dicy Anderson - issued November 24, 1790, Bondsman:
Robert Jones, SUMNER Co.

BRANTLEY, Phinebas to Rachel Graham - issued March 28, 1828, m. by:
E. R. Davis, J. P., March 28, 1828, KNOX Co.

BRANTLEY, Samuel F. to Bettie King - issued March 4, 1861, Bondsman:
A. G. Moore, Jos. H. Thompson, Clk. by N. F. Thompson, Dep. Clk.,
m. by: I. J. Patton, M. G., March 5, 1861, BEDFORD Co.

BRANTLEY, William to Mourning Morris - issued October 29, 1817, Bondsman:
William Harris, m. by: S. W. Blythe October 29, 1817, SUMNER Co.

BRASELTON, Jacob to Rachel Armstrong - February 2, 1795, Security:
John Haworth, GREENE Co.

BRASFIELD, Elizabeth to J. T. Newcomer - issued January 10, 1864,
Bondsman: Geo. F. Blakemore, Jos. H. Thompson, Clk., BEDFORD Co.

BRASHEARS, Isaac W. to Sally Trott - issued February 12, 1833, Bondsman:
Z. W. Bivins, RUTHERFORD Co.

BRASHEARS, Nathan to Lucinda Pearson - issued January 21, 1833, Bondsman: Robt. Sanders, m. by: Jordan Willeford, J. P., January 21, 1833, RUTHERFORD Co.

BRASHEARS, Robert to Salina E. Kelly - issued January 20, 1864, Bondsman: James P. Tays, LAWRENCE Co.

BRASHIERS, Isaac to Elizabeth Wilson - issued October 6, 1818, m. by: R. Cole, J. P. K. C., KNOX Co.

BRASIER, Isaac to Pricilla Travathan - issued January 2, 1845, m. by: David Herring, J. P., ROBERTSON Co.

BRASSELL, Benjamin to Rebecca Hall - issued August 11, 1824, Bondsman: William Winham, m. by: James Douglass August 11, 1824, SUMNER Co.

BRASSELL, H. T. to Louisa Evans - m. by: L. B. Evans September 5, 1836, SUMNER Co.

BRASSFIELD, Sue E. to Frank Lacy - issued June 10, 1862, Bondsman: A. McCroy, Test. M. E. W. Dunaway, Jos. H. Thompson, Clk. per M. E. W. Dunaway, Dep. Clk., BEDFORD Co.

BRASSFIELD, Thomas to Mary Davis - December 25, 1796, KNOX Co.

BRASWELL, Vincent to Lucinda A. Sick - issued August 5, 1850, m. by: J. W. Featherston, M. G., ROBERTSON Co.

BRASWELL, Wm. to N. N. Mason - issued November 27, 1851, m. by: G. B. Mason, J. P., ROBERTSON Co.

BRASWELL, Wm. F. to Malissa Eddings - issued December 27, 1830, Bondsman: J. S. Lester, WILSON Co.

BRATCHER, Farrell H. to Anna Eliza Newgent - issued December 11, 1847, m. by: R. B. C. Howell, M. G., December 12, 1847, DAVIDSON Co.

BRATON, Green I. to Naomi E. Cox - issued March 20, 1863, Bondsman: Benj. Pollock, Jos. H. Thompson, Clk., BEDFORD Co.

BRATTEN, Robt. to Matilda Jones Hulme - December 9, 1816, WILLIAMSON Co.

BRATTON, J. R. to Lennie E. Harriford - issued November 29, 1870, m. by: D. S. Long, J. P., December 1, 1870, FRANKLIN Co.

BRATTON, James to Betsy Wilson - issued December 14, 1805, Bondsman: James Wilson, SUMNER Co.

BRATTON, James M. to Charlotte T. Knight - issued August 29, 1860, m. by: Wm. W. Conn, M. G., August 30, 1860, FRANKLIN Co.

BRATTON, Joseph M. to Sarah Bennett - issued January 5, 1849, m. by: B. B. Knight, J. P., January 5, 1849, FRANKLIN Co.

BRATTON, Joseph N. to N. A. Borem (Boren) - issued January 18, 1845, m. by: D. N. Brakefield, J. P., January 22, 1845, FRANKLIN Co.

BRAWLEY, Hugh to Jemima Todd - issued August 17, 1821, m. by: Cullin Curlee, J. P., August 17, 1821, RUTHERFORD Co.

BRAWLEY, Leeroy to Sally McSpedden - issued March 14, 1810, Bondsman: Jno. McSpedden, WILSON Co.

BRAWLEY, Levi to Polly Glascocke - issued November 19, 1813, Bondsman: David Patton, RUTHERFORD Co.

BRAWLY, Sarah C. to J. M. Ledbetter - issued November 6, 1863, Bondsman: John Barkeen, Jos. H. Thompson, Clk., BEDFORD Co.

BRAY, Benjamin to Catharine Ogan - issued April 3, 1827, Bondsman:
    Joseph C. Bunch, m. by: J. C. Bunch, J. P., April 3, 1827,
    GRAINGER Co.

BRAY, Hagner to Sally Waters - issued August 12, 1814, Bondsman:
    Henry Bray, GRAINGER Co.

BRAY, Hugh to Elizabeth Hawry - May 23, 1798, KNOX Co.

BRAY, James to Rachel Smith - issued July 29, 1797, Bondsman:
    John Roberson, Witness: Peggy McClung, KNOX Co.

BRAY, James to Mary Martin - issued February 5, 1818, m. by:
    T. H. Nelson February 5, 1818, KNOX Co.

BRAY, James to Mary Lovin - m. October 4, 1834, SUMNER Co.

BRAY, John B. to Rebecca Hogan - November 29, 1860, m. by: W. T. Ussery,
    GILES Co.

BRAY, Joseph to Elizabeth Harvey - issued May 20, 1798, Bondsman:
    Jeremiah Leakey, Witness: Joseph Greer, KNOX Co.

BRAY, Samuel to Mary Langford - issued January 3, 1840, m. by:
    Lewis Adams, M. G., January 4, 1840, ROBERTSON Co.

BRAZELL, James to Matilda Liles - issued February 7, 1866, Bondsman:
    Larkin L. Liles. m. by: R. L. McLaren, J. P., February 8, 1866,
    LAWRENCE Co.

BRAZELTON, Abram to Margrett Noah - issued December 22, 1857, m. by:
    Wm. D. Faris, J. P., December 23, 1857, FRANKLIN Co.

BRAZELTON, Andrew Jackson to Francis C. England - issued October 22,
    1839, m. by: A. J. Steel October 22, 1839, FRANKLIN Co.

BRAZELTON, Green to Mary Holland - issued March 16, 1843, m. by:
    A. J. Steel, M. G., March 17, 1843, FRANKLIN Co.

BRAZELTON, Green to Mary Ann Sharp - issued February 27, 1845, m. by:
    Rev. A. J. Steel, FRANKLIN Co.

BRAZELTON, Jacob H. to Sanina Thurman - m. by: A. J. Steel, M. G.,
    January 7, 1842, FRANKLIN Co.

BRAZELTON, John G. to Ann Bledsoe - issued January 10, 1839, m. by:
    A. J. Steele, M. G., January 10, 1839, FRANKLIN Co.

BRAZELTON, W. G. to Mary J. Brazier - issued December 9, 1868,
    m. December 9, 1868, FRANKLIN Co.

BRAZELTON, William to Abigail Bales - February 4, 1835, JEFFERSON Co.

BRAZELTON, William (Jr.) to Manerva Faris - issued September 23, 1846,
    FRANKLIN Co.

BRAZELTON, William to Ann F. Faris - issued January 3, 1851, FRANKLIN Co.

BRAZELTON, Wm. to Hester A. R. Kirkendal - issued June 4, 1868, m. by:
    J. C. Mails June 29, 1868, FRANKLIN Co.

BRAZELTON (Brazleton), William W. to Charlott P. Sims - issued
    December 16, 1841, FRANKLIN Co.

BRAZELTON, William W. to Mary E. Buchanan - issued November 18, 1847,
    m. by: N. P. Modrall, M. G., November 18, 1847, FRANKLIN Co.

BRAZIER, Dyer to Drucilla Spear - issued January 20, 1866, Bondsman:
    Finley A. Houser, m. by: J. B. Clayton, J. P., January 21, 1866,
    LAWRENCE Co.

BRAZIER, James W. to M. J. Brown - issued November 3, 1868, m. by:
J. Hudgins, M. G., November 3, 1868, FRANKLIN Co.

BRAZIER, Sion S. to Mary L. Baker - issued November 22, 1841, m. by:
Reuben Strambler November 22, 1841, FRANKLIN Co.

BRAZIER, Zachariah to Mary S. Stone - issued December 3, 1836, Bondsman:
Josiah Rascoe, SUMNER Co.

BRAZIL, William to Sarah Sebastan - issued September 19, 1795, Bondsman:
Thomas Edwards, SUMNER Co.

BRAZLETON (Brazelton), William W. to Charlott P. Sims - issued
December 16, 1841, FRANKLIN Co.

BRAZZELL, Allen to Nancy Baker - issued February 11, 1842, m. by:
James M. Lloyd, J. P., February 13, 1842, DICKSON Co.

BRAZZELL, Jackson to Sarah Tatom - issued July 17, 1839, DICKSON Co.

BRAZZELL, Richmond to Any Evans - issued June 27, 1838, m. by:
Henry Goodrich, Esq., June 28, 1838, DICKSON Co.

BREED (or Bruce), Sarah to James Harrison - GREENE Co.

BREEDEN, Archebald to Mary Ann Heaston - issued September 2, 1845,
m. by: C. A. Hunt, J. P., September, 1845, FRANKLIN Co.

BREEDEN, D. A. to Martha Walker - issued May 29, 1846, STEWART Co.

BREEDEN, Edward to Eve Sowers - issued February 18, 1828, Bondsman:
John Willis, m. by: Alexander Hamilton, J. P., February 18, 1828,
GRAINGER Co.

BREEDEN, Isham to Martha Elizabeth Powers - issued December 10, 1852,
Bondsman: John Dillen, m. by: James Almon, J. P., December 14,
1852, MONTGOMERY Co.

BREEDEN, J. C. to Nancy Clark - issued September 23, 1848, Bondsman:
Jas. W. Weakly, m. by: A. Baggett, J. P., September 27, 1848,
MONTGOMERY Co.

BREEDEN, Reuben to Levina Murry - issued July 18, 1829, m. by:
Edward R. Davis, J. P., July 19, 1829, KNOX Co.

BREEDEN, Spencer to Sarah Lewis - April 20, 1798, Security:
John Bird, GREENE Co.

BREEDEN, W. A. to Nancy Ann Anderson - issued November 4, 1860, m. by:
John T. Slatter, J. P., November 8, 1860, FRANKLIN Co.

BREEDING, B. P. to Ann Sample - issued October 1, 1844, m. by:
Robert Williams October 3, 1844, MONTGOMERY Co.

BREEDLOVE, ___(?) to Nancy Breedlove - issued February 10, 1810, Bondsman:
Martin Breedlove, WILSON Co.

BREEDLOVE, A. B. to Mary Wood - issued August 11, 1819, Bondsman:
John Hunley, SUMNER Co.

BREEDLOVE, John to Susan Cheek - issued December 23, 1846, DAVIDSON Co.

BREEDLOVE, Thomas to Sally Travillion - issued March 24, 1818, Bondsman:
Drury Bettis, m. by: Elijah Maddox, M. G., March 26, 1818, WILSON Co.

BREESE, James to Sarah Larew - issued September 10, 1818, m. by:
John Haynie, M. G., September 10, 1818, KNOX Co.

BRENDES, George R. to A. E. Warfield - issued September 5, 1850, Bondsman:
R. S. Moore, MONTGOMERY Co.

148

BRENNON, Luke C. to Mary E. Young - issued December 29, 1846, m. by:
R. B. C. Howell, M. G., December 29, 1846, DAVIDSON Co.

BRENSFIELD (Brinsfield), John A. to Rebecca Johnson - issued May 28,
1859, m. by: B. Higgenbotham, J. P., May 28, 1859, FRANKLIN Co.

BRENT, Joseph A. to Almeda W. Stanfield - issued August 23, 1845,
DAVIDSON Co.

BRENT, William to Patty Chisolm - November 4, 1800, KNOX Co.

BRENTS, Thos. to Jenny McWhorter - January 5, 1808, WILLIAMSON Co.

BRESHEARS, Brazeal to Sally Head - March 24, 1811, Bondsman:
W. W. Thompson, MAURY Co.

BRETHETT, Edward to Pauline P. Eaton - July 25, 1815, WILLIAMSON Co.

BREVARD, Alfred A. to Mary B. Alexander - issued July 15, 1822,
Bondsman: Geo. Thompson, m. by: John Wiseman July 15, 1822,
SUMNER Co.

BREVARD, Cyrus W. to Polyanna Mills - issued January 22, 1827, Bondsman:
Horace Lawson, SUMNER Co.

BREVARD, John C. to Mary H. Bilbo - issued October 17, 1828, Bondsman:
C. Hart, m. by: Thos. Joyner October 17, 1828, SUMNER Co.

BREWER, C. B. to M. C. Watson - issued April 29, 1869, m. by:
John Chitwood, J. P., April 29, 1869, FRANKLIN Co.

BREWER, Claburn to Martha Jane Brown - issued May 2, 1861, Bondsman:
M. K. Reed, m. by: S. L. Poag, J. P., May 2, 1861, LAWRENCE Co.

BREWER, Ed to Nancy Choat - issued September 3, 1845, m. by:
Jas. Sprouse, J. P., September 4, 1845, ROBERTSON Co.

BREWER, Edward to Nancy Choat - issued September 3, 1845, m. by:
James Sprouse, J. P., October 4, 1845, ROBERTSON Co.

BREWER, Erasmus G. to Margrett Lynch - issued July 15, 1846, m. by:
Wm. G. Guinn, FRANKLIN Co.

BREWER, George to Rebecca Davis - issued December 28, 1859, m. by:
T. W. Bell, J. P., February 20, 1860, FRANKLIN Co.

BREWER, George to Francis Goff - issued October 24, 1865, m. by:
E. L. Best, J. P., October 25, 1865, FRANKLIN Co.

BREWER, George A. to Sarah Bullion - issued April 19, 1864, Bondsman:
James Christian, LAWRENCE Co.

BREWER, Hardy to Pennina Worrick - issued December 31, 1856, m. by:
J. H. Lawrence, J. P., January 1, 1857, COFFEE Co.

BREWER, I. N. to Priscilla E. George - issued June 9, 1855, m. by:
Benj. Gambill, J. P., ROBERTSON Co.

BREWER, J. L. to Rebecca Brewer - issued February 11, 1870, FRANKLIN Co.

BREWER, J. R. to Pameseda Lavender - issued December 20, 1855, m. by:
E. H. Campbell, M. G., December 27, 1855, COFFEE Co.

BREWER, James to Nancy A. Frey - issued October 18, 1841, m. by:
Richard Chowning April 4, 1842, ROBERTSON Co.

BREWER, James to Julia Roberts - issued May 29, 1874, m. by:
A. J. Skidmore, J. P., May 31, 1874, FRANKLIN Co.

BREWER, Jesse to Nancy A. Latham - issued August 24, 1847, Bondsman:
A. Ingram, m. by: J. C. Bryan, J. P., August 24, 1847, MONTGOMERY Co.

BREWER, John to Eliza Tims - issued June 11, 1840, Bondsman: Henry Adams,
WILSON Co.

BREWER, John to Nancy A. Forister - issued September 25, 1841, m. by:
W. Haley, J. P., September 26, 1841, ROBERTSON Co.

BREWER, John to Jane May - issued August 28, 1848, STEWART Co.

BREWER, Jonothan to Nancy Leggate - issued July 8, 1848, m. July 12,
1848, STEWART Co.

BREWER, L. B. to Sarah West - issued November 29, 1852, m. by:
Thomas West, Minister, December 1, 1852, ROBERTSON Co.

BREWER, Morris to Sally Shannon - issued December 6, 1814, Bondsman:
James Braden, WILSON Co.

BREWER, Oliver to Polly Henderson - January 10, 1804, KNOX Co.

BREWER, P. W. to Sarah M. Heath - issued February 1, 1858, m. by:
L. N. Simpson, J. P., February 5, 1858, FRANKLIN Co.

BREWER, Samuel to Margaret Moore - July 14, 1800, Security:
Daniel Rawlings, GREENE Co.

BREWER, Wm. to Jane Hill - issued August 20, 1867, m. by:
J. T. Moore, J. P., August 22, 1867, FRANKLIN Co.

BREWER, William C. to Miss J. C. Davis - issued June 25, 1860, m. by:
G. B. McComb, M. G., June 26, 1860, COFFEE Co.

BREWER, William E. to Judy Perry - issued May 7, 1842, DAVIDSON Co.

BREWINGTON, Sarah to Jackson Blount - BEDFORD Co.

BREWINGTON, Sarah to Thos. C. Jones - BEDFORD Co.

BRGAN, Lewis C. to Sarah A. D. Ring - issued October 12, 1843, m. by:
T. P. Neeley, M. G., October 18, 1843, DAVIDSON Co.

BRIANT, Burrel to Rebecca Elizabeth Lyle - issued July 16, 1853,
Bondsman: G. A. Harrell, m. by: A. Bagget, J. P., July 17, 1853,
MONTGOMERY Co.

BRIANT, David to Mary Lane - issued March 1, 1825, Bondsman: Richard
Hight, WILSON Co.

BRIANT, Jessee to Elizabeth Gamble - m. by: M. Catchings, J. P.,
May 6, 1851, FRANKLIN Co.

BRIANT, John H. to Elizabeth Puckett - issued December 28, 1819,
Bondsman: Leonard H. Sims, WILSON Co.

BRIANT, John O. to Elizabeth Walker - issued December 20, 1840,
Bondsman: James Jackson, m. by: R. S. Tate December 22, 1840,
WILSON Co.

BRIANT, Samuel to Harriet Mitchell - issued February 12, 1834, Bondsman:
Joseph C. Johnson, m. by: E. P. Horn, J. P., WILSON Co.

BRICE, Robt. to M. M. Driver - issued June 10, 1868, m. by: J. C. Mails
June 14, 1868, FRANKLIN Co.

BRICE, William C. to Lucinda Brannon - issued July 26, 1838, m. by:
Benjamin B. Knight, J. P., July 26, 1838, FRANKLIN Co.

BRICHAM, Lemuel to Polly Logan - issued February 28, 1812, Bondsman: David Logan, m. by: Ransom Gwyn, J. P., March 1, 1812, WILSON Co.

BRICHUN, Josiah to Sally Organ - issued January 21, 1815, Bondsman: James Brichun, WILSON Co.

BRICKLES, Benard to Hepsey B. Shaw - issued December 1, 1841, m. by: William Shaw, G. M., ROBERTSON Co.

BRIDEY, Hugh to Malinda Howard - issued March 9, 1861, Bondsman: J. L. White, m. by: O. C. Craig, J. P., March 10, 1861, LAWRENCE Co.

BRIDGEMAN, Martin to Anna Dyer - issued November 8, 1830, Bondsman: Elijah S. Harrell, m. vy: James Kennon, M. G., November 8, 1830, GRAINGER Co.

BRIDGERS, John to Dicy Hunt - issued February 8, 1805, Bondsman: Edmund Bridgers, SUMNER Co.

BRIDGES, Alexander to Elizabeth Rolls - issued August 17, 1829, Bondsman: Taylor Lindsay, m. by: John Beard, M. G., August 18, 1829, WILSON Co.

BRIDGES, Allen H. to Sarah Hancock - issued November 28, 1827, Bondsman: Joseph Freeman, m. by: Josiah S. McClain November 29, 1827, WILSON Co.

BRIDGES, Brinkley to Nicey McWhirter - issued December 28, 1814, Bondsman: William Young, WILSON Co.

BRIDGES, G. H. to E. R. McCord - issued January 1, 1859, FRANKLIN Co.

BRIDGES, Granville H. to Elizabeth McCord - issued January 1, 1859, FRANKLIN Co.

BRIDGES, Isaac to M. J. Smith - issued February 18, 1839, m. by: Wm. S. Smith, M. G., FRANKLIN Co.

BRIDGES, Jacob J. to Elizabeth Counts - issued December 1, 1857, FRANKLIN Co.

BRIDGES, James to Susannah Mays - issued February 24, 1798, Bondsman: James McCarty

BRIDGES, Jesse to Mary King - issued October 12, 1831, Bondsman: John T. Carr, m. by: John T. Carr, J. P., October 12, 1831, SUMNER Co.

BRIDGES, Joel to Lucy Eskew - issued January 25, 1830, Bondsman: C. Neal, WILSON Co.

BRIDGES, John to Nancy Amanda Calhoun - issued August 8, 1835, Bondsman: John L. Payne, m. by: E. S. Allen, M. G., August 12, 1835, WILSON Co.

BRIDGES, John O. to Olevia Hatchett - issued September 19, 1867, m. by: Thos. F. Moseley, J. P., September 19, 1867, FRANKLIN Co.

BRIDGES, John R. to Sally A. David - issued February 14, 1854, m. by: B. M. Stephens, M. G., February 16, 1854, ROBERTSON Co.

BRIDGES, Joseph to Elizabeth Gill - issued August 24, 1812, Bondsman: Thos. Bridges, WILSON Co.

BRIDGES, Oliver H. to Mary A. Nuckles - issued January 4, 1840, m. by: Wm. S. Smith, M. G., FRANKLIN Co.

BRIDGES, Perry to Rachel Mairs - June 11, 1808, WILLIAMSON Co.

BRIDGES, R. J. to M. E. Poston - issued April 23, 1867, m. by: Jas. Campbell, M. G., April 23, 1867, FRANKLIN Co.

BRIDGES, Russell B. to Mary Ann Morgan - issued October 22, 1856, FRANKLIN Co.

BRIDGES, Samuel to Rachiel Martin - issued August 11, 1842, m. by: Wm. T. Wells, M. G., August 11, 1842, FRANKLIN Co.

BRIDGES, Squire to Elizabeth Powel - issued February 29, 1824, Bondsman: Evan Smith, m. by: Robert Gaines, J. P., February 29, 1824, GRAINGER Co.

BRIDGES, Thomas to Lucinda Berry - m. by: J. Davis, J. P., March 21, 1835, SUMNER Co.

BRIDGES, Thursey to Jonathan Alexander - GREENE Co.

BRIDGES, Wm. D. to Nancy Morris - July 10, 1805, WILLIAMSON Co.

BRIDGEWATER, Chesley to Julia Ann Johnson - issued April 29, 1849, Bondsman: James A. Gorden, m. by: James T. Garnett, J. P., MONTGOMERY Co.

BRIDGEWATER, Richard to Fane A. Goby - issued November 11, 1847, Bondsman: George Melom, MONTGOMERY Co.

BRIDGEWAY, John H. to Mary A. Cole - issued April 9, 1842, FRANKLIN Co.

BRIELY, John W. to Lucinda Murphy - issued January 16, 1860, m. by: James Cook, J. P., ROBERTSON Co.

BRIEN, A. W. to Sally P. Stewart - issued October 26, 1835, Bondsman: Nathaniel L. Orand, m. by: J. Lester, V. D. M., WILSON Co.

BRIEN, Elisha to Elizabeth Johnson - issued September 20, 1818, Bondsman: O. G. Finley, m. by: Wm. Steele, J. P., September 27, 1818, WILSON Co.

BRIGANCE, Charles N. to Fanny Dyer - issued January 2, 1816, Bondsman: John Brigance, SUMNER Co.

BRIGANCE, J. M. to E. E. George - m. October 26, 1837, SUMNER Co.

BRIGANCE, Joel to Matilda Hollis - issued December 19, 1829, Bondsman: Ruben Hunter, m. by: Wm. Walton, J. P., December 19, 1829, SUMNER Co.

BRIGANCE, John to Rebekah Stuart - issued November 16, 1818, Bondsman: Isaac Looney, SUMNER Co.

BRIGANCE, John to Catherine Loving - issued December 22, 1830, m. by: Wm. Walton, J. P., December 22, 1830, SUMNER Co.

BRIGANCE, William H. to Ann Demcy - m. by: Josiah Walton, J. P., February 15, 1831, SUMNER Co.

BRIGE, Rebecca to Newton Ray - issued January 6, 1863, Bondsman: J. B. Cooper, Jos. H. Thompson, Clk. per James E. Neil, Dep. Clk., BEDFORD Co.

BRIGGANCE, A. to Nancy Ann Hollis - m. by: R. D. Hobday February 10, 1838, SUMNER Co.

BRIGGANCE, William to Jemima D. Briggance - issued July 14, 1832, Bondsman: Reuben Hunter, m. by: Demcy Ashford, J. P., July 14, 1832, SUMNER Co.

BRIGGS, A. H. to Leethy Warren - issued December 14, 1849, m. by: James Anderson, J. P., December 18, 1849, ROBERTSON Co.

BRIGGS, Charles M. to Elizabeth M. Rogers - issued January 19, 1848, Bondsman: Joseph G. Ward, MONTGOMERY Co.

BRIGGS, David C. to Sarah M. Whitscarver - issued April 3, 1843, m. by:
U. Young, J. P., ROBERTSON Co.

BRIGGS, G. W. to A. W. Jackson - issued June 29, 1860, m. by:
J. B. Anderson, M. G., July 3, 1860, ROBERTSON Co.

BRIGGS, Samuel to Mary Johnston - issued July 19, 1830, Bondsman:
James H. Ca'dwell, m. by: Martin B. Carter, J. P., July 21, 1830,
KNOX Co.

BRIGHAM, David to Sarah Mixon - issued July 15, 1852, Bondsman:
Francis M. Dilling, m. by: James Almon, J. P., July 15, 1852,
MONTGOMERY Co.

BRIGHAM, James to Priscilla Crabb - m. by: Joseph Pitt October 28,
1837, SUMNER Co.

BRIGHAM, James M. to Ann James - issued May 13, 1838, m. by:
James Wilson, J. P., May 16, 1838, STEWART Co.

BRIGHAM, James W. to Mary E. Askew - issued April 19, 1847, m. by:
Jesse Edwards, M. G., STEWART Co.

BRIGHT, Elias R. to Deborah Hankins - issued October 4, 1822, m. by:
Wm. B. Carns, J. P., October 10, 1822, KNOX Co.

BRIGHT, George to Martha Bowman - issued February 13, 1824, m. by:
J. C. Bunch, J. P., GRAINGER Co.

BRIGHT, George to Martha Boman - issued February 13, 1826, Bondsman:
Henry Holt, m. by: J. C. Bunch, J. P., February 13, 1826,
GRAINGER Co.

BRIGHT, George W. to Anne B. Sharp - WILLIAMSON Co.

BRIGHT, Hiram to Elizabeth Tims - issued October 2, 1838, Bondsman:
Asa Oneal, m. by: Jas. Baird, J. P., October 3, 1838, WILSON Co.

BRIGHT, James to Betsey Cower - issued July 5, 1832, Bondsman:
William Paty, WILSON Co.

BRIGHT, James W. to Nancy Kennedy - issued December 1, 1825, Bondsman:
John Kennedy, m. by: Joseph Wood, J. P., Witness: Hu Brown,
KNOX Co.

BRIGHT, Jr., John to Susan Pugh - issued August 13, 1835, Bondsman:
Terrence W. McAffy, m. by: James Crippen, J. P., August 18, 1835,
KNOX Co.

BRIGHT, Wm. to Susan Josephine Harris - issued August 20, 1852, Bondsman:
Chas. Rudolph Oats, m. by: James T. Garnett, J. P., August 30,
1852, MONTGOMERY Co.

BRIGHT, Wm. J. to Nancy H. Thorn - issued September 25, 1851, Bondsman:
John Bearden, m. by: John M. Nolen, M. G., September 28, 1851,
MONTGOMERY Co.

BRIGHTWELL, Alexander to Adaline Pitlow - issued August 15, 1840,
Bondsman: William W. McWhirter, WILSON Co.

BRIGHTWELL, Elgin to Eliza Armstrong - issued August 19, 1843, Bondsman:
John Gross, m. by: Jesse Martin, J. P., August 20, 1843, MEIGS Co.

BRIGHTWELL, Gainum to Nancy Walker - issued December 29, 1839, Bondsman:
Wm. P. Edds, m. by: B. F. McKenzie, J. P., December 29, 1839,
MEIGS Co.

BRIGS, John to Nelley Shockley - issued February 1, 1809, Bondsman:
Aaren Rook, GRAINGER Co.

BRILEY, Elisha to Mary O. Crabtree - issued January 17, 1859, m. by: James Cook, J. P., ROBERTSON Co.

BRILEY, Ishmael H. to Jane M. Addam - issued October 29, 1836, Bondsman: Henry Volentine, SUMNER Co.

BRILEY, James to Jane Bandy - issued March 21, 1817, Bondsman: William Briley, m. by: Dan'l Latimer, J. P., March 21, 1817, SUMNER Co.

BRILEY, Joshua to Nancy Howell - March 27, 1811, WILLIAMSON Co.

BRILEY, Marcus to Nancy A. Toliver - issued September 5, 1857, m. by: M. L. Covington, J. P., September 6, 1857, ROBERTSON Co.

BRILEY, William C. to Permelia Ragans - issued December 4, 1845, DAVIDSON Co.

BRILL, Solomon to Nancy Jacobs - issued March 25, 1809, Bondsman: Andrew Barid, WILSON Co.

BRILY, Elisha to Rebecca Harper - issued October 1, 1825, Bondsman: Thomas Summers, m. by: S. H. Turner, J. P., October 1, 1825, SUMNER Co.

BRIM, Andrew Jackson to Mary Jane Boyd - issued November 17, 1842, m. by: Jos. G. Hinson, J. P., November 22, 1842, DICKSON Co.

BRIM, John to Polly McLellan - May 16, 1811, WILLIAMSON Co.

BRIMAGE, John to Mary A. R. Tripp - issued November 9, 1852, m. by: Rev. J. Scivally November 9, 1852, FRANKLIN Co.

BRINE, David to Susannah Haleman - issued July 15, 1822, m. by: G. H. Bullard, J. P., July 27, 1822, WILSON Co.

BRINKLEY, James to Susan Hill - issued November 6, 1872, FRANKLIN Co.

BRINKLEY, John A. to Polly Golden - issued June 8, 1822, Bondsman: Samuel A. Bailey, m. by: S. S. Turner, J. P., June 8, 1822, SUMNER Co.

BRINKLEY, John K. to Lucy E. Ellison - issued January 10, 1855, m. by: C. F. Lucas, J. P., January 18, 1855, ROBERTSON Co.

BRINKLEY, Kendal to Hannah Davis - issued September 27, 1817, Bondsman: Robt. Cochran, m. by: David Webb, M. G., September 27, 1817, SUMNER Co.

BRINKLEY, Robt. C. to Ann C. Overton - issued October 18, 1841, m. by: Phillip Lindsley October 18, 1841, DAVIDSON Co.

BRINKLEY, William to Lucy Ann Jones - issued March 16, 1832, Bondsman: Martin Whitten, WILSON Co.

BRINKLY, Jno. R. to Jane E. Wynn - issued October 13, 1862, Bondsman: B. T. Sutton, Jos. H. Thompson, Clk., BEDFORD Co.

BRINSFIELD (Brensfield), John A. to Rebecca Johnson - issued May 28, 1859, m. by: B. Higgenbotham, J. P., May 28, 1859, FRANKLIN Co.

BRINSFIELD, Wm. to Mary Jane Miles - issued December 4, 1856, m. by: A. B. Cunningham, M. G., December 10, 1856, FRANKLIN Co.

BRINSON, Jesse to Susanah Moss - issued January 29, 1812, Bondsman: Jacob Cook, WILSON Co.

BRINSON, Josiah to Betsey Modglin - issued April 6, 1816, Bondsman: James Brinson, m. by: Abner Hill, M. G., April 7, 1816, WILSON Co.

BRINSON, Thomas M. to Mary Ruff - issued November 25, 1834, Bondsman:
A. S. Winford, m. by: E. P. Horn, J. P., WILSON Co.

BRISCO, John to Martha Scoggins - issued August 27, 1844, m. by:
Benjamin Sells, J. P., August 27, 1844, FRANKLIN Co.

BRISLEY, John to Rosey Clendening - issued June 10, 1805, Bondsman:
Robt. Campbell, SUMNER Co.

BRISON, Elizabeth to Hugh McAdams - June 9, 1800, Security: James Rankin,
GREENE Co.

BRISON, George to Easter Reed - issued July 21, 1825, Bondsman:
Levy Reed, m. by: John McMinn, J. P., August 2, 1825, WILSON Co.

BRISON, Samuel to Isbell Bogel - issued March 15, 1825, Bondsman:
George Brison, m. by: John McMinn, J. P., WILSON Co.

BRISON, William to Sally Davinport - issued July 21, 1825, m. by:
John McMinn, J. P., July 24, 1825, WILSON Co.

BRISTER, John H. to Asanath Collins - issued December 22, 1838, m. by:
Allen McCaskilly, J. P., December 23, 1838, STEWART Co.

BRISTOE, Nicholas to Huldy Clifton - issued February 24, 1849, Bondsman:
Asa W. Hooper, MONTGOMERY Co.

BRISTOW, Thomas to Peggy Claunch - issued December 19, 1809, Bondsman:
John Griffitts, Witness: John F. Jack, J. P., GRAINGER Co.

BRITAIN, James to Jane Gass - May 25, 1794, Security: John W. Bowers,
GREENE Co.

BRITAIN, William to Mary Hannah - December 10, 1791, Security:
Josiah Kidwell, GREENE Co.

BRITE, Alexander to Malinda Jennings - issued March 28, 1839, Bondsman:
W. J. McClain, WILSON Co.

BRITT, George C. to Frances E. Mason - issued June 25, 1838, Bondsman:
G. W. C. Bond, m. by: Archb. B. Duval, WILSON Co.

BRITT, John M. to Eliza Ann Powers - issued July 20, 1849, Bondsman:
Willis Davidson, m. by: A. Baggett, J. P., July 23, 1849,
MONTGOMERY Co.

BRITT, Thomas G. to Sally McCloud - issued June 13, 1818, m. by:
John Bayless, J. P. K. C., June 14, 1818, KNOX Co.

BRITT, William W. to Permelia A. Small - issued January 16, 1840,
m. by: U. Young, J. P., ROBERTSON Co.

BRITTAIN, David A. to Utilda Porterfield - issued August 29, 1832,
Bondsman: E. T. Loggins, WILSON Co.

BRITTAIN, W. W. to E. F. Lyon - issued December 13, 1871, m. by:
James Wagner, M. G., December 13, 1871, FRANKLIN Co.

BRITTEN, James to Lydia Stanfield - October 12, 1815, GREENE Co.

BRITTEN, William to Susan Thompson - issued January 22, 1832, Bondsman:
John L. Dillard, RUTHERFORD Co.

BRITTENHAM, John to Mary Miller - issued January 25, 1819, m. by:
Robt. Henderson January 25, 1819, RUTHERFORD Co.

BRITTINGHAM, James to Louisa Boyer - issued November 21, 1836, Bondsman:
Sims Crawford, KNOX Co.

BRITTLE, George W. to Melissy Dale - issued August 25, 1847, DAVIDSON Co.

BRITTLE, Milton P. to Winney Spring - issued December 21, 1818, Bondsman: Geo. L. Swan, WILSON Co.

BRITTON, Abraham to Mary Anne Crutcher - issued October 28, 1816, Bondsman: Harvey Douglass, m. by: Obadiah C. Finly, J. P., WILSON Co.

BRITTON, James H. to Sarah (?) M. Lauderdale - issued February 2, 1824, Bondsman: J, m. by: John Wiseman, M. G., February 2, 1824, SUMNER Co.

BRITTON, John to Martha (?) Smith - issued June 27, 1818, m. by: John Fulton, J. P., July 9, 1818, RUTHERFORD Co.

BRIZENDINE, Richard C. to Frances Ashford - issued July 26, 1827, Bondsman: Young P. Brizendine, m. by: Meredith Hodges, J. P., July 26, 1827, SUMNER Co.

BRIZENDINE, Young P. to Amy Woodall - issued September 24, 1828, Bondsman: Wm. Woodall, m. September 24, 1828, SUMNER Co.

BROADBENT, William to Sarah F. Harris - issued May 1, 1849, Bondsman: Wm. S. Buckner, MONTGOMERY Co.

BROADNAX, John P. to Jame Sharp - March 10, 1813, WILLIAMSON Co.

BROADRICK, Abraham to Louisa Krisles - issued October 8, 1842, m. by: James Woodard, J. P., ROBERTSON Co.

BROADWAY, James to Elizabeth Foster - issued January 14, 1807, Bondsman: Henry Foster, WILSON Co.

BROADWAY, Nancy Stephens to R. F. Stegal - issued June 23, 1863, Bondsman: Walter Stephens, Jos. H. Thompson, Clk., BEDFORD Co.

BROADWAY, Thomas to Elizabeth Thorogmorton - issued November 5, 1839, m. by: James Wilson, J. P., November, 1839, STEWART Co.

BROCK, Allen to Elisabeth Parker - issued September 22, 1803, Bondsman: Carnelious Archer, Witness: John Hall, J. P., GRAINGER Co.

BROCK, Allen to Sarah Trogden - issued August 18, 1851, m. by: Burill Howard, J. P., August 18, 1851, VAN BUREN Co.

BROCK, Allen to Luesa Mitchell - issued December 22, 1858, m. by: B. L. Simmons, J. P., December 22, 1858, VAN BUREN Co.

BROCK, C. W. to Adaline Galloway - issued November 25, 1861, Bondsman: J. M. Pennington, m. by: J. M. Pennington, J. P., November 25, 1861, LAWRENCE Co.

BROCK, David (or Prock) to Flora (Flava) Love - issued November 11, 1836, Bondsman: Tilman Cannon, m. by: Taylor G. Gilliam November 11, 1836, SUMNER Co.

BROCK, Durham to Ann Marshall - issued March 1, 1811, Bondsman: John Layne, SUMNER Co.

BROCK, George to Sarah Elkins - issued September 12, 1834, Bondsman: John Brock, GRAINGER Co.

BROCK, James to Elizabeth Beeler - issued November 29, 1817, Bondsman: Isaac Dyer, m. by: John Hall, J. P., GRAINGER Co.

BROCK, Jesse (or Joseph) to Elisabeth Clark - issued July 16, 1803, Bondsman: Peter Hammack, Witness: John Hall, J. P., GRAINGER Co.

BROCK, Jesse to Susan Roberds - issued March 2, 1842, VAN BUREN Co.

BROCK, John to __(?) Bowman - issued December 22, 1820, Bondsman:
Robert Bose, GRAINGER Co.

BROCK, John to Susana Shockley - issued December 25, 1844, m. by:
David Haston, J. P., December 25, 1844, VAN BUREN Co.

BROCK, Jr., John to Mary Staley - issued December 27, 1847, Bondsman:
Robert Steel, m. by: J. B. Green, J. P., December 29, 1847,
MONTGOMERY Co.

BROCK, John to Tabitha Miles - issued November·14, 1848, Bondsman:
John Fairfax, MONTGOMERY Co.

BROCK, Leonard to Elizabeth Sharp - issued October 4, 1810, Bondsman:
John Mynett, GRAINGER Co.

BROCK, Moses to Nancy Ashlock - issued August 22, 1820, Bondsman:
James Durham, SUMNER Co.

BROCK, Moses to Susan Richeson - issued April 18, 1822, Bondsman:
John Browning, m. by: Wm. Smith, J. P., April 18, 1822, SUMNER Co.

BROCK, Moses to Zephrona Dennis - issued May 10, 1822, Bondsman:
Edward Brock, m. by: Martin Cleveland, J. P., May 12, 1822,
GRAINGER Co.

BROCK, Moses to Mahala Dyer - issued September 20, 1833, Bondsman:
Thomas Brock, GRAINGER Co.

BROCK, Obediah to Nancy Vandergriff - issued June 1, 1815, Bondsman:
Jacob Vandergriff, GRAINGER Co.

BROCKER, Jerry to Nancy Culvyhouse - issued February 22, 1822 (or
February 27, 1822), Bondsman: Garland Norris, m. by:
Alexander Hamilton, J. P., GRAINGER Co.

BROCKER, Larvos to Rebecca Grant - issued October 9, 1824, Bondsman:
William Reeder, GRAINGER Co.

BROCKERS, John to Mary Smith - issued February 17, 1813, Bondsman:
John Simmons, GRAINGER Co.

BROCKERS, Thomas to Nancy Norris - issued October 19, 1817, Bondsman:
William Norris, m. by: William Lane, J. P., October 19, 1817,
GRAINGER Co.

BROCKMAN, John to Nancy Hardin - issued July 3, 1827, Bondsman:
Nathan L. Douglas, RUTHERFORD Co.

BROCKMAN, Samuel to Martha E. Scoboe (?) - issued June 21, 1847,
Bondsman: Wm. L. Coulter, m. by: Wm. Shelton, M. G., June 23,
1847, MONTGOMERY Co.

BROCKS, Thomas to Susannah Helton - issued December 24, 1817, Bondsman:
James Helton, m. by: Isaiah Midkiff, J. P., December 25, 1817,
GRAINGER Co.

BROCKUS, John to Sophia Dewitt - October 30, 1812, KNOX Co.

BROCKUS, William to Elizabeth Ramsey - issued March 15, 1819, Bondsman:
Jeremiah Lovell, m. by: William Lane, J. P., GRAINGER Co.

BRODAN, Annette to William Ross - BEDFORD Co.

BRODDUS, Joseph E. to Harriett J. Whittaker - issued March 21, 1853,
Bondsman: Jack M. Rice, m. by: J. T. Hendrick March, 1853,
MONTGOMERY Co.

BRODERICK, Joseph to Amanda Escue - issued July 16, 1853, m. by:
David Henry, J. P., July 17, 1853, ROBERTSON Co.

BRODIE, Lodowick to Matilda Anthony - issued November 26, 1821,
    Bondsman: Hardy Cryer, SUMNER Co.

BROGAN, Amsted to Sarah Thomas - issued December 5, 1835, Bondsman:
    A. H. Foster, WILSON Co.

BROGAN, Armstead to Jane Moor - issued May 9, 1829, Bondsman:
    Samuel Bell, WILSON Co.

BROGAN, John A. to Elizabeth Moore - issued May 4, 1832, Bondsman:
    E. W. Cartwright, WILSON Co.

BROGAN, John A. to Lucy Johnson - issued January 14, 1840, Bondsman:
    Jesse B. Pemberton, m. by: James Thomas, J. P., January 16, 1840,
    WILSON Co.

BROGAN, Raynolds to Nancey Black - issued February 3, 1800, Bondsman:
    John Grifits, GRAINGER Co.

BROGAN, Reynolds to Delpha Grady - issued July 3, 1834, Bondsman:
    Robert Mitchell, m. by: John Dotson, J. P., July 7, GRAINGER Co.

BROGAN, William to Nancy Ann Montgomery - issued October 6, 1837,
    Bondsman: William Hubbard, m. by: Elihu, __, J. P., October 12,
    1837, WILSON Co.

BROGDEN, John A. to Sacey Mitchell - issued September 17, 1852, m. by:
    M. G. Brocket, M. G., September 22, 1852, VAN BUREN Co.

BROILES, Amos to Clamenza L. Wilson - issued July 1, 1845, Bondsman:
    Mark H. Wilson, m. by: T. K. Munsey, Min., July 1, 1845, MEIGS Co.

BROILES, Jacob to Mary Vaught - April 19, 1802, Curety: George Broiles,
    BLOUNT Co.

BROKER, William to Barbary Devault - issued January 14, 1836, Bondsman:
    James Broker, GRAINGER Co.

BROMAGE, Alexander to Charity Winkler - issued September 1, 1852,
    m. by: G. W. Bowling, J. P., September 1, 1852, FRANKLIN Co.

BROMET, Arthur to Frances Tucker - issued March 7, 1842, STEWART Co.

BROMLEY, Wm. J. to M. C. Hughes - issued September 24, 1862, Bondsman:
    M. C. Davis, m. by: R. L. McLaren, J. P., September 28, 1862,
    LAWRENCE Co.

BROOK, Isaac W. to Martha Huddleston - issued February 2, 1818, Bondsman:
    Zedekiah Tate, WILSON Co.

BROOK, Pixon (?) to Sarah Gillespie - August 3, 1789, Security:
    Thomas Gillespie, GREENE Co.

BROOKE, Wm. to Emeline Krisel - issued March 19, ROBERTSON Co.

BROOKERS, William to Elizabeth Ramsey - issued March 15, 1832, Bondsman:
    Jeremiah Lovell, m. by: William Lane, J. P., GRAINGER Co.

BROOKMAN, Willima to Elza Wyles - issued May 14, 1842, m. by:
    W. E. Cartwright May 14, 1842, DAVIDSON Co.

BROOKS, A. J. to Mary Ann Warick - issued January 9, 1845, Bondsman:
    Thos. Branham, m. by: T. B. McElwee, J. P., January 12, 1845,
    MEIGS Co.

BROOKS, Athy to Letha Gibson - issued April 15, 1830, Bondsman:
    John Pyle, m. by: Thos. Anderson, J. P., April 15, 1830, SUMNER Co.

BROOKS, Betsey to Hugh Ross - MAURY Co.

158

BROOKS, Christopher to Betsey Bender - issued February 11, 1830, Bondsman: James McCollock, m. by: C. Crain February 11, 1830, SUMNER Co.

BROOKS, Christopher B. to Mary Jane Pinkerton - issued January 28, 1845, m. by: Wm. Cummings January 30, 1845, DAVIDSON Co.

BROOKS, Edmund to Mary Wright - issued October 17, 1826, Bondsman: Thomas James, SUMNER Co.

BROOKS, Frederick to Mollie Shelby - issued September 19, 1870, m. by: M. H. Bone, M. G., September 20, 1870, FRANKLIN Co.

BROOKS, H. P. to Mary A. Sanders - issued January 17, 1872, m. by: H. Sneed, Rector Trinity Parish, January 17, 1872, FRANKLIN Co.

BROOKS, Isaac W. to Martha Huddleston - issued February 2, 1818, m. by: Joshua Lester, V. D. M., February 5, 1818, WILSON Co.

BROOKS, James to Esther Hopkins - November 24, 1810, Bondsman: Samuel Crawford, MAURY Co.

BROOKS, James to Ferrely Stevens - January 24, 1814, WILLIAMSON Co.

BROOKS, Jeremiah to Rachel Spring - issued February 2, 1818, Bondsman: George Swan, WILSON Co.

BROOKS, John to Sally Parker - issued September 11, 1810, Bondsman: Noah Parker, SUMNER Co.

BROOKS, John to Jane Lambert - issued August 8, 1811, SUMNER Co.

BROOKS, John to Elizabeth Brooks - issued July 4, 1813, Bondsman: Charles Brooks, m. by: John Cocke, J. P., GRAINGER Co.

BROOKS, Jno. to Maria Armstrong - issued January 9, 1821, m. by: R. Houston, J. P., January 9, 1821, KNOX Co.

BROOKS, John to Nancy Kirkland - issued July 10, 1823, Bondsman: D. Swaggerty, m. by: R. A. Swan, J. P., July 10, 1823, Witness: Wm. Swan, KNOX Co.

BROOKS, John to Nancy Brisindine - issued December 1, 1827, Bondsman: J. B. Brizendine, m. by: Robert Norvell December 1, 1827, SUMNER Co.

BROOKS, John to Elizabeth Pierson - issued February 18, 1833, m. by: John Kidwell, M. G., February 19, GRAINGER Co.

BROOKS, John to Rebecca Hall - issued May 30, 1840, Bondsman: Nathan Qualls, m. by: John Sebourn, J. P., May 31, 1840, MEIGS Co.

BROOKS, Johnson to Elizabeth Brewer - issued March 21, 1840, DAVIDSON Co.

BROOKS, Joseph to Polly Atkinson - April 24, 1823, WILLIAMSON Co.

BROOKS, Joseph A. to Margaret A. McMillan - issued September 9, 1828, m. by: Tho. H. Nelson September 9, 1828, KNOX Co.

BROOKS, Leonard to Margaret Kerr - issued December 23, 1841, Bondsman: Mathias Shaver, m. by: D. L. Godsey, M. G., December 23, 1841, MEIGS Co.

BROOKS, Marcy to Greenham Dotson - January 9, 1808, Bondsman: Samuel Brooks, MAURY Co.

BROOKS, Mathew to Margaret Eagen - issued February 20, 1834, Bondsman: J. C. Spillens, m. by: Thos. Babb, J. P., February 21, 1834, WILSON Co.

BROOKS, Midget to Rebecca Oneal - issued August 24, 1820, Bondsman: Jeremiah Brooks, WILSON Co.

BROOKS, Moses to Nancy Tait - issued July 14, 1813, Bondsman: David Tate, WILSON Co.

BROOKS, Moses J. to Lidia Wilson - issued February 18, 1858, FRANKLIN Co.

BROOKS, Jr., Moses T. to Mary Sample - issued November 1, 1847, m. by: James P. Hagar, J. P., November 2, 1847, DAVIDSON Co.

BROOKS, Nancy to Thomas Bartlett - April 30, 1811, Bondsman: Andrew Forgey, MAURY Co.

BROOKS, O. C. to Elizabeth L. Allen - issued October 16, 1858, m. by: Jas. Woodard, ROBERTSON Co.

BROOKS, Pleasant to Sarah Christmas - issued January 2, 1826, Bondsman: John Brooks, m. by: Silas Potts, J. P., January 2, 1826, SUMNER Co.

BROOKS, Rebecca A. to Jacob H. Swing - issued August 14, 1862, Bondsman: J. M. Mullins, Jos. H. Thompson, Clk. per M. E. W. Dunaway, D. Clk., m. by: R. S. Dean, J. P., BEDFORD Co.

BROOKS, Sam (?) to Catherine Doyle - __(?) 13, 1800, KNOX Co.

BROOKS, Sarah A. to F. M. Pratt - issued January 8, 1863, Bondsman: J. Holt, Joseph H. Thompson, Clk., BEDFORD Co.

BROOKS, Stephen to Anne Earnest - March 8, 1793, Security: Felix Earnest, GREENE Co.

BROOKS, Stephen to Margaret Whitenberger - January 7, 1800, Security: Lawrence Earnest, GREENE Co.

BROOKS, Stephen to Maria Swiney - issued September 30, 1818, Bondsman: Jeremiah Brooks, WILSON Co.

BROOKS, Thos. N. to Mary R. Greer - issued October 10, 1855, m. by: S. D. Ogburn, M. G., ROBERTSON Co.

BROOKS, William to Malinda McClanahon - issued May 9, 1838, MEIGS Co.

BROOKS, William W. to Lousara Huddleston - Bondsman: Isaac W. Brooks, WILSON Co.

BROOKSHIRE, Benjamin to Elizabeth Bateman - issued November 17, 1817, m. by: George Uselton, J. P., November 26, 1817, RUTHERFORD Co.

BROOKSHIRE, Enock W. to Emisia Bradford - issued May 12, 1821, Bondsman: R. M. Boyers, m. by: S. Hunt May 12, 1821, SUMNER Co.

BROOKSHIRE, Mannering to Sally Shelton - issued November 25, 1816, m. by: William Keele, M. G., November 26, 1816, RUTHERFORD Co.

BROOKSHIRE, S. N. to Mary C. Poe - issued February 19, 1859, m. by: H. W. Carroll, J. P., February 20, 1859, COFFEE Co.

BROOKSHIRE, Thomas to Matilda Giles - issued March 25, 1816, m. by: John Rutherford March 25, 1816, SUMNER Co.

BROOME, Benjamin F. to Mary Williams - issued January 14, 1847, m. by: C. Brandon, J. P., January 17, 1847, STEWART Co.

BROOMFIELD, William J. to Ann C. Fortner - issued May 4, 1854, Bondsman: G. O. Anderson, m. by: James Lamb May 3, 1854, MONTGOMERY Co.

BROTHERS, James to Elizabeth Page - issued November 5, 1835, Bondsman: William B. Page, RUTHERFORD Co.

BROTHERS, Thomas to Polley Kelton - issued March 12, 1827, Bondsman:
John L. Lynch, RUTHERFORD Co.

BROUGH, George Allen to Mirah Bone - issued November 18, 1806, Bondsman:
William Bone, WILSON Co.

BROUGHAN (Brougham), John to Martha Roda - issued June 2, 1859, m. by:
W. W. Estill, G. M., June 2, 1859, FRANKLIN Co.

BROUGHTON, Abel to Eleanor Scaper - issued December 20, 1827, Bondsman:
James Gwin, m. by: William Barr, J. P., December 20, 1827, SUMNER Co.

BROUGHTON, Thomas to Lucy E. Weever - issued July 23, 1822, m. by:
G. W. Banton, J. P., July 25, 1822, RUTHERFORD Co.

BROWDER, David to Mary E. Evans - issued April 16, 1839, m. by:
John P. Moore, ROBERTSON Co.

BROWDER, David to Eliz. Irvin - issued November 7, 1842, m. by:
A. H. Redfern November 8, 1842, ROBERTSON Co.

BROWDER, James to Louisa E. Childress - issued December 19, 1843,
Bondsman: John H. Cowan, MEIGS Co.

BROWN, A. V. to Cynthia Saunders - issued September 15, 1845, m. by:
J. T. Wheat, Rr. of Ct. Ch., September 16, 1845, DAVIDSON Co.

BROWN, Aaron to Susan Stockett - December 7, 1821, WILLIAMSON Co.

BROWN, Alexander to Sarah Miller - issued January 15, 1830, Bondsman:
John Ball, SUMNER Co.

BROWN, Alexander to Polly Jonican - issued March 7, 1833, m. March 9,
1833, RUTHERFORD Co.

BROWN, Alexander to Louisiana Clark - issued July 31, 1851, VAN BUREN Co.

BROWN, Alexander to Arter Hughlett - issued February 3, 1858, m. by:
Samuel Umbarger, J. P., February 4, 1858, COFFEE Co.

BROWN, Andrew to Catharine Worsham - issued October 11, 1837, Bondsman:
William Bates, WILSON Co.

BROWN, Andrew to Anney Plumlee - issued October 19, 1846, m. by:
Micagh Simons, J. P., November 7, 1846, VAN BUREN Co.

BROWN, Andrew M. to Mary E. Bell - issued July 11, 1825, Bondsman:
H. G. Bishop, m. by: R. Houston, J. P., July 11, 1825, KNOX Co.

BROWN, Anne to Henry Morris - February 11, 1799, Security: Sparling
Bowman and William Kindal, GREENE Co.

BROWN, Augustin to Cinthia Warren - issued October 13, 1832, Bondsman:
James M. Steel, m. by: John Parker, L. D., October 13, 1832,
SUMNER Co.

BROWN, Avery to Sarah Marlow - issued September 22, 1806, Bondsman:
Rich Marlow, WILSON Co.

BROWN, Bartlett to Temperance White - issued February 24, 1841, m. by:
J. Thos. Wheat February 24, 1841, DAVIDSON Co.

BROWN, Barton to Elizabeth Parker - issued August 10, 1830, Bondsman:
Sam'l R. Anderson, m. by: John M. Holland August 10, 1830, SUMNER Co.

BROWN, Bassel C. to Hannah Rutland - issued March 14, 1836, m. by:
John Beard, M. G., March 16, 1836, WILSON Co.

BROWN, Benjamin to Nancy A. Wise - issued August 14, 1862, Bondsman: J. J. Reavis, Jos. H. Thompson, Clk. per M. E. W. Dunaway, D. Clk., BEDFORD Co.

BROWN, Bernard to Martha Hoskins - issued August 4, 1821, m. by: Joshua Lester, V. D. M., August 25, 1821, WILSON Co.

BROWN, Bernard to Elizabeth Franklin - issued December 14, 1829, Bondsman: George T. Brown, m. by: John Parker, L. D., December 14, 1829, SUMNER Co.

BROWN, Beverly (Brawn?) to Adaline Abernathy - March 27, 1823, m. by: H. H. Brown, GILES Co.

BROWN, Clement (Noel) to Mary Smith - issued March 9, 1833, m. by: M. Powell, J. P., March 13, 1833, ROBERTSON Co.

BROWN, Cornelius to Sally White - November 15, 1817, WILLIAMSON Co.

BROWN, Cynthia to Robt. Mosely - BEDFORD Co.

BROWN, Daniel to Elizabeth Vivrette - issued January 8, 1832, Bondsman: John B. Vivrette, WILSON Co.

BROWN, David to Elizabeth Johnson - July 24, 1799, Security: Philip Stout, GREENE Co.

BROWN, David to Betsey Sloan - June 16, 1800, Security: John McAlroy, BLOUNT Co.

BROWN, David to Patience Southerlin - issued September 5, 1803, Bondsman: Henry Bowen, Jun., GRAINGER Co.

BROWN, David G. to Anny Smith - issued September 25, 1817, m. by: Thomas Berry, J. P., October 2, 1817, RUTHERFORD Co.

BROWN, Dudley to Edness Henderson - issued May 30, 1812, Bondsman: Cornelius Organ, m. by: Isaac Winston, J. P., June 3, 1812, WILSON Co.

BROWN, E. H. to Ann Feribee - issued April 29, 1847, m. by: Zacheriah Jones, J. P., April 29, 1847, DAVIDSON Co.

BROWN, Edward to Ann Dyer - issued August 4, 1802, Bondsman: James Dyer Junior, GRAINGER Co.

BROWN, Edward to Sally Bandy - issued September 12, 1806, Bondsman: Richard Bandy, WILSON Co.

BROWN, Edward to Joanna Hill - issued February 25, 1828, Bondsman: Wm. Horn, m. by: J. Lewis February 26, 1828, KNOX Co.

BROWN, Edward to Sarah Ann Roberts - issued July 24, 1832, Bondsman: Henry Ligon, WILSON Co.

BROWN, Edward to Martha Swaner - issued May 25, 1840, Bondsman: H. C. Brown, m. by: B. Tarver, J. P., May 26, 1840, WILSON Co.

BROWN, Edward L. to Elizabeth B. Russell - issued May 26, 1831, m. by: Abner W. Landsden, V. D. M., May 26, 1831, KNOX Co.

BROWN, Eli to Mary Waddle - issued April 29, 1841, m. by: B. P. Morris. J. P., April 29, 1841, DAVIDSON Co.

BROWN, Elijah to Love Ritter - March 4, 1807, WILLIAMSON Co.

BROWN, Elijah to Susan Brown - issued October 17, 1857, m. by: C. Jernigan, M. G., October 21, 1857, COFFEE Co.

BROWN, Elisha to Polly Allen - issued 1806, Bondsman: Jesse Cage, WILSON Co.

BROWN, Elisha to Jane Booker - April 17, 1822, KNOX Co.

BROWN, Elisha to Judy Peak - issued January 10, 1833, Bondsman: William Mitchell, RUTHERFORD Co.

BROWN, Elisha R. to Nancy Rush - m. by: Jonathan Davis, J. P., February 14, 1835, SUMNER Co.

BROWN, Elizabeth to John Newberry - January 19, 1798, Security: James Brown, GREENE Co.

BROWN, F. M. to M. J. Easley - issued May 10, 1860, m. by: W. R. Saddler, J. P., ROBERTSON Co.

BROWN, Francis to Betsy Browing - issued December 29, 1818, m. by: Sam'l Sample, J. P. K. C., December 31, 1818, KNOX Co.

BROWN, Francis G. to Polly Bell - issued December 6, 1821, m. by: Robert Lindsey, J. P., December 6, 1821, KNOX Co.

BROWN, G. A. to Josephine C. Orr - issued December 10, 1874, FRANKLIN Co.

BROWN, G. E. to Elizabeth Rives - issued April 12, 1849, Bondsman: W. R. Brown, MONTGOMERY Co.

BROWN, G. W. to Nancy Hannah - issued January 23, 1841, m. by: William Greer, J. P., January 24, 1841, DAVIDSON Co.

BROWN, Gabriel R. to Elizabeth King - issued January 2, 1827, m. by: John Brown, J. P., January 3, 1827, KNOX Co.

BROWN, Garfield to Priscilla McBride - issued September 5, 1842, m. by: Micaya Simons, J. P., September 8, 1842, VAN BUREN Co.

BROWN, George to Mary Hunter - March 28, 1792, Security: Thomas Harmon, GREENE Co.

BROWN, George to Polly Thompson - issued April 10, 1806, Bondsman: Jony Williams, WILSON Co.

BROWN, George to Patsey Head - issued December 28, 1824, m. by: O. W. Crockett, J. P., December 29, 1824, RUTHERFORD Co.

BROWN, George C. to Lucinda V. Austin - issued June 26, 1847, DICKSON Co.

BROWN, George H. to Nancy Hamilton - issued April 4, 1836, m. by: William McMurry, J. P., April 4, 1836, RUTHERFORD Co.

BROWN, George W. to Laura J. E. Phillips - issued July 11, 1854, m. by: H. Schackleford, J. P., July 11, 1854, COFFEE Co.

BROWN, George W. to Sarah S. E. Hice - issued January 17, 1866, m. by: B. B. Brandon, L. D., January 17, 1866, FRANKLIN Co.

BROWN, George W. to Delila R. Renis - issued February 15, 1872, m. by: Thos. J. Shaw, M. G., February 15, 1872, FRANKLIN Co.

BROWN, Hannah to Philip Hattler - July 13, 1786, Security: Joseph Williams, GREENE Co.

BROWN, Henry to Rebecca Mitchell - issued August 7, 1823, Bondsman: Mitchell Taswell, m. by: John Bonner, J. P., August 12, 1823, WILSON Co.

BROWN, Hezekiah to Betsy Collings (a woman of color) - issued June 30, 1824, Bondsman: Anderson Evans, m. by: James Brennon, J. P., July 1, 1824, WILSON Co.

BROWN, Hiram to Martha A. Curle - issued December 15, 1842, m. by:
Wm. T. Wells, M. G., December 15, 1842, FRANKLIN Co.

BROWN, Hugh to Margaret Kelsey - 1790, Security: Joseph Brown, GREENE Co.

BROWN, Hugh to Clarissa Browning - issued November 10, 1828, m. by:
Wm. A. McCampbell November 11, 1828, KNOX Co.

BROWN, Hugh to Lucinda Booker - issued February 6, 1835, Bondsman:
Samuel Booker, m. by: Thomas Smith, M. G., WILSON Co.

BROWN, Hugh to Lamiza McCarroll - issued August 14, 1835, Bondsman:
John N. Roach, m. by: John Beard, M. G., August 20, 1835, WILSON Co.

BROWN, Hugh to Sarah Wood - issued April 20, 1837, m. by:
Richard Kayhill, J. P., April 20, 1837, KNOX Co.

BROWN, Irvin to Minerva Booker - issued August 12, 1830, Bondsman:
G. W. Bussard, Lemuel Loyd, WILSON Co.

BROWN, Isaac to Fanney Clark - issued May 26, 1802, Bondsman:
Aroon Roach and William Brown, GRAINGER Co.

BROWN, Isaac C. to Jane Wade - issued November 4, 1824, Bondsman:
Nathaniel Douglas, RUTHERFORD Co.

BROWN, J. E. to Elizabeth Sisk - issued May 31, 1860, m. by:
J. D. Lynch, J. P., June 3, 1860, FRANKLIN Co.

BROWN, J. F. to M. L. Smith - issued April 19, 1867, m. by:
W. M. Bean, J. P., April 21, 1867, FRANKLIN Co.

BROWN, J. G. to Mary L. Speller - issued December 22, 1858, m. by:
C. A. Howell, P. G., December 22, 1858, COFFEE Co.

BROWN, J. L. to Elizabeth Garner - issued May 26, 1860, m. by:
John D. Lynch, J. P., May 27, 1860, FRANKLIN Co.

BROWN, J. U. to Caroline Brennet - issued February 25, 1858, m. by:
Samuel Umbarger, J. P., February 25, 1858, COFFEE Co.

BROWN, Jacob to Dovy Foster - issued September 18, 1820, Bondsman:
Joseph Spradlin, m. by: Meredith Hodges, J. P., September 18,
1820, SUMNER Co.

BROWN, Jacob to Anna Tatum - issued January 16, 1823, Bondsman:
Asa Hodges, m. by: M. Hodges, J. P., January 16, 1823, SUMNER Co.

BROWN, Jacob to Nancy Funk - issued October 28, 1846, Bondsman:
A. M. Hooper, m. by: R. W. Morrison, J. P., October 28, 1846,
MONTGOMERY Co.

BROWN, Jacob C. to Nancy Miller - issued January 2, 1830, Bondsman:
L. Miller, WILSON Co.

BROWN, James to Jane Newberry - September 22, 1796, Security:
John Henderson, GREENE Co.

BROWN, James to Sylva Break - issued April 1, 1805, Bondsman:
James McKain, SUMNER Co.

BROWN, Jas. to Judy Walker - January 4, 1809, WILLIAMSON Co.

BROWN, James to Patsey Chappel - issued August 21, 1810, Bondsman:
Patrick Youree, SUMNER Co.

BROWN, James to Nancy Nobles - December 19, 1810, WILLIAMSON Co.

BROWN, James to Margaret Fraker - issued February 12, 1822, m. by:
Wm. B. Carns, J. P., February 14, 1822, KNOX Co.

BROWN, James to Elizabeth Kirkpatrick - issued August 23, 1825, Bondsman: Jeremiah Burgess, SUMNER Co.

BROWN, James to Casandra Norman - issued January 5, 1829, Bondsman: Theron Norman, m. by: Jno. Bayless, J. P., January 7, 1829, KNOX Co.

BROWN, James to Sarah Jonakin - issued December 30, 1829, Bondsman: William Brown, m. by: David Patton, J. P., December 30, 1829, RUTHERFORD Co.

BROWN, James to Polly Tuttle - m. by: Thomas Gilmore August 15, 1835, SUMNER Co.

BROWN, James to Ruth Sellers - issued December 5, 1839, m. by: Wm. White, J. P., December, 1839, DICKSON Co.

BROWN, James to Mary Link - issued February 27, 1845, m. by: John Eubank, J. P., February 27, 1845, DICKSON Co.

BROWN, James to Jane E. Carpenter - issued December 20, 1848, m. by: Isaac Steel, ROBERTSON Co.

BROWN, James to Jane Denton - issued October 2, 1856, m. by: L. W. Marbury, J. P., October 2, 1856, COFFEE Co.

BROWN, James A. to Lucy A. Rowland - issued December 20, 1836, Bondsman: Travis Windrow, RUTHERFORD Co.

BROWN, James M. to Celia Roach - issued July 28, 1825, Bondsman: James H. Barr, m. by: David Foster, M. G., August 4, 1825, WILSON Co.

BROWN, James M. to Esther Fleming - issued January 5, 1829, Bondsman: Wm. T. Christy, RUTHERFORD Co.

BROWN, James M. to Martha Jane Wynn - issued September 16, 1851, Bondsman: George W. Bagwell, m. by: G. Orgain September 18, 1851, MONTGOMERY Co.

BROWN, Jas. Percy to Lesinka Campbell - issued April 25, 1839, m. by: J. Thos. Wheat, Re. of Cr. Ch., April 25, 1839, DAVIDSON Co.

BROWN, James T. to Charlott T. Hammonds - issued December 20, 1838, DAVIDSON Co.

BROWN, Jane to Elias Veatch - GREENE Co.

BROWN, Jarrett to Rebecca Jane Weathers - issued October 1, 1859, m. by: M. A. Carden, J. P., October 1, 1859, COFFEE Co.

BROWN, Jeremiah to Molly Menuby - issued November 26, 1799, Bondsman: Jacob Boiler, Witness: A. White, KNOX Co.

BROWN, Jeremiah to Nancy Hodges - issued March 13, 1821, Bondsman: Holly Hodges, m. by: Anderson Darnel, M. G., March 13, 1821, SUMNER Co.

BROWN, Jesse to Ellen Pritchet - issued December 24, 1818, Bondsman: John Ralph, m. by: John McMurtry, M. P., December 24, 1818, SUMNER Co.

BROWN, Jessee E. to Jennie E. Wood - issued November 5, 1873, m. by: M. B. Clements, M. G., November 5, 1873, FRANKLIN Co.

BROWN, Jethro to Sarah Cutbirth - July 29, 1811, Bondsman: John M. Taylor, MAURY Co.

BROWN, John to Priscilla Essman - January 6, 1800, Security: Thos. Essman and Francis Antrison, GREENE Co.

BROWN, John to Nancy Allen - July 30, 1801, Security: John Bradley, BLOUNT Co.

BROWN, John to Nancy House - issued February 17, 1804, m. by: R. Houston, J. P. K. C., February 17, 1804, KNOX Co:

BROWN, John to Elizabeth Ball - issued July 29, 1805, Bondsman: Abner Ball, SUMNER Co.

BROWN, John to ___ (?) Bumpass - issued April 10, 1807, Bondsman: William McAdow, WILSON Co.

BROWN, John to Rachel Lomax - issued December 16, 1809, Bondsman: Jonathan Picket, WILSON Co.

BROWN, John to Octavia Conn - issued April 4, 1812, Bondsman: Sam'l Meredith, SUMNER Co.

BROWN, John to Rebeckah Cocke - issued December 11 (or 8?), 1815, Bondsman: William E. Cocke, m. by: Isaac Barton, J. P., GRAINGER Co.

BROWN, John to Betsy Wheeler - issued May 5, 1819, m. May 5, 1819, RUTHERFORD Co.

BROWN, John to Mahala Dennis - issued November 25, 1824, Bondsman: Joseph Dennis, GRAINGER Co.

BROWN, John to Sarah Wood - issued February 28, 1325, m. February 28, 1825, KNOX Co.

BROWN, John to Sarah Williams - issued April 4, 1825, Bondsman: George Benthall, WILSON Co.

BROWN, John to Beedy Wright - issued December 29, 1825, Bondsman: James B. Cole, m. by: B. Bridges, J. P., March 27, 1826, WILSON Co.

BROWN, John to Sara Foster - issued December 4, 1826, Bondsman: William Dorris, m. by: Meredith Hodges, J. P., December 4, 1826, SUMNER Co.

BROWN, John to Fanny Simons - issued January 4, 1827, Bondsman: Edw. Stratton, SUMNER Co.

BROWN, John to Margarett Gilliam - issued November 20, 1830, Bondsman: William Gilliam, m. by: Joshua Lester, V. D. M., WILSON Co.

BROWN, John to Eliza Wood - issued June 2, 1831, Bondsman: Zack Green, SUMNER Co.

BROWN, Jno. to Polly Gossett - issued July 24, 1833, m. by: Chas. Hall, J. P., July 25, 1833, KNOX Co.

BROWN, John to Nancy A. Jetton - issued September 10, 1834, Bondsman: Edmund Pendleton, m. by: H. Trott, J. P., September 10, 1834, RUTHERFORD Co.

BROWN, John to Mary Ann Jones - issued October 27, 1838, m. by: W. M. Smith, M. G., FRANKLIN Co.

BROWN, John to Lucinda McDaniel - issued November 29, 1842, m. by: David Ralston, J. P., November 30, 1842, DAVIDSON Co.

BROWN, John to Elizabeth Brooks - issued January 30, 1847, DAVIDSON Co.

BROWN, John to Rebaca ___(?) - issued December 19, 1856, VAN BUREN Co.

BROWN, John to Elizabeth J. Parker - issued May 17, 1862, m. by: M. A. Carden, J. P., May 17, 1862, COFFEE Co.

BROWN, John A. to Cyrena Jones - issued November 28, 1846, m. by:
John Byrom, M. G., November 30, 1846, FRANKLIN Co.

BROWN, John A. to Caroline Weaver - issued July 2, 1870, m. by:
B. B. Brandon July 4, 1870, FRANKLIN Co.

BROWN, John B. to Mary Dobson - issued May 24, 1847, m. by:
G. D. Fullmer, J. P., May 24, 1847, DAVIDSON Co.

BROWN, John F. to Margaret F. Seawell - issued September 16, 1817,
Bondsman: Mathew Dew, m. by: John Payne, WILSON Co.

BROWN, John G. to Sarah Scott - issued March 23, 1825, Bondsman:
Moses Brown, WILSON Co.

BROWN, John G. to Martha E. Read - issued November 25, 1841, m. by:
Philip Ball, M. G., November 25, 1841, DAVIDSON Co.

BROWN, John H. to Sarah Bass - issued January 14, 1835, Bondsman:
Robt. Lawrence, WILSON Co.

BROWN, John H. to Sarah A. Houndershall - issued March 2, 1836,
Bondsman: William Gray, m. by: Elisha Vaughan March 2, 1836,
SUMNER Co.

BROWN, John L. to M. A. McCarty - issued June 30, 1851, m. by:
Thomas Farmer, J. P., ROBERTSON Co.

BROWN, John R. to Sarah N. Harris - issued February 23, 1848, m. by:
W. B. Ross, J. P., February 23, 1848, DICKSON Co.

BROWN, John S. to Rachiel C. Weaver - issued January 29, 1866, m. by:
M. Tipps, J. P., January 30, 1866, FRANKLIN Co.

BROWN, John W. to Elizabeth Burrough - issued December 25, 1849,
FRANKLIN Co.

BROWN, Jordan to Sarah N. Hill - issued September 1, 1830, Bondsman:
A. W. Hicks, m. by: John M. Holland September 28, 1830, WILSON Co.

BROWN, Joseph to Mary Calbert - issued October 26, 1817, Bondsman:
Isaiah Simmons, m. October 26, 1817, SUMNER Co.

BROWN, Joseph to Sally Hilton - issued December 23, 1820, Bondsman:
James Bryant, m. by: Geo. Moody, J. P., December 26, 1820,
GRAINGER Co.

BROWN, Joseph to Edy Brown - issued July 1, 1836, Bondsman: Levi
Richmond, m. by: Thomas Gilmore July 1, 1836, SUMNER Co.

BROWN, Joseph to Mary Staggs - issued June 20, 1839, m. by:
R. B. C. Howell June 20, 1839, DAVIDSON Co.

BROWN, Joseph to Nancy Sullivan - issued February 1, 1842, m. by:
W. Hand, J. P., February 1, 1842, DICKSON Co.

BROWN, Joseph to Martha Roberson - issued September 20, 1850, m. by:
W. A. Breeden, J. P., September 21, 1850, FRANKLIN Co.

BROWN, Joseph F. to Susan Bass - issued August 1, 1831, Bondsman:
William Brown, m. by: B. Bridges, J. P., August 3, 1831, WILSON Co.

BROWN, Joseph W. to Susanna Markrum - m. by: Jonathan Davis, J. P.,
June 8, 1835, SUMNER Co.

BROWN, Joshua to Prudence McMin - issued June 27, 1808, Bondsman:
Solomon George, WILSON Co.

BROWN, Joshua to Francis Blakely - issued September 27, 1818, m. by:
John Bayless, J. P. K. C., September 30, 1818, KNOX Co.

BROWN, Joshua to Sarah Shasteen - issued August 10, 1870, FRANKLIN Co.

BROWN, Josiah C. to Cynthia L. Morris - issued August 30, 1855, m. by:
Wm. Frame, J. P., August 30, 1855, FRANKLIN Co.

BROWN, Josiah G. to Judith Scott - issued December 7, 1847, m. by:
R. B. C. Howell, M. G., December 8, 1847, DAVIDSON Co.

BROWN, Lazarus to Peggy McCarty - issued August 5, 1800, Bondsman:
Benjamin Davis, SUMNER Co.

BROWN, Lydda to James Hust - November 19, 1792, Security: Lewis Tadlock
and Thomas Brown, GREENE Co.

BROWN, Lytle to Jane Conger - issued August 19, 1836, Bondsman:
Robert Lawrence, m. by: Thos. Babb, J. P., August 20, 1834,
WILSON Co.

BROWN, Manaweather to Clarissa West - issued December 18, 1822,
m. December 18, 1822, SUMNER Co.

BROWN, Margaret to Thomas Beals - GREENE Co.

BROWN, Marion to Mary Bowens - issued February 20, 1854, m. by:
L. N. Simpson, J. P., February 25, 1854, FRANKLIN Co.

BROWN, Mathew J. S. to Elvira Epps - issued September 14, 1854, m. by:
D. B. Muse, J. P., September 14, 1854, FRANKLIN Co.

BROWN, Mathews to Elizabeth Walker - issued July 30, 1828, Bondsman:
John H. Coles, m. by: T. Kirkpatrick, J. P., WILSON Co.

BROWN, Moses to Tabitha Gardner - issued February 14, 1825, Bondsman:
Anderson Evans, m. by: Ezekiel Cloyd, M. G., February 17, 1825,
WILSON Co.

BROWN, Nathaniel to Sally Scott - issued January 24, 1810, Bondsman:
Thomas Donnell, WILSON Co.

BROWN, Nathaniel J. to Nancy A. Cook - issued January 7, 1850, m. by:
M. W. Watson, J. P., January 9, 1850, FRANKLIN Co.

BROWN, Neal S. to Mary A. Trimble - issued December 28, 1839, m. by:
Philip Lindsley December 26, 1839, DAVIDSON Co.

BROWN, Nicholas to __(?) - issued __(?) 7, 1838, DAVIDSON Co.

BROWN, Nimrod to Susanna T. Brown - issued September 22, 1823, Bondsman:
Reuben D. Brown, SUMNER Co.

BROWN, Paskel to Charlotte McCain - issued October 19, 1844, STEWART Co.

BROWN, Peggy to Francis Beard - August 12, 1811, Bondsman: Andrew Brown,
MAURY Co.

BROWN, Peter to Comfort Beard - December 11, 1815, WILLIAMSON Co.

BROWN, Peter to Rebecca Dunbar - issued December 1, 1840, m. by:
Jas. S. Cawley, J. P., December 1, 1840, FRANKLIN Co.

BROWN, Peter W. to Evaline Williams - issued December 8, 1865, Bondsman:
Jeremiah Henson, m. by: J. H. Strayhorn, M. G., December 10, 1865,
LAWRENCE Co.

BROWN, Phoebe to William Greene - GREENE Co.

BROWN, Pleasant to Phebie C. Parker - issued June 20, 1857, m. by:
J. A. Brantley, J. P., June 24, 1857, COFFEE Co.

BROWN, R. S. to Alice M. Booker - issued February 11, 1864, Bondsman: Jos. H. Thompson and Clerk, BEDFORD Co.

BROWN, Rebecca to Michael Waldrop (Waldross) - MAURY Co.

BROWN, Rederick P. to C. A. Cobble - issued November 16, 1870, m. by: J. F. Syler, J. P., October 12, 1870, FRANKLIN Co.

BROWN, Repps E. to Malenda Brown - issued September 8, 1853, m. by: D. D. Martin, Gospel Minister, September 8, 1853, COFFEE Co.

BROWN, Reuben S. to Kisiah Sarver - m. by: Meredith Hodges, J. P., March 15, 1823, SUMNER Co.

BROWN, Rezin S. to Martha I. Freeman - issued September 13, 1862, Bondsman: L. A. Freeman, Jos. H. Thompson, Clk., BEDFORD Co.

BROWN, Richard to Lucinda Landrum - issued November 15, 1826, Bondsman: Mathew Johnson, SUMNER Co.

BROWN, Richard to Mariah Lowry - issued December 12, 1827, Bondsman: F. P. Crockett, RUTHERFORD Co.

BROWN, Richard to Elizabeth P. Scruggs - issued October 8, 1831, Bondsman: W. P. McClain, WILSON Co.

BROWN, Riley to Nancy Smith - issued July 19, 1849, Bondsman: J. L. Crotzer, m. by: Stephen Cocke, J. P., July 19, 1849, MONTGOMERY Co.

BROWN, Robert to Hannah Brown - issued June 11, 1812, Bondsman: Robert Patton, SUMNER Co.

BROWN, Robert to Hanah Brown - issued June 12, 1812, Bondsman: Robert Patton, SUMNER Co.

BROWN, Robert to Mary Stewart - issued August 4, 1827, Bondsman: Hugh Smith, RUTHERFORD Co.

BROWN, Robt. to Sarah Jane Lewis - issued August 29, 1846, m. by: John J. Travis, J. P., August 30, 1846, FRANKLIN Co.

BROWN, Ross to Rosanah Brown - issued September 1, 1835, Bondsman: Thomas Robinson, WILSON Co.

BROWN, Ruben to Margarette Cathey - issued August 22, 1846, DICKSON Co.

BROWN, Samuel to June Watson - issued May 20, 1806, Bondsman: Abraham Pruit, GRAINGER Co.

BROWN, Samuel to Susannah Benthal - issued September 20, 1809, Bondsman: Robt. Patton, SUMNER Co.

BROWN, Samuel to Hanah Beals - March 9, 1817, Security: Newhope Quaker Meeting, GREENE Co.

BROWN, Samuel to Lucy Chandler - issued December 12, 1822, m. by: G. H. Bussard, J. P., WILSON Co.

BROWN, Samuel to Barshaba Evans - issued October 26, 1826, Bondsman: David Johnson, SUMNER Co.

BROWN, Samuel to Elizabeth Hightower - issued February 24, 1831, Bondsman: Thomas Hawley, GRAINGER Co.

BROWN, Samuel to Nancy McCombs - issued October 29, 1834, Bondsman: Owen Quenly, m. by: John Beard, M. G., October 30, 1834, WILSON Co.

BROWN, Samuel to Sarah E. Samuel - issued February 25, 1846, m. by: R. B. C. Howell, M. G., February 25, 1846, DAVIDSON Co.

BROWN, Saml. B. to Ann Baird - issued April 11, 1854, m. by:
Isaac Steel, ROBERTSON Co.

BROWN, Sarah to William H. Hill - September 18, 1810, Bondsman:
Jesse Brown, MAURY Co.

BROWN, Sarah C. to Elisha B. Williams - issued September 16, 1861,
Bondsman: James W. Chambers, Jos. H. Thompson, Clk. per
N. F. Thompson, D. Clk., BEDFORD Co.

BROWN, Spill C. to Mary Jane Armstrong - issued January 21, 1845,
m. by: B. Herndon, J. P., January 21, 1845, STEWART Co.

BROWN, Squire to Martha B. Flipping - issued January 3, 1831, Bondsman:
William Caldwell, SUMNER Co.

BROWN, Stephen to Milley Rhodes - issued October 21, 1800, Bondsman:
Edwin L. Moore, SUMNER Co.

BROWN, Stephen to Polly Crawford - issued January 31, 1816, Bondsman:
Sterling Bryant, WILSON Co.

BROWN, Susanna to Daniel B. Miller - MAURY Co.

BROWN, Thomas to Jane McElwee - February 16, 1801, KNOX Co.

BROWN, Thomas to Miriam Jone - October 24, 1810, Security: Newhope
Quaker Meeting, GREENE Co.

BROWN, Thomas to Rebecca Cooper - issued July 8, 1822, m. by:
Jas. Jones, J. P., July 11, 1822, RUTHERFORD Co.

BROWN, Thomas to Rebecca Smothers - issued November 27, 1823, Bondsman:
Archibald Stinson, m. by: Logan Henderson, J. P., November 30,
1823, RUTHERFORD Co.

BROWN, Thomas to Rebecca Boon - issued March 12, 1828, Bondsman:
Granville Edwards, WILSON Co.

BROWN, Thos. to Jane Gentry - issued December 17, 1844, m. by:
I. Porter, J. P., December 19, 1844, DICKSON Co.

BROWN, Thomas to Maria Jones - issued December 1, 1859, m. by:
Charles Coulson, J. P., December 1, 1859, COFFEE Co.

BROWN, Thos. C. to S. A. Bennett - issued January 16, 1849, m. by:
James Woodard, ROBERTSON Co.

BROWN, Volentine H. to Mary Pyle - issued March 1, 1836, Bondsman:
James L. McKoin, m. by: A. B. Duval March 1, 1836, SUMNER Co.

BROWN, W. A. to Eliza J. Kinner - issued December 24, 1863, Bondsman:
__(?), Jos. H. Thompson, Clk., BEDFORD Co.

BROWN, W. J. to Buena Vesta Freeman - issued November 13, 1863,
Bondsman: W. J. Miller, BEDFORD Co.

BROWN, W. R. to Sarah J. Walker - issued February 9, 1852, Bondsman:
G. W. Welker, m. by: Wm. Thompson, M. G., February 9, 1852,
MONTGOMERY Co.

BROWN, Westley to Mary Shackleford - issued November 19, 1858, m. by:
Jas. Woodard November 21, 1858, ROBERTSON Co.

BROWN, William to Polly Ann Moffet - April 12, 1800, Security:
Cornlius Bogart, BLOUNT Co.

BROWN, William to Rebecca Evans - issued September 30, 1807, KNOX Co.

BROWN, William to Polly Sherrel - issued August 26, 1814, Bondsman:
William Sherrel, GRAINGER Co.

BROWN, William to Anne Taylor - issued January 27, 1816, KNOX Co.

BROWN, William to Avarilla Malone - issued October 4, 1817, Bondsman:
John Brown, SUMNER Co.

BROWN, William to Rebecca Wigger - issued October 5, 1818, m. by:
Jas. Jones, J. P., October 6, 1818, RUTHERFORD Co.

BROWN, William to Delila Pate - issued February 11, 1819, Bondsman:
Sam'l Meredith, m. by: John W. Payton, J. P., February 20, 1819,
WILSON Co.

BROWN, William to Mary Johnson - issued August 12, 1819, Bondsman:
James Thomas, WILSON Co.

BROWN, William to Matilda Hawkins - issued January 18, 1820, Bondsman:
John Bryant, m. by: Jesse Sears, a Baptis Minister, January 18,
1820, GRAINGER Co.

BROWN, William to Elizabeth Brown - issued July 22, 1822, m. by:
Elijah Maddox, M. G., July 23, 1822, WILSON Co.

BROWN, William to Fanny Hodges - issued March 29, 1828, Bondsman:
Holly Hodges, SUMNER Co.

BROWN, William to May Curry - issued November 18, 1831, Bondsman:
William Jones, m. by: James Drennon, J. P., WILSON Co.

BROWN, William to Jane Hamilton - issued January 18, 1834, Bondsman:
Arthur McCrary, RUTHERFORD Co.

BROWN, Wm. to Mary Ann Lyles - issued November 3, 1835, Bondsman:
Lewis Lyles, Witness: Geo. M. White, KNOX Co.

BROWN, William to Elizabeth Brown - issued December 6, 1836, Bondsman:
George Brown, m. by: Levi Satterfield, M. G., GRAINGER Co.

BROWN, William to Margaret Turbeville - issued November 10, 1840,
DAVIDSON Co.

BROWN, Wm. to Nancy Stewart - issued March 7, 1842, m. March 8, 1842,
STEWART Co.

BROWN, William to Nancy Gilliam - issued June 23, 1842, m. by:
J. P. Walker June 23, 1842, FRANKLIN Co.

BROWN, Wm. to Eliza Radigins - issued December 1, 1858, m. by:
J. P. Wedington, J. P., December 2, 1858, FRANKLIN Co.

BROWN, William to Mary A. Cunningham - issued March 5, 1860, m. by:
F. W. Hazelwood, M. G., March 5, 1860, COFFEE Co.

BROWN, William to Mary Harpe - issued January 7, 1861, m. by:
D. H. Williams, Mins. of M. E. Church So., January 9, 1861,
COFFEE Co.

BROWN, Wm. B. to Sarah Russell - issued May 12, 1862, Bondsman:
Jos. H. Thompson, security and clerk, BEDFORD Co.

BROWN, William C. to Mary C. Johnson - issued December 24, 1839,
Bondsman: Elijah M. Holt, m. by: Melikijah L. Vaughn, M. G.,
WILSON Co.

BROWN, Wm. C. to Calidonia J. Hoover - issued June 22, 1863, Bondsman:
J. M. Moore, Security; Jos. H. Thompson, Clk., BEDFORD Co.

BROWN, Wm. E. to Margrett Richardson - issued August 11, 1874, m. by:
Jas. B. Hudgins, M. G., August 13, 1874, FRANKLIN Co.

BROWN, William F. to Martha Hiser - issued May 2, 1847, m. by:
T. W. Ruffin, J. P., ROBERTSON Co.

BROWN, William F. to Nancy Catharine Graves - December 22, 1852, m. by:
M. H. Butler, GILES Co.

BROWN, William G. to Nancy Steele - issued November 22, 1830, m. by:
James Charlton, J. P., November 22, 1830, SUMNER Co.

BROWN, William J. to Nancy C. Carroll - issued August 8, 1860, m. by:
R. S. McBride, J. P., August 9, 1860, COFFEE Co.

BROWN, William L. to Eliza Hightower - August 14, 1816, WILLIAMSON Co.

BROWN, William M. to Sarah Mitchell - issued July 6, 1844, m. by:
William L. Mitchell, J. P., July 7, 1844, VAN BUREN Co.

BROWN, William M. to Mary Ann Williams - issued July 9, 1860, m. by:
F. D. McBride, J. P., July 12, 1860, COFFEE Co.

BROWN, William P. to Elizabeth J. Hobbs - issued October 24, 1840,
DAVIDSON Co.

BROWN, William R. to Abigail Smith - January 31, 1827, Security:
Ira E. Brown, GILES Co.

BROWN, William S. to Elizabeth Wills - issued November 10, 1829,
Bondsman: John Taber, RUTHERFORD Co.

BROWN, William S. to Patcy Bruce - issued December 7, 1829, RUTHERFORD Co.

BROWN, William T. to Louisa Burns - issued October 30, 1817, m. by:
H. Robinson, J. P., November 2, 1817, RUTHERFORD Co.

BROWN, Willie to Peggy Wesnoe (Wisner) - October 8, 1807, WILLIAMSON Co.

BROWN, Willie to Kissiah Gambrel - issued October 12, 1829, Bondsman:
Jesse Brown, RUTHERFORD Co.

BROWN, Willis to Lucinda S. Meador - m. by: J. Hobday, J. P., February 25,
1834, SUMNER Co.

BROWNING, C. F. to Mary F. Gorrell - issued December 13, 1857, m. by:
Jas. Woodard, ROBERTSON Co.

BROWNING, C. H. to Amanda Porter - issued October 30, 1854, m. by:
David Henry, J. P., ROBERTSON Co.

BROWNING, Charles R. to L. L. Gorrell - issued November 28, 1848, m. by:
Jas. Woodard, ROBERTSON Co.

BROWNING, Clifton to Jane Williamson - issued December 10, 1832,
Bondsman: Jno. A. Williamson, WILSON Co.

BROWNING, Daniel to Vathle West - issued July 29, 1811, Bondsman:
David Browning, SUMNER Co.

BROWNING, George to Sally McIntosh - issued January 27, 1806, Bondsman:
Reuben Nowell, SUMNER Co.

BROWNING, Henry R. to Eliza Chilbourn (?) - issued October 9, 1832,
Bondsman: Milender Clibourne, m. by: D. Fleming, M. G., October 16,
1832, KNOX Co.

BROWNING, Jacob A. to Polly Beckman - issued December 19, 1818, Bondsman:
Edward Browning, SUMNER Co.

BROWNING, James G. to Polly Ann Neale - issued November 20, 1827,
Bondsman: Jno. Dobbins, m. November 20, 1827, SUMNER Co.

BROWNING, James T. to Elizabeth Crafford - issued September 7, 1841,
m. by: Isaiah Warren, J. P., ROBERTSON Co.

BROWNING, John to Abigail Rippey - issued September 10, 1823, m. by:
M. Hodges, J. P., September 10, 1823, SUMNER Co.

BROWNING, Jonathan to Elizabeth Stalcup - issued November 7, 1826,
Bondsman: Clifton G. Browning, SUMNER Co.

BROWNING, Wm. to Mary Leviny - issued February 14, 1848, Bondsman:
Thomas Doris and W. P. Lane, m. by: W. B. Carney, J. P., February 14,
1848, MONTGOMERY Co.

BROWNING, William P. to Mary Brown - issued November 12, 1836, Bondsman:
James Oglesby, m. by: Luke P. Allen November 12, 1836, SUMNER Co.

BROWNLOW, John to Julia Morris - issued December 21, 1843, m. by:
I. H. McEwen, J. P., December 21, 1843, DAVIDSON Co.

BROWNLOW, John P. to Hester J. Ussery - December 1, 1859, m. by:
William Peaton, J. P., GILES Co.

BROYLES, Aaron to Nancy Davis - December 2, 1797, Security:
Felix Earnest, GREENE Co.

BROYLES, Alfred to Susana Mankins - issued November 17, 1822, m. by:
William Keele November 19, 1822, RUTHERFORD Co.

BROYLES, Andrew to Anna Glaze - November 17, 1801, Security:
George Alexander and John Glaze, GREENE Co.

BROYLES, Eleanor to James Broyles - October 22, 1792, Security:
Matthias and Ephraim Broyles, GREENE Co.

BROYLES, Elizabeth to Horris (?) Medcalf - GREENE Co.

BROYLES, Elizabeth to David Bird - GREENE Co.

BROYLES, Elizabeth to Jacob Fox - GREENE Co.

BROYLES, Elizabeth to Adam Barnhart - GREENE Co.

BROYLES, Elizabeth to John Kindle - GREENE Co.

BROYLES, Eva to George Kindle - GREENE Co.

BROYLES, Ezekial to Caty Bays - November 13, 1802, Security:
Lewis Broyles, GREENE Co.

BROYLES, Frances to John Broyles - GREENE Co.

BROYLES, George to Catherine Vaut - June 16, 1796, Surety: Andrew Vaut,
BLOUNT Co.

BROYLES, James to Eleanor Broyles - October 22, 1792, Security:
Matthias and Ephraim Broyles, GREENE Co.

BROYLES, Jemima to Jacob Hoover - GREENE Co.

BROYLES, Jeremiah to Sarah Jones - July 27, 1796, Security: John Jones,
GREENE Co.

BROYLES, Joel to Mary Fox - issued July 24, 1835, Bondsman: Joseph Fox,
RUTHERFORD Co.

BROYLES, John to Frances Broyles - November 20, 1797, Security:
Thomas Williamson, GREENE Co.

BROYLES, Kezia to Thomas Williamson - August 31, 1790, Security: James Broyles, GREENE Co.

BROYLES, Lewis to Mary Cain - August 14, 1784, Security: Abraham Broyles, GREENE Co.

BROYLES, Lewis H. to Maria Sevier - October 19, 1818, GREENE Co.

BROYLES, Mary to David Bird - February 14, 1804, Security: Ephraim Broyles, GREENE Co.

BROYLES, Matthias to Nancy Smith - December 29, 1797, Security: Ephraim Broyles and Philip Smith, GREENE Co.

BROYLES, Michael to Margaret Newberry - April 2, 1805, Security: Aaron Broyles, GREENE Co.

BROYLES, Nile M. to Eleanor C. Wilson - issued May 20, 1845, Bondsman: W. H. Stockton, MEIGS Co.

BROYLES, Polly to John Wilhoit - GREENE Co.

BROYLES, Rebecca to Daniel Moore - GREENE Co.

BROYLES, Sally to Jacob Delaney - GREENE Co.

BROYLES, Simeon to Mary Fox - April 6, 1801, Security: Ephraim Broyles, GREENE Co.

BROYLES, Susanna to John M (?) - GREENE Co.

BROYLES, Thomas to Sarah Humbard - January 16, 1811, GREENE Co.

BRUBAKER, Garrett to Elizabeth Madison - issued December 21, 1830, Bondsman: John Crow, m. by: Henry Ridley, J. P., December 23, 1830, RUTHERFORD Co.

BRUCE, Charles to Sally Hawkins - issued January 9, 1834, m. by: N. L. Mabry, WILSON Co.

BRUCE, David to Lucy Bruce - issued December 24, 1808, Bondsman: James McKain, SUMNER Co.

BRUCE, Edward to Nelly Burns - issued March 30, 1807, Bondsman: John Burus, WILSON Co.

BRUCE, George W. to Lydia Dunnegan - issued February 15, 1841, m. February 16, 1841, DICKSON Co.

BRUCE, J. L. to Mollie P. Wiseman - issued September 30, 1868, FRANKLIN Co.

BRUCE, James to Peggy Lindsey - issued May 5, 1812, Bondsman: Isaac Lindsey, SUMNER Co.

BRUCE, James to Raney Stanley - issued September 1, 1830, Bondsman: Jefferson Bruce, m. by: Isaac Lindsey, M. G., September 1, 1830, SUMNER Co.

BRUCE, James H. to Zady Smith - issued May 16, 1835, Bondsman: James Castleman, RUTHERFORD Co.

BRUCE, James M. to Sarah Waggoner - issued March 8, 1845, DAVIDSON Co.

BRUCE, Jefferson to Mary Wallace - issued September 19, 1832, Bondsman: Frederick Dugger, SUMNER Co.

BRUCE, John to Betsey Williams - issued March 13, 1817, Bondsman: Daniel Montgomery, m. by: Wm. Montgomery, J. P., March 13, 1817, SUMNER Co.

BRUCE, John to Mary R. Henderson - issued May 8, 1821, m. by:
Robt. Henderson May 8, 1821, RUTHERFORD Co.

BRUCE, John to Elizabeth Seargent - issued January 14, 1869, m. by:
J. Seargent, J. P., January 14, 1869, FRANKLIN Co.

BRUCE, John W. to Eliza Kenedy - m. by: Robt. Patton, J. P., July 7,
1835, SUMNER Co.

BRUCE, Littleton to Jane Duff - issued April 2, 1821, Bondsman:
Adam Turner, m. by: Isaac Lindsey April 2, 1821, SUMNER Co.

BRUCE, Reuben to Jemima Brown - issued December 9, 1826, Bondsman:
Simon Bruce, m. by: Stephen R. Roberts, J. P., December 9, 1826,
SUMNER Co.

BRUCE, Robert to Susannah Cobb - issued October 3, 1817, Bondsman:
William McQuay, m. by: Douglas October 3, 1817, SUMNER Co.

BRUCE, Robert to Hannah Cantrell - issued February 27, 1830, Bondsman:
Wm. Jones, SUMNER Co.

BRUCE, Robert to Hannah Cantrell - issued February 27, 1831, m. by:
J. S. Swaney, J. P., February 27, 1831, SUMNER Co.

BRUCE, Robert to Mary T. Pryor - issued December 24, 1861, m. by:
John J. Pittman, M. G., December 24, 1861, COFFEE Co.

BRUCE (or Breed), Sarah to James Harrison - GREENE Co.

BRUCE, Thomas to Polly Turpin - issued May 5, 1817, Bondsman:
William Dorris, m. by: John McMurtry, J. P., May 5, 1817, SUMNER Co.

BRUCE, W. J. to Lucy Pepper - issued October 19, 1860, m. by:
Jo Hardaway, J. P., ROBERTSON Co.

BRUCE, Walter to Polly Smith - issued October 10, 1804, Bondsman:
D. Dugger, SUMNER Co.

BRUCE, William to Elizabeth Buchannon - issued November 6, 1832,
Bondsman: James Benton, m. by: Peter Ketring, J. P., November 6,
1832, SUMNER Co.

BRUCE, Wilson to Elizabeth Frazier - issued June 19, 1845, m. by:
J. P. Bellamy, L.E. of M.E. Church S, June 19, 1845, MONTGOMERY Co.

BRUICE, Archibald to Martha Leath - issued October 6, 1836, Bondsman:
Shelton Dalton, m. October 28, 1836, SUMNER Co.

BRUICE, S. C. to M. O. Smith - m. by: H. B. Hill August 15, 1837,
SUMNER Co.

BRUMBALOW, Lewis to Inisey Crutcher - issued June 2, 1851, m. by:
James Anderson, J. P., June 8, 1851, ROBERTSON Co.

BRUMBAUGH, A. C. to Jane Sheridan - issued October 26, 1854, Bondsman:
W. G. Beck, m. by: W. E. Beaumont, J. P., October 26, 1854,
MONTGOMERY Co.

BRUMBELOW, Archd. to Susanna Neely - issued November 9, 1838, DAVIDSON Co.

BRUMET, Lerry to Elizabeth M. Clay - issued August 25, 1842, m. by:
B. M. Barnes, J. P., August 25, 1842, DAVIDSON Co.

BRUMFIELD, Humphrey to Mary Ann King - issued February 20, 1826,
Bondsman: John Philips, GRAINGER Co.

BRUMLY, Augustine to Elizabeth Wagg - January 3, 1797, Security:
Barnet Brumly, GREENE Co.

BRUMLY, John to Mary Brumly - April 15, 1797, Security: Barnet and Augustine Brumly, GREENE Co.

BRUMLY, John, Jun. to Catherine Countz - February 12, 1798, Security: John, Sen. and Larkin Brumly, GREENE Co.

BRUMLEY, Mary to James Davis - GREENE Co.

BRUMLY, Mary to John Brumly - GREENE Co.

BRUMLY, William to Susanna Rayton - March 18, 1793, Security: John (?) Right, GREENE Co.

BRUMMIT, William to Rebecca Simpson - issued September 16, 1797, Bondsman: William Dunlap, Witness: Chas. McClung, KNOX Co.

BRUNSON, Asabel to Emily Smiley - issued February 7, 1839, m. by: J. T. Edgar February 7, 1839, DAVIDSON Co.

BRUNSON, Isaac K. to Elizabeth Heflin - issued September 18, 1848, m. by: W. B. Howell, J. P., September 18, 1848, STEWART Co.

BRUNSON, John to Polina Fuqua - issued December 21, 1847, m. December 24, 1847, STEWART Co.

BRUNSON, Smiley to Emily Smiley - issued February 7, 1839, m. by: J. T. Edgar February 7, 1839, DAVIDSON Co.

BRUNTY, James to Eliza Long - issued June 5, 1848, Bondsman: Wm. B. Collins, MONTGOMERY Co.

BRUTON, Berry to Patsy Casteel - Bondsman: J. P. Casteel, BEDFORD Co.

BRYAN, A. J. W. to Virginia C. Tate - issued January 13, 1850, Bondsman: M. W. Bryan, m. by: Mark Senter, M. G., January 15, 1850, MONTGOMERY Co.

BRYAN, Abner to Frances Powell - issued December 17, 1855, m. by: John Charles, J. P., December 17, 1855, COFFEE Co.

BRYAN, Agnes to Jacob Anderson - GREENE Co.

BRYAN, Andres to Mary Crosby - October 29, 1800, Security: James Hays and Thomas Crosby, GREENE Co.

BRYAN, Arthur to Margaret Kirk - issued October 26, 1850, Bondsman: Wm. S. Bryan, m. by: Stephen Cook October 27, 1850, MONTGOMERY Co.

BRYAN, Christopher to Mary T. Bryan - issued March 1, 1847, Bondsman: A. J. W. Bryan, m. by: W. B. CArney, J. P., March 1, 1847, MONTGOMERY Co.

BRYAN (or O'Bryan), Dennis to Anny Hamilton - issued June 16, 1795, Bondsman: John Hamilton, SUMNER Co.

BRYAN, Henry to Frances Ann Smith - issued January 23, 1843, m. by: R. Wilson, J. P., January 24, 1843, STEWART Co.

BRYAN, J. A. to V. M. Kelly - issued January 1, 1866, Bondsman: W. J. McAnally, m. by: R. L. McLaren, J. P., January 2, 1866, LAWRENCE Co.

BRYAN, J. C. to Sarah E. Holmes - issued November 26, 1860, m. by: William Wilson, M. G., November 27, 1860, COFFEE Co.

BRYAN, Jefferson to Fany Locke - issued February 21, 1830, m. by: James B. Taylor, J. P., WILSON Co.

BRYAN, Jesse H. to Sarah Myatt - m. by: David Gray, M. G., July 17, 1844, DICKSON Co.

BRYAN, John to Esther Anderson - issued September 10, 1794, Bondsman: James Anderson, Witness: Chas. McClung, C. K. C., KNOX Co.

BRYAN, John to Nancey Moore - issued December 6, 1809, Bondsman: Joseph Bryan, GRAINGER Co.

BRYAN, John A. to Charlotte E. Hampton - issued March 18, 1858, m. by: John Charles, J. P., March 21, 1858, COFFEE Co.

BRYAN, John W. to Martha France - December 16, 1837, m. by: J. M. Busick, J. P., GILES Co.

BRYAN, Joseph to Elizabeth Hill - issued February 15, 1820, Bondsman: Thomas D. Karling, m. by: William Lane, J. P., February 17, 1820, GRAINGER Co.

BRYAN, Josiah to Polley Redding - issued March 19, 1807, Bondsman: Mathew Redding and Richard Shelton, Witness: Henry Boatman, GRAINGER Co.

BRYAN, Lewis to Nancy Tallent - issued August 30, 1820, m. by: Amos Hardin, J. P. K. C., August 31, 1820, KNOX Co.

BRYAN, Nelson B. to Manerva Jane Waters - issued December 14, 1840, Bondsman: Thos. Waters, m. by: Joshua Lester, M. G., December 16, 1840, WILSON Co.

BRYAN, Thomas to Eliza Ore - issued June 10, 1813, Bondsman: Joseph Bryan, GRAINGER Co.

BRYAN, Thomas H. to Patsy Manifold - issued November 27, 1824, m. by: James McMillan, J. P., December 2, 1824, KNOX Co.

BRYAN, Thomas J. to Mahala Burnes - issued December 8, 1847, m. December 12, 1847, STEWART Co.

BRYAN, Thomas O. to Rebecca L. Cothran - issued January 3, 1844, m. by: J. W. Hunt, J. P., January 10, 1844, ROBERTSON Co.

BRYAN, William to Jenny Gillespie - issued May 1, 1794, Bondsman: George Roulstone, Witness: Hu L. White, KNOX Co.

BRYAN, William to Hester Walker - August 6, 1818, KNOX Co.

BRYAN, William A. G. to Elizabeth McMahan - issued October 3, 1860, m. by: A. J. Carl, L. D., October 3, 1860, COFFEE Co.

BRYAN, Wm. S. to Margaret A. Campbell - issued September 27, 1842, DAVIDSON Co.

BRYANT, Alexander to Catherine Johnson - issued February 28, 1859, m. by: L. D. Phillips, L. D., March 2, 1859, COFFEE Co.

BRYANT, Alfred to Nancy Hickman - issued March 30, 1820, Bondsman: Bryant T. Motley, m. by: Wm. Steele, J. P., March 31, 1820, WILSON Co.

BRYANT, Amelia Caroline to David Watson - BEDFORD Co.

BRYANT, Augustine to Mahala A. May - issued March 22, 1848, m. by: J. M. Stemmons March 23, 1848, ROBERTSON Co.

BRYANT, Calvin to Ann Keith - issued November 17, 1837, m. by: John Pryor November 17, 1837, KNOX Co.

BRYANT, David C. to Maryann Mase - issued January 10, 1855, m. by: G. W. Sparkman, J. P., January 28, 1855, VAN BUREN Co.

BRYANT, Ephram to Fannie Farris - issued September 18, 1873, m. by: James A. Hudgins, M. G., September 15, 1873, FRANKLIN Co.

BRYANT, George W. to Nancy Ross - issued July 22, 1845, m. by:
C. Travis, J. P., July 31, 1845, STEWART Co.

BRYANT, Hiram to Mary Wray - issued January 3, 1825, Bondsman:
Elisha Vaughn, m. by: Jas. T. Tompkins, M. G., January 5, 1825,
WILSON Co.

BRYANT, J. C. to Mary Jetton - issued June 15, 1871, m. by:
J. Campbell, M. G., June 15, 1871, FRANKLIN Co.

BYANT (?), Jesse to Virginia Grissom - issued October 24, 1849, m. by:
John Gillentine, J. P., October 25, 1849, VAN BUREN Co.

BRYANT, John to Nancy Monroe - issued May 1, 1847, Bondsman:
Asa W. Edwards, m. by: Wm. Dinwiddie, M. G., May 9, 1847,
MONTGOMERY Co.

BRYANT, John to Elizabeth W. Monroe - issued January 19, 1852, Bondsman:
George W. Bryant, m. by: John Gold, J. P., January 22, 1852,
MONTGOMERY Co.

BRYANT, John B. to Katarine Waters - issued October 17, 1836, Bondsman:
Thomas McKee, m. by: Joshua Lester, V. D. M., WILSON Co.

BRYANT, Levi to Nelly Hall - issued August 15, 1826, Bondsman:
Joseph Spradlin, SUMNER Co.

BRYANT, Lytle to Sarah Wilkerson - issued August 1, 1835, Bondsman:
Nathl. Cartwell, m. by: John Beard, M. G., August 13, 1835,
WILSON Co.

BRYANT, N. A. D. to Susan E. Joslin - issued November 24, 1845,
DICKSON Co.

BRYANT, Nicholas to Melinda J. Ainsworth - issued April 10, 1847,
m. by: B. F. Fraser, J. P., February 11, 1847, STEWART Co.

BRYANT, Robt. H. to Zoy Charton - issued August 27, 1874, FRANKLIN Co.

BRYANT, Samuel B. to Mary Manley - issued June 22, 1836, Bondsman:
Robt. S. Morris, m. by: Samuel S. Parrish, J. P., June 23, 1836,
RUTHERFORD Co.

BRYANT, Silas to Tabitha Fogg - issued March 25, 1847, DAVIDSON Co.

BRYANT, Thomas to Charlotta Jetton - issued June 5, 1837, Bondsman:
J. C. Spillars, WILSON Co.

BRYANT, William to Lucy Kirby - issued August 2, 1816, m. by:
Solomon Beesly, J. P., RUTHERFORD Co.

BRYANT, William to Ceyley Higdon - issued August 27, 1823, Bondsman:
James Allcorn, WILSON Co.

BRYANT, William to Martha Blakely - issued April 1, 1838, m. by:
A. L. Hughes, J. P., April 6, 1838, FRANKLIN Co.

BRYANT, William to Malinda B. Olliver - issued March 18, 1839,
FRANKLIN Co.

BRYANT, William Colton to Rebecca Ann Wilson - issued December 30,
1845, m. by: Samuel Taylor, J. P., December 30, 1845, FRANKLIN Co.

BRYANT, Wm. J. to Mary C. Reeves - issued September 25, 1851, m. by:
W. J. Fox, V. D. M., September 25, 1851, FRANKLIN Co.

BRYANT, William L. J. to Elizabeth A. Thomas - issued September 3,
1833, Bondsman: Alfred Whitfield, RUTHERFORD Co.

BRYANT, Wm. M. to Susan White - issued November 5, 1846, Bondsman:
S. C. Ransom, m. by: John Gold, J. P., November 5, 1846,
MONTGOMERY Co.

BRYANT, William T. to Jane Kerr - issued December 16, 1829, Bondsman:
Robert S. Morris, RUTHERFORD Co.

BRYAR, James J. to Nannie Brazelton - issued April 26, 1870, m. by:
M. H. Bone, M. G., April 29, 1870, FRANKLIN Co.

BRYLIE, Hiram to Patsey Wilet - m. by: G. Edward December 19, 1835,
SUMNER Co.

BRYLIE, Samuel to Nancy Summers - m. by: T. Y. Turner, J. P.,
December 29, 1835, SUMNER Co.

BRYNE, Milton S. to Fredonia R. Martin - issued January 2, 1840,
Bondsman: Wm. C. Winston, m. by: J. B. Lasater, J. P., WILSON Co.

BRYSON, Daniel to Martha Reed - issued October 28, 1833, m. by:
John McMinn, J. P., November 6, 1833, WILSON Co.

BRYSON, Elisha to Polly Ward - issued December 8, 1818, Bondsman:
John Leeck, m. by: John McMinn, J. P., December 10, 1818,
WILSON Co.

BRYSON, Hiram to Jemima A. Alexander - issued August 31, 1833, m. by:
John McMinn, J. P., August 3, 1833, WILSON Co.

BRYSON, John to Nancy Fuston - issued October 15, 1829, Bondsman:
George Bogle, WILSON Co.

BRYSON, John to Lottie Beech - issued September 29, 1835, Bondsman:
Mark Alexander, m. by: James Thomas, M. G., WILSON Co.

BRYSON, Joseph to Jane Bryson - issued August 1, 1827, Bondsman:
William Bryson, m. by: John McMinn, J. P., WILSON Co.

BRYSON, Peter to June Gillespie - issued August 1, 1809, Bondsman:
George Gillespie, SUMNER Co.

BRYSON, Robert to Sarah Stanley - issued August 9, 1833, m. by:
John McMinn, J. P., August 15, 1833, WILSON Co.

BRYSON, Samuel to Mary Milligan - issued February 3, 1826, Bondsman:
David Milligan, m. by: Christophis Cooper, M. G., February 4,
1826, WILSON Co.

BRYSON, Samuel B. to Elizabeth Davenport - issued November 7, 1836,
m. by: George Bogle, J. P., December 23, 1836, WILSON Co.

BRYSON, William to Lydia Stanley - issued August 24, 1816, Bondsman:
Andrew Kirkpatrick, WILSON Co.

BRYSON, William to Elizabeth Nicholson - issued August 20, 1822,
Bondsman: Samuel C. Odom, WILSON Co.

BRYSON, William to Sophia Matthews - issued September 8, 1830, Bondsman:
James Wilson, WILSON Co.

BRYSON, William to Elizabeth McGlothlin - issued May 18, 1844, m. by:
James A. Haston, J. P., May 19, 1844, VAN BUREN Co.

BUCALLO, William to Eleanor Holt - December 16, 1815, KNOX Co.

BUCHANAN, ___(?) to Araminta D. Bumpass - April 7, 1851, Security:
A. D. Smith, GILES Co.

BUCHANAN, Alexander to Margaret M. Matlock - issued May 31, 1845, m. by:
John Beard, M. G., June 5, 1845, DAVIDSON Co.

BUCHANAN, Benj. A. to Jane Ray - issued November 28, 1872, m. by:
James A. Hudgins, M. G., November 28, 1872, FRANKLIN Co.

BUCHANAN, Clay to Agness Peters - issued October 2, 1873, m. by:
W. P. DuBose December 16, 1873, FRANKLIN Co.

BUCHANAN, Daniel to Cathrine Presswood - issued September 18, 1858,
m. by: W. H. Byrom, J. P., September 19, 1858, FRANKLIN Co.

BUCHANAN, David B. to Lucenda Shepherd - issued November 22, 1852,
Bondsman: Robert E. Thacker, m. by: W. B. Walker, M. G.,
November 25, 1852, MONTGOMERY Co.

BUCHANAN, James to Mariah T. Ott - issued November 17, 1836, Bondsman:
Richard Lyons, RUTHERFORD Co.

BUCHANAN, John to Elizabeth Anderton (Anderson) - issued January 4,
1841, m. by: L. G. Simpson, J. P., January 5, 1841, FRANKLIN Co.

BUCHANAN, John to Martha Ford - issued January 1, 1845, STEWART Co.

BUCHANAN, John to Mary Hanks - issued December 1, 1857, m. by:
Thos. Finch, J. P., December 1, 1857, FRANKLIN Co.

BUCHANAN, John A. to Rebecca E. Womack - issued December 5, 1872,
m. by: James A. Hudgins, M. G., December 5, 1872, FRANKLIN Co.

BUCHANAN, M. H. to Sarah E. McAnally - issued September 20, 1865,
Bondsman: D. M. Foster, m. by: W. P. Warren, P. C., September 20,
1865, LAWRENCE Co.

BUCHANAN, Robt. to Sarah Hampton - October 12, 1807, WILLIAMSON Co.

BUCHANAN, W. J. to Sarah A. Curry - issued August 16, 1864, Bondsman:
M. H. Buchanan, LAWRENCE Co.

BUCHANAN, Wm. to Mary Clanton - issued April 23, 1858, FRANKLIN Co.

BUCHANAN, Wm. S. to Nancy Keith - issued August 1, 1850, m. by:
A. G. Gibson, M. G., August 1, 1850, FRANKLIN Co.

BUCHANNON, Cleton to Clarissa Spicer - STEWART Co.

BUCHANON, Addison to Sarah M. Fleming - issued March 8, 1847, m. by:
John Beard, M. G., March 9, 1847, DAVIDSON Co.

BUCHANON, John R. to Nancy E. Hays - issued May 27, 1841, m. by:
E. M. Patterson, J. P., May 26, 1841, DAVIDSON Co.

BUCHANON, William to Nancy Wortham - issued October 11, 1815, Bondsman:
B. W. McWhirter, WILSON Co.

BUCHINGHAM, Peter to Milley F. Dickens - issued October 1, 1862,
Bondsman: Stephen Batten, Jos. H. Thompson, Clk. per N. F. Thompson,
D. Clk., BEDFORD Co.

BUCK, John W. to Emiliza Garrett - m. by: John McLin April 4, 1837,
SUMNER Co.

BUCK, Thos. M. to Martha Hanks - issued January 30, 1839, m. by:
W. D. T. Sawrie, M. G., January 31, 1839, DAVIDSON Co.

BUCKALEW, James to Mahala Holt - issued August 25, 1824, Bondsman:
Joshua Jackson, KNOX Co.

BUCKER, Thos. G. to Susan E. Smith - issued May 11, 1865, FRANKLIN Co.

BUCKHAM, Andrew to Charlotte Taylor - issued July 15, 1808, Bondsman:
William McNutt and Joe Parrish, SUMNER Co.

BUCKHANNAN, Samuel D. to Susan H. Moss - issued October 12, 1847,
   Bondsman: A. J. Fortner, m. October 22, 1847, MONTGOMERY Co.

BUCKHANNAN, Wm. to Mariah Thomas - issued July 13, 1846, Bondsman:
   Wm. M. Shelton, m. by: H. McFall July 14, 1846, MONTGOMERY Co.

BUCKHART, Joseph to Sallie Lumpkin - August 11, 1812, KNOX Co.

BUCKHART, Peter to Anna Gillum - issued August 10, 1836, Bondsman:
   Thos. Frazier, m. by: Jno. Mynatt, J. P., August 14, 1836, KNOX Co.

BUCKINGHAM, Ann to William Walker - November 24, 1786, Security:
   Foseph Hardin, GREENE Co.

BUCKINGHAM, Thos. to Elizabeth Talbot - m. by: John Wiseman December 21,
   1833, SUMNER Co.

BUCKLEY, Embry to Susan Martin - m. by: John Wiseman November 4, 1837,
   SUMNER Co.

BUCKLEY, William to Polly Henneman - January 25, 1804, KNOX Co.

BUCKLEY, William to Rebecca Johnson - issued August 21, 1820, Bondsman:
   Oliver Johnson, m. by: Joshua __(?), V. D. M., August 22, 1820,
   WILSON Co.

BUCKLY, Henry J. to Nancy Miles - issued December 17, 1845, Bondsman:
   Carney Batson, m. by: J. Moore December 18, 1825, MONTGOMERY Co.

BUCKLY, Patrick H. to Frances Dickinson - issued June 30, 1825,
   Bondsman: James Taylor, SUMNER Co.

BUCKNER, D. L. to Mary S. Justin - issued October 28, 1873, FRANKLIN Co.

BUCKNER, E. D. to S. E. Johnson - issued May 22, 1862, Bondsman:
   H. M. Poplin, m. by: James W. Locke May 23, 1862, LAWRENCE Co.

BUCKNER, Henry to Bella (Cilly) Woodall - issued August 13, 1800,·
   Bondsman: Thomas Wittson, GRAINGER Co.

BUCKNER, James to Tompy Gibson - issued May 26, 1838, Bondsman:
   James T. Sims, WILSON Co.

BUCKNER, Joe to Vina Lynch - issued December 12, 1868, FRANKLIN Co.

BUCKNER, John K. to Sophiah Austell - issued April 25, 1857, m. by:
   J. F. L. Faris, J. P., May 3, 1857, COFFEE Co.

BUCKNER, Presley R. to Mary Bostick - issued November 4, 1856, m. by:
   Wm. W. Conn, M. G., November 6, 1856, FRANKLIN Co.

BUCKNER, Richmond L. to Sarah A. Perkins - issued April 7, 1849, m. by:
   A. Gilliam, P. G., April 7, 1349, FRANKLIN Co.

BUCKNER, Richmond T. to Nancy J. Perkins - issued December 11, 1843,
   m. by: D. N. Brakefield, J. P., December 12, 1843, FRANKLIN Co.

BUCKNER, S. W. to Mary K. Brakefield - issued March 10, 1874, m. by:
   Wm. Delzell, J. P., March 10, 1874, FRANKLIN Co.

BUCKNER, W. S. to Caroline S. Morn - issued April 28, 1849, Bondsman:
   T. M. Shelton, MONTGOMERY Co.

BUCKNER, Wilson to Mary S. Bass - issued May 23, 1872, m. by:
   Asa D. Oakley, M. G., May 23, 1872, FRANKLIN Co.

BUCLEW, George to Rachel Holt - issued August 10, 1816, KNOX Co.

BUDD, Thos. L. to Eliza Jane Moffett - issued November 9, 1839, m. by:
R. B. C. Howell, Pastor Baptist Ch., November 9, 1839, DAVIDSON Co.

BUFORD, James to Polly Giddens - October 6, 1812, WILLIAMSON Co.

BUFORD, John to Sarah Elliott - issued April ·3, 1824, Bondsman:
George W. Lee, RUTHERFORD Co.

BUGG, Arthur D. to Tabitha J. Smith - issued October 11, 1821, Bondsman:
Ethelbert Sanders, SUMNER Co.

BUGG, Bob to __(?) Seany __(?) - issued June 4, 1838, Bondsman:
William Twopence, m. by: Ben Gray June 4, 1838, SUMNER Co.

BUGG, John M. to Sarah Taylor - m. by: H. B. Hill February 14, 1838,
SUMNER Co.

BUGG, Richard G. to Prudence Chapill - issued December 13, 1824,
Bondsman: Thomas Gregory, m. by: J. H. Swaney, M. P., December 13,
1824, SUMNER Co.

BUGG, Samuel to Lucy Sweaney - issued June 7, 1838, m. by: H. W. Turner,
J. P., June 8, 1838, DICKSON Co.

BUGS, Willeby to Polly Wills - issued August 7, 1816, m. by:
Thomas Berry, J. P., August 8, 1816, RUTHERFORD Co.

BUKERSTAFF, Henry to Peggy Hannah - issued June 8, 1799, Bondsman:
David Head, Witness: H. L. White, KNOX Co.

BULL, George to Elizabeth Grayson - issued February 4, 1802, Bondsman:
John Bull, GRAINGER Co.

BULL, Jeremiah to Mary E. Horn - issued January 2, 1846, m. by:
E. Bishop, M. G., January 6, 1846, DICKSON Co.

BULL, John to Nelley Collins - issued November 23, 1800, Bondsman:
John Bull, Senr., Witness: Sm'l Yancey, GRAINGER Co.

BULL, John to Fetney Bean - issued April 3, 1806, Bondsman:
Bartley Marshall, GRAINGER Co.

BULL, Joseph to Nancey Bray - issued June 7, 1810, Bondsman:
Stagner Bray, GRAINGER Co.

BULL, Richard to Fanncy Bray - issued May 11, 1805, Bondsman: John Ogan,
GRAINGER Co.

BULL, William A. to Mary Anderson - issued September 20, 1820, Bondsman:
Ramsey L. Mason, m. by: Thos. Anderson, J. P., September 20, 1820,
SUMNER Co.

BULLA, James to Sally Carlisle - issued January 21, 1805, Bondsman:
James Carlisle, RUTHERFORD Co.

BULLARD, Ann to Moses Johnston - GREENE Co.

BULLARD, George H. to Elizabeth Spradlin - issued March 2, 1815,
Bondsman: John Harpole, WILSON Co.

BULLARD, John to Agnes Kinsey - January 4, 1786, Security: Luke Bowyer,
GREENE Co.

BULLARD, John to Rebecca Bumgarner - issued December 26, 1817, Bondsman:
Hezekiah Rhodes, m. by: George Uselton, J. P., December 27, 1817,
RUTHERFORD Co.

BULLARD, Mary to David Rutledge - GREENE Co.

BULLARD, Peter H. to Louiza Jane Herod - issued September 14, 1834, Bondsman: James R. Smith, RUTHERFORD Co.

BULLARD (Ballard), Phebe to James Carter - GREENE Co.

BULLEN, Joseph to Betsy Dolson - issued June 19, 1821, Bondsman: Joseph Beeler and Benjamin Fry, GRAINGER Co.

BULLIN, Isaac to Mary Dotson - issued November 3, 1829, Bondsman: Joseph Bullin, GRAINGER Co.

BULLION, Henry to Sarah Hambrick - issued August 21, 1844, m. by: Samuel Tate, J. P., August 22, 1844, DICKSON Co.

BULLOCH, Thomas to Francis Williams - issued June 14, 1829, Bondsman: John F. McCutchen, RUTHERFORD Co.

BULLOCK, Amos to Rachel Tompkins - January 9, 1805, WILLIAMSON Co.

BULLOCK, Elijah to Polley Norris - issued February 21, 1809, Bondsman: Jeremiah Norris, GRAINGER Co.

BULLOCK, Jonathon to Penelope Fly - April 9, 1821, MAURY Co.

BULLOCK, Nathan to Sarah Hays - April 22, 1806, WILLIAMSON Co.

BULLOUCK, Howel C. to Josephine Reynolds - December 11, 1861, m. by: G. D. Taylor, GILES Co.

BULLS, Barnabas to Elizabeth Deene - August 18, 1813, WILLIAMSON Co.

BUMGARNER, Peter to Nancy Gregory - issued September 29, 1817, m. by: George Uselton, J. P., October 1, 1817, RUTHERFORD Co.

BUMPAS, Robert H. to Eliza S. Craddock - issued January 24, 1837, Bondsman: Geo. Smith, m. by: John Whitlock, V. D. M., January 8, 1837, WILSON Co.

BUMPASS, George W. to Mary Ann Price - issued January 12, 1854, Bondsman: Buckner Killebrew, m. by: T. A. Jones, J. P., January 12, 1854, MONTGOMERY Co.

BUMPASS, John to Mary J. Jones - issued December 19, 1850, Bondsman: Sam'l Bumpass, m. by: C. Orgain December 18, 1850, MONTGOMERY Co.

BUMPASS, Joseph to Elizabeth N. Jones - issued January 1, 1851, Bondsman: Sampson Hart, m. by: E. Bishop January 5, 1851, MONTGOMERY Co.

BUMPASS, Robert H. to Martha Wade - issued July 30, 1821, m. by: R. Henderson July 31, 1821, RUTHERFORD Co.

BUMPASS, Samuel to Lucy D. Jones - issued December 10, 1845, Bondsman: Kinchen Bumpass, m. by: G. W. Martin December 10, 1845, MONTGOMERY Co.

BUMPASS, Wm. to Maranda Ogg - issued February 21, 1861, m. by: W. L. Adams February 27, 1861, ROBERTSON Co.

BUMPIS, John F. to Nancy J. Clark - issued December 11, 1848, m. by: John Richards, J. P., STEWART Co.

BUNCH, Mary to Peter Miller - GREENE Co.

BUNDY, David to Frances Martin - issued November 20, 1822, m. by: James Walton November 20, 1822, SUMNER Co.

BUNDY, James to Rebecca Williford - issued February 11, 1823, m. by: Wilson Hearn, M. G., February 13, 1823, WILSON Co.

BUNDY, John to Nancy Williford - issued January 21, 1834, Bondsman:
John Obrien, m. by: B. T. Mabry January 23, 1834, WILSON Co.

BUNDY, Nathan to Absilla Johnson - issued June 18, 1818, Bondsman:
Elijah Jones, m. by: John Dew, M. G., WILSON Co.

BUNDY, Nathan to Martha G. Mullin - issued September 23, 1839, Bondsman:
Allgood Woolard, m. by: Jas. C. Willeford, J. P., September 24,
1839, WILSON Co.

BUNN, Louisa to George Woodward - BEDFORD Co.

BUNNY, Samuel to Jane Davis - issued December 22, 1824, RUTHERFORD Co.

BUNTIN, Theodore to Mariah Tally - issued August 27, 1864, Bondsman:
Smith Batson, m. by: Wm. Frazer, J. P., August 27, 1854,
MONTGOMERY Co.

BUNTING, Thomas W. to Sarah Vaughn - issued February 9, 1847, Bondsman:
J. R. Watson, m. by: John E. Bond, February 4, 1847, MONTGOMERY Co.

BUNTNG, W. B. to Louisa E. McQuerry - issued January 15, 1850, Bondsman:
J. R. Watson, m. by: R. Ross, P. G., January 17, 1850,
MONTGOMERY Co.

BUNTON, James to Sindy H. Thomas - issued January 9, 1817, Bondsman:
James Thomas, m. by: Abner W. Bone, WILSON Co.

BUNTON, John W. to Mary H. Howell - m. by: J. W. Hall February 5, 1837,
SUMNER Co.

BUNTON, Thomas to Betsey Turner - issued April 27, 1819, Bondsman:
Robert Desha, m. April 27, 1819, SUMNER Co.

BUNTON, William R. to Elizabeth Cotton - issued December 31, 1842,
DAVIDSON Co.

BURAM, Henry to Nancy F. Badgett - issued December 18, 1832, Bondsman:
Jno. T. King, KNOX Co.

BURCHAM, William to Polly Durham - issued March 1, 1844, m. by:
Jas. Chambers, J. P., March 3, 1844, STEWART Co.

BURCHET, John to Susan Shepherd - m. by: Robt. Patton, J. P., April 14,
1834, SUMNER Co.

BURCHETT, Anderson to Sally Vernon - issued June 21, 1823, Bondsman:
Thomas Burchett, RUTHERFORD Co.

BURCHETT, Bradley to Elizabeth Burgess - issued December 23, 1834,
Bondsman: John Johnston, RUTHERFORD Co.

BURCHETT, Henry to Editha Stratton - issued May 12, 1848, m. by:
David M. Wells, J. P., May 18, 1848, ROBERTSON Co.

BURCHETT, J. W. to W. E. Lipford - issued November 16, 1860, m. by:
F. C. Plaster, M. G., ROBERTSON Co.

BURCHETT, Thomas to Sarah Petty - issued December 30, 1841, m. by:
D. Judd, L. E., December 30, 1841, DAVIDSON Co.

BURCHETT, William to Sally Doyal - issued May 28, 1806, Bondsman:
John Doyal, SUMNER Co.

BURCHETT, Wm. to Fanny Elsbery - issued July 8, 1847, m. by:
Josiah Ferriss, J. P., July 8, 1847, DAVIDSON Co.

BURD, A. W. to Nancy A. Doty - issued October 2, 1857, m. by:
H. H. Orndorff, J. P., ROBERTSON Co.

BURFORD, John H. to Nancy McCollester - issued March 24, 1817, Bondsman:
   Jesse Clark, SUMNER Co.

BURGE, Henry to Elizabeth Knox - issued November 4, 1824, Bondsman:
   William Faulkenbury, RUTHERFORD Co.

BURGE, Jeremiah to Zibeath Clemmons - issued February 20, 1816, m. by:
   G. W. Banton, J. P., February 22, 1816, RUTHERFORD Co.

BURGE, John F. to Frances Causby - December 20, 1860, Security:
   Thomas S. Pittard, GILES Co.

BURGE, Petermon to Elizabeth Palmer - issued February 26, 1817, Bondsman:
   James Slate, WILSON Co.

BURGE, Richard to Nancy Massey - issued April 30, 1818, Bondsman:
   William Faulkenberry, RUTHERFORD Co.

BURGESS, A. to Francis Stalls - issued February 25, 1843, STEWART C-.

BURGESS, Albert to Eliza Chilton - issued January 12, 1857, m. by:
   B. B. Batts, J. P., January 11, 1857, ROBERTSON Co.

BURGESS, Boling J. to Rachel C. Terry - issued January 30, 1840,
   m. by: Jeremiah Batts, J. P., ROBERTSON Co.

BURGESS, Edward to Mary Blanton - issued December 10, 1829, Bondsman:
   John Burgess, m. by: John Lane, RUTHERFORD Co.

BURGESS, James to Mary Ayres - issued November 3, 1861, m. by:
   J. W. Featherston, ROBERTSON Co.

BURGESS, James H. to Elizabeth A. Bassham - issued October 7, 1863,
   Bondsman: William Fondrin, LAWRENCE Co.

BURGESS, John to Nancy Johnson - issued June 10, 1825, m. by:
   Peyton Smith June 16, 1825, RUTHERFORD Co.

BURGESS, John to Phebee Watkins - issued December 28, 1839, m. by:
   W. B. Dotson, J. P., December 29, 1839, DICKSON Co.

BURGESS, John to Jane Gardner - January 8, 1850, m. by: J. W. Lee,
   M. G., GILES Co.

BURGESS, Joseph to Rebecca Mahan - issued April 19, 1845, m. by:
   I. C. Pullem, J. P., April 21, 1845, DICKSON Co.

BURGESS, Margaret to Joseph Matthews - GREENE Co.

BURGESS, Thomas to Sally Blanton - issued January 2, 1821, m. by:
   H. Robinson, J. P., January 3, 1821, RUTHERFORD Co.

BURGESS, William to Martha Murphy - issued May 8, 1851, m. by:
   R. G. Cole, J. P., May 9, 1851, ROBERTSON Co.

BURHAM, Mary to D. B. Burrow - DAVIDSON Co.

BURK, Arthur L. to Matilda M. Henry - issued October 3, 1842, m. by:
   Wm. L. Baldry, M. G., October 5, 1842, ROBERTSON Co.

BURK, Edward to Allis Hegarty - issued April 20, 1819, Bondsman:
   William Hartsfield, WILSON Co.

BURK, Elisha to Mary Robinson - issued August 25, 1792, Bondsman:
   William Miller, SUMNER Co.

BURK, Elmore to Bety Vaughn - issued September 29, 1870, m. by:
   G. S. Wedington, J. P., September 29, 1870, FRANKLIN Co.

BURK, Lewis to Elizabeth Letzinger - issued June 8, 1827, Bondsman:
Green L. White, SUMNER Co.

BURK, Thomas to Fanny Robertson - issued February 26, 1822, Bondsman:
Thos. McKnight, WILSON Co.

BURK, William to Rachel Cooper - issued December 31, 1795, Bondsman:
William Parner, SUMNER Co.

BURK, Wm. P. to Mary Denson - issued February 19, 1857, m. by:
John T. Slatter, J. P., February 19, 1857, FRANKLIN Co.

BURK, Arnold to Margaret Smith - issued May 18, 1827, Bondsman:
Thos. Burk, WILSON Co.

BURKE, Charles to Margaret Maynard - issued October 24, 1841, m. by:
E. S. Hall October 24, 1841, DAVIDSON Co.

BURKE, Feilding to Anna Cluck - issued March 13, 1837, Bondsman:
James Cluck, m. by: Wm. Alsup, J. P., March 15, 1837, WILSON Co.

BURKE, James M. to Caroline Braime - issued November 25, 1846, m. by:
John Gold, J. P., November 29, 1845, MONTGOMERY Co.

BURKE, John G. to Lucy M. Moore - issued December 30, 1846, m. by:
John Corbett, J. P., December 31, 1846, DAVIDSON Co.

BURKE, John H. to Caroline T. Vaughn - issued November 19, 1842,
DAVIDSON Co.

BURKE, Richard to Elizabeth Roeolin - issued May 20, 1805, Bondsman:
Ryland Burke, GRAINGER Co.

BURKE, Sam'l R. to Charity Halloway - issued January 20, 1840, m. by:
John Morton, DAVIDSON Co.

BURKES, Martin C. to Sally Osborn - issued September 21, 1838, m. by:
John Weaver October 4, 1838, FRANKLIN Co.

BURKES, Richard to Charlott Burkes - issued September 27, 1838,
FRANKLIN Co.

BURKES, Willis to Charlotte Miller - issued October 29, 1827, Bondsman:
John F. Howland, RUTHERFORD Co.

BURKIT, Daniel to Massey Honneycut - June 1, 1809, Bondsman: James Love,
MAURY Co.

BURKS, J. K. to Margaret E. Wiser - issued February 28, 1860, m. by:
Samuel Umbarger, J. P., February 28, 1860, COFFEE Co.

BURKS, James to Amy Lucas - issued December 26, 1839, m. by: L. R. Sims,
J. P., December 26, 1839, FRANKLIN Co.

BURKS, James to Mary Duncan - issued December 23, 1871, m. by:
J. L. Payne, M. G., December 23, 1871, FRANKLIN Co.

BURKS, John to Martha Lucas - issued June 28, 1839, m. by:
George Hudspeth, J. P., FRANKLIN Cc.

BURKS, John W. to Harriett Dousan - issued September 21, 1858, m. by:
John T. Slatter, J. P., September 22, 1858, FRANKLIN Co.

BURKS, Leroy to Rebecca Harbern - issued April 17, 1816, m. by:
George Uselton April 17, 1816, RUTHERFORD Co.

BURKS, Lorenso to Arena Lewis - issued March 19, 1839, m. by:
H. W. Turner, J. P., DICKSON Co.

BURKS, Margaret to Alexander Clark - BEDFORD Co.

BURKS, Obadiah to Sarah Miller - issued December 16, 1874, m. by:
M. Carter, M. G., December 20, 1874, FRANKLIN Co.

BURKS, Thomas M. to Mary C. Lucas - issued October 15, 1847, m. by:
C. L. Blanton, J. P., October 15, 1847, FRANKLIN Co.

BURKS, William to Martha Clark - issued December 5, 1860, m. by:
W. P. Keith, J. P., December 9, 1860, FRANKLIN Co.

BURKS, Willis to Lucinda Blakely - issued February 1, 1834, Bondsman:
William Ledbetter, RUTHERFORD Co.

BURLESON, Hilkay to Penelope Pope - issued September 22, 1810, Bondsman:
Ezekiel Pope, RUTHERFORD Co.

BURLESON, Joseph to Patience Ward - issued January 7, 1817, m. by:
David Gordon April 4, 1817, RUTHERFORD Co.

BURLISON, David to Ruthy Hobson - issued March 8, 1819, m. by:
Peyton Smith March 11, 1819, RUTHERFORD Co.

BURLISON, Jr., H. K. to Mary L. Cochran - issued May 21, 1865, Bondsman:
John J. Burlison, LAWRENCE Co.

BURLISON, Jr., Hillkiah to Mary L. Cochran - issued May 21, 1864,
Bondsman: John J. Burlison, m. by: J. M. Pennington, J. P.,
May 21, 1864, LAWRENCE Co.

BURLISON, Isaac to Fanny Morton - issued March 17, 1818, Bondsman:
Thos. G. Watkins, m. by: John Fulton, J. P., March 22, 1818,
RUTHERFORD Co.

BURMAN, Owen to Polly Hood - issued April 12, 1820, Bondsman:
James Hood, m. by: Peter Nance, J. P. K. C., April 13, 1820, KNOX Co.

BURNAM, Joshua to Anna McPherson - January 4, 1816, WILLIAMSON Co.

BURNES, Richard to Nancy Philips - issued January 9, 1847, m. by:
Asa D. Scarborough, J. P., January 9, 1847, STEWART Co.

BURNES, W. J. C. to Sarah J. Dickey - issued March 16, 1864, Bondsman:
W. G. Pennington, LAWRENCE Co.

BURNETT, Absalom to Sarah Catherine Roberts - issued April 27, 1837,
Bondsman: Josephus Alexander, m. by: Wm. Lindsay, J. P., April 27,
1837, KNOX Co.

BURNETT, Anderson to Alley Maney - issued August 7, 1830, Bondsman:
Sam'l Anderson, m. by: Elijah Johnson, J. P., August 8, 1830,
Witness: Wm. Swan, KNOX Co.

BURNETT, Berry (Bery) to Betsy Ellison - issued January 3, 1820,
m. by: Peter Nance, J. P. K. C., KNOX Co.

BURNETT, Berry to Nancy Payne - issued October 4, 1825, Bondsman:
James Allison, m. by: David Nelson, J. P., October 4, 1825,
KNOX Co.

BURNETT, Brooking J. to Lethi Moss - issued March 10, 1825, Bondsman:
Reynear H. Mason, WILSON Co.

BURNETT, Edward to Rachell Cheetwood - July 2, 1801, Security:
James Roddy, BLOUNT Co.

BURNETT, Henry to Parthenea Moss - issued January 9, 1826, Bondsman:
Reynor H. Mason, m. by: Jacob Sullivan January 10, 1826, WILSON Co.

BURNETT, Henry to Jennetta J. Davis - issued August 15, 1843, DAVIDSON Co.

BURNETT, Howell to Elizabeth Sherartz - issued May 31, 1825, Bondsman:
John Sherartz, KNOX Co.

BURNETT, James W. to Lucy Ann Lipford - issued December 10, 1859, m. by:
F. C. Plaster, M. G., December 12, 1859, ROBERTSON Co.

BURNETT, John to Demarius Jourdan - issued March 13, 1846, Bondsman:
E. Trice, m. by: John Mallory March 15, 1846, MONTGOMERY Co.

BURNETT, Joseph to Anna Beesley - issued March 22, 1819, m. by:
John Fulton, J. P., March 25, 1819, RUTHERFORD Co.

BURNETT, Joseph to Jane Martin - issued May 16, 1822, m. by: R. Houston
May 16, 1822, KNOX Co.

BURNETT, Joseph to Sally Brown - issued May 31, 1828, Bondsman:
Benj. Burnett, KNOX Co.

BURNETT, Lewis G. to Temperance A. Perry - issued March 5, 1836,
Bondsman: Andrew Finney, RUTHERFORD Co.

BURNETT, Michael to Rosy Alexander - issued September 10, 1833, m. by:
B. McNutt, J. P., September 11, 1833, KNOX Co.

BURNETT, Samuel to Rowena Pace - issued October 17, 1827, m. by:
J. A. Swan, J. P., KNOX Co.

BURNETT, Thomas M. to Mary J. Whitfield - December 4, 1843, Security:
James H. Strong, GILES Co.

BURNETT, Wm. W. to Martha Dowlen - issued August 3, 1842, m. by:
J. W. Hunt, J. P., August 4, 1842, ROBERTSON Co.

BURNETT, Zachariah to Mary Ford - issued September 20, 1830, Bondsman:
Joseph Burnett, m. by: Elijah Johnson, J. P., September 23, 1830,
KNOX Co.

BURNETTE, Lemuel to Jane Fisher - issued June 6, 1821, m. by:
Sam'l. Montgomery June 7, 1821, KNOX Co.

BURNEY, James H. to Purahan Jernigan - issued December 16, 1839, m. by:
E. J. Williams, J. P., December 18, 1839, ROBERTSON Co.

BURNEY, John C. to Nancy Brown - issued December 29, 1847, Bondsman:
W. L. Burney, m. by: W. R. Morrison, J. P., December 29, 1847,
MONTGOMERY Co.

BURNEY, John M. to Emily Kenedy - issued July 25, 1831, Bondsman:
Joshua Pyles, m. by: Greenberry Garrett, M. G., July 25, 1831,
SUMNER Co.

BURNEY, Robt. A. to Delila Stalcup - m. by: D. Ashford March 2, 1833,
SUMNER Co.

BURNEY, William to Anne Guthrie - issued July 7, 1812, Bondsman:
Isaac Armfield, SUMNER Co.

BURNHAM, Hezekiah to Susanna Hussong - issued February 9, 1826, KNOX Co.

BURNHAM, Joshua to Elizabeth Elliott - issued April 20, 1807, Bondsman:
Abner Elliott, GRAINGER Co.

BURNHAM, Wm. to Martha Fields - issued November 19, 1843, DAVIDSON Co.

BURNHART, Barbara to Adma Hardman (Harmon) - GREENE Co.

BURNISS, Jno. G. to Nancy Smotherman - issued November 6, 1863, Bondsman:
Jos. H. Thompson, BEDFORD Co.

BURNLEY, John to Levisa Carr - m. by: John T. Carr October 23, 1833, SUMNER Co.

BURNLY, James to Rachel Vance - issued December 19, 1831, Bondsman: Abraham Vance, SUMNER Co.

BURNS, Elida to Lucy Cugh - issued June 16, 1841, m. by: Benjamin Darrow, A. Bats. Preacher, June 17, 1841, DICKSON Co.

BURNS, George to Elizabeth Peach - July 31, 1811, WILLIAMSON Co.

BURNS, George to Marjory Day - issued August 14, 1824, Bondsman: Thomas Coddle, SUMNER Co.

BURNS, Hannah to George Bond - March 5, 1799, Security: David Parhine and John Reed, GREENE Co.

BURNS, Hugh to Sarah Jordan - issued January 27, 1848, m. by: O. L. V. Schmittou, J. P., January 27, 1848, DICKSON Co.

BURNS, James to Anny White - issued December 24, 1805, Bondsman: Stephen Cantrell, SUMNER Co.

BURNS, James to Massa Osteen - March 31, 1812, WILLIAMSON Co.

BURNS, James W. to Becksey E. A. Bryant - issued March 21, 1866, Bondsman: B. T. Yancey, LAWRENCE Co.

BURNS, Jesse to Petty Freeman - issued June 9, 1816, m. by: H. Robinson, J. P., June 10, 1816, RUTHERFORD Co.

BURNS, Mary L. to James B. Scott - BEDFORD Co.

BURNS, Michael to Margaret Gilliam - issued March 12, 1842, m. by: Richard P. Miles March 13, 1842, DAVIDSON Co.

BURNS, Rachel to Thomas Stanfield - MAURY Co.

BURNS, Wiley H. to Permelia Cantrell - issued May 10, 1853, m. by: David Throneberry, J. P., May 10, 1853, COFFEE Co.

BURNS, William to Frances Carroll - issued February 7, 1854, m. by: Harison Shackleford, J. P., February 8, 1854, COFFEE Co.

BURNSIDE, Jesse to Goweldor Green - issued August 14, 1838, m. by: William Ellis, J. P., August 16, 1838, STEWART Co.

BUROUGHS, Francis to Emelia Hell - June 14, 1811, WILLIAMSON Co.

BURPO, Joseph to Delila Baker - issued April 24, 1820, m. by: Jordan Willeford, J. P., April 28, 1820, RUTHERFORD Co.

BURR, C. O. to Mary J. Pitt - issued July 7, 1861, m. by: E. Burr, J. P., ROBERTSON Co.

BURRESS, J. W. to Sally Parks - issued June 24, 1873, m. by: A. F. Dix, M. G., June 24, 1873, FRANKLIN Co.

BURRIS, Dickison to Jane Fraley - issued August 10, 1826, Bondsman: Daniel Miers, SUMNER Co.

BURRIS, Dickson to Jane Fraley - m. by: Jonathan Davis, J. P., August 10, 1827, SUMNER Co.

BURRIS, Jacob to Mary Jane Branch - issued June 24, 1839, m. by: John Nugent, J. P., June 24, 1839, FRANKLIN Co.

BURRISS, Nancy M. to Wm. Loving - issued August 17, 1863, Bondsman: James Sanders, BEDFORD Co.

BURROUGH, John M. to Sarah S. Price - issued April 25, 1850, m. by:
Rev. A. J. Steel April 25, 1850, FRANKLIN Co.

BURROUGH, Joseph M. to Elizabeth Estill - issued December 8, 1840,
FRANKLIN Co.

BURROUGH, Jos. M. to Eliza A. Patrick - issued November 9, 1859, m. by:
W. W. Estill, M. G., November 10, 1859, FRANKLIN Co.

BURROUGHS, Michael to Polly Walker - August 6, 1812, WILLIAMSON Co.

BURROW, Caldonia to Willis Patterson - issued September 24, 1862,
Bondsman: A. Hunt, Jos. H. Thompson, Clk. per M. E. W. Dunaway,
Dep. Clk., BEDFORD Co.

BURROW, D. B. to Mary Burham - issued October 11, 1862, Bondsman:
R. F. Darnaby, Jos. H. Thompson, Clk. per N. F. Thompson, D. Clk.,
BEDFORD Co.

BURROW, Goodman to Rebecca Miller - issued March 18, 1854, m. by:
E. H. Ikard, J. P., March 19, 1854, FRANKLIN Co.

BURROW, Jesse D. to Mary Brights - issued July 19, 1846, STEWART Co.

BURRUS, Phillip J. to Martha W. Yandell - issued June 20, 1827, Bondsman:
John W. Childress, RUTHERFORD Co.

BURT, Alford to Elizabeth Brasford - issued July 4, 1840, m. by:
James F. Green, J. P., July 5, 1840, FRANKLIN Co.

BURT, Alford to Lucinda Franklin - issued December 22, 1848, m. by:
Joseph Smith, M. G., December 22, 1848, FRANKLIN Co.

BURT, Calvin C. to Nancy Parks - issued June 4, 1854, m. by:
L. N. Simpson, J. P., June 4, 1854, FRANKLIN Co.

BURT, Charles F. to Mary E. Eggleston - issued October 13, 1856, m. by:
Joseph Smith October 14, 1856, FRANKLIN Co.

BURT, Chas. H. to Catherine Wilson - issued May 27, 1863, Bondsman:
Jos. H. Thompson and Clerk, BEDFORD Co.

BURT, Gaston to Araminta M. Payne - issued July 30, 1855, m. by:
D. B. Muse, J. P., July 31, 1855, FRANKLIN Co.

BURT, J. H. to Lucretia Casteel - issued January 24, 1866, m. by:
B. Pennington, M. G., January 25, 1866, FRANKLIN Co.

BURT, J. J. to Nancy Smith - issued October 29, 1845, m. by:
B. D. Kelley, J. P., November 19, 1845, FRANKLIN Co.

BURT, Joseph G. to Nancy J. M. Haisless - issued August 22, 1857,
FRANKLIN Co.

BURT, Jos. G. to Nancy J. M. Harsley - issued August 23, 1858, m. by:
Allen Tribble August 23, 1858, FRANKLIN Co.

BURT, Sue E. to R. C. Swain - issued June 8, 1861, Bondsman: J. R. Bell,
Jos. H. Thompson, Clk. per N. F. Thompson, Dep. Clk., m. by:
R. H. Allen, M. G., BEDFORD Co.

BURT, William to Christian Thomas - issued April 16, 1823, Bondsman:
Jesse Angel, m. by: H. Robinson, J. P., April 16, 1823,
RUTHERFORD Co.

BURT, William T. to Martha A. Robertson - issued December 8, 1842,
m. by: W. H. Wharton December 8, 1842, DAVIDSON Co.

BURT, Wm. W. to Rachiel E. Smith - issued September 6, 1858, m. by:
D. D. Smith, J. P., September 8, 1858, FRANKLIN Co.

BURT, Willis to Elizabeth Rogers - issued February 4, 1853, m. by:
    D. D. Smith, J. P. February 8, 1853, FRANKLIN Co.

BURTHWRIGHT, Samuel A. to Eliza Vaughn - issued December 3, 1845,
    m. by: Josiah Ferriss, J. P., December 4, 1845, DAVIDSON Co.

BURTON, Allen to Polly Ann Adams - issued November 8, 1854, m. by:
    Uriah Sherrill, M. G., November 8, 1854, COFFEE Co.

BURTON, David to Ann Davis - issued October 8, 1807, Bondsman:
    Ebenezer Donelson, WILSON Co.

BURTON, David C. to Margaret Lucinda Elliott - issued July 29, 1858,
    m. by: John J. Pittman, M. G., COFFEE Co.

BURTON, Edmund to Amanda Louis - issued June 30, 1827, Bondsman:
    Josiah L. McClain, WILSON Co.

BURTON, Harvey to Polly Ann Fraser - issued March 12, 1845, m. by:
    P. Lynch, J. P., March 13, 1845, STEWART Co.

BURTON, Hugh to Elizabeth Chandler - issued February 10, 1832, Bondsman:
    William D. Tarver, m. by: Frances Jarratt, M. G., WILSON Co.

BURTON, Isaac to Nancy Ingram - issued November 22, 1827, m. by:
    Elijah M. Engleton, M. G., November 22, 1827, KNOX Co.

BURTON, James to Nancy Edwards - issued December 29, 1820, Bondsman:
    Edward D. Burton, m. by: James Gray, J. P., December 31, 1820,
    WILSON Co.

BURTON, John Henry to Rebecca Robbins - August 10, 1816, WILLIAMSON Co.

BURTON, Joseph W. to Susan E. Justis - issued December 28, 1850,
    Bondsman: H. N. Moseley, m. by: G. Orgain, J. P., December 30, 1850,
    MONTGOMERY Co.

BURTON, Morris G. to Polley Reading - issued February 13, 1811, Bondsman:
    Lewis Reading, WILSON Co.

BURTON, Richard to Mahulda Sanders - issued September 6, 1824, Bondsman:
    John Hudson, m. by: R. Warnick, J. P., September 7, 1824,
    RUTHERFORD Co.

BURTON, Robert A. to Elizabeth H. Donaldson - issued November 16, 1837,
    Bondsman: George S. Golladay, m. by: George Donnell, V. D. M.,
    WILSON Co.

BURTON, Thomas to Amanda Parham - issued December 16, 1835, Bondsman:
    Isaac Rutland, WILSON Co.

BURTON, William to Elizabeth Williams - m. by: Henry R. Winbourn
    November 11, 1833, SUMNER Co.

BURTZ, James to Susanna Petitt - issued July 15, 1843, Bondsman:
    Wm. McCarrell, m. by: Wm. Johns, J. P., July 15, 1843, MEIGS Co.

BURUM, Henry to Nancy F. King - issued May 31, 1827, m. by:
    Sam Flenniken, J. P., May 31, 1827, KNOX Co.

BURUS, Brantly to Celana Harrington - issued April 2, 1822, Bondsman:
    B. Modglin, m. by: G. H. Bussard, J. P., April 24, 1822, WILSON Co.

BUSBEY, M. to M. Brannon - issued December 15, 1868, m. by: J. S. Faris,
    J. P., December 18, 1868, FRANKLIN Co.

BUSBY, Anderson to Parizade Coleman - issued February 8, 1825, Bondsman:
    John Mitchell, SUMNER Co.

BUSBY, Elijah to Lucy Busby - issued January 29, 1822, Bondsman: Solomon Shoulders, SUMNER Co.

BUSBY, James H. to Malinda Roney - issued January 25, 1836, Bondsman: James Dinning, m. by: S. H. Turner January 25, 1836, SUMNER Co.

BUSBY, James J. to Sarah A. Wasson - issued September 20, 1864, Bondsman: A. M. Gillespie, m. by: A. M. Gillespie, M. G., September 20, 1864, LAWRENCE Co.

BUSBY, John to Polly Barrett - issued January 1, 1827, Bondsman: Arioch Thomas, SUMNER Co.

BUSBY, John to Cynthia J. Cluck - issued May 22, 1849, m. by: Benj. Sells, J. P., May 22, 1849, FRANKLIN Co.

BUSBY, John S. to Margaret E. Carrell - issued March 21, 1865, Bondsman: John C. Carrell, m. by: William A. Harris, Min., March 21, 1865, LAWRENCE Co.

BUSBY, Robt. to Elizabeth Ann Curry - issued December 15, 1847, STEWART Co.

BUSBY, Samuel S. to Mary J. Vick - issued May 7, 1866, Bondsman: Stephen Busby, m. by: Samuel Baker, M. G., May 8, 1866, LAWRENCE Co.

BUSBY, Stephen to Sally Hale - issued May 12, 1810, Bondsman: John Mitchell, SUMNER Co.

BUSH, Daniel to Maia Johnson - issued August 21, 1842, m. by: John A. Jones, M. G., M. E. C., August 25, 1842, STEWART Co.

BUSH, George to Elizabeth Marlin - issued November 27, 1806, Bondsman: Archibald Marlin, SUMNER Co.

BUSH, George to Cathrarine Stoode - issued September 4, 1824, Bondsman: Allen Gardner, SUMNER Co.

BUSH, George B. to Sarah E. Hill - issued December 23, 1852, Bondsman: Howard B. Bush, m. by: John Gold, J. P., December 30, 1852, MONTGOMERY Co.

BUSH, Greenberry to Rebecca Dorris - issued September 8, 1828, Bondsman: Lewis Dorris, SUMNER Co.

BUSH, John to Ellen Hommel - issued June 6, 1833, m. by: G. Fleming June 6, 1833, KNOX Co.

BUSH, John H. to Martha Williams - issued __(?) 29, 1830, Bondsman: Micajah Whitley, RUTHERFORD Co.

BUSH, Josiah to Caty Rider - issued March 2, 1825, Bondsman: William Bush, m. March 2, 1825, SUMNER Co.

BUSH, Oliver to Nancy Cravens - issued December 31, 1816, Bondsman: Jourdon Jackson, m. by: Edw. Douglass December 31, 1816, SUMNER Co.

BUSH, Oliver to Eliza Paul - m. by: J. Hobday, J. P., December 11, 1834, SUMNER Co.

BUSH, Stephen L. to Elizabeth Tate - issued September 8, 1834, Bondsman: James P. Hays, WILSON Co.

BUSH, Tenny to Hollen West - m. by: Wm. Montgomery October 17, 1828, SUMNER Co.

BUSH, William to Louiza Powell - issued September 4, 1819, Bondsman: Joseph Kirkpatrick, m. by: Hugh Kirkpatrick, M. G., September 4, 1819, SUMNER Co.

BUSH, Wm. to Elizabeth Groves - issued October 6, 1821, Bondsman:
     Arch Marlin, SUMNER Co.

BUSH, William to Sally Gardner - issued July 2, 1824, Bondsman:
     William Cooly, SUMNER Co.

BUSH, William to Jane Hammel - issued May 30, 1834, Bondsman:
     Henry Brown, GRAINGER Co.

BUSH, Zachariah to Lucinda Gilly - issued November 1, 1821, RUTHERFORD Co.

BUSHONG, Joseph to Elizabeth Owens - issued October 2, 1823, Bondsman:
     James Hines, m. by: Noah Jarnagin, J. P., October 2, 1823,
     GRAINGER Co.

BUSSEY, George to Mary Ann Lacy - issued May 17, 1848, STEWART Co.

BUSTER, Michael W. to Elizabeth Wan - issued December 24, 1845, Bondsman:
     James Small, m. by: William Green, M. G., December 25, 1845,
     MEIGS Co.

BUSTER, Saml. to M. A. Royster - issued August 15, 1839, Bondsman:
     James Wilhelm, m. by: Jacob Price, J. P., August 18, 1839, MEIGS Co.

BUSTER, Wm. to Nancy Price - issued January 17, 1839, Bondsman:
     Jas. Wilhelms, m. January 20, 1839, MEIGS Co.

BUTCHER, Ezekiel to Sarah Evans - issued January 21, 1826, Bondsman:
     Isaac Butcher, m. by: Valentine Molder, J. P., January 21, 1826,
     GRAINGER Co.

BUTCHER, Hasting to Margaret Oaks - issued January 26, 1831, Bondsman:
     Richard Oaks, m. by: Valentine Molder, J. P., GRAINGER Co.

BUTCHER, James to Jeany Huddleston - issued June 24, 1813, Bondsman:
     Robert Huddleston, GRAINGER Co.

BUTCHER, John to Nancy Sevard - issued May 25, 1809, Bondsman:
     Justice Null, GRAINGER Co.

BUTLER, Alexander to Tabitha Winnett - issued January 3, 1860, m. by:
     M. A. Carden, J. P., January 4, 1860, COFFEE Co.

BUTLER, Aron to Rosannah Bracken - issued February 11, 1804, Bondsman:
     Wm. Bracken, SUMNER Co.

BUTLER, Benjamin to Elizabeth Shoemaker - issued August 24, 1824,
     Bondsman: Thomas Butler, RUTHERFORD Co.

BUTLER, Calvin to Jane Crosslan - issued March 23, 1854, m. by:
     E. H. Roughton, J. P., March 23, 1854, COFFEE Co.

BUTLER, E. C. to Mary Turley - issued December 18, 1838, m. by:
     John W. Hanner December 18, 1838, DAVIDSON Co.

BUTLER, Edward to Nancy Holt - issued May 13, 1820, m. by: Amos Hardin,
     J. P. K. C., May 18, 1820, KNOX Co.

BUTLER, Edward to Ann Casey - issued October 22, 1841, m. by:
     C. W. Moorman, J. P., October 28, 1841, DAVIDSON Co.

BUTLER, Edward to Rebecca Gay - issued April 12, 1843, DAVIDSON Co.

BUTLER, Elijah to Elizabeth Doss - issued March 11, 1826, Bondsman:
     Joshua Doss, m. by: Samuel Davis, J. P., March 11, 1826, SUMNER Co.

BUTLER, Henry to Fanny Week - issued February 16, 1824, Bondsman:
     Daniel Allsup, m. by: Daniel Webb, M. G., February 16, 1824,
     SUMNER Co.

BUTLER, Jacob M. to Sarah Hardin - issued November 17, 1823, Bondsman:
Jas. H. Gallaher, KNOX Co.

BUTLER, James to Nancy Smith - issued July 21, 1813, m. by: John Miller,
J. P., July 22, 1813, RUTHERFORD Co.

BUTLER, James to Anne West - issued October 22, 1823, Bondsman:
Andrew Higdon, RUTHERFORD Co.

BUTLER, James to Matilda Bell - issued December 24, 1830, Bondsman:
Wm. Caldwell, m. by: Sam'l Davis, J. P., December 24, 1830,
SUMNER Co.

BUTLER, James to Unity Whitehead - issued August 21, 1836, Bondsman:
James Simmons, m. by: Wm. Carnutt, J. P., GRAINGER Co.

BUTLER, James to Malinda Bouden - issued May 29, 1844, Bondsman:
John Bouden, m. by: Mark Renfrow, J. P., May 29, 1844, MEIGS Co.

BUTLER, John to Betsy Hays - April 26, 1811, Bondsman: Jacob Daimwood,
MAURY Co.

BUTLER, John E. to Harriet Earhart - issued November 12, 1847,
DAVIDSON Co.

BUTLER, John L. to Caroline Skeen - issued January 29, 1831, Bondsman:
Kinion Skeen, m. by: Arch'd B. Duval January 29, 1831, SUMNER Co.

BUTLER, John W. to Sarah Greer Wilson - issued January 15, 1842, m. by:
John Thos. Wheat, Rr. of Ct. Ch., January 16, 1842, DAVIDSON Co.

BUTLER, L. C. to Rebecca E. Winnett - issued January 9, 1854, m. by:
R. W. Casey, J. P., January 10, 1854, COFFEE Co.

BUTLER, Peter to Nancy Jane Stacy - issued February 5, 1853, m. by:
R. W. Casey, J. P., February 5, 1853, COFFEE Co.

BUTLER, Robt. V. to Sarah R. Widener - issued January 2, 1872, m. by:
W. C. Tipps, J. P., January 3, 1872, FRANKLIN Co.

BUTLER, Samuel to Mary Hunt - m. by: Jonathan Davis, J. P., January 12,
1835, SUMNER Co.

BUTLER, Samuel to Mickey Earhart - issued July 9, 1845, m. by:
Jas. H. Hagen, J. P., July 10, 1845, DAVIDSON Co.

BUTLER, Samuel to Mrs. Peggy Wilkins - issued February 28, 1861, m. by:
D. J. Martin, J. P., March 4, 1861, FRANKLIN Co.

BUTLER, Stephen to Mary A. Shirley - issued September 27, 1829, Bondsman:
Endy E. Eaton, m. by: G. McDaniel, M. G., September 27, 1829,
GRAINGER Co.

BUTLER, Thomas to Polly Huff - issued October 22, 1816, m. by:
Jas. L. Jetton, J. P., October 25, 1816, RUTHERFORD Co.

BUTLER, Valentine to Polly Gideon (Gedion?) - September 26, 1800, KNOX Co.

BUTLER, W. H. to Rachael Winnett - issued March 21, 1859, m. by:
Samuel Umbarger, J. P., March 21, 1859, COFFEE Co.

BUTLER, William to Martha Hughes - issued December 16, 1822, Bondsman:
Jonathan Huggins, RUTHERFORD Co.

BUTLER, William to Susan Patton - issued August 23, 1836, Bondsman:
William Twopence, m. by: Jesse Harper August 23, 1836, SUMNER Co.

BUTLER, William to Ellen Ellis - m. by: J. H. House March 29, 1837,
SUMNER Co.

BUTLER, William to Jane West - issued August 18, 1859, m. by:
L. F. Dillard, J. P., August 18, 1859, COFFEE Co.

BUTLER, Wm. D. to Elizabeth Cavett - issued February 4, 1820, m. by:
Sam'l. Sample, J. P., February 7, 1820, KNOX Co.

BUTLER, William S. to Julia G. Marshall - issued December 9, 1823,
m. by: John Fletcher, J. P., December 14, 1823, RUTHERFORD Co.

BUTNER, E. L. D. to Jensey A. Ward - issued April 18, 1857, m. by:
L. Burnum, J. P., April 19, 1857, COFFEE Co.

BUTS, Craven to Delilah Carter - issued May 15, 1841, m. by:
B. P. Morrice, J. P., May 15, 1841, DAVIDSON Co.

BUTT, Cyrus E. to Milley Traughber - issued July 4, 1860, m. by:
E. Burr, J. P., July 8, 1860, ROBERTSON Co.

BUTT, Hazel to Cynthia Hunt - issued November 1, 1820, Bondsman:
Ruben Webb, WILSON Co.

BUTT, Hazel Green to Mary Ann Barker - m. by: Freeman Senter March 12,
1838, SUMNER Co.

BUTT, Henry to Emeline Fiser - issued October 21, 1841, m. by:
Robt. Draughon, J. P., October 24, 1841, ROBERTSON Co.

BUTT, John to Nancy Todd - m. by: John L. Swaney, J. P., November 29,
1823, SUMNER Co.

BUTT, Philip to Jincy Sadler - issued November 3, 1828, Bondsman:
Samuel Butt, m. by: John L. Swaney, J. P., November 3, 1828,
SUMNER Co.

BUTT, William A. to Emily Boren - issued June 12, 1832, Bondsman:
Alexander Pirkle, SUMNER Co.

BUTTER, Christopher to Mary McHaney - issued November 19, 1836, Bondsman:
James McHaney, m. by: Joshua Lester, V. D. M., WILSON Co.

BUTTERWORTH, Isham to Elizabeth Ross - issued January 1, 1825, Bondsman:
William W. Babb, m. by: Isaac Lindsey, E. M. G., January 6,
1825, WILSON Co.

BUTTHRWORTH, Jese to Sally Clay - issued August 7, 1819, Bondsman:
John Pervat, SUMNER Co.

BUTTERWORTH, John to Lucy Tally - issued March 17, 1819, Bondsman:
Zach Tally, Jr., m. by: Isaac Lindsey, M. G., March 17, 1819,
SUMNER Co.

BUTTERWORTH, John to A. R. Short - issued April 17, 1872, m. by:
H. H. Sneed April 18, 1872, FRANKLIN Co.

BUTTERWORTH, R. N. to Mary J. Brookman - issued October 31, 1850,
Bondsman: George W. Talley, m. by: R. P. Bowling November 10,
1849, MONTGOMERY Co.

BUTTON, Robert to Susan Davidson - issued June 28, 1836, Bondsman:
William P. Branch, SUMNER Co.

BUTTREY, Washington G. L. to Mary Lampley - issued August 23, 1841,
m. by: J. Hill, J. P., August 26, 1841, DICKSON Co.

BUTTRICK, David to Josephene Cook - issued April 25, 1865, FRANKLIN Co.

BUYERS, James to Cassy Overton - August 21, 1815, WILLIAMSON Co.

(BUYERS?) Byers, Susan to David Pickins - MAURY Co.

BUYFORD, William to Louisa Franklin - issued June 18, 1833, m. by:
Geo. S. Hooper, J. P., June 20, 1833, WILSON Co.

BUZBY, John to Peggy Martin - issued October 6, 1799, Bondsman:
David Shelton, Witness: Sm. Yancey, GRAINGER Co.

BYERLEY, David to Mary Johnston - issued November 22, 1817, Bondsman:
John Wright, KNOX Co.

BYERLEY, Jacob to Sally Brown - issued November 2, 1824, Bondsman:
John McFaddin, m. by: P. A. Swan, J. P., November 3, 1824, KNOX Co.

BYERLEY, Martin to Polly Roop - issued November 19, 1836, Bondsman:
Wm. Watkins, m. by: Jas. Rodgers, J. P., December 6, 1836, KNOX Co.

BYERLY, Isaac to Polly Hobbs - issued February 25, 1834, Bondsman:
James Courtney, KNOX Co.

BYERLY, James to Hallalujah Yarnell - issued December 7, 1830, Bondsman:
James Watkins, m. by: Wm. Morris, J. P., December 9, 1830,
Witness: Wm. Swan, KNOX Co.

BYERS (Buyers?), Susan to David Pickins - MAURY Co.

BYERS, Wm. H. to An'd Williams - November 14, 1846, m. by:
J. R. Graves, Pastor 2nd Baptist Church, November 15, 1846,
DAVIDSON Co.

BYFORD, Aron to Jane Franklin - issued May 6, 1829, Bondsman: Rich Holt,
RUTHERFORD Co.

BYFORD, David to Lear McGoigal - RUTHERFORD Co.

BYFORD, George to Jane Smith - issued August 3, 1817, m. by: A. McEwen,
J. P., August 3, 1817, RUTHERFORD Co.

BYFORD, Hardy to Mary Cooke - issued February 24, 1824, Bondsman:
James Sissum, m. by: B. B. Dickins, February 26, 1824, RUTHERFORD Co.

BYFORD, John to Sarah Elliott - issued April 3, 1824, Bondsman:
George W. Lee, RUTHERFORD Co.

BYFORD, William to Lear McGoigal - issued April 17, 1819, m. by:
B. L. McFerrin April 17, 1819, RUTHERFORD Co.

BYFORD, William to Sarah Lennox - issued July 26, 1837, Bondsman:
William Leigh, RUTHERFORD Co.

BYNUM, David W. to Sarah Morris - issued June 26, 1844, m. by:
Wm. B. Talliferro, J. P., June 27, 1844, FRANKLIN Co.

BYNUM, Jesse to Catharine Hedge - issued April 21, 1858, m. by:
R. J. Price, J. P., April 22, 1858, COFFEE Co.

BYNUM, William to Martha McCulloch - issued December 16, 1834, Bondsman:
J. W. McCulloch, m. by: B. B. Dickens, J. P., December 20, 1834,
RUTHERFORD Co.

BYRAM, Albert to Eliz McGuire - issued December 24, 1842, m. by:
C. Woodall, J. P., December 27, 1842, ROBERTSON Co.

BYRAM, Alexander W. to Melissa Williams - issued January 24, 1857,
m. by: Isaac Steel, M. G., January 25, 1857, ROBERTSON Co.

BYRAM, Lemuel to Francis Bradford - issued January 23, 1820, Bondsman:
Ashley Stanfield, SUMNER Co.

BYRAM, Lemuel to Francis Bradford - issued January 23, 1826, m. by:
Thomas Joyner January 23, 1826, SUMNER Co.

BYRAM, Levi to Mary Rigney - issued January 13, 1823, Bondsman:
Ebenezer Byram, m. by: Mordecai Yarnell, J. P., January 16, 1823,
Witness: Wm. Swan, KNOX Co.

BYRAM, Saml. to Ellen Jane Yates - issued October 19, 1852, m. by:
W. H. Rife, J. P., October 20, 1852, ROBERTSON Co.

BYRAM, Widen to Eliza Whitworth - issued August 31, 1829, Bondsman:
Lemuel Byram, m. by: Isaac Lindsey, M. G., August 31, 1829,
SUMNER Co.

BYRAN, Wm. S. to Eliza. G. Richardson - issued August 4, 1845, Bondsman:
W. E. Murphy, m. by: Thomas B. Ripley, M. G., August 6, 1845,
MONTGOMERY Co.

BYRD, Abraham to Betsy Gillespie - March 20, 1799, BLOUNT Co.

BYRD, Amos to Anne Gillespie - January 21, 1794, Witness: Chas. McClung,
KNOX Co.

BYRD, James M. to S. E. Smith - issued October 2, 1862, Bondsman:
S. G. Smith, m. by: R. L. McLaren, J. P., October 2, 1862,
LAWRENCE Co.

BYRD, John to Polly McCoy - issued August 2, 1801, Bondsman: Neal McCoy,
Witness: Sm'l. Yancey, GRAINGER Co.

BYRD, John to Virginia Nichols - issued April 18, 1854, Bondsman:
L. L. Whitfield, m. by: Lewis Lowe, M. G., April 18, 1854,
MONTGOMERY Co.

BYRD, John A. to Brinthy P. Wilkinson - issued August 17, 1846, m. by:
B. Henrdon, J. P., August 20, 1846, STEWART Co.

BYRD, Nathan to Prudence Smith - issued February 25, 1823, m. by:
Abner Hill, M. G., February 26, 1823, WILSON Co.

BYRD, Nathaniel to Mary Lea - November 7, 1836, KNOX Co.

BYRD, Stephen to Polly Gillespie - issued April 1, 1794, Bondsman:
Abraham Byrd, Witness: Chas. McClung, C. K. C., KNOX Co.

BYRD, Thos. to Budy Kemp - issued April 1, 1823, m. by: B. Bridges,
WILSON Co.

BYRD, Thomas to Mildred J. Morrison - issued May 27, 1863, Bondsman:
Chas. A. Smith, BEDFORD Co.

BYRD, William to Nancy Waters - issued February 25, 1823, m. by:
Abner Hill, M. G., February 26, 1823, WILSON Co.

BYRN, Allen to Nancy Gillespie - m. by: Richard Johnson December 9,
1834, SUMNER Co.

BYRN, Charles L. to Mary C. Davidson - issued November 23, 1816,
Bondsman: William Cantrill, SUMNER Co.

BYRN, David P. to Martha C. Kilpatrick - issued December 14, 1831,
Bondsman: George M. Bledsoe, m. by: L. M. Woodson December 14,
1831, SUMNER Co.

BYRN, James to Rebecca Word - issued March 23, 1807, Bondsman:
J. Jetton Thomas, WILSON Co.

BYRN, Peter J. to Evaline Harper - issued November 30, 1829, Bondsman:
Thos. Byson, SUMNER Co.

BYRN, Reason to Francis Craddock - issued October 13, 1808, Bondsman:
James Byrn, WILSON Co.

BYRNE, Neal W. to Martha Ann Norman - issued November 6, 1841, m. by:
Jas. Daniel, J. P., November 7, 1841, DICKSON Co.

BYRNE, Richard G. to Agnes Hanna - issued August 15, 1831, Bondsman:
Allen Byrne, SUMNER Co.

BYRNES, James G. to Aramiscia Dunn - issued November 1, 1849, m. by:
Benjamin Rawls, ROBERTSON Co.

BYRNS, Asberry to Anna Smith - April 17, 1811, WILLIAMSON Co.

BYRNS, John to Polly Pruett - issued December 24, 1817, Bondsman:
Amos Goyne and James Pruett, m. by: John Rutherford December 24,
1817, SUMNER Co.

BYRNS, John to Elizabeth Long - issued December 10, 1844, m. by:
William L. Perry, J. P., December 11, 1844, ROBERTSON Co.

BYRNS, Martin to Rebecca Yarbrough - issued November 30, 1821, Bondsman:
Wm. Mayberry, SUMNER Co.

BYRNS, Stephen to Mary Thompson - issued April 14, 1788, Bondsman:
James Byrns, SUMNER Co.

BYROM, Asbury M. to Fanny E. Morris - issued November 25, 1874, m. by:
Rev. H. J. Byrom, M. G., November 25, 1874, FRANKLIN Co.

BYROM, Benjamin to Eliza Hays - issued October 18, 1847, m. by:
Jeremiah Dean, M. G., October 19, 1847, FRANKLIN Co.

BYROM, E. B. to Emeline Holder - issued November 23, 1868, m. by:
Eld. J. A. Hudgins November 23, 1868, FRANKLIN Co.

BYROM, Edwin B. to A. C. Jordan - issued January   (?), 1861, m. by:
John H. Holt, M. G., January 10, 1861, FRANKLIN Co.

BYROM, Geo. S. to Sallie E. McElroy - issued February 23, 1870, m. by:
G. W. Henderson, M. G., February 24, 1870, FRANKLIN Co.

BYROM, Green H. to Margret A. Rice - issued October 7, 1854, m. by:
A. B. Cunningham, M. G., October 15, 1854, FRANKLIN Co.

BYROM, H. F. to Margret James - issued November 1, 1870, FRANKLIN Co.

BYROM, H. J. to T. E. Shasteen - issued December 22, 1866, m. by:
J. S. Erwin, M. G., December 22, 1866, FRANKLIN Co.

BYROM, H. L. to Elizabeth Jones (MB) - issued November 10, 1869, m. by:
Wm. Prince, FRANKLIN Co.

BYROM, Henry L. to Winney Smith - issued October 24, 1843, m. by:
John Byrom, J. P., October 25, 1843, FRANKLIN Co.

BYROM, J. A. to Mary A. Dean - issued October 12, 1869, m. October 12,
1869, FRANKLIN Co.

BYROM, J. W. to L. J. Curle - issued April 11, 1865, m. by:
James Brasier, J. P., April 13, 1865, FRANKLIN Co.

BYROM, Jas. J. P. to Arie E. Martin - issued December 28, 1871, m. by:
W. P. Cherry, M. G., December 28, 1871, FRANKLIN Co.

BYROM, James R. to Synthia Jones - issued August 9, 1842, m. by:
Stanford Lasater August 11, 1842, FRANKLIN Co.

BYROM, John A. to Malinda H. Crick - issued December 3, 1855, m. by:
D. B. Muse, J. P., December 5, 1855, FRANKLIN Co.

BYROM, John W. to Elizabeth Lewis - issued June 13, 1868, m. by:
B. B. Brandon, L. E., June 14, 1868, FRANKLIN Co.

BYROM, Milton L. to Jane E. Blake - issued July 8, 1856, m. by:
D. B. Muse, J. P., July 9, 1856, FRANKLIN Co.

BYROM, Noah to Mina (Illegible) - issued January 11, 1820, Bondsman:
Jamison Bandy, SUMNER Co.

BYROM, Richmond D. to Mary J. Powell - issued October 17, 1854, m. by:
J. M. P. Hickerson, V. D. M., October 19, 1854, COFFEE Co.

BYROM, T. H. to Elenore Hasty - issued March 17, 1863, Bondsman:
Campbell Tribble, Jos. H. Thompson, Clk., BEDFORD Co.

BYROM, Wm. H. to Nancy C. Byrom - issued June 4, 1852, m. by:
Joseph Smith, M. G., June 4, 1852, FRANKLIN Co.

BYRUM, George to Susan Harris - issued July 28, 1831, Bondsman:
John D. Harris, WILSON Co.

BYRUM, Isaac to Rabella Morris - issued July 28, 1856, m. by:
J. A. Silvertooth, J. P., July 29, 1856, FRANKLIN Co.

BYSON, Peter to Sally E. Saunders - issued July 23, 1817, Bondsman:
John H. Bower, SUMNER Co.

BYSOR, Thomas to Lemizer Parker - issued April 12, 1845, DAVIDSON Co.

CABBAGE, Adam to Catherine Long - issued August 20, 1819, Bondsman:
David Capps, m. by: Alexander Hamilton August 22, 1819, GRAINGER Co.

CABBAGE, Jacob to Frances Bolton - issued February 7, 1818, Bondsman:
Peter Bolton, m. by: Philip Sigler, J. P., February 7, 1818,
GRAINGER Co.

CABBAGE, John to Catherine Moyers - issued July 20, 1812, Bondsman:
John Moyers, GRAINGER Co.

CABE, John to Margaret Cooper - February 21, 1798, BLOUNT Co.

CABLER, Calvin to Sarah Newburn - issued August 26, 1843, m. by:
J. B. Walker, M. G., M. E. Ch., August 27, 1843, DAVIDSON Co.

CABLER, Frederick to Elizabeth Anderson - issued November 30, 1847,
m. by: Wilson Mullen, J. P., December 1, 1847, DAVIDSON Co.

CABLER, William D. to Louisa Harsh - issued May 1, 1845, m. by:
R. B. C. Howell, M. G., May 1, 1845, DAVIDSON Co.

CACYE, Thomas to Sarah Thomas - issued May 12, 1851, Bondsman:
P. A. Bondurant, m. by: John Gold, J. P., May 15, 1851,
MONTGOMERY Co.

CADZOW, Archibald D. to Agness B. Hunt - issued January 9, 1873, m. by:
A. F. Dix, M. G., July 9, 1873, FRANKLIN Co.

CACY, David S. to Lycinda Guanoway - issued August 15, 1843, m. by:
John Gillentine, J. P., August 16, 1843, VAN BUREN Co.

CAEMAN, John B. to Phoebe Waddle - issued November 2, 1838, m. by:
N. B. Butler, J. P., November 2, 1838, DAVIDSON Co.

CAFFEY, Alexander H. to Nancy E. Weatherly - issued August 2, 1828,
m. by: Amzi Bradshaw, M. G., August 14, 1828, RUTHERFORD Co.

CAFFEY, Medford to Rutha Ann Yardley - issued May 27, 1820,
m. June 1, 1820, RUTHERFORD Co.

CAFFREY, W. W. to Julia A. McFarlin - issued May 13, 1863, Bondsman:
W. H. Foster, BEDFORD Co.

CAFFRY, John to Eliza Bradford - issued January 10, 1820, Bondsman: Dixon Stroud, SUMNER Co.

CAGE, Edward to Malissa Young - issued December 27, 1831, m. by: James Charlton, J. P., December 27, 1831, SUMNER Co.

CAGE, John O. to Sarah Robb - issued January 12, 1836, Bondsman: John T. McClain, m. by: J. W. Hall January 12, 1836, SUMNER Co.

CAGE, Loftain to Naomi Gillespie - issued September 30, 1805, Bondsman: Jesse Cage, SUMNER Co.

CAGE, O. L. to L. E. Douglass - m. by: A. B. Duval October 17, 1838, SUMNER Co.

CAGE, Reuben to Polly Morgan - issued January 7, 1800, Bondsman: Wilson Cage, SUMNER Co.

CAGE, William to Nancy Morgan - issued June 19, 1792, Bondsman: David Shelby, SUMNER Co.

CAGE, William to Fanny Street - issued March 12, 1806, Bondsman: James Winchester, SUMNER Co.

CAGE, William G. to Julia G. Franklin - m. by: J. W. Hall May 13, 1834, SUMNER Co.

CAGE, Wilson to Mary Dalton - issued February 29, 1796, Bondsman: Ezekiel Douglass, SUMNER Co.

CAGE, Wilson to Polly Cunningham - m. by: G. W. Morris June 1, 1835, SUMNER Co.

CAGLE, George W. to Katherine Eledge - issued May 11, 1844, m. by: John Fleming, J. P., May 12, 1844, VAN BUREN Co.

CAGLE, Jno. to Clarissa Chasteen - issued October 12, 1850, Bondsman: Wm. R. Cagle, m. by: Jo Pollard, J. P., October 17, 1850, MONTGOMERY Co.

CAGLE, Jonathan to Elizabeth Miles - issued January 23, 1841, m. by: Charles Crafford P January 28, 1841, ROBERTSON Co.

CAGLE, Joseph V. to M. E. Kennedy - issued January 21, 1871, FRANKLIN Co.

CAGLE, Linsey to Caroline May - issued January 2, 1855, m. by: John Fleming, J. P., February 1, 1855, VAN BUREN Co.

CAGLE, Wm. W. to Keziah Elveritt - issued January 5, 1839, m. by: David Abernathy, J. P., January 8, 1839, DAVIDSON Co.

CAHAL, Joseph to Hannah Muttymine - issued May 6, 1848, Bondsman: Dennis Sullivant, m. by. Lewis Orengo, Pastor of Catholic Church, May 7, 1848, MONTGOMERY Co.

CAHAL, Terry H. to Ann Saunders - m. by: Jas. P. Smith March 9, 1837, SUMNER Co.

CAIGLAR, David to Nancy Miles - September 6, 1816, WILLIAMSON Co.

CAIN, Elisha G. to Mary Ann Sherrill - issued May 20, 1830, m. by: F. E. Pitts, M. G., WILSON Co.

CAIN, Elkainer to Martha Pyle - m. by: Jas. L. McKoin, J. P., February 4, 1834, SUMNER Co.

CAIN, George to Elizabeth Nevils - issued December 18, 1829, Bondsman: Henry R. Kirby, m. by: Henry Ridley, J. P., December 25, 1829, RUTHERFORD Co.

CAIN, George J. to Christiana G. Jones - issued September 22, 1821, Bondsman: George Smith, Jr., m. by: Joshua Lester, V. D. M., September 25, 1821, WILSON Co.

CAIN, Hugh to Lucinda Holston - issued September 5, 1827, Bondsman: Henry Holston, GRAINGER Co.

CAIN, Iredell M. to Nancy Johnson - issued August 4, 1839, m. by: E. Edwards, M. E. C., ROBERTSON Co.

CAIN, James to Karen Savely - issued August 13, 1825, Bondsman: Caleb Willis, SUMNER Co.

CAIN, John to Elizabeth Moore - June 16, 1787, Security: Moses Moore, GREENE Co.

CAIN, John B. to Arinda Hall - Bondsman: James Cain, MONTGOMERY Co.

CAIN, John B. to Arinda Hall - issued January 23, 1851, Bondsman: Jas. Cain, m. by: R. H. Weakley January 23, 1850, MONTGOMERY Co.

CAIN, Mary to Lewis Broyles - GREENE Co.

CAIN, Robt. I. to Hester Ann Harrison - issued August 16, 1849, Bondsman: H. Beardune, m. by: R. H. Weakley, J. P., September 16, 1849, MONTGOMERY Co.

CAIN, Wm. L. to Martha Ann Edmundson - issued September 11, 1845, m. by: J. T. Edgar September 11, 1845, DAVIDSON Co.

CAITS, Barry to Delia Briant - issued April 30, 1825, Bondsman: Claiborne Latham, m. by: J. C. Bunch, J. P., April 30, 1825, GRAINGER Co.

CAKE, John to Nancy C. Hooper - issued January 3, 1843, m. by: C. G. Lovell, J. P., January 5, 1843, DAVIDSON Co.

CALAHAN, Moses P. to Sarah R. Hearn - issued March 7, 1829, Bondsman: Wm. L. Sypert, WILSON Co.

CALAN, Thomas to Nancy Woods - issued May 29, 1828, m. by: John Lane, RUTHERFORD Co.

CALAS, Edward to Sarah Merchant - issued October 24, 1840, Bondsman: John R. Billingsley, m. by: B. Pyland, M. G., October 29, 1840, WILSON Co.

CALCOTE, James L. to Elizabeth S. Overton - issued March 17, 1846, m. by: J. G. Edgar March 17, 1846, DAVIDSON Co.

CALDWELL, Absalom to Hannah Hinds - issued January 11, 1808, Bondsman: James Caldwell, Witness: J. Purris, KNOX Co.

CALDWELL, Alexander to Isabella Moore - June 11, 1793, Security: Thomas Temple, GREENE Co.

CALDWELL, Amos to Sally Dodson - August 14, 1809, Bondsman: Allen C. Yates, MAURY Co.

CALDWELL, Bonepart to Martha Ann Leggate - issued July 4, 1844, m. by: R. Cooley, J. P., July 4, 1844, STEWART Co.

CALDWELL, Charles to Eliza Patton - m. by: Geo. Donnell, V. D. M., August 12, 1834, SUMNER Co.

CALDWELL, David to Molly Russell - January 21, 1791, Security: Vance Russell, BLOUNT Co.

CALDWELL, David to Elizabeth Kelly - issued May 6, 1794, Bondsman: Alexander Kelly, KNOX Co.

CALDWELL, David to Elizabeth Griffin - October 25, 1800, Security:
John Ewing, BLOUNT Co.

CALDWELL, David to Elizabeth P. Stanfield - issued February 2, 1828,
Bondsman: Josiah Stanfield, SUMNER Co.

CALDWELL, English to Amelia Rutherford - issued October 12, 1833, m. by:
Joseph Meek, J. P., October 17, 1833, KNOX Co.

CALDWELL, George to Juley (Juby?) Capell - March 13, 1810, Bondsman:
Amos Caldwell, MAURY Co.

CALDWELL, Hu to Lucretia Welsh - issued February 5, 1825, Bondsman:
Hezekiah Rhodes, m. by: Wm. Sawyers, J. P., February 6, 1825,
KNOX Co.

CALDWELL, Isaac to Betsey Hart (or Hurt) - issued December 14, 1795,
Bondsman: Absolum Hart (or Hurt), SUMNER Co.

CALDWELL, James to Polly Davis - issued December 16, 1809, Bondsman:
Abram Trigg, SUMNER Co.

CALDWELL, James to Louisa Ballard - issued May 19, 1834, Bondsman:
Banister Tally, m. by: John Beard, M. G., May 22, 1834, WILSON Co.

CALDWELL, Jas. A. to Mary McCampbell - issued March 11, 1819, m. by:
Jno. McCampbell, V. D. M., March 13, 1819, KNOX Co.

CALDWELL, James T. to Elizabeth J. Langhran - issued November 8, 1849,
Bondsman: J. A. Brown, MONTGOMERY Co.

CALDWELL, Jesse to Mary McCampbell - issued March 11, 1819, m. March 18,
1819, KNOX Co.

CALDWELL, John to Patsy C. Rutledge - June 5, 1809 (?), Bondsman:
James Rutledge, MAURY Co.

CALDWELL, John to Polly Ann Riggle - issued May 16, 1818, m. by:
William B. Carns, J. P. K. C., May 19, 1818, KNOX Co.

CALDWELL, John D. to Emeline Law - issued September 9, 1847, DAVIDSON Co.

CALDWELL, Patsey S. to Joseph Johnson - February 12, 1810, Bondsman:
Micajah Davis, MAURY Co.

CALDWELL, Robert to Elizabeth Clapp - issued October 30, 1837, Bondsman:
Daniel Graves, KNOX Co.

CALDWELL, Samuel to Eliza B. Thompson - issued January 10, 1839,
m. by: -- Howard, J. P., January 11, 1839, FRANKLIN Co.

CALDWELL, Samuel to Rachel Ewing - January 28, 1793, KNOX Co.

CALDWELL, Thomas to Jean McCulloch - issued December 16, 1793, Bondsman:
James McCulloch, Witness: Chas. McClung, C. K. C., KNOX Co.

CALDWELL, Thos. J. to Lucy Dardis - issued November 28, 1826, Bondsman:
Andrew Park - H. G. Crozier, KNOX Co.

CALDWELL, Thos. J. to Lucy Dardis - issued November 28, 1826, m. by:
Tho. H. Nelson, M. G., November 28, 1826, KNOX Co.

CALDWELL, Thomas M. to Elizabeth W. Bell - issued January 23, 1838,
m. by: Jesse Edwards, M. G., January 25, 1838, DICKSON Co.

CALDWELL, W. A. to N. A. Rogers - issued September 26, 1867, m. by:
A. J. Simpson, J. P., September 26, 1867, FRANKLIN Co.

CALDWELL, Wallace to Abigail Nicholson - issued April 11, 1821, Bondsman:
William T. Webb, m. by: Wm. Gray, J. P., April 13, 1821, WILSON Co.

CALDWELL, William to Eleanor Moor - August 30, 1791, Security:
David Moor, GREENE Co.

CALDWELL, William to Cinderilla Stanfield - issued February 13, 1825,
Bondsman: Wm. Murray, SUMNER Co.

CALDWELL, William to Mary Butler - issued January 3, 1831, Bondsman:
Quire (or Squire) Brown, m. by: Sam'l. Davis, J. P., January 3,
1831, SUMNER Co.

CALDWELL, William to Emily Hutchison - issued November 17, 1834,
Bondsman: Millington Harrell, m. by: E. MacGowan, M. G.,
November 18, 1834, RUTHERFORD Co.

CALDWELL, William to Martha Joslin - issued December 2, 1843, DICKSON Co.

CALDWILL, Robt. to Sarah Grimes - February 15, 1810, WILLIAMSON Co.

CALFEE, Henry to Tabitha Hazlewood - issued August 23, 1820, Bondsman:
Benj. Hazlewood, m. by: Sam'l Montgomery, J. P., August 23, 1820,
KNOX Co.

CALHOON, James to Winney Woodward - issued November 7, 1812, Bondsman:
Joseph Barton, WILSON Co.

CALHOON, Samuel to Martha H. Figures - issued July 15, 1824, Bondsman:
Thomas Bradley, m. by: John Jarratt July 20, 1824, WILSON Co.

CALHOON, Wilson to Piety Ogilvie - September 26, 1805, WILLIAMSON Co.

CALHOUN, Andrew M. to Seills Martin - issued October 25, 1835, Bondsman:
W. H. Crenshaw, m. by: John Provine, M. G., WILSON Co.

CALHOUN, E. F. to Lydia E. Brown - issued July 9, 1832, Bondsman:
C. P. McDaniel, SUMNER Co.

CALHOUN, James C. to Lulia Ann Bradley - issued February 3, 1840,
Bondsman: William Calhon, m. by: J. Robt. D. Bell, M.G., February 4,
1840, WILSON Co.

CALHOUN, Samuel to Martha King - issued January 27, 1820, Bondsman:
John Shelton, SUMNER Co.

CALHOUN, Wilson to Martha I. Erwin - issued February 1, 1864, Bondsman:
J. H. Halfield, Jos. H. Thompson, Clk., BEDFORD Co.

CALL, A. J. to Sarah C. Chapman - issued January 5, 1857, m. by:
Elijah Turner, M. G., January 7, 1857, COFFEE Co.

CALL, Caleb C. to Sophirias M. Lynch - issued September 1, 1841, m. by:
W. G. Guinn, M. G., September 1, 1841, FRANKLIN Co.

CALLAGHN, Micheal to Jane Roach - issued November 20, 1838, m. by:
John Wright, J. P., November 2, 1838, DAVIDSON Co.

CALLAHAN, David H. to Nancy Sherrill - issued November 8, 1855, m. by:
L. D. Phillips, M. G., November 8, 1855, COFFEE Co.

CALLAHAN, Moses P. to Sarah R. Hearn - issued March 7, 1830, m. by:
J. B. Lasiter, J. P., March 12, 1830, WILSON Co.

CALLAN, Archibald to Jane Evans - issued November 17, 1820, Bondsman:
Robert Shields, m. by: Sam'l Sample, J. P. K. C., December 7,
1820, KNOX Co.

CALLEN, Edward to Patsy Cates - issued March 11, 1824, Bondsman:
John Cates, m. March 11, 1824, KNOX Co.

CALLET, Reuben to Agga Jones - issued August 20, 1821, Bondsman:
James Pearson, m. by: Sam Montgomery August 21, 1821, KNOX Co.

CALLICO, Paskel to Janny Wheeler - issued October 17, 1820, Bondsman:
John Walton, WILSON Co.

CALLISON, James to Anne Gillespie - issued January 21, 1794, Bondsman:
William McNutt, Witness: H. L. White, KNOX Co.

CALLISON, Samuel to Elley Morgan - issued December 22, 1809, Bondsman:
William Morgan, GRAINGER Co.

CALLOWAY, Achills to Elizabeth McWaters - issued June 24, 1843, m. by:
W. C. Jones, J. P., June 24, 1843, STEWART Co.

CALLOWAY, David to Nancy Ferguson - issued December 15, 1820, Bondsman:
John Fuller, m. by: E. Cross, V. D. M., December 15, 1820

CALLOWAY, Shadrack to Mary Hendrix - issued June 20, 1835, Bondsman:
Thos. Calloway, m. by: Wm. Morris, J. P., June 21, 1835, KNOX Co.

CALLOWAY, Thomas to Celia Griffin - issued November 25, 1812, Bondsman:
James Coats, WILSON Co.

CALLOWAY, Thos. F. to Polly Cox - issued November 22, 1837, m. by:
J. C. England November 3, 1837, KNOX Co.

CALLUM, John to Cathrine Low - November 1, 1793, KNOX Co.

CALLY, George L. to Mary Fitzgerald - issued July 1, 1848, m. by:
T. S. Elliott, L. P., July 1, 1848, STEWART Co.

CALPIN, William M. to Patsy Wooton - July 17, 1807, WILLIAMSON Co.

CALVERT, Blufort to Catharine Kirtley - issued November 20, 1846,
Bondsman: Peyton S. Calvert, m. by: Joseph Sturdivant, J. P.,
November 20, 1846, MONTGOMERY Co.

CALVERT, Robt. to Nancy Porter - July 12, 1808, WILLIAMSON Co.

CALVIN, Edward to Eliza Ann Simons - issued January 3, 1848, Bondsman:
L. W. Glenn, m. by: W. B. Carney, J. P., July 3, 1848,
MONTGOMERY Co.

CALVIN, James to Elizabeth D. Lester - issued November 14, 1836,
m. by: Joshua Lester, V. D. M., WILSON Co.

CAMBREL, James L. to Nancy Simmons - issued April 6, 1861, m. by:
Peyton Wilkerson, J. P., April 6, 1861, FRANKLIN Co.

CAMERON, Abraham to Betsey Gallian - issued March 7, 1812, Bondsman:
John Stiffy, GRAINGER Co.

CAMERON, Alexander to Margaret Cameron - issued February 1, 1806,
Bondsman: William Leakey, Witness, Jno. A. Gamble, KNOX Co.

CAMERON, Elizabeth to Thomas Travis - September 9, 1799, Security:
John Reed and Alex. Hays, GREENE Co.

CAMERON, John to Mary Coffrey - issued November 27, 1854, m. by:
Rev. John M. Jacquet November 30, 1854, FRANKLIN Co.

CAMERON, Hardin to Elizabeth Ray - issued October 17, 1833, Bondsman:
Samuel West, GRAINGER Co.

CAMERSON, Jesse M. to Nancy Jane Bayer - issued November 1, 1848,
m. by: Christopher Brandon, J. P., November 1, 1848, STEWART Co.

CAMICK, Charles M. to Luvica McCain - issued October 22, 1841, m. by:
E. H. East, J. P., October 22, 1841, DAVIDSON Co.

CAMLIN, John to Sarah Green - issued August 2, 1847, m. by:
James H. Hagen August 26, 1847, DAVIDSON Co.

CAMP, Anderson A. to Rebecca Partin - issued October 3, 1855, m. by:
Lewis Anderson, J. P., October 4, 1855, FRANKLIN Co.

CAMP, George L. to Martha Willhite - issued July 14, 1842, m. by:
Wm. G. Guinn July 14, 1842, FRANKLIN Co.

CAMP, James to Lenora Graham - issued April 18, 1831, Bondsman:
Joseph Jackson, m. by: W. Lyon, J. P., April 21, 1831, KNOX Co.

CAMP, James to Hettey Bass - issued December 28, 1835, Bondsman:
Soloman Bass, WILSON Co.

CAMP, Thomas S. to Rachael Herriford - issued March 7, 1838, FRANKLIN Co.

CAMP, Vandrey to Loucinda Galloway - issued October 11, 1854, m. by:
John M. Billingsley, J. P., October 12, 1854, VAN BUREN Co.

CAMPBELL, A. to Mary Noah - issued December 28, 1840, m. by:
John R. Patrick, J. P., December 28, 1840, FRANKLIN Co.

CAMPBELL, A. S. A. to J. S. Vaughn - issued September 25, 1858, m. by:
Robert R. Enochs, J. P., September 26, 1858, COFFEE Co.

CAMPBELL, A. Z. to M. F. Pickney - issued November 22, 1873, m. by:
Geo. S. Wedington, J. P., November 22, 1873, FRANKLIN Co.

CAMPBELL, Alexander to Cindrilla Wills - issued January 5, 1825,
Bondsman: Jno. McCaleb, m. by: J. A. Mabry, J. P., January 13,
1825, KNOX Co.

CAMPBELL, Alexander H. to Isabella Carlisle - issued February 13,
1855, m. by: I. J. Patton February 14, 1855, COFFEE Co.

CAMPBELL, Alfred F. to Polly Huston - m. by: John McMurtry, J. P.,
January 7, 1835, SUMNER Co.

CAMPBELL, Andrew to Mary Reed - December 20, 1800, Security:
John McPharman and John Doan, GREENE Co.

CAMPBELL, Andrew to Sarah Shiplett - issued November 10, 1840,
Bondsman: Harrison Wood, m. by: John Seabern, J. P., November 12,
1840, MEIGS Co.

CAMPBELL, Archibald to Susan F. Nailly - issued December 20, 1821,
RUTHERFORD Co.

CAMPBELL, Archibald to Mary Noe - issued July 26, 1840, m. by:
A. L. Hyder, J. P., July 26, 1840, FRANKLIN Co.

CAMPBELL, Armstead to Mary Louisa Faris - issued September 14, 1846,
m. by: N. A. D. Bryant, M. G., September 16, 1846, FRANKLIN Co.

CAMPBELL, B. H. to Joanna C. Wright - issued September 21, 1861, m. by:
E. A. Rutledge, J. P., September 21, 1861, COFFEE Co.

CAMPBELL, Burrell to Martha Hill - issued November 9, 1838, FRANKLIN Co.

CAMPBELL, C. W. to Caroline Wilson - issued May 17, 1851, m. by:
Robert Green, J. P., ROBERTSON Co.

CAMPBELL, Charles to Sarah Burket - issued July 8, 1819, Bondsman:
John Stiffy, m. by: John Kkdwell, M. G., July 8, 1819, GRAINGER Co.

CAMPBELL, Charles to Janes Edwards - issued November 4, 1854, m. by:
Jesse B. White, J. P., November 5, 1854, ROBERTSON Co.

CAMPBELL, Daniel to Harriet L. Doyle - issued August 16, 1855, m. by:
A. Rose, J. P., ROBERTSON Co.

CAMPBELL, David to Jennet Lockard - December 11, 1785, Security:
James Willson, GREENE Co.

CAMPBELL, David to Mary Hamilton Campbell - issued May 14, 1800,
Bondsman: David Campbell, Witness: Chas. McClung, KNOX Co.

CAMPBELL, David to Sally Mayson - issued August 30, 1803, Bondsman:
John McElhanny (1926), GRAINGER Co.

CAMPBELL, David to Jenny Cowan - issued Spetember 13, 1803, Bondsman:
Sam'1 G. Ramsey, Witness, Chas. McClung, KNOX Co.

CAMPBELL, David to Catherine Bowen - issued April 10, 1806, Bondsman:
Jas. Desha, SUMNER Co.

CAMPBELL, David to Lucy Cooper - June 23, 1809, Bondsman:
John M. Armstrong, MAURY Co.

CAMPBELL, David to Jane G. Cowan - issued May 30, 1814, m. by:
Tho. H. Nelson May 30, 1814, KNOX Co.

CAMPBELL, David to Jane Smith - issued November 29, 1823, Bondsman:
Jno. T. Smith, m. by: Rd. H. King November 29, 1823, KNOX Co.

CAMPBELL, David to Mary Ann Lacky - issued October 4, 1826, Bondsman:
Colin Campbell, SUMNER Co.

CAMPBELL, Davis to Patsey James - issued November 5, 1821, Bondsman:
John James, m. by: Valentine Molder, J. P., GRAINGER Co.

CAMPBELL, E. F. to M. M. Jones - issued September 23, 1871, FRANKLIN Co.

CAMPBELL, Edward to Rachel Dobbins - July 29, 1813, WILLIAMSON Co.

CAMPBELL, Edward to Seanath Maxwell - issued December 21, 1827,
Bondsman: Edward Campbell, WILSON Co.

CAMPBELL, Eleanor to John Campbell - GREENE Co.

CAMPBELL, Fletcher to Elizabeth F. Gray - issued December 11, 1832,
Bondsman: Joseph C. Johnson, WILSON Co.

CAMPBELL, George to Margaret Gillis - August 7, 1800, Security:
Hoden Shanks, GREENE Co.

CAMPBELL, George to Seney Evans - issued January 8, 1827, Bondsman:
Pryor Harvey, GRAINGER Co.

CAMPBELL, George to Elizabeth Skean - issued December 25, 1838,
Bondsman: Mathew Skean, m. by: John Billingsly, J. P., December 26,
_____, WILSON Co.

CAMPBELL, George to Evirilda Winsett - issued February 12, 1864,
Bondsman: R. C. Garrett, Jos. H. Thompson, Clk., BEDFORD Co.

CAMPBELL, Harris to Sarenia Hambleton - issued February 8, 1825,
m. by: John Bonner, J. P., February 9, 1825, WILSON Co.

CAMPBELL, Harris to Sarena Hamilton - issued February 8, 1826, Bondsman:
William O Neal, WILSON Co.

CAMPBELL, Hiram to Polly Hilburn - February 21, 1816, WILLIAMSON Co.

CAMPBELL, Hugh to Sally Hern - issued May 24, 1816, Bondsman:
Woodson Webb, m. by: A. W. Bone, J. P., May 28, 1816, WILSON Co.

CAMPBELL, Hugh L. to Mary Tracy - issued September 16, 1831, Bondsman: John H. Vowell, m. by: William Phillips, J. P., September 27, 1831, WILSON Co.

CAMPBELL, Isaac to Mary Ann Fristoe - issued June 8, 1811, KNOX Co.

CAMPBELL, J. B. to Rebecca Whitford - issued November 18, 1841, m. by: W. M. Cherry, J. P., November 18, 1841, STEWART Co.

CAMPBELL, J. E. to E. E. Barnett - issued October 27, 1863, Bondsman: J. G. Russell, Jos. H. Thompson, Clk. per N. E. W. Dunaway, D. Clk., BEDFORD Co.

CAMPBELL, J. M. to Mary A. Fulton - issued September 24, 1850, m. by: W. B. Kelly, M. Gospel, September 27, 1850, ROBERTSON Co.

CAMPBELL, J. P. to Rebecca W. Sims - issued December 16, 1846, m. by: Nathan Green, Judge Supreme Court, December 16, 1846, DAVIDSON Co.

CAMPBELL, James to Elizabeth Hawkins - issued December 17, 1814, Bondsman: Peter Moses, GRAINGER Co.

CAMPBELL, James to Elizabeth Garrett - September 30, 1816, WILLIAMSON Co.

CAMPBELL, James to Betsey Pace - issued November 18, 1817, m. by: Jas. S. Jetton, J. P., November 20, 1817, RUTHERFORD Co.

CAMPBELL, James to Patsy Hazelwood - issued October 5, 1822, Bondsman: James H. Reagan, KNOX Co.

CAMPBELL, James to Hannah Phelps - issued December 19, 1823, Bondsman: William Allbright, m. by: Robt. Guthrie, M. G., December 19, 1823, SUMNER Co.

CAMPBELL, James to Sally Smith - issued March 19, 1824, m. by: R. H. King March 20, 1824, KNOX Co.

CAMPBELL, James to Polly Prichard - issued March 7, 1825, Bondsman: Benjamin Prichard, WILSON Co.

CAMPBELL, James to Charlotte Dardis - issued August 11, 1825, m. by: Tho. H. Nelson, M. G., August 11, 1825, KNOX Co.

CAMPBELL, James to Charlotte Dardis - issued August 11, 1825, Bondsman: E. R. Campbell, KNOX Co.

CAMPBELL, James to Margery Blain - issued May 29, 1830, Bondsman: Andrew C. Eaton, m. by: James Kennon, M. G., GRAINGER Co.

CAMPBELL, James to Happy Sexton - issued March 9, 1844, m. by: B. Herndon, J. P., March 14, 1844, STEWART Co.

CAMPBELL, James to Virginia A. Moore - issued September 16, 1848, m. by: C. A. Hunt, J. P., FRANKLIN Co.

CAMPBELL, James A. to Rebecca E. McNeill - issued October 8, 1838, Bondsman: R. M. Campbell, m. by: Joseph B. Wynne, M. G., WILSON Co.

CAMPBELL, James W. to Susan C. Morgan - issued May 21, 1829, Bondsman: Wm. Swan, KNOX Co.

CAMPBELL, Jane to William Stevenson - GREENE Co.

CAMPBELL, Jenny to Holden Shanks - GREENE Co.

CAMPBELL, John to Eleanor Campbell - September 15, 1789, Security: George Huntchison, GREENE Co.

CAMPBELL, John to Nancy Dobbins - February 2, 1808, WILLIAMSON Co.

CAMPBELL, John to Pheby Casady - issued November 2, 1808, Bondsman: Samuel Barton, WILSON Co.

CAMPBELL, John to Peggy Brown - issued October 25, 1811, KNOX Co.

CAMPBELL, John to Jane Reed - June 4, 1812, KNOX Co.

CAMPBELL, John to Mary Dodd - issued November 18, 1816, Bondsman: Simon Camper, m. by: John W. Payton, J. P., November 21, 1816, WILSON Co.

CAMPBELL, John to Judah A. Lambert - issued October 23, 1818, Bondsman: John Morrow, WILSON Co.

CAMPBELL, John to Mary E. Cowan - issued May 23, 1822, Bondsman: E. R. Campbell, KNOX Co.

CAMPBELL, Jno. to Mary E. Cowan - issued May 23, 1822, m. by: Tho. H. Nelson, M. G., May 23, 1822, KNOX Co.

CAMPBELL, John to Malinda Bone - issued September 6, 1825, Bondsman: Hugh Campbell, WILSON Co.

CAMPBELL, John to Levicy Williams - issued June 30, 1827, Bondsman: John McClain, RUTHERFORD Co.

CAMPBELL, John to Sarah Burnett - issued January 25, 1829, Bondsman: Josiah C. Bunch, m. by: J. C. Bunch, J. P., January 25, 1829, GRAINGER Co.

CAMPBELL, Jno. to Elizabeth Armstrong - issued June 29, 1829, m. by: B. McNutt, J. P., June 29, 1829, KNOX Co.

CAMPBELL, John to Minerva Jones - issued January 3, 1833, m. by: Isaac Lindsey, M. G., January 3, 1833, SUMNER Co.

CAMPBELL, John to Susan An Suddoth - issued September 22, 1846, m. by: D. G. Baird, J. P., ROBERTSON Co.

CAMPBELL, John to Susan Ann Luadth - issued September 22, 1846, m. by: D. G. Baird, J. P., ROBERTSON Co.

CAMPBELL, John to Anna Crunk - issued July 30, 1851, m. by: D. M. Wells, J. P., ROBERTSON Co.

CAMPBELL, John B. to Caroline McClanhon - issued January 21, 1836, Bondsman: Samuel O. Wood, m. by: Joseph McSpadin, M. G., January 21, 1846, MEIGS Co.

CAMPBELL, John P. to Elizabeth Ann Lambut - issued October 17, 1820, Bondsman: John Campbell, m. by: Geo. Clark, J. P., October 19, 1820, WILSON Co.

CAMPBELL, John S. to Jeanet Orr - January 10, 1808, WILLIAMSON Co.

CAMPBELL, John S. to Nancy Smith - issued February 2, 1828, Bondsman: Jno. T. Smith, m. by: Wm. Eagleton, M. G, February 7, 1828, KNOX Co.

CAMPBELL, John T. to Emeline R. Williams - issued July 9, 1839, m. by: A. L. P. Green, M. G., July 10, 1839, DAVIDSON Co.

CAMPBELL, Joseph to Milly Norris - issued January 13, 1813, Bondsman: David Green, m. by: S. Hunt, J. P., January 13, 1813, SUMNER Co.

CAMPBELL, Joseph to Emeline Counts - issued November 2, 1848, m. by: H. Y. Ganson, M. G., November 2, 1848, FRANKLIN Co.

SHADDEN, Martin to Ailey Dodson - July 13, 1807, WILLIAMSON Co.

CAMPBELL, Layton W. to Elizabeth May - issued January 30, 1856, m. by: T. W. Bell, J. P., January 30, 1856, FRANKLIN Co.

CAMPBELL, Lewellen to Lindsey Vaught - issued October 22, 1833, Bondsman: Richard Alman, RUTHERFORD Co.

CAMPBELL, Lewis to Elizabeth Samson (or Lawson) - issued April 17, 1833, Bondsman: John Campbell, GRAINGER Co.

CAMPBELL, Lewis to Barthena Lefever - issued January 1, 1835, Bondsman: John Campbell, GRAINGER Co.

CAMPBELL, Lewis to Peggy Washman - issued April 30, 1835, Bondsman: John Campbell, GRAINGER Co.

CAMPBELL, Maria W. to Joseph E. Miller - MAURY Co.

CAMPBELL, Marion to Polly Ann Campbell - issued June 15, 1858, FRANKLIN Co.

CAMPBELL, Mary to Samuel McFeron - GREENE Co.

CAMPBELL, Matthew to Jane Valentine - issued September 15, 1829, Bondsman: Berryman G. Hankins, RUTHERFORD Co.

CAMPBELL, Robert to Martha Hamilton - issued March 29, 1793, Bondsman: John Hamilton, SUMNER Co.

CAMPBELL, Robert to Tilley Stewart - issued November 3, 1809, Bondsman: Joseph Kirkpatrick, WILSON Co.

CAMPBELL, Robert to Betsey Gamble - issued August 26, 1811, Bondsman: William Campbell, KNOX Co.

CAMPBELL, Robt. M. to Mary E. McNiel - issued September 18, 1839, Bondsman: Fletcher Campbell, m. by: Joseph B. Wynns September 20, 1839, WILSON Co.

CAMPBELL, Samuel to V. L. Barker - issued June 3, 1851, m. by: Isaac Steele, ROBERTSON Co.

CAMPBELL, Sidney to Martha Rigsby - issued June 18, 1848, m. by: Thos. West, Minister of the Gospel, ROBERTSON Co.

CAMPBELL, Thomas to Fanny McHenry - issued March 26, 1804, Bondsman: Wm. King, SUMNER Co.

CAMPBELL, Thomas to Frances Culver - issued December 25, 1827, Bondsman: Thomas Williams, RUTHERFORD Co.

CAMPBELL, Thomas to Rachel Morris - issued August 3, 1848, m. by: James Sprouse, J. P., ROBERTSON Co.

CAMPBELL, Thomas to Rebecca C. Little - issued December 12, 1849, m. by: William Gale December 13, 1849, FRANKLIN Co.

CAMPBELL, Thomas A. to Louisiana Thomas - issued March 1, 1847, m. by: George Gill, J. P., March 3, 1847, DAVIDSON Co.

CAMPBELL, Thomas L. to Martha Jones - issued February 21, 1848, m. by: W. B. Kelly, M. G., February 22, 1848, ROBERTSON Co.

CAMPBELL, Thomas L. to Martha B. Frazier - issued March 19, 1857, m. by: E. H. Campbell, M. G., March 19, 1857, COFFEE Co.

CAMPBELL, W. A. to Josephine Wells - issued September 26, 1860, m. by: John W. Smith, J. P., September 27, 1860, ROBERTSON Co.

CAMPBELL, Washington B. L. to Elizabeth C. Frazier - issued August 20, 1856, m. by: E. H. Campbell, M. G., August 21, 1856, COFFEE Co.

CAMPBELL, William to Jenny Pentecost - issued May 15, 1809, Bondsman:
John Farley, SUMNER Co.

CAMPBELL, William to Betsy Goddard - issued July 20, 1815, KNOX Co.

CAMPBELL, William to Polly Warren - issued August 10, 1824, Bondsman:
Solomon Suggs, m. by: Joshua Lester, V. D. M., August 11, 1824,
WILSON Co.

CAMPBELL, William to Polly Rhea - issued October 28, 1834, Bondsman:
C. Williams, m. by: Williamson Williams, M. G., October 30, 1834,
WILSON Co.

CAMPBELL, Wilson to Frances Arnold - issued December 4, 1820, Bondsman:
Richard Harrison, m. by: Geo. L. Smith, J. P., December 20, 1820,
WILSON Co.

CAMPSEY, John to Elizabeth D. Peace - issued August 11, 1831, WILSON Co.

CAMRON, John to Mary Pollard - issued September 15, 1831, Bondsman:
James Pollard, m. by: Levi Satterfield, M. G., GRAINGER Co.

CANAHAN, Benja. to Rebecca McMinn - issued June 19, 1822, m. by:
Wesley Walker, M. G., WILSON Co.

CANE, Josiah to Nancy Wilkerson - issued July 27, 1811, Bondsman:
Joseph Barron, SUMNER Co.

CANE, William to Mary James - issued August 5, 1840, m. by: W. Hand,
J. P., August 6, 1840, DICKSON Co.

CANEDY (or Kennedy), Dempsey to Patsey Barnes - issued January 19,
1796, Bondsman: John Kennedy (or Canedy), SUMNER Co.

CANNADA, William T. to Susan Dwyer - issued February 18, 1829, Bondsman:
Jas. Riddle, WILSON Co.

CANNADY, Michael to Susan J. Long - issued October 3, 1866, FRANKLIN Co.

CANNON, Abraham W. to Mary Y. Sharpe - issued May 24, 1820, m. by:
Theos. A. Cannon, J. P., May 24, 1820, RUTHERFORD Co.

CANNON, Alanson to Elizabeth C. Sharp - m. by: J. W. Hall May 16, 1834,
SUMNER Co.

CANNON, Benj. B. to Eliza Tunnell - issued March 31, 1828, m. by:
Sam'l Fleming, J. P., April 3, 1828, KNOX Co.

CANNON, Charles D. to Martha Warmath - issued April 16, 1860, m. by:
W. C. Rawls, J. P., April 17, 1860, ROBERTSON Co.

CANNON, Clement to Susan Locke - issued August, 1810, Bondsman:
William White, RUTHERFORD Co.

CANNON, David to Sary Piles - issued December 20, 1825, Bondsman:
J. Carr, m. December 20, 1825, SUMNER Co.

CANNON, George to Phebe Pope - April 25, 1798, Security: John Newman,
GREENE Co.

CANNON, George to Lucinda Gaines - m. by: Jesse Gambling, J. P.,
January 15, 1835, SUMNER Co.

CANNON, Geo. R. to Mary Russell - issued January 26, 1824, m. by:
R. H. King January 28, 1824, KNOX Co.

CANNON, H. to Malinda Pellum - issued August 1, 1865, m. by:
M. Catchings, J. P., August 5, 1865, FRANKLIN Co.

CANNON, Hughes to Margaret Irby - issued October 27, 1824, Bondsman:
James Lewis, m. by: James Kennon, M. G., October 27, 1824,
GRAINGER Co.

CANNON, J. M. to Martha A. White - issued October 31, 1859, m. by:
Jesse B. White, J. P., ROBERTSON Co.

CANNON, James to Rebecca Bowen - issued May 31, 1816, Bondsman:
Humphrey Robertson, m. by: John Kidwell, M. G., June 2, 1816,
GRAINGER Co.

CANNON, John to Nancy Willon - January 29, 1800, Security: John Newman,
GREENE Co.

CANNON, John A. to M. M. M. Hamson - issued October 29, 1849, m. by:
Tho. W. Ruffin, J. P., November 2, 1840, ROBERTSON Co.

CANNON, John D. to Rebecka Wilkerson - issued March 4, 1831, Bondsman:
B. B. Cannon, m. by: Sam'l. Fleming, J. P., March 8, 1831,
KNOX Co.

CANNON, John O. to Caroline Nelson - issued October 25, 1827, Bondsman:
Andrew McMillan, m. by: Tho. H. Nelson October 25, 1827, KNOX Co.

CANNON, John T. to Sarah A. Harrison - issued July 15, 1829, Bondsman:
James D. Glinn, RUTHERFORD Co.

CANNON, Mary to Joseph Hall - BEDFORD Co.

CANNON, Nobles to Annis Chandler - issued July 11, 1818, Bondsman:
Byrd Guille, m. by: Joseph T. Williams, J. P., July 12, 1818,
WILSON Co.

CANNON, Patrick to Mary Cotter - January 30, 1795, Security:
Stephen Cotter, GREENE Co.

CANNON, Perry to Elizabeth Baldwin - issued November 19, 1861, m. by:
Wm. Draughon, J. P., ROBERTSON Co.

CANNON, Richd. to Malinda Young - issued December 23, 1841, m. by:
A. Justin, Justice of the Peace for R. County, ROBERTSON Co.

CANNON, Robert to Elizabeth Scales - November 25, 1822, WILLIAMSON Co.

CANNON, S. T. to Mary S. Coggins - issued January 2, 1862, Bondsman:
G. S. Phillips, Jos. H. Thompson, Clk. per N. F. Thompson, Dep.
Clk., m. by: H. F. Holt, J. P., BEDFORD Co.

CANNON, Samuel to Polly Alexander - issued August 21, 1809, Bondsman:
Robert Alexander, WILSON Co.

CANNON, Thomas to Elizabeth Garrett - issued June 25, 1822, m. by:
Edward Willis June 26, 1822, WILSON Co.

CANNON, Thompson to Elizabeth Kinnard - July 20, 1811, WILLIAMSON Co.

CANNON, William H. to Dorotha Payne - issued January 30, 1860, m. by:
J. B. White, J. P., ROBERTSON Co.

CANNON, Wm. W. to Elizabeth J. Nelson - issued March 4, 1852, m. by:
Joseph Smith, M. G., March 5, 1852, FRANKLIN Co.

CANOVER, H. E. to S. E. Trainum - issued October 28, 1859, m. by:
F. C. Plaster, M. G., October 29, 1959, ROBERTSON Co.

CANTRELL, Darby H. to Elmira W. Gillespie - issued January 14, 1829,
Bondsman: Wm. Montgomery, SUMNER Co.

CANTRELL, George C. to Mary Davenport - issued May 11, 1842, m. by:
J. B. McFerrin, M. G., May 11, 1842, DAVIDSON Co.

CANTRELL, James B. to Hannah Brown - issued May 13, 1820, Bondsman:
Jacob Brown, m. by: James Gwin, M. G., May 13, 1820, SUMNER Co.

CANTRELL, Ota to Sally Nolen - issued February 14, 1810, Bondsman:
----? Nolen, SUMNER Co.

CANTRELL, Ota to Nelton Cummins - issued July 27, 1818, Bondsman:
James Thompson, m. by: Robert Henderson, V. D. M., July 29, 1818,
RUTHERFORD Co.

CANTRELL, Stephen to Elizabeth Sturd (or Hurd) - issued May 11, 1809,
m. by: Sam'l. Yancey, J. P., GRAINGER Co.

CANTRELL, William to Joice E. Bugg - issued April 9, 1818, Bondsman:
Wm. Trousdale, SUMNER Co.

CANTRELL, Z. P. to Mary M. Sanderson - issued May 12, 1829, Bondsman:
J. J. Franklin, m. by: Wm. Hume, V. D. M., May 12, 1829, SUMNER Co.

CAPBELL, Harmon to Rebecca Clenton - issued September 8, 1844, m. by:
D. G. Baird, ROBERTSON Co.

CAPEL, Ruffins to Lucinda Eddins - issued January 13, 1829, m. by:
Geo. F. McWhirter, J. P., January 14, 1829, WILSON Co.

CAPERTON, Ryon to Elizabeth Webb - issued December 21, 1846, m. by:
Madison Williams, J. P., December 21, 1846, FRANKLIN Co.

CAPELL, John to Eliza Freeman - December 2, 1809, WILLIAMSON Co.

CAPELL, Juley (Juby?) to George Caldwell - MAURY Co.

CAPERTON, Ryon to Susan Williams - issued February 15, 1840, FRANKLIN Co.

CAPLES, Ruffin C. to Sarah Eddins - issued December 7, 1836, m. by:
L. Fisher, M. G., WILSON Co.

CAPLINER, William to Harriet Nelson - issued November 14, 1832,
Bondsman: Christopher Corley, m. by: William Algood, M. G.,
December 20, 1832, WILSON Co.

CAPLINGER, John to Catherine Harpole - issued July 24, 1812, Bondsman:
Adam Harpole, WILSON Co.

CAPLINGER, Samuel to Rebecca March - issued October 29, 1827, Bondsman:
John Swan, WILSON Co.

CAPLINGER, Samuel to Martha Carter - issued March 20, 1833, m. by:
A. J. McDonell, J. P., March 21, 1833, WILSON Co.

CAPLINGER, Solomon to Martha Masey - issued September 18, 1821,
Bondsman: _____(?) Douglas, WILSON Co.

CAPP, Caleb to Peggy Hood - July 18, 1818 (?), KNOX Co.

CAPPS, Ewing S. to Polly Pitt - m. by: S. H. Turner, J. P., July 18,
1835, SUMNER Co.

CAPPS, John to Patience Barry - issued May 21, 1830, Bondsman:
Thomas Frazor, SUMNER Co.

CAPPS, Mary to Mary Evans - issued July 17, 1824, Bondsman: John Long,
m. by: John Harris, J. P., July 17, 1824, GRAINGER Co.

CAPPS, Robert to Sarah Fudge - issued June 12, 1841, m. by:
John McRobertson June 12, 1841, DAVIDSON Co.

CAPPS, William to Lucy Fly - October 9, 1815, WILLIAMSON Co.

CAPS, David to Barbary Long - issued September 2, 1818, Bondsman:
John Long, m. by: Martin Cleveland, J. P., September 3, 1818,
GRAINGER Co.

CAPS, Jacob to Jemima Long - issued October 20, 1818, Bondsman:
Peter Boulton, GRAINGER Co.

CAPSHAW, Thomas to Catherine Sensebaugh - issued July 31, 1822,
Bondsman: Wm. Tarwater, m. by: Robert McBath, Esq., August 1,
1822, Witness: Wm. Swan, KNOX Co.

CAPSHAW, West Walker to Mary Magdeine Sensebaugh - issued October 28,
1830, m. by: B. B. Cannon, J. P., October 28, 1830, KNOX Co.

CAPSHAW, William to Nancy Guinn - issued January 8, 1840, m. by:
M. Catchings, J. P., FRANKLIN Co.

CAR, Thomas to Nancy Williams - issued November 14, 1835, Bondsman:
Henry Car, m. by: G. B. Mitchell, J. P., GRAINGER Co.

CARAWAY, Elihu to Mary D. Richmond - issued December 3, 1836, m. by:
Henry Truett, J. P., December 11, 1836, WILSON Co.

CARAWAY, John to Narcissa Allen Rogers - issued October 10, 1820,
Bondsman: Tyloames Merritt, WILSON Co.

CARAWAY, Lovet to Peggy Shannon - issued March 13, 1825, Bondsman:
Merit Caraway, WILSON Co.

CARAWAY, Merritt to Nancy Sherrell - issued November 17, 1830, Bondsman:
Silas Ragsdale, m. by: James Somers, J. P., November 25, 1830,
WILSON Co.

CARAWAY, Willis to Susanna Clemmons - issued September 25, 1818,
Bondsman: Herrod Merrett, m. by: Edward Harris October 1, 1818,
WILSON Co.

CARDEN, Goldman B. to Rosanah Monroe - issued December 22, 1835,
Bondsman: Samuel Gill, GRAINGER Co.

CARDEN, James to Pherbia Simpson - issued January 18, 1855, m. by:
R. W. Casey, J. P., January 18, 1855, COFFEE Co.

CARDEN, James A. to Nancy Barton - issued February 28, 1856, m. by:
R. W. Casey, J. P., March 2, 1856, COFFEE Co.

CARDEN, John to Sally McPhetridge - issued September 23, 1827, Bondsman:
John F. Huddleston, m. by: Eli Clark, J. P., GRAINGER Co.

CARDIN, William T. to Winford Dyer - issued September 16, 1820,
Bondsman: Owen Dyer, m. by: William Lane, J. P., September 21,
1820, GRAINGER Co.

CARDON, Henry J. to Elizabeth J. Seaton - issued December 21, 1855,
m. by: Wm. W. Conn, M. G., December 23, 1855, FRANKLIN Co.

CARDWELL, Anthony to Mary Perrimon - issued November 14, 1822, m. by:
John Kidwell, M. G., GRAINGER Co.

CARDWELL, Daniel to Elizabeth Abbott - issued May 11, 1818, Bondsman:
Stephen Cocke, m. by: James Moore, J. P., May 19, 1818, GRAINGER Co.

CARDWELL, Daniel to Martha Easley - issued December 31, 1821, Bondsman:
T. D. Knight, GRAINGER Co.

CARDWELL, James H. to Clarissa Graves - issued January 14, 1834,
Bondsman: A. G. Jackson, m. by: Jacob Nutty, M. G., January 15,
1834, KNOX Co.

CARDWELL, James W. to Martha A. P. Nugent - issued October 2, 1839, m. by: Jno. W. Hannah, M. G., October 2, 1839, DAVIDSON Co.

CARDWELL, John to Sarah Smith - issued February 20, 1830, Bondsman: Clements York, m. by: Levi Satterfield, M. G., GRAINGER Co.

CARDWELL, Joseph T. to Thensa E. Ragsdale - issued April 4, 1863, Bondsman: Wm. Howlin, Jos. H. Thompson, Clk., BEDFORD Co.

CARDWELL, Nelson to Nancy Hughs - issued November 30, 1816, Bondsman: William Stovall, m. by: C. Ballard November 30, 1816, SUMNER Co.

CARDWELL, Nelson to Polly Bennett - issued October 3, 1835, Bondsman: R. M. Boyers, SUMNER Co.

CARDWELL, Perrin to Eliza Norris - issued November 26, 1836, Bondsman: Andrew P. Mitchell, m. by: William Hinkle, M. G., GRAINGER Co.

CARDWELL, Robert to Leigh Ore - issued December 17, 1833, Bondsman: John Cox, m. by: Levi Satterfield, M. G., GRAINGER Co.

CARDWELL, Robert to Nancy Mayes - issued October 23, 1837, Bondsman: James Cardwell, m. by: Clisbe Austin, L. D. of the M. E. C., October 23, 1837, GRAINGER Co.

CARDWELL, Thos. to B. Lewis - m. by: J. A. Browning June 25, 1838, SUMNER Co.

CARDWELL, Thomas G. to Sarah Easley - issued May 5, 1823, Bondsman: Wesley Barton, m. by: Joseph B. Wymms, M. G., May 5, 1823, GRAINGER Co.

CARDWELL, Thomas G. to Martha Acklin - issued March 15, 1835, Bondsman: Sam'l B. Tinsley, RUTHERFORD Co.

CARDWELL, William to Calia Harper - issued January 7, 1820, Bondsman: John Cardwell, m. by: John Harris, J. P., GRAINGER Co.

CARDWELL, Wm. L. to Mary Ann G. Bittle - issued December 15, 1829, Bondsman: Robt. Masengill, GRAINGER Co.

CAREL, Robert to Sally Cochran - issued December 24, 1811, Bondsman: Thos. Carrel, SUMNER Co.

CARELESS, Benjamin to Sally Rascoe - issued December 10, 1816, Bondsman: William House, m. by: Hardy M. Cryer December 10, 1816, SUMNER Co.

CAREY, John H. D. to Frances Sanders - issued July 4, 1826, Bondsman: Richard H. P. Carey, SUMNER Co.

CAREY, Thomas to Martha Brewster - issued April 16, 1818, Bondsman: James Adams, m. by: W. C. Ballard, M. G., April 16, 1818, SUMNER Co.

CARGILE, H. to Amanda J. Cunningham - issued July 25, 1859, m. by: R. J. Price, J. P., July 26, 1859, COFFEE Co.

CARGILE, John R. to Elizabeth Cox - issued January 15, 1845, m. by: P. Lynch, J. P., January 15, 1845, STEWART Co.

CARGILL, Peyton C. to Mahala Melvin - issued April 17, 1847, DAVIDSON Co.

CARITHERS, John to Elizabeth Clark - issued April 18, 1810, Bondsman: Andrew Carithers, KNOX Co.

CARITHERS, John G. to Charlotte Dyer - issued May 14, 1816, m. by: Edm's Jones May 16, 1816, RUTHERFORD Co.

CARLILE, Wilson to Ann C. Huston - issued October 20, 1838, m. by: W. H. Hunt, J. P., October 2, 1839, DAVIDSON Co.

CARLIN, Hugh to Patsey Pemberton - issued May 4, 1819, Bondsman:
John Pemberton, WILSON Co.

CARLIN, Spencer to Manerva Hogan - issued February 26, 1831, m. by:
James C. Willifort, J. P., February 28, 1831, WILSON Co.

CARLIN, William to Sarah Johnson - issued October 13, 1818, Bondsman:
John Cox, WILSON Co.

CARLIN, Zach H. to Sally Hill - issued November 9, 1822, m. by:
Elijah Maddox, M. G., November 12, 1822, WILSON Co.

CARLISLE, Henry to Mary Ann Fletcher - issued February 15, 1860, m. by:
J. W. Featherston February 16, 1860, ROBERTSON Co.

CARLISLE, James S. to Mary Warrick - issued September 22, 1860, m. by:
G. W. Jackson, M. G., September 23, 1860, COFFEE Co.

CARLISLE, N. R. M. to Elizabeth Douglass - issued November 26, 1857,
m. by: W. B. Watterson, M. G., November 26, 1857, COFFEE Co.

CARLISLE, William to Martha Hubbard - issued December 28, 1853, m. by:
J. J. Patton, M. G., December 28, 1853, COFFEE Co.

CARLOCK, Ebenezer to Nancy Pemberton - issued September 5, 1820,
Bondsman: George Donnell, WILSON Co.

CARLTON, J. M. B. to A. E. Brazelton - issued March 23, 1869, m. by:
S. M. Cowan, V. D. M., March 23, 1869, FRANKLIN Co.

CARLTON, William to Emily Rucker - issued May 23, 1832, m. by:
O. W. Crockett, J. P., RUTHERFORD Co.

CARLOUGH (?), Abraham to Abigail Ozborn - December 30, 1790, Security:
Hugh Rodgers, GREENE Co.

CARLOUGH, Catherine to John Coons (Coonee) - GREENE Co.

CARMACK, G. W. to Amanda Fortsom - issued August 11, 1849, Bondsman:
E. Johnson, MONTGOMERY Co.

CARMAN, Isiah to Martha Eagan - issued February 3, 1836, Bondsman:
Thomas Tiller, m. by: Francis Johnson February 3, 1836, SUMNER Co.

CARMAN, Larkin to Elizabeth Barton - issued November 5, 1817, Bondsman:
Elijah Barton, SUMNER Co.

CARMEN, Elisha to Alley Carmen - issued December 13, 1832, Bondsman:
Stephen Parsley, RUTHERFORD Co.

CARMICAL, Daniel to Prudance Howell - issued May 10, 1826, Bondsman:
Joshua Hickey, m. by: James Kennon, M. G., May 10, 1826, GRAINGER Co.

CARMICHAEL, Alexander to Esther Vance - April 26, 1791, Security:
Samuel Vance, GREENE Co.

CARMICHAEL, Hugh to Nancy Tindell - issued December 25, 1801, Bondsman:
Wm. Covey, Witness: A. White, KNOX Co.

CARMICHAEL, Isabella to Andrew Donaldson - GREENE Co.

CARMICHAEL, Pumroy to Nancy Bell - issued November 6, 1807, Bondsman:
William Bell, Witness: Jno. Gamble, KNOX Co.

CARMICHAL, William B. to Margaret Patterson - issued November 7, 1829,
Bondsman: Thomas Patterson, m. by: Elijah M. Eagleton, J. P.,
November 12, GRAINGER Co.

CARMON, Larkin to Elizabeth Cochran - issued August 16, 1827, Bondsman:
James Cochran, SUMNER Co.

CARNAHAN, Abraham to Cynthia Price - issued February 3, 1829, Bondsman: Archibald Tenison, RUTHERFORD Co.

CARNAHAN, Hugh to Elizabeth Thompson - issued June 21, 1806, Bondsman: Abraham Thompson, RUTHERFORD Co.

CARNEAL, John to Mary Jane Tally - issued February 27, 1854, Bondsman: L. Vaughn, m. by: M. G. Carney, M. G., MONTGOMERY Co.

CARNEAL, Josiah to Lucy Jane McQuery - issued August 13, 1853, Bondsman: Joshua Brown, m. by: A. H. Alsup, M. G., August 16, 1853, MONTGOMERY Co.

CARNES, A. C. to Nancy Wood - issued July 14, 1852, m. by: S. Erchleaum, M. G., July 16, 1852, VAN BUREN Co.

CARNES, James to Betsy Mitchell - issued August 15, 1803, Bondsman: James Dodd, Witness: Chas. McClung, Clerk, KNOX Co.

CARNEY, C. N. to Margaret C. Lynes - issued May 6, 1848, Bondsman: David Heflin, m. by: R. W. Morrison, J. P., May 17, 1848, MONTGOMERY Co.

CARNEY, Elijah to Marcilla Brandon - issued May 12, 1847, m. by: Wm. Ellis, J. P., May 12, 1847, STEWART Co.

CARNEY, George G. to Lucresa Mables - issued March 26, 1847, m. by: W. Crocket, J. P., April 4, 1847, DAVIDSON Co.

CARNEY, Isaac T. to Mariah Boyd - issued April 11, 1845, m. by: W. Crockett, J. P., April 12, 1845, DAVIDSON Co.

CARNEY, J. S. to S. A. J. Blanton - issued June 11, 1862, Bondsman: James Green, Jos. H. Thompson, Clk. per James H. Neil, Dep. Clk., BEDFORD Co.

CARNEY, John to Elizabeth Chamberling (Chamberlain) - issued December 1, 1821, Bondsman: John Combs, m. by: Isaac Barton, M. G., December 6, 1821, GRAINGER Co.

CARNEY, John to Mary Vess - issued August 8, 1832, Bondsman: Sam Henderson, WILSON Co.

CARNEY, John to Sally A. Young - issued November 22, 1844, m. by: Jesse Edwards, M. G., November 22, 1844, STEWART Co.

CARNEY, Joshua to Mary Charlton - issued December 21, 1825, Bondsman: Olive Dickerson, SUMNER Co.

CARNEY, Marion G. to Mary Tate - issued January 5, 1846, Bondsman: C. N. Carney, m. by: Drury C. Stephens, G. M., January 15, 1846, MONTGOMERY Co.

CARNEY, Rebecca to John McCormick - GREENE Co.

CARNEY, Samuel to Mary Frack - issued October 2, 1929, Bondsman: John Carney, SUMNER Co.

CARNEY, Shelton to Susan Charlton - issued February 24, 1824, m. by: James Walton, J. P., February 24, 1824, SUMNER Co.

CARNEY, Thomas to Mary Jane Haley - issued August 7, 1837, Bondsman: William Vantrease, m. by: Sion Bass, M. G., WILSON Co.

CARNEY, Wm. V. to Martha Copher - issued May 12, 1845, m. by: Wm. S. Baldry, M. G., May 20, 1845, DAVIDSON Co.

CARNS, Alexander B. to Cynthia M. Gowen - issued May 9, 1832, m. by: Tolbert Fannin, Eld. C. C., May 10, 1832, RUTHERFORD Co.

CARNS, Alexander C. to Elizabeth Israel - issued June 19, 1834, m. by:
Jno. Mynatt, J. P., June 22, 1834, KNOX Co.

CARNSACK, Joseph to Pennina Allen - issued August 6, 1854, Bondsman:
Jame Bowers, m. by: A. Outlaw, J. P., August 6, 1854, MONTGOMERY Co.

CARNSHAN, Andrew to Sarah Helten - February 5, 1808, WILLIAMSON Co.

CARNUTT, David to Drucilla Johnston - issued February 20, 1829,
Bondsman: William Carnutt, m. by: Robert Gaines, J. P., GRAINGER Co.

CARNUTT, William to Lucindia Dent - issued December 2, 1817, Bondsman:
David Smith, GRAINGER Co.

CAROTHERS, Andrew to Polly Stanley - July 23, 1817, WILLIAMSON Co.

CAROTHERS, James to Jane Irwin - issued January 29, 1800, Bondsman:
Hugh Carothers, SUMNER Co.

CAROTHERS, John to Polly Carothers - May 29, 1809, WILLIAMSON Co.

CAROTHERS, Thomas to Sally Holland - issued October 23, 1804, Bondsman:
James Carothers, SUMNER Co.

CAROTHERS, William to Sally Carothers - February 6, 1808, WILLIAMSON Co.

CARPENTER, Asa to Elizabeth Mason - issued September 23, 1815, m. by:
John Hoover, J. P., September 25, 1815, RUTHERFORD Co.

CARPENTER, Asa to Eleanor Stephens - issued December 20, 1838, Bondsman:
John M. Payton, WILSON Co.

CARPENTER, Conrad to Eliza Ann Quarles - issued March 5, 1827, Bondsman:
J. L. Lester, m. by: Joshua Lester, V. D. M., WILSON Co.

CARPENTER, Frederick to Lucinda Chambers - issued January 21, 1822,
Bondsman: James Alderson, m. by: Addison Foster, J. P., January 21,
1822, SUMNER Co.

CARPENTER, J. E. R. to Jane S. Wilson - issued August 17, 1864,
Bondsman: J. D. Massey, m. by: J. Simpson Frierson August 18,
1864, LAWRENCE Co.

CARPENTER, Jacob to Polly Kerr - issued August 17, 1825, Bondsman:
Isaac M. Steel, m. by: W. B. A. Ramsey, J. P., August 18, 1825,
KNOX Co.

CARPENTER, James to Elizabeth Crank - issued January 30, 1828, Bondsman:
Andrew McMillan, m. by: Wm. Sawyers, J. P., February 7, 1828,
KNOX Co.

CARPENTER, John to Mary O'Neal - February 10, 1787, Security:
Hugh Veard, GREENE Co.

CARPENTER, Jn. to Penny McAfee - May 21, 1808, WILLIAMSON Co.

CARPENTER, Leeroy to Prudence Walker - issued December 7, 1829, m. by:
John McMillan, J. P., December 7, 1829, KNOX Co.

CARPENTER, Maggie A. to John Hansel - issued December 9, 1863, Bondsman:
John F. Neil, Jos. H. Thompson, Clk., BEDFORD Co.

CARPENTER, Thomas to Mary Ann Shock - issued June 13, 1801, Bondsman:
George Carpenter, Witness: H. L. White, KNOX Co.

CARPENTER, William to Isabella McCline - issued February 18, 1822,
m. by: James McMillan, J. P., February 21, 1822, KNOX Co.

CARPENTER, Wm. to Abigail Knott - issued May 21, 1840, m. by:
C. D. Elliopt, M. G., May 21, 1840, DAVIDSON Co.

CARPENTER, William to Margaret Putnam - issued August 27, 1857, m. by:
F. M. Yell, J. P., October 16, 1857, COFFEE Co.

CARPER, Green to Mary Petty - issued April 26, 1838, m. by:
Daniel Judd, L. E., April 30, 1838, DAVIDSON Co.

CARR, Alason G. to Eliza Young - m. by: Arch'd. B. Duval February 18,
1834, SUMNER Co.

CARR, Allen to Polly Crocker - issued August 27, 1834, m. by:
T. P. Holman, J. P., WILSON Co.

CARR, Benjamin to Huldah Beard - issued July 29, 1826, Bondsman:
Jno. Owens, m. by: Sam Flenniken, J. P., July 31, 1826, Witness:
Wm. Swan, KNOX Co.

CARR, David to Sally Guthrie - issued November 4, 1819, Bondsman:
Robert Guthrie, m. by: Hugh Kirkpatrick, M. G., November 4, 1819,
SUMNER Co.

CARR, David to Leannah Ball - m. September 9, 1837, SUMNER Co.

CARR, Elijah to Britan Decabor - issued May 10, 1816, Bondsman:
Walter Carr, m. by: Abner Hill, M. G., May 11, 1816, WILSON Co.

CARR, Harrison T. to Ann W. Estill - issued January 15, 1856, m. by:
A. D. Trimble, M. G., January 15, 1856, FRANKLIN Co.

CARR, James to Elizabeth Williams - issued July 15, 1825, Bondsman:
Wm. Kennedy, m. by: John McMurtry, J. P., July 15, 1825, SUMNER Co.

CARR, James C. to Harriett Belote - issued September 25, 1827, Bondsman:
Lucilius Winchester, m. by: John Parker, L. D., September 25,
1827, SUMNER Co.

CARR, Jesse to Maria E. Sanford - issued March 14, 1836, Bondsman:
J. A. Carr and H. F. Anderson, SUMNER Co.

CARR, John to Sally Cage - issued November 23, 1791, Bondsman:
King Carr and James Frazier, SUMNER Co.

CARR, Jr., John to Hannah Carr - issued May 10, 1809, Bondsman:
King Carr, SUMNER Co.

CARR, John to Polly Orr - August 14, 1810, WILLIAMSON Co.

CARR, John to Mary Riddle - issued January 3, 1828, Bondsman:
William Gentry, m. by: John Jarratt, WILSON Co.

CARR, John to Sarah Parsons - issued November 29, 1830, m. by:
J. Higgason, J. P., November 29, 1830, SUMNER Co.

CARR, John to Nancy Perrin - issued March 29, 1834, Bondsman:
Giles J. Bledsoe, GRAINGER Co.

CARR, John to Phoebe Marshall - m. by: John F. Carr, J. P., December 19,
1835, SUMNER Co.

CARR, John S. to Martha Hanna - issued October 7, 1823, m. by:
Wm. Smith, J. P., October 7, 1823, SUMNER Co.

CARR, Jordon to Lucy Ann Burnley - issued December 19, 1829, Bondsman:
Alexander Brown, SUMNER Co.

CARR, Joseph to Rebecka M. Yates - issued December 30, 1832, Bondsman:
Thomas Miller, m. by: Tho. H. Nelson December 31, 1832, KNOX Co.

CARR, King to Anne Hamilton - issued January 24, 1789, Bondsman:
Richard Carr, SUMNER Co.

CARR, Richard to Jemimah Glenn - issued January 27, 1827, Bondsman:
Wm. Steele, m. by: Elijah Maddox, M. G., January 28, 1827,
WILSON Co.

CARR, Richard to Barbary Miller - issued January 15, 1831, m. January 15,
1831, SUMNER Co.

CARR, Richardson to Joanna Dwyne - issued October 27, 1834, Bondsman:
W. M. Carr, m. by: Thos. P. Holman, J. P., January 24, 1835,
WILSON Co.

CARR, Thomas to Mahala Donelson - issued December 19, 1829, Bondsman:
William Shaw, SUMNER Co.

CARR, Thomas H. to O. S. Mathew - issued December 26, 1836, Bondsman:
Andrew J. Graham, m. by: James Charlton December 26, 1836,
SUMNER Co.

CARR, Richardson to Milly Sawyers - issued September 6, 1809, Bondsman:
Thomas Carr, WILSON Co.

CARR, Walter to Sarah McDaniel - issued October 11, 1821, m. by:
E. Maddox, M. G., WILSON Co.

CARR, Walter to Sarah Daniel - issued October 11, 1828, Bondsman:
H. L. Douglas, WILSON Co.

CARR, William C. to Minerva Willis - issued December 16, 1830, Bondsman:
A. F. Young, m. by: Thomas Joyner December 16, 1830, SUMNER Co.

CARR, William H. to Eliza H. Jones - issued December 7, 1831, Bondsman:
A. Mills, m. by: John T. Carr, J. P., December 7, 1831, SUMNER Co.

CARR, William P. to Peggy Reed - issued March 29, 1820, Bondsman:
J. W. Byrn, SUMNER Co.

CARR, Wilson L. to Jane L. Baskerville - issued May 8, 1826, Bondsman:
James B. Hanner, SUMNER Co.

CARREL, Wiley to Elizabeth G. Gilpin - issued July 30, 1808, Bondsman:
James G. Sloan, SUMNER Co.

CARRELL, Geo. to Becky Shook - issued April 30, 1832, KNOX Co.

CARRELL, James R. to Rachael E. Ross - issued August 17, 1865, Bondsman:
James Roberts, m. by: William C. Davis, J. P., August 17, 1865,
LAWRENCE Co.

CARRELL, John C. to Nancy K. Meek - issued October 18, 1864, Bondsman:
A. F. Springer, m. by: William A. Harris, Min. M. E. Ch. So.,
October 18, 1864, LAWRENCE Co.

CARRELL, John T. to Margaret E. Green - issued April 4, 1866, Bondsman:
W. A. Rochiell, m. by: Geo. O. W. White, J. P., April 4, 1866,
LAWRENCE Co.

CARRELL, William J. to Eliza Ann Simms - issued September 16, 1865,
Bondsman: William P. Pickard, m. by: John W. Pennington, J. P.,
September 17, 1865, LAWRENCE Co.

CARREY, G. W. J. to Emily D. Martin - issued September 10, 1846, m. by:
Robt. A. Lapsley September 10, 1846, DAVIDSON Co.

CARRICK, Addison to Rebeccah Gamble - issued November 5, 1812,
Bondsman: Will Purris, KNOX Co.

CARRICK, Montgomery to Elizabeth Vance - February 1, 1797, Security:
Robert Wyly, GREENE Co.

CARRICK, Samuel to Annie McClelland - January 27, 1794, KNOX Co.

CARRICK, Thomas to Sarah Smith - issued January 5, 1825, m. by:
J. Higgins, J. P., January 6, 1825, RUTHERFORD Co.

CARRINGER, Marry to Jesse Smith - GREENE Co.

CARROL, James to Polly Bond - issued September 1, 1820, Bondsman:
John Carrol, m. by: John Harris, J. P., GRAINGER Co.

CARROL, Meshack to Martha Carrol - issued September 7, 1819, Bondsman:
John Cooper, m. by: Isaac Linslay September 9, 1819, WILSON Co.

CARROL, Minor to Lucinda Browning - issued September 26, 1838,
FRANKLIN Co.

CARROL, William to Nancy Ludewell - issued June 25, 1838, FRANKLIN Co.

CARROLL, Addison to Lucretta R. Thomason - issued November 26, 1838,
Bondsman: E. B. Summerhill, m. by: Moses Ellis, J. P., November 28,
1838, WILSON Co.

CARROLL, Ellingston A. to Sally Collins - issued February 21, 1853,
m. by: G. Orgain, J. P., February 24, 1853, MONTGOMERY Co.

CARROLL, Ellington to Sarah E. Daniel - issued January 17, 1743,
m. by: W. Hand, J. P., January 28, 1843, DICKSON Co.

CARROLL, George to Susan Blankenship - issued January 27, 1835,
Bondsman: Saml H. Porterfield, m. by: J. Lester, V. D. M.,
WILSON Co.

CARROLL, George W. to Mary Matthews - issued July 8, 1843, m. by:
M. R. Mann, J. P., July 9, 1843, FRANKLIN Co.

CARROLL, James to Eleanor Gregory - m. by: James Charlton August 28,
1833, SUMNER Co.

CARROLL, James G. to Elizabeth Caroline Ross - issued July 13, 1853,
m. by: R. C. Farris, Mins., July 13, 1853, COFFEE Co.

CARROLL, John to Rebecca Baker - issued August 5, 1830, Bondsman:
Edmund York, WILSON Co.

CARROLL, John J. to Mary Lowery - issued February 11, 1845, m. by:
W. Ellis, J. P., February 13, 1845, STEWART Co.

CARROLL, John L. to Margaret F. Pollard - issued July 31, 1852, Bondsman:
N. B. Whitfield, m. by: R. W. Nixon, M. G., August 1, 1852,
MONTGOMERY Co.

CARROLL, John O. to Niny Barnes - issued March 9, 1849, m. by:
Madison Williams, J. P., March 9, 1849, FRANKLIN Co.

CARROLL, Levi P. to Margrett S. Knight - issued October 18, 1873,
m. by: J. L. Payne, M. G., October 19, 1873, FRANKLIN Co.

CARROLL, M. C. to Jane E. Poe - issued December 26, 1857, m. by:
H. W. Carroll, J. P., December 26, 1857, COFFEE Co.

CARROLL, Michum to Oney Bryant - issued May 24, 1817, m. by:
David Gordon, RUTHERFORD Co.

CARROLL, Robert to Peggy Stuart - issued April 10, 1817, Bondsman:
George Elliott, SUMNER Co.

CARROLL, Robert to Elizabeth Everett - issued February 24, 1847,
DICKSON Co.

CARROLL, Samuel to Manerva Taylor - issued November 9, 1855, m. by:
    H. W. Carroll, J. P., November 9, 1855, COFFEE Co.

CARROLL, Stephen to Anne Locke - issued March 31, 1810, Bondsman:
    Henry Boyer, RUTHERFORD Co.

CARROLL, Thos. B. to Eliza B. Ham - issued May 30, 1840, m. by:
    J. T. Edgar June 2, 1840, DAVIDSON Co.

CARROLL, Wily to Clarenda P___(?) - May 29, 1818, KNOX Co.

CARROLL, William to Cecelia M. Bradford - issued September 1, 1813,
    Bondsman: Henry Bradford, SUMNER Co.

CARROLL, William to Jenoma Flowers - issued May 8, 1832, Bondsman:
    William F. Lindsey, m. by: Isaac Lindsey, E. M. G., May 8, 1832,
    SUMNER Co.

CARROLL, William to Mary Rush - issued September 4, 1832, Bondsman:
    Jacob Woods, m. by: James Lacey, M. G., September 4, 1832,
    GRAINGER Co.

CARROLL, William to Catherine Williams - issued November 18, 1844,
    m. by: C. Rooker, S. L. Meth. E. Ch., November 19, 1844, DICKSON Co.

CARROLL, Wm. F. to Margaret M. Morrow - May 7, 1855, m. by: John M.
    Hewitt, J. P., GILES Co.

CARROLL, William H. to Eliza H. Breath - issued November 5, 1838,
    m. by: J. T. Edgar November 5, 1838, DAVIDSON Co.

CARROLL, Z. N. to Mary J. Miller - issued September 7, 1865, m. by:
    James M. Darwin, M. G., September 7, 1865, FRANKLIN Co.

CARRUTH, Eli S. to Elizabeth Hunter - issued September 25, 1833, m. by:
    Stephen McDonald, J. P., WILSON Co.

CARRUTH, James to Sally Williams - issued March 20, 1807, Bondsman:
    W. Bradley, WILSON Co.

CARRUTH, James C. to Mildred C. Davis - issued August 14, 1820,
    Bondsman: Foster G. Crutcher, m. by: Wm. Steele, J. P., August 16,
    1820, WILSON Co.

CARRUTH, James T. to Nancy Williams - issued January 26, 1825, Bondsman:
    Thomas Guthrie, m. by: Walter Evrett, J. P., January 27, 1825,
    WILSON Co.

CARRUTH, Sam'l C. to Mary C. Lane - issued December 3, 1832, Bondsman:
    John Barnfield, WILSON Co.

CARRUTH, Walter to Nancy Keath - issued January 10, 1827, Bondsman:
    Thomas Dean, m. by: Stephen McDonald, J. P., January 11, 1827,
    WILSON Co.

CARRUTH, William to Elizabeth Davis - issued April 21, 1825, Bondsman:
    Jesse Jackson, WILSON Co.

CARRUTHERS, William to Rachel Moore - issued November 27, 1831,
    Bondsman: Stephen Moore, m. by: G. B. Mitchell, J. P., GRAINGER Co.

CARSON, David A. to Elizabeth J. Shelton - issued December 17, 1846,
    Bondsman: G. Watwood, m. by: B. F. Williamson, J. P., December 30,
    1846, MONTGOMERY Co.

CARSON, Elizabeth to Joseph Steele - GREENE Co.

CARSON, James to Nancy S. Stewart - issued December 19, 1791, Bondsman:
    Joseph Waller, SUMNER Co.

CARSON, James to Ellendor Taylor - June 18, 1813, WILLIAMSON Co.

CARSON, Jane to David Henderson - GREENE Co.

CARSON, John to Anne Lister - October 26, 1789, Security: John Lister,
    GREENE Co.

CARSON, John to Sally Estes - issued December 5, 1801, Bondsman:
    John Estes, GRAINGER Co.

CARSON, John to Cynthia Spilman - issued August 4, 1819, Bondsman:
    Christopher Spilman, KNOX Co.

CARSON, Jno. to Cynthia Spilman - issued August 4, 1819, m. by:
    Jeremiah King, M. G., August 5, 1819, KNOX Co.

CARSON, John to Hester A. Palmer - issued October 8, 1848, m. by:
    I. Hardin, J. P., October 8, 1848, DICKSON Co.

CARSON, John B. to Elizabeth Walker - April 20, 1831, WILLIAMSON Co.

CARSON, John M. to Martha A. Hodge - issued November 16, 1861, Bondsman:
    James Cyfert, m. by: W. C. Davis, J. P., November 17, 1861,
    LAWRENCE Co.

CARSON, Joseph to Rebecca Wilson - November 30, 1808, WILLIAMSON Co.

CARSON, Mary to James Taylor - GREENE Co.

CARSON, Robert to Martha Shaw - issued March 12, 1849, m. by:
    A. Gilliam, P. G., March 12, 1849, FRANKLIN Co.

CARSON, Ruth to William Carosn, Jun. - GREENE Co.

CARSON, Samuel to Sally Bradley - October 16, 1811, WILLIAMSON Co.

CARSON, Thomas to M. E. Wilhoite - issued December 14, 1861, Bondsman:
    John Wilhoite, Jos. H. Thompson, Clk. per M. E. W. Dunaway,
    Dep. Clk., BEDFORD Co.

CARSON, W. L. R. to S. E. Scivally - issued April 17, 1869, FRANKLIN Co.

CARSON, William, Jun. to Ruth Carson - October 25, 1785, Security:
    William Carson, Sen., GREENE Co.

CARSON, William to Margaret Brazell - issued September 28, 1830,
    Bondsman: J. L. Warner, m. by: Wm. Walton, J. P., September 28,
    1830, SUMNER Co.

CARSON, William to Ann McCallum - January 15, 1837, KNOX Co.

CARSON, William H. to Mary Goff - September 10, 1828, WILLIAMSON Co.

CARSON, Willis to Peggy Burgess - December 19, 1811, WILLIAMSON Co.

CARTER, Alexander to Rhody Benthal - issued April 23, 1809, Bondsman:
    Webb Bloodworth, SUMNER Co.

CARTER, Amos to Nancy Luttrell - issued March 11, 1819, Bondsman:
    Jozadak Roberts, KNOX Co.

CARTER, Anna to Samuel Hanna - GREENE Co.

CARTER, Banard to Rasey Benthal - issued March 23, 1811, Bondsman:
    Benthal, WILSON Co.

CARTER, Brackstone to Lavicey Morton - November 23, 1821, WILLIAMSON Co.

CARTER, Burwell to Nancy Burgess - issued October 13, 1830, Bondsman:
    Henry D. Ransom, RUTHERFORD Co.

CARTER, Caleb to Phebe Williams - March 17, 1798, Security:
    Joseph Carter, GREENE Co.

CARTER, Cullin to Emily C. Bloodworth - issued August 5, 1834, m. by:
    Thos. Sanders, J. P., August 5, 1834, RUTHERFORD Co.

CARTER, Daniel to Anne Jones - February 11, 1795, Security:
    Robert Campbell, GREENE Co.

CARTER, Edward to Penelope Condway - issued March 21, 1851, m. by:
    F. C. Plaster, ROBERTSON Co.

CARTER, Elizabeth to Ellis King - GREENE Co.

CARTER, Enochl to Susan Wilkison - February 27, 1794, Security:
    William Wilkison, GREENE Co.

CARTER, Enos to Celia Osburn - issued November 27, 1837, Bondsman:
    Solomon Carter, m. by: Moses Woollen, J. P., November 28, 1837,
    WILSON Co.

CARTER, Ezekiel to Martha Stanly - November 27, 1800, Security:
    Abraham Carter, GREENE Co.

CARTER, Flivoas J. to Sarah E. Parker - issued August 15, 1850,
    m. by: Patrick Martin, L. E., ROBERTSON Co.

CARTER, Fountaine B. to Polly A. Atkinson - June 28, 1823, WILLIAMSON Co.

CARTER, Granville to Martha Jones - issued December 9, 1845, DICKSON Co.

CARTER, Gideon to Lydia Case - issued March 10, 1828, Bondsman:
    Snodon Hickman, m. by: John Beard, M. G., March 11, 1828, WILSON Co.

CARTER, Gideon to Martha Devault - issued March 28, 1825, Bondsman:
    Abraham Carter, m. by: James Drennon, J. P., March 31, 1825,
    WILSON Co.

CARTER, Gideon to Betsy Swaney - issued May 15, 1813, Bondsman:
    Joseph Carter, SUMNER Co.

CARTER, Geo. W. to Lucinda Gillaspy - issued July 1, 1844, m. by:
    Lewis Adams, M. G., ROBERTSON Co.

CARTER, Francis M. to Narcissa Hannah - issued September 10, 1842,
    DAVIDSON Co.

CARTER, G. M. W. to Prissey Lewis - issued June 7, 1849, m. by:
    John Gillentine, J. P., June 7, 1849, VAN BUREN Co.

CARTER, Gabriel to Elizabeth Wilhoit - April 17, 1804, Security:
    Wm. Carter and Wm. Majors (?), GREENE Co.

CARTER, George G. to M. A. Martin - issued January 18, 1853, m. by:
    Thomas Martin, M. G., ROBERTSON Co.

CARTER, Hannah to Nathan Carter - GREENE Co.

CARTER, Henry to Mary E. Hardeman - issued November 16, 1833, Bondsman:
    Walker Peak, RUTHERFORD Co.

CARTER, Hiram C. to Elizabeth McDowell - issued September 26, 1837,
    m. by: G. T. Henderson, E. M. E. C., September 26, 1837,
    RUTHERFORD Co.

CARTER, Hiram J. to Rachiel Gray - issued September 28, 1872, m. by:
    Wm. H. Matlock, J. P., October 1, 1872, FRANKLIN Co.

CARTER, Huth to Sarah Ross - March 9, 1789, Security: Seth Babb,
    GREENE Co.

CARTER, J. W. to Annie Moseley (MB) - issued November 2, 1869,
m. by: W. Bryant November 4, 1869, FRANKLIN Co.

CARTER, James to Phebe Bullard (Ballard) - May 2, 1791, Security:
Isaac Ballard, GREENE Co.

CARTER, James to Polly Davidson - issued January 23, 1807, Bondsman:
Moses Carter and John Brown, WILSON Co.

CARTER, James to Polly Morris - issued November 8, 1824, Bondsman:
John Morris, m. by: John Parker, L. D., November 8, 1824, SUMNER Co.

CARTER, James to Jane Crosswell - issued January 9, 1843, m. by:
Jesse Edwards, M. G., STEWART Co.

CARTER, James to Emily Atkinson - issued September 26, 1843, Bondsman:
David D. Beegles, MEIGS Co.

CARTER, James to Susannah Morris - issued September 4, 1847, DICKSON Co.

CARTER, James to M. E. Carter - issued November 6, 1848, m. by:
G. W. Martin, G. M., November 9, 1848, ROBERTSON Co.

CARTER, James M. to Rebecka Johnston - issued July 24, 1833, Bondsman:
M. B. Carter, m. by: Thos. Stringfield July 30, 1833, KNOX Co.

CARTER, James M. to Eliza M. Lock - January 29, 1860, m. by:
W. N. Watkins, J. P., GILES Co.

CARTER, Jarrett to Sally Tuttle - issued April 4, 1825, Bondsman:
Gideon Carter, m. by: W. Smith, J. P., April 4, 1825, SUMNER Co.

CARTER, Jesse to Susanna Harmon - January 9, 1798, Security:
Thomas Harmon, GREENE Co.

CARTER, Joel to Hannah Stockton - issued November 6, 1809, Bondsman:
John Campbell, KNOX Co.

CARTER, John to Narcissa Gibson - issued January 31, 1830, m. by:
Joshua Woollen, M. G., February 1, 1830, WILSON Co.

CARTER, John to Narcissa Gibson - issued January 31, 1831, Bondsman:
Thos. Weber, WILSON Co.

CARTER, John to Lithey Morris - issued March 7, 1832, Bondsman:
John Morris, m. by: Wm. M. Carter, J. P., March 7, 1832, SUMNER Co.

CARTER, John to Nancy Silliman - issued December 4, 1834, Bondsman:
A. E. Donnell, m. by: Walter Carruth, J. P., WILSON Co.

CARTER, John to Elizabeth Webb - issued July 15, 1845, m. by:
Jesse Edwards, M. G., July 15, 1845, STEWART Co.

CARTER, John B. to M. E. Chowning - issued January 17, 1850, m. by:
J. Sprouse, J. P., ROBERTSON Co.

CARTER, John P. to Mary Lackey - issued April 28, 1827, Bondsman:
Jesse Medley, WILSON Co.

CARTER, Joseph to Betsey Mallard - issued June 30, 1813, Bondsman:
Gideon Carter, SUMNER Co.

CARTER, Joseph to Mary E. Francis - issued April 24, 1851, m. by:
Rev. A. L. Steel, FRANKLIN Co.

CARTER, Joseph to Julia Henderson - issued September 20, 1853, m. by:
W. J. Fox, V. D. M., September 20, 1853, FRANKLIN Co.

CARTER, Joseph to Nancy Stephens - issued October 19, 1865, FRANKLIN Co.

CARTER, Joseph W. to Nancy White - issued September 20, 1830, Bondsman:
Wm. Carter, SUMNER Co.

CARTER, Joseph W. to Mary L. Estill - issued November 18, 1847, m. by:
N. P. Modrall, M. G., November 18, 1847, FRANKLIN Co.

CARTER, Kinchin to Mary Benthall - issued February 25, 1804, Bondsman:
James Haynes, SUMNER Co.

CARTER, Landon I. to Nancy Carter - m. by: Thomas Gilmore April 5,
1837, SUMNER Co.

CARTER, Littleton N. to Charity D. Garrison - issued February 23,
1837, Bondsman: John Hearn, m. by: John Hearn, J. P., WILSON Co.

CARTER, Marshall to Priscilla Clifton - issued December 13, 1834,
Bondsman: John W. Wynne, WILSON Co.

CARTER, Martha Ann to Jacob Noblett - issued September 6, 1861,
Bondsman: Wiley Richards, Jos. H. Thompson, Clk. per N. F. Thompson,
Dep. Clk., BEDFORD Co.

CARTER, Martin B. to Martha Epps - issued October 29, 1825, Bondsman:
Wm. Molden, m. by: James McMillan, J. P., November 1, 1825,
KNOX Co.

CARTER, Mary to John Kelller - GREENE Co.

CARTER, Micajah to Ann Stockton - August 28, 1784, Security: Caleb
Carter, GREENE Co.

CARTER, Miller to Pheby Philips - issued June 21, 1817, Bondsman:
Benjamin Philips, m. by: O. G. Finley June 22, 1817, WILSON Co.

CARTER, Nancy to George Weems - February 6, 1797, Security:
Daniel Duggan and Daniel Rawlings, GREENE Co.

CARTER, Nancy to William Myers - GREENE Co.

CARTER, Nathan to Hannah Carter - July 1, 1786, Security: William Shores,
GREENE Co.

CARTER, Nathan W. to Mary Thompson - issued December 20, 1836, Bondsman:
Joseph Flowers, m. by: John M. Williams, J. P., December 22,
1836, RUTHERFORD Co.

CARTER, Nathaniel G. to Kiseah H. Johnson - issued January 9, 1816,
Bondsman: Elijah Brien, m. by: James Foster, J. P., January 11,
1816, WILSON Co.

CARTER, P. M. to L. A. Carter - issued October 14, 1850, m. by:
Tho. Martin, L. E., October 15, 1850, ROBERTSON Co.

CARTER, Peter to Sally Medly - issued October 12, 1805, Bondsman:
John Sharp, Witness: W. Park, KNOX Co.

CARTER, Rachel to John Hartly - GREENE Co.

CARTER, Randal to Polly Johnson - issued May 11, 1811, Bondsman:
Harrison Akin, WILSON Co.

CARTER, Rebekah to John Hardin - GREENE Co.

CARTER, Redman to Mary Welch - issued July 4, 1832, Bondsman:
Isaac Peake, m. by: James Drennon, J. P., July 5, 1832, WILSON Co.

CARTER, Richard to Sallie Windrew - August 23, 1809, WILLIAMSON Co.

CARTER, Richard to Elizabeth Lones - January 17, 1811, KNOX Co.

CARTER, Richard to Dolly Ann Norvell - issued February 8, 1831, m. by:
_____ (?), J. P., February 8, 1831, SUMNER Co.

CARTER, Robert to Elizabeth Todd - issued December 28, 1830, Bondsman:
Alexander A. Neisbett, RUTHERFORD Co.

CARTER, Robert to Mary Hill - issued April 26, 1864, Bondsman:
Newt. Templeton, BEDFORD Cc.

CARTER, Samuel P. to Elizabeth Andrews - issued May 31, 1862, Bondsman:
James P. Stewart, m. by: M. C. Davis, J. P., May 31, 1862,
LAWRENCE Co.

CARTER, Solomon to Ann H. Stewart - issued October 21, 1834, Bondsman:
John Carter, m. by: R. Gwyn, J. P., October 22, 1834, WILSON Co.

CARTER, Stephen to Mary A. Lenehan - issued February 26, 1849, m. by:
Rev. A. J. Steel, FRANKLIN Co.

CARTER, Stephen B. to Mary J. Williams - issued December 31, 1872,
m. by: James Seargent, J. P., December 31, 1872, FRANKLIN Co.

CARTER, Susanna to Absalom Templeton - GREENE Co.

CARTER, Thomas to Louisa T. Hawkins - issued June 8, 1848, m. by:
W. L. Baldry, G. M., June 11, 1848, ROBERTSON Co.

CARTER, Thomas T. to Mary E. Haynes - October 11, 1860, m. by:
D. V. Vandiveer, M. G., GILES Co.

CARTER, William to Elizabeth Jones - August 3, 1793, Security:
John Jones, GREENE Co.

CARTER, William to Charity Baker - issued March 25, 1801, Bondsman:
Cornelius Hickey, Witness: A. White, KNOX Co.

CARTER, William to Ruthey Boan - issued July 18, 1801, Bondsman:
Washington Boan, GRAINGER Co.

CARTER, Wm. to Ruthy Bean - issued July 18, 1802, Bondsman:
Washington Bean, GRAINGER Co.

CARTER, William to Susan Ferguson - issued May 26, 1817, Bondsman:
Lewis Luttrell and Stephen Ferguson, m. by: Sam'l Sample, J. P.,
May 27, 1817, KNOX Co.

CARTER, William to Polly Duncan - issued February 21, 1820, Bondsman:
W. H. Hart, SUMNER Co.

CARTER, William to Nancy Rickman - issued July 29, 1822, Bondsman:
John Dalton, m. by: James Carr, J. P., July 29, 1822, SUMNER Co.

CARTER, William to Elizabeth Stanley - issued September 7, 1830,
Bondsman: Robert Carter, RUTHERFORD Co.

CARTER, William to Mary Moore - issued April 21, 1835, Bondsman:
Alexander Neisbet, RUTHERFORD Co.

CARTER, William to Nancy Napper - issued June 1, 1861, Bondsman:
B. M. Tillman, Jos. H. Thompson, Clk. per James H. Neil, Dep. Clk.,
BEDFORD Co.

CARTER, Wm. C. to Francis A. Graham - issued October 12, 1848, Bondsman:
G. O. Newman, MONTGOMERY Co.

CARTER, William F. to Sarah Denney - issued February 8, 1844, m. by:
Robert K. Richley, J. P., VAN BUREN Co.

CARTER, William O. to Eliza A. Hawkins - issued January 1, 1845,
    m. by: John T. Slatter, J. P., January 1, 1845, FRANKLIN Co.

CARTER, William W. to Izabella Roan - issued November 20, 1828,
    Bondsman: Wm. M. Chapman, WILSON Co.

CARTER, Wm. W. to Susan A. Jenkins - issued April 8, 1857, m. by:
    John T. Slatter, J. P., April 9, 1857, FRANKLIN Co.

CARTER, Winston to Susannah Luttrell - issued June 1, 1821, Bondsman:
    Abram D. White, Witness: Will Swan, KNOX Co.

CARTHY, Andrew to Suky Mitchell - issued July 13, 1807, Bondsman:
    John Menefee, KNOX Co.

CARTMELL, Martin to Margaret E. Neil - issued October 20, 1820, m. by:
    Jemiah Hendrick, J. P., October 23, 1820, WILSON Co.

CARTRIGHT, Dan'l to Polly Hailey - July 15, 1807, WILLIAMSON Co.

CARTWRIGHT, Alexander to Patsey P. Rawlings - issued December 24,
    1806, Bondsman: James Rutherford, SUMNER Co.

CARTWRIGHT, Benajah to Delila Davis - issued June 26, 1823, Bondsman:
    William Taylor, m. by: Nace Overall, M. G., July 3, 1823,
    RUTHERFORD Co.

CARTWRIGHT, David to Sarah Pitt - issued September 17, 1832, Bondsman:
    Richard G. Thompson, SUMNER Co.

CARTWRIGHT, Edward W. to Dicy H. Crutchfield - issued February 19,
    1833, m. by: E. J. Allen, M. G., February 27, 1833, WILSON Co.

CARTWRIGHT, Hezekiah to Elizabeth Maholland - issued September 2,
    1808, Bondsman: Matthew Cartwright, WILSON Co.

CARTWRIGHT, Hezekiah to Mary Brown - issued January 7, 1823, m. by:
    John Bass, J. P., January 8, 1823, WILSON Co.

CARTWRIGHT, Hezekiah to Sally Maholland - issued October 16, 1827,
    Bondsman: William Davidson, m. by: German Baker October 17, 1827,
    WILSON Co.

CARTWRIGHT, Hezekiah to Delila Searcy - issued June 6, 1828, Bondsman:
    John Cox, m. by: James B. Taylor, J. P., WILSON Co.

CARTWRIGHT, Hezekiah to Nancy H. Grissim - issued October 8, 1834,
    Bondsman: T. C. Grissim, WILSON Co.

CARTWRIGHT, Isaac to Sally Morris - issued March 15, 1806, Bondsman:
    Frederick White, RUTHERFORD Co.

CARTWRIGHT, James to Martha Ann Coleman - issued June 18, 1838,
    Bondsman: Joseph Collier, m. by: Elihu Jewel June 19, 1838,
    WILSON Co.

CARTWRIGHT, James to Eliza Sutton - issued January 30, 1846, m. by:
    Thomas N. Cotton, J. P., February 3, 1846, DAVIDSON Co.

CARTWRIGHT, John to Polly Dillard - issued March 16, 1810, Bondsman:
    W. P. Pool, WILSON Co.

CARTWRIGHT, Richard to Ann Waters - issued November 6, 1815, Bondsman:
    Wilson T. Waters, WILSON Co.

CARTWRIGHT, Robt. to Elizabeth Warson - October 1, 1808, WILLIAMSON Co.

CARTWRIGHT, Robert to Elizabeth Vinson - issued December 2, 1810,
    Bondsman: Charles Thompson, SUMNER Co.

CARTWRIGHT, Saml to Letty Moore - issued March 20, 1810, Bondsman: Jno. Tipet and Saml Harris, WILSON Co.

CARTWRIGHT, Thomas to Agness Christian - issued January 22, 1791, Bondsman: Thomas Masten, SUMNER Co.

CARTWRIGHT, Thomas to Patsey Davidson - issued November 1, 1819, Bondsman: Alexander Braden, m. by: Wm. Steele, J. P., November 4, 1819, WILSON Co.

CARTWRIGHT, Thomas to Mary Fisher - issued January 3, 1838, Bondsman: Thomas Hankins, m. by: Shelah Waters, J. P., January 4, 1838, WILSON Co.

CARTWRIGHT, Thomas to Elizabeth Hooper - issued January 18, 1838, DAVIDSON Co.

CARTWRIGHT, Thomas D. to Mary Ann Sudden - issued November 28, 1846, m. by: Thomas N. Cotton, J. P., November 29, 1846, DAVIDSON Co.

CARTWRIGHT, Thomas W. to Elizabeth Cook - issued July 14, 1825, Bondsman: John Stanford, SUMNER Co.

CARTWRIGHT, William to Patsey Fuller - issued June 3, 1809, Bondsman: William Draper, WILSON Co.

CARTWRIGHT, William to Elizabeth Goodall - issued February 13, 1811, Bondsman: Ambrose Porter, SUMNER Co.

CARTWRIGHT, Wilson T. to Elizabeth Tracy - issued December 10, 1839, Bondsman: R. H. Cartwright, WILSON Co.

CARUTH, James to Polly Donnell - issued August 29, 1816, Bondsman: Josiah Donnell, m. by: Samuel Donnell, V. D. M., WILSON Co.

CARUTH, Walter to Sarah Prior - issued May 17, 1833, m. by: F. Carter, J. P., May 27, 1833, WILSON Co.

CARUTHERS, A. M. to Martha Robinson - m. by: John Wiseman July 20, 1837, SUMNER Co.

CARUTHERS, Robert to Sally Saunders - issued January 15, 1827, Bondsman: Baily Payton, SUMNER Co.

CARUTHERS, William to Sally Giles - m. by: John McLin August 30, 1838, SUMNER Co.

CARUTHERS, Woodson to Louisa Abernathy - November 21, 1860, m. by: C. W. McMillian, J. P., GILES Co.

CARVER, Archibald to Mary Ann Swingley - issued February 3, 1840, Bondsman: Andrew J. Spickard, m. by: John Kelly, M. G., February 6, 1840, WILSON Co.

CARVER, Benjamin to Nancy Lumpkin - issued February 6, 1822, Bondsman: Jas. C. Drake, m. by: J. F. Davis, J. P., WILSON Co.

CARVER, Henry to Elizabeth A. Hamblen - issued December 23, 1840, Bondsman: Wm. L. Martin, m. by: John Kelly, M. G., December 24, 1840, WILSON Co.

CARVER, Isaac to Mary Hugh - issued October 11, 1817, Bondsman: William Carver, m. by: John Williamson, J. P., October 12, 1817, WILSON Co.

CARVER, J. C. to Eliza F. Ford - issued August 4, 1860, m. by: M. M. Speer, J. P., August 5, 1860, ROBERTSON Co.

CARVER, J. J. to Phareby Crossland - issued March 22, 1858, m. by: B. H. Adams, J. P., March 22, 1858, COFFEE Co.

CARVER, Samuel to Pamelia Lumpkin - issued February 24, 1834, Bondsman:
    William T. Eatherly, m. by: Ezekiel Cloyd, M. G., February 7,
    1834, WILSON Co.

CARVER, Thomas to Margaret Donelson - issued December 4, 1809, Bondsman:
    Humphry Donelson, WILSON Co.

CARVIN, George W. to Brunette P. Rice - issued December 5, 1838,
    Bondsman: Thomas C. Osborn, WILSON Co.

CARVIN, James to Sarah Martin - issued August 21, 1845, Bondsman:
    David Fox, m. by: Wm. Johns, J. P., August 25, 1845, MEIGS Co.

CARVIN, Philow to Peggy Teague - issued February 7, 1845, Bondsman:
    James Carvin, m. by: J. Locke, Min. G., February 10, 1845, MEIGS Co.

CARY, Robbert to Martha Howard - issued June 17, 1846, m. by:
    Preston Dulaney, J. P., June 18, 1846, VAN BUREN Co.

CASE, Alexander E. to Lucender Ray - issued August 26, 1837, m. by:
    Edward Tate, J. P., GRAINGER Co.

CASE, Eleakin to Nancy Grimes - issued February 6, 1812, Bondsman:
    Enos Hamers, GRAINGER Co.

CASE, Henry T. to Georgia A. White - issued February 10, 1870,
    FRANKLIN Co.

CASEDY, Rueben to Rachel McCoy - issued October 14, 1805, Bondsman:
    William Johnson and Daniel Hoffar, Witness: W. Park, KNOX Co.

CASEY, Andrew to Polly Cagle - issued August 2, 1846, m. by:
    Charles Crafford, J. P., ROBERTSON Co.

CASEY, Andrew to Polly Cagle - issued August 19, 1846, m. by:
    Charles Crafford, J. P., August 22, 1846, ROBERTSON Co.

CASEY, Charles S. to Mary Earthman - issued July 4, 1842, m. by:
    Josiah Ferriss June 7, 1842, DAVIDSON Co.

CASEY, Elizabeth to William Blackwood - GREENE Co.

CASEY, James to Mary D. McNish - issued January 22, 1842, m. by:
    P. P. Neely, M. G., January 25, 1842, DAVIDSON Co.

CASEY, John to Elow Melton - issued June 17, 1829, Bondsman:
    Thos. Bradley, WILSON Co.

CASEY, Joseph to Elizabeth Blackwood - February 20, 1788, GREENE Co.

CASEY, Samuel to Ann Bealor (or Beatas) - issued February 20, 1798,
    Bondsman: John Casey, Witness: Sm'l Yancey, GRAINGER Co.

CASH, Benjamin to Betsy Burnett - issued March 8, 1823, Bondsman:
    G. Brown, Witness: Wm. Swan, KNOX Co.

CASH, Benj. to Betsy Burnett - issued March 8, 1825, m. by:
    Sam'l Sample, J. P., March 9, 1825, KNOX Co.

CASH, Benjamin to Louisa Rodes - issued March 18, 1846, Bondsman:
    Peter Thornberry, m. by: John Seabourn, J. P., March 19, 1846,
    MEIGS Co.

CASH, Jesse to Debian Nix - issued December 7, 1848, m. by:
    N. G. Morris, J. P., December 7, 1848, STEWART Co.

CASH, John to Mary Ann Linton - issued January 7, 1862, m. by:
    J. F. L. Faris, J. P., January 9, 1862, COFFEE Co.

CASH, Polly to John Carrigin - MAURY Co.

CASH, Shadrack to Elizabeth Shrink - issued April 7, 1829, m. by:
Eli King, J. P., April 14, 1829, KNOX Co.

CASHION, Temple J. to Dana Pitcock - issued November 25, 1856,
FRANKLIN Co.

CASHION, Wm. A. to Sarah C. Wiseman - issued December 23, 1871,
FRANKLIN Co.

CASHON, James to Mary Wade - issued January 3, 1852, m. by:
Lemuel Brandon, J. P., January 4, 1852, FRANKLIN Co.

CASICK, Catherine to James Adams - GREENE Co.

CASILMAN, John to Martha Bell - issued August 15, 1823, Bondsman:
John J. Bell, WILSON Co.

CASKEY, Joseph to Caty Scobel - issued January 15, 1817, Bondsman:
Joseph Weir, m. by: J. I. Johnson, J. P., January 16, 1817,
WILSON Co.

CASNER, Mary to Fred'k Louder (Souder) - GREENE Co.

CASNFY, John to Nancy Summars - issued March 27, 1827, m. by:
Ed. Edwards March 27, 1827, SUMNER Co.

CASON, Elijah to Martha A. Clopton - issued May 9, 1837, Bondsman:
J. B. Rutland, m. by: James Bond, V. D. M., May 11, 1837,
WILSON Co.

CASON, James to Jane McKnight - issued February 6, 1822, Bondsman:
Albert Wynne, m. by: Jas. Bond, V. D. M., February 14, 1822,
WILSON Co.

CASON, John to Elmira Miles - issued December 19, 1832, Bondsman:
C. W. Cummings, WILSON Co.

CASON, Joseph T. to Joanna Jarmon - issued February 23, 1839, Bondsman:
J. D. Scott, WILSON Co.

CASON, William to Mary McKnight - issued September 2, 1826, Bondsman:
George Smith, m. by: James Bond, V. D. M., September 7, 1826,
WILSON Co.

CASSADA, John to Margaret Caldwell - issued December 19, 1832, m. by:
Joseph Anderson, J. P., December 20, 1832, KNOX Co.

CASSADY, Richard to Mary Walker - issued September 7, 1824, Bondsman:
Andrew Cassaday, m. by: Wm. Sawyers, J. P., September 9, 1824,
KNOX Co.

CASSEL, Ruffin to Lucinda Eddins - issued June 13, 1828, Bondsman:
Allen W. Vicks, WILSON Co.

CASSELMAN, _____ (?) to Jane Jenkins - issued August 12, 1837, Bondsman:
Burrell P. Casselman, WILSON Co.

CASSELMAN, Jacob to Anne Moore - issued August 29, 1811, Bondsman:
Benjamin Casselman, WILSON Co.

CASSELMAN, Lazirus to Jane E. Summers - issued August 7, 1839, Bondsman:
Jacob Casselman, WILSON Co.

CASSLEMAN, Robert to Ardminta Reed - issued November 26, 1834,
Bondsman: Thomas Pentecost, m. by: Levi Holloway, J. P.,
November 27, 1834, WILSON Co.

CASSIDY, Andrew to Barbara Milteberger - issued October 1, 1828, m. by: Wm. Sawyers, J. P., October, 1828, KNOX Co.

CASTEEL, Abednigo to Agnes Hensely - issued April 26, 1808, Bondsman: Daniel Casteel, Witness: Jno. A. Gamble, KNOX Co.

CASTEEL, David to Sarah Mitchell - issued May 3, 1798, Bondsman: Morris Mitchell, Witness: H. L. White, KNOX Co.

CASTEEL, Elijah to Sally Fairchild - issued August 30, 1823, Bondsman: Jeremiah Johnson, m. by: Robert McBath September 2, 1823, Witness: Wm. Swan, KNOX Co.

CASTEEL, James to Susannah Underwood - issued August 7, 1833, Bondsman: Isaac Bond, Witness: Chas. Scott, KNOX Co.

CASTEEL, John W. to Eliza A. Liles - issued September 12, 1853, m. by: John Nugent, J. P., September 13, 1853, FRANKLIN Co.

CASTEEL, Margary to John Melone - GREENE Co.

CASTEEL, Naomi to Abner Aires - GREENE Co.

CASTEEL, Patsy to Berry Bruton - BEDFORD Co.

CASTEEL, Peter to Susanna Richardson - May 8, 1800, Security: Larkin Brumly and Shadrach McNew, GREENE Co.

CASTEEL, Rachel to Jachariah (Zachariah) Melone - GREENE Co.

CASTERWOOD, John to Manerva Franklin - issued April 11, 1870, m. by: G. W. Bowling, J. P., April 11, 1870, FRANKLIN Co.

CASTLEBERRY, Franklin to Eveline Tennessee Hackney - January 13, 1841, m. by: Richard Abernathy, J. P., GILES Co.

CASTLEBERRY, J. M. to Fanny Wiley - issued June 29, 1872, m. by: C. C. Rose, J. P., July 4, 1872, FRANKLIN Co.

CASTLEMAN, Abraham to Sally Hicks - February 13, 1813, WILLIAMSON Co.

CASTLEMAN, Benjamin to Polly McFarlin - issued September 7, 1809, Bondsman: Sam'l Meredith, WILSON Co.

CASTLEMAN, Bery to Elizabeth Carrington - issued September 24, 1839, m. by: B. N. Barnes, J. P., September 24, 1839, DAVIDSON Co.

CASTLEMAN, Burrell P. to Gennetta Brooks - issued January 18, 1841, m. by: Jas. H. Cook, J. P., January 18, 1841, DAVIDSON Co.

CASTLEMAN, Ira to Indiana Sears - issued June 26, 1847, DICKSON Co.

CASTLEMAN, John to Lurena Lankford - issued April 28, 1843, m. by: I. Porter, J. P., April 30, 1843, DICKSON Co.

CASTLEMAN, Joseph to Susanna Smith - issued April 13, 1816, m. by: G. W. Banton, J. P., April 21, 1816, RUTHERFORD Co.

CASTLEMAN, Lewis to Lucinda Starkey - issued March 12, 1836, Bondsman: Josiah H. Castleman, m. by: Burwell Perry, J. P., April 30, 1836, RUTHERFORD Co.

CASTLEMAN, Robert B. to Anna E. Woods - issued December 18, 1845, m. by: W. H. Wharton December 18, 1845, DAVIDSON Co.

CASTLEMAN, William S. to Susannah Sanders - issued July 13, 1836, Bondsman: Joseph Flowers, m. by: John M. Williams, J. P., July 14, 1836, RUTHERFORD Co.

CASY, Joshua to Alley Harris - issued December 23, 1815, Bondsman:
Samuel Richardison, m. by: David Tate, J. P., January 14, 1816,
GRAINGER Co.

CATCHOART, David to Rhoda Anderson - issued April 28, 1815, Bondsman:
Samuel Roberts, m. by: P. Nance, J. P., KNOX Co.

CATCHINGS, A. J. to Elizabeth Parsons - issued March 21, 1859, m. by:
Simpson West, J. P., March 28, 1859, FRANKLIN Co.

CATCHINGS, Benj. to Malisa Ann Rose - issued August 12, 1844, m. by:
John D. Lynch, J. P., FRANKLIN Co.

CATCHINGS, Meredith to Tempy Singleton - FRANKLIN Co.

CATCHINGS, Meredith to Mahala Barnes - issued December 9, 1853, m. by:
Thos. Finch, J. P., December 11, 1853, FRANKLIN Co.

CATCHINGS, S. A. to Mary Reynolds - issued December 11, 1867, m. by:
B. B. Brandon, L. E., December 12, 1867, FRANKLIN Co.

CATCHINGS, W. A. to Jane Sexton - issued November 16, 1858, m. by:
A. J. Wiseman, J. P., November 17, 1858, FRANKLIN Co.

CATE, Alfred to Nancy Thomas - issued August 14, 1845, Bondsman:
Lafayett Norman, m. by: Ezekiel Ward, Senr. Min., August 14, 1845,
MEIGS Co.

CATE, Jesse to Rachel Pyror - issued August 8, 1815, Bondsman:
Sam'l Henry, m. by: Thos. H. Nelson August 8, 1815, KNOX Co.

CATE, Joseph H. to Margaret Tillery - issued September 1, 1842,
Bondsman: William Lillard, m. by: J. Locke, M. G., September 1,
1842, MEIGS Co.

CATE, Samuel to Malinda McClure - issued June 15, 1822, Bondsman:
Samuel McClure, KNOX Co.

CATES, Anderson to Elizabeth Combs - issued December 27, 1823. Bondsman:
Samuel B. Tate, m. by: John Kidwell, M. G., December 27, 1823,
GRAINGER Co.

CATES, Charles to Elizabeth Loyd - issued April 4, 1826, Bondsman:
Robert Loyd, m. by: James Kennon, M. G., April 4, 1826, GRAINGER Co.

CATES, Daniel H. to Rachael Smith - issued October 1, 1835, m. by:
Joseph Dyer, J. P., GRAINGER Co.

CATES, John to Alley Johnson - issued June 17, 1828, Bondsman:
Thomas Chamberland, WILSON Co.

CATES, M. M. to M. E. Cobb - issued September 25, 1865, FRANKLIN Co.

CATES, Norman to Jane Williams - issued July 27, 1841, m. by:
__(?) Harress ___(?), 1841, FRANKLIN Co.

CATES, Richard M. to Lucinda Williams - issued February 9, 1848, m. by:
John Byrom, M. G., February 11, 1848, FRANKLIN Co.

CATES, S. A. to W. H. Davis - issued February 11, 1863, Bondsman:
Wm. Hime, Jos. H. Thompson, Clk., BEDFORD Co.

CATES, Samuel to Mary Richardson - issued July 9, 1818, Bondsman:
John Richardson, m. by: Francis Moore, J. P., July 19, 1818,
GRAINGER Co.

CATES, Stephen to Elizabeth Cassady - issued August 8, 1823, Bondsman:
James Cassady, m. by: James Harris, J. P., August 8, 1823,
GRAINGER Co.

CATES, Wm. to Amanda Missimon - issued June 25, 1829, Bondsman: Joel Nance and Jno. Missimon, m. by: Wm. Morris, J. P., June 25, 1829, KNOX Co.

CATHAM, Edmond to Betsy Longwutt (?) - August 16, 1827, KNOX Co.

CATHELL, Nancy to Eleazar Kilpatrick - MAURY Co.

CATHER, Reuben M. to Charlotte K. Collier - issued March 1, 1832, Bondsman: Wm. Solomon, m. by: Wm. Edwards, J. P., March 1, SUMNER Co.

CATHEY, Alex to Mary Malone - issued April 8, 1806, Bondsman: Thos. Malone, SUMNER Co.

CATHEY, Alexander to Mary Locke - issued August 1, 1805, Bondsman: Alexander McKnight, RUTHERFORD Co.

CATHEY, Daniel to Mary Goodwin - issued October 18, 1838, DICKSON Co.

CATHEY, George W. to Zelleaum Vickers - issued August 14, 1843, STEWART Co.

CATHEY, Griffith to Susannah Cathey - issued March 15, 1803, Bondsman: Griffith W. Rutherford, SUMNER Co.

CATHEY, James to Sally Oliver - issued May 8, 1817, Bondsman: John Darrah, RUTHERFORD Co.

CATHY, John G. to Rebecca Vickers - issued August 2, 1847, STEWART Co.

CATHEY, John R. to Rebecca Spicer - issued September 30, 1847, DICKSON Co.

CATHEY, Martin to Louise Creech - issued December 22, 1840, m. by: L. Russell, J. P., December 23, 1840, DICKSON Co.

CATHEY, Samuel to Lucinda Edwards - issued August 16, 1844, DICKSON Co.

CATHEY, William to Elizabeth Cathey - issued February 5, 1805, Bondsman: Wm. Cathey, SUMNER Co.

CATHEY, William to Betsey Gale - issued April 2, 1806, Bondsman: Alex Cathey, SUMNER Co.

CATO, Elisha to Jency Anderson - issued May 25, 1824, Bondsman: James H. Hunt, m. by: Hardy Hunt, J. P., May 29, 1824, WILSON Co.

CATO, George to Euphama Rife - issued December 31, 1821, m. by: Brinkley Bridges, J. P., March 28, 1822, WILSON Co.

CATO, George to Euphenia Rife - issued December 31, 1821, Bondsman: John R. Rutherford, WILSON Co.

CATO, George W. to Elizabeth Jordan - issued February 29, 1848, m. by: Wm. Morris, J. P., February 29, 1848, STEWART Co.

CATO, Green H. to Rhody Alley - issued July 1, 1827, m. by: Sam'l Gwin, J. P., July 1, 1827, SUMNER Co.

CATO, Robert to Frances J. Waters - issued June 29, 1824, Bondsman: James Allcorn, m. by: Hardy Hunt, J. P., July 2, 1824, WILSON Co.

CATO, Robert M. to Elizabeth A. Derickson - issued March 24, 1838, DAVIDSON Co.

CATO, William to Martha Peobles - issued January 1, 1839, m. by: Wm. Shelton, J. P., January 6, 1839, DAVIDSON Co.

CATON, Abner to Elizabeth Johnson - issued January 24, 1824, Bondsman: James Dickey, m. by: L. Landers, J. P., January 24, 1824, SUMNER Co.

CAUDLE, Aaron to Sarah Stringer - issued October 26, 1849, m. by:
Isaac Steel October 27, 1849, ROBERTSON Co.

CAUDLE, Geo. W. to Middy Ally - issued March 8, 1845, m. by:
J. W. Hunt March 9, 1845, ROBERTSON Co.

CAUDLE, James K. to Mary E. Alsbrook - issued June 5, 1841, m. by:
J. W. Ferguson, J. P., June 6, 1841, ROBERTSON Co.

CAULEY, Stephen to Patsey Tally - issued February 8, 1819, Bondsman:
Woodson Layne, WILSON Co.

CAUSBY, Lewis to Sarrah Galloway - March 22, 1860, m. by: A. H. Berry,
GILES Co.

CAVANAH, Charles W. to Elizabeth Lacy - issued November 16, 1847,
Bondsman: W. Trice, m. by: N. F. Trice, J. P., November 16, 1847,
MONTGOMERY Co.

CAVANAUGH, Hugh to Jane McFaren - March 31, 1784, Security: John Blair,
GREENE Co.

CAVEN, Robt. to Malinda Jolly - issued February 22, 1854, m. by:
John Nugent, J. P., February 23, 1854, FRANKLIN Co.

CAVENESS, William to Polly Bruce - issued December 16, 1806, Bondsman:
John Chapman, SUMNER Co.

CAVENESS, William to Rhody Walker - m. by: John W. Spradlin May 26,
1838, SUMNER Co.

CAVERT, John to Mary Grayham - issued March 14, 1800, Bondsman:
George Hallmark, KNOX Co.

CAVIN, Francis to Mahala Rail - issued October 14, 1843, m. by:
John Roleman, J. P., October 14, 1843, FRANKLIN Co.

CAVIN, James to Nancy McCarver - issued March 29, 1856, m. by:
James Seargent, J. P., March 30, 1856, FRANKLIN Co.

CAVIN, Peter to Sarah Jane Warren - issued June 8, 1859, m. by:
L. D. Phillips, Mins., June 9, 1859, COFFEE Co.

CAVITT, Claibourne to Nancy Cornelius - issued April 7, 1828, Bondsman:
James Briley, m. by: Scaton Turner, J. P., April 7, 1828,
SUMNER Co.

CAVITT, J. W. to Margaret C. Caldwell - issued February 19, 1839,
m. by: John A. Jones, M. G., February 19, 1839, STEWART Co.

CAVITT, Moses to Elizabeth Tinnin - issued October 19, 1812, Bondsman:
William Tinnin, SUMNER Co.

CAVITT, N. Y. to S. A. Bailey - issued September 13, 1854, Bondsman:
J. W. Bailey, m. by: Reuben Ross, P. E., September 19, 1854,
MONTGOMERY Co.

CAVITT, Richard to Peggy Barrow - issued August 4, 1812, Bondsman:
Samuel Piper, SUMNER Co.

CAVITT, Wesley to Sarah Horton - issued December 17, 1856, m. by:
R. H. Harrison December 18, 1856, ROBERTSON Co.

CAWLING, Joseph to Permelia Camp - issued January 13, 1841, m. by:
Elder J. P. Walker January __, 1841, FRANKLIN Co.

CAWOOD, Thomas to Ruth Ford - issued December 22, 1841, m. by:
B. F. McKenzie, J. P., December 23, 1841, MEIGS Co.

CAWTHON, James to Sally Peak - issued September 29, 1812, Bondsman:
John Cawthon, WILSON Co.

CAWTHON, James to Nancy McDowell - issued March 17, 1834, Bondsman:
Joseph E. Basham, m. by: B. Baker March 20, 1834, RUTHERFORD Co.

CAWTHON, James H. to Margaret A. Patterson - issued August 5, 1843,
m. by: John Beard August 10, 1843, DAVIDSON Co.

CAWTHON, Joab P. to Delanta A. E. J. Robbins - issued November 16,
1840, Bondsman: James Cawthon, m. by: Thomas Kirkpatrick, J. P.,
November 23, 1840, WILSON Co.

CANTHON, John H. to Nancy Rece - issued August 9, 1820, Bondsman:
James H. Cawthon, m. by: Ransom Gwyn, J. P., August 10, 1820,
WILSON Co.

CAWTHON, Martin B. to Nancy Elliott - issued April 16, 1823, m. by:
H. Robinson, J. P., April 16, 1823, RUTHERFORD Co.

CAWTHON, Pleasant to Jane Robinson - issued December 14, 1823, m. by:
B. L. McFerrin, J. P., December 23, 1823, RUTHERFORD Co.

CAWTHON, Thomas to Susan Daniel - issued July 17, 1816, Bondsman:
James Cawthon, WILSON Co.

CAWTHON, Vincen to Rosanah Irwin - issued February 1, 1819, Bondsman:
Thomas Cawthon, WILSON Co.

CAWTHORN, John R. to Ruth Alford - issued November 18, 1833, m. by:
B. Graves, J. P., WILSON Co.

CAYCE, Fleming to Cynthia Little - November 12, 1816, WILLIAMSON Co.

CAYCE, Thomas to Hannah Standley - October 14, 1815, WILLIAMSON Co.

CAYTON, Elijah to Elizabeth W. Roch - issued November 11, 1813,
Bondsman: John W. Roch, GRAINGER Co.

CELLEGHAR, Philip to Mary Ann Carroll - issued August 29, 1848,
Bondsman: Wm. White, m. by: P. Preistly, J. P., August 29, 1848,
MONTGOMERY Co.

CENTER, Phinnis W. to Matilda E. Farris - issued August 12, 1874,
m. by: G. D. Guinn, M. G., August 18, 1874, FRANKLIN Co.

CENTER, Richard to Betsey Hunt - issued July 9, 1808, Bondsman:
Moses Gains, SUMNER Co.

CEPHART, Perry A. to Christiana M. Charlton - issued (July 27, 1847)
September 22, 1847, m. by: James G. Hinson, J. P., July 27,
1847, DICKSON Co.

CERLY, John B. to Lucinda Stelle - issued December 16, 1841, m. by:
W. H. Wilkes December 16, 1841, DAVIDSON Co.

CEROW, Dausey to Lucinda Hail - issued June 11, 1840, Bondsman:
Hartwell Miser, m. by: Prior Neil, J. P., June 11, 1840, MEIGS Co.

CESSNA (?), John to Elizabeth Neilson - September 7, 1798, Security:
Henry Farnsworth, GREENE Co.

CHADBOURNE, John to Tabith Brassell - issued July 13, 1818, Bondsman:
John Bell, SUMNER Co.

CHADOWIN, J. J. to Harriet E. Roe - issued October 10, 1859, m. by:
Ruebin Elmore, J. P., ROBERTSON Co.

CHADWELL, John A. to Miranda E. Wright - issued January 20, 1842,
DAVIDSON Co.

CHADWELL, Lydda to William Skyles - GREENE Co.

CHADWELL, Payton to Esther Jane Rickets - issued July 25, 1839,
    Bondsman: John T. Rickets, m. by: G. A. Huddleston, J. P.,
    July 29, 1839, WILSON Co.

CHADWELL, Robert to Mary Ann Burge - issued January 22, 1845, m. by:
    J. T. Edgar January 23, 1845, DAVIDSON Co.

CHADWELL, Thomas to Mary A. Childress - issued July 18, 1846, m. by:
    R. B. C. Howell, M. G., July 20, 1846, DAVIDSON Co.

CHAFFIN, J. C. to Susan D. Childress - issued October 7, 1863, Bondsman:
    F. P. Scott, m. by: Wm. A. Harris, M. G., October 8, 1863,
    LAWRENCE Co.

CHAFIN, Jas. H. to Charity A. Aldman - issued November 12, 1858,
    FRANKLIN Co.

CHAFIN, John H. to Charity Ann Oldman - issued November 12, 1858,
    m. by: E. S. Jones, L. D., November 14, 1858, FRANKLIN Co.

CHAMBERLAIN, Andrew to Mary Cardwell - issued October 11, 1830,
    Bondsman: Robert Boza, m. by: Levi Satterfield, M. G., GRAINGER Co.

CHAMBERLAIN, James H. to Abiah Hawkins - issued October 13, 1856,
    m. by: Jesse B. White, J. P., ROBERTSON Co.

CHAMBERLAN, Thompson to Nancy (?) West - issued July 25, 1818, Bondsman:
    John Braom, m. by: Isaac Barton, M. G., July 28, 1818, GRAINGER Co.

CHAMBERLIN, Charles C. to Jane Clifton - issued January 13, 1830,
    Bondsman: Robert McKee, WILSON Co.

CHAMBERLIN, John B. to Rebecca Rolan - issued November 16, 1838,
    m. by: L. B. Davidson, J. P., November 18, 1838, DAVIDSON Co.

CHAMBERS, Alexander to Jane Hunter - issued January 25, 1838, Bondsman:
    Robert J. Garrison, m. by: John Borum January 28, 1838, WILSON Co.

CHAMBERS, Daniel to Nancy Simmons - issued September 25, 1817,
    Bondsman: Joel Smith, GRAINGER Co.

CHAMBERS, Daniel W. to Sarah Coffey - issued October 14, 1843,
    Bondsman: Robert Coffey, m. by: Jesse Martin, J. P., October 14,
    1843, MEIGS Co.

CHAMBERS, Edward to Eliza E. Hunter - issued September 11, 1834,
    Bondsman: Joseph Astor, m. by: Stephen McDonald, J. P., WILSON Co.

CHAMBERS, Eli to Caroline Hendricks - issued August 11, 1856, m. by:
    A. J. Wiseman, J. P., August 14, 1856, FRANKLIN Co.

CHAMBERS, Elijah R. to Missouri Bird - issued January 15, 1845, m. by:
    P. Lynch, J. P., January 15, 1845, STEWART Co.

CHAMBERS, James E. to Jane Mangrum - issued January 27, 1858, m. by:
    M. A. Carden, J. P., January 27, 1858, COFFEE Co.

CHAMBERS, James J. to Sally Ann Seal - issued August 6, 1840, m. by:
    Benjamin Rawls, G. M., ROBERTSON Co.

CHAMBERS, Jas. W. to Lucy W. Bell - issued September 18, 1860, m. by:
    J. B. Anderson, Minister of the Gospel, October 2, 1860,
    ROBERTSON Co.

CHAMBERS, John to Anne McKey - January 14, 1807, WILLIAMSON Co.

CHAMBERS, John to Edney Johnson - issued December 15, 1830, Bondsman:
    Thi. T. Gray, WILSON Co.

CHAMBERS, John M. to Mary E. Seal – issued July 27, 1839, m. by:
Richd. W. Mantle, J. P., July 28, 1839, ROBERTSON Co.

CHAMBERS, Moses to Mary Tadlock - December 16, 1786, Security:
John Tadlock, GREENE Co.

CHAMBERS, Nicholas to Elizabeth McDonald - issued June 25, 1834,
Bondsman: Joel Algood, WILSON Co.

CHAMBERS, Nicholas to Elizabeth Norris - issued October 28, 1840,
Bondsman: John Chambers, m. by: John Borum October 29, 1840,
WILSON Co.

CHAMBERS, Nicholas to Mary A. Jackson - issued September 14, 1837,
Bondsman: John E. Bell, WILSON Co.

CHAMBERS, William to Rhoda Cannady - June 29, 1813, WILLIAMSON Co.

CHAMBERS, William W. to Eveline Donoho - issued December 6, 1823,
Bondsman: George Thompson, m. December 6, 1823, SUMNER Co.

CHAMBLESS, Lewis H. to Malinda C. Hollis - issued December 24, 1857,
m. by: J. T. Craig, J. P., ROBERTSON Co.

CHAMBLESS, Mark to Mary V. Alley - issued February 28, 1844, m. by:
J. W. Hunt, J. P., March 2, 1844, ROBERTSON Co.

CHAMBLISS, Robert to Susannah Johnson - issued December 1, 1836,
WILSON Co.

CHAMBLISS, Wm. B. to Sarah A. Chaudoin - issued December 19, 1848,
m. by: Banja. Rawls, ROBERTSON Co.

CHAMNES, Asbury to Mary Harris - issued August 19, 1819, m. August 23,
1819, GRAINGER Co.

CHAMP, Pleasant R. to Sarah Hogan - issued September 30, 1843, m. by:
Wm. Ellis, J. P., October 1, 1843, STEWART Co.

CHAMP, Sutherlin to Jane Copeland - October 1, 1817, WILLIAMSON Co.

CHAMPION, Jr., Daniel to Louisa A. Young - issued July 18, 1842, m. by:
J. P. Walker July 20, 1842, FRANKLIN Co.

CHAMPION, Daniel to Polly Champion - issued November 21, 1845, m. by:
Elder J. P. Walker, __, 1845, FRANKLIN Co.

CHAMPION, Daniel to Margret A. Sewell - issued October 4, 1856,
m. by: Ira E. Douthit, M. G., October 5, 1856, FRANKLIN Co.

CHAMPION, Henry to Catherine Singleton - issued June 9, 1842, m. by:
J. B. McFerrin, M. G., June 9, 1842, DAVIDSON Co.

CHAMPION, J. R. to W. F. McKelvy - issued March 25, 1869, FRANKLIN Co.

CHAMPION, John F. to Rebecca Cross - issued March 9, 1863, Bondsman:
Abram Evans, Jos. H. Thompson, Clk., BEDFORD Co.

CHAMPION, Joseph to Mary Jane Sells - issued November 17, 1870, m. by:
Payton Wilkerson November 20, 1870, FRANKLIN Co.

CHAMPION, William to Adaline Jackson - issued October 23, 1848, m. by:
J. C. Montgomery, J. P., October 24, 1848, FRANKLIN Co.

CHAMPION, Wm. to Margrett Mahathy - issued August 21, 1869, m. by:
R. D. Shook August 29, 1869, FRANKLIN Co.

CHANCE, B. S. to Nancy J. Dycus - issued May 26, 1858, m. by:
F. R. Gooch, M. G., May 31, 1858, ROBERTSON Co.

CHANCE, James to Mary Nichols - issued November 18, 1820, Bondsman:
Henry C. Nichols, m. by: Thomas S. Green, J. P., November 21,
1820, WILSON Co.

CHANCE, Joseph B. to Nancy Braden - issued November 13, 1820, Bondsman:
Elijah Chance, m. by: Edward Harris, J. P., November 14, 1814,
WILSON Co.

CHANCE, Robert C. to Julia Birdwell - issued January 13, 1846, Bondsman:
P. H. Dillin, m. by: H. McFall, J. P., January 14, 1846,
MONTGOMERY Co.

CHANDLER, Andrew to Ann Hutchison - issued September 15, 1821, Bondsman:
John Boyd, SUMNER Co.

CHANDLER, Archills to Cloe Dew - issued July 31, 1827, Bondsman:
Thomas Cox, m. by: Wm. Steele, J. P., August 2, 1827, WILSON Co.

CHANDLER, B. F. to L. P. Cook - issued January 10, 1849, m. by:
James Sprouse, J. P., January 11, 1849, ROBERTSON Co.

CHANDLER, David to Nancy E. Pride - issued May 7, 1833, m. by:
R. S. Tate, M. G., WILSON Co.

CHANDLER, David to S. S. Simmons - issued December 20, 1852, m. by:
Wm. Thomas Chowning, J. P., ROBERTSON Co.

CHANDLER, Eddins to Huldy Sherwool - issued January 11, 1811, Bondsman:
Sam'l Meredith, WILSON Co.

CHANDLER, Gabriel to Jenney Thomas - issued January 30, 1810, Bondsman:
Samuel Sherrill, WILSON Co.

CHANDLER, Green to Betsy Lumpkin - issued January 6, 1824, Bondsman:
William Chandler, WILSON Co.

CHANDLER, Henry to Elizabeth Dew - issued June 20, 1822, m. by:
Wm. Steele, WILSON Co.

CHANDLER, J. M. to Lutitia Wilson - issued December 10, 1849, m. by:
James Sprouse, J. P., December 13, 1849, ROBERTSON Co.

CHANDLER, John to Catherine Nicely - issued December 31, 1832,
Bondsman: Jonas Nicely, GRAINGER Co.

CHANDLER, John to Eliza Jane Terry - issued March 10, 1863, Bondsman:
B. M. Green, Jos. H. Thompson, Clk, BEDFORD Co.

CHANDLER, John M. to Mary Ann Belcher - issued February 26, 1831,
m. by: H. W. Pickett, V. M. G., March 3, 1831, WILSON Co.

CHANDLER, John N. to Lucinda G. Rogers - issued December 2, 1839,
Bondsman: J. B. Murray, m. by: Wm. Barton, M. G., December 5,
1839, WILSON Co.

CHANDLER, Jordon to Elizabeth Avery - issued December 16, 1817,
Bondsman: William Avery, WILSON Co.

CHANDLER, Joseph to Vashtie Chandler - issued January 7, 1832,
Bondsman: Christopher Lane, WILSON Co.

CHANDLER, Marshall M. to Mary J. Lawrence - issued October 12, 1859,
m. by: J. J. Patton, M. G., October 12, 1859, COFFEE Co.

CHANDLER, Obadiah to Nancy A. Crabtree - issued November 26, 1860,
m. by: W. B. Kelly, M. G., November 28, 1860, ROBERTSON Co.

CHANDLER, Obediah to Rebecca A. Crabtree - issued January 6, 1853,
m. by: Wm. Thomas Chowning, J. P., ROBERTSON Co.

CHANDLER, Parkes to Louisia Allen - issued May 1, 1816, Bondsman: Ryland Chandler, WILSON Co.

CHANDLER, Pitts to Permilia Hinderson - issued May 11, 1811, Bondsman: Wm. Moss, WILSON Co.

CHANDLER, Rhoda to Joseph Bowman - GREENE Co.

CHANDLER, Robert to Margaret Calhoon - issued December 27, 1824, Bondsman: John Dew, WILSON Co.

CHANDLER, Thomas to Hannah Fletcher - issued August 27, 1818, Bondsman: Robert McMillan, m. by: Martin Cleveland, J. P., August 27, 1818, GRAINGER Co.

CHANDLER, Tobias H. to Louisa H. Rogers - issued January 1, 1840, Bondsman: A. H. Russell, m. by: Wm. Barton, M. G., January 2, 1840, WILSON Co.

CHANDLER, William to Rachel Shannon - issued December 28, 1819, Bondsman: Tobias Henderson, WILSON Co.

CHANDLER, William to Elizabeth Wadkins - issued September 5, 1834, Bondsman: Alexander Belcher, m. by: Robt. H. Ellis, M. G., September 17, 1834, WILSON Co.

CHANDLER, William to Matilda J. Crabtree - issued January 13, 1857, m. by: James Cook, J. P., ROBERTSON Co.

CHANDLER, William J. to Nancy J. Pepper - issued December 22, 1853, m. by: David Henry, J. P., ROBERTSON Co.

CHANDLERS, Asbury to Mary Hall (?) - issued August 19, 1809, Bondsman: Robert Massengill, GRAINGER Co.

CHANDLY, William to Sarah Prather - November 19, 1799, Security: Sparling Bowman, GREENE Co.

CHANEY, Charles J. to Sarah Ann Morgan - issued December 12, 1839, m. by: J. T. Edgar December 13, 1839, DAVIDSON Co.

CHANEY, George to Susan Dinkens - issued December 30, 1832, Bondsman: Hardin T. Garretson, m. by: Robert Norvell December 30, 1832, SUMNER Co.

CHANEY, James to Sarah Bull - issued April 27, 1822, Bondsman: Nathan Shipley, m. by: John Davis, J. P., April 29, 1822, GRAINGER Co.

CHANEY, John R. to Missouri Gregory - m. by: Elisha Vaughn, M. G., May 8, 1834, SUMNER Co.

CHANNEL, Thomas F. to Harriett F. McNeal - issued April 21, 1854, Bondsman: D. A. McKown, m. by: Robert Williams, M. G., April 25, 1854, MONTGOMERY Co.

CHANNELL, Elisha J. to Manerva Powell - issued January 22, 1849, Bondsman: Jesse Sikes, m. by: T. Nanny, J. P., January 23, 1849, MONTGOMERY Co.

CHANNELL, William to Allena Smith - issued January 7, 1851, Bondsman: John Powers, m. by: A. Baggett, J. P., January 9, 1851, MONTGOMERY Co.

CHAPEL, Asahel to Martha Woodruff - issued July 30, 1849, Bondsman: Jas. Miller, m. by: P. Priestly, J. P., July 28, 1849, MONTGOMERY Co.

CHAPELL, Robert to Elizabeth Brown - issued February 25, 1828,
    Bondsman: Baker Walsh, m. by: S. R. Roberts, J. P., February 25,
    1828, SUMNER Co.

CHAPMAN, Alfred to Martha Edward - issued January 24, 1846, ROBERTSON Co.

CHAPMAN, Arch to Mattie Hart - September 19, 1799, KNOX Co.

CHAPMAN, Archibald to Polly McGuire - issued March 15, 1823, Bondsman:
    Hanson Hunt, SUMNER Co.

CHAPMAN, Asabel to Matty Hart - issued September 19, 1797, Bondsman:
    Patrick Burns, Witness: A. White, KNOX Co.

CHAPMAN, Benjamin to Abigale Haris - issued June 30, 1816, Bondsman:
    James Eason, WILSON Co.

CHAPMAN, Benjamin to Rebecca Bull - issued August 6, 1827, Bondsman:
    Joseph McReynolds, m. August 6, 1827, SUMNER Co.

CHAPMAN, Charles P. to Mary B. Thompson - issued March 4, 1837,
    Bondsman: James Dunlap, m. by: G. S. White, M. G., March 9, 1937,
    KNOX Co.

CHAPMAN, Daniel to A. P. Thompson - issued December 9, 1840, m. by:
    J. M. Gunn, J. P., December 10, 1840, ROBERTSON Co.

CHAPMAN, E. to C. Redfearn - issued November 27, 1847, m. by:
    W. B. Kelly, M. G., November 28, 1847, ROBERTSON Co.

CHAPMAN, Fayette W. to Mary Keys - issued December 26, 1825, Bondsman:
    Joseph Jackson, m. by: James McMillan, J. P., December 27, 1825,
    KNOX Co.

CHAPMAN, George to Elizabeth Thompson - issued August 11, 1823,
    Bondsman: Hugh Boyle, m. by: Robt. Norvell, M. G., August 11,
    1823, SUMNER Co.

CHAPMAN, Harrey to Nancy Chapman - issued February 27, 1847, m. by:
    James Woodard, J. P., ROBERTSON Co.

CHAPMAN, Isaiah to Polly Crabb - issued March 5, 1817, Bondsman:
    Joseph Crabb, m. by: Robt. Lindsay, J. P., March 5, 1817, KNOX Co.

CHAPMAN, James L. to Mary Bettis - issued December 10, 1835, Bondsman:
    Saml. C. Anderson, WILSON Co.

CHAPMAN, John to Peggy Baldridge - issued November 26, 1821, Bondsman:
    Enos Vinson, m. November 26, 1821, SUMNER Co.

CHAPMAN, John to Ellen Legg - issued January 3, 1829, m. by:
    W. A. McCampbell, M. G., January 6, 1829, KNOX Co.

CHAPMAN, John to Sally Durnal - issued June 30, 1830, Bondsman.
    Solomon Shoulders, m. by: Robert Norvell June 30, 1830, SUMNER Co.

CHAPMAN, John to Winny Abel - issued September 25, 1836, Bondsman:
    Stephen A. Gilliam, m. by: T. G. Gilliam September 25, 1836,
    SUMNER Co.

CHAPMAN, John to Eliz C. Thompson - issued March 5, 1842, m. by:
    W. Holland, J. P., ROBERTSON Co.

CHAPMAN, John to Elizabeth Thompson - issued March 5, 1842, m. by:
    W. Holland, J. P., ROBERTSON Co.

CHAPMAN, John to Rachel Morris - issued December 25, 1846, m. by:
    David M. Wells, J. P., ROBERTSON Co.

CHAPMAN, John L. to Eleanor Warnick - issued February 17, 1819, m. by:
John Haynie, M. G. Methodist Ch., February 17, 1819, KNOX Co.

CHAPMAN, Jno. M. to Catharine Ann Carns - issued January 2, 1830,
Bondsman: Wm. Barnwell, m. by: W. A. McCampbell, M. V. D.,
January 5, 1830, KNOX Co.

CHARLES, Jno. P. to Harriett E. Stewart - issued April 3, 1863,
Bondsman: Jno. L. Haney, Jos. H. Thompson, Clk., BEDFORD Co.

CHAPMAN, Joseph to Elizabeth Walker - issued May 18, 1824, Bondsman:
Joseph Dyer, m. by: Joseph Dyer, J. P., May 18, 1824, GRAINGER Co.

CHAPMAN, Joseph to Martha V. Gorham - issued April 25, 1857, m. by:
John W. Smith, J. P., April 26, 1857, ROBERTSON Co.

CHAPMAN, Joseph M. to Nancy J. Moore - issued January 5, 1852,
FRANKLIN Co.

CHAPMAN, L. A. to N. M. Roton - issued August 23, 1865, m. by:
Allen Tribble August 24, 1865, FRANKLIN Co.

CHAPMAN, Mary to Thomas Crawford - GREENE Co.

CHAPMAN, Miles to Nancy Burk - issued January 24, 1810, Bondsman:
Thomas Chapman, m. by: R. Houston, J. P., January 24, 1810,
KNOX Co.

CHAPMAN, Nelson to Sarah Sumners - June 13, 1807, WILLIAMSON Co.

CHAPMAN, Phillip to Celia C. Hamilton - m. by: J. W. Hall February 25,
1834, SUMNER Co.

CHAPMAN, Robert to Frances Russell - issued September 4, 1865,
Bondsman: Cliper, m. by: C. B. Davis, M. G., September 4, 1865,
LAWRENCE Co.

CHAPMAN, Thomas to Patsey Jones - issued June 13, 1809, Bondsman:
Richard Roseygrant, Witness: Jno N. Gamble, KNOX Co.

CHAPMAN, Thomas to Rachel Garrison - issued October 25, 1824, Bondsman:
James G. Elliss, m. by: John McMurtry, J. P., October 25, 1824,
SUMNER Co.

CHAPMAN, Thomas to Verinda Snow - issued August 16, 1838, Bondsman:
William Coggins, WILSON Co.

CHAPMAN, Jr., Thos. H. to Ann Crabb - issued August 7, 1828, Bondsman:
Joseph Crabb, KNOX Co.

CHAPMAN, William to Margaret Bull - issued January 15, 1823, m. by:
Thos. Anderson, J. P., January 15, 1823, SUMNER Co.

CHAPPELL, Drury to Rebecca Henry - issued August 5, 1840, m. by:
Wm. White, J. P., August 5, 1840, DICKSON Co.

CHAPPELL, Humphrey to Charity Johnson - issued November 13, 1818,
Bondsman: John Coe, WILSON Co.

CHAPPELL, John to Mary F. Smith - issued August 2, 1834, Bondsman:
Jas. F. Fletcher, RUTHERFORD Co.

CHAPPELL, Samuel to Musa Henderson - issued June 21, 1819, Bondsman:
Nath'l Prince, m. by: Sam'l Gibson, E. C., June 21, 1819,
SUMNER Co.

CHAPPELL, Thomas to Nancy Jones - issued January 6, 1829, Bondsman:
Jos. Davenport, WILSON Co.

CHAPPLE, William to Elizabeth Walker - issued March 1, 1820, Bondsman: Solomon Walker, m. by: J. F. Davis March 2, 1820, WILSON Co.

CHAPPLE, William to Elizabeth Redding - issued May 5, 1820, Bondsman: Nathan Redding, m. by: James Gray, J. P., May 7, 1820, WILSON Co.

CHARLES, Isaac to Jane M. Tucker - issued July 27, 1856, m. by: John Charles, J. P., July 28, 1856, COFFEE Co.

CHARLES, Oliver to Tealy Gilles - issued February 16, 1853, m. by: L. Phillips, M. G., March 1, 1853, COFFEE Co.

CHARLES, Thomas L. to Martha S. Burroughs - issued February 7, 1854, m. by: Rev. C. D. Meador February 8, 1854, COFFEE Co.

CHARLTON, Abner to Polly Anglea - issued December 21, 1824, Bondsman: Jarratt Taylor, SUMNER Co.

CHARLTON, Isaac to Elizabeth Black - issued March 24, 1822, Bondsman: Shadrick Finn, m. by: Jonathan Williams, J. P., March 24, 1822, SUMNER Co.

CHARLTON, James W. to Mary Elizabeth Harvey - issued February 23, 1847, Bondsman: R. M. Baxter, m. by: J. B. Green, J. P., February 16, 1847, MONTGOMERY Co.

CHARLTON, Jennings to Anna Robertson - issued August 16, 1819, Bondsman: Francis Day, SUMNER Co.

CHARLTON, Oscar to Elizabeth Greer - issued April 23, 1845, m. by: Wm. Greer, Jr., April 24, 1845, DAVIDSON Co.

CHARLTON, Wm. to Hannah Graham - issued November 26, 1845, m. by: J. T. Edgar December 26, 1845, DAVIDSON Co.

CHARLTON, Willis L. to Mary S. Evans - issued December 26, 1840, DAVIDSON Co.

CHASTAIN, John S. to Amanda Bradley - issued November 21, 1840, Bondsman: Isaac Bradley, m. by: John Borum, M. G., November 27, 1840, WILSON Co.

CHASTAIN, Jonathan K. to Jane L. Stone - issued August 21, 1843, Bondsman: Leroy P. Capemon, m. by: William Green, M. G., August 20, 1843, MEIGS Co.

CHASTAIN, Joseph L. to Eliz. A. Hill - issued September 10, 1844, m. by: U. Young, J. P., ROBERTSON Co.

CHASTAIN, Thos. W. to Jane Mathews - issued December 10, 1857, m. by: J. A. Edmondson, M. G., December 13, 1857, FRANKLIN Co.

CHASTEEN, Andron to Sarah E. Helton - issued November 20, 1858, m. by: James Brasings, J. P., November 30, 1858, FRANKLIN Co.

CHASTEEN, Chas. W. to Sophia Graves - issued September 27, 1855, m. by: Lemuel Brandon, M. G., September 27, 1855, FRANKLIN Co.

CHASTEEN, R. H. to Elizabeth Foster - issued December 20, 1859, m. by: T. W. Bell, J. P., December 23, 1859, FRANKLIN Co.

CHASTIN, George to Betsy Lisby - March 10, 1837, KNOX Co.

CHATHAM, Thomas to Mary Wyatt - January 27, 1800, Security: Thomas Wyatt, GREENE Co.

CHAUDION, Joel to Martha A. Felts - issued August 31, 1841, m. by: Benjamin Rawls, G. M., September 2, 1841, ROBERTSON Co.

CHAUDOIN, Henry to Lucretia Pool - issued September 25, 1849, m. by: W. H. Bugg, J. P., September 28, 1849, ROBERTSON Co.

CHAUDOIN, Reuben to Matilda Hooper - issued May 19, 1841, m. by: W. Crockett, J. P., May 22, 1841, DAVIDSON Co.

CHAVIS, James to Catharine Chavis - issued March 14, 1815, Bondsman: John Garner, Witness: A. Hutcheson, KNOX Co.

CHAVOUSE, Abraham to Eliza Weaver - issued July 28, 1843, DAVIDSON Co.

CHAWNING, Moses P. to Pernina T. Smiley - issued March 28, 1843, m. by: J. B. McFerrin, M. G., March 28, 1843, DAVIDSON Co.

CHEASMAN, George to Malinda Mayfield - April 2, 1823, KNOX Co.

CHEATHAM, Edward S. to Jane Eleanor Foster - issued October 19, 1841, m. by: J. Thos. Wheat, Rector Cr. Ch., October 19, 1841, DAVIDSON Co.

CHEATHAM, George to Malinda Mayfield - issued April 2, 1825, m. by: J. A. Swan, J. P., April 7, 1825, KNOX Co.

CHEATHAM, Geo. to Eliza Bunch - issued December 12, 1837, Bondsman: Wm. Hickman, Witness: M. M. Swan, KNOX Co.

CHEATHAM, John A. to Anne McLin - issued October 11, 1836, m. by: Burwell Perry, J. P., October 11, 1836, RUTHERFORD Co.

CHEATHAM, Joseph to Nancy Hines - issued August 10, 1836, Bondsman: D. F. Dearmond, m. by: J. Johnson, J. P., August 16, 1836, KNOX Co.

CHEEK, James to Margaret Ann Carroll - m. by: John McMurtry, J. P., July 16, 1834, SUMNER Co.

CHEEK, John to Patsey Perdew - m. by: Robert Norvell April 26, 1837, SUMNER Co.

CHEEK, Littleton R. to Elizabeth Harris - issued April 14, 1838, DAVIDSON Co.

CHEEK, Milton to Patsy McCarroll - issued December 31, 1825, Bondsman: John Jennings, GRAINGER Co.

CHEEK, Philip to Lucinda Acre - issued October 13, 1831, Bondsman: A. C. Gains, SUMNER Co.

CHEEK, Thomas H. to Julia A. Glenn - issued January 13, 1840, Bondsman: Benjamin H. Glenn, m. by: Solomon Caplinger, J. P., WILSON Co.

CHEEK, William to Lucindia Dyer - issued December 2, 1817, Bondsman: Lenord Brock, m. by: John Hall, J. P., GRAINGER Co.

CHELWOOD, Mattheas to Susannah Winstead - June 21, 1815, WILLIAMSON Co.

CHENAULT, Felix to Nancy Anne Trigg - issued November 11, 1826, Bondsman: David M. Sanders, SUMNER Co.

CHENNAULT, F. B. to M. E. Mitchell - issued June 30, 1863, Bondsman: Isaac Chennault, LAWRENCE Co.

CHENOWITH, Geo. W. to Nancy Nester - issued August 26, 1835, Bondsman: Sam'l P. Bell, m. by: Sam'l. White, J. P., August 27, 1835, KNOX Co.

CHERRY, Albert G. to Eliza W. Bradley - issued September 12, 1833, WILSON Co.

CHERRY, Benjamin to Rebecca Hawkins - issued March 2, 1846, m. by: John Nugent, J. P., March 2, 1846, FRANKLIN Co.

CHERRY, Benj. to Emily E. Nugent - issued April 27, 1854, m. by:
John Hendley, J. P., April 27, 1854, FRANKLIN Co.

CHERRY, Cutter to Cornelia ___ (?) - issued June 2, 1870, m. by:
H. H. Sneed, M. G., June 2, 1870, FRANKLIN Co.

CHERRY, Daniel B. to Margaret J. Kenedy - issued July 5, 1848, m. by:
B. W. Howell, J. P., July 5, 1848, STEWART Co.

CHERRY, Elijah to Jenney Chadock - issued July 31, 1813, m. by:
Thos. Calhoon, August 29, 1813, WILSON Co.

CHERRY, Ezekiel to Jane Wilson - issued November 5, 1812, Bondsman:
Robert Collier, SUMNER Co.

CHERRY, George to Susan Mildred Herring - issued February 11, 1848,
Bondsman: G. B. Hill, m. by: Wm. Shelton, M. G., February 11,
1848, MONTGOMERY Co.

CHERRY, James M. to Elizabeth Jackson - issued July 5, 1840, m. by:
Edward Smith, Esqr., July 18, 1840, STEWART Co.

CHERRY, James M. to Lyda Frezell - issued May 16, 1843, m. by:
Fenell, J. P., May 16, 1843, STEWART Co.

CHERRY, John to Elizabeth Boyer - issued January 26, 1818, Bondsman:
Thomas Bragg, m. by: Daniel Travers, E. C. C., January 29, 1818,
RUTHERFORD Co.

CHERRY, Lewis D. to Martha McCanoe - issued November 6, 1839, m. by:
E. Goodrich, J. P., November 8, 1839, DAVIDSON Co.

CHERRY, Mary J. to John Pope - BEDFORD Co.

CHERRY, Philip E. to Mary Brunson - issued January 1, 1846, m. by:
Thos. Elliott February 1, 1846, STEWART Co.

CHERRY, Pierce W. to Mary Ann Gleaves - issued January 17, 1846,
DAVIDSON Co.

CHERRY, Silas M. to Elizabeth J. Tally - issued December 17, 1846,
Bondsman: M. D. Simmons, m. by: B. F. Williamson, J. P.,
December 17, 1846, MONTGOMERY Co.

CHERRY, Thomas to Amy Justice - issued August 29, 1825, Bondsman:
Mark Justice, m. by: Samuel Cochran, J. P., August 29, 1825,
SUMNER Co.

CHERRY, W. B. to Sally Eliza West - issued March 24, 1842, m. by:
Rev. James T. Morris March 24, 1842, STEWART Co.

CHERRY, William to Charlotte Ettinage - issued October 28, 1842,
m. by: Isaac Steel, G. M., ROBERTSON Co.

CHERRY, William D. to Malinda Head - issued February 22, 1847, m. by:
James M. Cherry, M. G., February 25, 1847, ROBERTSON Co.

CHERRY, Wm. L. to E. A. Martin - issued September 18, 1873, m. by:
James A. Hudgins, M. G., September 18, 1873, FRANKLIN Co.

CHERSHER, Thomas to Matilda Smith - issued December 21, 1815, Bondsman:
Fredrick Smith, m. by: James Moore, J. P., GRAINGER Co.

CHESER, Mathew W. to Amanda W. Franklin - issued July 22, 1858, m. by:
F. R. Gooch, Minister of the Gospel, ROBERTSON Co.

CHESHER, Dennis to Betsy Ault - issued February 28, 1822, Bondsman:
Henry Havron, m. by: John Haynie, M. G., February 28, 1822,
KNOX Co.

CHESHIR, Thornton to Memey Gibson - issued March 8, 1808, Bondsman:
Samuel Ousley, GRAINGER Co.

CHESHIRE, John L. to Martha Ann Sandifer - issued July 8, 1853,
Bondsman: B. J. Cheshire, m. by: M. G. Carney, G. M.,
MONTGOMERY Co.

CHESNEY, John to Sarah Scaggs - November 3, 1815, KNOX Co.

CHESNEY, John to Ruthy Lain - issued January 9, 1835, Bondsman:
Wortham Easley, m. by: Wm. Hickle, M. G., GRAINGER Co.

CHESNEY, Nathaniel to Sally Rodgers - issued December 16, 1836,
Bondsman: Jno. Seabolt, m. by: Thos. Annwood, J. P., December 20,
1836, Witness: M. M. Swan, KNOX Co.

CHESTER, Henry J. to Elizabeth Thueatt - issued September 21, 1844,
m. by: C. Travis, J. P., September 29, 1844, STEWART Co.

CHESTER, Joseph H. to Mary White - issued July 18, 1844, m. by:
John Brown, J. P., July 19, 1844, DICKSON Co.

CHESTER, William to Sophia M. Hogg - issued February 12, 1820, m. by:
John Wiseman, WILSON Co.

CHESTER, William to Sophia M. Hogg - issued February 12, 1824, Bondsman:
R. M. Burton, WILSON Co.

CHESTNUT, Joacob to Margaret Blake - February 27, 1797, Security:
Ewen Allison, GREENE Co.

CHESTNUT, John to Elizabeth Blake - April 19, 1794, Security:
James Campbell, GREENE Co.

CHICHESTER, Cyrus to Jane Mallory - issued July 5, 1848, m. by:
Allen Nesbitt, J. P., July 5, 1848, DICKSON Co.

CHICK, Burrell to Eleanor Sanders - issued December 26, 1835, Bondsman:
James Sanders, WILSON Co.

CHILDEN (?), Mitchell to Juliet B. Tarpley - issued August 12, 1835,
Bondsman: Nathan G. Jarratt, m. by: John C. Parker, WILSON Co.

CHILDERS, James to Susannah Thompson - issued November 15, 1796,
Bondsman: George Hays, KNOX Co.

CHILDERS, Robert to Polly Lucas - issued November 8, 1805, Bondsman:
John Childers, Witness: James Park, KNOX Co.

CHILDERS, West W. to Maria Muse - issued January 12, 1839, m. by:
Thos. Howard, J. P., January 17, 1839, FRANKLIN Co.

CHILDERS, William to Betsey Jordan - issued November 24, 1821, m. by:
Cullen Curlee, J. P., November 24, 1821, RUTHERFORD Co.

CHILDRESS, David to Susan Smith - issued January 24, 1826, m. by:
Peyton Smith February 3, 1826, RUTHERFORD Co.

CHILDRESS, Edward H. to Sophia C. McEwin - issued September 24, 1845,
m. by: A. L. P. Green, M. G., September 25, 1845, DAVIDSON Co.

CHILDRESS, Henry to Nancy Harris - issued April 20, 1830, Bondsman:
Travis Watts, RUTHERFORD Co.

CHILDRESS, James to Polly Ayres - issued November 7, 1808, Bondsman:
John Childs, KNOX Co.

CHILDRESS, James to Lockey Johnson - issued January 20, 1813, m. by:
Jeremiah King, M. G., January 24, 1813, KNOX Co.

CHILDRESS, James to Rebecca Kinkade - issued May 28, 1818, m. by:
H. Trott, J. P., May 28, 1818, RUTHERFORD Co.

CHILDRESS, John to Mary Curtney - November 8, 1796, BLOUNT Co.

CHILDRESS, John to Levina Wray - issued August 7, 1837, m. by:
W. H. Murray, J. P., August 8, 1837, RUTHERFORD Co.

CHILDRESS, Joseph to Sara Crawford - issued August 11, 1827, Bondsman:
Joseph Sursa, m. by: Jordan Willeford, J. P., August 15, 1827,
RUTHERFORD Co.

CHILDRESS, Lindsay to Mary M. Karnes - issued November 21, 1837,
Bondsman: Wm. Dunlap, m. by: Nathan Alldridge, J. P., November 21,
1837, KNOX Co.

CHILDRESS, Logan to Elizabeth Seymore - issued September 23, 1829,
Bondsman: Walter Lowe, RUTHERFORD Co.

CHILDRESS, Mitchell to Frances Dowell - issued September 28, 1809,
Bondsman: Josiah Armstrong, KNOX Co.

CHILDRESS, Mitchell to Rachael Hendrix - issued March 1, 1815,
Bondsman: William Morrow, Witness: A. Hutcheson, D. C., KNOX Co.

CHILDRESS, Richard to Becka White - issued May 21, 1819, m. by:
James I. Haise, J. P., May 25, 1819, KNOX Co.

CHILDRESS, Robt. L. to Leah Cox - issued February 16, 1830, m. by:
Robt. Tindell, J. P., February 16, 1830, KNOX Co.

CHILDRESS, Jr., Robt. L. to Hannah Lacey - issued October 12, 1832,
m. by: Lindsay Childress, J. P., October 18, 1832, KNOX Co.

CHILDRESS, Stephen to Sally Hall - issued June 16, 1810, Bondsman:
Mitchell Childress, KNOX Co.

CHILDRESS, Thos. to Lucinda Walker - December 31, 1825, WILLIAMSON Co.

CHILDRESS, William to Betsey Jordan - issued November 24, 1821, m. by:
Cullin Curlee, J. P., November 29, 1821, RUTHERFORD Co.

CHILDRESS, Wm. to Elizabeth Wade - issued September 29, 1830, Bondsman:
Wm. Brown, m. by: Elijah Johnson, J. P., September 29, 1830,
Witness: Wm. Swan, KNOX Co.

CHILDRESS, William to Evaline Childress - issued May 1, 1835, m. by:
Tandy Munday, J. P., May 10, 1835, KNOX Co.

CHILDRESS, William to Elizabeth Bryant - issued May 4, 1835, Bondsman:
Samuel Jones, m. by: Jordan Willeford, J. P., May 5, 1835,
RUTHERFORD Co.

CHILDRESS, Wm. to Sophia Taylor - issued September 19, 1841, Bondsman:
David Bricker, m. by: Peach Taylor, J. P., September 19, 1841,
MEIGS Co.

CHILDRESS, Wm. M. to Lidia Ann Stanly - issued November 13, 1841,
Bondsman: Wm. Childress, m. by: James Witten, M. G., December 2,
1841, MEIGS Co.

CHILDS, Garland to Francis Head - issued April 16, 1947, Bondsman:
T. W. Wisdom, MONTGOMERY Co.

CHILDS, John to Ann Arm - issued July 7, 1831, Bondsman: Claibourn
Haley, m. by: G. B. Mitchell, J. P., July 7, GRAINGER Co.

CHILES, Micajah to Elizabeth Wilkens - July 29, 1826, KNOX Co.

CHILES, Rowling to Elizabeth Greer - issued February 4, 1833, Bondsman:
Hardin Willis, m. by: G. B. Mitchell, J. P., February 8, GRAINGER Co.

CHILTON, James M. to Caroline M. Smith - issued April 29, 1843, m. by:
W. H. Wharton April 30, 1843, DAVIDSON Co.

CHILTON, John W. to Martha L. Burgess - issued January 10, 1857, m. by:
B. B. Batts, J. P., ROBERTSON Co.

CHILTON, Joseph to Dorothy A. Dennison - issued February 22, 1850,
Bondsman: J. O. Shackleford, m. by: J. T. Hendrickson, V. D. M.,
February 22, 1850, MONTGOMERY Co.

CHILTON, L. F. to Sarah W. Killebrew - issued October 15, 1851,
MONTGOMERY Co.

CHILTON, Levi A. to Frances C. E. Sartin - issued November 25, 1845,
m. by: R. W. Bell, J. P., ROBERTSON Co.

CHILTON, Richard to Suffey Nuckles - issued April 2, 1867, m. by:
John Armstrong, J. P., April 3, 1867, FRANKLIN Co.

CHILTON, Thomas L. to Mary M. Jones - issued October 19, 1857, m. by:
Wm. W. Conn, M. G., October 20, 1857, FRANKLIN Co.

CHILTON, W. B. to E. A. Baird - issued December 23, 1836, Bondsman:
Aron S. Neel, m. by: John Beard December 23, 1836, SUMNER Co.

CHILTON, Wesley W. to Elizabeth R. Wiggins - issued November 18, 1857,
m. by: A. B. Cummings, M. G., November 26, 1857, FRNAKLIN Co.

CHILTON, Wm. L. to Annie Dortch - issued April 27, 1847, Bondsman:
A. Chilton, m. by: William C. Crane, Rector Trinity Church,
April 27, 1847, MONTGOMERY Co.

CHILTON, Wm. O. to Ellen S. Bechnoll - issued November 12, 1845,
m. by: J. T. Wheat, Rr. of Ct. Ch., November 13, 1845, DAVIDSON Co.

CHINN, Reuben to Lottie Eddington - February 16, 1837, KNOX Co.

CHINN, Richard M. to Sarah Ann Crew (or Cruise) - issued November 23,
1833, Bondsman: H. T. Scott, KNOX Co.

CHINOWITH, Richard to Ellen Hammer - issued January 14, 1823, Bondsman:
Mordecai Yarnell, m. by: Mordecai Yarnell, J. P., January 14,
1823, KNOX Co.

CHISM, Walter A. to Mary E. Caudill - issued November 23, 1846,
m. by: Isaac Steel, ROBERTSON Co.

CHISM, William to Patsey Griffin - issued July 21, 1817, Bondsman:
John Griffin, m. by: John W. Payton, J. P., July 22, 1817,
WILSON Co.

CHITWOOD, Joel to Sarah Duncan - issued January 21, 1843, m. by:
W. M. B. Talliferro, J. P., January 22, 1843, FRANKLIN Co.

CHITWOOD, John to Francis L. Martin - issued December 8, 1838, m. by:
B. B. Knight, J. P., December 25, 1838, FRANKLIN Co.

CHITWOOD, John to Elizabeth F. Rhew - issued July 31, 1871, m. by:
John Armstrong, J. P., August 2, 1871, FRANKLIN Co.

CHIZENHALL, John to Rhoda Pinson - issued August 17, 1821, m. by:
Carey James, RUTHERFORD Co.

CHOAT, Edward to Sally Ascum - issued June 4, 1813, Bondsman:
Christopher Woodall, SUMNER Co.

CHOAT, Edward to Martha Ann Shannon - issued August 15, 1846, m. by:
R. G. Cole, J. P., August 16, 1846, ROBERTSON Co.

CHOAT, Edward to Martha Ann Shannon - issued August 16, 1846, m. by:
R. G. Cole, J. P., ROBERTSON Co.

CHOAT, Gabriel to Jane Brewer - issued October 16, 1841, m. by:
Rich. Chowning, J. P., October 17, 1841, ROBERTSON Co.

CHOAT, John to Barbary Bell - issued January 23, 1841, m. by:
L. Adams, Min. of the Gos., January 24, 1841, ROBERTSON Co.

CHOAT, John W. to Cine Simmons - issued February 18, 1857, m. by:
James Cook, J. P., ROBERTSON Co.

CHOAT, Stephen to Rhoda Warren - issued January 6, 1851, m. by:
R. G. Cole, J. P., June 7, 1851, ROBERTSON Co.

CHOAT, Thos. J. to A. J. Williams - issued July 20, 1845, m. by:
David Jones, J. P., ROBERTSON Co.

CHOAT, William to Elizabeth Doyal - issued June 24, 1856, m. by:
A. Rose, J. P., June 26, 1856, ROBERTSON Co.

CHOATE, John I. to Chris__(?) Hassell - issued December 1, 1819,
Bondsman: A. H. Douglas, SUMNER Co.

CHOATE, Thomas D. to Josephine Pullen - issued December 16, 1865,
Bondsman: George K. Welch, m. by: R. L. McLaren, J. P., December 24,
1865, LAWRENCE Co.

CHOCKLEY, John W. to Frances Ann Parker - issued July 16, 1861,
Bondsman: Isaac Green, Jos. H. Thompson, Clk. per N. F. Thompson,
Dep. Clk., m. by: H. F. Holt, J. P., BEDFORD Co.

CHOOTE, G. W. to Mary Jane Gibbs - issued July 8, 1848, m. by:
Wm. Hill, J. P., July, 1848, DICKSON Co.

CHOWNING, John to Caroline Cannon - issued October 5, 1846, m. by:
J. W. Judkins, J. P., ROBERTSON Co.

CHOWNING, Lemuel to Amanda J. Cole - issued November 30, 1850, m. by:
O. H. Morrow, M. G., December 1, 1850, ROBERTSON Co.

CHOWNING, R. to Milly Brewer - issued February 24, 1845, m. by:
"Solemnized though not certified," ROBERTSON Co.

CHOWNING, Wm. T. to Sarah A. Frey - issued December 24, 1844, m. by:
David Jones, J. P., December 26, 1844, ROBERTSON Co.

CHRISMAN, George to Malinda Smith - issued February 23, 1846, DICKSON Co.

CHRISMAN, Joseph to Margaret Northren - issued July 19, 1838, m. by:
James Daniel, J. P., July 19, 1938, DICKSON Co.

CHRISP, Ezechial to Margaret Greer - issued September 5, 1838, m. by:
S. B. Davidson, J. P., September 5, 1838, DAVIDSON Co.

CHRISP, William to Mary Elder - issued April 4, 1821, m. by:
Peyton Smith, M. G, April 12, 1821, RUTHERFORD Co.

CHRISTA, James to Sarah Speers - issued April 8, 1832, Bondsman:
James W. Speers, m. by: Sam'l Davis, J. P., April 8, 1832,
SUMNER Co.

CHRISTIAN, Allen C. to Rhoda Ann Sewell - issued July 9, 1855, m. by:
James B. Foster, J. P., August 9, 1855, FRANKLIN Co.

CHRISTIAN, Andrew to __(?) Robertes - issued September 26, 1855,
VAN BUREN Co.

CHRISTIAN, George to Eliza McCormack - issued June 1, 1803, Bondsman: William McCormack, Witness: Chas. McClung, Clerk, KNOX Co.

CHRISTIAN, George W. to Jane Haston - issued July 20, 1846, m. by: David Haston, J. P., July 21, 1846, VAN BUREN Co.

CHRISTIAN, John A. to Sarah W. Bishop - issued December 19, 1825, Bondsman: Jno. M. McCampbell, m. by: John Bayless, J. P., December 20, 1825, Witness: Wm. Swan, KNOX Co.

CHRISTIAN, John S. to Mary C. Roberson - issued October 17, 1851, Bondsman: Wm. P. Miller, m. by: J. C. Bryan, J. P., October 17, 1851, MONTGOMERY Co.

CHRISTIAN, Milton to Jane Perry - issued December 26, 1837, m. by: Joseph Meek, J. P., January 2, 1837, KNOX Co.

CHRISTIAN, Peyton to Peggy Pace - issued February 4, 1833, Bondsman: James Pace, RUTHERFORD Co.

CHRISTIE, Granville to Margaret Crawley - issued September 6, 1832, Bondsman: James W. Speers, SUMNER Co.

CHRISTOPHER, Jesse to Susan Shoemaker - issued July 31, 1831, m. by: Joshua Woollen, M. G., August 9, 1832, WILSON Co.

CHRISTOPHER, John to Jiney Carter - issued June 23, 1818, Bondsman: James Baldridge, m. by: L. Davis, J. P., June 26, 1818, RUTHERFORD Co.

CHRISTOPHER, John to Elizabeth Jones - issued December 30, 1824, m. by: Jacob Payne, J. P., December 30, 1824, RUTHERFORD Co.

CHRISTOPHER, Joseph to Rebecka Coleman - issued November 1, 1806, Bondsman: Thomas Groves, SUMNER Co.

CHRISTOPHER, Joshua to Rosamond Rutledge - issued April 11, 1822, m. by: Jacob Payne, J. P., April 12, 1822, RUTHERFORD Co.

CHRISTY, Wm. T. to Ellen P. Morgan - issued July 12, 1832, Bondsman: William Park, m. by: Tho. H. Nelson July 12, 1832, KNOX Co.

CHRONISTER, A. R. to R. L. Kirk - issued November 30, 1861, Bondsman: Levi Voss, m. by: J. M. Pennington, J. P., December 3, 1861, LAWRENCE Co.

CHUMBLEY, Claborn to Judith Hale - issued March 7, 1838, Bondsman: William Hale, m. by: H. A. Belote March 7, 1838, SUMNER Co.

CHUMLEA, John to Susanah Legg - issued August 11, 1828, Bondsman: Thos. G. Cardwell, m. by: Sam'l Love, M. G., August 14, 1828, KNOX Co.

CHUMLEE, Wm. W. to Jane E. Anderson - issued December 20, 1827, m. by: W. A. McCampbell, V. D. A., December 27, 1827, KNOX Co.

CHUMLEY, Beverly to Martha Bell - issued June 20, 1837, Bondsman: John Cumming, m. by: Wm. Lawrence, J. P., June 22, 1837, WILSON Co.

CHUMLEY, Claiborne to Elizabeth Cavet - issued September 20, 1822, Bondsman: David Thompson, KNOX Co.

CHUMLEY, Claiborne to Elizabeth Cavet - issued September 20, 1822, m. by: Rob't Tunnell, J. P., September 22, 1822, KNOX Co.

CHUMNEY, Pleasant to Betsey Panter - issued July 1, 1837, Bondsman: James Panter, m. by: W. G. Bailey, J. P., July 2, 1837, WILSON Co.

CHUMNEY, William to Elizabeth Fossy - issued December 12, 1817, Bondsman: Richard Chumney, m. by: Abner W. Bone, J. P., December 23, 1817, WILSON Co.

CHUMNEY, Wm. to Matilda Burnett - issued December 19, 1831, Bondsman: Jno. McCullough, KNOX Co.

CHURCH, Henderson to Sophia C. Hise - issued August 9, 1854, m. by: A. J. Wiseman, J. P., August 9, 1854, FRANKLIN Co.

CHURCH, Henderson to Mary M. Neal - issued November 28, 1859, m. by: B. Higgenbotham, J. P., FRANKLIN Co.

CHURCH, Jacob to Nancy Ray - issued July 5, 1865, m. by: M. Tipps, J. P., July 7, 1865, FRANKLIN Co.

CHURCH, John A. to Margaret L. Ramsey - issued December 16, 1819, m. by: John L. Jetton, J. P., December 16, 1819, RUTHERFORD Co.

CHURCH, John F. to Charlotte Limbaugh - issued September 15, 1859, m. by: B. Higgenbotham, J. P., September 18, 1859, FRANKLIN Co.

CHURCH, Nancy Hannah to Joseph Fox - MAURY Co.

CHURCH, Robert to Amanda Bryant - issued March 3, 1835, Bondsman: James Ramsey, m. March 3, 1835, RUTHERFORD Co.

CHURCH, Samuel to Eve Weaver - issued January 6, 1848, m. by: Rev. J. Scivally January 9, 1848, FRANKLIN Co.

CHURCH, William to Eliza J. Neal - issued June 13, 1867, m. by: J. C. Mials, M. G., June 13, 1867, FRANKLIN Co.

CHURCH, William to Ellen Wagner - issued May 14, 1870, m. by: Lewis Anderson, J. P., May 16, 1870, FRANKLIN Co.

CHURCHMAN, Jackson to Rachel Kindar - issued September 21, 1837, Bondsman: James B. Boyd, m. by: Levi Satterfield, M. G., September 21, 1837, GRAINGER Co.

CHURCHMAN, James S. to Mary Young - issued July 25, 1834 (or July 27), Bondsman: Enos Hammer, m. by: James B. Boyd, J. P., GRAINGER Co.

CHURCHMAN, Reubin to Marget (Margaret) Eaton - issued January 1, 1802, Bondsman: Joseph Eaton, GRAINGER Co.

CHURCHMAN, Thomas to Margaret Williams - issued June 21 (or 29), 1816, m. by: Geo. Moody, J. P., GRAINGER Co.

CHURCHWELL, Geo. W. to R. E. Montgomery - issued May 26, 1825, Bondsman: R. G. Dunlap, KNOX Co.

CHURCHWELL, Geo. W. to R. E. Montgomery - issued May 26, 1825, m. by: Geo. Atkin, M. G., May 26, 1825, KNOX Co.

CHURCHWELL, Geo. W. to Sophia M. Park - issued September 14, 1836, m. by: Tho. H. Nelson September 15, 1836, KNOX Co.

CHURCHWELL, Geo. W. to Sophia N. Park - issued September 14, 1836, Bondsman: And. R. Humes, KNOX Co.

CHURCHWELL, William to Peggy Ayres - December 26, 1870, MAURY Co.

CISER, Michael to Nancy Julian - issued January 11, 1806, Bondsman: Abner Parr, Witness: Jno. Ferris (?), KNOX Co.

CIVILS, John to Fredonia Heathcock - issued June 17, 1854, m. by: S. A. Nesbitt, J. P., June 18, 1854, MONTGOMERY Co.

CLABORN, J. S. to R. B. Wilson - issued June 29, 1874, m. by:
A. B. Cummings, M. G., June 30, 1874, FRANKLIN Co.

CLACK, Elijhah to Myrum Alderson - m. by: Robert Norvell April 12,
1833, SUMNER Co.

CLACK, John to Sarah May - issued November 24, 1825, m. by:
O. W. Crockett, J. P., November 24, 1825, RUTHERFORD Co.

CLACKSTON, Mary to Josiah Kidwell - GREENE Co.

CLAIBORNE, Jno. W. to Ann Pyland - issued December 21, 1863, Bondsman:
Hiram H. Hopper, Jos. H. Thompson, Clk., BEDFORD Co.

CLAIBORNE, Leonard to Emeline Claiborne - issued November 9, 1835,
m. by: Joseph Meek, J. P., November 10, 1835, KNOX Co.

CLAIBORNE, Susan to S. J. Sutton - BEDFORD Co.

CLAIBORNE, Wm. C. C. to Clarice Duralde - October 25, 1806

CLAIBOURNE, Ephraim to Polly Brown - issued December 20, 1809, Bondsman:
Joseph Blackley, KNOX Co.

CLAIBOURNE, Ouseley to Frances H. Robertson - issued September 5,
1829, Bondsman: David Robertson, m. September 5, 1829, SUMNER Co.

CLAIR, Henry to Nancy Dunlap - issued January 25, 1812, Bondsman:
James Harbison, KNOX Co.

CLAIRY, Andrew to Polly Blackard - issued November 25, 1819, Bondsman:
John McMurtry, m. by: John McMurtry, J. P., November 25, 1819,
SUMNER Co.

CLAMPEL, Jonathan to Priscella Rogers - issued September 17, 1800,
Bondsman: King Carr, SUMNER Co.

CLAMPET, John to Sally Carey - issued May 22, 1819, Bondsman:
John R. Wilson, m. by: John Williamson, J. P., June 10, 1819,
WILSON Co.

CLAMPETT, Nathan A. to Amanda Ann Gillespie - issued June 14, 1834,
Bondsman: Josiah Strange, WILSON Co.

CLANTON, George W. to Sarah A. Mickle - issued October 24, 1854,
Bondsman: H. H. Hopson, MONTGOMERY Co.

CLANTON, Hy to Blanchy Dilliard - July 2, 1807, WILLIAMSON Co.

CLANTON, Susan to James Anderson - BEDFORD Co.

CLANTON, Wesley to Mary Claxton - issued April 18, 1858, FRANKLIN Co.

CLANTON, William T. to Bethana Robertson - June 13, 1844, Security:
Hezekiah Jackson, GILES Co.

CLAP, Adam to Rebecca Roberts - September 17, 1822, KNOX Co.

CLAPP, Boston to Polly Tannyhill - issued April 13, 1819, m. by:
John Thompson, J. P., April 15, 1819, KNOX Co.

CLAPP, David to Sarah Rutherford - ___(?) 25, 1817, KNOX Co.

CLAPP, Solomon to Teaberry Smith - issued September 1, 1815, Bondsman:
McC. Frost, KNOX Co.

CLARDY, Benjamin to Lucinda B. Avrett - issued September 5, 1836,
Bondsman: John G. Averitt, m. by: John Wiseman September 5, 1836,
SUMNER Co.

CLARDY, Harriett to Stephen D. Green - issued July 24, 1863, Bondsman: William Pinkerton, BEDFORD Co.

CLARDY, Louisa T. to Jessee C. Wheeler - BEDFORD Co.

CLARDY, Patrick H. to Rachael Abernathy - issued February 10, 1842, m. by: B. M. Barnes, J. P., February 20, 1842, DAVIDSON Co.

CLARDY, Thomas M. to Elizabeth Lazenberry - issued August 18, 1846, m. by: J. B. McCutchen, J. P., August 18, 1846, DAVIDSON Co.

CLARK, A. J. to Hellon Bailey - issued January 23, 1843, m. by: B. Herndon, J. P., February 5, 1843, STEWART Co.

CLARK, Abraham to Mary Ann Edgmon - issued November 9, 1840, Bondsman: Jno. A. Clark, m. by: James Patterson, J. P., November 12, 1840, MEIGS Co.

CLARK, Alexander R. to Lucy Young - August 13, 1833, WILLIAMSON Co.

CLARK, Alexander to Milley Lane - issued February 17, 1849, m. by: John Gillentine, J. P., May 24, 1849, VAN BUREN Co.

CLARK, Alexander to Margaret Burks - issued January 3, 1862, Bondsman: James P. Bell, Jos. H. Thompson, Clk. per N. F. Thompson, Dep. Clk., m. by: Rich Phillips, J. P., BEDFORD Co.

CLARK, Anderson A. to Nancy C. Robb - issued June 7, 1836, Bondsman: Thomas P. Clark, m. by: John Allison, V. D. M., June 7, 1836, RUTHERFORD Co.

CLARK, Andrew to Polly Wilson - issued November 3, 1812, Bondsman: Montetion W. Wilson, SUMNER Co.

CLARK, Andrew to Mary Taylor - issued July 16, 1831, Bondsman: James Taylor, WILSON Co.

CLARK, Benjamin to Polly Grissom - issued October 21, 1846, m. by: Preston Dulaney, J. P., October 22, 1846, VAN BUREN Co.

CLARK, Benj. to Mary E. Sisk - issued December 18, 1858, m. by: E. B. Crisman December 22, 1858, FRANKLIN Co.

CLARK, Benjamin to Charlotta Koger - issued November 7, 1868, m. by: W. W. Simmons, M. G., November 12, 1868, FRANKLIN Co.

CLARK, Ben. P. to Henrietta H. Morgan - issued May 20, 1846, m. by: J. G. Edgar May 20, 1846, DAVIDSON Co.

CLARK, Beverly to Quintilla Atkinson - MONTGOMERY Co.

CLARK, Bird to Sarah Williams - issued May 24, 1858, m. by: John Fleming, J. P., May 29, 1858, VAN BUREN Co.

CLARK, Boling to Susan Travilion - issued December 18, 1843, m. by: Leonard Burnett December 19, 1843, DAVIDSON Co.

CLARK, Boon to Mary Ann Beard - May 31, 1857, m. by: Hardin Griggs, J. P., GILES Co.

CLARK, Bowlin to T. K. Corn - issued October 14, 1868, m. by: E. L. Best, J. P., October 15, 1868, FRANKLIN Co.

CLARK, C. M. to Elizabeth Young - issued December 24, 1873, m. by: Jas. A. Hudgins, M. G., December 25, 1873, FRANKLIN Co.

CLARK, Clabourn to Sarah Neal - issued August 2, 1828, Bondsman: Isaac Neal, WILSON Co.

CLARK, David to Susan Bain - issued May 25, 1830, Bondsman:
   Joshua Rickmond, m. by: John Parker, J. P., May 25, 1830,
   SUMNER Co.

CLARK, Edward G. to Mary C. Felts - issued December 18, 1847, m. by:
   Jas. Woodard December 23, 1847, ROBERTSON Co.

CLARK, Eli to Polly Hollinsworth - issued May 1, 1813, Bondsman:
   Levi Clark, GRAINGER Co.

CLARK, Elisha B. to Ann Dickinson - issued January 21, 1817, Bondsman:
   Thos. Washington, m. by: J. Burns, RUTHERFORD Co.

CLARK, Ellick to Elizabeth Church - issued August 25, 1846, FRANKLIN Co.

CLARK, George to Nancy Kirk - issued March 8, 1808, Bondsman:
   William Kirk, GRAINGER Co.

CLARK, Harry to Rhody Vinson - issued September 11, 1809, Bondsman:
   James McKain, SUMNER Co.

CLARK, Henry to Mariah Morris - issued October 25, 1855, m. by:
   Thos. Finch, J. P., October 25, 1855, FRANKLIN Co.

CLARK, Hugh M. to Mary Smith - issued March 5, 1827, m. by:
   Wm. Morris, J. P., March 6, 1827, KNOX Co.

CLARK, Isaac to Nancy Bounds - August 6, 1794, KNOX Co.

CLARK, Isaac N. to Martha A. Roberts - issued July 30, 1851, m. by:
   John Fleming, J. P., July 31, 1851, VAN BUREN Co.

CLARK, Isham to Isabell Jeffre - issued April 21, 1800, Bondsman:
   Joseph Clerk, GRAINGER Co.

CLARK, J. I. to Frances Winters - issued November 30, 1854, m. by:
   B. W. Bradley, J. P., December 5, 1854, ROBERTSON Co.

CLARK, J. W. to Nancy Chapman - m. October 19, 1837, SUMNER Co.

CLARK, James to Leah Gilleland - issued September 24, 1800, Bondsman:
   William Morrison, SUMNER Co.

CLARK, James to Edy Lowry - issued August 18, 1804, Bondsman:
   David Stuart, SUMNER Co.

CLARK, James to Elizabeth Daniel - issued February 17, 1810, Bondsman:
   James Conn, GRAINGER Co.

CLARK, James to Polly Stubblefield - issued September 25, 1824,
   Bondsman: Joseph Stubblefield, GRAINGER Co.

CLARK, James to Nelly Burks - issued August 13, 1836, Bondsman:
   Leroy Burks, RUTHERFORD Co.

CLARK, James M. to Asenath Jetton - issued August 27, 1835, Bondsman:
   William B. Holloway, RUTHERFORD Co.

CLARK, James P. to Susan McCarry - issued June 27, 1820, m. by:
   Isaac Anderson, M. G., June 27, 1820, KNOX Co.

CLARK, Jasper N. to Clara E. Baggett - issued May 17, 1854, m. by:
   James Cook, J. P., May 18, 1854, ROBERTSON Co.

CLARK, Jesse to Nancy Bowlding - issued February 23, 1846, m. by:
   G. D. Fullman, J. P., February 23, 1846, DAVIDSON Co.

CLARK, Jesse to Sally A. Chambers - issued June 13, 1850, m. by:
   J. W. Hunt, J. P., June 15, 1850, ROBERTSON Co.

CLARK, Jesse J. to Mary Allen - issued March 24, 1838, m. by:
Charley Brooks, Minister, March 25, 1838, STEWART Co.

CLARK, John to Letitia Sharp (Harp) - January 29, 1801, Security:
James Gillespie, BLOUNT Co.

CLARK, John to Patsey Moore - July 15, 1807, WILLIAMSON Co.

CLARK, John to Sally Rains - August 13, 1808, WILLIAMSON Co.

CLARK, John to Sally Alsup - issued June 23, 1812, WILSON Co.

CLARK, John to Mary Young - issued June 20 (or 28), 1812, Bondsman:
Nathan Humphrey, m. by: George Moody, J. P., GRAINGER Co.

CLARK, John to Catey Moats - March 14, 1814, KNOX Co.

CLARK, John to Frances Acuff - issued February 3, 1823, Bondsman:
Joseph Clark, m. by: Jas. Kenmore, M. G., February 3, 1823,
GRAINGER Co.

CLARK, John to Mary E. Sims - issued January 10, 1844, m. by:
J. Crawford January 11, 1844, FRANKLIN Co.

CLARK, John to Nancy Sides - issued July 12, 1869, FRANKLIN Co.

CLARK, John to Armildrice Rountree - issued August 22, 1844, m. by:
Robert Green, J. P., ROBERTSON Co.

CLARK, John to Elizabeth Wray - issued April 13, 1848, Bondsman:
John M. Burgess, m. by: N. F. Trice, J. P., April 13, 1848,
MONTGOMERY Co.

CLARK, John to Jane Crownover - issued September 26, 1874, m. by:
D. S. Long, J. P., September 27, 1874, FRANKLIN Co.

CLARK, John A. to Jane Thompson - issued March 6, 1838, DAVIDSON Co.

CLARK, John A. to Margaret Beard - issued August 3, 1838, Bondsman:
James H. Branch, m. by: J. A. Young, J. P., WILSON Co.

CLARK, John A. to Drusanna Edgemon - issued November 22, 1843,
Bondsman: Alxr. Clark, m. by: Richd. Simpson, M. G., November 23,
1843, MEIGS Co.

CLARK, John C. to Beneta Hughes - issued February 4, 1820, Bondsman:
Nmbleton Gregory, SUMNER Co.

CLARK, John C. to Lydia Mitchell - issued January 6, 1849, VAN BUREN Co.

CLARK, Jno. D. to L. L. Davidson - issued September 15, 1849, Bondsman:
C. H. Sanders and J. H. Bailey, m. by: E. L. Knight September 16,
1849, MONTGOMERY Co.

CLARK, John E. to Jane Parker - issued November 27, 1841, m. by:
John Gillentine, J. P., November 28, 1841, VAN BUREN Co.

CLARK, John E. to Caroline More - issued July 25, 1855, m. by:
William Worthington, J. P., July 26, 1855, VAN BUREN Co.

CLARK, John F. to Matilda Wormington - issued October 13, 1821,
Bondsman: John J. King, SUMNER Co.

CLARK, John H. to Elizabeth Kemper - issued December 1, 1842, m. by:
A. L. P. Green, M. G., December 1, 1842, DAVIDSON Co.

CLARK, John M. to Rebecka W. Crawford - issued July 29, 1820, Bondsman:
James Kennedy, m. by: John McCampbell August 3, 1820, KNOX Co.

CLARK, John N. to Caroline McFadden - issued January 11, 1837, Bondsman: William R. McFadden, RUTHERFORD Co.

CLARK, John P. to Elizabeth Wileman - issued August 17, 1854, m. by: W. G. Gwinn, M. G., August 17, 1854, COFFEE Co.

CLARK, Joseph to Susan Latham - issued December 10, 1823, Bondsman: William Clark, GRAINGER Co.

CLARK, Joseph to Martha Grove - issued January 10, 1833, Bondsman: Archibald P. Greer, m. by: Wm. E. Cocke, J. P., GRAINGER Co.

CLARK, Jos. to Lucinda Gillaspie - issued October 6, 1859, m. by: A. J. Wiseman, J. P., October 6, 1859, FRANKLIN Co.

CLARK, Joseph J. to Mary E. Sutor - issued March 9, 1850, Bondsman: Joseph A. Collashau, m. by: Elisha Vaughn March 10, 1850, MONTGOMERY Co.

CLARK, Joshua to Sarah Allen - issued August 13, 1829, m. by: Benjn. Maddox, M. G., August 30, 1829, WILSON Co.

CLARK, Joshua to Sarah Allen - issued August 17, 1829, Bondsman: Wm. M. Chapman, WILSON Co.

CLARK, Josiah to Nancy Bowers - issued January 31, (1827?), Bondsman: William Hartsfield, WILSON Co.

CLARK, Jourdin to Elizabeth Brewer - issued August 7, 1837, Bondsman: Ezekiel Morrison, RUTHERFORD Co.

CLARK, Levi to Susana McVay - issued August 27, 1814, Bondsman: Elisha Hall, GRAINGER Co.

CLARK, Levin to Patsey Doak - issued December 26, 1811, Bondsman: Thos. Bradley, WILSON Co.

CLARK, Mark to Mary Ann Abbott - issued December 1, 1816, Bondsman: Thos. Scurry and Edw. Douglas, SUMNER Co.

CALRK, Mary A. to Joshua Dean - BEDFORD Co.

CLARK, Milly to Birney McNichol - issued March 27, 1863, Bondsman: Jordan C. Holt, Jos. H. Thompson, Clk., BEDFORD Co.

CLARK, Richard to Betsey Jones - issued March 2, 1825, Bondsman: Richard Philips, m. by: Jonathan Davis, J. P., March 2, 1825, SUMNER Co.

CLARK, Robert to Mary York - February 13, 1816, WILLIAMSON Co.

CLARK, S. E. P. to Victoria Hamlin - issued June 21, 1863, Bondsman: G. W. Cox, BEDFORD Co.

CLARK, Samuel to Betsey Dial - issued October 9, 1807, m. by: John Love, Esq., KNOX Co.

CLARK, Samuel to Sarah U. Coleman - issued September 9, 1851, Bondsman: Sam'l P. Wyatt, m. by: John Gold, J. P., September 9, 1851, MONTGOMERY Co.

CLARK, Thomas to Sally Diggins - issued March 27, 1800, Bondsman: Vachel Clark and James Trousdale, SUMNER Co.

CLARK, Thomas to Elizabeth Craig - issued June 18, 1829, m. by: Wm. Morris, J. P., June 30, 1829, KNOX Co.

CLARK, Thos. to Sarah Bradford - issued September 25, 1847, m. by: J. T. Green, J. P., September 26, 1847, FRANKLIN Co.

CLARK, Thomas to Elizabeth Hampton - issued March 22, 1848, m. by:
    Wm. Garrett, J. P., March 22, 1848, DICKSON Co.

CLARK, Thomas to Nancey Parker - issued April 24, 1854, VAN BUREN Co.

CLARK, Thos. A. to Naoma C. Darrell - issued April 20, 1858, m. by:
    J. T. Slatter, J. P., April 20, 1858, FRANKLIN Co.

CLARK, Thomas A. to Naoma A. Darrell - issued April 20, 1858,
    FRANKLIN Co.

CLARK, Thomas H. to Martha Ann Hale - issued January 12, 1853,
    Bondsman: G. Orgain, m. by: G. Orgain, J. P., January 12, 1853,
    MONTGOMERY Co.

CLARK, W. A. to E. McGuire - issued June 14, 1849, m. by:
    N. M. Henry, J. P., ROBERTSON Co.

CLARK, Warren H. to Sarah Mason - issued December 25, 1872, m. by:
    Meredith Garner, M. G., December 26, 1872, FRANKLIN Co.

CLARK, William to Abagail Gardner - issued July 13, 1805, Bondsman:
    James Clark and Hugh T. Dunn, SUMNER Co.

CLARK, William to Nancy White - issued November 11, 1813, Bondsman:
    Jno. Armstrong, KNOX Co.

CLARK, William to Elizabeth Jennings - issued June 10, 1823, Bondsman:
    Joseph Clark, GRAINGER Co.

CLARK, William to Elizabeth Conley - issued December 12, 1826, Bondsman:
    Silas Conley, m. by: Sam'l Fleming, J. P., December 12, 1826,
    Witness: Chas. McClung, KNOX Co.

CLARK, William to Emily Kelton - issued September 17, 1835, Bondsman:
    Reuben Curry, RUTHERFORD Co.

CLARK, William to Eliza Mallicoat - issued May 19, 1836, Bondsman:
    Jackson Churchman, GRAINGER Co.

CLARK, William to Susan Clark - issued January 3, 1837, Bondsman:
    Jno. Neal, m. by: James C. England, J. P., January 5, 1837, KNOX Co.

CLARK, Wm. C. to Nancy J. Hail - issued October 17, 1865, Bondsman:
    John S. Roberts, m. by: W. C. Davis, J. P., October 19, 1865,
    LAWRENCE Co.

CLARK, William F. to Emma Douglass - issued March 22, 1831, Bondsman:
    David M. Fulton, SUMNER Co.

CLARK, Wm. J. to Mary S. Ralston - issued June 2, 1836, m. by:
    J. D. Bennett, J. P., June 2, 1836, KNOX Co.

CLARK, Wilson H. to Betheny Morris - issued March 22, 1849, m. by:
    Solomon Sparks, J. P., March 22, 1849, FRANKLIN Co.

CLARKE, George to Susan Burchett - issued March 1, 1823, Bondsman:
    John Hall, RUTHERFORD Co.

CLARKE, Joseph M. to Nancy McCampbell - issued January 19, 1813, m. by:
    Tho. H. Nelson, Pres. Church, January 20, 1813, KNOX Co.

CLARKE, Sally to Joseph Holt - GREENE Co.

CLARKSTON, Joshua to Delila Hand - issued October 15, 1838, m. by:
    D. S. Ford, J. P., October 16, 1838, DICKSON Co.

CLARY, Elijah to Polly Barnes - issued February 20, 1793, Bondsman:
    Peter Looney, SUMNER Co.

CLARY, J. W. to Martha Ogilvie - issued January 20, 1864, Bondsman:
W. T. Clary, Jos. H. Thompson, Clk., BEDFORD Co.

CLARY, James to Penny Stephens - issued November 25, 1830, Bondsman:
Loyd Richmond, m. by: B. S. Hattles, J. P., WILSON Co.

CLARY, Spencer to Winney Daniel - issued November 30, 1816, Bondsman:
Elisha Clary, SUMNER Co.

CLARY, William to Nancy Mercer - issued April 3, 1794, Bondsman:
Peter Looney, SUMNER Co.

CLASPILL, Jacob S. to Rebecca Hays - issued (?) November 13, 1826,
Bondsman: Jo. C. Guild, SUMNER Co.

CLASOP, William to Patsey Cox - issued September 8, 1806, m. by:
Sm'l. Yancey, J. P., GRAINGER Co.

CLAUSON, Peter to Ruth Bailes - issued July 17, 1798, m. by:
Sm'l Yancey, J. P., July 17, 1798, Witness: Sm'l Yancey, GRAINGER Co.

CLATER, Sophia W. to W. T. Neil - BEDFORD Co.

CLAWGER, William R. to Mary Lambeth - issued March 6, 1832, Bondsman:
Wm. Lambeth, m. by: Arch B. Duval March 6, 1832, SUMNER Co.

CLAXTON, D. C. to Eliza Taylor - issued August 1, 1849, Bondsman:
C. Shelton, m. by: J. Nolen August 8, 1849, MONTGOMERY Co.

CLAXTON, Isaac to Jane Self - April 12, 1857, m. by: S. A. Parson,
J. P., GILES Co.

CLAXTON, James to Polly Martin - issued March 3, 1817, Bondsman:
Thomas Scurry, m. by: Sam'l Gibson, E. C. C., March 3, 1817,
SUMNER Co.

CLAXTON, Joshua to Susannah Rice - issued October 3, 1810, Bondsman:
James Claxton, SUMNER Co.

CLAXTON, Rush to America J. Nash - issued June 5, 1858, FRANKLIN Co.

CLAY, Charles to Rebecca Douglass - issued July 3, 1833, Bondsman:
James Rochelle, m. by: H. Hobson, J. P., WILSON Co.

CLAY, Eleazar to Mary Dumvelle - issued January 19, 1802, Bondsman:
William Clay, GRAINGER Co.

CLAY, James M. to Nancy M. Lamb - issued June 9, 1843, m. by:
Wm. S. Smith, M. G., June 9, 1843, FRANKLIN Co.

CLAY, John to Harriet Andrews - issued September 26, 1831, Bondsman:
Samuel N. Ross, WILSON Co.

CLAY, John to Martha Davis - issued October 10, 1831, Bondsman:
Ebenezer Gilbert, m. by: Henry Hobson, J. P., WILSON Co.

CLAY, John to Sally L. Davis - issued December 24, 1834, Bondsman:
William C. Ross, WILSON Co.

CLAY, John R. to Elizabeth Haws - issued July 17, 1848, m. by:
James C. Handly, J. P., July 17, 1848, FRANKLIN Co.

CLAY, Joseph W. to Sarah Fletcher - issued December 31, 1839, m. by:
J. T. Edgar December 31, 1839, DAVIDSON Co.

CLAY, Joshua to Eliza Still - issued May 16, 1840, m. by: C. D. Elliott,
M. G., May 19, 1840, DAVIDSON Co.

CLAY, Robert T. to Sarah Edwards - issued December 26, 1843, DICKSON Co.

CLAY, Samuel T. to Martha Ann Edwards - issued November 2, 1822, RUTHERFORD Co.

CLAY, Sydney to Clara Barnett - issued September 6, 1833, Bondsman: John Barnett, m. by: R. H. Mason, J. P., September 6, 1833, RUTHERFORD Co.

CLAY, William to Tilley Hays - issued October 9, 1787, Bondsman: Peter Looney, SUMNER Co.

CLAY, William H. to Nancy Ann Thrower - issued March 24, 1861, m. by: W. M. Brewer, J. P., March 24, 1861, COFFEE Co.

CLAY, Wooday to Sallie Sarmons - July 12, 1815, WILLIAMSON Co.

CLAYBROOKE, John S. to Mary E. Perkins - April 20, 1834, WILLIAMSON Co.

CLAYTON, Benjamin to Lockey Quarls - issued March 26, 1817, Bondsman: Edward Clayton, m. by: Joshua Lester, V. D. M., March 27, 1817, WILSON Co.

CLAYTON, Daniel to Nancy P. Willis - issued September 7, 1848, m. by: D. G. Baird, J. P., ROBERTSON Co.

CLAYTON, David to Caroline Mason - issued June 6, 1833, Bondsman: Wm. Fields, Jr., m. by: D. Fleming June 6, 1833, KNOX Co.

CLAYTON, G. B. to Olive Smith - issued December 31, 1853, m. by: J. C. Barbee, J. P., January 1, 1854, ROBERTSON Co.

CLAYTON, L. C. to M. A. Dorris - issued October 26, 1851, m. by: D. G. Baird, J. P., ROBERTSON Co.

CLAYTON, Richd. L. to Elizabeth Willis - issued September 24, 1844, m. by: D. G. Baird, J. P., September 26, 1844, ROBERTSON Co.

CLAYTON, Robt. to Rutha Morris - June 18, 1805, WILLIAMSON Co.

CLAYTON, Robert to Elizabeth Hommel - issued August 16, 1833, m. by: Michael Davis, J. P., August 22, 1833, KNOX Co.

CLAYTON, Stephen to Nancy Hill - November 15, 1808, WILLIAMSON Co.

CLAYTON, Thornton to Fanny Beardon - issued March 6, 1813, Bondsman: John Bently, SUMNER Co.

CLAYTON, W. H. to S. E. Willis - issued May 23, 1848, m. by: Isaac Steel May 24, 1848, ROBERTSON Co.

CLAYTON, William to Rosannah Norman - issued January 26, 1808, Bondsman: Pritchard Alexander, RUTHERFORD Co.

CLAYTON, William C. to Elizabeth Norman - issued February 13, 1833, Bondsman: J. B. Jones, m. by: I. J. Miller, J. P., February 14, 1833, RUTHERFORD Co.

CLAYTON, Wm. to Henrietta Woodfins - issued January 24, 1839, m. by: Jno. W. Hannah January 24, 1839, DAVIDSON Co.

CLEAR, Peter to Peggy Damewood - issued August 16, 1809, Bondsman: Kinsey Coats, Witness: John F. Jack, J. P., GRAINGER Co.

CLEARWATER, Ann to Jesse Wright - GREENE Co.

CLEARWATER, Dorcas to John Moore - GREENE Co.

CLEARWATER, Jacob to Hannah Fisher - January 28, 1800, Security: James Dinwoddie, GREENE Co.

CLEAVELAND, A. C. to E. Barnes - issued July 8, 1867, m. April 20, 1867, FRANKLIN Co.

CLEAVLAND, Moses to Francis Mullin - issued August 23, 1858, m. by: Joseph Smith, M. G., August 22, 1858, FRANKLIN Co.

CLEEK, Sarah E. to John W. Lynch - BEDFORD Co.

CLEINENTS, Wm. C. to Mary Frances Kay - issued December 21, 1843, m. by: Jno. M. Nolin, M. G., December 21, 1843, STEWART Co.

CLEMEN, John to Mrs. M. Coggins - issued March 18, 1871, m. by: John Nugent, J. P., March 19, 1871, FRANKLIN Co.

CLEMENTS, John G. to Charity Sharpe - issued October 23, 1827, Bondsman: Alfred Bell, RUTHERFORD Co.

CLEMENTS, Stephen to Mary Foster - issued December 23, 1841, m. by: D. P. Harris, M. G., December 23, 1841, DAVIDSON Co.

CLEMMENS, James to Nancy R. Casselman - issued August 20, 1839, Bondsman: William Clemmons, m. by: John Billingsley, J. P., September 3, 1839, WILSON Co.

CLEMMENT, John to Jane Pullem - issued September 27, 1808, Bondsman: Samuel Barton, WILSON Co.

CLEMMONS, Alford to Elizabeth Young - issued November 23, 1825, Bondsman: Allen Clemmons, m. by: Jacob Sullivan November 25, 1825, WILSON Co.

CLEMMONS, Allen to Jimey Young - issued October 14, 1823, Bondsman: William Russell, m. by: Joshua Woolard, M. G., October 16, WILSON Co.

CLEMMONS, Edwin to Susannah Woodrum - issued March 2, 1833, m. by: John Beard, M. G., March 7, 1833, WILSON Co.

CLEMMONS, Edwin to Patience Harris - issued March 21, 1838, Bondsman: Thos. Robertson, m. by: Jas. Baird March 22, 1838, WILSON Co.

CLEMMONS, James to Elizabeth Lee - issued February 26, 1822, Bondsman: William Clemmons, m. by: James Bone, V. D. M., March 6, 1822, WILSON Co.

CLEMMONS, James to Mavis Parton - issued May 7, 1825, Bondsman: Etheldred Clemmons, m. by: Edward Harris, J. P., April 10, 1825, WILSON Co.

CLEMMONS, Jeptha to Margarett Truett - issued __(?) 28, 1835, Bondsman: William Clemmons, WILSON Co.

CLEMMONS, Richard to Elizabeth Brown - issued August 29, 1806, Bondsman: William Brown, GRAINGER Co.

CLEMMONS, Samuel T. to Sayly Teague - issued December 8, 1813, Bondsman: James Clemmons, WILSON Co.

CLEMMONS, William to Rachael Truett - issued December 26, 1833, Bondsman: John Fields, WILSON Co.

CLEMON, Eli to Elizabeth Griffis - issued January 19, 1843, m. by: Josiah Ferriss, J. P., January 19, 1843, DAVIDSON Co.

CLEMONONS, Eli to Nancy Rear - issued January 23, 1841, m. by: John Wright, J. P., January 23, 1841, DAVIDSON Co.

CLEMONS, John to Elizabeth McHenry - issued September 3, 1838, Bondsman: Jesse Christopher, m. by: G. A. Huddleston September 5, 1838, WILSON Co.

CLEMONS, John to Susannah Mavity - issued July 8, 1845, Bondsman:
Jesse Mavity, m. by: B. F. McKenzie, J. P., July 8, 1845, MEIGS Co.

CLEMONS, William to Nancey Bowman - issued December 23, 1852, VAN BUREN Co.

CLEMONS, William H. to Mary C. Earthman - issued December 9, 1840,
m. by: F. B. McFerrin, M. G., December 10, 1840, DAVIDSON Co.

CLENARD, Philip W. to Sarah Reynolds - issued December 19, 1846, m. by:
B. F. Fraser, J. P., December 24, 1846, STEWART Co.

CLENDENAN, John to Elizabeth Herndon - issued April 6, 1825, m. by:
Jesse Alexander, V. D. M., April 13, 1825, RUTHERFORD Co.

CLENDENING, James to Betsy Bledsoe - issued June 10, 1789, Bondsman:
William Neely, SUMNER Co.

CLENDENNING, Charles to Cauley Honeycut - issued October 15, 1832,
Bondsman: Hugh Johnston, m. by: Peter Ketring, J. P., October 15,
1832, SUMNER Co.

CLENDENNING, Charles F. to Polly Frazier - m. by: Charles Watkins
November 16, 1833, SUMNER Co.

CLENDENNING, John to Margaret Frazor - issued August 24, 1829, Bondsman:
Wm. Kirkpatrick, m. by: Wm. Montgomery August 24, 1829, SUMNER Co.

CLENDENNING, Thomas B. to Elizabeth Frazor - issued July 5, 1824, m. by:
Joseph Kirkpatrick July 5, 1824, SUMNER Co.

CLENDENNON, John to Mary Meadors - issued September 4, 1837, m. by:
Stokely White, J. P., September 5, 1837, RUTHERFORD Co.

CLENDENON, Joseph G. to Hannah Kirkpatrick - issued June 11, 1823,
Bondsman: William Mackentire, m. by: William Grey, J. P., June 12,
1823, WILSON Co.

CLENNY, Henry to Martha Bugg - m. by: Rich'd Johnson October 8, 1834,
SUMNER Co.

CLENSMAN, Albert to Rena C. Palham - issued February 3, 1874, m. by:
William Prince, J. P., February 3, 1874, FRANKLIN Co.

CLEPTON, Ansel to Louisa Barnes - issued January 3, 1859, FRANKLIN Co.

CLEVELAND, Champion C. to Malinda E. Moore - issued December 10, 1857,
m. by: L. N. Simpson, J. P., December 10, 1857, FRANKLIN Co.

CLEVELAND, H. P. to Lucinda Alderson - issued January 1, 1840, m. by:
R. B. C. Howell, Pastor Baptist Ch., January 1, 1840, DAVIDSON Co.

CLEVELAND, John to Mary Martin - issued May 3, 1807, Bondsman:
James Magee, m. by: R. Houston, J. P., May 3, 1807, Witness:
Jno. H. Gamble, KNOX Co.

CLEVELAND, Martin to An McPheters - issued October 9, 1832, Bondsman:
Joseph Clark, m. by: Joseph Clark, J. P., GRAINGER Co.

CLEVELAND, Nancy to William Dawson - GREENE Co.

CLEVELAND, William to J. English - issued September 5, 1863, Bondsman:
Henry Riddell, m. by: J. M. Powell September 7, 1863, LAWRENCE Co.

CLEVENGER, John to Harriet Steel - issued March 8, 1842, m. by:
T. W. Felts, Minister, ROBERTSON Co.

CLEVINS, Atwood to Mary Oliver - issued January 13, 1853, m. by:
John C. Chitwood, J. P., January 18, 1853, FRANKLIN Co.

CLIBORN, Larenzo D. to Peggy E. Anderson - issued October 2, 1823,
   Bondsman: James Anderson, Witness: Wm. Swan, KNOX Co.

CLIBURN, Henderson to Martha Wilkes (or Welks) - issued July 23, 1829,
   m. by: Samuel Love, M. G., July 23, 1829, KNOX Co.

CLIBURN, James (or Jones) to Betsy Doran - issued March 7, 1829, m. by:
   Wm. A. McCampbell, J. P., March 8, 1829, KNOX Co.

CLIBURN, John to Sarah Lusby - issued July 23, 1829, m. by:
   Samuel Love, M. G., July 27, 1829, KNOX Co.

CLIBURN, Lasley to Cynthia Hopper - issued October 27, 1821, Bondsman:
   James Human, m. by: Wm. A. McCampbell, J. P., October 27, 1821,
   KNOX Co.

CLIBURN, Malinder to Sally Brown - issued January 6, 1829, KNOX Co.

CLICK, G. W. to Mary Hughs - issued April 4, 1839, Bondsman:
   G. W. Houseley, m. by: John Taff, J. P., April 4, 1839, MEIGS Co.

CLICK (Cleek), Malachai to Elizabeth Shally - May 6, 1795, Security:
   Martin Cleek, GREENE Co.

CLICK, Malachi to Rachel Laney - January 29, 1798, Security:
   Martin Click, GREENE Co.

CLICK, Mathias B. to Nancy Moss - issued May 6, 1817, Bondsman:
   William Moss, WILSON Co.

CLIFT, Sen., James to Patsy Knipper - issued September 28, 1833,
   Bondsman: Chas. W. Price, m. by: Eli King, J. P., September 29,
   1833, KNOX Co.

CLIFT, Joseph to Christiana Hayworth - issued November 13, 1826,
   Bondsman: Barnes Crawford, KNOX Co.

CLIFT, Wm. to Nancy Brooks - issued April 15, 1823, Bondsman:
   Wm. Walker, KNOX Co.

CLIFT, Wm. to Nancy Brooks - issued April 15, 1823, m. by:
   Tho. H. Nelson, M. G., April 15, 1823, KNOX Co.

CLIFTON, A. to Mary Garner - issued June 29, 1859, m. by: Wm. Prince
   June 29, 1859, FRANKLIN Co.

CLIFTON, B. M. to Mary Ann Wells - issued July 28, 1853, Bondsman:
   George Alwell, m. by: J. G. Ward, J. P., July 25, 1853,
   MONTGOMERY Co.

CLIFTON, Benjamin to Hannah Clifton - issued June 30, 1823, Bondsman:
   Lawrence Sypert, m. by: Howard Harris, J. P., July 1, 1823,
   WILSON Co.

CLIFTON, Benjamin to Nancy Johnson - issued December 21, 1836, m. by:
   B. S. Mabry, M. G., February 22, 1837, WILSON Co.

CLIFTON, G. W. to Louisa Box (Poore) - issued June 9, 1861, m. by:
   Geo. W. Trenary, ROBERTSON Co.

CLIFTON, Harry to Sarah Michie - issued March 11, 1816, Bondsman:
   William Michie, m. by: Christopher Cooper, J. P., March 13, 1816,
   WILSON Co.

CLIFTON, James to Lucinda Oliver - issued January 21, 1859, m. by:
   E. L. Jones, L. D., January 20, 1859, COFFEE Co.

CLIFTON, Jesse to Sally Smith - issued January 4, 1819, Bondsman:
   James B. Guthrie, WILSON Co.

CLIFTON, John to E. R. Sadlers - issued December 31, 1843, Bondsman: Pleasant Ray, m. by: Daniel Cate, J. P., December 31, 1843, MEIGS Co.

CLIFTON, Leven to Hannah Skean - issued November 8, 1826, Bondsman: George Tucker, m. by: Obadiah Freeman, M. G., WILSON Co.

CLIFTON, Nathaniel to Susan E. Houser - issued December 14, 1863, Bondsman: James M. Stribling, m. by: J. B. Clayton, J. P., December 14, 1863, LAWRENCE Co.

CLIFTON, Samuel to Mary Pennebaker - issued July 15, 1837, m. by: Jas. Willeford, J. P., July 16, 1837, WILSON Co.

CLIFTON, Thomas to Letty Rogers - issued December 22, 1806, Bondsman: John Tucker, WILSON Co.

CLIFTON, Thomas to Nancy Seat - issued September 7, 1825, Bondsman: Spencer W. Tally, WILSON Co.

CLIFTON, Wm. to Elizabeth Perdue - issued September 10, 1849, Bondsman: Allen Teasley, m. by: Lewis Lowe, Minister, September 11, 1849, MONTGOMERY Co.

CLIFTON, William to Dilly Everett - issued September 2, 1854, Bondsman: J. W. Gupton, MONTGOMERY Co.

CLIMER, Aaron to Rebecca Sullivan - issued September 20, 1813, Bondsman: James Ozment, m. by: Jacob Sulivan September 23, 1814, WILSON Co.

CLIMER, Milton to Polly Martin - issued May 2, 1836, WILSON Co.

CLIMER, Milton to Adaline Cowthon - issued May 1, 1837, Bondsman: Wm. Graves, WILSON Co.

CLIMER, Thomas to Sally Kemp (?) - issued December 18, 1832, Bondsman: James S. Swain, m. by: John Shane, J. P., December 20, 1832, WILSON Co.

CLIMER, William to Jane Lane - issued May 8, 1828, Bondsman: Anderson Perry, m. by: Benjamin Graves, J. P., May 9, 1828, WILSON Co.

CLIMER, William to Elizabeth Wilkinson - issued November 1, 1834, m. by: Thomas Somers, J. P., November 7, 1834, WILSON Co.

CLINARD, B. C. to N. P. Rawles - issued November 3, 1847, m. by: Alex Lowe, Minister, ROBERTSON Co.

CLINARD, Bradford to Nancy Justice - issued October 23, 1841, m. by: William D. Baldwin, Minister of the Gospel, October 24, 1841, ROBERTSON Co.

CLINARD, Brown to Eliza Parker - issued May 12, 1859, m. by: Benj. Rawls, M. G., ROBERTSON Co.

CLINARD, James A. to Sarah Street - issued September 22, 1856, m. by: J. T. Craig, J. P., ROBERTSON Co.

CLINARD, John to Malinda C. Hollis - issued April 16, 1847, m. by: A. Justice, J. P., April 21, 1847, ROBERTSON Co.

CLINARD, Josiah to Harriet A. Parker - issued October 1, 1860, m. by: J. L. Hollis, J. P., November 4, 1860, ROBERTSON Co.

CLINARD, Lewis to Haldah Justice - issued November 2, 1839, m. by: T. W. Felts November 3, 1839, ROBERTSON Co.

CLINARD, Robert H. to Mary Gullege - issued March 23, 1844, m. by: D. G. Baird, J. P., March 25, 1844, ROBERTSON Co.

CLINARD, Simeon to Julia Parker - issued December 26, 1854, m. by:
B. Rawls, M. G., ROBERTSON Co.

CLINARD, William to Catherine A. Parker - issued November 1, 1855,
m. by: J. S. Hollis, J. P., ROBERTSON Co.

CLINARD, William to Thirsey Fuqua - issued September 10, 1860, m. by:
W. C. Rawls, J. P., September 23, 1860, ROBERTSON Co.

CLINE, Adam to Sarah Black - issued November 29, 1813, Bondsman:
John Cline, SUMNER Co.

CLINE, Andrew to Polly Sikes - m. by: Henry S. Anthony December 3,
1833, SUMNER Co.

CLINE, John to Polly Miltebarger - issued March 13, 1813, Bondsman:
Jacob Miltebarger, Witness: John N. Gamble, KNOX Co.

CLINE, John to Lydia Hunter - issued February 7, 1831, m. by: __(?),
J. P., February 7, 1831, SUMNER Co.

CLINE, Michael to Nancy Rippy - issued February 27, 1827, Bondsman:
John Rippy, SUMNER Co.

CLINE, William to Hetty Rippy - issued February 2, 1832, Bondsman:
Edward Bracken, m. by: J. Davis, J. P., February 2, 1832, SUMNER Co.

CLINTON, Samuel to Mary Ann Rogers - August 13, 1862, m. by:
Jas. C. Stevenson, GILES Co.

CLIPPER, Joseph to Nancy Beverly - issued August 15, 1829, Bondsman:
Isaac Kline, GRAINGER Co.

CLOAR, Absalom to Ann Cockran - issued July 18, 1810, Bondsman:
John Hubert, SUMNER Co.

CLOAR, Calvin to Ann Woodson - m. by: John Wiseman, M. G., September 10,
1834, SUMNER Co.

CLOAR, John to Sally Turner - issued October 19, 1805, Bondsman:
John Hubert, SUMNER Co.

CLOAR, William to Polly Hubbard - issued March 27, 1804, Bondsman:
Isaac Bledsoe, SUMNER Co.

CLODDY, Pleasant J. to Charlotte Lazenbury - issued December 8, 1840,
m. by: B. M. Barnes, J. P., December 8, 1840, DAVIDSON Co.

CLOE, Elijah to Betsey Cloe - issued January 5, 1809, Bondsman:
William Cloe, SUMNER Co.

CLOE, Elijah to Patsey Lane - issued December 28, 1824, Bondsman:
Patrick Buckley, WILSON Co.

CLOEY, Jesse to Elizabeth Aust - issued January 9, 1833, m. by:
Henry Hobson, J. P., January 10, 1833, WILSON Co.

CLOPTON, John to Matilda Drake - issued March 25, 1830, Bondsman:
Jno. Bussard, m. by: Ezekiel Cloyd April 3, 1830, WILSON Co.

CLOPTON, John A. to Elizabeth Ann Hurd - issued November 10, 1831,
Bondsman: Isaac Barnett, WILSON Co.

CLOPTON, Jr., Walter to Martha Ann Duffer - issued August 12, 1825,
m. by: Joshua Lester, V. D. M., August 17, 1825, RUTHERFORD Co.

CLOPTON, William A. to Elizabeth Medlin - issued October 21, 1833,
m. by: Joshua Lester, V. D. M., WILSON Co.

CLOSE, William to Eliza Herron - issued November 19, 1807, Bondsman: Abner Witt, Witness: Jno. Ferris (?), KNOX Co.

CLOUD, Reuben to Elizabeth Stout - issued July 15, 1834, m. by: Wm. Rodgers, J. P., July 17, 1834, KNOX Co.

CLOUD, Reuben to Elizabeth Stout - issued July 15, 1834, Bondsman: Joseph Scott, KNOX Co.

CLOUD, Samuel to Betsey Cabbage - issued April 9, 1821, Bondsman: Isaac Mayes, GRAINGER Co.

CLOUD, Saml. O. to Martha W. Roberts - issued October 4, 1850, m. by: D. G. Baird, J. P., October 5, 1850, ROBERTSON Co.

CLOUSE, Geo. to Nancy McInterf - issued December 29, 1836, Bondsman: Jesse Sherrod, KNOX Co.

CLOW, Robert I. to Eveline Ball - issued September 4, 1838, m. by: Robert Boyt C. Howell September 4, 1838, DAVIDSON Co.

CLOWDIS, Radford R. to Catharine Marley - issued March 19, 1833, m. by: Wm. Morris, J. P., March 21, 1833, KNOX Co.

CLOWEN, Daniel to Polley Fargerson - issued November 16, 1809, Bondsman: Robert Gaines, GRAINGER Co.

CLOWER, Elijah to Nicy Sutton - issued October 4, 1830, Bondsman: Mathew Dew, WILSON Co.

CLOWER, Elisha to Martha Tucker - issued December 24, 1829, Bondsman: Geo. H. Bussard, WILSON Co.

CLOWER, Elizabeth to Gideon Thompson - GREENE Co.

CLOWES, James to Polly Sharp - issued December 9, 1815, Bondsman: Thomas Griffin, GRAINGER Co.

CLOYD, David to Nancy Wilson - issued May 22, 1819, Bondsman: Osburn Thompson, WILSON Co.

CLOYD, Ezekiel to Nancy White - issued July 18, 1825, Bondsman: Edward White, m. by: David Foster, M. G., July 21, 1825, WILSON Co.

CLOYD, Ezekeil to Agnes S. Cambell - issued August 13, 1845, DAVIDSON Co.

CLOYD, James M. to Margaret C. Sharpe - issued October 18, 1829, m. by: Jesse Alexander, V. D. M., October 20, 1829, WILSON Co.

CLOYD, John to Lettis Alexander - issued May 13, 1814, Bondsman: Samuel Meredith, WILSON Co.

CLOYD, John to Elizabeth Griffet - issued September 11, 1826, Bondsman: John Nunner, m. by: John Williams, J. P., September 13, 1826, WILSON Co.

CLOYD, John W. to Sarah W. Brooks - issued November 11, 1840, m. by: John Beard, M. G., November 12, 1840, DAVIDSON Co.

CLOYD, Joseph to Caty Alexander - issued May 12, 1817, Bondsman: Wm. I. Alexander, m. by: Jesse Alexander, V. B. D., M. A., May 15, 1817, WILSON Co.

CLOYD, Newton to Elizabeth Williamson - issued January 7, 1824, Bondsman: John Williamson, m. by: John Williamson, J. P., January 8, 1824, WILSON Co.

CLOYD, Stephen to Polly Wilson - issued June 8, 1811, Bondsman: Edmund Cruther, WILSON Co.

CLOYD, William S. to Ann W. Jones - issued December 24, 1840, m. by:
A. G. Goodlet December 25, 1840, DAVIDSON Co.

CLUCK, Adam to Marinda Howel - issued March 17, 1817, Bondsman:
William Alsup, WILSON Co.

CLUCK, Daniel to Jane Kidwell - issued October 26, 1817 (or 1816),
Bondsman: David Kidwell, m. by: Isaiah Midkiff, J. P., October 30,
1817, GRAINGER Co.

CLUCK, Henry to Hannah Kidwell - issued April 4, 1818, Bondsman:
Daniel Cluck, m. by: Felps Read, J. P., April 10, 1818, GRAINGER Co.

CLUCK, Henry to Mary Robertson - issued July 19, 1828, Bondsman:
Thomas Burk, WILSON Co.

CLUCK, Henry to Sally Upchurch - issued September 14, 1840, Bondsman:
Leven Woollen, WILSON Co.

CLUCK, James J. to Rachel Robertson - issued February 22, 1838, Bondsman:
Jonathan Hall, m. by: John Bond, V. D. M., February 23, 1838,
WILSON Co.

CLUCK, John to Mary Martin - issued February 24, 1824, Bondsman:
Thomas Martin, WILSON Co.

CLUCK, John to Mary Martin - issued February 24, 1825, m. by:
Jacob Martin, J. P., February 27, 1825, WILSON Co.

CLUCK, John to Jane Robinson - issued August 10, 1833, Bondsman:
James Daniel, GRAINGER Co.

CLUCK, Uriah to Elizabeth Hall - issued November 19, 1839, Bondsman:
William Hall, m. by: John Bond, M. G., November 20, 1839, WILSON Co.

CLUCK, Wm. to Narcissa A. Donaldson - issued August 7, 1858, m. by:
R. C. Smith, J. P., August 10, 1858, FRANKLIN Co.

CLYMER, William to Darcus Bristow - issued March 21, 1846, Bondsman:
David Burton, m. by: R. W. Morrison, J. P., March 26, 1846,
MONTGOMERY Co.

CLYNARD, Henderson to Eliza June Wilkerson - issued February 19, 1845,
DAVIDSON Co.

CLYNE, Michael to Margaret Ogle - issued November 26, 1818, Bondsman:
Wm. Alderson, SUMNER Co.

COALMAN, Daniel to Mary Chumbley - November 2, 1810, KNOX Co.

COAPLAND, Wilson to Milly Rhea - issued June 17, 1829, Bondsman:
Henry Williams, m. by: Williamson Williams, J. P., June 18, 1829,
WILSON Co.

COARTON, James to Amanda Hendley - issued November 7, 1865,
m. November 24, 1865, FRANKLIN Co.

COATES, Shepheard to Elisabeth Haston - issued September 1, 1850,
VAN BUREN Co.

COATS, Armstead to Nancy Brown - issued October 20, 1825, m. by:
J. Higgins, J. P., October 27, 1825, RUTHERFORD Co.

COATS, Austin M. to Lucinda Dismuke - issued November 14, 1824,
Bondsman: Thos. W. Royster, SUMNER Co.

COATS, Benjamin to Elizabeth Brock - issued September 9, 1801, Bondsman:
John Margran, GRAINGER Co.

COATS, Benjamin to Hannah Chandler - issued June 19, 1834, Bondsman:
Claibourn Johnson, m. by: Joseph Clark, GRAINGER Co.

COATS, David to Jency Lee - December 2, 1810, KNOX Co.

COATS, David to Jincy Lee - issued December 24, 1816, m. by:
Amos Hardin, J. P., December 26, 1816, KNOX Co.

COATS, David to Mary Hinshaw - issued October 23, 1819, Bondsman:
Josiah Grasty (Jonah Grasly), m. by: Robert Ganes, J. P.,
October 24, 1819, GRAINGER Co.

COATS, Jesee to Nancy Hammock - issued December 17, 1825, Bondsman:
Presley Barret, GRAINGER Co.

COATS, John to Sarah Rogers - January 12, 1796, Surety: James Houston,
BLOUNT Co.

COATS, John H. to Harriett S. A. Duncan - issued February 27, 1826,
Bondsman: Richard P. Hall, SUMNER Co.

COATS, Kinsey to Sinthey Merchant - issued February 10, 1807, GRAINGER Co.

COATS, Lewis to Parthena Hynds - issued October 20, 1827, Bondsman:
James Campbell, m. by: S. M. Hawkins, J. P., October 20, 1827,
GRAINGER Co.

COATS, Peyton H. to Elizabeth Richardson - issued August 31, 1825,
m. by: J. Higgins, J. P., September 5, 1825, RUTHERFORD Co.

COATS, Thomas to Alsey Lee - July 21, 1812, KNOX Co.

COATS, William to Patsey Tracy - issued April 12, 1817, Bondsman:
J. B. Taylor, m. by: James Davidson April 15, 1817, WILSON Co.

COATS, Wilson to Caty Rule - issued February 8, 1790, Bondsman:
John Cravins, SUMNER Co.

COBB, Christopher to Sally Underhill - issued April 21, 1829, Bondsman:
John Langley, WILSON Co.

COBB, Fountain H. to Sarah Surlock - issued January 1, 1840, Bondsman:
H. F. Johnson, m. by: Wm. Walker, J. P., January 2, 1840, WILSON Co.

COBB, George to Sarah Burnley - issued April 17, 1819, Bondsman:
James Carr, m. by: James Carr April 17, 1819, SUMNER Co.

COBB, George W. to Mary Arnold - issued January 12, 1849, m. by:
W. W. Watson January 12, 1849, FRANKLIN Co.

COBB, J. R. to Sarah Hasty - issued February 9, 1842, m. by:
L. G. Simpson, J. P., February 10, 1842, FRANKLIN Co.

COBB, James to Sallie Harper - May 7, 1811, KNOX Co.

COBB, James H. to Martha J. Boyce - issued May 21, 1841, m. by:
J. T. Edger May 23, 1841, DAVIDSON Co.

COBB, James P. to Susannah E. Darrow - issued August 29, 1856, m. by:
W. H. Anthony, M. G., August 29, 1856, FRANKLIN Co.

COBB, Jesse to Nancy Mullins - issued January 30, 1821, Bondsman:
Alexander Bearden (Alex. Rankin), GRAINGER Co.

COBB, Joseph to Sarah Blair - issued December 29, 1797, Bondsman:
John Smith, GRAINGER Co.

COBB, Joseph to Eliza A. Jernigan - issued January 13, 1853, m. by:
D. M. Wells, J. P., ROBERTSON Co.

COBB, Josephus to Mary S. Crutcher - issued December 28, 1858, m. by:
W. W. Wynn, M. G., December 30, 1858, ROBERTSON Co.

COBB, Lebbicus to Margaret Simpson - issued September 20, 1831,
Bondsman: Samuel McCann, SUMNER Co.

COBB, Lebbins to Margaret L. Simpson - issued September 20, 1830, m. by:
J. Davis, J. P., September 20, 1830, SUMNER Co.

COBB, M. D. to Sarah C. T. Binkley - issued February 15, 1860, m. by:
J. T. W. Davis, Minister, February 16, 1860, ROBERTSON Co.

COBB, Milton to Jane H. Dickey - issued September 11, 1828, Bondsman:
James Godfrey, KNOX Co.

COBB, Robt. to Caroline Williams - issued December 8, 1845, m. by:
C. Brandon, J. P., December 11, 1845, STEWART Co.

COBB, Thomas to Eliza G. Pearson - issued January 8, 1820, m. by:
John Clark, J. P., January 13, 1820, RUTHERFORD Co.

COBB, Thomas C. to Martha M. Darden - issued November 15, 1847, m. by:
J. L. Ellis, J. P., November 18, 1847, ROBERTSON Co.

COBB, W. F. to S. M. Darden - issued September 15, 1849, m. by:
Robert Draughon, J. P., September 16, 1849, ROBERTSON Co.

COBB, William to Catharine Jackson - issued December 21, 1819, Bondsman:
Harrison Irby, WILSON Co.

COBBLE, A. W. to Nancy C. Morris - issued December 27, 1865, m. by:
B. B. Brandon, L. D., December 28, 1865, FRANKLIN Co.

COBBLE, Jackson H. to Mary J. Jones - issued May 7, 1851, m. by:
Joseph Smith, M. G., May 8, 1851, FRANKLIN Co.

COBBLE, John to Mary A. Stewart - issued January 10, 1857, m. by:
A. J. Wiseman, J. P., January 11, 1857, FRANKLIN Co.

COBBLE, John to Louisa Branch - issued December 1, 1860, m. by:
A. J. Simpson, J. P., December 2, 1860, FRANKLIN Co.

COBBLE, William to Nancy Webb - issued July 19, 1854, m. by:
A. J. Wiseman, J. P., July 23, 1854, FRANKLIN Co.

COBBLER, Martin H. to Mary Ann Smith - issued May 27, 1840, m. by:
Jesse Edwards, M. G., May 28, 1840, DICKSON Co.

COBBS, T. E. H. to Abigil Matilda Gray - issued September 3, 1848,
Bondsman: B. S. Fox, MONTGOMERY Co.

COBBS, William A. to Nancy J. Dunn - issued June 26, 1846, m. by:
Thomas Martin, M. G., ROBERTSON Co.

COBLER, Frederick to Rachel Cobler - issued November 29, 1841, m. by:
W. E. Cartwright November 29, 1841, DAVIDSON Co.

COBUN, William J. to Elizabeth Wyatt - issued January 3, 1846, m. by:
Allen McCaskill, J. P., STEWART Co.

COCHRAN, A. D. to Nancy Brown - issued February 12, 1838, m. by:
L. Russell, J. P., February 17, 1838, DICKSON Co.

COCHRAN, Abner to Mary Stringfield - issued March 16, 1807, Bondsman:
Gideon Reynolds, Witness: Jno. Gamble, KNOX Co.

COCHRAN, Charles P. to Elizabeth Estill - issued May 24, 1855, m. by:
N. J. Fox, V. D. M., May 24, 1855, FRANKLIN Co.

COCHRAN, Daniel to Ellinor Moore - March 1, 1796, BLOUNT Co.

COCHRAN, Edward A. to Elizabeth Wade - issued July 16, 1825, m. by:
Peyton Smith July 17, 1825, RUTHERFORD Co.

COCHRAN, Elizabeth to David Johnson - GREENE Co.

COCHRAN, F. D. to Martha J. Green - issued January 18, 1864, Bondsman:
Luke King, m. by: J. M. Powell, J. P., January 19, 1864, LAWRENCE Co.

COCHRAN, Hugh L. to Margaret Reagan - September 4, 1797, Surety:
George Blackburn, BLOUNT Co.

COCHRAN, Isaac to Polly Kelly - April 10,20, 1799, BLOUNT Co.

COCHRAN, James to Mary A. Segraves - October 14, 1852, m. by:
Peter Shulen, J. P., GILES Co.

COCHRAN, James B. to Martha R. Williamson - October 7, 1860, m. by:
H. K. Shields, M. G., GILES Co.

COCHRAN, James E. to Rebecca Harvey - issued October 18, 1853, Bondsman:
David P. Hodges, m. by: Thos. H. Batson, J. P., October 20, 1853,
MONTGOMERY Co.

COCHRAN, John W. to Nancy D. Hudgins - issued May 15, 1850, m. by:
A. Rose, M. G., May 16, 1850, ROBERTSON Co.

COCHRAN, Samuel to Milly Brown - m. by: M. Hodges, J. P., December 3,
1822, SUMNER Co.

COCHRAN, William to Sally Corder - June 20, 1807, WILLIAMSON Co.

COCK, William to Elizabeth Hubbard - issued December 27, 1824, Bondsman:
Solomon Thomas, WILSON Co.

COCKE, Benjamin to Mary Cocke - issued October 4, 1850, Bondsman:
Jno. W. Hale, m. by: Jas. Majors, J. P., October 9, 1850,
MONTGOMERY Co.

COCKE, Flemming to Martha Williams - issued March 23, 1825, Bondsman:
William Gray, m. by: J. S. McCall, J. P., March 24, 1825, WILSON Co.

COCKE, Henry to Elizabeth Tipton - issued November 21, 1808, Bondsman:
Joshua Tipton, WILSON Co.

COCKE, James W. to Caroline E. Howell - issued January 15, 1835,
Bondsman: William T. Roberts, m. by: William Eagleton, V. D. M.,
January 15, 1835, RUTHERFORD Co.

COCKE, Jarratt to Martha Simpson - issued November 18, 1822, m. by:
Joshua Lester, V. D. M., November 21, 1822, WILSON Co.

COCKE, Senr., John to Elizabeth H. Williams - issued February 25, 1817,
Bondsman: William C. Collings, m. by: Joshua Lester, V. D. M.,
WILSON Co.

COCKE, John to Elizabeth Harris - issued February 17, 1818, Bondsman:
Leonard H. Sims, m. by: Joshua Lester, V. D. M., WILSON Co.

COCKE, John to Margaret J. Fouste - issued September 1, 1853, Bondsman:
C. C. Cocke, m. by: G. Orgain, J. P., September 1, 1853,
MONTGOMERY Co.

COCKE, John A. to Sarah Ann Williams - issued September 11, 1849,
Bondsman: Wm. G. Norris, m. by: R. P. Bowling, L. E. of M. E.
Church S., June 3, 1849, MONTGOMERY Co.

COCKE, Joseph to Sarah W. Winston - issued December 16, 1817, Bondsman:
William C. Collings, WILSON Co.

COCKE, Richard to Elenor Desha - issued July 1, 1806, Bondsman:
Thomas Cocke, SUMNER Co.

COCKE, Stephen to Elizabeth Ransdale - issued December 30, 1853,
Bondsman: Robert McCordie, m. by: R. W. Morrison, J. P., December 7,
1853, MONTGOMERY Co.

COCKE, Thos. J. to Ann E. George - issued November 17, 1845, Bondsman:
Pleasant Bagwell, m. by: Drury C. Stephens, G. M., November 18,
1845, MONTGOMERY Co.

COCKE, William J. to Manerva Bloodworth - issued November 7, 1831,
Bondsman: Jonathan Tipton, WILSON Co.

COCKE, William M. to Sarah F. Cocke - issued January 9, 1835, Bondsman:
David Barton, GRAINGER Co.

COCKERHAM, John to Annis Prowell - December 21, 1811, WILLIAMSON Co.

COCKRAN, Massey to Rachel Churchman - issued October 3, 1825, m. by:
J. Kennon, J. P., GRAINGER Co.

COCKRAN, James to Margaret Grainger - m. by: John Graves March 15, 1837,
SUMNER Co.

COCKRILL, James Thomas to Louisa Phelps - issued August 29, 1839, m. by:
Fountain E. Pitts, M. G., August 29, 1839, DAVIDSON Co.

COCKRUM, Loyd to Sarah Kinder - issued August 10, 1836, Bondsman:
Jackson Churchman, m. by: Levi Satterfield, M. G., GRAINGER Co.

COCKS, Isaac M. to Mary Ann Cunningham - issued March 5, 1846,
DAVIDSON Co.

CODY, John F. to Martha J. Garnett - issued April 10, 1865, m. by:
M. B. Clement, M. G., April 10, 1865, FRANKLIN Co.

CODY, Pierce to Delmah Floyd - issued September 1, 1831, Bondsman:
Robert Floyd, m. by: Levi Satterfield, M. G., GRAINGER Co.

COE, Isaac to Patsey Rather - issued August 1, 1811, Bondsman:
James Rather, WILSON Co.

COE, John to Patsey Parmer - issued December 27, 1825, Bondsman:
Alfred H. Harris, m. by: William Sypert, J. P., December 29, 1825,
WILSON Co.

COEN, John W. to Charlotte Monday - issued July 1, 1823, m. by:
Mordecai Yarnell, J. P., July 1, 1823, KNOX Co.

COFER, John to Nancy J. Shiflett - issued July 30, 1845, Bondsman:
Jacob J. Zeigler, m. by: John Seabourn, J. P., July 30, 1845,
MEIGS Co.

COFER, Joseph to Mary Ann Shiflet - issued July 28, 1842, Bondsman:
Joseph Jiles, m. by: John Seabern, J. P., July 25, 1842, MEIGS Co.

COFFEE, Cobby to Mary Adams - issued May 22, 1830, Bondsman:
John Rucker, GRAINGER Co.

COFFEE, James to Sally Fielding - issued December 14, 1825, Bondsman:
John Coffee, m. by: J. Kennon, M. G., December 14, 1825, GRAINGER Co.

COFFEE, Joel to Elizabeth Grubb - issued February 5, 1829, Bondsman:
Jacob Grubb, m. by: Jas. Kennon, M. G., GRAINGER Co.

COFFEL, James to Sarah Wyatt - August 27, 1796, Security: Samuel Wyatt,
GREENE Co.

COFFER (Coffee?), John to Rebecah Ragsdel (Ragsdale?) - issued
    February 24, 1821, Bondsman: Jacob Arnett, m. by: David Tate,
    J. P., February 27, 1821, GRAINGER Co.

COFFETT, Rebecca to John Bible - GREENE Co.

COFFEY, Michael W. to Anna Williams - issued April 8, 1842, Bondsman:
    Susan Graves, m. by: B. F. McKenzie, J. P., April 11, 1842,
    MEIGS Co.

COFFEY, Leven S. to Celia Perry - issued December 24, 1844, Bondsman:
    L. M. Stokes, m. by: Drury L. Godsey, M. G., December 24, 1844,
    MEIGS Co.

COFFEY, Phililia to James Turbow - MAURY Co.

COFFIMAN, William to Polly Wirick - issued March 22, 1819, Bondsman:
    Peter Boulton, m. by: Martin Cleveland, J. P., March 23, 1819,
    GRAINGER Co.

COFFIN, Chas. A. to Eliza Park - issued January 3, 1837, Bondsman:
    A. R. Humes, KNOX Co.

COFFIN, Charles H. to Eliza Park - issued January 3, 1837, m. by:
    T. H. Nelson, M. G., January 4, 1837, KNOX Co.

COFFMAN, Andrew to Anny Kirkpatrick - issued September 7, 1819, Bondsman:
    Thomas Coffman, m. by: John Kidwell, M. G., September 9, 1819,
    GRAINGER Co.

COFFMAN, Andrew P. to Elizabeth Clark - issued February 1, 1836,
    Bondsman: Enos Hammers, m. by: James Kenon, M. G., GRAINGER Co.

COFFMAN, Barton to Polly White - issued March 5, 1828, Bondsman:
    David Counts, m. March 5, 1828, GRAINGER Co.

COFFMAN, David to Susanah Bunch - issued August 20, 1813, Bondsman:
    Philip Free, GRAINGER Co.

COFFMAN, Jacob to Sarah James - issued October 17, 1862, Bondsman:
    Jos. H. Thompson, Security and Clerk, BEDFORD Co.

COFFMAN, James to Sarah Chumbley - May 23, 1833, KNOX Co.

COFFMAN, John to Moody Ann Sullivan - issued January 11, 1856, m. by:
    G. B. Mason, J. P., ROBERTSON Co.

COFFMAN, John N. to Rebecca A. Stark - issued August 12, 1858, m. by:
    J. F. Hardaway, J. P., ROBERTSON Co.

COFFMAN, Michael to Polly Henderson - issued May 9, 1813, Bondsman:
    Thomas Ogle, GRAINGER Co.

COFFMAN, Rhinehart to Sarah Beeler - issued January 22, 1831, Bondsman:
    Leanard Coffman, GRAINGER Co.

COFFMAN, Samuel to Jane Spratt - January 28, 1800, Security: John Newman,
    GREENE Co.

COFIRED, Willis to Maria McDonald - issued October 10, 1821, Bondsman:
    Stephen McDonald, WILSON Co.

COGGENS, Robert to Priscilla Merritt - issued December 24, 1832, m. by:
    J. Melton December 26, 1832, WILSON Co.

COGGINS, Eli to Nancy Ragsdale - issued December 19, 1835, Bondsman:
    John L. Casilman, m. by: G. H. Huddleston, J. P., December 22,
    1835, WILSON Co.

COGGINS, Eli to Polly Penny - issued June 3, 1839, Bondsman:
John F. Hancock, m. by: John Billingsley, J. P., June 25, 1839,
WILSON Co.

COGGINS, Mary S. to S. T. Cannon - BEDFORD Co.

COGHILL, Ambrose G. to Jemima Fuquay - issued September 19, 1844,
m. by: Isaac Steel, ROBERTSON Co.

COGLE, Mathew J. J. to Rebecca Bone - issued January 7, 1847, DICKSON Co.

COGWELL, James H. to Sarah Ethridge - issued July 1, 1840, Bondsman:
William Turner, WILSON Co.

COHEA, Alexander to Adeline Draughon - issued September 20, 1856, m. by:
G. Benton, J. P., ROBERTSON Co.

COHEA, H. to M. Pitt - issued November 19, 1851, m. by: David Hering,
J. P., ROBERTSON Co.

COHEA, Perry to Mary Benton - issued December 23, 1850, m. by:
D. Hering, J. P., ROBERTSON Co.

COHEE, Green W. to Martha F. Fort - issued October 28, 1845, m. by:
Thomas Martin, ROBERTSON Co.

COHEN, Elizabeth to Barnabas Gable - GREENE Co.

COIN, Elkainer to Martha Pyles - issued February 4, 1836, Bondsman:
V. H. Brown, SUMNER Co.

COINBR-?, Jamima to Francis Harbison - January 5, 1785, Security:
Alex. McCaughlan, GREENE Co.

COKE, Sterling (or Stirling Cocke) to Eliza Massingill - issued
August 25, 1814, m. by: Isaac Barton, J. P., September 6, 1814,
Witness: John Cocke, Clk., GRAINGER Co.

COKER, J. C. to Mary Richardson - issued March 5, 1866, m. by:
D. S. Long, J. P., March 5, 1866, FRANKLIN Co.

COKER, James to Polly McCammon - issued October 27, 1819, m. by:
Peter Nance, J. P., October 29, 1819, KNOX Co.

COKER, James R. to Margaret McTeer - issued January 3, 1837, Bondsman:
Chas. Lones, m. by: Wm. Billue, M. G., January 3, 1837, KNOX Co.

COKER, Joel to Susan McCampbell - issued June 9, 1807, Bondsman:
Philip Taylor, Witness: Jno. Purris, KNOX Co.

COKER, John to Sally Ferguson - issued December 16, 1826, m. by:
Sam'l Flenniken, J. P., December 17, 1826, KNOX Co.

COKER, John to Elizabeth Comings - issued May 9, 1849, m. by:
John Nugent, J. P., May 9, 1849, FRANKLIN Co.

COKER, Jno. P. to Bertha (or Rutha) Caldwell - issued June 16, 1836,
Bondsman: Leonard Coker, m. by: Jas. D. Murray, J. P., June 16,
1836, KNOX Co.

COKER, John T. to Anna Kirley - issued September 24, 1836, Bondsman:
Dan'l. Griggs, m. by: Taylor G. Gilliam September 24, 1836,
SUMNER Co.

COKER, Leonard to Elizabeth Williams - issued February 26, 1828,
Bondsman: James Coker, m. by: Wm. Lyon, J. P., February 28, 1828,
KNOX Co.

COKER, Melmuth to Milly Gipson - issued November 1, 1841, m. by:
J. P. Walker November, 1841, FRANKLIN Co.

COKER, Valentine to Thiny Lee - issued June 24, 1826, Bondsman:
Joseph T. Bell, m. by: Abner Hill, M. G., June 26, 1826, WILSON Co.

COKER, Warren to Polly Cunningham - issued September 28, 1808, Bondsman:
Joel Coker, Witness: Jno. A. Gamble, KNOX Co.

COKER, William to Jane Cumins - issued April 4, 1843, m. by:
D. N. Brakefield, J. P., April 5, 1843, FRANKLIN Co.

COKER, Willie to Eliza Taylor - February 1, 1817, KNOX Co.

COLBREN, John to E. A. Conn - issued October 30, 1851, m. by:
A. Rose, M. G., ROBERTSON Co.

COLBURN, John to C. C. Deckerd - issued November 23, 1866, FRANKLIN Co.

COLBY, Solon to Susan Cox - issued August 21, 1838, m. by:
John Corbitt, J. P., August 21, 1838, DAVIDSON Co.

COLDWELL, Edward to Elizabeth I. Durard - issued July 23, 1848, m. by:
J. Hardin, J. P., July 23, 1848, DICKSON Co.

COLDWELL, I. A. to Mary C. Turner - issued December 12, 1867, m. by:
J. Campbell, M. G., December 12, 1867, FRANKLIN Co.

COLDWELL, John to Sophia Knight - issued February 12, 1868, m. by:
James Seargent, J. P., February 13, 1868, FRANKLIN Co.

COLDWELL, John H. to Donna M. Christian - issued March 5, 1848, m. by:
Allen Nesbitt, J. P., March 5, 1848, DICKSON Co.

COLE, Andrew to Priscilla Woolsey - September 29, 1798, Security:
Philip Cole, GREENE Co.

COLE, Andrew to Sally Crafton - September 22, 1812, WILLIAMSON Co.

COLE, Andrew J. to Ellen Villines - issued June 8, 1850, m. by:
Wm. H. Rife, J. P., June 9, 1850, ROBERTSON Co.

COLE, Bartholemeu, to Amelia Witzel - issued April 25, 1843, DAVIDSON Co.

COLE, Benjamin to Polly Walker - March 21, 1821, KNOX Co.

COLE, Caleb to Polly G. Wright - issued March 16, 1815, Bondsman:
Byrd Izel, Witness: A. Hutcheson, KNOX Co.

COLE, Champ T. to Polly Covington - issued October 1, 1840, m. by:
W. Hailey P October 8, 1840, ROBERTSON Co.

COLE, Crawford to Elizabeth Whitemill - issued December 23, 1841,
m. by: Benja. Gambill, J. P., ROBERTSON Co.

COLE, David to Diley Pike - issued February 21, 1821, Bondsman:
Tobias Henderson, WILSON Co.

COLE, Dixon to Sally Tucker - December 3, 1811, WILLIAMSON Co.

COLE, Elisha to Elizabeth Moss (Mays) - issued November 19, 1800,
Bondsman: William Howorth and John Arnwine, Witness: Robert Yancey,
GRAINGER Co.

COLE, Henderson to Malinda Cole - issued March 30, 1840, m. by:
William Haley, J. P., March 31, 1840, ROBERTSON Co.

COLE, Henry to Frances Johnson - issued April 21, 1841, DICKSON Co.

COLE, Henry A. to Elizabeth H. Garland - issued November 11, 1846,
Bondsman: C. B. Haskins, m. by: W. C. Crane, Rector, Trinity
Church, Clarksville, November 11, 1846, MONTGOMERY Co.

COLE, Isham to Nelly Reed - December 26, 1806, WILLIAMSON Co.

COLE, J. B. to Jennetta Corner - issued May 3, 1856, m. by:
E. W. Gunn, M. G., May 4, 1856, ROBERTSON Co.

COLE, J. M. to E. Henry - issued December 2, 1847, m. by: James Sprouse,
J. P., ROBERTSON Co.

COLE, James to Jane Underwood - m. by: Lewis Hiett September 2, 1837,
SUMNER Co.

COLE, James to Susan Graybill - issued November 14, 1871, m. by:
J. B. Hudgins, J. P., November 16, 1871, FRANKLIN Co.

COLE, James B. to Jacout Bridges - issued July 27, 1826, Bondsman:
Aaron Britton, m. by: B. Bridges, J. P., July 30, 1826, WILSON Co.

COLE, Jas. F. to Harriet Stark - issued July 7, 1860, m. by: E. Burr,
J. P., July 8, 1860, ROBERTSON Co.

COLE, John to Polly Mizer - issued March 13, 1820, Bondsman: Wm. Allen,
m. by: Jno. Haynie, D. M. E., March 13, 1820, KNOX Co.

COLE, John to Lucy Parker - issued June 23, 1836, Bondsman:
Joseph Parker, m. by: B. McNutt, J. P., June 23, 1836, KNOX Co.

COLE, John to Sophia A. Burcham - issued June 18, 1844, Bondsman:
Wm. Wan, Jr., m. by: D. L. Godsey, M. G., June 20, 1844, MEIGS Co.

COLE, John N. to Eliza Jane Walker - issued October 31, 1843, m. by:
Wm. H. Hamblin, J. P., November 2, 1843, DAVIDSON Co.

COLE, Joseph to Nancy Simmons - October 22, 1812, WILLIAMSON Co.

COLE, Joshua P. to Rachiel J. Moore - issued October 12, 1841, m. by:
John Roleman, J. P., October 12, 1841, FRANKLIN Co.

COLE, Philip to Rebecca English - February 20, 1794, Security:
James English, GREENE Co.

COLE, Sally to John Robinson, Jr. - GREENE Co.

COLE, Sam'l to Polly Deal - April 14, 1807, WILLIAMSON Co.

COLE, Samuel to Anna Johnston - September 9, 1818, GREENE Co.

COLE, Samuel P. to Rosanna M. Baker - issued September 1, 1841,
FRANKLIN Co.

COLE, Stephen to Dosha Turner - issued January 15, 1848, m. by:
J. W. Judkins, J. P., January 18, 1848, ROBERTSON Co.

COLE, Thomas to Margaret Tillery - issued September 27, 1827, m. by:
Mordecai Yarnell, J. P., September 27, 1827, KNOX Co.

COLE, Thos. to Nellie Ellison - issued August 26, 1861, m. by:
A. Cook, J. P., ROBERTSON Co.

COLE, W. P. to M. C. Riddle - issued October 14, 1869, FRANKLIN Co.

COLE, William to Peggy McWilliams - March 9, 1811, Bondsman:
Hugh McWilliams, MAURY Co.

COLE, William to Fanny Law - issued October 15, 1825, Bondsman:
Joseph Cole, m. by: Sam'l Davis, J. P., October 15, 1825, SUMNER Co.

COLE, Wm. to Mathiah Ashley - issued April 2, 1836, Bondsman:
Wm. Mourfield, Witness: Geo. M. White, KNOX Co.

COLE, William to Mary Osborn - issued November 2, 1852, m. by: Lemuel Brandon, M. G., November 2, 1852, FRANKLIN Co.

COLE, William to Angeline Irvin - issued October 8, 1856, m. by: John Crawford, J. P., October 9, 1856, ROBERTSON Co.

COLE, Wm. to Sarah Woods - issued November 24, 1863, Bondsman: Alfred Devins, Jos. H. Thompson, Clk., BEDFORD Co.

COLE, William A. to Elanor L. Moss - issued July 7, 1860, m. by: Jas. N. Thornhill, J. P., July 9, 1860, ROBERTSON Co.

COLE, William Temple to Mary Brown - issued September 19, 1800, Bondsman: James Bentley, SUMNER Co.

COLE, Willie W. to Gertrude McMahan - issued September 16, 1846, DAVIDSON Co.

COLEMAN, Abram K. to Frances M. Lee - issued December 12, 1844, m. by: Wm. Burr, M. G., December 12, 1844, STEWART Co.

COLEMAN, Alexander to Nancy Jane Newton - October 6, 1852, m. by: J. A. Beall, J. P., GILES Co.

COLEMAN, Alfred to Alpha Thomas - issued February 7, 1844, m. by: Thos. S. Elliott, M. G., February 16, 1844, STEWART Co.

COLEMAN, Baley to Cathrine Miller - issued July 14, 1851, m. by: John Roleman, J. P., July 14, 1851, FRANKLIN Co.

COLEMAN, Charles A. to Sarah M. Moseley - issued December 27, 1852, m. by: B. Franks, L. D., December 28, 1852, FRANKLIN Co.

COLEMAN, Chastain A. to Lucy Smith - issued December 11, 1829, Bondsman: Jesse Roberts, m. by: John Lane December 14, 1829, RUTHERFORD Co.

COLEMAN, Daniel to Sarah Higgins, J. P. - issued January 23, 1854, Bondsman: Frank S. Beaumont, m. by: J. C. Bryan, J. P., MONTGOMERY Co.

COLEMAN, Downden H. to Patsey Hall - issued March 13, 1827, Bondsman: James Coleman, SUMNER Co.

COLEMAN, Edward L. to M. C. Small - m. by: N. B. Lewis, M. G., October 29, 1846, ROBERTSON Co.

COLEMAN, Grief to Rebecca Coleman - issued July 30, 1824, Bondsman: Ephraim Meadors, m. by: Wm. Vinson, J. P., July 30, 1824, RUTHERFORD Co.

COLEMAN, Henry to Frances Burns - issued December 25, 1843, m. by: M. Berry, M. G., December 26, 1843, DICKSON Co.

COLEMAN, James to Sally Hickey - issued May 1, 1822, Bondsman: Jacob Lones, m. by: James C. Luttrell, J. P., May 2, 1822, KNOX Co.

COLEMEN, James to Leather Shoemake - issued March 28, 1832, Bondsman: Edward Lee, m. by: Dan'l McAulay, J. P., March 28, 1832, SUMNER Co.

COLEMAN, James I. to Margaret J. Harrison - issued November 23, 1850, m. by: Benjamin Rawls, M. G., ROBERTSON Co.

COLEMAN, Jas. L. to Catharine A. Lester - October 2, 1856, m. by: G. D. Talor, GILES Co.

COLEMAN, Jesse to Elizabeth Bivins - issued October 26, 1836, Bondsman: Wiley Harman, m. by: J. D. Rogers, J. P., November 24, 1836, RUTHERFORD Co.

COLEMAN, Jesse to Priscilla L. Terry - issued December 24, 1838, m. by:
L. Russell, J. P., December 24, 1838, DICKSON Co.

COLEMAN, John to Nancy Lewis - issued August 13, 1818, Bondsman:
Ansil D. Bugg, SUMNER Co.

COLEMAN, John to Temperance W. Harris - issued April 5, 1827, Bondsman:
Joel Neal, RUTHERFORD Co.

COLEMAN, John to Milley Coleman - issued September 25, 1833, Bondsman:
Charles A. Frensley, RUTHERFORD Co.

COLEMAN, John W. to Elizabeth Gray - issued September 23, 1842, m. by:
J. C. Pullen, J. P., September 25, 1842, DICKSON Co.

COLEMAN, Jordan to Nancy Anderson - issued December 18, 1809, Bondsman:
James H. Gambill, RUTHERFORD Co.

COLEMAN, Jordan P. to Senith Turner - m. by: J. W. Hall December 25,
1838, SUMNER Co.

COLEMAN, Joseph to Temperance Rogers - issued June 7, 1824, m. by:
Jacob Payne, J. P., June 17, 1824, RUTHERFORD Co.

COLEMAN, L. E. to M. B. Muse - issued October 20, 1862, Bondsman:
Wm. Thompson, Security, Jos. H. Thompson, Clerk per James H. Neil,
Dep. Clk., BEDFORD. Co.

COLEMAN, L. E. to W. T. Thompson - issued September 15, 1863, Bondsman:
Jno. F. T. Jones, Jos. H. Thompson, Clk. per James H. Neil,
Dep. Clk., BEDFORD Co.

COLEMAN, Mordecai to Elizabeth Coleman - issued December 6, 1834,
Bondsman: D. Caldwell, RUTHERFORD Co.

COLEMAN, Richard H. to Susan Ann Weatherford - issued October 12, 1852,
Bondsman: John H. Johnson, m. by: Wm. Dinwiddie October 19, 1852,
MONTGOMERY Co.

COLEMAN, Stephen H. to Nancy P. Harrisson - issued August 29, 1825,
Bondsman: Joshua Harrison, m. by: James T. Tompkins, D. D.,
September 1, 1825, WILSON Co.

COLEMAN, Thomas to Eliza D. Cage - issued October 19, 1826, Bondsman:
G. N. Douglas, SUMNER Co.

COLEMAN, William to Sophy Perryman - issued November 8, 1823, Bondsman:
Henry Condry, m. by: Alexander Hamilton, J. P., November 8, 1823,
GRAINGER Co.

COLEMAN, William to Susan Lewis - issued November 20, 1833, Bondsman:
Lewelling Williams, m. by: James Sanford December 10, 1833,
RUTHERFORD Co.

COLEMAN, William to Elizabeth Hodge - issued __(?) 12, 1834, Bondsman:
Wm. A. Coleman, RUTHERFORD Co.

COLEMAN, Wm. D. to Mary E. Seay - issued October 21, 1850, Bondsman:
John Hollman, MONTGOMERY Co.

COLEMAN, William L. to Lucy I. Bryant - issued September 2, 1841,
m. by: Robert Green, P., ROBERTSON Co.

COLEMAN, Wm. W. to Mary R. Johston - July 23, 1832, WILLIAMSON Co.

COLES, Isaac G. to Mary Ann Walters - issued May 14, 1823, Bondsman:
John Walters, m. by: N. Sanders, J. P., May 14, 1823, SUMNER Co.

COLES, Isaac G. to Mary E. Gillum - issued May 17, 1860, m. by:
W. W. Pepper, Judge 10th Circuit of Tenn., ROBERTSON Co.

COLES, John H. B. to Elizabeth White - issued October 17, 1829, Bondsman: George Apperson, WILSON Co.

COLES, Samuel to Calister Walker - issued March 10, 1828, Bondsman: John Davis, m. by: Dnl. Moser, J. P., March 11, 1828, WILSON Co.

COLES, Samuel to Sally Walker - issued July 2, 1829, Bondsman: John James, m. by: Elijah Boddie, J. P., July 2, 1829, SUMNER Co.

COLES, William T. F. to Lititia Shepherd - issued June 24, 1839, Bondsman: Daniel Barley, m. by: Melkizah S. Vaughn, M. G., June 25, 1839, WILSON Co.

COLEWICK, William to Margarette Steele - issued August 7, 1823, Bondsman: B. Taylor, WILSON Co.

COLEY, Berry to Jane Frisby - issued July 27, 1827, Bondsman: Jno. McDonough, m. by: J. A. Swan, J. P., July 27, 1827, KNOX Co.

COLEY, William to Rosey Perry - issued June 2, 1828, Bondsman: Benjamin Crews, m. June 2, 1828, SUMNER Co.

COLLET, Rebecca to Jesse O'Neil - GREENE Co.

COLLETT, Abraham to Nancy Ellis - March 23, 1802, Security: John Ellis, GREENE Co.

COLLETT, Abraham to Jane Sutton - October 23, 1804, Security: Henry Earnest, GREENE Co.

COLLEY, Charles to Polley Lissick - issued December 28, 1840, m. by: P. B. Morris, J. P., December 28, 1840, DAVIDSON Co.

COLLEY, Thos. H. to Sarah E. Howard - issued June 9, 1849, Bondsman: Wm. S. Bradley, m. by: John Gold June 9, 1849, MONTGOMERY Co.

COLLEY, Thomas S. to Emily V. Shackleford - issued May 18, 1854, m. by: R. M. Haggard, M. G., May 18, 1854, COFFEE Co.

COLLIER,   (?) to David Hays - October 9, 1793, Security: Hugh Hays, GREENE Co.

COLLIER, Eleanor to Thomas Johston - March 12, 1799, Security: John Collier, GREENE Co.

COLLIER, Hugh to Martha Jane Turner - issued January 4, 1854, Bondsman: M. J. Allison, m. by: M. G. Carney, M. G., January 4, 1854, MONTGOMERY Co.

COLLIER, Ingram B. to Martha Covington - issued December 13, 1817, m. by: Sol. Beesley, J. P., December 24, 1817, RUTHERFORD Co.

COLLIER, Isaac to Jane Bowman - issued December 27, 1826, Bondsman: Dan'l Escue, m. by: James Charlton, J. P., December 27, 1826, SUMNER Co.

COLLIER, J. to Elizabeth Bowers - issued January 20, 1851, Bondsman: John M. Bowers, MONTGOMERY Co.

COLLIER, Jane to Robert Hays - GREENE Co.

COLLIER, P. P. to Susan D. Bryan - issued July 21, 1830, m. by: Peyton Smith July 22, 1830, RUTHERFORD Co.

COLLIER, Richard to Lucinda Wooldridge - issued April 7, 1842, DAVIDSON Co.

COLLIER, Susanna to Hugh Hays - GREENE Co.

COLLIER, Thomas to Susan Donnell - issued December 29, 1824, Bondsman: William Parker, m. by: John Parker, L. D., December 29, 1824, SUMNER Co.

COLLIER, Thomas to Mary Shelton - issued November 22, 1838, DAVIDSON Co.

COLLIERS, Abner to Elerna Milam - issued February 17, 1809, Bondsman: L. Sims, SUMNER Co.

COLLINGS, Charles to Elizabeth Sanders - issued March 10, 1821, Bondsman: Elisha Collings, WILSON Co.

COLLINGS, George to Nancy Renshaw - issued September 15, 1821, Bondsman: Jeremiah Collings, WILSON Co.

COLLINGS, Jeremiah to Gilly Evans - issued August 26, 1824, Bondsman: Lemuel Nickings, m. by: James Drennon, J. P., WILSON Co.

COLLINGS, John C. to Mahaly Wortham - issued March 20, 1819, Bondsman: James Howard, WILSON Co.

COLLINGSWORTH, Addison to Francis Combs - issued December 11, 1825, Bondsman: Robert Loyd, m. by: J. Kennon, M. G., December 11, 1825, GRAINGER Co.

COLLINS, A. J. to Nancy C. Lane - issued June 23, 1863, Bondsman: Howell Williams, BEDFORD Co.

COLLINS, A. W. to S. L. Metcalf - issued February 26, 1868, m. by: G. W. Bowling, J. P., February 26, 1868, FRANKLIN Co.

COLLINS, Alexander to Emely Gressom - issued August 8, 1836, Bondsman: Moses Collins, GRAINGER Co.

COLLINS, Alfred to Mary A. Campbell - issued September 9, 1842, m. by: Wm. Little, J. P., September 12, 1842, FRANKLIN Co.

COLLINS, Allen to Biddy Collins - issued October 24, 1827, Bondsman: Moses Collins, m. October 24, 1827, GRAINGER Co.

COLLINS, Ann to David Hinds - MAURY Co.

COLLINS, Barbee to Louisa C. Hicks - issued January 22, 1850, m. by: R. C. Smith, J. P., January 24, 1850, FRANKLIN Co.

COLLINS, Conley to Comfort Nickles - issued April 26, 1828, Bondsman: Winston Painter, GRAINGER Co.

COLLINS, Crafford to Polly Collins - issued September 26, 1829, Bondsman: James Nickens, WILSON Co.

COLLINS, Crofford to Polly Collins - issued September 20, 1828, m. by: Joshua Woollen, M. G., September 27, 1828, WILSON Co.

COLLINS, David to Mary Dodson - issued February 6, 1801, Bondsman: Charles McEnelly, GRAINGER Co.

COLLINS, Dowell to Mary Ennis - issued September 22, 1806, Bondsman: Griffin Collins, GRAINGER Co.

COLLINS, Edmond to Delpha Drennon - issued January 13, 1819, Bondsman: Henry Belote, WILSON Co.

COLLINS, Erastus T. to Martha North - December 13, 1817, WILLIAMSON Co.

COLLINS, George to Mariah Carback - issued June 7, 1828, Bondsman: Thomas Carback, m. by: David Tate, J. P., GRAINGER Co.

COLLINS, George W. to Catharine J. Diddley - issued March 3, 1863, Bondsman: A. V. Tomme, Jos. H. Thompson, Clk. per M. E. W. Dunaway, Dep. Clk., BEDFORD Co.

COLLINS, Ira D. to Nancy Sikes - issued June 19, 1848, m. by:
Allen McCaskill, J. P., June 20, 1848, STEWART Co.

COLLINS, Isaiah to Betsy (or Elizabeth) Mason - issued November 20,
1805, Bondsman: David McAnally, Esqr., GRAINGER Co.

COLLINS, James to Elizabeth Martin - issued January 17, 1825, Bondsman:
William Benney, m. by: Jno. Bunch, J. P., January 17, 1825,
GRAINGER Co.

COLLINS, James to Elizabeth Keane - m. by: Jas. L. Martin, J. P.,
May 10, 1834, SUMNER Co.

COLLINS, James to Jane Rigg - issued September 13, 1843, Bondsman:
James A. Carven, m. by: B. F. McKenzie, J. P., September 14, 1843,
MEIGS Co.

COLLINS, James to Lucinda E. Church - issued May 28, 1852, m. by:
Allison Akin, M. G., May 30, 1852, FRANKLIN Co.

COLLINS, James to Martha McDowell - issued January 3, 1855, m. by:
James W. Williams, Local Preacher, January 8, 1855, COFFEE Co.

COLLINS, James B. to Martha Ann Foster - issued March 21, 1843,
DAVIDSON Co.

COLLINS, James G. to Sarah P. Breeden - issued October 3, 1840, m. by:
John R. Patrick, J. P., October 4, 1840, FRANKLIN Co.

COLLINS, James H. to Caledonia Forbsbee - issued December 17, 1871,
FRANKLIN Co.

COLLINS, James H. to Sarah Garner - issued October 13, 1873, m. by:
C. C. Rose, J. P., October 16, 1873, FRANKLIN Co.

COLLINS, Jas. S. to Harkles P. Thompson - issued January 11, 1827,
Bondsman: John Smothers, RUTHERFORD Co.

COLLINS, Jesse to Irin Wynne - issued September 30, 1829, Bondsman:
George Thomas, WILSON Co.

COLLINS, Jesse to Julia Collins - issued December 1, 1830, Bondsman:
William Patrick, WILSON Co.

COLLINS, Jessee to Sarah Thomas - issued February 8, 1851, m. by:
J. J. Travis, J. P., February 9, 1851, FRANKLIN Co.

COLLINS, John to Lydia Toner - issued October 8, 1821, Bondsman:
Griffin Collins, GRAINGER Co.

COLLINS, John to Nancy Drew - issued April 2, 1829, Bondsman:
William Patrick, m. by: Joshua Woollen, M. G., April 3, 1829,
WILSON Co.

COLLINS, John to Minerva Chapman - issued February 13, 1830, m. by:
Wm. A. McCampbell, M. V. D., February 16, 1830, KNOX Co.

COLLINS, John to Charlotte Nelson - issued March 2, 1848, m. by:
W. M. Sells, J. P., March 2, 1848, FRANKLIN Co.

COLLINS, John to Canzada Pack - issued September 23, 1867, m. by:
Wm. Prince, J. P., September 23, 1867, FRANKLIN Co.

COLLINS, Josiah to Mary Pearson - issued September 6, 1844, m. by:
M. Catchings, J. P., FRANKLIN Co.

COLLINS, Lewis to Catherine Baughman - issued August 25, 1831, Bondsman:
Samuel Widner, m. by: J. Godwin, J. P., GRAINGER Co.

COLLINS, Lewis D. to Sally Ann Hickerson - issued July 10, 1839, m. by:
John Eubanks, J. P., July 14, 1839, DICKSON Co.

COLLINS, M. to J. F. Piant - issued October 8, 1861, Bondsman:
H. R. Green, Jr., Jos. H. Thompson, Clk. per N. F. Thompson,
Dep. Clk., BEDFORD Co.

COLLINS, M. D. J. to Martha S. P. Mangrum - issued August 31, 1863,
Bondsman: Jos. H. Thompson, Clk. per M. E. W. Dunaway, Dep. Clk.,
m. by: A. N. Vincent, J. P., August 31, 1863, BEDFORD Co.

COLLINS, P. M. to Sarah Ann Garner - issued October 13, 1873, m. by:
C. C. Rose, J. P., October 13, 1873, FRANKLIN Co.

COLLINS, Rice to Elizabeth Shaw - issued December 12, 1870, FRANKLIN Co.

COLLINS, Snoch to Susan J. Phillips - issued December 11, 1841,
DAVIDSON Co.

COLLINS, W. D. to A. E. Gipson - issued May 25, 1874, m. by:
C. C. Rose, J. P., March 31, 1874, FRANKLIN Co.

COLLINS, William to Patsy McAfee - March 19, 1808, WILLIAMSON Co.

COLLINS, William to Mary Ann Carter - issued July 2, 1837, Bondsman:
Enos Dalton, m. by: Benjamin Lewis, M. G., July 2, 1837, GRAINGER Co.

COLLINS, William C. to Sarah Wortham - issued July 2, 1817, Bondsman:
Joseph Cocke, WILSON Co.

COLLINS, Wm. J. to Eliza J. Myrick - issued October 13, 1856, m. by:
R. C. Smith, J. P., October 14, 1856, FRANKLIN Co.

COLLINS, William J. to Martha L. Wilson - issued August 9, 1861,
Bondsman: Howell Williams, Jos. H. Thompson, Clk. per James H. Neil,
Dep. Clk., BEDFORD Co.

COLLINS, William L. to Mary J. Bickley - issued December 3, 1860,
m. by: David Lipscomb, M. G., December 11, 1860, FRANKLIN Co.

COLLINGSWORTH, Benjamin F. to Elizabeth Mason - issued September 19,
1825, m. by: John Lane, RUTHERFORD Co.

COLLIS, Henry to Elizabeth Farrington - issued September 23, 1830,
Bondsman: William Dollner, m. by: James Foster, J. P., WILSON Co.

COLLISHAW, John H. to Sarah Elizabeth Baker - issued February 28, 1854,
Bondsman: James A. Pennington, MONTGOMERY Co.

COLLISHAW, Joseph A. to Sarah A. Riggins - issued January 12, 1854,
Bondsman: A. H. Judkins, MONTGOMERY Co.

COLLISON, John to Nancy Grove - issued September 1, 1836, Bondsman:
James McFarland, m. by: Wm. E. Cocke, J. P., GRAINGER Co.

COLLISSEN, Jr., James to Elizabeth Young - issued July 17, 1800,
Bondsman: John Collison, Senr., Witness: Robert Yancey, GRAINGER Co.

COLLUM, Ezekiah Barnes (or Ezekiah Collum Barnes) to Dotia Stone -
issued August 23, 1817, Bondsman: John Moore, m. by: James Douglas,
J. P., August 23, 1817, SUMNER Co.

COLSON, Tamar to John Ellis - GREENE Co.

COLTON, E. N. to Caroline Crabtree - issued December 23, 1868, m. by:
James Campbell, G. M., December 24, 1868, FRANKLIN Co.

COLTON, J. M. to S. S. Green - issued February 14, 1870, FRANKLIN Co.

COLVILLE, Joseph to Martha Smartt - December 21, 1802, Surety:
Gideon Blackburn, BLOUNT Co.

COLVIN, Elijah to Susan Moulder - issued December 3, 1822, Bondsman:
Hayman Claridge, m. by: Valentine Moulder, J. P., December 3, 1822,
GRAINGER Co.

COLVIN, James to Barcary Phipps - issued December 14, 1826, Bondsman:
James Phipps, m. by: Thos. Brown, J. P., December 14, 1826,
GRAINGER Co.

COLWELL, William to Polly Curry - issued May 19, 1806, Bondsman:
John Curry, RUTHERFORD Co.

COLYAR, Arther S. to Agnes E. Estill - issued December 9, 1847, m. by:
N. P. Modrall December 9, 1847, FRANKLIN Co.

COLYAR, James S. to M. A. Provine - issued August 28, 1840, m. by:
George Hudspeth, J. P., FRANKLIN Co.

COMAR, John to Peggy McCarty - issued March 18, 1805, Bondsman:
Elijah Pruett, SUMNER Co.

COMBS, Henry to Judith Smith - May 20, 1815, WILLIAMSON Co.

COMBS, J. J. to Mary E. McKelvey - issued October 28, 1873, m. by:
John W. Bragg October 28, 1873, FRANKLIN Co.

COMBS, John to Jinney Jackson - issued July 15, 1807, Bondsman:
Lewis Combs, GRAINGER Co.

COMBS, John to Dorcus Cox - issued September 11, 1826, Bondsman:
John Talbot, m. by: Jas. Kennon, M. G., September 11, 1826,
GRAINGER Co.

COMBS, John A. to Margret Goldin - issued December 17, 1843, FRANKLIN Co.

COMBS, Lewis to Jinny Smith - issued July 5, 1803, GRAINGER Co.

COMBS, Pleasant to Mary Hayworth - issued February 16, 1830, Bondsman:
Joseph Combs, m. by: Jas. Kennon, J. P., GRAINGER Co.

COMBS, Thomas to Anna Anderson - issued May 30, 1829, Bondsman:
John Anderson, m. May 30, 1829, SUMNER Co.

COMBS, Thomas to M. C. Anderson (MB) - issued November 8, 1869,
FRANKLIN Co.

COMBS, William to Elizabeth Luton - issued April 19, 1829, Bondsman:
John J. King, SUMNER Co.

COMER, Aaron to Levina Bell - issued February 27, 1833, Bondsman:
Francis G. Brown, m. by: Mordecai __(?), J. P., February 28, 1833,
KNOX Co.

COMER, Jas. to Sarah Ellison - issued December 2, 1828, Bondsman:
John L. Allison, WILSON Co.

COMER, James B. to Martha Shanon - issued January 21, 1835, Bondsman:
James Johns, m. by: Levi Holloway, J. P., January 22, 1835,
WILSON Co.

COMER, Robert to Sarah E. McMasters - September 7, 1858, m. by:
Thos. H. Noblett, J. P., GILES Co.

COMER, Sam'l R. to Mahala Marrs - issued October 12, 1830, m. by:
Jno. F. Doak, J. P., WILSON Co.

COMER, Samuel R. to Jane Jackson - issued August 20, 1835, Bondsman:
A. H. Foster, m. by: James Foster, J. P., WILSON Co.

COMER, Stephen E. to Anna Marrs - issued October 22, 1836, Bondsman:
Sam R. Comer, WILSON Co.

COMER, Stephen E. to Anna Marrs - issued October 22, 1836, m. by:
R. Comer, J. P., October 28, 1836, WILSON Co.

COMPERRI, W. B. to Lucinda Simms - issued June 27, 1847, Bondsman:
W. B. Carney, m. by: W. B. Carney, J. P., June 27, 1847,
MONTGOMERY Co.

COMPTON, Alexander J. to Martha Wood - issued September 4, 1827,
Bondsman: Mathew Compton, WILSON Co.

COMPTON, Allen to Mary Bettis - issued January 8, 1832, Bondsman:
Allison Sypert, m. by: Henry Hobson, J. P., January 13, 1832,
WILSON Co.

COMPTON, Braxton to Polly Underwood - issued September 3, 1838,
Bondsman: William Acols, m. by: J. W. Locke, J. P., September 4,
1838, WILSON Co.

COMPTON, Charles to Nancy Hancock - issued July 9, 1831, Bondsman:
Northern Nooner, m. by: William Philips, J. P., August 23, 1831,
WILSON Co.

COMPTON, Dewitt C. to Nancy M. Gibson - December 6, 1855, m. by:
Wm. Peaton, J. P., GILES Co.

COMPTON, Edward to Mason Booker - issued February 20, 1836, m. by:
Sion Bass, M. G., WILSON Co.

COMPTON, John to Lucinda Travilion - issued June 9, 1812, Bondsman:
Wm. Harris, WILSON Co.

COMPTON, John to Cathrine Awatt (Awalt) - issued October 3, 1849, m. by:
J. J. Travis, J. P., October 4, 1849, FRANKLIN Co.

COMPTON, Nancy to John Leaper - MAURY Co.

COMPTON, Robert to Elizabeth Warren - issued January 4, 1839, Bondsman:
Lofton Echols, m. by: Wm. S. Wallis, J. P., January 5, 1839,
WILSON Co.

COMPTON, Thomas to Susan Murphy - issued March 30, 1846, m. by:
R. B. C. Howell, M. G., March 31, 1846, DAVIDSON Co.

COMPTON, Vincent to Mary Scurlock - issued December 20, 1832, Bondsman:
Thos. Sypert, m. by: Henry Hobson, J. P., WILSON Co.

COMPTON, William to Eliza Coe - issued August 29, 1831, Bondsman:
John Barbee, WILSON Co.

COMPTON, William to Martha Ferrell - issued December 21, 1836, m. by:
Wm. __(?), WILSON Co.

COMPTON, William to Rachel M. Nunn - issued October 11, 1837, Bondsman:
Mosses Atwood, m. by: Sion Bass, M. G., WILSON Co.

CON, James N. to Elizabeth McMurry - issued January 25, 1834,
RUTHERFORD Co.

CONATSER, Nicholas to Sally L. Wherry - issued September 4, 1823,
Bondsman: Eli Nicholas, m. September 4, 1823, RUTHERFORD Co.

CONAWAY, Daniel to Betsy Night - issued March 2, 1846, m. by:
Benj. Sells, J. P., March 2, 1846, FRANKLIN Co.

CONDON, James to Ellen Adams - issued February 22, 1839, m. by:
C. G. Macpherson February 27, 1839, DAVIDSON Co.

CONDRAY, Mathius to Rebecca Anderson - issued January 5, 1812, Bondsman: James Seamore, GRAINGER Co.

CONDREY, Pherney to Peggy Condrey - issued July 27, 1821, Bondsman: George Moulder, m. by: Valentine Moulder, J. P., GRAINGER Co.

CONDRY, Homar to Myra Branson - issued September 15, 1827, Bondsman: Lathim Blackburn, m. by: Owen Dyer, J. P., September 15, 1827, GRAINGER Co.

CONDRY, Isaac to Rebeccah Haynes - issued April 9, 1825, Bondsman: William Easley, m. by: John Wood, D. D., April 9, 1825, GRAINGER Co.

CONDRY, James to Esther Hibbert - March 3, 1789, Security: Michael Harrison, GREENE Co.

CONDRY, Pherncy to Sarah Moulder - issued March 23, 1820, Bondsman: G. W. L. Moulder, m. by: Valentine Moulder, J. P., GRAINGER Co.

CONDRY, William to Mancy Stanley - issued November 15, 1804, Bondsman: Mathew Talley, GRAINGER Co.

CONE, Colier to Elizabeth Goldin - issued March 10, 1845, DAVIDSON Co.

CONEY, Patrick to Mary Bryant - issued June 9, 1944, m. by: James Woodard, J. P., ROBERTSON Co.

CONGER, Adam to Kizziah Davis - issued December 29, 1817, Bondsman: Abner Harpole, m. by: Elijah Maddox, M. G., December 30, 1817, WILSON Co.

CONGER, John to Susanah Spradling - issued October 30, 1819, Bondsman: Cornemus Buck, m. by: Abner Hill, M. G., November 5, 1819, WILSON Co.

CONGER, John to Meecy Hill - issued April 3, 1821, Bondsman: Walter Carr, m. by: Wm. Peace, J. P., WILSON Co.

CONGER, Samuel to Elizabeth Kenedy - issued April 20, 1822, Bondsman: John Conger, m. by: Abner Hill, M. G., April 25, 1822, WILSON Co.

CONGER, Thos. to Sally Aust - issued July 5, 1823, Bondsman: John Conger, m. by: G. H. Bussard, J. P., August 20, 1823, WILSON Co.

CONGER, William to Aggey Arrington - issued March 3, 1814, Bondsman: Philip Bryen, WILSON Co.

CONGERS, Thomas W. to Martha Walker - issued December 16, 1835, Bondsman: Little Berry Wright, m. by: Henry Hobson, J. P., December 17, 1835, WILSON Co.

CONGILL, Martin to Sally Perry - issued November 19, 1827, m. by: Wm. Walton, J. P., November 19, 1827, SUMNER Co.

CONGILL, Washington to Vilet Hager - issued October 22, 1833, m. by: John Beard, M. G., October 23, 1833, WILSON Co.

CONLAN, James W. to Catherine A. Wiert - issued August 26, 1839, m. by: J. T. Edgar August 27, 1839, DAVIDSON Co.

CONLEE, Daniel to Susanna Randolph - December 10, 1800, Security: Isaac Conlee, GREENE Co.

CONLEY, Abram to Sally Hoskins - issued August 28, 1830, Bondsman: Richard Conley, m. by: B. B. Cannon, J. P., August 29, 1830, Witness: Wm. Swan, KNOX Co.

CONLEY, Daniel to Francis Kulin - issued April 2, 1855, m. by: Rev. Jno. M. Jacquet April 9, 1855, FRANKLIN Co.

CONLEY, James M. to Nancy Coker - issued July 21, 1836, m. by:
   R. H. Lindsay, M. G., July 21, 1836, KNOX Co.

CONLEY, John B. to Susan Virginia Conley - February 16, 1858, m. by:
   W. G. Hensley, M. G., GILES Co.

CONLEY, Richard to Rosanah Stout - issued January 26, 1829, Bondsman:
   John Threewitts, m. by: James Suton, J. P., January 26, 1829,
   Witness: Chas. McClung, KNOX Co.

CONN, George A. to Martha A. Dillard - issued July 24, 1822, m. by:
   William Keele July 25, 1822, RUTHERFORD Co.

CONN, James to Jain Henderson - issued October 17, 1810, Bondsman:
   William Windham, GRAINGER Co.

CONN, James to Nancy Angel - issued December 5, 1855, m. by:
   H. W. Carroll, J. P., December 5, 1855, COFFEE Co.

CONN, Josephus H. to Jane C. McFerrin - issued August 4, 1822, m. by:
   R. L. Fagan August 6, 1822, RUTHERFORD Co.

CONN, R. G. to S. C. Knight - issued July 30, 1868, FRANKLIN Co.

CONNALLY, John to Polly Cavannaugh - November 28, 1807, WILLIAMSON Co.

CONNEEL, John to Sally Verhain (or Verhine, Verhian) - issued
   February 26, 1848, m. by: J. P., Bellemy, L. E., February 27,
   1848, STEWART Co.

CONNELL, Enoch P. to Nancy Walton - issued July 4, 1812, Bondsman:
   Will Trigg, Jr., SUMNER Co.

CONNELL, W. W. to M. C. Goodman - issued October 13, 1856, m. by:
   W. R. Sadler, J. P., October 19, 1856, ROBERTSON Co.

CONNELL, Jacob to Mary Kirby - issued September 10, 1847, m. by:
   Isaac Steel September 11, 1847, ROBERTSON Co.

CONNELL, William to Narcissa Ann Mathews - issued February 10, 1843,
   m. by: A. G. Goodlett February 22, 1843, DAVIDSON Co.

CONNELL, William B. to Ollivia Walton - issued April 19, 1826, Bondsman:
   George Million, m. by: Hugh Kirkpatrick, M. G., April 19, 1826,
   SUMNER Co.

CONNELLY, George W. to Rebecca Young - issued December 5, 1821, m. by:
   Jas. Jones, J. P., December 6, 1821, RUTHERFORD Co.

CONNELLY, Hardy S. to Elizabeth B. Read - issued July 8, 1824, Bondsman:
   Robert C. Owen, m. by: Peyton Smith July 8, 1824, RUTHERFORD Co.

CONNELLY, James B. to Elizabeth W. Tweedy - issued March 12, 1818, m. by:
   Jas. Jones, J. P., March 12, 1818, RUTHERFORD Co.

CONNELLY, John to Eliza Jane Davis - issued December 25, 1832, Bondsman:
   Jno. Hill and Isaac Haynes, KNOX Co.

CONNELLY, John W. to Sally Nichols - issued November 24, 1824, Bondsman:
   Caleb Ballew, RUTHERFORD Co.

CONNELLY, John W to Angelica R. West - issued September 15, 1841,
   DAVIDSON Co.

CONNELLY, Thomas J. to Stacy Hewitt - issued January 21, 1834, Bondsman:
   R. Blair, m. by: Wm. H. Davis January 21, 1834, RUTHERFORD Co.

CONNELLY, William to Racheal Quinn - issued June 4, 1839, m. by:
   C. G. Macpherson June 5, 1839, DAVIDSON Co.

CONNER, Amos L. to Mary Ann Beals - issued February 2, 1838, m. by:
E. P. Connell, J. P., January 4, 1838, DAVIDSON Co.

CONNER, D. A. to Mary Askins - issued February 4, 1840, m. by:
I. T. Hines, J. P., FRANKLIN Co.

CONNER, Daniel to Jane Holden - issued May 28, 1829, Bondsman:
Josiah Mullins, m. by: W. Lyon, J. P., May 28, 1829, Witness:
Wm. Swan, KNOX Co.

CONNER, James to R. J. Clemmons - issued April 26, 1863, Bondsman:
W. R. Love, m. by: J. M. Powell, J. P., April 28, 1863, LAWRENCE Co.

CONNER, James M. to Ellen F. Crawford - issued February 13, 1855,
m. by: F. C. Plaster, Minister of Baptist Church, February 15,
1855, ROBERTSON Co.

CONNER, John to Mariah Kern - issued April 5, 1842, m. by:
Jas. L. Henning, M. G., April 7, 1842, STEWART Co.

CONNER, John to Mary Jane Turner - issued August 27, 1845, m. by:
W. D. F. Sawrie, M. G., August 27, 1845, DAVIDSON Co.

CONNER, Jno. M. to Polly Haskew - issued September 21, 1829, Bondsman:
R. Cox, m. by: Robt. Tindell, J. P., September 24, 1829, KNOX Co.

CONNER, Lewis to Nancy Preston - issued January 4, 1826, Bondsman:
Robert Crocket, SUMNER Co.

CONNER, Matison to Cristan Fraisure - issued December 15, 1853,
VAN BUREN Co.

CONNER, Sampson to Sally Knight - issued May 9, 1821, Bondsman:
James Hollingsworth, m. by: James McAdow, J. P., May 20, 1821,
WILSON Co.

CONNER, Samuel to Patsy Hickey - issued January 12, 1819, Bondsman:
Josiah Armstrong, m. by: Wm. Alldredge, J. P., January 14, 1819,
KNOX Co.

CONNER, Samuel to Margaret Kime - issued November 29, 1825, m. by:
B. McNutt, J. P., December 1, 1825, KNOX Co.

CONNER, William to Sally Case - issued December 30, 1805, Bondsman:
Mordicai Yarnell, Witness: W. Park, KNOX Co.

CONNER, Wm. R. to Martha Gammon - issued February 28, 1832, m. by:
Thomas Frazier March 1, 1832, KNOX Co.

CONNER, John to Fanny Atkins - issued July 16, 1823, Bondsman:
Enos Hammer, m. by: Jas. Kennore, M. G., July 16, 1823, GRAINGER Co.

CONNOR, William E. to Mary E. Carter - October 5, 1858, m. by:
E. Hanks, M. G., GILES Co.

CONOLY, Archibald to Mary S. A. Price - July 31, 1832, m. by:
Elias Tidwell, J. P., GILES Co.

CONROD, John to Caty Morris - issued April 22, 1820, Bondsman:
Bazil Davis, WILSON Co.

CONSIDINE, Thos. to Hanora Davet - issued July 3, 1858, m. by:
L. Haste, Catholic Priest, July 5, 1858, ROBERTSON Co.

CONWAY, C. to M. Sayle - issued November 14, 1850, m. by: I. Steele,
ROBERTSON Co.

CONWAY, Charles to Elizabeth Robertson - issued October 19, 1796,
Bondsman: David Robertson, Witness: Hu. Law. White, KNOX Co.

CONWAY, Christopher to Martha Warren - June 4, 1793, Security: Joseph Lask, GREENE Co.

CONWAY, Dennie to Mary Marcheall - issued April 1, 1804, Bondsman: Jackson Smith, GRAINGER Co.

CONWAY, Elizabeth to John Sevier, Jr. - GREENE Co.

CONWAY, Henderson H. to Rebecca E. Neil - issued November 4, 1856, m. by: F. C. Plaster, M. G., ROBERTSON Co.

CONWAY, James to Jane Nipper - issued March 13, 1836, m. by: Eli King, J. P., March 22, 1836, KNOX Co.

CONWAY, Saml. to Rachel C. Green - issued December 21, 1854, m. by: Samuel D. Ogburn, ROBERTSON Co.

CONWAY, Susanna to Thomas Conway - GREENE Co.

CONWAY, Thomas to Susanna Conway - February 9, 1792, Security: Alex Culton (Cuttan), GREENE Co.

CONWAY, Thomas, Sen. to Nancy Ruton (Rector) - April 11, 1792, Security: Thomas Conway, Jr., GREENE Co.

CONYEARS, Thomas to Zilpha McLendon - issued March 10, 1845, m. by: G. W. Wharton, J. P., March 13, 1845, DAVIDSON Co.

CONYER, John H. to Mary Harrington - issued May 28, 1839, Bondsman: Truman Harrington, m. by: G. H. Bussard, J. P., WILSON Co.

CONYERS, Thomas to Jane Wills - issued September 10, 1787, Bondsman: James Frazier, SUMNER Co.

COOK, Alexander C. to Sally A. Stark - issued December 12, 1841, m. by: Benjamin Gambill, J. P., ROBERTSON Co.

COOK, Andrew J. to Eva J. Burchett - issued September 9, 1854, m. by: David Henry, J. P., September 10, 1854, ROBERTSON Co.

COOK, Archibald to Charlotte Lockheart - issued April 3, 1846, m. by: Jas. Chambers, J. P., April 7, 1846, STEWART Co.

COOK, Benjamin to Nancy Barnes - issued May 7, 1825, Bondsman: Solomon Sholders, SUMNER Co.

COOK, C. C. to R. C. Morris - issued February 9, 1856, m. by: J. P., Wedington, J. P., February 10, 1856, FRANKLIN Co.

COOK, David to Sarah Patten - issued March 21, 1845, m. by: David Jones, J. P., ROBERTSON Co.

COOK, David to M. A. Chowning - issued February 22, 1849, m. by: James Sprouse, J. P., ROBERTSON Co.

COOK, Dempsey to Polly Watkins - issued November 12, 1827, Bondsman: Philip Watkins, SUMNER Co.

COOK, Eli to Sarah J. Swift - issued November 7, 1859, m. by: John Crawford, J. P., November 8, 1859, ROBERTSON Co.

COOK, Eli T. to Louisa Fletcher - issued May 3, 1845, m. by: R. W. Bell, J. P., May 4, 1845, ROBERTSON Co.

COOK, Ellis P. to Louisa Y. Stother - issued October 16, 18--(?), m. by: E. Edwards, M. E. C., October 16, 1839, ROBERTSON Co.

COOK, Ezekiel to Lucy Jones - issued November 27, 1843, m. by: John T. Edgar November 27, 1843, DAVIDSON Co.

COOK, Flute to Nancy Harris - issued December 27, 1822, m. by:
Joshua Lester, V. D. M., WILSON Co.

COOK, George W. to Mary Mathenia - issued June 14, 1819, m. by:
John Hoover, J. P., June 16, 1819, RUTHERFORD Co.

COOK, George W. to Rachel Ingram - issued September 14, 1848, m. by:
H. G. Townsen, J. P., September 14, 1848, STEWART Co.

COOK, Henry to Amelia A. Wa--(?) - issued June 29, 1861, m. by:
W. J. ___(?), June 30, 1861, COFFEE Co.

COOK, Hezekiak to Lucinda Watson - issued June 17, 1806, Bondsman:
Aron Rook, GRAINGER Co.

COOK, Isaac to Delila Lovel - issued August 25, 1824, Bondsman:
Jarred Norris, m. by: Alexander Hamilton, J. P., GRAINGER Co.

COOK, Isaac to Polly A. Young - issued July 21, 1842, m. by: M. R. Mann,
J. P., July 21, 1842, FRANKLIN Co.

COOK, Isaac to Sarah Hodge - issued July 11, 1871, FRANKLIN Co.

COOKE, James to Margaret Gould - January 22, 1801, Security:
James Sloan, BLOUNT Co.

COOK, James to Mary Duvall - m. by: Sam'l Gwin, J. P., January 2, 1828,
SUMNER Co.

COOK, James to Mary Smith - issued January 30, 1837, m. by: J. D. Rogers
February 2, 1837, RUTHERFORD Co.

COOK, James to Elizabeth Sneed - issued March 12, 1839, m. by:
B. Herndon, J. P., March 17, 1839, STEWART Co.

COOK, James to Martha J. Overstreet - issued September 20, 1842,
ROBERTSON Co.

COOK, James A. to Ann French - issued November 14, 1840, m. by:
Allen McCaskill, J. P., STEWART Co.

COOK, James C. to Catherine A. Mockbee - issued August 22, 1846, m. by:
James Chambers, J. P., August 23, 1846, STEWART Co.

COOK, James H. to Angeline Reed - issued March 5, 1858, m. by:
J. P. Wedington, J. P., March 7, 1858, FRANKLIN Co.

COOK, James W. to Cynthia A. Walker - issued July 23, 1844, m. by:
J. Eubank, J. P., DICKSON Co.

COOK, Jesse to Mary Clay - issued July 29, 1829, Bondsman:
Joseph Freeman, WILSON Co.

COOK, John to Alvina Kearns - issued August 20, 1820, GRAINGER Co.

COOK, John to Annis S. Mentheny - issued December 4, 1820, Bondsman:
Job Mentheny, m. by: James Gray, J. P., December 20, 1820, WILSON Co.

COOK, John to Anna Teel - issued November 20, 1830, Bondsman:
Hardy Byford, RUTHERFORD Co.

COOK, John to Martha Huddleston - issued August 9, 1833, m. by:
Geo. S. Hooper, J. P., WILSON Co.

COOK, John to Sarah T. Brewer - issued January 14, 1842, m. by:
Richd. Chowning, J. P., April 4, 1842, ROBERTSON Co.

COOK, John to Sarah Coop - issued October 21, 1863, Bondsman:
F. M. Cortner, Joseph H. Thompson, Clk., BEDFORD Co.

COOK, John E. to Frances M. Williams - issued December 18, 1843, m. by:
Josiah Ferriss, J. P., December 18, 1843, DAVIDSON Co.

COOK, John F. to Caroline A. Duvall - issued October 14, 1841,
DAVIDSON Co.

COOK, Joseph to Mary Ferguson - issued May 7, 1818, m. by:
Jas. S. Jetton, J. P., May 8, 1818, RUTHERFORD Co.

COOK, Joseph to Elizabeth Roberson - issued January 10, 1845, m. by:
John Morris, J. P., FRANKLIN Co.

COOK, Joseph C. to Martha Anderson - issued September 10, 1838, m. by:
Wm. N. Taylor, J. P., FRANKLIN Co.

COOK, Lewis to Synthia Stratton - issued January 4, 1836, Bondsman:
Joseph Barber, m. by: John Hobday January 4, 1836, SUMNER Co.

COOK, Matthew to Mary McNairy - issued April 24, 1843, DAVIDSON Co.

COOK, Nathaniel to Elizabeth Sypert - issued January 1, 1840, Bondsman:
Joseph J. Strong, WILSON Co.

COOK, Noah to Ann Swain - issued August 12, 1857, m. by: Thos. Finch,
J. P., August 12, 1857, FRANKLIN Co.

COOK, Pleasant to Lucy Ann Tate - issued October 21, 1856, m. by:
G. M. Featherston, M. G., ROBERTSON Co.

COOK, Robert G. to Mary J. England - issued September 23, 1853, m. by:
W. L. Chowning, J. P., ROBERTSON Co.

COOK, Stokeley to Amanda Lucas - issued November 17, 1854, m. by:
David Henry, J. P., November 19, 1854, ROBERTSON Co.

COOK, Thomas to Delila Belt - issued December 11, 1832, Bondsman:
Thomas Campbell, m. by: Thomas Smith, M. G., WILSON Co.

COOK, Thomas to Karon Smith - issued January 16, 1835, Bondsman:
William Forbs, m. by: Cary James, D. M. E. C., January 23, 1835,
RUTHERFORD Co.

COOK, Thomas to Sarah Carter - issued October 5, 1846, m. by:
G. D. Fullmer, J. P., October 5, 1846, DAVIDSON Co.

COOK, Thornton H. to Eleanor B. Copton - issued June 5, 1834, Bondsman:
William A. Clopton, m. by: William P. Smith, M. G., WILSON Co.

COOK, Turner to Betsey Durham - issued September 27, 1817, Bondsman:
Allen Meirs, SUMNER Co.

COOK, Valentine L. to Ann Martin - issued May 24, 1830, m. by:
Barton Brown, M. G., May 24, 1830, SUMNER Co.

COOK, Wiett W. to Mariah Clark - issued February 3, 1830, Bondsman:
George Jones, RUTHERFORD Co.

COOK, Wiley to Betsey Barns - issued May 5, 1822, Bondsman:
John Underwood, SUMNER Co.

COOK, William A. to Susan M. Gorham - issued February 2, 1853, m. by:
David Henry, J. P., February 3, 1853, ROBERTSON Co.

COOK, Yerby to Elinor Morris - issued January 4, 1809, Bondsman:
Mathias Mouch, SUMNER Co.

COOKE, Green to Polly Nicholson - issued April 11, 1814, Bondsman:
Thos. Bradley, WILSON Co.

COOKE, Green to Lurainy Nixon - issued July 20, 1822, m. by:
John Fulton, J. P., July 28, 1822, RUTHERFORD Co.

COOKE, John D. to Christian Mullins - issued November 17, 1825, m. by:
John Lane November 17, 1825, RUTHERFORD Co.

COOKSEY, Benjamin to Lydia Wier - issued February 21, 1838, Bondsman:
James Allen, m. by: Moses Ellis, J. P., WILSON Co.

COOKSEY, Joseph to Lucinda Satterfield - issued March 2, 1835, Bondsman:
Alfred Pride, WILSON Co.

COOKSEY, William H. to Melville Jett - issued July 5, 1854, Bondsman:
Wm. Heathman, m. by: John M. Nolen July 6, 1854, MONTGOMERY Co.

COOLEN, Henry to Mary Lee Moore - issued June 12, 1865, m. by:
J. L. Payne, M. G., June 13, 1865, FRANKLIN Co.

COOLEY, George to Rebecka Howard - issued November 23, 1820, m. by:
Peter Nance, J. P., November 23, 1820, KNOX Co.

COOLEY, Josiah to Nancy Maney - issued December 26, 1821, Bondsman:
Samuel Badgett, m. by: P. Nance, J. P., December 26, 1821, KNOX Co.

COOLEY, Levi to Lucinda Bettis - issued June 20, 1862, Bondsman:
Elijah Logan, Jos. H. Thompson, Clk. per N. F. Thompson, D. Clk.,
m. by: H. F. Holt, J. P., BEDFORD Co.

COOLEY, Rich W. to Caroline Webster - issued September 12, 1847, m. by:
W. T. Weston, J. P., September 12, 1847, STEWART Co.

COOLEY, Samuel to Emeline Booth - issued July 7, 1844, m. by:
W. A. Martin, J. P., STEWART Co.

COOLEY, Thomas F. to Mary T. Pollard - issued October 2, 1844, STEWART Co.

COOLEY, W. J. to Martha W. Batts - issued October 3, 1855, m. by:
F. R. Gooch, M. G., October 4, 1855, ROBERTSON Co.

COOLEY, William to Eliza Hassell - m. by: A. B. Duvall April 27,
1837, SUMNER Co.

COOLEY, William to Tabitha Boott - issued April 6, 1842, m. by:
H. W. Smith, J. P., April 6, 1842, STEWART Co.

COOLY, Henry to Malinda Lunce - issued December 22, 1827, Bondsman:
Gray Medling, m. by: B. Bridges, J. P., WILSON Co.

COOLY, Stephen to Eliza Ann Cuffman - issued December 22, 1831,
Bondsman: John Bell, SUMNER Co.

COOPER, A. H. to Elizabeth Frazier - issued June 1, 1849, MONTGOMERY Co.

COOPER, A. S. to Harriett E. Large - issued April 29, 1861, m. by:
Thos. A. Morris, M. G., April 29, 1861, FRANKLIN Co.

COOPER, Bedford C. to Elizabeth J. Turner - issued August 25, 1836,
Bondsman: William K. Wilson, m. by: G. T. Henderson, E. M. E. C.,
August 30, 1836, RUTHERFORD Co.

COOPER, Benjamin B. to Rebecca Owen - issued December 4, 1824, Bondsman:
Warren Davenport, WILSON Co.

COOPER, Charles D. to Elizabeth V. Lindsay - issued October 31, 1835,
Bondsman: Richard Ledbetter, RUTHERFORD Co.

COOPER, Cornelius to Jane Taylor - issued March 27, 1841, FRANKLIN Co.

COOPER, Cornleus to Frances Gee - issued November 16, 1844, m. by:
Allen Elliott, M. G., November 16, 1844, STEWART Co.

COOPER, Cornelius to Jane Adair - issued September 21, 1841, STEWART Co.

COOPER, Ebenezar to Nancy Brown - issued June 28, 1815, m. by:
Tho. H. Nelson June 28, 1815, KNOX Co.

COOPER, Edward to Celia Wheeler - issued March 24, 1825, Bondsman:
Richard Lennox, m. by: David Patton, J. P., March 25, 1825,
RUTHERFORD Co.

COOPER, Eli P. to Drucilla Stiles - issued June 8, 1850, m. by:
Geo. W. Bowling, J. P., June 8, 1850, FRANKLIN Co.

COOPER, Frances to Ann Thomas - issued October 31, 1820, Bondsman:
James Reed, m. by: John McMinn, J. P., November 5, 1820, WILSON Co.

COOPER, George to Martha Dillard - issued May 26, 1818, Bondsman:
James Browning, m. by: John Page May 28, 1818, WILSON Co.

COOPER, Houston to Peggy Snoddy - issued September 23, 1809, Bondsman:
David Snoddy, SUMNER Co.

COOPER, James to Emeline Simpson - issued August 17, 1849, FRANKLIN Co.

COOPER, James to W. E. Touman - issued October 22, 1853, m. by:
G. B. Mason, J. P., October 24, 1853, ROBERTSON Co.

COOPER, Jinny to Pryor Kyle - MAURY Co.

COOPER, John to Susanna Howell - issued June 5, 1797, Bondsman:
Henry Howell, GRAINGER Co.

COOPER, John to Lucy Graves - issued November 1, 1797, Bondsman:
John Byrd, KNOX Co.

COOPER, John to Susanna Howel - issued June 5, 1799 (see 1797),
Witness: Sm'l. Yancey, GRAINGER Co.

COOPER, John to Piney Rogers - issued December 6, 1813, Bondsman:
W. Woodward, WILSON Co.

COOPER, Jno. to Nancy Love - August 24, 1808, WILLIAMSON Co.

COOPER, John to Levicy Goodin - issued November 6, 1824, Bondsman:
Jacob Davis, m. by: Cullin Curlee, J. P., November 7, 1824,
RUTHERFORD Co.

COOPER, John B. to Jane McGuffin - issued June 22, 1835, Bondsman:
Charles D. Cooper, RUTHERFORD Co.

COOPER, John L. to Frances C. Lindsey - issued April 21, 1834, Bondsman:
Thomas Edwards, m. by: G. W. Morris, E. M. E. C., April 21, 1834,
RUTHERFORD Co.

COOPER, Jonathan to Elizabeth Duffie - September 9, 1809, WILLIAMSON Co.

COOPER, Joseph to Beth Chiles - issued October 27, 1836, m. by:
Wm. Lindsay, J. P., October 27, 1836, KNOX Co.

COOPER, Kerncheon to Mariah Kidd - issued September 3, 1847, STEWART Co.

COOPER, Laten to Sarah Prewit - issued January 20, 1843, m. by:
B. Sells, J. P., January 22, 1843, FRANKLIN Co.

COOPER, Levi to Pricilla W. Horn - issued February 22, 1851, Bondsman:
Isaac Robertson, m. by: John Mallory, M. G., February 23, 1851,
MONTGOMERY Co.

COOPER, Lucy to David Campbell - MAURY Co.

COOPER, Mary W. to James A. Slaughter - issued June 20, 1861, Bondsman: A. A. Cooper, Jos. H. Thompson, Clk. per N. F. Thompson, Dep. Clk., m. by: Elder T. D. Jones, BEDFORD Co.

COOPER, Micajah T. to Sarah A. Vinson - issued March 31, 1829, Bondsman: Joseph Hollis, RUTHERFORD Co.

COOPER, Nathan to Christiana Hughes - August 1, 1791, Security: John McDonald, GREENE Co.

COOPER, Nelson to Eliza Jacobs - issued December 24, 1833, Bondsman: Jonathan Owen, RUTHERFORD Co.

COOPER, Nixon to Hulda Nichols - issued August 1, 1846, m. by: Wm. Bell, J. P., August 2, 1846, STEWART Co.

COOPER, Noah to Eliza M. Farr - issued October 20, 1835, Bondsman: E. L. Farr, RUTHERFORD Co.

COOPER, Richard to Elizabeth Miller - issued April 23, 1804, Bondsman: William Nash and Samuel Wilson, RUTHERFORD Co.

COOPER, Thomas to Mary A. Boyd - issued January 24, 1838, m. by: B. M. Barnes, J. P., January 25, 1838, DAVIDSON Co.

COOPER, W. B. to Ann Litton - issued January 17, 1839, m. by: A. L. P. Green, M. G., January 17, 1839, DAVIDSON Co.

COOPER, William to Mary Moore - issued March 16, 1801, Bondsman: Isaac Cooper, GRAINGER Co.

COOPER, William to Mary Blaylock - issued January 17, 1812, Bondsman: Eli T. Hunt, WILSON Co.

COOPER, William to Margrett Windsor - issued March 19, 1840, m. by: James F. Green, J. P., March 19, 1840, FRANKLIN Co.

COOPER, William to Sallena Simpson - issued December 11, 1848, m. by: W. M. Watson, J. P., December 13, 1848, FRANKLIN Co.

COOPER, William to Caroline Smith - issued September 4, 1850, Bondsman: David I. Cooper, MONTGOMERY Co.

COOTS, J. M. to Susan Herrington - issued June 2, 1874, m. by: Martin Mason, J. P., June 3, 1874, FRANKLIN Co.

COPE, Iddoa to Nancy Lambuth - issued December 30, 1829 (see card as of year 1830), Bondsman: Pitt M. House, m. by: A. D. Duvall, J. P., December 30, 1829, SUMNER Co.

COPE, Iddoce to Nancy Lambert - issued December 30, 1830, m. by: A. D. Duvall (see Iddoa Cope and Nancy Lambuth card, year 1829), SUMNER Co.

COPE, James to Annis Murdin - issued October 29, 1824, Bondsman: Henry Sarver, SUMNER Co.

COPE, Richard to Keziah Best - issued September 7, 1819, Bondsman: Thomas White, m. by: James Gwin, M. G., September 7, 1819, SUMNER Co.

COPE, Salem P. to Rebecca L. Grant - issued May 12, 1852, Bondsman: J. W. Breathell, m. by: John Gold, J. P., May 12, 1852, MONTGOMERY Co.

COPE, Thomas to Sally Ann Waggoner - issued September 10, 1845, Bondsman: Washington Dukes, m. by: W. B. Carney, J. P., September 10, 1845, MONTGOMERY Co.

COPEHEART, John W. to Mary Reeves - issued August 6, 1835, Bondsman: __(?) Newbern, WILSON Co.

COPELAND, Andrew to Elizabeth Bell - December 21, 1813, KNOX Co.

COPELAND, David to Susannah Craig - June 25, 1800, Security:
James Craig, BLOUNT Co.

COPELAND, David D. to Nancy Combs - issued September 21, 1824, m. by:
Wm. B. Carns, J. P., September 21, 1824, KNOX Co.

COPELAND, Hugh S. to Francis Bibbs - issued March 28, 1832, m. by:
Thomas Frazier, J. P., March 29, 1832, KNOX Co.

COPELAND, James to Ann Cameron - September 11, 1800, Security:
James Craig, BLOUNT Co.

COPELAND, Joel to Rebecka Huchison - September 14, 1798, Surety:
John Huchison, BLOUNT Co.

COPELAND, John to Elizabeth Fielding - issued August 11, 1830, Bondsman:
Andrew Chamberlain, m. by: Levi Satterfield, M. G., GRAINGER Co.

COPELAND, John M. to Lourinda Eatherly - issued December 2, 1843,
m. by: J. W. Judkins, J. P., December 6, 1843, ROBERTSON Co.

COPELAND, Thomas to Elizabeth Mount - issued July 16, 1824, Bondsman:
Joshua Copeland, WILSON Co.

COPELAND, Thomas to Jane Beazley - issued June 5, 1846, m. by:
T. Fagundus, J. P., June 10, 1846, DAVIDSON Co.

COPELAND, Thomas J. to Nancy Cummings - issued February 8, 1866,
Bondsman: Jacob Sanders, m. by: Thos. J. Frazier, J. P.,
February 8, 1866, LAWRENCE Co.

COPLAND, Anthony to Nancy Craig - issued March 24, 1806, Bondsman:
David Craig, WILSON Co.

COPLAND, John to Sarah Short - issued March 25, 1798, Bondsman:
John Smith (a), GRAINGER Co.

COPLEY, Wm. to Katty Peeler - issued November 28, 1826, Bondsman:
Berry Peeler, m. by: J. A. Swan, J. P., KNOX Co.

COPLIN, James to Nancy Lowry - issued March 23, 1820, m. by:
B. L. McFerrin, J. P., March 23, 1820, RUTHERFORD Co.

COPPAGE, Charles to Ann Kennedy - issued January 27, 1836, WILSON Co.

COPPAGE, Charles to Harriet Brown - issued May 25, 1837, Bondsman:
Thomas L. Coppage, WILSON Co.

COPPAGE, William to Mary T. Davis - issued December 1, 1830, Bondsman:
Charles Coppage, WILSON Co.

COPPEDGE, James M. to Elizabeth Miller - issued February 3, 1829,
Bondsman: John O'Neal, m. by: E. P. Horn, J. P., February 5, 1829,
WILSON Co.

COPPOCK, Aaron to Margaret Tucker - February 9, 1797, Security:
Newhope Quaker Meeting, GREENE Co.

CORAM, Thornton to Anna Gaines - issued March 9, 1827, Bondsman:
Milton Yate, m. by: Greenberry Mitchell, J. P., GRAINGER Co.

CORBAN, Burrell to Sally Ann Andrews - issued August 21, 1851, Bondsman:
Uriah Smith, m. August 21, 1851, MONTGOMERY Co.

CORBEN, Burrel to Martha Allen - issued August 3, 1847, m. by:
Jesse Edwards, M. G., STEWART Co.

CORBETT, J. M. to Sarah M. Bayliss - issued February 17, 1846, Bondsman: Josiah Ogburn, m. by: Moses Steele, J. P., February 19, 1846, MONTGOMERY Co.

CORBETT, Joseph to Agnus Biggers - issued December 30, 1828, Bondsman: Mason Carr, m. by: F. E. Pitts December 30, 1828, SUMNER Co.

CORBIN, Charnel to Celia Barns - issued October 30, 1800, Bondsman: Elisha Clary, SUMNER Co.

CORBITT, Allen T. to Mary E. Harrison - issued July 25, 1838, DAVIDSON Co.

CORBITT, David W. to Louisa A. Withers - issued November 6, 1856, m. by: J. W. Cullum, M. G., ROBERTSON Co.

CORBITT, Nicholas P. to Frances Wills - issued August 17, 1839, m. by: W. D. F. Sawrie, M. G., August 18, 1839, DAVIDSON Co.

CORBITT, Samuel R. to Caroline Smith - issued November 2, 1841, m. by: W. E. Cartwright November 4, 1841, DAVIDSON Co.

CORCSON (Coresan), James Will to Mary J. Warren - issued June 17, 1866, FRANKLIN Co.

CORDEL, Jno. W. to B. A. Gossett - issued August 28, 1848, m. by: W. M. C. Barr, J. P., ROBERTSON Co.

CORDER, Azariah to Viney Shaw - issued February 24, 1819, Bondsman: Hugh Park, m. by: Joseph T. Bell, J. P., February 25, 1819, WILSON Co.

CORDER, James L. to Elizabeth Trout - issued March 15, 1828, Bondsman: Samuel Trout, m. March 15, 1828, SUMNER Co.

CORDER, Lewis to Rebecca Phillips - issued September 11, 1817, Bondsman: Ebben Phillips, SUMNER Co.

CORDER, Martha to Job Jacob - GREENE Co.

CORDER, Orpha to Robert Montgomery - GREENE Co.

CORDER, Orpha to James Seers - GREENE Co.

CORDER, Ruth to Isaac Allen - GREENE Co.

CORDER, Solomon to Martha Brown - issued February 12, 1818, Bondsman: Jesse Shaw, m. by: John Bonner, J. P., February 15, 1818, WILSON Co.

CORDER, William to Martha Stone - issued November 10, 1821, Bondsman: James Stone, m. by: Abner Hill, M. G., November 11, 1821, WILSON Co.

CORDER, William C. to Margaret Prichette - issued January 23, 1834, Bondsman: Benjamin Corder, m. by: M. T. Cartwright January 23, 1834, WILSON Co.

CORE, Jonathan to Debarha Carrel - March 15, 1817, WILLIAMSON Co.

CORESAN (Corcson), James Will to Mary J. Warren - issued June 17, 1866, FRANKLIN Co.

CORHEIN, Aaron to Eliza Ann Yarbrough - March 6, 1812, WILLIAMSON Co.

CORKIEFF, Madison W. to Martha Ann Walthall - issued January 31, 1854, Bondsman: Oscar L. Shropshire, MONTGOMERY Co.

CORKLE (McCorkle), William to Jenny Graham - issued June 9, 1800, Bondsman: Griffeth Rutherford, SUMNER Co.

CORLEN, Wm. D. to Martha Harper - issued October 14, 1847, Bondsman: C. H. Morrison, m. by: Jas. E. Douglass, MONTGOMERY Co.

CORLETT, James to Elizabeth Whayle - June 8, 1816, WILLIAMSON Co.

CORLEW, John to Susan Leech - issued December 5, 1839, DICKSON Co.

CORLEY, Austin to Milley Turner - issued April 12, 1823, Bondsman: Benjamin Johnson, m. by: Rich'd Johnson April 12, 1823, SUMNER Co.

CORLEY, Bartlet to Letitia Hallum - issued January 8, 1838, m. by: W. Garrett, M. G., January 8, 1838, DAVIDSON Co.

CORLEY, Edmund to Clankey Beasley - issued December 18, 1832, Bondsman: John Ward, WILSON Co.

CORLEY, Nathan to Sarah Terry - issued October 28, 1836, m. by: J. A. McDonald, J. P., WILSON Co.

CORLEY, Nathaniel to Nancy Turner - issued July 30, 1824, Bondsman: Michael Yerger, m. by: Geo. Clark, J. P., September 9, 1824, WILSON Co.

CORLEY, Robert to Maryan Adams - issued March 22, 1828, Bondsman: Samuel Corley, WILSON Co.

CORLEY, Samuel to Esther Priestly - issued July 13, 1829, Bondsman: Hallum Priestly, WILSON Co.

CORLEY, William to Eliza Jane Neelson - issued January 9, 1839, Bondsman: Montgomery J. Corley, m. by: P. Y. Davis, M. G., WILSON Co.

CORMAC, Charles to Mary Pain - issued October 4, 1854, m. by: Patrick Moore, M. G., October 4, 1854, VAN BUREN Co.

CORN, Benj. W. to Elizabeth A. Graham - issued March 19, 1849, m. by: Henry Hunt, M. G., March 20, 1849, FRANKLIN Co.

CORN, George W. to Nancy C. Muse - issued August 22, 1850, m. by: Thos. Finch, J. P., August 22, 1850, FRANKLIN Co.

CORN, J. B. to T. T. Duncan - issued December 22, 1868, m. by: J. L. Payne December 23, 1868, FRANKLIN Co.

CORN, Jessee B. to Sarah C. Wood - issued November 1, 1853, m. by: John Chitwood, J. P., November 3, 1853, FRANKLIN Co.

CORN, Jessee B. to Eliza W. Embry - issued September 2, 1858, m. by: Wm. Hill, M. G., September 2, 1858, FRANKLIN Co.

CORN, John to Susan Warren - issued November 19, 1853, m. by: John Chitwood, J. P., November 19, 1853, FRANKLIN Co.

CORN, John A. to Sarah Corn - issued December 27, 1845, m. by: William B. Taliferro, J. P., December 27, 1845, FRANKLIN Co.

CORN, Lafayette to Susan Wiseman - issued June 13, 1865, m. by: E. P. Armstrong, M. G., June 15, 1865, FRANKLIN Co.

CORN, M. to Mary A. Corn - issued February 26, 1870, FRANKLIN Co.

CORN, Payton S. to Terrissa K. Duncan - issued September 12, 1850, m. by: Henry Hunt, M. G., September 12, 1850, FRANKLIN Co.

CORN, Richard S. to Malissa Corn - issued March 28, 1842, m. by: Henry Hunt, M. G., March 31, 1842, FRANKLIN Co.

CORN, Richard S. to Adaline McNeil - issued October 29, 1846, m. by: Henry Hunt, M. G., October, 1846, FRANKLIN Co.

CORN, Samuel to Mary Moore - issued July 1, 1828, m. by: John McMinn,
J. P., WILSON Co.

CORN, William to Ede Hunt - issued August 3., 1840, m. by: Henry Hunt,
M. G., August 6, 1840, FRANKLIN Co.

CORN, Wm. H. to Winford Knight - issued July 25, 1859, m. by:
Wm. G. Guinn July 28, 1859, FRANKLIN Co.

CORNELIUS, Richard to Betsey Reynolds - issued April 28, 1827,
Bondsman: John Crumpler, SUMNER Co.

CORNELIUS, William to Sarah Ingram - issued January 12, 1846, FRANKLIN Co.

CORNING, D. B. to L. E. Smith - issued March 10, 1866, m. March 10,
1866, FRANKLIN Co.

CORNNANT, Joseph to A. J. Partin - issued November 3,. 1873, m. by:
R. F. Oakley, J. P., November 4, 1873, FRANKLIN Co.

CORNSTOCK, William to Ida Sherman - issued January 29, 1867, m. by:
W. B. Watterson, M. G., January 29, 1867, FRANKLIN Co.

CORNUT, John to Savary Moser - issued February 19, 1827, Bondsman:
Wm. Carnut, m. by: Robert Gaines, J. P., February 19, 1827,
GRAINGER Co.

CORNWALL, Elijah to Elizabeth Poindexter - issued July 13, 1814,
Bondsman: Richard Bragg, GRAINGER Co.

CORRETHERS (Carrithers), John to Elizabeth Hankins - issued October 18,
1803, Bondsman: John Hankins, GRAINGER Co.

COUCH, David to Elizabeth Reed - issued June 13, 1822, Bondsman:
Wm. Moore, m. by: Wm. Morris, J. P., June 13, 1822, KNOX Co.

COUCH, David to Clarinda Moulden - issued September 25, 1845, m. by:
Isaac Denton, M. G., September 25, 1845, VAN BUREN Co.

COUCH, Elizabeth to Joab Moore - GREENE Co.

COUCH, George to Mary Milsaps - June 26, 1800, Security: John Moyer,
GREENE Co.

COUCH, George W. to Lucinda Tindal - issued September 10, 1838, m. by:
John Wright, J. P., September 10, 1838, DAVIDSON Co.

COUCH, Isaac N. to Melvina Green - issued November 22, 1858, m. by:
W. P. Cherry, M. G., November 25, 1858, COFFEE Co.

COUCH, Marshall to Amelia A. Head - issued August 27, 1840, m. by:
S. S. Yarbrough, M. C., August 27, 1840, DAVIDSON Co.

COUCH, Mary to Thomas Shella - GREENE Co.

COUCH, Newton to Susan Emline Calloway - issued August 30, 1866, m. by:
G. W. Bowling, J. P., August 31, 1866, FRANKLIN Co.

COUCH, Nicholas to Mary Roach - July 26, 1787, Security: Edmund Roberts,
GREENE Co.

COUCH, Peter to Ann Haley - issued October 18, 1838, m. by: N. B. Butler
October 18, 1838, DAVIDSON Co.

COUCH, Susanna to Jacob Moyer - GREENE Co.

COUCH, William to Susan Anglin - issued May 30, 1834, Bondsman:
Anderson Anglin, RUTHERFORD Co.

COUCH, Wm. to Sophia Davidson - issued October 17, 1878, Bondsman:
Jno. L. Brandon, BEDFORD Co.

COUCH, Wm. W. to Emily E. Welch - issued July 4, 1866, Bondsman:
C. C. Brewer, m. by: R. L. McLaren, J. P., July 5, 1866,
LAWRENCE Co.

COUEN, Richard to Louisa Chapman - issued December 16, 1845, DICKSON Co.

COUK, Greenberry to Pheby Olinger - issued March 11, 1835, Bondsman:
Wm. Arts, m. by: Michael Davis, J. P., March 11, 1835, KNOX Co.

COULEE, Isaac to Hannah Jones - April 14, 1800, Security: John Jones,
GREENE Co.

COULSON, David to Malissa Alexander - issued November 23, 1853, m. by:
J. J. Comer, Mins., November 23, 1853, COFFEE Co.

COULSON, David to Lydia L. Cunningham - issued January 20, 1859, m. by:
B. H. Adams, J. P., January 22, 1859, COFFEE Co.

COULSON, N. H. to Ellen Sims - issued April 29, 1839, m. by: Henry Hart,
M. G., April 30, 1839, FRANKLIN Co.

COULSON, Wm. to Margaret Slatery - issued December 28, 1831, Bondsman:
John Herndon, m. by: Michael David, J. P., December 29, 1831,
Witness: Wm. Swan, KNOX Co.

COULTER, Asa to Barbara Everett - issued August 30, 1821, m. September 10,
1821, RUTHERFORD Co.

COULTER, Mary to George Sample - GREENE Co.

COULTER, Richard to Minner Kitchin - June 19, 1799, BLOUNT Co.

COUNCE, Peter to Anna Green - issued July 18, 1861, Bondsman:
S. A. Carrell, m. by: S. A. Carrell, J. P., July 18, 1861, LAWRENCE Co.

COUNCIL, John D. to Elizabeth Dority - issued May 7, 1854, Bondsman:
W. P. Brockman, m. by: John M. Pope, J. P., May 7, 1854,
MONTGOMERY Co.

COUNTS, David to Sarah Spoon - issued January 26, 1832, Bondsman:
Abraham Spoon, m. by: Joseph Rich, J. P., GRAINGER Co.

COUNTS, George to Sally Rich - issued July 23, 1806, Bondsman:
Thomas Rich, RUTHERFORD Co.

COUNTS, George S. to Nancy A. Hays - issued May 20, 1834, Bondsman:
James Pybass, m. by: Martin Clark, E. M. E. C., May 20, 1834,
RUTHERFORD Co.

COUNTS, Henry to Mary Campbell - issued November 17, 1824, Bondsman:
John Brown, m. by: Jas. Kennon, M. G., November 17, 1824,
GRAINGER Co.

COUNTS, James to Nancy Stiles - issued April 22, 1856, m. by:
T. W. Bell, J. P., April 22, 1856, FRANKLIN Co.

COUNTS, Jessee to Easter Campbell - issued December 21, 1824, Bondsman:
Benjamin Craighead, GRAINGER Co.

COUNTS, Jesse to Margaret Holloway - issued April 3, 1834, Bondsman:
William Davis, RUTHERFORD Co.

COUNTS, Jessee S. to Julia A. Arledge - issued December 20, 1854,
m. by: J. Campbell, M. G., December 21, 1854, FRANKLIN Co.

COUNTS, John to Mary M. Bell - issued January 11, 1847, m. by:
Aaron Alexander January 12, 1847, FRANKLIN Co.

COUNTS, Phillip to Rebecca T. Ore - issued May 19, 1797, Bondsman: Martin Ashburn, GRAINGER Co.

COUNTS, William to Sara Freeman - issued December 13, 1804, Bondsman: Geo. Counts, RUTHERFORD Co.

COUNTS, William to Elizabeth Forkner - issued February 17, 1836, Bondsman: Andrew Forkner, m. by: Wm. E. Cocke, J. P., GRAINGER Co.

COUNTZ, Arron to Ruth Hammers - issued September 23, 1817, Bondsman: Winphrey Robertson, GRAINGER Co.

COUNTZ, Catherine to John Brumly, Jr. - February 12, 1798, Security: John, Sen. and Larkin Brumly, GREENE Co.

COUNTZ, David to Elizabeth Howell - issued November 8, 1806, Bondsman: Henry Bowen, Witness: Sm'l Yancey, GRAINGER Co.

COUNTZ, (Counts), Isaac to Patsey M. Murry (Patsy McMurray) - issued March 14, 1803, Bondsman: John Countz and James Bowen, GRAINGER Co.

COUNTZ, Nicholas to Patsey Hammers - issued August 29, 1813, Bondsman: Zachariah Keith, GRAINGER Co.

COUNTZ, Peter to Martha Russell - October 25, 1794, Security: James Russell, GREENE Co.

COUNTZ, William to Anney Bean - issued September 10, 1798 (or Sept. 11), Bondsman: John Countz and Robert Blair, m. by: Samuel Yancey, J. P., GRAINGER Co.

COURSEY, Chasteen to Elizabeth J. Crabtree - issued February 14, 1844, m. by: U. Young, J. P., ROBERTSON Co.

COURSEY, William to Catherine Gregory - issued January 26, 1835, Bondsman: Anglen Anglen, m. by: John Landrum January 29, 1835, RUTHERFORD Co.

COURTIS, Mary to Nehemiah Woosey - GREENE Co.

COURTNEY, George to Nancy Atwood - issued December 4, 1832, Bondsman: William Spring, WILSON Co.

COURTNEY, James to Elizabeth Henson - issued January 2, 1833, Bondsman: Arthur Robertson, m. by: Wm. Lyons, J. P., January 3, 1833, Witness: Chas. Scott, KNOX Co.

COURTNEY, James to Mary Matthis - issued August 16, 1841, m. by: C. W. Moorman, J. P., August 21, 1841, DAVIDSON Co.

COURTNEY, John to Nancy Robison - issued October 29, 1822, Bondsman: Wm. Courtney, m. by: P. Nance, J. P., October 30, 1822, KNOX Co.

COURTNEY, John to Patsy Williams - issued November 30, 1826, Bondsman: John Haskins, KNOX Co.

COURTNEY, Jonathan to Mary Goadus - issued October 15, 1805, Bondsman: James Dyer, Witness: A. White, KNOX Co.

COURTNEY, Mathew to Hannah Carroll - issued March 19, 1858, m. by: Thomas Finch, J. P., March 20, 1858, FRANKLIN Co.

COURTNEY, Samuel to Susan Luttrell - issued July 5, 1819, Bondsman: John Luttrell, KNOX Co.

COURTS, Charles to Clary Hudspeth - October 14, 1808, MAURY Co.

COUSSENS, John H. to Mary Royster - issued December 24, 1840, m. by: T. Fanning, C. T., December 24, 1840, DAVIDSON Co.

COUTS, A. B. to Susan C. Green - issued October 10, 1857, m. by:
Benjamin Rawls, M. G., October 11, 1857, ROBERTSON Co.

COUTS, Archer B. to Martha J. Couts - issued June 7, 1847, m. by:
Benjamin Rawls, M. G., June 8, __(?), ROBERTSON Co.

COUTS, Jno. F. to Eliz. A. Davis - issued December 16, 1849, m. by:
Lewis Adams, M. G., ROBERTSON Co.

COUTS, W. H. to Lydia A. Moore - issued June 22, 1852, m. by:
David Herring, J. P., June 23, 1852, ROBERTSON Co.

COUTS, William to Martha Moon - issued August 28, 1847, m. by:
Jas. Woodard, J. P., August 29, 1847, ROBERTSON Co.

COVENDER, Benjamin to Sally Nance - issued December 26, 1827, Bondsman:
Martin Vineyard, m. by: G. B. Mitchell, J. P., GRAINGER Co.

COVENTON, Washington to Eliza Hughes - issued September 19, 1827,
m. September 19, 1827, SUMNER Co.

COVENTON, William to Priscilla Bloodworth - issued February 28, 1806,
Bondsman: Webb Bloodworth, SUMNER Co.

COVEY, Russell R. to Rachel Davis - November 21, 1810, Bondsman:
John D. Love, MAURY Co.

COVEY, William to Mary A. Swann - issued January 12, 1857, m. by:
Wm. W. Conn, M. G., January 13, 1857, FRANKLIN Co.

COVINGTON, C. S. to Nancy M. Carr - issued February 2, 1857, m. by:
W. T. Chowning, J. P., March 3, 1857, ROBERTSON Co.

COVINGTON, Daniel to Narcissa Pitner - issued May 7, 1835, Bondsman:
Jno. T. Palm, m. by: J. Johnson, J. P., May 7, 1835, KNOX Co.

COVINGTON, David to Judith Kindrick - issued January 29, 1817, m. by:
John Fulton, J. P., January 30, 1817, RUTHERFORD Co.

COVINGTON, Edmund to Emelia D. Underwood - issued December 20, 1830,
Bondsman: Ellis Hankins, m. by: O. W. Crockett, J. P., RUTHERFORD Co.

COVINGTON, Henry L. to Mary M. B. Tate - issued December 30, 1846,
m. by: Rev. Russell Eskew, ROBERTSON Co.

COVINGTON, Henry L. to Margaret N. Tate - issued December 30, 1846,
m. by: Rev. Rassel Eskew, ROBERTSON Co.

COVINGTON, Hiram to Lucy Payne - issued January 19, 1825, Bondsman:
Wm. Wydner, m. by: Sam'l Montgomery, J. P., January 20, 1825,
Witness: Mat. McClung, KNOX Co.

COVINGTON, J. A. to Mary Grimes - issued October 15, 1857, m. by:
R. Elmore, J. P., October 18, 1857, ROBERTSON Co.

COVINGTON, Jackson to Mary Corder - issued February 3, 1835, Bondsman:
N. C. Goodloe, m. by: D. R. Gooch, J. P., February 4, 1835,
RUTHERFORD Co.

COVINGTON, Jacob F. to Evaline M. Luten - issued May 30, 1857,
ROBERTSON Co.

COVINGTON, Jesse to Levica Beesley - issued October 22, 1816, m. by:
H. Robinson, J. P., October 24, 1816, RUTHERFORD Co.

COONROOD, William to Patsey Rogers - issued April 2, 1822, Bondsman:
James Grisim, WILSON Co.

COONS (Coonee), John to Catherine Carlough - November 19, 1791, Security:
H. Carlough, GREENE Co.

COOP, Sarah to John Cook - issued October 21, 1863, Bondsman:
F. M. Cortner, Joseph H. Thompson, Clk., BEDFORD Co.

COOPE, David to Kity Niamon - March 18, 1802, Security:
Abraham Philips, BLOUNT Co.

COOPER, A. A. to Mary Singleton - issued October 7, 1862, Bondsman:
John G. Webster, Jos. H. Thompson, Clk., BEDFORD Co.

COON, George to Nancy Wallace - issued December 24, 1842, m. December 25,
1842, DICKSON Co.

COON, John to Lovey Etherage - issued August 1, 1841, m. by:
Benja. Gambill, J. P., ROBERTSON Co.

COONCE, Christopher to Polly Brinson - issued January 27, 1806,
Bondsman: Amos Small, WILSON Co.

COONEY, Joshua to Judy I. Demumbraum - issued October 27, 1845,
DAVIDSON Co.

COONROD, John to Matilda Wheeler - issued April 5, 1828, Bondsman:
Enoch Davis, WILSON Co.

CORRIGAR, Hugh to Elizabeth Lynhart - issued August 17, 1797, Bondsman:
Thomas Henderson, GRAINGER Co.

CORTNEY (or Cartney), William to Rachel McClure - issued December 20,
1820, Bondsman: John Craighead, m. by: Peter Nance, J. P.,
December 20, 1820, KNOX Co.

CORUM, Martin to Rebecca Carruthers - issued November 10, 1827,
Bondsman: Thornton Corum, m. by: Robert Gaines, J. P., GRAINGER Co.

CORZINE, Shelby to Sallie Kinnard - September 4, 1813, WILLIAMSON Co.

COSBEY, Alfred G. to Sarah McKinley - issued July 28, 1836, Bondsman:
Robert S. Morris, m. by: Martin Clark, E. M. E. C., July 28,
1836, RUTHERFORD Co.

COSBEY, Williamson to Mary Ann Cook - issued December 2, 1836, Bondsman:
A. D. Marshall, m. by: Jesse Alexander, V. D. M., December 15,
1836, RUTHERFORD Co.

COSBY, Wallace to Sarah Rankin - issued January 12, 1823, Bondsman:
Richard Neill, m. by: Wm. H. Davis, J. P., January 23, 1823,
RUTHERFORD Co.

COTHERN, Daniel to Martha Nimro - issued August 5, 1841, m. by:
Isaac Steele, G. M., ROBERTSON Co.

COTHERN, Dow to Sarah Spears - issued March 10, 1853, m. by:
David Simpson, J. P., March 10, 1853, COFFEE Co.

COTHILL, Rubin to Judith Dickerson - issued July 24, 1805, m. by:
Sm'l. Yancey, J. P.,

COTHON, John to Perthana W. Rutland - issued November 18, 1805, WILSON Co.

COTNER, Martin to Sally Ballard - issued February 6, 1813, Bondsman:
Nathan Ballard, GRAINGER Co.

COTRILL, Ralien to Judith Dickerson - issued July 24, 1806, GRAINGER Co.

COTTEL (?), Margaret to James Kenney - GREENE Co.

COTTER, Mary to Patrick Cannon - GREENE Co.

COTTLE, William to Margaret Kelley - September 6, 1811, Bondsman:
Robert Johnston, MAURY Co.

COTTON, Abner to Polly Crosslin - issued April 23, 1805, Bondsman: Wm. Crass, RUTHERFORD Co.

COTTON, Charles to Betsy Lyons - February 2, 1806, WILLIAMSON Co.

COTTON, Henry F. to Elizabeth Cotton - issued March 26, 1836, Bondsman: William Rice, m. by: Jesse Gambling March 26, 1836, SUMNER Co.

COTTON, Hiram S. to Martha Ellis - issued May 23, 1840, DAVIDSON Co.

COTTON, Hugh to Patience Edwards - issued January 26, 1830, Bondsman: John Strother, SUMNER Co.

COTTON, Hugh to Patience Edwards - issued January 26, 1831, m. by: Josiah Walton, J. P., January 26, 1831, SUMNER Co.

COTTON, James A. to Mary Jane Doss - Bondsman: A. M. Lyles, m. by: J. T. Hendrick, C. P., September 4, 1851, MONTGOMERY Co.

COTTON, John to Fanny Hamilton - issued January 4, 1791, Bondsman: Ephraham Payton and Lazrus Cotton, SUMNER Co.

COTTON, John to Jennet Crafford - issued November 22, 1800, Bondsman: Moore Cotton, SUMNER Co.

COTTON, John to Fanny Blackwell - issued June 24, 1811, Bondsman: Jonathan White, SUMNER Co.

COTTON, Kezia to John Evans - GREENE Co.

COTTON, Lee to Anna E. Wright - issued August 6, 1872, FRANKLIN Co.

COTTON, Moor to Levy Edwards - issued January 10, 1825, Bondsman: Bright Harris, m. by: Josiah Walton, J. P., January 10, 1825, SUMNER Co.

COTTON, Peter to Lebinah Tucker - issued May 20, 1806, Bondsman: Jeremiah Tucker, WILSON Co.

COTTON, Thos. L. to Louisa A. M. Buckner - issued May 6, 1854, Bondsman: W. D. Landes, m. by: James Lamb May 3, 1854, MONTGOMERY Co.

COTTRELL, George W. to Lydia M. Barnett - issued February 3, 1866, Bondsman: Joseph A. Roper, LAWRENCE Co.

COTTRELL, Joshua to Betsy Chesser - issued January 25, 1826, Bondsman: Jason Williams, Witness: Wm. Swan, KNOX Co.

COTTRELL, Sam'l. to Eliza Summers - issued October 8, 1829, m. by: Jno. Brown, J. P., October 9, 1829, KNOX Co.

COTTRELL, Samuel to Eliza Summers - issued October 8, 1829, Bondsman: Geo. C. Berry, Witness: Wm. Swan, KNOX Co.

COTTRELL, Thomas to Lydia Cheesman - December 27, 1821, KNOX Co.

COTTRELL, Thomas to Lydia Chesher - issued December 27, 1821, m. by: P. Nance, J. P., KNOX Co.

COTTRELL, Wm. to Nancy Williams - issued June 14, 1831, Bondsman: Edward Maney, m. by: Elijah Johnson, J. P., June 14, 1831, Witness: Wm. Swan, KNOX Co.

COUCH, Catherine to John Moyers - GREENE Co.

COUCH, Christopher C. to Permelia A. Meadows - issued November 14, 1860, m. by: W. B. M. Williams, Mins. M. E. Church So., November 15, 1860, COFFEE Co.

COTTRELL, Thomas to Lydia Cheesman - December 27, 1821, KNOX Co.

COTTRELL, Thomas to Lydia Chesher - issued December 27, 1821, m. by:
P. Nance, J. P., KNOX Co.

COTTRELL, Wm. to Nancy Williams - issued June 14, 1831, Bondsman:
Edward Maney, m. by: Elijah Johnson, J. P., June 14, 1831, Witness:
Wm. Swan, KNOX Co.

COUCH, Catherine to John Moyers - August 16, 1789, Security:
George Couch, GREENE Co.

COUCH, Christopher C. to Permelia A. Meadows - issued November 14,
1860, m. by: W. B. M. Williams, Mins. M. E. Church So., November 15,
1860, COFFEE Co.

COVINGTON, John to Jane Marlin - issued February 19, 1824, Bondsman:
Raiford Crawford, m. by: S. Beesley, J. P., February 19, 1824,
RUTHERFORD Co.

COVINGTON, John to Polly Crews - issued March 29, 1828, Bondsman:
Josiah Bloodworth, m. by: Josiah Walton, J. P., March 29, 1828,
SUMNER Co.

COVINGTON, Larkin to Ann Minifee - issued March 12, 1817, Bondsman:
Andrew Griffin, m. by: Sol. Beesley, J. P., March 13, 1817,
RUTHERFORD Co.

COVINGTON, R. M. to Mary E. Freeland - issued June 2, 1860, ROBERTSON Co.

COVINGTON, S. S. to Eveline E. McMillon - issued July 15, 1854, m. by:
W. T. Chowning, J. P., July 16, 1854, ROBERTSON Co.

COWAN, James to Margaret Montgomery - April 22, 1800, Surety:
Samuel Cowan, BLOUNT Co.

COWAN, James A. to Jane Collins - issued July 24, 1844, Bondsman:
W. S. Miller, m. July 25, 1844, MEIGS Co.

COWAN, James H. to Lucinda Dickenson - issued November 25, 1830,
Bondsman: B. M. Wallace, KNOX Co.

COWAN, James H. to Lucinda Dickenson - issued November 25, 1830, m. by:
Isaac Anderson, V. D. M., November 26, 1830, KNOX Co.

COWAN, James P. to Nancy Stephens - issued March 4, 1861, m. by:
W. R. Francis, J. P., March 5, 1861, FRANKLIN Co.

COWAN, James W. to Jennie M. Williams - issued February 14, 1872,
FRANKLIN Co.

COWAN, John to Agnes Martin - August 2, 1788, Security: Moses Moore,
GREENE Co.

COWAN, John to Polly Kirkum (?) - March 24, 1794, KNOX Co.

COWAN, John to Ann Gillespie - August 28, 1797, BLOUNT Co.

COWAN, Joseph to Jane Cowan Graham - August 27, 1804, WILLIAMSON Co.

COVINGTON, William to Sarah Hunter - issued March 13, 1827, m. by:
Demcy Ashford, J. P., March 13, 1827, SUMNER Co.

COW, Wm. G. to M. J. Herndon - issued April 11, 1841, m. by:
Isaac Steel, G. M., ROBERTSON Co.

COWAN, Alford E. to Susan Newberry - issued October 12, 1853, m. by:
J. C. Montgomery, J. P., October 13, 1853, FRANKLIN Co.

COWAN, Alfred E. to Susan Newberry - issued October 12, 1853, m. by:
J. C. Montgomery, J. P., October 13, 1853, FRANKLIN Co.

COWAN, Henry to Elizabeth Franklin - issued September 28, 1839, m. by:
J. G. Simpson September 29, 1839, FRANKLIN Co.

COWAN, Letitia to Jacob Gillespie - BEDFORD Co.

COWAN, Mathew to Katy Trousdale - issued March 8, 1800, Bondsman:
Edward Hogin, SUMNER Co.

COWAN, Robert to Nancy Martin - August 20, 1797, Surety: James Martin,
BLOUNT Co.

COWAN, Robt. H. to Hannah Thurman - issued December 19, 1872, FRANKLIN Co.

COWAN, Ross B. to Mary H. Hazelton - issued December 8, 1840, FRANKLIN Co.

COWAN, Ross B. to Mary Garrett - issued March 12, 1857, m. by:
John G. Biddle March 12, 1857, FRANKLIN Co.

COWAN, Samuel H. to Mary E. Moore - issued March 25, 1840, FRANKLIN Co.

COWAN, Varner D. to Margaret Jetton - issued June 7, 1824, Bondsman:
William Ledbetter, m. by: Robert Henderson June 11, 1824,
RUTHERFORD Co.

COWAN, Varner D. to Susan B. Johns - issued June 28, 1827, Bondsman:
Wm. T. Christy, m. by: Peyton Smith June 28, 1827, RUTHERFORD Co.

COWAN, W. H. to Julia A. Seargent - issued March 31, 1868, m. by:
J. M. Cowan, V. D. M., FRANKLIN Co.

COWAN, William to Sally Wallace - December 18, 1809, Bondsman:
Elias Frierson, MAURY Co.

COWAN, William to Mary E. Johns - issued April 23, 1833, Bondsman:
D. B. Molloy, m. by: G. Baker, M. G., August 23, 1833, RUTHERFORD Co.

COWAN, William to Elizabeth Lewis - issued October 4, 1842, m. by:
M. J. Simpson, J. P., October 27, 1842, FRANKLIN Co.

COWAN, Wm. to Indianna Williams - issued November 6, 1867, m. by:
M. B. Watterson, J. P., November 7, 1867, FRANKLIN Co.

COWAN, William B. to Nancy Sublett - issued July 2, 1823, m. by:
David Gordon July 2, 1823, RUTHERFORD Co.

COWAN, William M. to Mary M. Briant - issued March 10, 1832,
RUTHERFORD Co.

COWAN, William M. to Mary F. Bledsoe - issued March 11, 1857, m. by:
J. B. Foster, J. P., March 11, 1857, FRANKLIN Co.

COWAN, Wm. M. to S. C. Farris - issued December 14, 1870, FRANKLIN Co.

COWAN, William Wallace to Polly Flenniken - issued March 26, 1806,
Bondsman: James Campbell and Samuel Givens, Witness:
Stephen Hillis, KNOX Co.

COWANS, N. S. to Josie B. Kelley - issued September 25, 1867, m. by:
James Seargent, J. P., September 25, 1867, FRANKLIN Co.

COWARD, John to Sally Yarnell - issued May 22, 1827, m. by:
Wm. Morris, J. P., KNOX Co.

COWDEN, John J. to Eleanor F. Bradford - issued August 13, 1840, m. by:
T. Fanning August 13, 1840, DAVIDSON Co.

COWDEN, William to Elizabeth Sulivan - issued March 20, 1809, Bondsman:
Robert Simpson, SUMNER Co.

COWDEN, William to Elizabeth Scott - February 8, 1810, Bondsman:
James Scott, MAURY Co.

COWEN, George to Margaret Carothers - issued April 13, 1819, Bondsman:
Elmore Harris, SUMNER Co.

COWEN, James to Nancy Walker - issued January 12, 1826, Bondsman:
Mathew Horn, m. by: Elijah Maddox, M. G., WILSON Co.

COWEN, William M. to Mary M. Moseley - issued September 20, 1826,
Bondsman: James Allcorn, WILSON Co.

COWGER, John (see Conger, John)

COWGILL, Daniel to Eliza Stephens - issued October 3, 1831, Bondsman:
James Kigsley, m. by: W. Watson, J. P., October 3, 1831, SUMNER Co.

COWGILL, Martin to Sally Brooks - issued September 24, 1821, Bondsman:
Thos. Brooks, SUMNER Co.

COWGILL, Martin to Sally Perry - issued November 19, 1826, Bondsman:
Zack W. Baker, SUMNER Co.

CONGILL, Thompson to Rebecca Hallum - issued June 8, 1841, m. by:
Jas. H. Cook, J. P., June 9, 1841, DAVIDSON Co.

COX, A. M. to Susan E. Fowler - issued December 21, 1865, m. by:
I. N. Martin, J. P., December 21, 1865, FRANKLIN Co.

COX, Abraham to Mary W. Calloway - issued July 10, 1833, Bondsman:
Thos. F. Calloway, m. by: Wm. Morris, J. P., July 11, 1833, KNOX Co.

COX, Alexander to Rebecca Hutchison - issued June 3, 1813, Bondsman:
Samuel Martin and William Rodgers, KNOX Co.

COX, Anderson to Sally Palmer - issued June 17, 1819, Bondsman:
Thomas Cox, WILSON Co.

COX, Angenal (alias Doss) to Sarah Antoinett Edwards - December 29,
1850, m. by: W. G. Hensley, Deacon M. E. Church, GILES Co.

COX, Benjamin to Nancy Hearn - issued March 13, 1816, Bondsman:
Harry L. Douglas, m. by: Joseph T. Williams, J. P., March 14, 1816,
WILSON Co.

COX, C. C. to Nancy Lacy - issued September 21, 1835, m. October 1,
1835, KNOX Co.

COX, Charles to Martha Palmer - issued June 20, 1825, Bondsman:
John Cox, m. by: Jas. Johnson, J. P., June 24, 1825, WILSON Co.

COX, Elisha to Malinda Coker - issued April 1, 1828, Bondsman:
James H. Edington, KNOX Co.

COX, Elisha to Frances W. Via - issued December 17, 1835, Bondsman:
Isaac Ledbetter, m. December 19, 1835, RUTHERFORD Co.

COX, Ephraim to Anne Bell - issued April 6, 1825, m. by: Joseph Mason,
J. P., April 12, 1825, RUTHERFORD Co.

COX, Ezekiel to Mary L. Watson - issued July 14, 1835, Bondsman:
Richard Ledbetter, RUTHERFORD Co.

COX, Fountain to Zerilda Smith - issued December 2, 1843, m. by:
Thos. N. Cotton, J. P., December 3, 1843, DAVIDSON Co.

COX, George to Rachel Moffett - issued July 4, 1804, Bondsman:
Ben Grayson, Witness: Chas. McClung, KNOX Co.

COX, George to Mary Miles - issued December 11, 1846, m. by:
J. B. McCutchen, J. P., December 14, 1846, DAVIDSON Co.

COX, Dr. George W. to Amanda C. Moore - March 1, 1859, m. by:
W. L. Tarbut, D. V. M., GILES Co.

COX, Henry to Elizabeth Gwin - issued October 2, 1820, m. by:
Jno. Gass, J. P., October 3, 1820, KNOX Co.

COX, Henry R. to Purlena Shorter - issued November 11, 1826, Bondsman:
William Cox, WILSON Co.

COX, Henry R. to Maria Clifton - issued March 26, 1830, Bondsman:
E. D. Foster, m. by: Jas. C. Willford, J. P., March 31, 1830,
WILSON Co.

COX, Hiram to Elizabeth Ridgeway - issued March 21, 1814, Bondsman:
John Ridgeway, RUTHERFORD Co.

COX, Hiram to Elizabeth Chisenhall - issued November 15, 1823, Bondsman:
William Warren, RUTHERFORD Co.

COX, Hopkins to Eliza Ore - issued September 18, 1816, Bondsman:
Richard Braden, GRAINGER Co.

COX, J. R. to Zielha E. Bower - issued October 23, 1843, Bondsman:
Maradith Cox, m. by: A. King, M. G., October 24, 1843, MEIGS Co.

COX, James to Nancy Owens - January 16, 1805, WILLIAMSON Co.

COX, James to Ferrelly Allen - March 8, 1807, WILLIAMSON Co.

COX, James to Betsey Gammon - issued October 8, 1810, Bondsman:
William Conner, KNOX Co.

COX, James to Lusy Cox - issued November 11, 1826, Bondsman:
William Cox, WILSON Co.

COX, James to Martha Still - issued July 15, 1839, m. by:
Jas. Whitsitt July 17, 1839, DAVIDSON Co.

COX, James to Susan Wilson - issued April 1, 1844, FRANKLIN Co.

COX, James I. to Rebecca W. Chisenhall - issued November 17, 1834,
Bondsman: Alexr. S. Dickson, RUTHERFORD Co.

COX, James L. to Susan Porterfield - issued January 31, 1835, Bondsman:
James H. Alexander, RUTHERFORD Co.

COX, Jane to John Jones - GREENE Co.

COX, Jesse to Margery Cox - September 25, 1789, Security: Benjamin Cox,
GREENE Co.

COX, Jesse to Feariby (?) Leahy - July 13, 1812, KNOX Co.

COX, Jesse to Elizabeth Brown - January 11, 1816, WILLIAMSON Co.

COX, John to Alice Gammon - issued October 16, 1815, Bondsman:
John Goss, Witness: A. Hutcheson, D. C., KNOX Co.

COX, John to Elizabeth Palmer - issued October 13, 1818, Bondsman:
William Carlin, m. by: John W. Payton October 20, 1818, WILSON Co.

COX, John to Elizabeth Hampton - issued February 2, 1821, m. by:
Wm. Sawyers, J. P., KNOX Co.

COX, John to Betsey Edwards - issued August 26, 1824, Bondsman:
Alexander Rutledge, WILSON Co.

COX, John to Zeda Edwards - issued June 20, 1829, Bondsman:
Thomas Taylor, m. by: J. B. Taylor, J. P., WILSON Co.

COX, John to Susan Baker - issued August 30, 1853, m. by:
W. B. Cummings, J. P., August 30, 1853, VAN BUREN Co.

COX, John A. to Fannie Leonnard (Leonard) - issued February 15, 1867,
m. by: W. W. Hawkins, M. G., February 15, 1867, FRANKLIN Co.

COX, Jonathan to Mary Ann Galliher - issued October 25, 1819, m. by:
Amos Hardin, J. P., November 4, 1819, KNOX Co.

COX, Joseph M. to Delila May - issued February 15, 1837, Bondsman:
Thos. B. Cox, m. by: John Mynatt, J. P., February 16, 1837, KNOX Co.

COX, Lewis to Emily Holt - issued November 9, 1809, Bondsman:
William Park, KNOX Co.

COX, Margery to Jesse Cox - GREENE Co.

COX, Moses to Polly Conner - issued October 26, 1824, Bondsman:
John Gass, m. by: John Gass, J. P., October 28, 1824, KNOX Co.

COX, Naomi E. to Green I. Braton - issued March 20, 1863, Bondsman:
Benj. Pollock, Jos. H. Thompson, Clk., BEDFORD Co.

COX, Peter to Margaret Marshill - October 3, 1805, JEFFERSON Co.

COX, Peter to Thurza Phillips - issued December 14, 1839, Bondsman:
Henry Phillips, m. by: Solomon Caplinger, J. P., January 14, 1840,
WILSON Co.

COX, Richardson to Polly Julian - issued May 30, 1825, Bondsman:
Jonathan Williams, m. by: Robt. Tindel, J. P., May 30, 1825,
KNOX Co.

COX, Robert to Rebecca Rowton - issued March 20, 1824, Bondsman:
Anderson Cox, m. by: John Grary, J. P., March 23, 1824, WILSON Co.

COX, Sam'l. to Clotilda Darden - March 14, 1805, WILLIAMSON Co.

COX, Samuel to Margaret Crippen - issued December 9, 1807, Bondsman:
Matthias Talley, m. by: Jno. Purris, KNOX Co.

COX, Samuel to Polly Ann Jackson - February 3, 1859, m. by:
James A. Warren, J. P., GILES Co.

COX, Thomas to Nancy Baily - issued December 22, 1834, Bondsman:
Sam'l Yerger, m. by: Moses Ellis, J. P., January 1, 1835, WILSON Co.

COX, Thomas to Rhoda A. Jones - issued September 21, 1854, m. by:
Thos. Finch, J. P., September 21, 1854, FRANKLIN Co.

COX, Thos. B. to Caroline Calloway - issued April 12, 1829, m. by:
Mordecai Yarnell, J. P., April 12, 1829, KNOX Co.

COX, Thomas W. to Millanda D. Bradford - issued August 22, 1823,
Bondsman: Ralph McFadden, RUTHERFORD Co.

COX, Whitner to Rachel Miller - issued December 16, 1822, m. by:
John Bayless, J. P., December 19, 1822, KNOX Co.

COX, William to Mary Gass - October 7, 1797, Security: James Gass,
GREENE Co.

COX, William to Evalina Reese - issued May 16, 1818, Bondsman:
James Turner, m. by: Wm. Steele, J. P., May 21, 1818, WILSON Co.

COX, William to Holland Greer - issued July 25, 1821, Bondsman:
Britton Drake, WILSON Co.

COX, Wm. to Salina Bannon - issued June 18, 1844, m. by: Isaac Steel, G. M., ROBERTSON Co.

COX, William to Elizabeth Harris - issued January 20, 1848, m. by: Robert Green, J. P., ROBERTSON Co.

COX, Wm. C. to Ellen H. Jestin - issued December 8, 1853, m. by: Thos. Finch, J. P., December 8, 1853, FRANKLIN Co.

COXE, John to Peggy Hamilton - October 30, 1805, KNOX Co.

COYLE, Wm. R. to Martha E. Scudder - issued March 27, 1848, Bondsman: Philander P. Scudder, m. by: Jo. Pollard, J. P., March 30, 1848, MONTGOMERY Co.

COZBY, John to Abigail McBee - issued August 10, 1808, Bondsman: Wm. Smith, KNOX Co.

CRABB, Hiram G. N. to Elizabeth J. Sparkman - issued February 20, 1866, Bondsman: W. H. Sexton, m. by: Thos. J. Frazier February 20, 1866, LAWRENCE Co.

CRABB, Stephen to Delila Daniel - issued August 13, 1798, Bondsman: John Rhea, Witness: Sm'l. Yancey, GRAINGER Co.

CRABTREE, M. L. to Eliza Holcomb - issued November 26, 1866, m. by: Wm. Elliott, J. P., December 12, 1866, FRANKLIN Co.

CRABTREE, Benjamin to Sally Brewer - issued May 14, 1842, m. by: Thos. Cook, J. P., ROBERTSON Co.

CRABTREE, Benj. F. to Sarah E. Hugh - issued May 4, 1866, FRANKLIN Co.

CRABTREE, G. M. to Amanda M. Brown - issued May 22, 1866, FRANKLIN Co.

CRABTREE, George to Susannah Berry - issued July 8, 1841, m. by: M. Catchings, J. P., July 8, 1841, FRANKLIN Co.

CRABTREE, George to Susannah J. Suiter - issued August 12, 1849, m. by: M. Catchings, J. P., August 12, 1849, FRANKLIN Co.

CRABTREE, George W. to America M. Holder - issued December 27, 1873, m. by: William Sells, J. P., January 1, 1873, FRANKLIN Co.

CRABTREE, Jacob to Patsey Binley - issued December 28, 1819, Bondsman: Wm. Hadley, SUMNER Co.

CRABTREE, Jacob P. to Mary Jane Briley - issued December 20, 1856, m. by: James Cook, J. P., December 21, 1856, ROBERTSON Co.

CRABTREE, Jas. to Mary Colman - issued September 2, 1843, m. by: A. D. Scarborough, J. P., September 2, 1843, STEWART Co.

CRABTREE, James to Mary A. Chandler - issued December 30, 1856, m. by: James Cook, J. P., ROBERTSON Co.

CRABTREE, James M. to Lawrence J. Trice - issued August 5, 1847, Bondsman: C. H. Saunders, m. by: Wm. Shelton August 3, 1847, MONTGOMERY Co.

CRABTREE, John to Susan Wilson - issued December 28, 1846, m. by: W. B. Kelly, M. G., December 28, 1846, STEWART Co.

CRABTREE, John M. to Nancy Gifford - m. by: J. B. Rogers, J. P., December 25, 1856, FRANKLIN Co.

CRABTREE, Joseph to Hannah Carr - issued September 10, 1787, Bondsman: James Frazier, SUMNER Co.

CRABTREE, Joseph to Sally Holdman - issued April 10, 1795, Bondsman: Nathan Holdman, SUMNER Co.

CRABTREE, L. D. to Winney Medling - issued April 3, 1820, Bondsman: Harbird Young, WILSON Co.

CRABTREE, L. D. to Winney Medling - issued April 3, 1829, m. by: Wm. Willis, J. P., April 16, 1829, WILSON Co.

CRABTREE, Martin to Mary Richards - issued June 18, 1874, m. by: R. F. Oakley, J. P., June 18, 1874, FRANKLIN Co.

CRABTREE, Thomas to Mary A. Morgan - issued January 27, 1847, m. by: W. B. Richmon, J. P., January 28, 1847, ROBERTSON Co.

CRACKEN, Saml. W. to Margaret M. Guire - December 20, 1807, WILLIAMSON Co.

CRADDOCK, David to Rachel Oatey - November 12, 1788, Security: Cornelius Newman, GREENE Co.

CRADDOCK, Elijah H. to Sarah Hulett - issued June 19, 1838, m. by: Chas. W. Moorman, J. P., June 20, 1838, DAVIDSON Co.

CRADDOCK, Elicum to Anne Sutherland - issued November 2, 1829, Bondsman: Oliver M. Crutchfield, RUTHERFORD Co.

CRADDOCK, John to Ruth E. Hicks - issued June 14, 1823, Bondsman: Jesse Jennings, m. by: Joshua Lester, V. D. M., WILSON Co.

CRADDOCK, John to Lucrecia Arnold - issued January 12, 1824, Bondsman: Robert Bumpas, WILSON Co.

CRADDOCK, John N. to Anne Edmondson - issued August 10, 1829, Bondsman: John G. Keeble, m. by: Peyton Smith August 13, 1829, RUTHERFORD Co.

CRADDOCK, R. S. to M. E. Holand - issued September 30, 1846, DAVIDSON Co.

CRADDOCK, Richard to Polly Alsup - issued September 15, 1830, Bondsman: James Adams, m. by: J. Lester, V. D. M., WILSON Co.

CRADDOCK, Robert to Elizabeth King - issued June 20, 1836, m. by: Anthony Owing, WILSON Co.

CRADDOCK, Simon to Maria Jane Vick - issued July 14, 1840, Bondsman: Leonard Walker, m. by: James Thomas, M. G., July 16, 1840, WILSON Co.

CRADDOCK, William to Polly Wortham - issued September 24, 1816, Bondsman: George Glegly, WILSON Co.

CRAFFORD, James to Nancy Brumbelow - issued December 11, 1844, m. by: Wm. D. Baldwin, M. G., December 15, 1844, ROBERTSON Co.

CRAFFORD, James to Sarah Henrey - issued March 26, 1854, m. by: M. Catchings, J. P., March 26, 1854, FRANKLIN Co.

CRAFFORD, James H. to Martha I. Wallace - issued February 8, 1853, m. by: J. Sprouse, J. P., ROBERTSON Co.

CRAFFORD, John to Sally Pepper - issued June 19, 1841, m. by: Isaiah Warren June 20, 1841, ROBERTSON Co.

CRAFFORD, John to Martha Brakefield - issued March 30, 1850, m. by: W. L. Baldry, Gospel Minister, April 1, 1850, ROBERTSON Co.

CRAFFORD, John L. to Margaret Bennett - issued November 8, 1847, m. by: Isaac Steel, ROBERTSON Co.

CRAFFORD, Jno W. to Celia Tinson - issued February 3, 1846, m. by: Wm. D. Baldwin, M. G., ROBERTSON Co.

CRAFTON, Hezekiah to Sally Massey - issued August 15, 1826, m. by:
Silas Polk August 15, 1826, SUMNER Co.

CRAFTON, James to Mary Caudle - issued February 24, 1854, m. by:
W. M. C. Barr, J. P., February 28, 1854, ROBERTSON Co.

CRAFTON, Jospeh to Sarah Moore - issued July 12, 1852, Bondsman:
J. S. Moore, m. by: R. P. Bowling, J. P., July 12, 1852,
MONTGOMERY Co.

CRAIG, Alexander to Susann Logan - May 28, 1800, Security: Sugh Ferguson,
BLOUNT Co.

CRAIG, Andrew to Jemima Crafton - October 23, 1810, WILLIAMSON Co.

CRAIG, Benjamin R. to Mary G. Lewis - issued March 20, 1839, DICKSON Co.

CRAIG, David to Mrs. F. C. Colley - issued October 21, 1861, m. by:
W. H. Bugg, J. P., ROBERTSON Co.

CRAIG, Elizabeth to Robert Murphy - GREENE Co.

CRAIG, Gilbert C. to Eliza Swan - issued March 1, 1836, Bondsman:
Robt. Carns., KNOX Co.

CRAIG, J. H. to Cynthia A. Pennington - issued July 31, 1865, Bondsman:
R. A. Kelsey, m. by: W. P. Warren, P. C., August 1, 1865,
LAWRENCE Co.

CRAIG, James to Elizabeth Garner - issued February 20, 1843, m. by:
Sam'l Taylor, J. P., February 23, 1843, FRANKLIN Co.

CRAIG, James to Elizabeth Redding - issued June 30, 1852, m. by:
A. B. Soyars, J. P., July 1, 1852, ROBERTSON Co.

CRAIG, James T. to Nancy A. Reasing - issued July 15, 1841, m. by:
Reverend Thomas Martin, ROBERTSON Co.

CRAIG, James W. to Rebecka Low - issued February 9, 1828, Bondsman:
James H. Cowan, m. by: Geo. Donnell, M. G., February 14, 1828,
KNOX Co.

CRAIG, John to Betsey Monry (Money?) - October 12, 1809, Bondsman:
John Raggan, MAURY Co.

CRAIG, John to Nancy Cowan - issued January 22, 1823, Bondsman:
Absolom Stout, RUTHERFORD Co.

CRAIG, Lewis Y. to Mary E. Lowry - issued July 5, 1843, m. by:
R. B. C. Howell, M. G., July 6, 1843, DAVIDSON Co.

CRAIG, Rebecca to William Adams - MAURY Co.

CRAIG, Robert to Elizabeth Jones - issued August 13, 1828, Bondsman:
Archibald Wells, KNOX Co.

CRAIG, Rob't. to Elizabeth Jones - issued August 13, 1828, m. by:
Geo. Donnell, M. G., August 14, 1828, KNOX Co.

CRAIG, Susanna to James Montgomery - MAURY Co.

CRAIG, Thomas to Jane Thompson - May 25, 1816, WILLIAMSON Co.

CRAIG, Thomas to Mary Ann Pope - issued January 7, 1819, Bondsman:
Jonathan Dale, GRAINGER Co.

CRAIG, Thos. to Susan Graves - issued September 28, 1836, Bondsman:
Nathaniel Byrd, m. by: Duerrett Everett, Esq., September 29,
1836, Witness: Geo. M. White, KNOX Co.

CRAIG, William to Esther Montgomery - July 5, 1802, Security:
Alexander Mongomery, BLOUNT Co.

CRAIG, Wm. to Ann A. G. Seaton - issued November 24, 1835, m. by:
W. A. McCampbell, M. V. D., November 26, 1835, KNOX Co.

CRAIG, William B. to Elizabeth Gordon - November 26, 1846, m. by:
Jehu Nave, J. P., GILES Co.

CRAIG, William J. to Virginia B. Abernathy - November 19, 1850, m. by:
W. T. Plummer, M. G., GILES Co.

CRAIGHEAD, Benjamin to Orlena P. Bunch - issued November 11, 1828,
Bondsman: Wm. L. Cardwell, m. by: Jas. Kennon, M. G., November 11,
1828, GRAINGER Co.

CRAIGHEAD, Thomas to Polly Galespie - issued December 23, 1803,
Bondsman: Robert Craighead, Witness: A. White, KNOX Co.

CRAIGHEAD, Thos. G. to Rutclid Armstrong - issued August 18, 1828,
Bondsman: Jno. Campbell, m. by: Elijah M. Eagleton August 19,
1828, KNOX Co.

CRAIGUE, Nicholas to Nancy Thomison - issued December 1, 1847,
VAN BUREN Co.

CRAIN, Aron G. to Mary Ann Deaton - issued September 4, 1855, m. by:
James Moore, M. G., September 7, 1855, VAN BUREN Co.

CRAIN, Benjimin to Jenny Shelton - issued June 13, 1801, Bondsman:
Micajah Terry, Witness: A. White, KNOX Co.

CRAIN, Buswell J. to Harriet Tucker - issued March 7, 1839, m. by:
Geo. Childress, J. P., ROBERTSON Co.

CRAIN, Charles to Margret Trogdon - issued October 10, 1815, Bondsman:
Charles Crain, Senr., m. by: J. S. Moore, J. P., October 10,
1815, GRAINGER Co.

CRAIN, Davis to Sarah Beckham - issued November 21, 1832, Bondsman:
John Crain, m. by: H. Allsur, J. P., GRAINGER Co.

CRAIN, Jesse to Laxis Phillips - issued December 2, 1852, m. by:
W. B. Huddleston, M. G., December 2, 1852, VAN BUREN Co.

CRAIN, Jr., John to Elizabeth Lemmons - issued March 11, 1827, Bondsman:
Thomas Ray, Jr., m. by: D. Tate, J. P., March 11, 1827, GRAINGER Co.

CRAIN, Newel to Margret Lewis - issued August 23, 1849, m. by:
M. Y. Brocket, M. G., August 23, 1849, VAN BUREN Co.

CRAIN, Sparkes to Zelley Phillips - issued January 23, 1850, VAN BUREN Co.

CRAIN, Sparkes to Zelly Phillips - issued February 27, 1850, m. by:
John Gillentine, J. P., February 27, 1850, VAN BUREN Co.

CRANE, Oliver C. to Francis Ballard - issued February 21, 1844, m. by:
Uriah York, J. P., February 22, 1844, VAN BUREN Co.

CRANE, W. G. to Mollie M. Cole - issued September 22, 1871, m. by:
E. P. Anderson, M. G., September 22, 1871, FRANKLIN Co.

CRANE, William to Nancy Rascoe - issued August 7, 1817, Bondsman:
Philip Turner, SUMNER Co.

CRANK, James to Nancy George - issued January 17, 1826, Bondsman:
Thos. Crank, m. by: John Bayless, J. P., January 22, 1826,
Witness: Wm. Swan, KNOX Co.

CRANK, Jesse to Eliza George - issued January 30, 1829, Bondsman:
Stephen George, m. by: Jno. Bayless, J. P., February 5, 1829,
Witness: Wm. Swan, KNOX Co.

CRANK, Thomas to Anna Human - issued April 4, 1820, Bondsman:
James Human, m. by: Wm. A. McCampbell April 5, 1820, KNOX Co.

CRASSAN, Wm. to Elizabeth Spillman - issued February 10, 1834, m. by:
Saml. White, J. P., February 10, 1834, KNOX Co.

CRASSLIN, William to Sarah George - issued September 27, 1859, m. by:
Benjamin Gambill, J. P., September 29, 1859, ROBERTSON Co.

CRATON, James to Jenney Wamack - issued December 31, 1808, Bondsman:
Richard, Diskill, WILSON Co.

CRAVENS, Gersham to Zerilda Darnell - issued October 14, 1845, m. by:
John Gold, J. P., October 14, 1845, MONTGOMERY Co.

CRAVENS, James to Anne Love - December 20, 1797, Security: George Gordon,
GREENE Co.

CRAVENS, Richard to Rebecca Darnell - issued January 8, 1846, m. by:
John Gold, J. P., January 8, 1846, MONTGOMERY Co.

CRAVINS, Williams to Cyntha A. Billingsley - issued March 1, 1860,
m. by: B. L. Simmons, J. P., VAN BUREN Co.

CRAWFORD, A. T. to A. E. Hall - issued March 20, 1869, m. by:
E. P. Anderson, M. G., March 21, 1869, FRANKLIN Co.

CRAWFORD, Adam to Cathrina Scott - January 18, 1833, KNOX Co.

CRAWFORD, Alexander to Esther Alexander - December 20, 1808, Bondsman:
Wilson Henderson (?), MAURY Co.

CRAWFORD, Alexander M. to Polly McClure - issued August 7, 1841,
m. by: Geo. Hudspeth, FRANKLIN Co.

CRAWFORD, Andrew to Sally Meeke - issued May 22, 1823, Bondsman:
T. L. Williams, m. by: Geo. Atkin, M. G., May 22, 1823, KNOX Co.

CRAWFORD, Andrew to Catherine O. Riley - issued October 17, 1839,
m. by: J. Thos. Wheat, Rec. of Cr. Ch., October 17, 1839,
DAVIDSON Co.

CRAWFORD, Arthur to Nancy Tarver - issued November 24, 1829, m. by:
Elijah M. Eagleton November 26, 1829, KNOX Co.

CRAWFORD, Barnes to Amanda Lavin (Louise or Lones?) - issued December 4,
1837, Bondsman: David Lyon, m. by: J. M. Kelley, M. G., December 5,
1837, KNOX Co.

CRAWFORD, C. W. to Elvira R. Anglin - issued August 26, 1854, m. by:
John K. Woodson, M. G., August 27, 1854, ROBERTSON Co.

CRAWFORD, Charles B. to Mary I. Clayton - issued November 24, 1835,
Bondsman: Jas. W. Leiper, RUTHERFORD Co.

CRAWFORD, Counsel L. to Aristem L. Hill - issued January 2, 1839,
Bondsman: Jeptha Clemmons, m. by: Jas. T. Tompkins, WILSON Co.

CRAWFORD, David to Elizabeth Casey - issued January 21, 1805, Bondsman:
James Carlisle, RUTHERFORD Co.

CRAWFORD, Edmant to Elizabeth Smith - issued December 16, 1829,
Bondsman: Gilbert Young, m. by: John Beard, M. G., December 17,
1829, WILSON Co.

CRAWFORD, Edwin to Polly Webster - issued March 9, 1833, Bondsman:
Hugh Jones, m. by: M. B. Carter, J. P., March 9, 1833, KNOX Co.

CRAWFORD, Henry to Betsy Hickson - issued November 9, 1836, m. by:
Martin L. Mynatt, J. P., November 10, 1836, KNOX Co.

CRAWFORD, Henry to Eliza Henshaw - issued October 29, 1839, m. by:
James F. Green, J. P., October 29, 1839, FRANKLIN Co.

CRAWFORD, Henry to Cathrine Denson - issued February 25, 1860, m. by:
James C. Handley, J. P., February 29, 1860, FRANKLIN Co.

CRAWFORD, Hugh to Patty Worker - issued February 8, 1824, Bondsman:
Moore Cotton, m. by: Charles Watkins February 8, 1824, SUMNER Co.

CRAWFORD, Hugh to Catharine Mynatt - issued August 27, 1827, KNOX Co.

CRAWFORD, Hugh to Catharine Mynatt - issued August 27, 1827, m. by:
Geo. Graves, J. P., August 30, 1827, KNOX Co.

CRAWFORD, James to Anny Thrower - issued April 20, 1811, Bondsman:
William Crawford, WILSON Co.

CRAWFORD, James J. to Elizabeth T. Hogan - issued March 17, 1841, m. by:
A. L. P. Green, M. G., March 18, 1841, DAVIDSON Co.

CRAWFORD, James L. to Lutendy Kelly - issued September 19, 1844,
m. by: D. G. Baird, J. P., ROBERTSON Co.

CRAWFORD, John to Elizabeth Rutherford - February 25, 1808, WILLIAMSON Co.

CRAWFORD, John to Betsey Payne - issued November 10, 1810, Bondsman:
Hugh Finley, SUMNER Co.

CRAWFORD, John to Mrs. Susan Green - issued September 15, 1869,
FRANKLIN Co.

CRAWFORD, Joseph to Betsy Brock - issued April 10, 1799, Bondsman:
James Brock, Witness: A. White, KNOX Co.

CRAWFORD, Joseph A. to Margaret L. Austell - issued November 4, 1856,
m. by: L. Payne, Minister, November 4, 1856, COFFEE Co.

CRAWFORD, Josiah to Lydia Sears - issued August 26, 1819, Bondsman:
Elishia Long, m. by: J. Rutherford August 26, 1819, SUMNER Co.

CRAWFORD, Micajah to Mary F. Jackson - issued November 20, 1837,
Bondsman: G. M. Hazen, m. by: Jacob Nutty, T. D., November 20,
1837, KNOX Co.

CRAWFORD, Moses to Melinda Churchman - issued December 29, 1823,
Bondsman: Dotson Morgan, m. by: David Tate, J. P., December 30,
1823, GRAINGER Co.

CRAWFORD, N. D. to Elizabeth D. Neely - issued October 8, 1862,
Bondsman: E. T. Mallard, Jos. H. Thompson, Clk. per N. F. Thompson,
Dep. Clk., BEDFORD Co.

CRAWFORD, Thomas to Mary Chapman - October 20, 1784, Security:
Seabert Sollers (?), GREENE Co.

CRAWFORD, Thomas to Maria Harris - issued September 20, 1825, Bondsman:
John Hickle, m. by: John Bayless, J. P., September 20, 1825,
KNOX Co.

CRAWFORD, William to Sally Terry - issued December 7, 1801, Bondsman:
Jesse Terry, Witness: Wm. C. Blount, KNOX Co.

CRAWFORD, Wm. to Matilda Churchman - issued February 18, 1824, m. by:
Wm. Sawyers, J. P., February 19, 1824, KNOX Co.

CRAWFORD, William to Nancy Bell - issued January 5, 1837, m. by:
John R. Sullivan, J. P., January 5, 1837, RUTHERFORD Co.

CRAWFORD, William C. to Mary Anne Killiam - issued December 17, 1824,
Bondsman: John Crawford, m. by: John H. B. E. Warren December 17,
1824, RUTHERFORD Co.

CRAWFORD, Wm. H. to Elizabeth Barger - issued March 21, 1833, Bondsman:
Nicholas Barger, m. by: Sam'l. White, J. P., March 24, 1833,
Witness: Wm. Swan, KNOX Co.

CRAWLEY, James H. to Anna E. Oakley - issued May 14, 1867, m. by:
Thomas F. Moseley, J. P., May 14, 1867, FRANKLIN Co.

CRAWLEY, Samuel to Margaret Hay - September 20, 1808 (?), MAURY Co.

CRAWLY, Henry to Delia Graham - issued December 30, 1853, m. by:
W. B. Cummings, J. P., December 30, 1853, VAN BUREN Co.

CRAYTON, Gland to Mary Hiles - December 3, 1806, WILLIAMSON Co.

CRAZE, Abner G. to Mary Sullivan - issued October 17, 1828, Bondsman:
Samuel Rutter, m. by: Wm. M. Swain, J. P., October 24, 1828,

CREACH, Jno. W. to Nancy Jane Bell - issued July 7, 1842, m. by:
John Beard, M. G., July 7, 1842, DAVIDSON Co.

CREACH, Wm. to Sarah White - issued June 20, 1838, m. by: John Eubank,
J. P., June, 1838, DICKSON Co.

CREAL, John B. to Mary Williams - issued December 1, 1846, m. by:
Allen Knight December 2, 1846, DAVIDSON Co.

CREAMER, Daniel to Sarah Wilson - December 7, 1790, Security:
William Caldwell, GREENE Co.

CREAMER, Jeremiah to Catharine T. Simms - issued May 9, 1846, Bondsman:
H. R. Jenkins, m. by: N. F. Trice, J. P., MONTGOMERY Co.

CREASEY, John to Nancy Hill - February 10, 1807, WILLIAMSON Co.

CRECIATE, Henry to Louisa A. Burnett - issued February 24, 1872,
m. by: W. P. DuBose, Chaplain University of the South, February 28,
1872, FRANKLIN Co.

CRECK, George to Sally Glass - November 6, 1811, WILLIAMSON Co.

CREECH, Thomas to Alamanza Green - issued March 17, 1842, m. by:
W. E. Cartwright March 17, 1842, DAVIDSON Co.

CREECY, Jesse to Sarah Jane Goold - December 2, 1850, m. by: W. T. Lee,
GILES Co.

CREEK, John to Frances Calton - issued July 23, 1836, Bondsman:
James Hill, m. by: John Landrum July 28, 1836, RUTHERFORD Co.

CREEK, M. B. to Mary Montgomery - m. by: Rev. Hugh L. Montgomery
November 1, 1857, COFFEE Co.

CREENSHAW, William to Polly Edwards - issued December 31, 1809,
Bondsman: David Edwards, SUMNER Co.

CREIGHTON, Joseph to Nancy Travillion - issued July 21, 1843, m. by:
L. Burnett, J. P., July 26, 1843, DAVIDSON Co.

CRENSHAW, A. J. to Amy Lathum - issued December 19, 1833, m. by:
B. C. Seawell, J. P., December 19, 1833, SUMNER Co.

CRENSHAW, Benjamin O. to Mary E. Gunn - issued November 21, 1844,
m. by: Joel Whitten, ROBERTSON Co.

311

CRENSHAW, Charles to Elizabeth Wright - April 2, 1811, WILLIAMSON Co.

CRENSHAW, Chesteen to Sarah Crenshaw - November 15, 1831, WILLIAMSON Co.

CRENSHAW, Daniel to Ruth Anderson - June 20, 1829, WILLIAMSON Co.

CRENSHAW, James to Eliza Winslow - April 8, 1811, WILLIAMSON Co.

CRENSHAW, John to Betsey Parker - issued May 18, 1812, Bondsman:
    Richard Gillespie, SUMNER Co.

CRENSHAW, John to Mary Stewart - m. by: Thos. Joyner May 14, 1834,
    SUMNER Co.

CRENSHAW, Meredith to Elizabeth Pharr - issued January 2, 1816,
    Bondsman: Enos Vinson, m. by: John Rutherford January 2, 1816,
    SUMNER Co.

CRENSHAW, Nathaniel to Harriett Rice - issued September 10, 1810,
    Bondsman: John Edwards, SUMNER Co.

CRENSHAW, Oliver to Elizabeth Crawford - July 11, 1814, WILLIAMSON Co.

CRENSHAW, Vincent to Ann King - issued August 30, 1839, m. by:
    Lewis Garrett September 1, 1839, DAVIDSON Co.

CRENSHAW, William H. to Delia Ann Hall - issued December 9, 1835,
    Bondsman: Edmund B. Drake, m. by: Geo. Donnell, M. G., WILSON Co.

CRESWELL, Andrew to Anna Brown - issued February 6, 1810, Bondsman:
    Wm. Holbrook, WILSON Co.

CRESWELL, Andrew J. to Frances Lane - issued October 22, 1838, Bondsman:
    Hardy B. Griffin, WILSON Co.

CRESWELL, Halem to Elizabeth Johnson - issued August 29, 1821, Bondsman:
    David Brown, m. by: E. Maddox, M. G., WILSON Co.

CRESWELL, John A. to Martha Mays - issued June 13, 1820, Bondsman:
    Alexander Kirkpatrick, m. by: William Gray, J. P., June 14, 1820,
    WILSON Co.

CRESWELL, John A. to Nancy Mays - issued September 7, 1840, Bondsman:
    Isaac G. Caler, m. by: Melkijah L. Vaughn, M. G., September 8,
    1840, WILSON Co.

CRESWELL, Martin to Harriet Eagan - issued January 5, 1839, Bondsman:
    Minor Creswell, m. by: Thos. Burk, J. P., January 6, 1839,
    WILSON Co.

CRESWELL, Samuel to Sarah Mays - issued September 5, 1827, Bondsman:
    James Edding, m. by: J. Kirkpatrick, J. P., September 6, 1827,
    WILSON Co.

CREVAT, Moses to Nancy West - issued January 15, 1829, m. by:
    Jno. Tindel, M. G., January 15, 1829, KNOX Co.

CREW, Pleasant to Margaret Layton - issued June 7, 1819, m. by:
    John Haynie June 7, 1819, KNOX Co.

CREW, Pleasant to Roberta S. Parham - issued October 8, 1835, Bondsman:
    Sam'l. R. Rodgers, KNOX Co.

CREWDON, Geo. to Eliza I. Thompson - issued December 22, 1847, m. by:
    Isaac Steel December 23, 1847, ROBERTSON Co.

CREWGAR, George to Ellen Corn - issued April 18, 1866, m. by:
    John Armstrong, J. P., April, 1866, FRANKLIN Co.

CREWS, Archibald to Margaret Brown - issued February 8, 1836, Bondsman:
A. J. Brown, m. by: Richard Keyhill, J. P., February 8, 1836,
KNOX Co.

CREWS, Benjamin to Susan Crenshaw - issued October 30, 1819, Bondsman:
Richard Higgason, SUMNER Co.

CREWS, David to Polly Smith - issued October 4, 1823, Bondsman:
Levi McCloud, m. by: William B. Carns, J. P., October 5, 1823,
KNOX Co.

CREWS, Edward to Sally Bently - issued December 20, 1826, Bondsman:
James Anglea, SUMNER Co.

CREWS, George W. to Margaret T. Howard - issued October 25, 1865,
Bondsman: Jonathan Crews, m. by: William Clayton, M. G.,
October 26, 1865, LAWRENCE Co.

CREWS, Henry to Jane Hankins - issued June 14, 1824, Bondsman:
Thomas Hawley, m. by: Henry Hawkins June 14, 1824, GRAINGER Co.

CREWS, Howell to Sarah O. Kirkham - issued June 28, 1825, Bondsman:
Rase Bowen, GRAINGER Co.

CREWS, John to Rushia Bloodworth - issued March 5, 1825, Bondsman:
Wm. Griffin, m. by: C. Crane March 5, 1825, SUMNER Co.

CREWS, Pleasant to Elizabeth Lavender - issued March 21, 1808, Bondsman:
John Jones, SUMNER Co.

CREWS, Pleasant to Mary Trusley - issued November 21, 1848, Bondsman:
M. Musgrove, m. by: R. H. Weakley, J. P., November 23, 1848,
MONTGOMERY Co.

CREWS, Robert to Mary Ann Bivinham - issued April 3, 1823, m. by:
Rob't. McBath, Esq., April 16, 1823, KNOX Co.

CREWS, Robert to Elizabeth M. Broadie - issued May 16, 1846, Bondsman:
J. Hester, MONTGOMERY Co.

CREWS, Squire to Piety Prewitt - issued August 21, 1819, Bondsman:
Wm. Rawlins, RUTHERFORD Co.

CREWS, Tarlton to Jane Day - issued February 28, 1832, Bondsman:
Willis Crews, m. by: Wm. C. Carter, J. P., February 28, 1832,
SUMNER Co.

CREWS, Walter to Nancy Walker - issued April 13, 1821, m. by:
Robt. McBath, Esq., April 26, 1821, KNOX Co.

CREWS, Wm. J. to Mary J. Simms - issued September 27, 1865, Bondsman:
George W. Crews, m. by: J. B. Clayton, J. P., September 28,
1865, LAWRENCE Co.

CREWS, Willis to Nancy Thurmond - m. September 2, 1828, SUMNER Co.

CREWS, Willis to Margery Byrn - issued February 28, 1832, Bondsman:
William B. Stovall, m. by: Wm. M. Carter, J. P., February 28,
1832, SUMNER Co.

CREWSE, Wm. to Elizabeth Hood - issued April 26, 1825, Bondsman:
Shadrack Massey, m. by: Robt. McBath April 26, 1825, Witness:
Wm. Swan, KNOX Co.

CREYTON, John to Agnes Dalton - issued June 10, 1815, Bondsman:
William Clark, GRAINGER Co.

CRICK, Christina to Wm. H. H. Haynes - BEDFORD Co.

CRICKMORE, William to Nancy Hickman - issued December 19, 1857, m. by:
Benjamin Gambill, J. P., December 20, 1857, ROBERTSON Co.

CRIDDLE, Smith to Lucy Whitfield - September 4, 1832, WILLIAMSON Co.

CRIDDLE, Smith to Belle Ann Bremaker - issued October 16, 1839, m. by:
R. B. C. Howell, Pastor Baptist Ch., October 16, 1839, DAVIDSON Co.

CRIPPEN, James to Patsy Hall - issued March 28, 1808, Bondsman:
Joseph Giron, Witness: Jno. A. Gamble, KNOX Co.

CRIPPEN, John to Elizabeth Allen - issued December 28, 1809, Bondsman:
Wm. Harrelson, m. by: R. Houston, J. P., December 28, 1809,
KNOX Co.

CRIPPENS, Wm. P. to Dice Tindell - issued November 21, 1833, m. by:
Lewis Luttrell, J. P., November 21, 1833, KNOX Co.

CRISBY, John to Betsey Lafin - issued July 25, 1808, Bondsman:
Griffy Griffitts, GRAINGER Co.

CRISCO, David to Mary E. Gill - issued April 5, 1857, m. by:
E. L. Jones, L. D., April 12, 1857, COFFEE Co.

CRISMAN, Charles to Senil Lewis - issued October 20, 1853, m. by:
Rev. N. T. Power October 21, 1853, FRANKLIN Co.

CRISMAN, Jr., Isaac to Isabella Pursley - issued October 27, 1825,
Bondsman: Fleming Pursley, m. by: James McMillan, J. P., October 27,
1825, KNOX Co.

CRISMAN, William B. to Anna Alexander - issued July 31, 1860, m. by:
Rev. A. J. Baird July 31, 1860, FRANKLIN Co.

CRISP, Elias to Mary Walding - issued September 3, 1838, Bondsman:
B. H. Taylor, m. by: Prior Neil, J. P., September 9, 1838, MEIGS Co.

CRISTOL, Ritchard to Elisabeth Rhea - issued February 2, 1797, Bondsman:
John Lebow, GRAINGER Co.

CRISWELL, Francis G. to George Ann Thomas - issued July 26, 1853, m. by:
J. M. Gunn, J. P., ROBERTSON Co.

CRISWELL, Mathew to Jane Gray - issued December 1, 1832, m. by:
Elisha Vaughn, WILSON Co.

CRISWELL, Mathew to Jane Gray - issued December 1, 1832, Bondsman:
William Gray, WILSON Co.

CRISWELL, Minor to Catharine Gray - issued January 1, 1837, Bondsman:
Fletcher Campbell, WILSON Co.

CRISWELL, Robert to Rebecca Thomas - issued July 12, 1831, Bondsman:
David Thomas, m. by: B. Bridges, J. P., July 13, 1831, WILSON Co.

CRISWELL, William T. to Matilda Lane - issued December 1, 1838,
Bondsman: Hardy P. Griffin, m. by: R. S. Tate December 5, 1838,
WILSON Co.

CRITZ, James M. to Ann Eliza Scales - issued October 15, 1845, m. by:
R. B. C. Howell, M. G., October 15, 1845, DAVIDSON Co.

CROCKER, Benjaman F. to Elizabeth Watson - issued December 14, 1846,
m. by: Samuel Edmonson December 15, 1846, DAVIDSON Co.

CROCKER, Henderson J. to L. E. Doss - issued December 2, 1850, m. by:
B. Randolph, J. P., December 4, 1850, ROBERTSON Co.

CROCKER, Jas. M. to Ellen Brook - issued October 7, 1848, Bondsman:
Jonas Gray, MONTGOMERY Co.

CROCKER, Jesse to Jane Kirkpatrick - issued June 23, __(?), Bondsman: John O'Neal, m. by: John Jarrett, M. G., WILSON Co.

CROCKER, John T. to Eliza Winston - issued June 19, 1834, m. by: Wm. Vinson, J. P., June 19, 1834, RUTHERFORD Co.

CROCKER, Lambert to Lucy Williams - issued October 4, 1830, Bondsman: Moses B. Wadley, RUTHERFORD Co.

CROCKETT, Fountain O. to Julia G. Smith - issued December 5, 1820, m. by: Robt. Henderson, V. D. M., December 5, 1820, RUTHERFORD Co.

CROCKETT, Granville S. to Sarah Sims - issued May 16, 1821, m. by: Peyton Smith, M. G., May 16, 1821, RUTHERFORD Co.

CROCKETT, J. W. to Harriet Rawls - issued January 18, 1854, m. by: Benj. Rawls, M. G., January 22, 1854, ROBERTSON Co.

CROCKETT, Jackson to Eliz Fiser - issued December 29, 1842, m. by: W. Seal, J. P., ROBERTSON Co.

CROCKETT, James to Nancy W. Menees - issued November 12, 1839, m. by: J. W. Ferguson, J. P., ROBERTSON Co.

CROCKETT, Jane to George Hisaw - GREENE Co.

CROCKETT, Joseph to Polly Crockett - December 1, 1812, WILLIAMSON Co.

CROCKETT, Judge W. to Polly Wall - issued March 31, 1840, m. by: W. Hand, J. P., April 2, 1840, DICKSON Co.

CROCKETT, Leftwich to Huldy Davidson - issued August 2, 1849, Bondsman: Jno. C. Breedon, m. by: A. Baggett, J. P., August 3, 1849, MONTGOMERY Co.

CROCKETT, Overton W. to Evalina A. Smith - issued November 24, 1815, Bondsman: L. Anderson, RUTHERFORD Co.

CROCKETT, Robert M. to Ann Tinsley - issued October 2, 1854, Bondsman: Wm. A. Williams, m. by: Wm. Frazier, J. P., October 4, 1854, MONTGOMERY Co.

CROCKETT, Samuel to Frances B. Dudley - January 26, 1815, WILLIAMSON Co.

CROCKETT, W. B. E. J. to Martha Jane Boyd - issued January 11, 1843, m. by: Josiah Ferriss, J. P., January 11, 1843, DAVIDSON Co.

CROFORD, Elizabeth to Joseph Stockard - MAURY Co.

CROMWELL, Beverly A. to Mary Young - issued February 18, 1840, Bondsman: C. T. Harris, m. by: Robt. D. Bell, M. G., WILSON Co.

CROMWELL, Napoleon to Elizabeth J. Sharp - issued August 16, 1843, FRANKLIN Co.

CRON, John to M. C. Johnson - issued December 19, 1836, Bondsman: Abner Luckadoo, SUMNER Co.

CROOK, Barbara to Jacob Limebough (?) - GREENE Co.

CROOK, Robertson to Seleny Eatheridge - issued April 5, 1820, Bondsman: Charles Nicholson, WILSON Co.

CROOK, William to Susan Rutledge - issued August 15, 1831, Bondsman: John Scoggins, m. by: J. L. Swaney, J. P., August 15, 1831, SUMNER Co.

CROOK, William M. to Rebecca Lasiter - issued November 23, 1824, Bondsman: Isaac Shark, WILSON Co.

CROOK, Z. V. to Mary H. Pullin - issued April 15, 1861, Bondsman:
George K. Welch, m. by: William Lackey April 18, 1861, LAWRENCE Co.

CROOMS, James to Charity Tait - issued March 27, 1816, Bondsman:
Hugh Harris, m. by: John Williamson, J. P., March 28, 1816,
WILSON Co.

CROPPER, James to Peggy Purvine - issued August 17, 1808, Bondsman:
John Purvine, WILSON Co.

CROPPER, Jame to Rhoda Holland - issued December 28, 1824, Bondsman:
Reed A. Holland, WILSON Co.

CROPPER, James to Malinda Dellis - issued February 29, 1836, m. by:
B. T. Mottley, J. P., March 1, 1836, WILSON Co.

CROPPER, James P. to Malinda Bass - issued June 11, 1832, Bondsman:
J. C. Green, WILSON Co.

CROPPER, John to Isabel Harney - issued January 3, 1838, Bondsman:
Henry T. Cropper, m. by: Robert H. Ellis, J. P., WILSON Co.

CROPPER, Tho. H. to Elizabeth Dellis - issued March 19, 1832, Bondsman:
Michael Jones, m. by: B. T. Mottley, J. P., March 20, 1832,
WILSON Co.

CROPPER, Thomas H. to Lerzah Telford - issued August 29, 1838, Bondsman:
Henry S. Cropper, m. by: John Beard, M. G., WILSON Co.

CROSBY, Mary to Andres Bryan - GREENE Co.

CROSEDAY, James to Winnie Joyner - issued September 3, 1838, Bondsman:
Abram B. Joyner, m. by: Robt. Patton, J. P., September 3, 1838,
SUMNER Co.

CROSIER, James to Miss M. C. Johnson - issued November 3, 1849,
Bondsman: Jno. R. Payne, m. by: J. T. Hendrick November 4, 1849,
MONTGOMERY Co.

CROSLIN, Wright W. to Catharine Byron - issued December 17, 1832,
Bondsman: Joseph Hondyshell, SUMNER Co.

CROSNER, George to Catey Houck - issued November 26, 1804, Bondsman:
George Grimes, SUMNER Co.

CROSS, Benjamin J. J. to Martha J. Tarewater - issued July 21, 1856,
m. by: H. W. Carroll, J. P., July 17, 1856, COFFEE Co.

CROSS, David to Rebecca Wilkins - issued September 24, 1857, m. by:
G. B. Mason, J. P., ROBERTSON Co.

CROSS, Gibbons to Jenney Hill - issued July 13, 1808, Bondsman:
Henry Matlock, GRAINGER Co.

CROSS, John to Elizabeth West - issued July 31, 1815, Bondsman:
Joshua Anderson, WILSON Co.

CROSS, John to Mary D. Joy - issued December 1, 1835, Bondsman:
Thomas Boyd, RUTHERFORD Co.

CROSS, Mary to Mitchell Fuller - issued May 2, 1864, Bondsman:
H, C. Ferguson, BEDFORD Co.

CROSS, Noah to Nancy Van Rutledge - m. by: I. M. Hedge, J. P., May 29,
1845, DICKSON Co.

CROSS, Rebecca to John F. Champion - BEDFORD Co.

CROSS, William to Sarah Smith - November 29, 1859, m. by: H. K. Shields,
M. G., GILES Co.

CROSS, Zachariah to Esther Johnston - issued August 11, 1790, Bondsman:
John Frederick Morgan, SUMNER Co.

CROSSLAN, Jacob to Jane Mankins - issued March 9, 1854, m. by:
Samuel Umbarger, J. P., March 12, 1854, COFFEE Co.

CROSSLAN, James to Jane Jones - issued September 21, 1861, m. by:
Samuel W. Hall, J. P., September 21, 1861, COFFEE Co.

CROSSLAN, Thomas to Emily Crew - issued December 22, 1859, m. by:
W. B. M. Williams, M. E. Mins., December 22, 1859, COFFEE Co.

CROSSLIN, Gilbert to Sarrah C. Anderson - issued January 28, 1861,
m. by: W. M. Brewer, J. P., January 29, 1861, COFFEE Co.

CROSSTHWAIT, George D. to Frances E. Burton - issued October 11, 1836,
Bondsman: Wm. H. Sneed and John W. Jetton, m. by: Rev. Wm. Eagleton,
V. D. M., October 12, 1836, RUTHERFORD Co.

CROSSTON, Edward to Elizabeth Garrison - July 29, 1789, Security:
James Goodin, GREENE Co.

CROSSWELL, Obidiah to Martha A. Mizell - issued June 27, 1846, m. by:
Allen McCaskill, J. P., STEWART Co.

CROSSWY, James C. to Nancy Draper - issued July 16, 1840, DAVIDSON Co.

CROSTHWAITE, J. H. to Sarah Fisher - issued April 28, 1865, Bondsman:
J. C. Chaffin, m. by: Samuel Baker, M. G., April 29, 1865,
LAWRENCE Co.

CROTZER, Jas. to Rachel Smith - issued January 11, 1849, Bondsman:
W. H. Crotzer, m. by: Stpehen Cocke, J. P., January 18, 1849,
MONTGOMERY Co.

CROTZER, Joshua to Nancy J. Myres - issued February 6, 1851, Bondsman:
George Welker, m. by: J. H. Majors, J. P., February 6, 1851,
MONTGOMERY Co.

CROUCE, Henry to Polly Greer - issued January 23, 1805, Bondsman:
John Winyard, GRAINGER Co.

CROUCH, William H. to Margaret J. Rudolph - issued August 18, 1846,
Bondsman: Jas. G. Woodson, MONTGOMERY Co.

CROUCHER, Larkin to Julia Pratt - May 29, 1812, WILLIAMSON Co.

CROUSE, Gideon to Nelly Douglass - issued January 15, 1850, m. by:
R. C. Durham, J. P., January 16, 1850, VAN BUREN Co.

CROUSE, Gidian to Neley Douglass - issued January 15, 1850, m. by:
R. C. Durham, J. P. January 16, 1850, VAN BUREN Co.

CROUSE, John to Elizabeth Hynds - issued April 24, 1832, Bondsman:
William Walker, m. by: J. Bunch, J. P., April 24, 1832, GRAINGER Co.

CROUSE, Matthias to Mary Hunt - issued October 27, 1827, Bondsman:
James Pybass, m. by: H. Trott, J. P., RUTHERFORD Co.

CROUSE, Nemoe to Margaret Swaggerty - issued July 28, 1830, Bondsman:
Armstead Clark, m. by: Jacob Godwin, J. P., GRAINGER Co.

CROUSE, Spencer to Derindia Hunt - issued December 20, 1830, Bondsman:
P. G. Noland, m. by: Lee Nolen, J. P., RUTHERFORD Co.

CROW, Allen G. to Nancy Adcocke - issued January 8, 1846, m. by:
J. C. Pullem, J. P., January 8, 1846, DICKSON Co.

CROW, Betsy to Thomas McLaughlin - GREENE Co.

CROW, John to Nancy Martin - issued August 15, 1824, m. by:
Charley Simmons August 15, 1824, SUMNER Co.

CROW, John to Mary Tidwell - issued November 22, 1842, m. by:
John Brown, J. P., November 22, 1842, DICKSON Co.

CROW, Rachel to James Williams - GREENE Co.

CROW, Richard J. to Sarah Ann Hawks - issued October 7, 1855, m. by:
Robert Brown, J. P., September 7, 1855, COFFEE Co.

CROW, Robert to Westy Wade - issued February 16, 1855, m. by:
Samuel Umbarger, J. P., February 18, 1855, COFFEE Co.

CROW, Thomas to Rhoda Jackson - issued September 22, 1828, Bondsman:
Wm. Jackson, m. by: Samuel Love, M. G., September 22, 1828,
Witness: Wm. Swan, KNOX Co.

CROW, William to Sarah Taylor - issued October 19, 1822, Bondsman:
Marrel M. Midkiff, GRAINGER Co.

CROW, William to Lucy Ann Morris - issued September 1, 1853, Bondsman:
Jas. Linebaugh, m. by: J. C. Bryan, J. P., September 1, 1853,
MONTGOMERY Co.

CROWDER, B. J. to Rebecca M. Elliott - issued October 8, 1845, Bondsman:
Wm. Stewart, m. by: Lemuel Cherry, J. P., October 9, 1845,
MONTGOMERY Co.

CROWDER, Cage to Mary Rogers - issued December 8, 1825, Bondsman:
Thos. James, m. by: Thos. Anderson, J. P., December 8, 1825,
SUMNER Co.

CROWDER, David to Elizabeth Pugh - issued March 14, 1827, Bondsman:
Lewis Vick, WILSON Co.

CROWDER, Jesse to Elizabeth Lee - issued September 22, 1823, Bondsman:
Hezekiah Watkins, m. by: Logan Henderson, J. P., September 25,
1823, RUTHERFORD Co.

CROWDER, Larkin T. to Fanny Lawhorn - issued September 27, 1832,
Bondsman: Addison Wilson, SUMNER Co.

CROWDER, Nathaniel to Nancy Neisbet - issued February 5, 1827, Bondsman:
Allen Gowen, RUTHERFORD Co.

CROWDER, Robt. to Jezaleel Pinkerton - July 14, 1807, WILLIAMSON Co.

CROWDER, Stephen to Milly Dav s - May 5, 1809, WILLIAMSON Co.

CROWDER, Thomas to Elizabeth Nemo - issued September 18, 1816, Bondsman:
Amos McCarther, SUMNER Co.

CROWDER, Thomas to Martha Brandon - issued April 28, 1853, ROBERTSON Co.

CROWDER, William to Ann Rebecca Poacher - issued January 17, 1854,
Bondsman: J. W. Barbee, MONTGOMERY Co.

CROWELL, Charles to Mary Earheart - issued August 13, 1861, Bondsman:
John Paschell, Jos. H. Thompson, Clk. per N. F. Thompson, Dep.
Clk., m. by: L. T. Williams, J. P., BEDFORD Co.

CROWELL, Joshua to Mary C. Gordon - issued May 3, 1864, Bondsman:
Joseph Thompson, BEDFORD Co.

CROWELL, Mary to Wm. A. Mann - issued August 18, 1863, Bondsman:
Jas. H. Locke, BEDFORD Co.

CROWLEY (?), David to Elizabeth Dulaney - August 27, 1785, Security:
Richard Woods, GREENE Co.

CROWNOVER, Benjamin to Sarah Pane - m. by: Simpson West, J. P.,
    May 15, 1857, FRANKLIN Co.

CROWNOVER, Charles P. to Deboriah McBee - issued August 16, 1846,
    m. by: John D. Lynch, J. P., August 16, 1846, FRANKLIN Co.

CROWNOVER, James C. to Elizabeth Roan - m. by: Simpson West, J. P.,
    May 29, 1856, FRANKLIN Co.

CROWNOVER, Jonathan to Feby Taylor - issued January, 1842, m. by:
    M. Catchings, J. P., January 10, 1842, FRANKLIN Co.

CROWNOVER, Joseph to Mary J. Montgomery - issued September 11, 1867,
    m. by: John Nugent, J. P., September 11, 1867, FRANKLIN Co.

CROWNOVER, William to Hannah Berry - issued March 19, 1845, m. by:
    John D. Lynch, J. P., March 19, 1845, FRANKLIN Co.

CROWNOVER, Wm. to Malissa Kitchens - issued January 13, 1872, m. by:
    J. T. Merritt, J. P., January 13, 1872, FRANKLIN Co.

CROWNOVER, William to Laura Montgomery - issued January 22, 1874,
    m. by: C. C. Rose, J. P., January 25, 1874, FRANKLIN Co.

CROZIER, John to Hannah Barton - issued January 2, 1799, Bondsman:
    Thomas N. Clark, Witness: H. L. White, KNOX Co.

CRUDJINGTON, Wm. to Nancy Pharis - issued May 13, 1838, m. by:
    Wm. Green May 13, 1838, MEIGS Co.

CRUDUP, John to Elizabeth Graves - issued October 23, 1837, Bondsman:
    C. B. Lumpkins, WILSON Co.

CRUDUP, Robert to Caroline Harkreader - issued September 28, 1835,
    Bondsman: Samuel Walker, WILSON Co.

CRUDUPE, Elisha B. to Louisina Alford - issued April 14, 1827, Bondsman:
    Lamuel Booth, m. by: John Williamson, J. P., April 16, 1827,
    WILSON Co.

CRUDUPE, Robert to Polly Gwyll - issued June 19, 1821, Bondsman:
    Samuel Sperry, m. by: J. F. Davis June 24, 1821, WILSON Co.

CRUISE, John B. to Anna Cunningham - issued February 7, 1824, Bondsman:
    Robert M. Landrum, m. by: James Kennon, M. G., February 7, 1824,
    GRAINGER Co.

CRUISE, William to Elizabeth Wright - issued June 27, 1841, m. by:
    Jackson Dyer, J. P., June 27, 1841, VAN BUREN Co.

CRUIZE, Hardeman to Esther Maney - issued April 11, 1807, Bondsman:
    Wm. Harrelson, KNOX Co.

CRUM, Elizabeth to Solomon Wolford (?) - GREENE Co.

CRUMBLY, Abrahm to Elizabeth Marshall - February 20, 1817, Security:
    Newhope Quaker Meeting, GREENE Co.

CRUMP, Fendall to Martha Pope - April 15, 1815, WILLIAMSON Co.

CRUMP, John C. to Louisa Jane Wilkinson - issued Apirl 24, 1845, m. by:
    B. Herndon, J. P., April 24, 1845, STEWART Co.

CRUMP, Lewis W. to Susan Clenny - issued January 17, 1824, m. by:
    Thomas Anderson, J. P., January 17, 1824, SUMNER Co.

CRUMP, Robert H. to Lydia M. Bledsoe - m. by: John Wiseman January 9,
    1838, SUMNER Co.

CRUMP, W. H. to E. J. May - m. by: A. B. Duval October 4, 1838,
SUMNER Co.

CRUMPLER, John G. to Elizabeth Coldwell - issued May 16, 1840, DICKSON Co.

CRUMPTON, Thomas D. M. to Eliza A. Doxey - issued January 17, 1836,
Bondsman: Willie Vinson, m. by: J. W. Hall January 17, 1836,
SUMNER Co.

CRUMSTOCK, Isaac to Anna Curtis - March 17, 1796, Security: Thomas Woolsy,
GREENE Co.

CRUNK, John to Betsey Conner - issued January 19, 1822, Bondsman:
Ezekeil Young, SUMNER Co.

CRUNK, John M. to Sarah J. Armstrong - issued November 28, 1853,
Bondsman: W. Crunk, m. by: T. A. Jones, J. P., November 28, 1853,
MONTGOMERY Co.

CRUSE, Edward to Sally Nelson - issued March 17, 1813, KNOX Co.

CRUSE, Gilbert to Susan Havely - issued December 24, 1816, Bondsman:
John Cruize, m. by: S. Montgomery December 24, 1816, Witness:
C. A. C. White, KNOX Co.

CRUSE, James to Lannice Childress - issued October 22, 1816, m. by:
Jeremiah King, M. G., October 22, 1816, KNOX Co.

CRUSE, Redmon to S. E. Duboise - issued October 14, 1869, m.: October 14,
1869, FRANKLIN Co.

CRUSE, Walter to Lavin Tucker - issued February 5, 1819, Bondsman:
James Coker, m. by: Jas. A. Haise, J. P., February 5, 1819,
KNOX Co.

CRUSE, William to Lucy Childress - April 19, 1813, KNOX Co.

CRUSH, John to Lydia Bales - issued June 5, 1830, m. by: Isaac Lewis
June 6, 1830, KNOX Co.

CRUTCHER, Caswell to Serona Stanley - issued August 1, 1839, m. by:
James Sprouse, J. P., August 8, 1839, ROBERTSON Co.

CRUTCHER, Edmund to Jenny Allcorn - issued September 23, 1800, Bondsman:
William Gillespie, SUMNER Co.

CRUTCHER, George to Mary Brumbelon - issued January 26, 1846,
ROBERTSON Co.

CRUTCHER, James M. to Susan M. Horton - issued November 8, 1848, m. by:
Henry Larkin November 9, 1848, FRANKLIN Co.

CRUTCHER, John to Jane McCraken - December 4, 1810, WILLIAMSON Co.

CRUTCHER, John to Keziah Stanley - issued July 15, 1839, m. by:
James Sprouse, J. P., July 17, 1839, ROBERTSON Co.

CRUTCHER, T. P. to J. A. Bedwell - issued February 13, 1850, m. by:
Benj. Rawls, M. G., ROBERTSON Co.

CRUTCHER, Thomas to Carline McMurry - issued December 9, 1846, m. by:
Wm. D. Baldwin, J. P., ROBERTSON Co.

CRUTCHER, William to Martha Cagle - issued April 15, 1845, m. by:
Charles Crafford, J. P., April 17, 1845, ROBERTSON Co.

CRUTCHFIELD, George to Amy Hancock - issued January 9, 1827, Bondsman:
James Allcorn, m. by: Obadiah Freeman, WILSON Co.

CRUTCHFIELD, Gideon to Marcia Walker - issued March 7, 1818, Bondsman: Zachriah P. Bell, RUTHERFORD Co.

CRUTCHFIELD, James to Martha Spain - issued May 26, 1837, Bondsman: Thomas Brown, m. by: Jas. Baird, J. P., May 28, 1837, WILSON Co.

CRUTCHFIELD, James M. to Elizabeth B. Lain - issued October 8, 1834, Bondsman: Albert G. Williamson, m. by: John Beard, M. G., October 9, 1834, WILSON Co.

CRUTCHFIELD, Samuel to Nancy Mcholand - issued August 29, 1814, Bondsman: John Cartwright, WILSON Co.

CRUTCHFIELD, Susan to John Iseley - BEDFORD Co.

CRUTCHFIELD, Thomas to Lotey Valentine - issued July 17, 1821, Bondsman: Benjamin Parrish, m. by: McMurry July 17, 1821, SUMNER Co.

CRUTCHFIELD, William to Hannah Mabry - issued March 4, 1805, Bondsman: John Jarratt, SUMNER Co.

CRUZE, Drury to Elizabeth Crenshaw - issued November 26, 1821, Bondsman: Josiah Lauderdale, m. by: Richard Johnson November 26, 1821, SUMNER Co.

CRUZE, Elison to Sally Gillespie - issued August 3, 1809, Bondsman: Robert Bayless, Witness: Thos. A. Rogers, KNOX Co.

CRYER, Elijah to Elizabeth Lassiter - November 7, 1853, Security: J. W. Hargroves, GILES Co.

CRYER, Hardy M. to Elizabeth L. Rice - issued November 6, 1812, Bondsman: James Douglas, SUMNER Co.

CUDDY, Lee to Elizabeth Vinegarden - June 11, 1813, WILLIAMSON Co.

CUFF, John W. to Susanna Baker - issued July 3, 1820, m. by: Carey James, D. M. E. C., July 11, 1820, RUTHERFORD Co.

CUFMAN, Pavatt to Jinny Gunsaw - issued February 15, 1808, Bondsman: Geo. G. Chapman, SUMNER Co.

CULAN, Thomas to Nancy Wood - issued May 29, 1828, m. by: John Lane, M. G., RUTHERFORD Co.

CULBEESTON, James to S. J. Fryer - issued October 22, 1856, m. by: J. B. White, J. P., ROBERTSON Co.

CULBERTSON, Benj. to Anna Elliott - August 22, 1810, WILLIAMSON Co.

CULBERTSON, John W. to Marthy P. Frey - issued November 6, 1858, m. by: John Crawford, J. P., November 7, 1858, ROBERTSON Co.

CULBERTSON, Thomas to Sarah Guthry - issued December 22, 1825, Bondsman: George Wills, m. by: James Guthrie, M. G., December 22, 1825, SUMNER Co.

CULBRETH, John to Mary Burton - issued January 3, 1833, Bondsman: Arthur B. Duval, SUMNER Co.

CULLAM, Elliston M. to Angeline Dozier - issued October 16, 1843, m. by: James C. Anderson, M. G., October 17, 1843, DAVIDSON Co.

CULLEN, Jno. M. to Rachel Craighead - issued May 30, 1810, Bondsman: Jno. N. Gamble, KNOX Co.

CULLEY, M. E. to E. B. Phillips - issued February 9, 1864, Bondsman: R. A. Coldwell, Jos. H. Thompson, Clk., BEDFORD Co.

CULLEY, Robert to Emily Work - issued October 27, 1843, m. by:
    C. W. Nance, J. P., October 27, 1843, DAVIDSON Co.

CULLINS, J. W. to Rebecca A. Adams - issued April 6, 1867, m. by:
    Thos. F. Mosley, J. P., April 9, 1867, FRANKLIN Co.

CULLUM, Alexander to Caroline Lowry - issued May 30, 1840, m. by:
    John McRobertson, J. P., June 14, 1840, DAVIDSON Co.

CULLUM, Lovell H. to Martha Greer - issued September 17, 1840, m. by:
    John McRobertson, J. P., September 17, 1840, DAVIDSON Co.

CULLUM, William H. to Hicksy Simmons - October 8, 1817, WILLIAMSON Co.

CULLY, Wm. to Mary A. Holt - issued October 25, 1862, Bondsman:
    Jos. H. Thompson and clerk, BEDFORD Co.

CULNER, Thos. to Tennessee Nippers - issued June 28, 1871, m. by:
    S. Kennedy, M. G., June 28, 1871, FRANKLIN Co.

CULTON, James to Peggy Weir - January 20, 1801, BLOUNT Co.

CULVAHOUSE, John to Frances Smith - issued December 23, 1826, Bondsman:
    Frederick Smith, GRAINGER Co.

CULVEHOUSE, Edward to Nancy Gooly - issued December 12, 1821, Bondsman:
    Gallant Harris, m. by: William Lane, J. P., December 13, 1821,
    GRAINGER Co.

CULVEHOUSE, Lewis to Francis Smith - issued March 29, 1828, Bondsman:
    Nathan Grear, GRAINGER Co.

CULVER, T. W. to Sarah Partlow - issued December 31, 1872, m. by:
    J. F. Brown, M. G., January 2, 1873, FRANKLIN Co.

CULVERHOUSE, Emiline to W. H. Gordon - BEDFORD Co.

CULVERHOUSE, John to Elizabeth Dale - issued September 14, 1827,
    Bondsman: Charles Hume, m. by: Henry Hawkins, J. P., September 14,
    1827, GRAINGER Co.

CULVERHOUSE, Sarah I. to Franklin L. Knott - BEDFORD Co.

CULVERS, Fleming to Jane Isbell - issued November 30, 1866, m. by:
    Thos. Finch, J. P., November 30, 1866, FRANKLIN Co.

CULWELL, David to Malinda Davis - m. by: Bartlet Turner October 1, 1837,
    SUMNER Co.

CUMMINGS, A. B. to Mrs. Sarah Highamer - issued January 29, 1861,
    m. by: John H. Holt, M. G., November 29, 1861, FRANKLIN Co.

CUMMINGS, Arthur to Mary McFarland - issued October 9, 1832, Bondsman:
    James M. Willis, WILSON Co.

CUMMINGS, Charles W. to Eliza W. Foster - issued November 19, 1828,
    Bondsman: Benj. T. Motley, m. by: J. Provine, M. G., WILSON Co.

CUMMINGS, Corum to Susan Irby - m. by: D. Ashford, J. P., February 7,
    1835, SUMNER Co.

CUMMINGS, G. C. to Mary T. Johnston - issued January 29, 1850, m. by:
    Lewis Adams, M. G., ROBERTSON Co.

CUMMINGS, G. M. to Martha Morgan - issued May 19, 1860, m. by:
    Joseph Cumings, J. P., May 20, 1860, VAN BUREN Co.

CUMMINGS, George to Martha D. Foster - issued April 13, 1825, Bondsman:
    John Hearn, m. by: John Provine, M. G., WILSON Co.

CUMMINGS, Henry to Martha A. Henley - issued December 27, 1844, m. by: J. M. Garland, M. G., ROBERTSON Co.

CUMMINGS, James C. to Nancy Haley - issued February 24, 1843, m. by: Z. T. Simmons, J. P., March 26, 1843, VAN BUREN Co.

CUMMINGS, Joseph W. to Dolly Ann Rideout - issued August 3, 1840, Bondsman: Nat Bell, m. by: Saml. H. Porterfield, J. P., August 6, 1840, WILSON Co.

CUMMINGS, Margaret to Berney Morris - issued March 14, 1861, Bondsman: B. K. Coble, Jos. H. Thompson, Clk., m. by: N. J. Fox, V. D. M., March 16, 1861, BEDFORD Co.

CUMMINGS, Uriah to Talitha Smith - issued December 24, 1832, Bondsman: Jas. S. Whiteman, Witness: Wm. Swan, KNOX Co.

CUMMINGS, William to Elizabeth J. Boggs - issued August 19, 1852, m. by: John Nugent, J. P., August 25, 1852, FRANKLIN Co.

CUMMINGS, William to Mary Powell - issued November 1, 1855, m. by: J. Batts, J. P., ROBERTSON Co.

CUMMINS, Benjamin to Parmely Gray - issued May 2, 1833, Bondsman: Micajah Thompson, RUTHERFORD Co.

CUMMINS, Robert to Elizabeth A. McFarlin - issued November 20, 1830, m. November 23, 1830, RUTHERFORD Co.

CUMMINS, Robert G. to Isabela McKnight - issued October 9, 1823, Bondsman: James Wilson, m. by: Jesse Alexander, V. D. M., October 14, 1823, RUTHERFORD Co.

CUMMINS, Samuel to Rachel Dobbins - February 24, 1805, WILLIAMSON Co.

CUMMINS, Sam'l to Jane C. Bullard - issued May 23, 1848, Bondsman: G. Rayburn, m. by: James Almund, J. P., May 24, 1848, MONTGOMERY Co.

CUMMINS, Uriah to Margaret Smith - issued July 27, 1816, m. by: John Hoover, J. P., July 29, 1816, RUTHERFORD Co.

CUMMINS, William to Peggy Stalcup - issued January 22, 1829, Bondsman: Joseph Pitt, m. by: Josiah Walton, J. P., January 22, 1829, SUMNER Co.

CUMSTOCK, Jasper W. to Nancy Keys - issued July 27, 1820, m. by: William Sawyers, J. P., August 6, 1820, KNOX Co.

CUMMINGHAM, John to Sally Warren - issued July 30, 1825, Bondsman: Moses Cunningham, WILSON Co.

CUNINGHAM, Jesse to Rossey Beasley - issued June 30, 1806, Bondsman: Dillard Beasley, WILSON Co.

CUNNINGHAM, Aaron to Elizabeth Hopkins - November 23, 1796, Security: Matthew Cunningham, GREENE Co.

CUNNINGHAM, Alexander to Frances Smith - issued September 1, 1822, Bondsman: James Baker, SUMNER Co.

CUNNINGHAM, Andrew to Elizabeth Anderson - issued November 11, 1824, Bondsman: John Stirling, KNOX Co.

CUNNINGHAM, Andrew to Bedy White - issued November 9, 1848, m. by: John Brown, J. P., November 9, 1848, DICKSON Co.

CUNNINGHAM, B. M. V. to R. A. Boswell - issued September 30, 1863, Bondsman: J. F. Blackman, m. by: Nicholas Gower, M. G., September 30, 1863, LAWRENCE Co.

CUNNINGHAM, Charlotte to George Turnley - GREENE Co.

CUNNINGHAM, Daniel to Ann Roberts - issued December 9, 1865, m. by:
D. S. Long, J. P., December 10, 1865, FRANKLIN Co.

CUNNINGHAM, David to Prissy Dennis - January 13, 1798, Surety:
Miles Cunningham, BLOUNT Co.

CUNNINGHAM, David to Jane Cunningham - issued May 30, 1798, Bondsman:
Francis Cunningham, Witness: Joseph Greer, KNOX Co.

CUNNINGHAM, Eppa to Caroline Lassiter - issued November 10, 1827,
m. by: Robt. Patton November 10, 1827, SUMNER Co.

CUNNINGHAM, F. C. to Sarah A. Coulson - issued December 31, 1873,
m. by: Asa D. Oakley, M. G., January 1, 1874, FRANKLIN Co.

CUNNINGHAM, Hiram to Maria E. Banks - issued January 29, 1856, m. by:
Samuel Umbarger, J. P., January 29, 1856, COFFEE Co.

CUNNINGHAM, Hiram to Nancy E. Banks - issued December 7, 1861, m. by:
M. A. Carden, J. P., December 8, 1861, COFFEE Co.

CUNNINGHAM, Hugh to Margaret Wear - October 14, 1796, Security:
John Wear

CUNNINGHAM, Isaac to Margaret Hannah - April 23, 1793, KNOX Co.

CUNNINGHAM, J. T. to Caroline M. Dunn - issued February 22, 1860,
m. by: J. K. L. Faris, J. P., February 23, 1860, COFFEE Co.

CUNNINGHAM, J. T. to Martha J. Morrow - issued September 22, 1862,
Bondsman: J. C. Blackwell, m. by: J. B. Clayton, J. P., September 24,
1862, LAWRENCE Co.

CUNNINGHAM, J. W. to Nancy E. Turner - issued January 6, 1862, m. by:
E. A. Rutledge, J. P., January 7, 1862, COFFEE Co.

CUNNINGHAM, Jacob to Elizabeth Wilhoit - October 29, 1794, Security:
Matthew Cunningham, GREENE Co.

CUNNINGHAM, James to Margaret Hannah - issued April 3, 1793, Bondsman:
James Telford and James McKinney, Witness: David Craig, KNOX Co.

CUNNINGHAM, James to Susannah Craig - issued April 24, 1794, Bondsman:
John McClellan, Witness: Chas. McClung, C. K. C., KNOX Co.

CUNNINGHAM, James to Rachel Thorn - issued January 12, 1820, m. by:
J. P. Browning, R. G. M., January 20, 1820, RUTHERFORD Co.

CUNNINGHAM, James to Peggy Anderson - issued September 3, 1823,
Bondsman: S. Jarnagin, m. by: Robert McBath September 4, 1823,
KNOX Co.

CUNNINGHAM, James to Elizabeth Patterson - issued August 31, 1825,
Bondsman: William F. Alexander, m. by: Joshua Lester, V. D. M.,
WILSON Co.

CUNNINGHAM, Jas. H. to Virginia S. Mooney - issued September 4, 1851,
FRANKLIN Co.

CUNNINGHAM, Jesse to Betsy Newman (?) - July 18, 1826, KNOX Co.

CUNNINGHAM, Jesse to Betsy Newman - issued July 18, 1827, Bondsman:
John Cunningham, m. by: J. Cunningham, M. G., July 20, 1827,
Witness: Wm. Swan, KNOX Co.

CUNNINGHAM, Jesse I. to Mary A. E. Williams - issued November 30, 1838,
m. by: E. S. Hall, J. P., November 30, 1838, DAVIDSON Co.

CUNNINGHAM, John to Rosannah Shinpock - issued November 16, 1810, Bondsman: Wm. Harrelson, KNOX Co.

CUNNINGHAM, Jno. to Mary Ann Wilson - issued April 30, 1836, m. by: T. G. Craighead, J. P., May 30, 1836, KNOX Co.

CUNNINGHAM, John to Mary Cole - issued January 8, 1842, m. by: Wm. H. Hamblin, J. P., January 18, 1842, DAVIDSON Co.

CUNNINGHAM, John T. to Alametia Jane Lusk - issued August 6, 1856, m. by: R. J. Price, J. P., August 7, 1856, COFFEE Co.

CUNNINGHAM, Joseph to Anny Knox - issued November 29, 1817, m. by: Jesse Alexander, V. D. M., December 2, 1817, RUTHERFORD Co.

CUNNINGHAM, Joseph to Mary E. Nichols - issued December 8, 1854, m. by: Samuel Umbarger, J. P., December 10, 1854, COFFEE Co.

CUNNINGHAM, Martin to Martha Sullivan - issued January 25, 1844, Bondsman: Ezekiel Sullivan, MEIGS Co.

CUNNINGHAM, Mary A. to Wiley Singleton - BEDFORD Co.

CUNNINGHAM, Miles to Elizabeth Davis - June 8, 1792, Security: James Davis, GREENE Co.

CUNNINGHAM, Miles to Mary Denning - November 19, 1795, Security: John Dinning, GREENE Co.

CUNNINGHAM, Miles to Mary Donney (?) - May 22, 1797, BLOUNT Co.

CUNNINGHAM, Moses to Mary Simpson - June 3, 1794, KNOX Co.

CUNNINGHAM, Moses to Margaret Long - June 29, 1795, Security: John McDonad and Aaron Cunningham, GREENE Co.

CUNNINGHAM, Moses to Polly Cropper - issued July 19, 1816, Bondsman: Robert Seat, m. by: John W. Payton, J. P., July 25, 1816, WILSON Co.

CUNNINGHAM, Moses to Esther T. Dearmond - issued September 23, 1824, Bondsman: John Dearmond, m. by: Geo. Atkin, M. G., September 23, 1824, KNOX Co.

CUNNINGHAM, Paul to Mary Ford - issued November 11, 1824, m. by: Robt. McBath November 11, 1824, KNOX Co.

CUNNINGHAM, Robert to Narcissa Hamlet - issued October 23, 1938, DAVIDSON Co.

CUNNINGHAM, Sam'l. to Eleanor F. Houston - issued October 25, 1821, Bondsman: John Davis, KNOX Co.

CUNNINGHAM, Sam'l. to Eleanor F. Houston - issued October 25, 1821, m. by: R. Houston, J. P., October 25, 1821, KNOX Co.

CUNNINGHAM, Samuel H. to Jean Flannagan - issued January 15, 1806, Bondsman: John Dearmond and Edward Mason, Witness: W. Park, KNOX Co.

CUNNINGHAM, Samuel N. to Jean Flannagan - January 15, 1804 (or 06?), KNOX Co.

CUNNINGHAM, Thomas to Sarah E. Farris - issued January 31, 1861, m. by: S. M. Cherry January 31, 1861, FRANKLIN Co.

CUNNINGHAM, Timothy to Viton Cooly - issued February 13, 1837, Bondsman: Daniel McMullen, m. by: Jno. T. King, J. P., February 15, 1837, KNOX Co.

CUNNINGHAM, Volentine E. to Mary P. Steel - issued April 20, 1829,
Bondsman: R. L. Warner, SUMNER Co.

CUNNINGHAM, W. F. to Mary J. Baldry - issued January 12, 1854, m. by:
W. L. Baldry, M. G., ROBERTSON Co.

CUNNINGHAM, William to Sarah E. Banks - issued March 19, 1853, m. by:
David Simpson, J. P., March 20, 1853, COFFEE Co.

CUNNINGHAM, William M. to Sarah Louisa Dunn - issued October 9, 1860,
m. by: J. F. L. Faris, J. P., October 9, 1860, COFFEE Co.

CUNNINGHAM, Wilson to Mary Callehan - issued February 25, 1871,
FRANKLIN Co.

CUPP, George to Celia Purkepile - issued April 25, 1831, Bondsman:
John Estes, Jr., m. by: John Harris, J. P., April 28, GRAINGER Co.

CURD, Aaron B. to Nancy Wooldridge - issued January 7, 1815, Bondsman:
John Cottles, WILSON Co.

CURD, Aaron B. to Nancy Wooldrid - issued January 7, 1815, WILSON Co.

CURD, James to Susan Everett - issued November 26, 1829, Bondsman:
William Curd, WILSON Co.

CURD, John S. to Mary E. Price - issued July 17, 1843, m. by:
U. Young, J. P., ROBERTSON Co.

CURD, Knight to Mary Couts - issued March 11, 1856, m. by:
J. W. Cullum, M. G., ROBERTSON Co.

CURD, Price to Elizabeth Hall - issued November 25, 1837, Bondsman:
William Curd, WILSON Co.

CURD, Thomas to Melcenia E. Rutland - issued October 12, 1836, m. by:
Wm. T. Luck, WILSON Co.

CURD, William to Susan Davis - issued November 21, 1832, Bondsman:
John Curd, m. by: Ezekiel Cloyd, M. G., November 22, 1832,
WILSON Co.

CURENBERRY, Thomas to M. J. Sears - issued November 6, 1847, m. by:
Isaac Steel December 23, 1847, ROBERTSON Co.

CURFMAN, James to Sarah Belcher - issued October 28, 1842, DAVIDSON Co.

CURL, C. C. to Sarah Clark - issued March 18, 1873, m. by:
Aldrich Brown, M. G., June 29, 1873, FRANKLIN Co.

CURL, William H. to Anna Jarnagin - issued September 22, 1828, Bondsman:
William Aldridge, GRAINGER Co.

CURLE, D. R. to A. E. Jefferson - m. by: Lewis Hill October 12, 1837,
SUMNER Co.

CURLE, Portland J. to Milly Marshall - issued June 15, 1819, m. by:
Jer. Burns, V. D. M., June 17, 1819, RUTHERFORD Co.

CURLE, W. J. to N. E. Shasteen - issued November 14, 1866, FRANKLIN Co.

CURLESS, William to Permelia A. Dorris - m. by: John McMurtry, J. P.,
December 16, 1834, SUMNER Co.

CURN, William to Cathrine Sofey - issued April 5, 1872, m. by:
J. T. Moore, J. P., April 5, 1872, FRANKLIN Co.

CURRAY, Moses M. to Margaret Dobson - issued February 13, 1837, Bondsman:
Isaac N. Currey, m. by: J. Hooker, M. G., February 14, 1837,
WILSON Co.

CURREN, Jonathan to Elizabeth Jenkins - December 14, 1813, WILLIAMSON Co.

CURREY, Moses to Joanna Osteen - March 31, 1812, WILLIAMSON Co.

CURREY, Richard O. to Rachel J. Estin - issued May 25, 1842, m. by:
    Robt. A. Lapsley May 26, 1842, DAVIDSON Co.

CURRIER, Adam to Mary Lethgo - issued November 15, 1837, Bondsman:
    Jonathan Marley, m. by: Wm. Rodgers, J. P., November 16, 1837,
    Witness: M. M. Swan, KNOX Co.

CURRIER, James to Anne Stockton - issued March 9, 1806, Bondsman:
    Isaac Bond, Witness: Chas. McClung, Clk., KNOX Co.

CURRIER, James to Sarah Bearden - issued July 14, 1833, Bondsman:
    Seth Lea, m. by: Sam'l. White, J. P., July 14, 1833, Witness:
    Charles McClung, KNOX Co.

CURRIER, William to Martha Fryar - issued November 7, 1806, Bondsman:
    William Fryar, Witness: Chas. McClung, KNOX Co.

CURRIN, Robt. S. to Sophronia Williams - issued July 30, 1845, m. by:
    J. T. Edgar July 31, 1845, DAVIDSON Co.

CURRY, Alfred to Mary White - January 16, 1844, Security:
    William M. (x) Clark, GILES Co.

CURRY, Benjamin to Elizabeth Acree - issued June, 1842, m. by:
    E. W. Smith, J. P., June 17, 1842, STEWART Co.

CURRY, Elijah to Margret Law - issued July 16, 1813, Bondsman:
    Robert Telford, m. by: David Foster July 20, 1813, WILSON Co.

CURRY, Ezekiel S. to Rebecca McDaniel - issued September 22, 1836,
    m. by: John Beard, M. G., September 28, 1836, WILSON Co.

CURRY, Isaac N. to Jane Dobson - issued March 25, 1835, Bondsman:
    Samuel B. Gibson, m. by: J. Hooker, M. G., WILSON Co.

CURRY, James to Rebecca Hoshone - issued June 15, 1814, m. by:
    H. Hamilton June 16, 1814, RUTHERFORD Co.

CURRY, James to Elizabeth White - issued January 7, 1830, Bondsman:
    Sam'l McGee, m. by: James Walton, J. P., January 7, 1830, SUMNER Co.

CURRY, John to Margaret Cowen - issued October 16, 1816, Bondsman:
    John McElurath, SUMNER Co.

CURRY, Robert B. to Ann Baker - issued July 4, 1840, Bondsman:
    William W. Huddleston, m. by: Wm. J. Bonner, M. G., July 15, 1840,
    WILSON Co.

CURRY, Wm. P. tc S. Pennington - issued August 11, 1862, Bondsman:
    J. N. Curry, LAWRENCE Co.

CURTIS, Anna to Isaac Cumstock - GREENE Co.

CURTIS, Anthony to Rebecca Williams - November 11, 1812, WILLIAMSON Co.

CURTIS (x), Isaiah to Nancy Barr - March 24, 1841, Security:
    Philip Manuel, GILES Co.

CURTIS, Isaiah to Nancy Doyle - March 24, 1841, m. by: Nehemiah Howard,
    J. P., GILES Co.

CURTIS, John to Elizabeth Colyar - issued January 21, 1842, m. by:
    J. B. Hollis, M. G., January 23, 1842, FRANKLIN Co.

CURTIS, P. N. to Mary E. Wilkerson - issued October 22, 1873, m. by:
    W. P. DuBose, M. G., October 22, 1873, FRANKLIN Co.

CURTIS, William to Nancy Staggs - October 11, 1815, WILLIAMSON Co.

CURTIS, William to Eliza Ann Gower - issued January 21, 1841, m. by:
    John McRobertson, J. P., January 28, 1841, DAVIDSON Co.

CURTISS, Francis A. E. to Thos. J. Dysart - BEDFORD Co.

CUSHMAN, Abiol to Elizabeth Ann Bryant - issued December 11, 1848,
    Bondsman: W. T. Hargrove, m. by: J. G. Ward December 12, 1848,
    MONTGOMERY Co.

CUSICK, Elizabeth to John Harris, Jr. - GREENE Co.

CUSICK, Joseph to Jean Blackburn - January 31, 1793, KNOX Co.

CUSOCK, John B. to Hulda Durham - October 9, 1799, BLOUNT Co.

CUSTER, Elbert W. to Louisa Adaline Caraway - issued October 19, 1841,
    m. by: Wm. T. Well, M. G., October 25, 1841, FRANKLIN Co.

CUTBIRTH, Sarah to Jethro Brown - July 29, 1811, Bondsman:
    John M. Taylor, MAURY Co.

CUTCHEN, Lemuel to Jane Drennon - issued April 2, 1827, Bondsman:
    Thomas Drennon, m. by: James Drennon, J. P., April 4, 1827,
    WILSON Co.

CUTHBERTSON, Wm. B. to Lucy Carlass - issued October 9, 1835, Bondsman:
    Wm. Pryor, m. by: Michael Davis, J. P., October 9, 1835, KNOX Co.

CUTHREL, Joseph to Margaret Spring - issued September 12, 1823,
    Bondsman: Milton W. Grissom, WILSON Co.

CUTRALL, Midget to Fanny Swan - issued October 16, 1830, Bondsman:
    John Swan, WILSON Co.

CUTRELL, Midget (see Cutrall, Midget)

CUTRELL, Charles N. to Mary Ann Lewis - issued April 27, 1837, Bondsman:
    John Rieff, m. by: John Seay, M. G., May 4, 1837, WILSON Co.

CUTTER, Seth to Elizabeth Easley - issued June 16, 1808, Bondsman:
    Frederick Mayers, GRAINGER Co.

CUTTER, Timothy T. to Martha J. Stalcup - issued August 8, 1846, m. by:
    Benj. Sharpe, J. P., August 8, 1846, DAVIDSON Co.

CYRUS, Enock to Rebecca Cook - issued August 31, 1816, Bondsman:
    Nimrod Cyrus, GRAINGER Co.

DABBS, James to Louise Cheek - issued August 18, 1842, DAVIDSON Co.

DABBS, James W. to Margarett Lee - issued January 15, 1848, m. by:
    James Chambers, J. P., January 18, 1848, STEWART Co.

DABBS, Joseph W. to Mary D. Menees - issued August 15, 1842, DAVIDSON Co.

DABBS, Samuel to Elizabeth Martin - issued January 7, 1834, Bondsman:
    George W. Smith, m. by: Ezekiel Cloyd, M. G., January 8, 1834,
    WILSON Co.

DABNEY, Abram to Martina Pin - issued September 4, 1832, Bondsman:
    Henry Ault, m. by: M. G. Carter, J. P., September 5, 1832, KNOX Co.

DABNEY, Charles A. to Nancy Wall - July 17, 1815, WILLIAMSON Co.

DABNEY, George Francis to Louise Dabney - issued January 20, 1853,
    Bondsman: W. A. Quarles, MONTGOMERY Co.

DABNEY, Wm. to Eliza Hicks - June 29, 1808, WILLIAMSON Co.

DAGGETT, Miller to Cynthia Jane Moore - September 25, 1849, Security:
Samuel E. Foust, GILES Co.

DAGLEY, John to Sarah Boyd - November 29, 1808, Bondsman: Jacob Lindsey,
MAURY Co.

DAILEY, James C. to Elizabeth H. Taylor - issued September 17, 1853,
Bondsman: Joseph N. H. Goe, m. by: G. H. Alsup September 18, 1853,
MONTGOMERY Co.

DAILWOOD, John to Nancy Reed - issued July 30, 1804, Bondsman:
William Reed, SUMNER Co.

DAKES, Alfred to Nancy Bradshaw - issued January 9, 1828, Bondsman:
Joshua Peak, WILSON Co.

DALE, Abner to Jane McDaniel - issued April 19, 1813, Bondsman:
Solomon Skaggs, Witness: H. Hutchison, KNOX Co.

DALE, Abner to Jane McDaniel - April 19, 1818, KNOX Co.

DALE, Alexander to Lea Harner - issued December 30, 1797, Bondsman:
William Belton, Witness: H. L. White, KNOX Co.

DALE, Charles C. to Susan Harris - issued October 27, 1838, Bondsman:
Charles Scott, WILSON Co.

DALE, Isaac A. to Nancy F. Long - issued October 6, 1846, m. by:
J. B. Graves, M. G. 2nd Baptist Ch., October 8, 1846, DAVIDSON Co.

DALE, James to Nancy McDonald - August 30, 1817, KNOX Co.

DALLEY, Abram to Easther Darwin - issued February 14, 1873, m. by:
D. S. Long, J. P., February 14, 1873, FRANKLIN Co.

DALLIS, Benjamin S. to Susan Allen - issued December 11, 1839, Bondsman:
James E. Cropper, m. by: Robert E. Ellis, J. P., WILSON Co.

DALE, Jonathan to Polley Cotton - issued March 22, 1808, Bondsman:
David Ethons, GRAINGER Co.

DALE, John P. to Elizabeth R. Harris - issued June 24, 1840, Bondsman:
Charles C. Dale, WILSON Co.

DALE, James G. to Elizabeth C. Kellingsworth - issued December 3, 1861,
Bondsman: Z. Roberts, m. by: John G. Bledsoe, M. G., BEDFORD Co.

DALLIS, Thomas to Nancy D. Chappell - issued July 10, 1838, Bondsman:
Josiah Griffin, m. by: Moses Ellis, J. P., WILSON Co.

DALTEN, Carter to Polly Viditoe - issued February 25, 1822, Bondsman:
Charlton Dyer, m. by: Martin Cleveland, J. P., February 26, 1822,
GRAINGER Co.

DALTON, Carter J. to Mary Coffee - issued September 2, 1833, Bondsman:
Timothy Daulton, m. by: H. Williams, L. D., GRAINGER Co.

DALTON, David to Polly Dyer - issued August 16, 1817, Bondsman:
Joshua Washman, m. by: Thomas Brown, J. P., August 17, 1817,
GRAINGER Co.

DALTON, John to Malinda Patterson - issued June 11, 1821, Bondsman:
Alexander Sadler, SUMNER Co.

DALTON, John to Eliza J. Parrish - issued September 28, 1837, Bondsman:
Edwin Rowton, RUTHERFORD Co.

DALTON, John H. to Latitia McConnell - issued January 5, 1830, Bondsman:
R. Dalton, SUMNER Co.

DALTON, John R. to Elizabeth Wooton - issued March 5, 1824, m. by:
John Wiseman, M. G., March 5, 1824, SUMNER Co.

DALTON, Josiah to Elizabeth Pruett - issued March 10, 1822, Bondsman:
Jonathan Davis, m. by: Jonathan Williams, J. P., March 10, 1822,
SUMNER Co.

DALTON, Larkin to Elizabeth Thornton - issued November 11, 1812,
Bondsman: W. H. Douglas, SUMNER Co.

DALTON, Meridia to Dolphy Rucker - issued February 3, 1813, Bondsman:
Rubin Dalton, GRAINGER Co.

DALTON, Jr., Reubin to Nancy Shockley - issued January 4, 1808,
Bondsman: Reubin Dalton, Senr., GRAINGER Co.

DALTON, Robert to Lucinda Harris - issued October 18, 1822, m. by:
G. H. Bussard, J. P., October 19, 1822, WILSON Co.

DALTON, Roisdon R. to Jane Bell - issued January 9, 1832, Bondsman:
Jas. L. McKoin, m. by: J. Talley, J. P., January 9, 1832, SUMNER Co.

DALTON, S. W. to Sarah J. Mason - issued January 6, 1857, m. by:
John W. Smith, J. P., January 7, 1857, ROBERTSON Co.

DALTON, Samuel to Rebecca Stanfield - September 22, 1800, Security:
Philip Stout, GREENE Co.

DALTON, Shelton to Patsey Walton - issued December 15, 1817, Bondsman:
Matthew Cathey, m. by: John Wiseman, J. P., December 15, 1817,
SUMNER Co.

DALTON, Tandy to Matilda Coffee - issued August 27, 1835, Bondsman:
Carter Dalton, GRAINGER Co.

DALTON, Thomas to Martha McCay - issued October 22, 1832, m. by:
Jas. F. Fletcher October 23, 1832, RUTHERFORD Co.

DALTON, Timothy to Dilpha Coffee - issued December 29, 1828, Bondsman:
Meredith Dalton, GRAINGER Co.

DALTON, Timothy to Susannah Adams - issued August 18, 1830, Bondsman:
William Dalton, GRAINGER Co.

DALTON, Tolbert L. to Angeline Mathews - issued September 13, 1841,
m. by: Robt. Draughon, J. P., ROBERTSON Co.

DALTON, Wyatt to Matilda Rowling - issued February 13, 1827, Bondsman:
Francis Duffy, SUMNER Co.

DALWOOD, John to Marthy Hynight - issued June 7, 1806, Bondsman:
William Laughlin and Peter Devault, RUTHERFORD Co.

DALZELL, John to Margaret McFaren - July 7, 1785, Security:
Robert Houston, GREENE Co.

DAME, Milton to Sarah E. Elliott - issued December 29, 1859, m. by:
J. B. Anderson, M. G., ROBERTSON Co.

DAMERON, Joseph to Mary Neal - issued October 29, 1870, m. by:
H. R. Moore, J. P., November 1, 1870, FRANKLIN Co.

DAMEWOOD, Isaac to Sally Norris - issued October 7, 1817, m. by:
John Thompson, J. P., October 9, 1817, KNOX Co.

DAMEWOOD, Isaac to Mildred Seamore - issued September 22, 1825,
Bondsman: James Damewood, m. by: William Lane, J. P., September 22,
1825, GRAINGER Co.

DAMEWOOD, James to Rachel Seamore - issued July 7, 1824, Bondsman:
    Ebben Dale, m. by: William Lane, J. P., GRAINGER Co.

DAMRELL, George B. to Elizabeth Nelson - issued January 19, 1859,
    m. by: D. D. Smith January 19, 1859, FRANKLIN Co.

DAMRON, Edley to Ann Stovall - issued September 17, 1872, m. by:
    H. R. Moore, J. P., September 19, 1872, FRANKLIN Co.

DAMRON, James to Susan Riddle - issued January 3, 1868, m. by:
    T. F. Moseley, J. P., January 8, 1868, FRANKLIN Co.

DAMRON, John to Sarah A. Syler - issued October 27, 1859, FRANKLIN Co.

DAMRON, John to Rebecca Isely - issued January 4, 1862, Bondsman:
    John Isley, test. B. G. Greer, Jos. H. Thompson, Clk., m. by:
    L. T. Williams, J. P., BEDFORD Co.

DAMRON, John to Sarah Syler - issued October 27, 1866, m. by:
    N. T. Power, M. G., October 28, 1866, FRANKLIN Co.

DAMRON, John W. to Elizabeth C. Metcalf - issued April 24, 1855,
    m. by: Rev. N. L. Power April 24, 1855, FRANKLIN Co.

DAMRON, Thomas to Jane Blythe - issued June 12, 1855, m. by:
    Joseph Smith, M. G., June 13, 1855, FRANKLIN Co.

DAMRON, William to Cathrine Damron - issued May 10, 1855, m. by:
    D. D. Smith, J. P., May 10, 1855, FRANKLIN Co.

DANIEL, Benjamin to Martha Ann Washburn - issued April 3, 1846,
    STEWART Co.

DANIEL, Calloway to Matilda Vanzant - issued June 26, 1851, FRANKLIN Co.

DANIEL, Edward to Precilla Mays - issued December 22, 1811, Bondsman:
    John McCarty, GRAINGER Co.

DANIEL, Edward to Phebe Mays - issued July 23, 1814, Bondsman:
    John Daniel, m. by: Geo. Moody, J. P., July 24, 1814, GRAINGER Co.

DANIEL, Edward to Melvina Trogan - issued March 24, 1835, m. by:
    James Whitlock, M. G., GRAINGER Co.

DANIEL, Elisha to Sally Alsup - issued January 22, 1821, m. January 23,
    1821, RUTHERFORD Co.

DANIEL, Ephraim to Martha Johnson - issued December 18, 1834, m. by:
    Richard Keyhill, J. P., December 22, 1834, KNOX Co.

DANIEL, Ephraim to Polly Wright - issued March 12, 1836, m. by:
    Richard Keyhill, J. P., March 12, 1836, KNOX Co.

DANIEL, F. K. to Malissa Green - issued October 17, 1859, m. by:
    R. W. Casey, J. P., October 18, 1859, COFFEE Co.

DANIEL, Isaac to Phebe Mayes - issued February 5, 1831, Bondsman:
    James McCarty, m. by: Jas. Kennon, M. G., GRAINGER Co.

DANIEL, J. to Phebie Ann Coocksey - issued December 29, 1846, DICKSON Co.

DANIEL, James to Eliza Smith - issued June 17, 1826, Bondsman:
    Josiah McClain, m. by: Josiah S. McClain, J. P., June 22, 1826,
    WILSON Co.

DANIEL, James to Elizabeth Alsup - issued August 29, 1827, Bondsman:
    Edward Daniel, RUTHERFORD Co.

DANIEL, James to Martha Kennon - issued August 12, 1833, Bondsman:
    John Kennon, GRAINGER Co.

DANIEL, Jesse to Ann Cotton - issued January 23, 1821, Bondsman:
Jesse Gambling, SUMNER Co.

DANIEL, Jesse to Sarah Elney - issued July 19, 1858, m. by:
John Byrom, M. G., July 21, 1858, FRANKLIN Co.

DANIEL, John L. to S. B. Hopkins - issued March 4, 1843, FRANKLIN Co.

DANIEL, John L. to Elizabeth J. Mathis - issued December 6, 1847,
Bondsman: Buckner Mathis, MONTGOMERY Co.

DANIEL, Joseph to Rebecca Hodges - issued December 21, 1806, Bondsman:
John Pratt and Thos. Turley, GRAINGER Co.

DANIEL, Joseph to Mary Long - issued December 13, 1820, Bondsman:
Sterling Cocke, GRAINGER Co.

DANIEL, Joseph to Elizabeth Bird - issued April 30, 1846, m. by:
B. M. Ellis, M. G., April 30, 1846, STEWART Co.

DANIEL, Joseph R. to Mary E. Randolph - issued May 30, 1836, Bondsman:
William C. J. Burrus, m. by: G. Baker May 31, 1836, RUTHERFORD Co.

DANIEL, Lewis to Betsey Hilton - issued February 4, 1837, Bondsman:
Daniel Noe, GRAINGER Co.

DANIEL, Mark to Martha May - issued February 18, 1834, Bondsman:
Frederic May, m. by: D. Carmical, J. P., GRAINGER Co.

DANIEL, R. A. to Caroline Smith - issued December 24, 1845, m. by:
D. B. Kelley, J. P., December 24, 1845, FRANKLIN Co.

DANIEL, R. B. to E. A. Tollarson - issued August 14, 1860, m. by:
D. K. Moreland, Pastor Harmony Church, August 16, 1860, ROBERTSON Co.

DANIEL, Robert to Elizabeth Grant - issued October 22, 1828, Bondsman:
W. Bradshaw, GRAINGER Co.

DANIEL, Simon to Rebecca Ann Sexton - issued April 14, 1847, m. by:
John Randle, J. P., April 14, 1847, STEWART Co.

DANIEL, Solomon L. to Mary C. Holt - issued November 19, 1873, m. by:
Jas. A. Hudgins, M. G., November 20, 1873, FRANKLIN Co.

DANIEL, Stephen to Abigail Allsup - issued August 29, 1827, Bondsman:
Edward Daniel, RUTHERFORD Co.

DANIEL, Stephen to Abigal Clounch - issued January 27, 1831, Bondsman:
David Clounch, m. by: I. Latham, J. P., GRAINGER Co.

DANIEL, Stephen H. to Elizabeth Daniel - issued November 10, 1845,
m. by: U. Young November 13, 1845, ROBERTSON Co.

DANIEL, Thomas to Judy Thornhill - issued April 10, 1816, Bondsman:
Michiel Green, m. by: Thos. Anderson, J. P., April 10, 1816,
SUMNER Co.

DANIEL, Thomas to Mary Bartlett - issued February 4, 1851, m. by:
J. S. Davis, M. G., February 6, 1851, FRANKLIN Co.

DANIEL, Thomas to Rebecca Putman - issued February 2, 1860, FRANKLIN Co.

DANIEL, Tilman M. to Mary E. Meredith - November 13, 1855, m. by:
C. P. Reece, GILES Co.

DANIEL, W. R. to T. C. Holt - issued September 23, 1869, m. by:
James A. Hudgins September 23, 1869, FRANKLIN Co.

DANIEL, Walter W. to Jane A. Berry - issued August 25, 1835, Bondsman:
John C. Berry, RUTHERFORD Co.

DANIEL, William to Martha Mayse - issued November 3, 1821, Bondsman:
William E. Cocke, m. by: Geo. Moody, J. P., November 4, 1821,
GRAINGER Co.

DANIEL, William to Justice Claunch - issued October 25, 1836, Bondsman:
Wenright Atkins, m. by: John Latham, J. P., GRAINGER Co.

DANIEL, Wyatt W. to Lucenda Caroline Buckhannon - issued October 1,
1855, m. by: James Stevens, J. P., October 2, 1855, COFFEE Co.

DANIELL, Dixan to Maryann Williams - issued September 19, 1838,
m. September 29, 1838, STEWART Co.

DANIS (Davis), Mc H. to Lyddia J. Rice - issued February 16, 1872,
m. by: Meredith Carter, M. G., February 18, 1872, FRANKLIN Co.

DANIS (Davis), W. M. to P. E. Parks - issued February 1, 1871,
FRANKLIN Co.

DANLEY, Jerome to Susan Edwards - issued January 3, 1856, m. by:
G. Benton, J. P., ROBERTSON Co.

DANNALY, Andrew to Janie Inman - January 22, 1812, WILLIAMSON Co.

DANNER, Jacob to Sarah Watson - issued December 20, 1815, Bondsman:
Henery Watson, m. by: John Hall, GRAINGER Co.

DANNER, John to Sally Young - issued December 23, 1844, m. by:
Thos. Elliott, M. G., December 24, 1844, STEWART Co.

DANNINGTON, Ephriam M. to Rebecca E. Wrights - issued February 15,
1856, m. by: Thomas West, M. G., February 19, 1856, ROBERTSON Co.

DARDEN, D. to Sarah Culbertson - issued July 22, 1858, m. by:
Jesse B. White, J. P., ROBERTSON Co.

DARDEN, J. A. to A. M. Fiser - issued March 15, 1860, m. by:
J. T. W. Davis, M. G., ROBERTSON Co.

DARDEN, Jacob H. to S. E. Polk (Sarah) - issued February 3, 1849,
m. by: James Burns, acting J. P., February 4, 1849, ROBERTSON Co.

DARDEN, James to Susan C. Frey - issued December 17, 1859, m. by:
J. T. W. Davis, M. G., December 18, 1859, ROBERTSON Co.

DARDEN, Thomas N. to Susan F. Davis - issued October 26, 1858, m. by:
J. P. Campbell, M. G., October 27, 1858, ROBERTSON Co.

DARDEN, W. J. to Mary E. Gardner - issued March 14, 1861, m. by:
A. Atkins, J. P., ROBERTSON Co.

DARDIS, W. T. to Mary E. Gray - issued February 23, 1842, FRANKLIN Co.

DARELL, A. P. to Louisa Ward - issued August 6, 1839, m. by:
Joseph Smith August 6, 1839, FRANKLIN Co.

DARNABY, Wm. A. to Elizabeth G. Sublett - issued March 10, 1855, m. by:
John Chitwood, J. P., March 11, 1855, FRANKLIN Co.

DARNELL, George W. to Miss Martha Barbee - issued July 23, 1850,
Bondsman: Bartell Barbee, m. by: James T. Garnett, J. P., July 21,
1850, MONTGOMERY Co.

DARNELL, James J. to Permelia Ann Coleman - issued June 1, 1857, m. by:
J. A. George, J. P., June 2, 1857, COFFEE Co.

DARNELL, John J. to Malinda J. Abney - issued April 13, 1852, Bondsman:
S. S. Ingram, m. by: Wilie Smith, J. P., April 13, 1852,
MONTGOMERY Co.

DARNELL, Joseph to Cordelia Jones - issued August 31, 1867, m. by:
D. D. Smith, M. G., August 1, 1867, FRANKLIN Co.

DARNELL, Logan to Mary Ferrell - issued September 5, 1859, m. by:
M. A. Carden, J. P., September 5, 1859, COFFEE Co.

DARNUL, William to Candice Freeman - issued December 12, 1820,
m. December 14, 1820, RUTHERFORD Co.

DARRELL, A. B. to Louisa E. Brown - issued April 11, 1844, m. by:
J. Thomas Slatter, J. P., April 11, 1844, FRANKLIN Co.

DARRELL, August P. to Martha J. McCoy - issued April 19, 1854, m. by:
Thos. Finch, J. P., April 19, 1854, FRANKLIN Co.

DARRINGTON, Allen to Francis E. Lathan - issued March 17, 1848,
Bondsman: Smith Gibson, m. by: W. B. Carney, J. P., March 17,
1848, MONTGOMERY Co.

DARRINGTON, Thomas to Sarah Laurence - issued September 24, 1829,
Bondsman: Daniel Oxford, m. by: Robert Norvell, M. G., September 24,
1829, SUMNER Co.

DARROW, Benjamin to Mary Murphy - issued January 18, 1844, m. by:
Wm. Adkins, J. P., January 31, 1844, DICKSON Co.

DARROW, Joseph to Chastina Henderson - issued September 15, 1846,
DAVIDSON Co.

DARWIN, Francis M. to Nancy Singleton - issued February 11, 1846,
m. by: Wm. G. Guinn February 12, 1846, FRANKLIN Co.

DARWIN, James M. to Eliza A. Oakley - issued July 15, 1852, m. by:
John S. Slatter, J. P., July 16, 1852, FRANKLIN Co.

DARWIN, John P. to Rebecca A. Stroud - issued January 6, 1851, m. by:
Robt. Hines, J. P., January 6, 1851, FRANKLIN Co.

DARWIN, P. B. to M. A. Phillips - issued August 22, 1868, FRANKLIN Co.

DARWIN, Payton B. to Louisa J. Phillips - issued July 19, 1873, m. by:
Rev. J. H. Hessey July 20, 1873, FRANKLIN Co.

DARWIN, Powell to Nancy Kennerly - issued January 14, 1839, FRANKLIN Co.

DARWIN, Robt. to Mary M. Knight - issued April 22, 1847, m. by:
Madison Williams, J. P., April 22, 1847, FRANKLIN Co.

DARWIN, Thos. J. to Amanda M. McCollum - issued September 18, 1850,
m. by: John T. Slatter, J. P., September 19, 1850, FRANKLIN Co.

DARWIN, W. P. to N. J. Beasley - issued February 18, 1868, FRANKLIN Co.

DASHILL, Richard R. to Louisa Jane Kizer - issued June 26, 1841,
m. by: Wm. Ellis, J. P., June 27, 1841, STEWART Co.

DAUB, Asa to Prudence Turner - issued August 27, 1849, m. by:
W. H. Bugg, J. P., August 28, 1849, ROBERTSON Co.

DAUGHERTY, George W. to ___ (?) - issued March 10, 1846, m. by:
Jas. L. Adams, J. P., March 11, 1846, ROBERTSON Co.

DAUGHERTY, James to Luvina White - issued January 10, 1841, DICKSON Co.

DAUGHERTY, John to Malinda Burt - issued August 18, 1852, m. by:
J. M. P. Hickerson, M. G., August 19, 1852, FRANKLIN Co.

DAUGHERTY, Sam'l. to Civey Garrett - November 18, 1815, WILLIAMSON Co.

DAUGHTRY, Jeremiah to Martha Mankin - issued March 1, 1837, Bondsman: Jesse Mankin, RUTHERFORD Co.

DAUGHTRY, Starkey to Lydia Forrester - issued December 8, 1812, Bondsman: Abram Trigg, SUMNER Co.

DAUGHTY, William to Dolly Spoon - issued January 26, 1826, Bondsman: John Spoon, GRAINGER Co.

DAULTON, Colby to Elizabeth McGinnis - issued December 20, 1833, Bondsman: David McCoy, m. by: John Eaton, J. P., December 22, GRAINGER Co.

DAULTON, Enoch to Jane Harrell - issued September 2, 1833, Bondsman: Timothy Daulton, m. by: W. Williams, J. P., GRAINGER Co.

DAULTON, James M. to Nancy C. Cole - issued November 14, 1843, m. by: John Roleman, J. P., November 16, 1843, FRANKLIN Co.

DAULTON, Richard to Poley Taylor - issued July 13, 1825, Bondsman: Andrew Taylor, m. July 13, 1825, SUMNER Co.

DAVENPORT, George to Jane Kilpatrick - issued May 23, 1836, Bondsman: Joseph Bogle, m. by: Wm. Thomas, J. P., May 24, 1836, RUTHERFORD Co.

DAVENPORT, James to Nancy Mobias - issued October 5, 1825, Bondsman: James M. Irwin, m. by: John Provine, M. G., WILSON Co.

DAVENPORT, James M. C. to Mary Hasty - issued December 7, 1844, m. by: Benj. D. Kelley, J. P., December 8, 1844, FRANKLIN Co.

DAVENPORT, Lewis to Mary Harris - issued April 25, 1829, Bondsman: Edward Sanderson, SUMNER Co.

DAVENPORT, Matthew to Lydia Preston - issued June 25, 1831, Bondsman: Felix R. Chenault, m. by: Isaac Lindsey June 25, 1831, SUMNER Co.

DAVENPORT, Matthew to Sarah B. Hopkins - August 1, 1832, m. by: Albin (Allen?) Hill, GILES Co.

DAVENPORT, Reuben to Ruth M. Sauls - issued March 28, 1825, Bondsman: John Sauls, RUTHERFORD Co.

DAVENPORT, Reubin to Susan Richardson - issued June 13, 1820, Bondsman: Frances Cooper, m. by: John McMinn, J. P., June 15, 1820, WILSON Co.

DAVENPORT, Thos. H. to Sally Thomas - issued December 16, 1829, Bondsman: James Allison, m. by: Jno. Brown, J. P., December 17, 1829, Witness: Wm. Swan, KNOX Co.

DAVENPORT, Warren to Susey Whitlock - issued February 25, 1825, Bondsman: James S. Leech, m. by: John McMinn, J. P., February 26, 1825, WILSON Co.

DAVENPORT, William to Nancy Boyer - issued March 4, 1819, Bondsman: John Mitchel, SUMNER Co.

DAVENPORT, Willie to Lucinda Ward - issued September 8, 1823, Bondsman: John Sauls, m. by: John McMinn, J. P., September 9, 1823, WILSON Co.

DAVID, A. R. to Sarah L. Cowan - issued April 5, 1847, m. by: H. Larkin April 6, 1847, FRANKLIN Co.

DAVID, Benjamin to Franky Vessor - m. by: Alexander McEwen, J. P., August 22, 1817, RUTHERFORD Co.

DAVID, Elizabeth to Moses Moore - GREENE Co.

DAVID, Isiah B. to Elizabeth Hays - issued September 24, 1838,
    Bondsman: Gaben Dollarhede, m. by: H. W. Puckett, M. G., September 27,
    1838, WILSON Co.

DAVIDSON, A. D. to Tabitha Rosson - issued January 22, 1848, m. by:
    Robert Williams, G. M., February 23, 1848, ROBERTSON Co.

DAVIDSON, Abner to Anney Evans - issued August 18, 1802, Bondsman:
    Joseph Davidson, GRAINGER Co.

DAVIDSON, Alexander to Patsy Smith - issued November 17, 1803,
    GRAINGER Co.

DAVIDSON, Briant to Sarah Janes - issued November 17, 1816, Bondsman:
    John Davidson, m. by: William Lane November 17, 1816, GRAINGER Co.

DAVIDSON, Butler to Elizabeth Brownlow - May 15, 1826, Security:
    George M. Gibson, GILES Co.

DAVIDSON, Edward to Polly King - issued October 24, 1829, Bondsman:
    Anderson King, m. by: Demcey Ashford, J. P., October 24, 1829,
    SUMNER Co.

DAVIDSON, Elijah to Mary Hudson - issued October 31, 1840, m. by:
    K. Myatt, J. P., October 31, 1840, DICKSON Co.

DAVIDSON, Elizabeth J. to W. J. Freeman - issued November 7, 1862,
    Bondsman: John W. Moore, Jos. H. Thompson, Clk. per N. F. Thompson,
    Dep. Clk., BEDFORD Co.

DAVIDSON, Francis to Sally Leek - May 18, 1808, WILLIAMSON Co.

DAVIDSON, Francis to Jane M. Cartwright - issued September 23, 1829,
    Bondsman: W. P. Davidson, m. by: A. Provine March 22, 1830,
    WILSON Co.

DAVIDSON, Francis P. to Sarah Hearn - issued December 18, 1826,
    Bondsman: Thomas Cox, WILSON Co.

DAVIDSON, George to Barsheba Tompkins - November 17, 1807, WILLIAMSON Co.

DAVIDSON, George W. to Lydia Jane Dodson - September 17, 1838, GILES Co.

DAVIDSON, Howell A. to Sarah Davidson - issued March 14, 1838, m. by:
    L. Russell, J. P., March 15, 1838, DICKSON Co.

DAVIDSON, J. D. to Alice Brown - issued September 30, 1863, Bondsman:
    J. H. Jones, m. by: C. B. Porter, G. M., October 1, 1863,
    LAWRENCE Co.

DAVIDSON, Jacob to Sarah Selvage - issued January 20, 1814, Bondsman:
    James Selvage, GRAINGER Co.

DAVIDSON, James to Nancy Braden - issued November 18, 1820, Bondsman:
    William Davidson, m. by: Valentine Moulder, J. P., GRAINGER Co.

DAVIDSON, James to Kiziah Davis - issued October 15, 1841, m. by:
    M. B. Stuart, J. P., October 21, 1841, DICKSON Co.

DAVIDSON, James L. to Rachael Jacobs - issued April 5, 1862, Bondsman:
    Samuel C. Carter, LAWRENCE Co.

DAVIDSON, James M. to Sarah Jane Luther - issued February 17, 1841,
    m. by: K. Myatt, J. P., February 28, 1841, DICKSON Co.

DAVIDSON, John to Fanny Bradley - May 6, 1807, WILLIAMSON Co.

DAVIDSON, Jno. to Fanny Brady - May 6, 1807, WILLIAMSON Co.

DAVIDSON, John to Rachal Carson - issued July 3, 1816, Bondsman:
David Billings, m. by: Thos. Calhoon, M. G., July 4, 1816,
WILSON Co.

DAVIDSON, John to Nancy Potts - October 4, 1817, WILLIAMSON Co.

DAVIDSON, John to Elizabeth Brown - issued October 11, 1817, Bondsman:
Henry H. Howel, m. by: John W. Payton, J. P., October 14, 1814,
WILSON Co.

DAVIDSON, John to Mary Hare - issued July 30, 1829, Bondsman:
Benjamin H. Billings, RUTHERFORD Co.

DAVIDSON, John to Martha Barnett - issued April 28, 1855, m. by:
Jas. Woodard, ROBERTSON Co.

DAVIDSON, John E. to Mary Neil Holmes - May 30, 1810, Bondsman:
Samuel J. Rogers, MAURY Co.

DAVIDSON, Jonah to Mary Finch - issued January 26, 1825, m. by:
Joseph Mason, J. P., January 27, 1825, RUTHERFORD Co.

DAVIDSON, Joseph to Rebecca Irwin - June 15, 1815, WILLIAMSON Co.

DAVIDSON, Mathew B. to Virginia Hendley - issued March 2, 1867, m. by:
D. S. Long, J. P., March 4, 1867, FRANKLIN Co.

DAVIDSON, Richard to Elizabeth Toombs - issued February 26, 1821,
m. by: John Fulton, J. P., March 1, 1821, RUTHERFORD Co.

DAVIDSON, Ruthy to Abraham Whiteside - August 5, 1809, Bondsman:
William Pillow, MAURY Co.

DAVIDSON, Samuel to Elizabeth Russell - issued June 10, 1835, Bondsman:
Henry Lonas, m. by: Sam'l. Dickey, J. P., June 11, 1835, KNOX Co.

DAVIDSON, Sophia to Wm. Couch - BEDFORD Co.

DAVIDSON, Thomas A. to Louisa Snell - issued September 4, 1861,
Bondsman: Jos. H. Thompson, Clk., BEDFORD Co.

DAVIDSON, Wilie L. to Sarah Ann Rye - issued May 30, 1846, Bondsman:
John H. Rye, MONTGOMERY Co.

DAVIDSON, William to Hannah Oaks - issued January 16, 1804, Bondsman:
Henry Ballenger, GRAINGER Co.

DAVIDSON, William to Susan Cartwright - issued November 1, 1819,
Bondsman: George Swann, m. by: Wm. Steele, J. P., November 2,
1819, WILSON Co.

DAVIDSON, Wm. to Patsy Luther - issued January 2, 1846, m. by:
I. C. Anglin, J. P., January 4, 1846, DICKSON Co.

DAVIDSON, William to Lucy Lears - issued February 9, 1861, Bondsman:
Edmund Winters, m. by: L. M. Sanford, J. P., February 9, 1861,
LAWRENCE Co.

DAVIE, A. F. to Sophronia A. Davis - issued May 13, 1850, Bondsman:
W. J. Lunsford, MONTGOMERY Co.

DAVIE, Joseph to Amie Demoss - March 27, 1806, WILLIAMSON Co.

DAVIS, A. to Lucinda Simpson - issued May 4, 1866, m. by:
A. J. Simpson, J. P., May 7, 1866, FRANKLIN Co.

DAVIS, A. J. to Mary Mulcaster - issued March 13, 1848, Bondsman:
M. A. Hodges, m. by: A. Vaughn, J. P., March 19, 1848, MONTGOMERY Co.

337

DAVIS, Jr., Abel to Tabitha Daniel - issued January 4, 1836, Bondsman:
W. G. Parrish, m. by: Jas. F. Fletcher, J. P., January 5, 1836,
RUTHERFORD Co.

DAVIS, Acquilla to Mary F. Morton - issued July 14, 1835, Bondsman:
Benj. W. Avent, m. by: Martin Clark, E. M. E. C., July 16,
1835, RUTHERFORD Co.

DAVIS, Alex to Polly Tipton - issued February 21, 1822, Bondsman:
Edward Burk, m. by: William Gray, J. P., WILSON Co.

DAVIS, Alexander to Anny Courtney - April 1, 1818 (?), KNOX Co.

DAVIS, Alexander to E. Couch - issued November 25, 1859, FRANKLIN Co.

DAVIS, Almire to P. L. Wade - issued October 4, 1862, Bondsman:
W. H Haile, Jos. H. Thompson, Clk. per N. F. Thompson, Dep. Clk.,
m. by: James G. Bledsoe October 12, 1862, BEDFORD Co.

DAVIS, Amos to Betsy Wood - April 28, 1809, WILLIAMSON Co.

DAVIS, Anderson to Narcissa Campbell - issued February 2, 1860,
Bondsman: J. S. Wamack, WILSON Co.

DAVIS, Andrew to Mary Ann Cassey - issued May 14, 1852, Bondsman:
Benj. Baggett, MONTGOMERY Co.

DAVIS, Andrew F. to Elizabeth R. Nukkles - issued August 10, 1815,
Bondsman: Joshua Nuckles, RUTHERFORD Co.

DAVIS, Anna to Andrew Hixon - GREENE Co.

DAVIS, Archibald to Elizabeth McBride - issued August 26, 1803,
Bondsman: David Stuart, SUMNER Co.

DAVIS, Benjamin to Nancy Mitchell - issued September 1, 1818, Bondsman:
Jesse Lysles, WILSON Co.

DAVIS, Benjamin to Elizabeth Spraggins - issued August 23, 1820,
m. August 25, 1820, RUTHERFORD Co.

DAVIS, Benjamin M. to Casander Taylor - issued August 16, 1817,
Bondsman: William H. Moore, m. by: Wm. B. Elgin, E. M. E. C.,
August 19, 1817, WILSON Co.

DAVIS, Charles to Catharine Overton - issued May 30, 1814, Bondsman:
Thomas Brasfield, KNOX Co.

DAVIS, Charles to Ellen Anderson - issued April 26, 1843, m. by:
W. Crocket, J. P., May 4, 1843, DAVIDSON Co.

DAVIS, Claiborne F. to Eliza Ann Wilson - issued September 16, 1845,
m. by: W. D. F. Sawrie, M. G., September 17, 1845, DAVIDSON Co.

DAVIS, Cliborne to Lavista (?) Damewood - issued December 14, 1833,
m. by: Isaac Bayless, J. P., December 26, 1833, KNOX Co.

DAVIS, D. J. to Sarah Wiggins - issued February 24, 1859, m. by:
D. D. Smith, M. G., March 8, 1859, FRANKLIN Co.

DAVIS, Daniel to Elizabeth Miller - issued May 21, 1841, VAN BUREN Co.

DAVIS, David to Betsy Tays - October 2, 1815, KNOX Co.

DAVIS, David to Mary Martin - issued September 27, 1825, m. by:
Joseph Mason, J. P., September 28, 1825, RUTHERFORD Co.

DAVIS, Davie to Martha Baggett - issued February 21, 1849, Bondsman:
Wm. Baggett, m. by: T. Ramey, J. P., February 22, 1849, MONTGOMERY Co.

DAVIS, Eaton to Deborah Moore - issued July 2, 1825, m. by:
O. W. Crockett, J. P., July 8, 1825, RUTHERFORD Co.

DAVIS, Edmond to Mary Ann Marthana Lefew - issued May 7, 1823,
Bondsman: Alexander Davis, Witness: Wm. Swan, KNOX Co.

DAVIS, Edmund to Sally Hannon - issued November 16, 1829, Bondsman:
Alexander Davis, m. by: Elijah Johnson, J. P., November 17, 1829,
Witness: Wm. Swan, KNOX Co.

DAVIS, Edmund to Jane Jones - issued December 16, 1837, Bondsman:
William Bunch, m. by: Edward Tate, J. P., December 16, 1837,
GRAINGER Co.

DAVIS, Edward to Rhody Sanders - issued April 14, 1824, m. by:
John Haynie April 14, 1824, KNOX Co.

DAVIS, Edward to Nancy Battle - issued February 26, 1829, Bondsman:
Charles Guyger, RUTHERFORD Co.

DAVIS, Edward to Amanda Mercer - issued October 19, 1849, m. by:
James T. Garnett, J. P., October 19, 1849, MONTGOMERY Co.

DAVIS, Eli to Mary Allen - issued July 3, 1832, Bondsman:
Jonathan L. Fare, WILSON Co.

DAVIS, Elias to Margaat Cockrun - issued June 15, 1802, Bondsman:
John Stiffee and George McCombs, GRAINGER Co.

DAVIS, Elijah to Abbey Ligget - October 19, 1793, Security:
William Galbraith, GREENE Co.

DAVIS, Elizabeth to Miles Cunningham - GREENE Co.

DAVIS, Elizabeth to Robert O'Neal - GREENE Co.

DAVIS, Elliott C. to Martha A. Nash - issued July 26, 1855, m. by:
W. W. Harris, M. G., July 26, 1855, FRANKLIN Co.

DAVIS, Ellis to Mary Minor - issued December 29, 1826, m. by:
J. B. Lasater, J. P., January 14, 1826, WILSON Co.

DAVIS, Elnathan to Jane Harris - issued December 28, 1831, Bondsman:
George B. Burns, m. by: H. O. Taylor, M. G., GRAINGER Co.

DAVIS, Elza to Mildred Gaines - issued August 2, 1833, Bondsman:
Bales E. Gaines, m. by: W. P. Humbard, J. P., August 8, GRAINGER Co.

DAVIS, Enoch to Elizabeth Clerk (or Clark) - issued August 21, 1798,
Bondsman: Joab Hill, Witness: Sm'l Yancey, GRAINGER Co.

DAVIS, Ezekiel to Jane Lee - m. by: Henry S. Anthony July 18, 1833,
SUMNER Co.

DAVIS, F. J. to E. F. Mitchell - Bondsman: J. P. Hornaday, BEDFORD Co.

DAVIS, Fanny to David Reynolds - GREENE Co.

DAVIS, Ferrell to Frances J. Joplin - issued November 2, 1829, Bondsman:
John Davis and John Joplin, m. by: Williamson Williams, J. P.,
November 3, 1829, WILSON Co.

DAVIS, Francis to Eleanor Lyons - April 20, 1797, KNOX Co.

DAVIS, G. W. to E. J. Connel - issued February 24, 1852, m. by:
Joseph Willis, M. G., ROBERTSON Co.

DAVIS, George to Margaret McCall - December 6, 1792, Security:
Moes Rodgers, GREENE Co.

DAVIS, George to Anne Delany - March 6, 1799, Security: John Delany, GREENE Co.

DAVIS, George to Cynthia Dearmond - issued September 13, 1814, KNOX Co.

DAVIS, George to Nancy Moore - issued February 5, 1848, VAN BUREN Co.

DAVIS, George to Mary Francis Bradshaw - issued April 9, 1852, Bondsman: W. C. Suter, m. by: Elisha Vaughn, M. G., April 11, 1852, MONTGOMERY Co.

DAVIS, George W. to Sarah Rucker - issued April 1, 1837, m. by: Anthony North, J. P., April 13, 1837, RUTHERFORD Co.

DAVIS, George W. to Catharine Mohorn - issued August 24, 1854, m. by: R. H. Weakley, J. P., August 24, 1854, MONTGOMERY Co.

DAVIS, George W. D. to Samantha E. Speck - issued September 5, 1856, m. by: R. C. Smith, J. P., September 9, 1856, FRANKLIN Co.

DAVIS, Gideon to Lucy J. Cloudy - issued January 10, 1847, DICKSON Co.

DAVIS, Goodman to Henrietta Pryor - issued September 14, 1834, Bondsman: Thomas Smith, RUTHERFORD Co.

DAVIS, Henry to Revecca Hampton - February 11, 1806, WILLIAMSON Co.

DAVIS, Henry to Ann Sullivan - issued April 7, 1818, Bondsman: Thomas Price, RUTHERFORD Co.

DAVIS, Henry to Susanna Dowell - issued April 17, 1820, Bondsman: Francis M. Weathered, SUMNER Co.

DAVIS, Henry to Rachel Hunter - issued November 21, 1825, Bondsman: Amos Carter, m. by: James McMillan, J. P., November 24, 1825, KNOX Co.

DAVIS, Henry N. to Sarah Ann Holder - issued July 15, 1856, m. by: L. W. Marbury, J. P., July 17, 1856, COFFEE Co.

DAVIS, Henry W. to Sally Winchester - issued February 27, 1839, m. by: E. S. Hall, J. P., February 27, 1839, DAVIDSON Co.

DAVIS, Hezekiah to Nancy Wilson - issued October 23, 1824, Bondsman: Millner Walker, WILSON Co.

DAVIS, Hiram to Polly Ford - issued September 11, 1825, Bondsman: Thomas Coddle, m. by: Wm. Smith, J. P., September 11, 1825, SUMNER Co.

DAVIS, Hiram to Elizabeth Wyatt - issued February 12, 1850, Bondsman: Jas. M. Mathis, m. by: P. Priestly, J. P., February 12, 1850, MONTGOMERY Co.

DAVIS, Isaac to Elizabeth Mulky - issued August 21, 1802, Bondsman: John Hutton, GRAINGER Co.

DAVIS, Isaac to Lucy Via - issued January 28, 1826, m. by: John A. Hoover, J. P., January 30, 1826, RUTHERFORD Co.

DAVIS, Isaac to Priscilla Craig - issued September 28, 1841, VAN BUREN Co.

DAVIS, Isham F. to Rachel S. Hays - issued October 10, 1809, Bondsman: Sam'l Meredith, WILSON Co.

DAVIS, Isham F. to Sally Curd - issued July 2, 1821, Bondsman: William McGrigor, WILSON Co.

DAVIS, J. H. to E. A. Villines - issued June 22, 1848, m. by: Jno. M. Harry, J. P., June 25, 1848, ROBERTSON Co.

DAVIS, J. T. W. to Mary E. Batts - issued October 31, 1860, m. by:
Jerome B. Anderson, M. G., November 1, 1860, ROBERTSON Co.

DAVIS, James to Mary Brumely - August 29, 1786, Security:
Barnabas Brumley, GREENE Co.

DAVIS, James to Mary Bowers - February 3, 1797, Security:
William Patterson, GREENE Co.

DAVIS, James to Nancy Golding - October 7, 1798, ·KNOX Co.

DAVIS, James to Ellenore Woods - issued August 5, 1803, Bondsman:
Jesse and James Daniel Pew, GRAINGER Co.

DAVIS, James to Betsey Russell - January 27, 1813, WILLIAMSON Co.

DAVIS, James to Dicey Pigg - October 4, 1816, WILLIAMSON Co.

DAVIS, James to Penelope Drake - issued October 10, 1818, Bondsman:
Thomas Scudder, m. by: J. T. Davis, WILSON Co.

DAVIS, James to Luise Cockrum - issued April 13, 1821, Bondsman:
John Davis, m. by: David Tate, J. P., April 22, 1821, GRAINGER Co.

DAVIS, James to Ibby Booker - issued May 20, 1823, Bondsman:
Nicholas Gibbs, m. by: John Bayless, J. P., May 22, 1823, KNOX Co.

DAVIS, James to Hannah Helton - issued January 24, 1825, Bondsman:
John Davis, GRAINGER Co.

DAVIS, James to Rachel Read - issued September 27, 1827, Bondsman:
John Hicks, m. by: Jordan Willeford October 4, 1827, RUTHERFORD Co.

DAVIS, Jr., James to Polly Stalsworth - issued July 15, 1828, Bondsman:
Samuel Holston, m. by: Henry Alsup, J. P., GRAINGER Co.

DAVIS, James to Susan Tippett - issued September 4, 1834, Bondsman:
Dabney Carr, m. by: M. T. Cartwright, J. P., WILSON Co.

DAVIS, James to Sarah Kimbro - issued December 27, 1834, Bondsman:
Jefferson Giffin, m. by: Robt. H. Snoddy, M. G., December 28,
1834, Witness: Geo. M. White, KNOX Co.

DAVIS, James to Susa Howard - issued February 14, 1841, m. by:
Jackson Dyer, J. P., February 14, 1841, VAN BUREN Co.

DAVIS, James to Fany Dukes - issued July 25, 1841, m. by:
Isaac Howard, J. P., July 26, 1841, VAN BUREN Co.

DAVIS, James to Rodey McGuffey - issued September 9, 1847, VAN BUREN Co.

DAVIS, James to Elizabeth Davis - issued September 27, 1865, Bondsman:
Robert C. Blair, m. by: C. P. Porter, G. M., September 29, 1865,
LAWRENCE Co.

DAVIS, James A. to Malinda Chaners - issued February 10, 1858, m. by:
John Handly, J. P., February 10, 1858, FRANKLIN Co.

DAVIS, James A. to Hattie Shearwood - issued September 26, 1863,
Bondsman: J. A. King, Jos. H. Thompson, Clk. per James H. Neil,
Dep. Clk., m. by: J. C. Martin, J. P., September 27, 1863,
BEDFORD Co.

DAVIS, James B. to Martha D. Shearman - issued November 23, 1830,
Bondsman: Malcomb R. Nelson, m. by: Peyton Smith, RUTHERFORD Co.

DAVIS, James E. to Polly Taylor - issued April 15, 1809, Bondsman:
Jones Hudson, WILSON Co.

DAVIS, James H. to Mary S. Garner - issued July 12, 1842, FRANKLIN Co.

DAVIS, James L. to Evalina Jane McMillan - issued November 15, 1832, m. by: Tho. H. Nelson November 15, 1832, KNOX Co.

DAVIS, James L. to Letitia M. Thomas - issued November 25, 1854, m. by: W. W. Pepper, Judge and c, November 26, 1854, ROBERTSON Co.

DAVIS, James M. to Sarah Weir - issued December 7, 1840, Bondsman: Wm. B. Pursey, m. by: Moses Ellis, J. P., December 8, 1840, WILSON Co.

DAVIS, James M. to Jane Hart - issued November 15, 1847, Bondsman: E. C. Collins, m. by: R. W. Morrison, J. P., November 18, 1847, MONTGOMERY Co.

DAVIS, James N. to Elizabeth McAdow - issued January 3, 1823, m. by: Abner W. Bond, J. P., WILSON Co.

DAVIS, James R. to Eliza Hughlett - issued July 17, 1854, m. by: Benjamin Gambell, J. P., July 20, 1854, ROBERTSON Co.

DAVIS, James T. to Narcissa Moss - issued January 14, 1841, m. by: Wm. R. Hooten, M. G., January 27, 1841, DAVIDSON Co.

DAVIS, James W. to Jemima Gregory - issued September 3, 1855, m. by: J. A. Silvertooth, J. P., September, 1855, FRANKLIN Co.

DAVIS, Jarome to Winey M. Marlow - July 21, 1859, m. by: S. A. Parsons, J. P., GILES Co.

DAVIS, Jesse to Elizabeth Hill - issued January 6, 1817, Bondsman: Andrew McHaffie, KNOX Co.

DAVIS, Jesse to Henrietta Vick - issued December 3, 1843, m. by: Lewis Adams, M. G., December 4, 1843, ROBERTSON Co.

DAVIS, Jesse M. to Sarah C. E. Featherston - issued March 29, 1841, m. by: Jeremiah Batts, J. P., ROBERTSON Co.

DAVIS, John to Elizabeth Johnson - issued February 1, 1799, Bondsman: Elijah Johnson, Witness: H. L. White, KNOX Co.

DAVIS, John to Matty Meneeby - issued November 25, 1800, Bondsman: Isaac Meneeby, Witness: A. White, KNOX Co.

DAVIS, John to Sarah Gossage - February 10, 1808, WILLIAMSON Co.

DAVIS, John to Polly McAlpen - issued March 14, 1808, Bondsman: Jesse Holt, WILSON Co.

DAVIS, John to Priscilla Floyd - November 15, 1808, WILLIAMSON Co.

DAVIS, John to Dicy Tombs - June 10, 1809, Bondsman: Reuben Parks, MAURY Co.

DAVIS, John to Sally Goodin - issued June 21, 1809, Bondsman: Wallace Kirkpatrick, SUMNER Co.

DAVIS, John to Betsey Shaw - issued June 25, 1809, Bondsman: Robt. Shaw, SUMNER Co.

DAVIS, John to Theodelia Marton - issued April 16, 1810, Bondsman: Nathaniel Davis, WILSON Co.

DAVIS, John to Franky Chatman - November 24, 1812, WILLIAMSON Co.

DAVIS, John to Margaret Griffitts - issued August 7, 1817, Bondsman: Ninion Riggs, m. by: Isaiah Midkiff, J. P., August 14, 1817, GRAINGER Co.

DAVIS, John to Nancy Johnston - issued July 22, 1820, Bondsman:
Hugh B. Maget, KNOX Co.

DAVIS, Jno. to Nancy Johnston - issued July 22, 1820, m. by:
Thos. Wilkerson, M. G., July 22, 1820, KNOX Co.

DAVIS, John to Sally Crosland - issued December 14, 1822, m. by:
Elijah Maddox, M. G., December 19, 1822, WILSON Co.

DAVIS, John to Mary Bryant - issued September 17, 1825, m. by:
James T. Tompkins, D. D., September 19, 1825, WILSON Co.

DAVIS, John to Elizabeth Goins - issued August 18, 1829, Bondsman:
Henry Alsup, m. by: Henry Alsup, J. P., August 19, GRAINGER Co.

DAVIS, John to Mary Ann Manley - issued December 12, 1829, Bondsman:
Madison Kirk, m. by: David Tate, J. P., December 13, GRAINGER Co.

DAVIS, John to Elizabeth Hearn - issued July 27, 1836, m. by:
John Hearn, J. P., WILSON Co.

DAVIS, John to Catharine Hearn - issued November 4, 1839, Bondsman:
John W. Wynne, WILSON Co.

DAVIS, John to Polly Adams - issued December 19, 1840, Bondsman:
James Dyer, m. by: Elder (?), MEIGS Co.

DAVIS, John to Celia Ann Richards - issued March 9, 1842, m. by:
C. W. Nance, J. P., March 10, 1842, DAVIDSON Co.

DAVIS, John to Nancy Ashley - issued August 23, 1855, FRANKLIN Co.

DAVIS, John to Mary Roberson - issued September 12, 1857, m. by:
L. N. Simpson, J. P., September 13, 1857, FRANKLIN Co.

DAVIS, John L. to Jane Smith - January 4, 1811, WILLIAMSON Co.

DAVIS, John M. to Jane Scott - issued December 23, 1824, m. by:
Tho. H. Nelson December 23, 1824, KNOX Co.

DAVIS, John M. to Eliza Turnor - issued October 21, 1387, Bondsman:
William A. Holbrook, WILSON Co.

DAVIS, John P. to Anny Sullivan - issued April 13, 1816, Bondsman:
James Sullivan, RUTHERFORD Co.

DAVIS, Jno. R. to Polly McCarrell - issued October 23, 1833, Bondsman:
Michael Davis, m. by: Elijah Johnson, J. P., October 24, 1833,
KNOX Co.

DAVIS, John S. to Francis L. Burt - issued March 31, 1842, m. by:
Wm. T. Wells, M. G., March 31, 1842, FRANKLIN Co.

DAVIS, John T. to Eliz McNeilly - issued October 31, 1841, m. by:
D. R. Harris, G. M., ROBERTSON Co.

DAVIS, Jonathan to Caty Hunt - issued January 6, 1812, Bondsman:
Thomas Hunt, SUMNER Co.

DAVIS, Jonathan H. to Pelitha Q. Williams - issued May 21, 1840,
m. by: I. T. Hines, J. P., May 21, 1840, FRANKLIN Co.

DAVIS, Joseph H. to Amanda M. Jarnagin - issued December 7, 1837,
Bondsman: James H. Jones, m. by: Jas. Kennon, M. G., December 7,
1837, GRAINGER Co.

DAVIS, Josiah to Charity Mitchell - January 10, 1816, WILLIAMSON Co.

DAVIS, Kezia to George Sterns (Sturms) - GREENE Co.

DAVIS, Levi to Patsy Caudle - issued September 26, 1845, m. by: A. Justen, J. P., ROBERTSON Co.

DAVIS, Levy to Synthy Hurdle - issued March 23, 1809, Bondsman: Wm. Morris and John Sutton, Witness: Jo Love, KNOX Co.

DAVIS, Lewis to Nancy McHenry - issued January 11, 1815, Bondsman: Geo. Brandon, KNOX Co.

DAVIS, Luckett to Eliza J. M. Jones - issued December 29, 1835, Bondsman: James W. Morton, RUTHERFORD Co.

DAVIS, M. to Sallie A. Hill - issued February 26, 1870, FRANKLIN Co.

DAVIS (Danis), Mc H. to Lyddia J. Rice - issued February 16, 1872, m. by: Meredith Carter, M. G., February 18, 1872, FRANKLIN Co.

DAVIS, Manard to Martha Green - issued September 11, 1862, Bondsman: James M. Davis, m. by: W. C. Davis, J. P., September 11, 1862, LAWRENCE Co.

DAVIS, Margaret to Elijah G. Lovell - issued April 17, 1864, Bondsman: Wynn F. Lovell, BEDFORD Co.

DAVIS, Mary to William K. Alexander - GREENE Co.

DAVIS, Matha to Louisa Roberts - issued November 6, 1854, m. by: Peter Carter, J. P., November 8, 1854, VAN BUREN Co.

DAVIS, Matha to Hannah E. L. Harrison - issued December 28, 1854, m. by: G. W. Sparkman, J. P., December 29, 1854, VAN BUREN Co.

DAVIS, Maulda to Coleman Mullins - issued July 22, 1861, Bondsman: Noel Davis, Jos. H. Thompson, Clk. per James H. Neil, Dep. Clk., BEDFORD Co.

DAVIS, Maye (Masse?) to Aaron Reynolds - December 24, 1810, Bondsman: Thomas Mitchell, MAURY Co.

DAVIS, Micager to Louisa J. Kindrick - issued February 14, 1864, Bondsman: Henry P. Day, m. by: S. A. Carrell, J. P., February 14, 1864, LAWRENCE Co.

DAVIS, Micajah C. to Polly Johnson - February 4, 1811, Bondsman: Samuel Word, MAURY Co.

DAVIS, Moses to Winefred (?) Wallen - issued January 26, 1799

DAVIS, Moses to Mary A. Dame - issued December 24, 1862, Bondsman: Harvey Dame, m. by: Samuel Baker, M. G., December 24, 1862, LAWRENCE Co.

DAVIS, Nancy to Aaron Broyles - GREENE Co.

DAVIS, Nancy to John Baker - GREENE Co.

DAVIS, Nathan to Eliza Rogers - issued March 30, 1811, Bondsman: David Bell, SUMNER Co.

DAVIS, Nathan to Lucinda Grant - issued March 31, 1855, m. by: L. N. Simpson, J. P., April 1, 1855, FRANKLIN Co.

DAVIS, Nathaniel to Sally Hannah - issued April 27, 1797, Bondsman: Samuel Hannah, Witness: Andw. White, KNOX Co.

DAVIS, Nathaniel to Elizabeth McFarlin - issued April 16, 1810, Bondsman: John Davis, WILSON Co.

DAVIS, Nelly to William Martin - July 5, 1809, Bondsman: William Dearing, MAURY Co.

DAVIS, Oliver to M. J. Cavin - issued April 29, 1860, FRANKLIN Co.

DAVIS, Orlander M. to Gracey L. Lander - issued January 31, 1852,
Bondsman: James T. Killebrew, m. by: N. F. Trice, J. P.,
January 31, 1852, MONTGOMERY Co.

DAVIS, Patience to John Kennedy - GREENE Co.

DAVIS, Peter to Polly Crafton - issued August 13, 1826, Bondsman:
Thomas Davis, m. by: Silas Potts, J. P., August 13, 1826, SUMNER Co.

DAVIS, Philander Y. to Eleanor Gwyn - issued December 20, 1837,
Bondsman: C. W. Jackson, WILSON Co.

DAVIS, Philip to Mary McAdams - issued April 24, 1840, Bondsman:
Samuel Davis, m. by: William Green, M. G., April 26, 1840, MEIGS Co.

DAVIS, Priscilla Gilaland to Anthony Walsh - GREENE Co.

DAVIS, Rachel to Russell R. Cove - MAURY Co.

DAVIS, Ranse to Elisabeth Mark - issued March 4, 1850, m. by:
Abraham Drake, J. P., March 6, 1850, VAN BUREN Co.

DAVIS (?), Rebecca to John Young - GREENE Co.

DAVIS, Reuben to Polly Moseley - issued May 3, 1847, m. by:
Robert Carey, M. G., May 3, 1847, VAN BUREN Co.

DAVIS, Richard to Lucy Lantern - issued May 11, 1833, m. by:
R. Gwyn, J. P., May 12, 1833, WILSON Co.

DAVIS, Richard A. to L. A. Polk - issued April 21, 1851, m. by:
J. W. Featherston, ROBERTSON Co.

DAVIS, Robert to Priscilla Sebastian - issued October 9, 1810,
Bondsman: Robert Shaw, SUMNER Co.

DAVIS, Robert to Sarah Doyle - October 8, 1812, KNOX Co.

DAVIS, Robert to Martha Haley - issued March 17, 1819, m. by:
Tho. H. Nelson March 17, 1819, KNOX Co.

DAVIS, Robert to Mary Shorter - issued May 15, 1834, Bondsman:
Jesse Jackson, m. by: B. Pyland, M. G., WILSON Co.

DAVIS, Robt. to Manerva J. Kitchens - issued August 6, 1849, m. by:
J. J. Travis, J. P., August 9, 1849, FRANKLIN Co.

DAVIS, Robert R. to Hariet C. Boggess - issued October 31, 1843,
Bondsman: John McReynolds, m. by: Robert Stockton, J. P.,
November 2, 1843, MEIGS Co.

DAVIS, Ruben to Martha Adair - issued August 23, 1860, m. by:
Simon P. Dotson, J. P., August 26, 1860, VAN BUREN Co.

DAVIS, Sampson to Saraphine Warren - issued April 2, 1857, m. by:
C. Farthing, J. P., ROBERTSON Co.

DAVIS, Samuel to Gressy Ross - April 3, 1798, Security: George Davis,
GREENE Co.

DAVIS, Samuel to Peggy Page - issued December 30, 1798, Bondsman:
Paul Harrolson, Witness: H. L. White, KNOX Co.

DAVIS, Samuel to Hannah Heavenridge - January 5, 1804, Security:
Newhope Quaker Meeting, GREENE Co.

DAVIS, Samuel to Liddy Murphy - issued February 22, 1820, m. by:
David Tate, J. P., February 27, 1820, GRAINGER Co.

DAVIS, Samuel to Margaret Steele - issued October 7, 1835, Bondsman: Thos. E. Everett, WILSON Co.

DAVIS, Samuel to Phebe Harvey - issued November 5, 1842, Bondsman: Prior Neil, m. by: Robert Stockton, J. P., November 5, 1842, MEIGS Co.

DAVIS, Soloman to Jane Davis - November 1, 1809, WILLIAMSON Co.

DAVIS, Spates to Emely Everett - issued December 8, 1843, m. December 9, 1843, STEWART Co.

DAVIS, Thomas to Sarah Walker - April 7, 1795, Security: James Brumley, GREENE Co.

DAVIS, Thomas to Polley Yeats - issued August 12, 1807, Bondsman: Thomas Ray, GRAINGER Co.

DAVIS, Thomas to Clounda Eckols - issued August 4, 1808, Bondsman: John Pendergast, SUMNER Co.

DAVIS, Thomas to Elizabeth Robertson - issued November 25, 1817, Bondsman: John Porter, m. by: John Williamson, J. P., WILSON Co.

DAVIS, Thomas to Jane Donnell - issued December 15, 1827, Bondsman: Calvin Donnell, m. by: Amzi Bradshaw December 20, 1827, WILSON Co.

DAVIS, Thomas to Martha Hogins - issued February 28, 1829, Bondsman: William Potts, RUTHERFORD Co.

DAVIS, Thomas to Amanda J. Donalson - issued July 3, 1852, Bondsman: Wm. L. Mallory, m. by: S. S. Mallory, M. G., July 4, 1852, MONTGOMERY Co.

DAVIS, Thomas to Mary E. Phillips - issued March 26, 1862, Bondsman: Henry J. Wise, Thomas B. Laird Test., Jos. H. Thompson, Clk. per M. E. W. Dunaway, Dep. Clk., BEDFORD Co.

DAVIS, Thos. to Emeline Griffard - issued February 21, 1867, FRANKLIN Co.

DAVIS, Thomas A. to Judith E. Brunson - issued February 28, 1848, Bondsman: Thomas H. Carter, m. by: John Gold, J. P., February 24, 1848, MONTGOMERY Co.

DAVIS, Thomas C. to Susan E. Kilpatrick - issued November 22, 1865, Bondsman: Henry Barton, m. by: Wm. A. Harris November 23, 1865, LAWRENCE Co.

DAVIS, Thomas D. to Arey Johnson - issued June 7, 1827, Bondsman: Moses Lynch, RUTHERFORD Co.

DAVIS, Thomas E. to Nancy H. Marshall - Bondsman: W. F. Dickens, BEDFORD Co.

DAVIS, Thomas E. to Amanda M. Reasons - issued April 15, 1847, Bondsman: W. D. Moss, m. by: J. C. Bryan, J. P., May 6, 1847, MONTGOMERY Co.

DAVIS, Thos. M. to Eliza E. Kitchens - issued December 17, 1853, m. by: J. W. Holmes, M. G., FRANKLIN Co.

DAVIS, Thomas P. to Lucinda Beesley - issued June 25, 1830, Bondsman: James McDowell, m. by: John Lane, RUTHERFORD Co.

DAVIS, Thomas P. to Lucinda Wright - issued March 7, 1834, Bondsman: A. J. Hoover, m. by: Carey James, D. M. E. C., March 8, 1834, RUTHERFORD Co.

DAVIS, Thomas P. to Nancy Popp - issued August 19, 1836, Bondsman: Richard B. Allison, m. by: John D. Rogers, J. P., August 25, 1836, RUTHERFORD Co.

DAVIS, Timothy to Frances Ross - issued November 30, 1805, Bondsman: Norton Gum, RUTHERFORD Co.

DAVIS, W. G. to M. J. Norvill - issued October 25, 1858, m. by: J. R. Smotherman, M. G., October 28, 1858, COFFEE Co.

DAVIS, W. H. to S. A. Cates - issued February 11, 1863, Bondsman: Wm. Hime, Jos. H. Thompson, Clk., BEDFORD Co.

DAVIS, W. H. to Mary Ann Farris - issued December 2, 1874, m. by: J. A. Hudgins, M. G., December 3, 1874, FRANKLIN Co.

DAVIS (Danis), W. M. to P. E. Parks - issued February 1, 1871, FRANKLIN Co.

DAVIS, W. S. to N. A. M. Brown - issued November 21, 1865, m. by: M. Tipps, J. P., November 22, 1865, FRANKLIN Co.

DAVIS, Waid to Patsey Drewney - issued May 23, 1813, Bondsman: Fielden Hankins, SUMNER Co.

DAVIS, Walter to Jane Scarborough - issued April 23, 1839, STEWART Co.

DAVIS, Wesley to Rebecca Wilcher - issued August 13, 1845, FRANKLIN Co.

DAVIS, Wiley to Nancy Crow - issued September 8, 1844, m. by: Empson Bishop, M..G., September 9, 1844, DICKSON Co.

DAVIS, William to Susanna Hixon - August 27, 1794, Security: Sparling Bowman, GREENE Co.

DAVIS, William to Nancy Cotton - issued November 15, 1806, Bondsman: James Cryer, SUMNER Co.

DAVIS, William to Polly Sebastan - issued January 6, 1808, Bondsman: John Davis, SUMNER Co.

DAVIS, William to Elizabeth Webb - issued October 17, 1820, m. by: Joshua Lester, V. D. M., WILSON Co.

DAVIS, William to Martha Trimble - issued February 10, 1821, m. by: William Bumpass, M. G., February 15, 1821, RUTHERFORD Co.

DAVIS, Wm. to Betsy Hunter - issued February 10, 1823, Bondsman: Wm. Swan, KNOX Co.

DAVIS, William to Barbary Johnson - issued July 17, 1824, Bondsman: Joseph Wyrick, m. by: William Laine, J. P., July 17, 1824, GRAINGER Co.

DAVIS, William to Sarah White - issued July 15, 1828, m. by: James T. Tompkins, M. G., July 17, 1828, WILSON Co.

DAVIS, William to Lucy Stewart - issued September 7, 1830, Bondsman: John Webb, WILSON Co.

DAVIS, Wm. to Susan Graves (or Groves) - issued December 7, 1832, m. by: M. B. Carter, J. P., December 11, 1832, KNOX Co.

DAVIS, William to Harriet Walker - issued July 5, 1833, Bondsman: B. B. Sypert, m. by: H. Hobson, J. P., July 9, 1833, WILSON Co.

DAVIS, William to Mary Ann Harrison - March 4, 1837, Security: James Harrison, GILES Co.

DAVIS, William to Nancy Darnaby - issued January 27, 1841, m. by: M. R. Mann, J. P., January 28, 1841, FRANKLIN Co.

DAVIS, William to Elizabeth Dunn - issued January 21, 1845, m. by: B. Fraser, J. P., January 22, 1845, STEWART Co.

DAVIS, William to Elizabeth Bennett - issued September 10, 1845,
    Bondsman: David Gennoe, m. by: Thomas V. Atchley, J. P., MEIGS Co.

DAVIS, William to Elizabeth Reagin - issued August 2, 1853, m. by:
    W. Denson, J. P., FRANKLIN Co.

DAVIS, Wm. to Ardema Simpson - issued December 18, 1859, FRANKLIN Co.

DAVIS, Wm. to Sarah Perry - issued August 24, 1865, m. by:
    Simpson West, J. P., September 15, 1865, FRANKLIN Co.

DAVIS, Wm. to Martha Weaver - issued August 6, 1873, m. by:
    W. C. Tipps, J. P., August 6, 1873, FRANKLIN Co.

DAVIS, William C. to Mary V. Kitchens - issued September 22, 1857,
    m. by: J. J. Ellis, R. M. G., September 22, 1857, FRANKLIN Co.

DAVIS, William H. to Susanna Mitchell - issued August 17, 1837,
    Bondsman: Elija Davis, m. by: Joseph Clark, J. P., August 17,
    1837, GRAINGER Co.

DAVIS, William H. to Kate Marks - issued January 4, 1873, m. by:
    M. H. Bone, M. G., January 15, 1873, FRANKLIN Co.

DAVIS, William L. to ___(?) - ROBERTSON Co.

DAVIS, William R. to Eliza J. Ashby - issued October 31, 1874, m. by:
    Martin Mason, J. P., November 2, 1874, FRANKLIN Co.

DAVIS, William T. to Louisa F. Curley - issued June 9, 1831, Bondsman:
    John Curley, m. by: Calbe Crain June 9, 1831, SUMNER Co.

DAVIS, Williford to Francis C. Pyland - issued December 2, 1857, m. by:
    Joseph Smith, M. G., December 3, 1857, FRANKLIN Co.

DAVIS, Wilson C. to Nancy G. Key - issued July 27, 1830, Bondsman:
    Geo. C. Thurmond, SUMNER Co.

DAVIS, Zachariah to Elizabeth Hill - issued November 30, 1815, Bondsman:
    James Johnson, WILSON Co.

DAVISON, Absolam to Margaret Stephens - issued March 23, 1847, Bondsman:
    W. G. Smith, m. by: R. W. Morrison, J. P., March 25, 1846,
    MONTGOMERY Co.

DAVISON, Bleir (or Blair) to Danius (?) Cunningham - issued November 8,
    1800, Bondsman: James Davison, Witness: Nelson Ore, GRAINGER Co.

DAVISON, James to Harriett Lokey - issued January 7, 1841, m. by:
    J. Byrom January 7, 1841, FRANKLIN Co.

DAVISON, James to Clarissa Parks - issued December 22, 1852, m. by:
    John Nugent, J. P., December 23, 1852, FRANKLIN Co.

DAWDY, John to Polly Moss - issued September 28, 1797, Bondsman:
    Howell Dawdy and Jepho Moss, Witness: Chas. McClung, Clk., KNOX Co.

DAWSON, Elisha to E. J. Boyt - issued February 20, 1839, m. by:
    Jno. Randal, J. P., February 20, 1839, STEWART Co.

DAWSON, Ezekiel to Hannah McFadden - July 19, 1808, WILLIAMSON Co.

DAWSON, Geo. to Polly Adams - August 18, 1807, WILLIAMSON Co.

DAWSON, George P. to Mary J. Overstreet - issued December 16, 1843,
    m. by: W. C. Richmond, acting J. P., ROBERTSON Co.

DAWSON, Henry to Sally Wright - issued December 5, 1810, Bondsman:
    Ebenezer Gilbert, WILSON Co.

DAWSON, Mary to William Mosely - GREENE Co.

DAWSON, William to Nancy Cleveland - September 23, 1800, Security:
Thomas Palmer and John Kennedy, GREENE Co.

DAWSON, William N. to Martha Jane Hartsfield - issued December 19,
1838, Bondsman: John W. Wynne, WILSON Co.

DAY, Chas. M. to Miss Mary C. Bell - issued December 4, 1851, Bondsman:
Samuel Lands, m. by: J. T. Hendrick December 4, 1851, MONTGOMERY Co.

DAY, George W. to Emily Hopkins - issued July 9, 1842, m. by:
John Roleman, J. P., July 10, 1842, FRANKLIN Co.

DAY, Isaac to Elizabeth Scott - issued December 17, 1827, Bondsman:
Francis Day, SUMNER Co.

DAY, John to Polly Ford - August 20, 1811, KNOX Co.

DAY, Moses C. to Lucy S. Lane - issued February 15, 1862, Bondsman:
___ (?), Jos. H. Thompson, Clk. per N. F. Thompson, Dep. Clk.,
BEDFORD Co.

DAY, Philip to Betsey Burns - issued December 10, 1822, m. by:
Wm. Smith, J. P., December 10, 1822, SUMNER Co.

DAY, Samuel to Arena Day - issued October 22, 1828, Bondsman:
Joyn Rawlings, SUMNER Co.

DAY, Solomon to Elizabeth Gillespie - issued January 6, 1823, Bondsman:
Green Daniel, m. by: Wm. Smith, J. P., January 6, 1823, SUMNER Co.

DAY, Stephen to Eliza Blair - issued July 15, 1829, Bondsman:
Hugh H. Luttrell and Wm. Luttrell, m. by: Jno. McMillan, J. P.,
July 16, 1829, Witness: Wm. Swan, KNOX Co.

DAY, Thomas to Elizabeth Thomas - issued September 30, 1828, Bondsman:
Stephen Norton, SUMNER Co.

DAY, Thomas to Mary A. Hart - issued March 19, 1832, Bondsman:
John Parker, SUMNER Co.

DAYS, Lewis to Nancy E. Adams - issued March 7, 1842, m. by:
A. L. P. Green, M. G., March 9, 1842, DAVIDSON Co.

DAYS, Sylvester to Mary G. Arledge - issued April 2, 1867, m. by:
Wm. M. Green, M. G., April 2, 1867, FRANKLIN Co.

DEADERICK, David to E. Jane Crozier - issued July 21, 1831, m. by:
Tho. H. Nelson July 21, 1831, KNOX Co.

DEADERICK, David A. to Elizabeth Jane Crozier - issued July 21, 1831,
Bondsman: W. B. A. Ramsey, KNOX Co.

DEADERICK, Geo. M. to Terrissa Huffman - issued December 26, 1839,
m. by: Wm. J. Drake, J. P., December 26, 1839, DAVIDSON Co.

DEAKINS, John to Elizabeth Watson - issued March 13, 1807, Bondsman:
Robert Watson, GRAINGER Co.

DEAL, Henry to Ann M. Cole - issued June 15, 1838, m. by:
E. P. Connell, J. P., June 20, 1838, DAVIDSON Co.

DEAL, James A. to Eliza Russell - issued February 3, 1841, m. by:
Wm. Shelton, J. P., February 4, 1841, DAVIDSON Co.

DEAL, Joseph to Elisabeth Cole - May 3, 1806, WILLIAMSON Co.

DEAN, E. U. to Nancy Jane Bailey - issued July 4, 1854, Bondsman:
M. M. Green, m. by: J. G. Ward, M. G., July 4, 1854, MONTGOMERY Co.

DEAN, Francis A. L. to Rosanah Melton - issued December 27, 1856,
m. by: M. A. Carden, J. P., December 27, 1856, COFFEE Co.

DEAN, Fredrick T. to Jane Ray - issued August 6, 1853, m. by:
Jeremiah Dean, M. G., August 8, 1853, FRANKLIN Co.

DEAN, Jane to Hugh Smotherman - issued August 1, 1862, Bondsman:
Adam Comer, Jos. H. Thompson, Clk. per James H. Neil, Dep. Clk.,
BEDFORD Co.

DEAN, Jerry to Telitha Ivey - issued July 20, 1868, FRANKLIN Co.

DEAN, John W. to Sarah M. Cook - issued November 19, 1846, m. by:
R. B. Rose, J. P., November 19, 1846, ROBERTSON Co.

DEAN, Joshua to Mary A. Clark - issued August 15, 1863, Bondsman:
Thomas Rudd, BEDFORD Co.

DEAN, Musadon to J. C. Grubbs - issued July 7, 1862, Bondsman:
John Q. Davidson, Jos. H. Thompson, Clk., BEDFORD Co.

DEAN, Peggy to Neill Johnson - MAURY Co.

DEAN, Robt. to Sarah M. Ray - issued December 27, 1859, m. by:
J. H. Holt, M. G., November 28, 1859, FRANKLIN Co.

DEAN, Robert to E. C. Grant - issued December 3, 1866, FRANKLIN Co.

DEANE, P. J. to Sarah C. Starnes - issued December 25, 1843, Bondsman:
John Bladden, m. by: B. F. McKenzie, J. P., December 24, 1843,
MEIGS Co.

DEARIN, John to Elizabeth Holloway - m. by: Thomas Gilmore February 27,
1837, SUMNER Co.

DEARMAN, Joseph to Mary Mansker - issued April 15, 1826, Bondsman:
William Shaw, m. by: Ed. Edwards April 15, 1826, SUMNER Co.

DEARMOND, John to Nellie Moore - September 26, 1798, KNOX Co.

DEARMOND, John to Annie Burnett - June 4, 1811, KNOX Co.

DEARMOND, Richard J. to Lucy Masterson - issued October 24, 1827,
m. by: Sam Flenniken, J. P., October 25, 1827, KNOX Co.

DEARMOND, Wm. to Polly Wandless - issued March 6, 1805, KNOX Co.

DEARMOND, Wm. to Jane Campbell - issued December 16, 1834, Bondsman:
Allen Perry, m. by: Richard Tindell, J. P., December 17, 1834,
KNOX Co.

DEASON, John to Sally Arnold - issued December 16, 1815, m. by:
J. Burns December 21, 1815, RUTHERFORD Co.

DEATON (Deatson), George W. to Francis Sparks - issued April 10, 1848,
m. by: C. A. Hunt, J. P., FRANKLIN Co.

DEATON, James A. to Mary Chavors - issued September 30, 1851, m. by:
Thos. Finch, J. P., October 2, 1851, FRANKLIN Co.

DEATON, Simeon to Senillia Stiles - issued December 22, 1854, m. by:
M. M. D. Farris, J. P., December 24, 1854, FRANKLIN Co.

DEATON, William to Peggy Masengil - November 23, 1820, GREENE Co.

DEATSON (Deaton), George W. to Francis Sparks - issued April 10, 1848,
m. by: C. A. Hunt, J. P., FRANKLIN Co.

DEAVERS, Amos to Polly Dellender - January 12, 1813, WILLIAMSON Co.

DEAVERS, William S. to Sarah Roberts - issued July 30, 1863, Bondsman:
George Wilsford, m. by: Winston McAnally, J. P., July 30, 1863,
LAWRENCE Co.

DEBAUPORT, Thomas to Carline Turner - issued August 16, 1848, m. by:
Thomas Farmer, J. P., August 17, 1848, ROBERTSON Co.

DEBOARD, Solomon to Polly Franklin - issued March 9, 1818, Bondsman:
George Reed, m. by: John McMurtry, J. P., March 9, 1818, SUMNER Co.

DEBORD, William to Merine Ball - issued September 10, 1802, Bondsman:
Joseph O'Riley, GRAINGER Co.

DEBOW, Bird to Ann Crawford - issued November 10, 1825, Bondsman:
John L. Blackwell, m. by: Charles Watkins, J. P., November 10,
1825, SUMNER Co.

DEBS, Samuel C. to Mary C. Cannon - issued October 24, 1836, Bondsman:
Jas. R. Cannon, RUTHERFORD Co.

DEBUSK, David B. to Gerusha E. Ruder - issued December 28, 1821,
Bondsman: Elisha Desun, m. by: P. Nance, J. P., December 28,
1821, KNOX Co.

DECHERD, John H. to Jemima C. Estill - issued August 5, 1851, m. by:
W. J. Fox, V. D. M., August 5, 1851, FRANKLIN Co.

DECHERD, William to Sarah Guthery - issued December 24, 1850, m. by:
Madison Williams, J. P., December 25, 1850, FRANKLIN Co.

DECHER, William I. to Elzira Lynch - issued August 20, 1848, m. by:
M. Catchings, J. P., August 20, 1848, FRANKLIN Co.

DECKER, William W. to Rhoda P. Franklin - issued December 23, 1846,
m. by: W. B. Wagner, J. P., December 24, 1846, FRANKLIN Co.

DECKS, George to Cynthia C. Cato - issued April 19, 1841, m. by:
H. H. Gorin, STEWART Co.

DEEN, Elijah to Penelope Taylor - issued December 28, 1843, m. by:
Jas. Woodard, J. P., __(?) 28, 1843, ROBERTSON Co.

DEEN, John M. to Minerva Barbee - issued July 3, 1845, m. by:
W. L. Baldry, M. G., July 31, 1845, ROBERTSON Co.

DEEN, John M. to Minerva Barbee - issued July 31, 1845, m. by:
Wm. T. Baldry, G. M., ROBERTSON Co.

DEEN, Wm. R. to Harriet Aikin - issued July 17, 1842, m. by:
Jas. Woodard, J. P., July 18, 1842, ROBERTSON Co.

DEENS, David to Nancy Williams - June 12, 1816, WILLIAMSON Co.

DEER, James to Margaret Frye - issued August 17, 1830, Bondsman:
Jacob Shoats, GRAINGER Co.

DEFFENDAFFER, Dewis A. to Christina G. Dick - issued January 17, 1854,
Bondsman: C. M. Hiter, m. by: J. T. Hendrick, M. G., MONTGOMERY Co.

DEFORD, Risden D. to Mary F. McDougal - issued August 2, 1865, Bondman:
James J. Davis, m. by: C. B. Porter, G. M., Augsut 3, 1865,
LAWRENCE Co.

DEFREES, Ricely to Elizabeth Holloway - issued December 21, 1821,
Bondsman: Hiram Duncan, m. by: Smith, J. P., December 21, 1821,
SUMNER Co.

DEFRIECE, Joseph to Maryann Day - issued May 3, 1821, Bondsman:
Robert Fleming, m. by: Smith, J. P., May 3, 1821, SUMNER Co.

DEFRIESE, Jno. M. to Sarah Parmer - issued September 28, 1836, m. by:
D. Everett, Esq., September 29, 1836, KNOX Co.

DEGMAN, Margaret to John Goldman - GREENE Co.

DEGRAFFENRIED, Charles to Mary Herndon - issued October 13, 1825,
Bondsman: John Roberson, SUMNER Co.

DEGRAFFENREID, Metcalf to Claudia J. Pope - WILLIAMSON Co.

DEHART, Andrew to Caty Emmett - issued December 31, 1825, m. by:
Wm. Morris, J. P., January 3, 1826, KNOX Co.

DEJARNET, William T. to Sarah Ann Pemberton - issued October 6, 1834,
Bondsman: Williamson B. Bandy, WILSON Co.

DELANEY, Elizabeth to David Paulson - GREENE Co.

DELANEY, Hyram F. to Nancy Farquharson - issued February 12, 1828,
m. by: Tho. H. Nelson February 12, 1828, KNOX Co.

DELANEY, Jacob to Sally Broyles - July 25, 1810, Security: John Delaney,
GREENE Co.

DELANY, Jesse to Anne Keener - issued September 7, 1808, KNOX Co.

DELANEY, Sarah to William McBride - February 24, 1800, Security:
Joseph McCoy, GREENE Co.

DELANY, Anne to George Davis - March 6, 1799, Security: John Delany,
GREENE Co.

DELANY, Jane to Henry Dycke, Jr. - GREENE Co.

DELL, Thomas to Agness Hopson - issued July 3, 1806, Bondsman:
John Harpole, WILSON Co.

DELLIS, Morgan to Elizabeth Allen - issued January 14, 1832, Bondsman:
Jefferson Bell, m. by: B. S. Motley, J. P., WILSON Co.

DELOACH, Simon to Ginnette (or Jinnette) Biter - issued July 13, 1848,
m. by: W. S. Coleman, J. P., July 13, 1848, DICKSON Co.

DELOACH, Solomon to Rachal Searcy - issued September 12, 1814, Bondsman:
Claibourn Whitworth, WILSON Co.

DELOATH, Boykin to Sally Bell - issued February 6, 1816, m. by:
Joshua Lester, V. D. M., February 8, 1816, RUTHERFORD Co.

DELZELL, William to Nancy McKelvey - issued December 8, 1852, m. by:
Wm. G. Guinn December 7, 1852, FRANKLIN Co.

DEMCY, William to Elizabeth Mitchell - issued January 25, 1831, m. by:
Josiah Walton, J. P., January 25, 1831, SUMNER Co.

DEMENT, Abraham to Mary Nance - issued March 28, 1821, m. by:
L. Davis, J. P., March 29, 1821, RUTHERFORD Co.

DEMENT, Allen to Catherine Robertson - issued February 18, 1824,
Bondsman: William Dickson, RUTHERFORD Co.

DEMENT, Cader to Mary M. Andrews - issued October 27, 1821, m. by:
Robt. Henderson October 31, 1821, RUTHERFORD Co.

DEMENT, Charles to Sarah H. Tarpley - issued March 1, 1820, m. by:
John Hoover, J. P., March 2, 1820, RUTHERFORD Co.

DEMENT, David to Elizabeth Kirkpatrick - issued November 5, 1805,
     Bondsman: Thomas Dement, SUMNER Co.

DEMENT, James to Rosannah Posey - issued June 5, 1835, Bondsman:
     Josephus Moore, RUTHERFORD Co.

DEMENT, John to Cecelia W. Lowe - issued September 27, 1820, m. by:
     John Hoover, J. P., September 28, 1820, RUTHERFORD Co.

DEMENT, Thomas M. to Elizabeth Bowler - issued March 3, 1813, Bondsman:
     David Dement, SUMNER Co.

DEMERY, David to Sally Murry - issued June 23, 1814, Bondsman:
     Mark Murry, WILSON Co.

DEMOMBRAUM, John to Barbara Quimby - issued May 9, 1846, m. by:
     W. E. Cartwright May 28, 1846, DAVIDSON Co.

DEMOSS, Jesse S. to Elvira Woodward - issued April 24, 1840, DAVIDSON Co.

DEMOSS, Jesse S. to Delilah Pack - issued May 3, 1842, DAVIDSON Co.

DEMOSS, Thomas to Mary Prowell - December 27, 1812, WILLIAMSON Co.

DEMPSEY, David C. to Mary Ann Porter - issued September 12, 1842,
     Bondsman: Joseph Lisles, m. by: John Seabern, J. P., September 12,
     1842, MEIGS Co.

DEMPSEY, James to Susan Clark - issued March 3, 1825, Bondsman:
     Edy Jacobs, m. by: Richard Harrison, J. P., March 3, 1825,
     SUMNER Co.

DEMPSEY, James to Elizabeth Hutson - issued August 3, 1836, Bondsman:
     Charles Mathis, SUMNER Co.

DEMPSEY, William to Glopha Stipe - issued March 6, 1855, m. by:
     John Pain, J. P., April 6, 1855, VAN BUREN Co.

DEMPSY, George to Polly Brigance - issued October 6, 1803, Bondsman:
     James Brigance, SUMNER Co.

DEMUMBER, William to Mary Patton - issued January 9, 1819, m. by:
     H. Trott, J. P., January 9, 1819, RUTHERFORD Co.

DEMUMBRA, Samuel to Mary Ann Rose - issued December 29, 1843,
     DAVIDSON Co.

DEMUMBRE, Andrew J. to Mary E. Glover - issued May 25, 1859, m. by:
     B. W. Bradley, J. P., May 26, 1859, ROBERTSON Co.

DEMUNBRO, R. S. to Sarah L. Binkley - issued February 20, 1854, m. by:
     B. F. Binkley, M. G., February 25, 1854, ROBERTSON Co.

DENEN, Hiram A. to Martha Hill - issued September 5, 1829, Bondsman:
     Finney Vaden, RUTHERFORD Co.

DENERANT, Wilson C. to Polly Waddle - issued November 17, 1823,
     Bondsman: John Henderson, m. by: John Harris, J. P., November 17,
     1823, GRAINGER Co.

DEREHORN (?), Philip to Rebecca Goin - issued December 22, 1812,
     Bondsman: Baxter Ivie, GRAINGER Co.

DENNEY, Austain to Martha Sparkman - issued October 30, 1854, m. by:
     W. B. Cummings, J. P., November 5, 1854, VAN BUREN Co.

DENNEY, Robert A. to Clementine C. Bobbitt - issued November 13, 1837,
     m. by: William D. Nelson, J. P., November 16, 1837, RUTHERFORD Co.

DENNEY, William L. to Susan Wise - issued July 8, 1826, Bondsman:
James Biggs, SUMNER Co.

DENNING, Grandville J. to Malvina Cooper - issued November 18, 1842,
m. by: C. Woodall, J. P., ROBERTSON Co.

DENNING, Mary to Miles Cunningham - GREENE Co.

DENNING, William to Mary Ann Cox - issued November 2, 1841, m. by:
Daniel Judd, L. E., November 4, 1841, DAVIDSON Co.

DENNIS, Edward to Ruth Beason - issued May 21, 1812, Bondsman:
John Dennis, GRAINGER Co.

DENNIS, Edward to Betsey More - issued December 6, 1813, Bondsman:
Joseph Hall, GRAINGER Co.

DENNIS, Henry to Mary A. Fletcher - issued September 15, 1852, m. by:
Thos. Finch, J. P., September 19, 1852, FRANKLIN Co.

DENNIS, John to Letty Fields - issued August 1, 1818, Bondsman:
William Dennis, m. by: Martin Cleveland, J. P., August 6, 1818,
GRAINGER Co.

DENNIS, John to Jane Dalton - issued August 31, 1822, Bondsman:
John Harris, SUMNER Co.

DENNIS, John to Catherine Starnes - issued August 8, 1831, Bondsman:
Eli Clark, m. by: Levi Satterfield, M. G., August 11, 1831,
GRAINGER Co.

DENNIS, Jr., John to Matilda Harrelson - issued September 28, 1833,
Bondsman: Levi Dennis, m. by: John Chesney, J. P., September 29,
GRAINGER Co.

DENNIS, John W. to O. J. King - issued January 7, 1861, Bondsman:
I. N. Craig, m. by: O. A. Williams, J. P., January 10, 1861,
LAWRENCE Co.

DENNIS, Joseph to Anne Irvine - issued May 25, 1821, Bondsman:
John Irvine, m. by: Alexander Hamilton, J. P., June 10, 1821,
GRAINGER Co.

DENNIS, Joseph to Polly Brown - issued March 6, 1823, Bondsman:
Meredith Sharp, m. by: William Lane, J. P., March 6, 1823,
GRAINGER Co.

DENNIS, Jr., Joseph to Bohamas Hardin - issued February 25, 1828,
Bondsman: David Bowers, m. by: Thos. Brown, J. P., February 25,
1828, GRAINGER Co.

DENNIS, Levi to Delila Dunnahew - issued November 25, 1830, Bondsman:
Samuel Jack, m. by: Joseph Clark, J. P., GRAINGER Co.

DENNIS, Owen C. to Deborah Green - issued June 20, 1821, Bondsman:
Isaac Green, m. by: William Gray, J. P., June 22, 1821, WILSON Co.

DENNIS, Thomas to Juliann Shaw - issued March 31, 1842, m. by:
James T. Morris, STEWART Co.

DENNIS, William to Mary Fields - issued August 4, 1813, Bondsman:
Joseph Fields, GRAINGER Co.

DENNIS, William to Ruth Pettie - February 29, 1819, KNOX Co.

DENNIS, William to Hannah Dyer - issued June 10, 1829, Bondsman:
Isaac Damewood, m. by: Wm. Lane, J. P., GRAINGER Co.

DENNIS, William to Ann Jackson - issued December 15, 1848, STEWART Co.

DENNISON, James to Emeline Milliken - issued June 29, 1833, m. by:
Elihu Milliken, M. G., GRAINGER Co.

DENNISON, John to Matilda C. Smith - issued May 30, 1855, m. by:
G. W. Chapman, M. G., May 30, 1855, COFFEE Co.

DENNISTON, Robert to Nancy Bradshaw - issued August 21, 1814, Bondsman:
William Davidson, GRAINGER Co.

DENNON, John to Lify Hodge - issued November 5, 1821, Bondsman:
William McGill, m. by: Isaiah Midkiff, J. P., November 15, 1821,
GRAINGER Co.

DENNY, A. to Nancy B. Morris - issued September 2, 1845, Bondsman:
A. F. Haskins, m. by: W. B. Carney, J. P., September 2, 1845,
MONTGOMERY Co.

DENNY, Austin to Sarah Bryant - issued October 11, 1851, m. by:
W. B. Cumings, J. P., October 12, 1851, VAN BUREN Co.

DENNY, John to Sally Beavers - issued December 27, 1804, Bondsman:
John Dodson, GRAINGER Co.

DENNY, Robert to Elizabeth Davis - issued September 16, 1816, Bondsman:
Thos. Scurry, m. by: Wm. Montgomery, J. P., September 16, 1816,
SUMNER Co.

DENNY, Robert to Lucy Farmer - issued August 12, 1830, Bondsman:
Jas. R. Cox, RUTHERFORD Co.

DENNY, Samuel to Jane Davis - issued December 22, 1824, Bondsman:
Evan Taylor, m. by: Nace Overall, M. G., December 22, 1824,
RUTHERFORD Co.

DENSON, John W. to M. E. Robertson - issued May 10, 1860, m. by:
J. T. Slatter, J. P., May 10, 1860, FRANKLIN Co.

DENSON, W. L. to Francis E. Finch - issued September 14, 1867,
m. September 15, 1867, FRANKLIN Co.

DENT, James to Francis Liles - issued July 14, 1844, m. by:
John D. Lynch, J. P., July 14, 1844, FRANKLIN Co.

DENT, John to Nancy Nemoe - issued November 20, 1823, Bondsman:
Martin Vinyard, m. by: Robert Gaines, J. P., November 20, 1823,
GRAINGER Co.

DENTON, Charles to Mary Anne Parsley - issued June 23, 1827, Bondsman:
Jesse Garner, RUTHERFORD Co.

DENTON, Edward to Rebeccah Dillard - issued April 2, 1821, Bondsman:
Thomas Denton, WILSON Co.

DENTON, Edward to Susan Smith - issued October 13, 1831, Bondsman:
Joseph Simmons, m. by: Silas Tarver, J. P., WILSON Co.

DENTON, Hardin to ___(?) - issued October 6, 1847, m. by:
T. E. Hutson, M. G., October 7, 1847, VAN BUREN Co.

DENTON, James H. to Nancy Hillsman - issued May 10, 1832, Bondsman:
Alexander W. Winter, m. by: Silas Tarver, J. P., WILSON Co.

DENTON, Leric B. to Lourama Carter - issued September 5, 1852,
VAN BUREN Co.

DENTON, Reuben to Nancy Busby - issued December 24, 1821, Bondsman:
Wm. Busby, SUMNER Co.

DEPEE, Aaron to Emely Jane Ferrell - issued January 13, 1845, m. by:
Allen Elliott, M. G., January 16, 1845, STEWART Co.

DEPRIEST, Charles C. to Polly T. Edwards - issued November 7, 1817, Bondsman: Charles B. Turley, RUTHERFORD Co.

DEPRIEST, Hugh to Mary Amanda Vanlandingham - issued June 5, 1843, m. by: I. Porter, J. P., June 8, 1843, DICKSON Co.

DERIFIELD, William to Syntha Moore - issued January 12, 1846, m. by: James Herd, M. G., January 15, 1846, VAN BUREN Co.

DERMOTT, Robt. to Martha Warren - issued August 11, 1866, FRANKLIN Co..

DERR, James to Sally Keiser - issued September 21, 1812, Bondsman: Joseph Blair, SUMNER Co.

DERRETT, Clabourn to E. J. Long - issued October 25, 1843, m. by: David Jones, J. P., ROBERTSON Co.

DERRETT, Joseph R. to Luiza White - issued October 14, 1863, Bondsman: J. C. R. Williams, LAWRENCE Co.

DERRETT, William to Martha Jones - issued May 23, 1859, m. by: H. L. Covington, J. P., May 24, 1859, ROBERTSON Co.

DERRICK, Jesse C. to Jane F. Wror - issued June 28, 1838, m. by: B. F. McKenzie, J. P., June 28, 1838, MEIGS Co.

DERRIN, S. M. to S. M. Nelson - issued September 1, 1863, Bondsman: Wm. Gusby, BEDFORD Co.

DERRYBERRY, Jacob to Margaret Long - March 6, 1806, WILLIAMSON Co.

DERRYBERRY, Michael to Mariah McCormack - issued February 5, 1828, Bondsman: Josiah Walton, m. by: Josiah Walton, J. P., February 5, 1828, SUMNER Co.

DERRYBERRY, Sarah M. to Wm. T. Saddler - issued October 7, 1861, Bondsman: J. H. Derryberry, Jos. H. Thompson, Clk. per N. F. Thompson, Dep. Clk., m. by: H. F. Holt, J. P., BEDFORD Co.

DESAIN, Elisha to Sally Johnston - issued December 15, 1819, Bondsman: James Badgett, m. by: Peter Nance, J. P., KNOX Co.

DESHA, Benjamin to Telitha Stams - issued May 31, 1819, Bondsman: Asahel W. Reese, SUMNER Co.

DESHA, Joseph to Peggy Bledsoe - issued December 29, 1789, SUMNER Co.

DESHA, Robert to E. (?) Garrett - issued June 24, 1836, Bondsman: Thomas Donoho, m. by: W. Hall June 24, 1836, SUMNER Co.

DESHIELDS, Joel to Sharlotta T. Jolly - issued January 11, 1851, m. by: J. R. Brown, M. G., January 11, 1851, FRANKLIN Co.

DEVAULT, David to Ann McCrory - issued September 2, 1816, Bondsman: Stephen Byrn, m. by: John Hannah, J. P., September 5, 1816, WILSON Co.

DEVAULT, Henry to Susan Jackson - issued May 1, 1830, Bondsman: Snoden Hickman, WILSON Co.

DEVEAUL, David to Susanna Guest (or Guist) - issued March 19, 1800, Bondsman: John Six, Witness: Sm'l Yancey, GRAINGER Co.

DEVENPORT, Hardy to Martha Bryson - Bondsman: Abram Cooper, WILSON Co.

DEVENPORT, William to Polly Huchland - December 20, 1802, Security: Terrance Conner, BLOUNT Co.

DEVERET, James A. to C. J. Goddard - issued February 1, 1868, m. by: J. W. Williams, J. P., February 1, 1868, FRANKLIN Co.

DEVIN, Wm. to Margertt Dumpley - issued February 26, 1851, m. by:
    Rev. Mr. John M. Jacquet February 26, 1851, FRANKLIN Co.

DEVINNY, Charles to Ann Gilliam - issued September 15, 1845, m. by:
    Benj. Sharpe, J. P., September 15, 1845, DAVIDSON Co.

DEVINNY, Charles B. to Esther Rose - issued August 6, 1846, m. by:
    R. B. C. Howell, M. G., August 6, 1846, DAVIDSON Co.

DEW, Arther W. to Nancy Hallum - issued July 4, 1821, Bondsman:
    Anderson Cook, m. by: John Dew, V. D. M., July 6, 1821, WILSON Co.

DEW, David S. to Elizabeth Rutherford - issued March 3, 1834, Bondsman:
    William B. Kerley, WILSON Co.

DEW, George W. to Mary Ann Ward - issued August 16, 1834, m. by:
    Robert Joyner, J. P., August 16, 1834, SUMNER Co.

DEW, Jose C. to Nancy Hunter - issued October 20, 1818, Bondsman:
    Mathew Dew, m. by: John Dew, M. G., October 22, 1818, WILSON Co.

DEW, Joseoh A. to Elizabeth M. Green - issued February 2, 1826,
    Bondsman: John H. Dew, m. by: Thos. Joyner February 2, 1826,
    SUMNER Co.

DEW, Mathew T. to Jane Bradley - issued February 23, 1819, Bondsman:
    John L. Wlynne, m. by: Thomas Calhoon, V. D. M., WILSON Co.

DEWBERRY, Henry to Martha Hadley - May 23, 1816, WILLIAMSON Co.

DEWEY, William to Elizabeth Mitchell - issued January 25, 1830,
    Bondsman: Solomon Sholder, SUMNER Co.

DEWIT, Jas. W. to Elizabeth Lambuth - issued October 23, 1849, Bondsman:
    R. S. Ware, MONTGOMERY Co.

DEWITT, Wm. E. to R. A. Campbell - issued May 10, 1860, m. by:
    E. B. Crisman, M. G., May 10, 1860, FRANKLIN Co.

DEWRY, Stephen to Elizabeth Allen - issued August 4, 1815, Bondsman:
    Frederick Walkins, m. by: Isaac Winston, J. P., August 6, 1815,
    WILSON Co.

DEWS, James B. to Sally Blair - issued February 9, 1826, Bondsman:
    Francis E. Garrett, m. February 9, 1826, SUMNER Co.

DEWS, John to Mary Rord - issued February 19, 1845, m. by:
    W. B. Carpenter February 20, 1845, DAVIDSON Co.

DEWS, Nathaniel to Patsey Bumpass - issued March 26, 1816, Bondsman:
    Thomas Bradley, m. by: Wm. Bumpass, D. D., WILSON Co.

DEWS, William to Mary Harrison - issued September 4, 1845, m. by:
    W. D. F. Sawrie, M. G., September 4, 1845, DAVIDSON Co.

DEYTON, Zachariah to Catherine Goddard - issued November 7, 1843,
    m. by: Harmon York, J. P., November 9, 1843, VAN BUREN Co.

DIAL, Hasten to Emily Hill - issued June 29, 1850, m. by: Thos. Finch,
    J. P., June 29, 1850, FRANKLIN Co.

DIAL, Isaac to Caroline Jones - issued September 3, 1846, m. by:
    John Nugent, J. P., September 3, 1846, FRANKLIN Co.

DIAL, Jackson to Sarah Bennett - issued December 13, 1853, m. by:
    John Nugent, J. P., December 13, 1853, FRANKLIN Co.

DIAL, Jacob D. to Sarah Simmons - issued July 17, 1850, m. by:
    R. C. Smith, J. P., July 18, 1850, FRANKLIN Co.

DIAL, Jacob D. to Martha J. Newton - issued February 21, 1866, Bondsman: Parris L. Simms, m. by: Stanford Clayton, M. G., February 21, 1866, LAWRENCE Co.

DIAL, James to Polly Finney - issued July 3, 1844, m. by: John Nugent, J. P., July 5, 1844, FRANKLIN Co.

DIAL, James to Mary E. Martin - issued December 27, 1853, m. by: David Thompson, J. P., December 28, 1853, COFFEE Co.

DIAL, James to Caldonia Tucker - issued March 21, 1874, m. by: Jas. Seargent, J. P., March 21, 1874, FRANKLIN Co.

DIAL, John C. to Mary Johnson - issued August 23, 1832, m. by: J. P. Miller, J. P., August 28, 1832, RUTHERFORD Co.

DIAL, Ruben to Zilphy Medlin - issued August 1, 1818, Bondsman: B. Bridges, m. by: Jas. T. Williams August 2, 1818, WILSON Co.

DICE, Henry K. to Elizabeth Springs - issued December 15, 1827, Bondsman: Daniel Bennett, WILSON Co.

DICK, Henry to Rebecca McMond - issued November 10, 1836, Bondsman: Hugh L. Brown, m. by: Eli King, J. P., November 10, 1836, KNOX Co.

DICK, Hiram H. to Caroline R. Allen - issued May 22, 1844, m. by: Isaac Steel, G. M., ROBERTSON Co.

DICK, Jacob to Patsy McBee - issued July 22, 1826, Bondsman: Benj. I. Wilson, m. by: Thomas Wilkerson July 27, 1826, KNOX Co.

DICKASON, Fielding to Polly Todd - issued July 15, 1824, Bondsman: Wm. L. Harris, m. by: J. L. Swaney, J. P., July 15, 1824, SUMNER Co.

DICKASON, Jr., George W. to W. Turner - issued August 2, 1816, Bondsman: Walter Dickason, SUMNER Co.

DICKASON, Griffith to Matilda Williams - issued November 29, 1816, Bondsman: J. W. Weatherred, SUMNER Co.

DICKASON, John to Polly Gillespie - issued November 23, 1819, Bondsman: William Dickason, SUMNER Co.

DICKASON, John B. to Sarah White - issued December 20, 1823, m. by: John L. Swaney, J. P., December 20, 1823, SUMNER Co.

DICKASON, Livingston to Frances Turner - issued June 11, 1823, m. by: John L. Swaney, J. P., June 11, 1823, SUMNER Co.

DICKASON, William T. to Janette Watts - issued May 25, 1836, Bondsman: Sam'l K. Henderson, m. by: James Charlton May 23, 1836, SUMNER Co.

DICKENS, Bradford to Nancy Jarrell - issued August 31, 1833, m. by: E. P. Horn, J. P., September 5, 1833, WILSON Co.

DICKENS, Edward G. to Sarah Sulivan - issued January 18, 1830, Bondsman: L. Kimbrough, m. by: Frances Jarrett, J. P., January 18, 1830, SUMNER Co.

DICKENS, George S. to Mary A. Laughmiller - issued December 10, 1873, m. by: S. O. Woods, M. G., December 11, 1873, FRANKLIN Co.

DICKENS, Hiram to Charity Reese - issued April 10, 1838, Bondsman: J. W. Barton, WILSON Co.

DICKENS, James H. to Lydia Pitner - issued September 19, 1829, Bondsman: Norflet B. Nelms, WILSON Co.

DICKENS, Milley F. to Peter Buchingham - issued October 1, 1862,
Bondsman: Stephen Batten, Jos. H. Thompson, Clk. per N. F. Thompson,
Dep. Clk., BEDFORD Co.

DICKENS, Samuel to Nancy Chandler - issued June 16, 1830, m. by:
Wm. White, M. G., June 17, 1830, WILSON Co.

DICKENS, William to Martha J. Price - issued November 10, 1859, m. by:
F. M. Jackson, Mins., November 10, 1859, COFFEE Co.

DICKENSON, John R. to Elizabeth D. Brown - issued November 17, 1828,
m. by: Richd Johnson November 17, 1828, SUMNER Co.

DICKENSON, Thomas J. to Lucinda L. Walker - issued October 10, 1831,
Bondsman: David Padgett, m. by: Austin Johnson October 10, 1831,
SUMNER Co.

DICKERSON, Augustine to Rachel Pace - February 29, 1852, m. by:
Peter Shulen, J. P., GILES Co.

DICKERSON, B. W. to Ann E. Russell - issued October 15, 1856, m. by:
John W. Smith, J. P., ROBERTSON Co.

DICKERSON, Cosby to Leathy Grey - issued October 6, 1823, Bondsman:
Sumpter Turner, m. by: J. C. Cook, J. P., October 6, 1823,
SUMNER Co.

DICKERSON, David N. to Elizabeth Bently - issued August 3, 1830,
Bondsman: Thomas Hughes, m. by: James Charlton, J. P., August 3,
1830, SUMNER Co.

DICKERSON, J. W. to E. W. Richerson - issued November 21, 1849,
m. by: John Forbes, J. P., ROBERTSON Co.

DICKERSON, James to Sarah New - issued November 29, 1839, Bondsman:
David W. Dickerson, m. by: H. B. Hill, M. G., December 3, 1839,
WILSON Co.

DICKERSON, John to Mary Compesry - issued March 8, 1851, m. by:
Thomas B. Mathews March 9, 1851, ROBERTSON Co.

DICKERSON, Martin T. to Elizabeth L. Cloar - issued December 23, 1830,
Bondsman: Clifton R. Jones, m. by: L. M. Woodson December 23,
1830, SUMNER Co.

DICKERSON, Richardson to Matilda Black - m. by: Austin Johnson
February 20, 1833, SUMNER Co.

DICKERSON, William to Elizabeth Blakemore - m. by: Francis A. Jarratt
October 19, 1833, SUMNER Co.

DICKERSON, Wire to Polly Etherly - issued August 24, 1803, Bondsman:
Zacheus Wilson, SUMNER Co.

DICKEY, Binoni (Benoni) to Margaret G. __(?) - June 23, 1809, Bondsman:
William Frierson, MAURY Co.

DICKEY, David D. to Margaret Ellis - issued January 20, 1829, Bondsman:
Robt. Davidson, KNOX Co.

DICKEY, George to Sarah W. Armstrong - July 12, 1810, Bondsman:
Binony Dickey, MAURY Co.

DICKY, George H. to Ann Stone - December 26, 1808, Bondsman:
Tilman Specner, MAURY Co.

DICKEY, James to Mary Wells - issued October 23, 1810, RUTHERFORD Co.

DICKEY, James M. to Polly Douglas - issued November 1, 1817, Bondsman:
Wm. Douglas, m. by: R. H. King (?) November 4, 1817, KNOX Co.

DICKEY, John to Nancy Page - January 19, 1807, WILLIAMSON Co.

DICKEY, John L. to Martha B. Taylor - issued April 18, 1827, Bondsman:
Amon Boring, RUTHERFORD Co.

DICKEY, John M. to Elizabeth C. Hale - January 20, m. by: James Brownlow,
M. G., GILES Co.

DICKEY, Matthew to Marah Jourdan - issued May 18, 1814, RUTHERFORD Co.

DICKEY, Nathan H. to Margrett E. Campbell - issued April 27, 1853,
m. by: H. Larkin, M. G., April 28, 1853, FRANKLIN Co.

DICKEY, Robert W. to Nancy H. Prior - January 27, 1858, m. by:
J. V. Vandiveer, M. G., GILES Co.

DICKINGS, James to George McWhirter - issued February 27, 1810,
Bondsman: George McWhirter, WILSON Co.

DICKINGS, Lemuel to Martha Holton - issued December 19, 1820, Bondsman:
O. G. Finley, m. by: Abner Hill, M. G., December 25, 1820,
WILSON Co.

DICKINGS, Lewis to Hannah Ashford - issued August 26, 1812, Bondsman:
Moses Ashford, WILSON Co.

DICKINGS, Samuel to Clampet - issued April 11, 1806, Bondsman:
Henry Truet, WILSON Co.

DICKINGS, Samuel to Nancy Heflin - issued July 28, 1807, Bondsman:
Jacob McDermet, WILSON Co.

DICKINGS, Samuel to Ann Enoch - issued December 21, 1818, Bondsman:
James Dickings, m. by: Elijah Maddox, M. G., December 22, 1818,
WILSON Co.

DICKINS, Baxter to Nancy Holton - issued February 14, 1820, m. by:
William Keele, M. G., February 17, 1820, RUTHERFORD Co.

DICKINS, Jesse to Polly McDerment - issued September 10, 1812, Bondsman:
Adam Vinyard, WILSON Co.

DICKINS, William to Elizabeth Adams - issued September 1, 1818,
m. by: H. Trott, J. P., September 1, 1818, RUTHERFORD Co.

DICKINSON, Alfred to Elizabeth Hall - issued October 3, 1836, m. by:
Nace Overall, M. G., October 4, 1836, RUTHERFORD Co.

DICKINSON, Charles to Mary Matilda Pentecost - issued September 3,
1860, m. by: W. M. Winters, J. P., September 6, 1860, ROBERTSON Co.

DICKINSON, David S. to Mary Ann Rollow - issued December 19, 1851,
Bondsman: W. W. Grady, m. by: B. H. Williams, J. P., December 19,
MONTGOMERY Co.

DICKINSON, Elija to Sarah Blackemore - issued January 3, 1831, m. by:
Austin Johnson January 3, 1831, SUMNER Co.

DICKINSON, Gallant D. to Isabella McCrary - issued November 3, 1828,
m. November 6, 1828, RUTHERFORD Co.

DICKINSON, Griffith to Mary Badgett - issued October 13, 1832,
Bondsman: Richardson Dickinson, m. October 13, 1832, SUMNER Co.

DICKINSON, Henry to Ann E. McGavock - issued April 28, 1845, m. by:
J. T. Edgar April 28, 1845, DAVIDSON Co.

DICKINSON, Isham S. to Sarah Warren - issued December 23, 1825, m. by:
David Batton, J. P., RUTHERFORD Co.

DICKINSON, John B. to Lucy Epperson - m. by: John Wiseman November 20, 1833, SUMNER Co.

DICKINSON, John E. to Susannah N. Sims - issued April 23, 1838, Bondsman: T. J. Sims, WILSON Co.

DICKINSON, Olive to Sarah Stubblefield - issued September 17, 1832, Bondsman: William Burnley, SUMNER Co.

DICKINSON, Samuel to Agnes Pallet - issued March 30, 1820, m. by: B. L. McFerrin, J. P., March 30, 1820, RUTHERFORD Co.

DICKINSON, Waller W. to Mildred Dickinson - issued January 9, 1828, Bondsman: Robert Dickenson, m. by: J. L. Swaney, J. P., January 9, 1828, SUMNER Co.

DICKINSON, William to Elizabeth Adams - issued September 1, 1818, Bondsman: George Adams, RUTHERFORD Co.

DICKS, William to Mary Haymer - issued March 21, 1840, m. by: H. Baldridge, M. G., March 22, 1840, DAVIDSON Co.

DICKSON, Alexander S. to Rebecca Patterson - issued January 6, 1835, Bondsman: Mark C. Alexander, m. by: John McMinn, J. P., January 8, 1835, WILSON Co.

DICKSON, Amos to Elizabeth Monday - issued May 23, 1814, Bondsman: Francis Monday, RUTHERFORD Co.

DICKSON, David to Anny Owen - issued December 31, 1833, Bondsman: A. M. Hamilton, RUTHERFORD Co.

DICKSON, E. F. to M. J. Holder - issued September 9, 1868, m. by: J. B. Hudgins September 10, 1868, FRANKLIN Co.

DICKSON, Enos H. to Cynthia Howell - issued April 20, 1824, Bondsman: Samuel Nelson, m. by: James Green April 21, 1824, RUTHERFORD Co.

DICKSON, Ezekiel to Rebecca L. Davis - issued October 21, 1820, m. by: Wm. H. Davis, J. P., RUTHERFORD Co.

DICKSON, George to Anny Nipper - issued May 6, 1835, Bondsman: Wm. McMillan, m. by: Eli King, J. P., May 14, 1835, Witness: Geo. M. White, KNOX Co.

DICKSON, James A. to Eliza I. Griffith - issued November 21, 1863, Bondsman: Geo. E. Calhoun, Jos. H. Thompson, Clk., BEDFORD Co.

DICKSON, John to Maryan Edmodson - October 30, 1802, Security: Samuel Hendley, BLOUNT Co.

DICKSON, John to Margaret G. Wills - issued September 25, 1820, Bondsman: John Wills, KNOX Co.

DICKSON, John B. to Nancy L. Binkley - issued February 4, 1846, m. by: I. Moore, M. G., February 5, 1846, DICKSON Co.

DICKSON, Joseph to Mary Hare - issued May 30, 1821, m. by: Jas. S. Jetton, J. P., May 31, 1821, RUTHERFORD Co.

DICKSON, Joseph R. to Catharine L. Alexander - issued August 31, 1829, Bondsman: James M. Cloyd, m. by: Jesse Alexander, V. D. M., September 1, 1829, WILSON Co.

DICKSON (or Decker?) , Stephen to Margaret Buch (?) - issued April 14, 1835, Bondsman: Wm. Dunn, m. by: Eli King, J. P., April 16, 1835, Witness: Geo. M. White, KNOX Co.

DICKSON, Thomas S. to Elizabeth Hollinsworth - issued December 31, 1840, Bondsman: Freeman R. Jackson, WILSON Co.

DICKSON, Thomas Y. to Cora G. C. Marable - issued January 9, 1854,
Bondsman: Thos. McCullock, MONTGOMERY Co.

DICKSON, William to Nelly Gordon - November 30, 1807, WILLIAMSON Co.

DICKSON, William to Perminty Reeves - issued May 23, 1825, m. by:
William Bumpass, M. G., May 20, 1825, RUTHERFORD Co.

DICKSON, William R. to Rody F. Johns - issued March 19, 1827, Bondsman:
Varner D. Cowan, m. by: Peyton Smith March 22, 1827, RUTHERFORD Co.

DICSON, Alfred to Elizabeth Hall - issued October 3, 1836, Bondsman:
Levi Jones, RUTHERFORD Co.

DIDDLEY, Catharine J. to George W. Collins - issued March 3, 1863,
Bondsman: A. V. Tomme, Jos. H. Thompson, Clk. per M. E. W. Dunaway,
Dep. Clk., BEDFORD Co.

DIEL, Calvin D. to Mary McDaniel - issued January 10, 1849, m. by:
A. Gilliam, P. G., FRANKLIN Co.

DIEN, Cabar to Martha Gunter - issued September 16, 1846, DICKSON Co.

DIES, Lovick to Matilda Johnson - issued April 2, 1828, m. by:
P. Douglas, J. P., April 3, 1828, WILSON Co.

DIGGINS, John to Nancy Hutchinson - issued April 28, 1853, m. by:
R. C. Smith, J. P., April 28, 1853, FRANKLIN Co.

DIGS, John to Rachel Walker - issued August 19, 1837, Bondsman:
Geo. G. Hardin, KNOX Co.

DILANEY, Agnes to Henry Maniwell (?) - GREENE Co.

DILBAY, Joseph D. to Anney McAuley - issued October 5, 1844,
m. October 5, 1844, STEWART Co.

DILL, John B. to Mary Jarroll - August 25, 1833, m. by: Thos. P. Holma,
J. P., WILSON Co.

DILL, Joseph to Nancy K. Wilson - May 21, 1835, m. by: Nace Overall,
M. G., RUTHERFORD Co.

DILL, Marvell, M. to Mary Ann Sanders - May 12, 1831, m. by: L. Nolen,
J. P., RUTHERFORD Co.

DILL, Newton C. to Narcissa (?) Kerr - February 8, 1827, Bondsman:
Simeon Hogue, RUTHERFORD Co.

DILL, Noah W. to Martha (?) A. Harwell - December 14, 1837, m. by:
Thos. Nelson, J. P., RUTHERFORD Co.

DILL, Richard to Elizabeth Douglass - August 17, 1836, WILSON Co.

DILL, Wm. to Eve Houck - September 18, 1804, Bondsman: Philip Kiser,
SUMNER Co.

DILL, William to Eliza Neely - January 11, 1841, Bondsman:
Eperson Bandy, WILSON Co.

DILLAHUNTY, Joseph S. to Elizabeth D. Burton - issued November 29,
1842, DAVIDSON Co.

DILLARD, Allen R. to Emma B. Taylor - issued January 3, 1822, Bondsman:
Harry Jackson, m. by: John Provin, M. G., WILSON Co.

DILLARD, Edward to Martha S. Gold - issued December 11, 1826, Bondsman:
A. W. Wynne, WILSON Co.

DILLARD, Henry to Rebecca Meholand - issued June 17, 1833, Bondsman:
Joseph Nasworthy, WILSON Co.

DILLARD, John to Sarah Jacobs - issued July 18, 1820, Bondsman:
Shadrach Owens, m. by: Abner Hill, M. G., July 19, 1820, WILSON Co.

DILLARD, John to Sarah Garland - issued August 28, 1841, m. by:
Joseph Hellam, J. P., September 2, 1841, DAVIDSON Co.

DILLARD, Joshua to Catharine Quinn - issued October 9, 1813, Bondsman:
Alexander Chambers, WILSON Co.

DILLARD, L. F. to Sarah S. Anderson - issued March 23, 1857, m. by:
Benjamin Gambill, J. P., March 29, 1857, ROBERTSON Co.

DILLARD, Stephen to Sarah A. Huffman - issued April 18, 1863, Security:
Lewis Bowers, BEDFORD Co.

DILLARD, William to Jane Scruggs - January 11, 1816, WILLIAMSON Co.

DILLARD, William to Elizabeth Corder - issued June 15, 1818, Bondsman:
James Browning, WILSON Co.

DILLARD, Wm. L. to Virginia E. Noblett - issued January 22, 1848,
Bondsman: John A. Reece, m. by: Allison Akin, M. G., January 27,
1848, MONTGOMERY Co.

DILLARD, William M. to Elizabeth F. Corley - issued September 3, 1826,
Bondsman: Robert Corley, m. by: William Algood September 5, 1826,
WILSON Co.

DILLENG, John to Barbary Thomas - issued October 26, 1844, m. by:
Allen McCaskill, J. P., October 5, 1845, STEWART Co.

DILLEY, James to Elizabeth Stark - issued January 14, 1832, Bondsman:
Wm. H. McInger, m. by: Isaac Lindsey, G. M. E., January 14, 1832,
SUMNER Co.

DILLIARD, Gabriel to Sarah Jones - issued May 31, 1820, Bondsman:
Ezekiel Crain, m. by: Hugh Kirkpatrick, M. G., May 31, 1820,
SUMNER Co.

DILLIHAY, Alfred to Mary Newman - issued October 30, 1841, m. by:
Jas. Daniel, J. P., November 5, 1841, DICKSON Co.

DILLIN, Chas. R. to Julia Q. Cautes - issued March 15, 1845, m. by:
W. B. Carpenter March 15, 1845, DAVIDSON Co.

DILLING, P. H. to Sarah P. Bullard - issued July 25, 1848, Bondsman:
J. W. Lockert, MONTGOMERY Co.

DILLING, Wm. H. to Elizabeth Cummings - issued November 10, 1846,
Bondsman: John Dilling, m. by: Judson Horn, J. P., November 11,
1846, MONTGOMERY Co.

DILLION, Allen to Lucy Loftin - issued June 15, 1836, Bondsman:
Samuel Winston, m. by: Martin Clark, E. M. E. C., June 16, 1836,
RUTHERFORD Co.

DILLON, Carter to Caroline Sparkman - issued December 15, 1846, m. by:
Thomas E. Hutson, M. G., December 27, 1846, VAN BUREN Co.

DILLON, Garret to Margaret Edmundson - April 5, 1797, Security:
Newhope Quaker Meeting, GREENE Co.

DILLON, Edmund to Hannah Tally - issued April 2, 1838, Bondsman:
William A. Jennings, m. by: John Lester, V. D. M., April 2, 1838,
WILSON Co.

DILLON, Isaac to Polly Kilbrath - issued September 19, 1806, Bondsman:
Tarlton Boren, SUMNER Co.

DILLON, Isaac to Polly Vaughn - issued May 8, 1823, Bondsman:
Edmund Alvis, m. May 8, 1823, SUMNER Co.

DILLON, James to Katharine Word - issued July 30, 1832, Bondsman:
Elisha G. Cain, m. by: Joshua Lester, V. D. M., WILSON Co.

DILLON, James to Winney Sparkman - issued November 26, 1846, m. by:
Thomas E. Hutson, M. G., November 27, 1846, VAN BUREN Co.

DILLON, Jemima to George Smith - GREENE Co.

DILLON, Nathan to Sarah Green - issued December 9, 1826, Bondsman:
William Nipper, WILSON Co.

DILLON, Phebe to John Rees - GREENE Co.

DILLON, Sarah to John Stanfield - GREENE Co.

DILLON, Thomas to Harriet Roane - issued October 18, 1830, Bondsman:
Andrew Roane, WILSON Co.

DILLON, Thomas to Mary Arbuckle - issued August 20, 1834, Bondsman:
Hall J. Winsett, m. by: J. Lester, V. D. M., August 20, 1834,
WILSON Co.

DILLON, William to Susannah Edmundson - October 29, 1806, Security:
Newhope Quaker Meeting, GREENE Co.

DILLON, William to Elizabeth Tracy - issued December 19, 1822, m. by:
Jonathan Williams, J. P., December 19, 1822, SUMNER Co.

DILLON, William to Dovey Jarmen - issued November 11, 1833, m. by:
J. Lester, V. D. M., WILSON Co.

DILLYARD, Bryant to Elizabeth Garland - issued December 18, 1841,
m. by: William Harris, M. G., December 23, 1841, DAVIDSON Co.

DILLYHAY, Robert to Sarah Ann Self - issued February 15, 1843, m. by:
Jas. Daniel, J. P., February 16, 1843, DICKSON Co.

DINKINS, William C. to Lucinda Harrison - issued August 30, 1838,
Bondsman: John W. Dinkins, m. by: Freeman Senters August 30,
1838, SUMNER Co.

DINNES, Benjamin H. to Rhoda Sanders - issued September 22, 1825,
Bondsman: Johnson Vaughn, m. by: James Drennon, J. P., October 13,
1825, WILSON Co.

DINNING, Andrew to Polly Groves - issued September 15, 1806, Bondsman:
Thomas Groves, SUMNER Co.

DINNING, Anthony to Sarah Webb - issued June 17, 1829, Bondsman:
William Dinning, m. by: Sam Cochran, J. P., June 17, 1829,
SUMNER Co.

DINNING, Anthony to Elizabeth Patterson - issued September 20, 1848,
Bondsman: N. P. Hogwood, m. by: G. Orgain, J. P., October 1,
1848, MONTGOMERY Co.

DINNING, Bowles to Martha Bowles - issued December 18, 1819, Bondsman:
Andrew Dinning, SUMNER Co.

DINNING, Bowles to Mahala Kirby - issued August 11, 1828, m. by:
Sam Thackson, J. P., August 11, 1828, SUMNER Co.

DINNING, James to Mary Hollis - m. by: Jesse Gambling, J. P., March 24,
1836, SUMNER Co.

DINNING, James to Sally Cooper - m. by: Freeman Senter July 4, 1837, SUMNER Co.

DINNING, John to Elizabeth Whitworth - issued August 11, 1806, Bondsman: Joseph McGlothin, m. by: Thomas Groves, Jr., J. P., August 21, 1806, SUMNER Co.

DINNING, John Richard to Fanny Kirby - issued March 22, 1824, Bondsman: David Kirby, m. by: Robt. Norvell, M. G., March 22, 1824, SUMNER Co.

DINNING, Thomas G. to Susan Busby - m. August 14, 1834, SUMNER Co.

DINNING, William to Betsey Roney - issued December 16, 1805, Bondsman: Sam'l Roney, SUMNER Co.

DINNING, William to Nancy Moody - issued July 15, 1816, Bondsman: Burwell Hunter, m. by: Edward Gwin, J. P., July 15, 1816, SUMNER Co.

DINNING, William to Lucky Alderson - issued April 17, 1818, Bondsman: Wm. Alderson, SUMNER Co.

DIRE, Lea to Caroline Ore - issued April 12, 1832, Bondsman: Henry Alsup, m. by: Thos. West, J. P., April 18, GRAINGER Co.

DIRIKSON, David S. to May L. Wilson - issued January 16, 1836, Bondsman: Robert H. Cate, RUTHERFORD Co.

DIRT, Francis R. to Jane Latimer - m. by: Ed. Edwards August 12, 1833, SUMNER Co.

DISHMAN, Daniel G. to Mary Ann Hutchins - issued July 6, 1843, m. by: W. C. Richmond, acting J. P., ROBERTSON Co.

DISHROOM, G. I. to Amanda A. Farris - issued June 5, 1867, m. by: E. S. Best, J. P., June 5, 1867, FRANKLIN Co.

DISMUKES, Elisha to Fanny Petty - issued December 8, 1816, Bondsman: Thomas Stone, m. by: Jas. Johnson, J. P., WILSON Co.

DISMUKES, Thomas U. to Mary Jane Hager - issued October 5, 1836, m. by: John W. Bowen October 6, 1836, RUTHERFORD Co.

DISON, Reuben to Harriett Baites - issued January 17, 1838, m. by: A. D. Oakley, J. P., January 17, 1838, FRANKLIN Co.

DIXON, Ephriam to Catherine Thompson - issued August 31, 1816, Bondsman: William White, SUMNER Co.

DIXON, Henry O. to Ann Maria Patterson - issued November 16, 1841, m. by: Jno. W. Hannah November 16, 1841, DAVIDSON Co.

DIXON, Izaiah to Margaret Hains (or Harris) - m. by: Francis Johnston November 20, 1838, SUMNER Co.

DIXON, Jackson C. to Frances Welch - issued February 28, 1838, m. by: M. Woollen, J. P., March 1, 1838, WILSON Co.

DIXON, James B. to Sarah M. Wilson - issued September 5, 1863, Bondsman: W. A. Smith, BEDFORD Co.

DIXON, Jeremiah to Grace Ellis - issued September 4, 1806, Bondsman: Philip Free, GRAINGER Co.

DIXON, Jeremiah to Pincey Beaver - issued September 3, 1823, m. by: Wm. Alexander, J. P., September 3, 1823, SUMNER Co.

DIXON, John to Jean Willson - July 26, 1786, Security: Joseph Willson, GREENE Co.

DIXON, Joseph to Catherine Lovin - issued August 6, 1789, Bondsman:
James Ruse, SUMNER Co.

DIXON, Joseph to Polly Clark - issued July 23, 1806, Bondsman:
Spencer Bevers, WILSON Co.

DIXON, Josiah to Dusty Williams - issued April 29, 1806, Bondsman:
David Stafford, SUMNER Co.

DIXON, Matthew to Polly Hill - issued September 18, 1804, Bondsman:
Jas. Reason, SUMNER Co.

DIXON, Robert to Nancy Adams - issued August 7, 1819, Bondsman:
William Roberts, m. by: James Gray, J. P., August 8, 1819,
WILSON Co.

DIXON, W. H. to L. J. McClure - issued October 25, 1854, m. by:
B. Franks, L. D., October 25, 1854, FRANKLIN Co.

DIXON, Warren G. to Martha S. Sneed - issued October 15, 1840, m. by:
Jesse Cox, M. G., October 15, 1850, DAVIDSON Co.

DIXON, William to Eliza Douglas - December 12, 1800, Security:
William Dewoody, GREENE Co.

DOAK, Alanson F. to Adaline Donnell - issued July 11, 1826, Bondsman:
T. S. Donnell, m. by: James Foster, J. P., July 18, 1826, WILSON Co.

DOAK, Hardy M. to Mary Charlotte - issued October 15, 1838, Bondsman:
James B. Rutland, WILSON Co.

DOAK, John F. to Coloe Harrison - issued April 4, 1827, Bondsman:
Leo Donald, m. by: Amzi Bradshaw April 5, 1827, WILSON Co.

DOAK, John Foster to Elizabeth Hunter - issued January 10, 1822,
Bondsman: Foster Crutcher, m. by: Wm. Steele, J. P., WILSON Co.

DOAK, Jonathan to Isabel Donnell - issued January 25, 1820, Bondsman:
Josiah Donnell, WILSON Co.

DOAK, Joseph to Maria T. Stovall - issued May 9, 1822, m. by:
B. L. McFerrin, J. P., May 16, 1822, RUTHERFORD Co.

DOAK, Nelson to Jane Smith - issued January 20, 1830, Bondsman:
Sam'l C. Smith, WILSON Co.

DOAK, Robert to Jane Wilson - issued May 25, 1822, m. by:
Robt. Henderson, May 25, 1822, RUTHERFORD Co.

DOAK, Sam'l to Nancy Word - issued November 7, 1824, Bondsman:
Valentine Ligon, m. by: Joshua A. Lester, V. D. M., WILSON Co.

DOBB, Alexander to Milly Smith - issued February 27, 1821, Bondsman:
James Smith, m. by: Isiah Bunch, J. P., GRAINGER Co.

DOBB, John to Sarah Anderson - issued May 6, 1813, Bondsman:
William Wygal, SUMNER Co.

DOBBIN, James to Mary Lenora Armstrong - August, 1810, Bondsman:
John Dobbin, MAURY Co.

DOBBINS, Carson to Betsey McMurry - issued March 4, 1812, Bondsman:
James McMurry, SUMNER Co.

DOBBINS, Cornelius to Polly Smith - June 16, 1814, KNOX Co.

DOBBINS, Henry to Sophia Allen - issued October 27, 1823, Bondsman:
Alexander B. Dobbins, m. by: Richard Beard, M. G., October 27,
1823, SUMNER Co.

DOBBINS, John to Elizabeth Shaw - issued May 24, 1806, Bondsman:
Jonathan Trousdale, SUMNER Co.

DOBBINS, Robert B. to Jane Bratney - issued March 30, 1818, Bondsman:
Thos. C. Beard, SUMNER Co.

DOBBINS, Robert D. to Nancy C. McLin - m. by: Francis Johnson, M. G.,
March 1, 1834, SUMNER Co.

DOBBINS, Sam'l to Minerva Bowls - issued December 3, 1832, Bondsman:
John Dobbins, m. by: D. Ashford, J. P., December 3, 1832, SUMNER Co.

DOBBINS, Thomas C. to Ann Beard - issued October 18, 1826, Bondsman:
John Dobbins, m. by: Robert Guthrie October 18, 1826, SUMNER Co.

DOBBS, Asa to Amy Bartlett - issued August 10, 1839, m. by:
Richd. W. Mantlo, J. P., August 11, 1839, ROBERTSON Co.

DOBBS, Asa S. to Martha Smart - issued October 19, 1838, m. by:
R. B. C. Howell October 21, 1838, DAVIDSON Co.

DOBBS, Jesse W. to Margaret Calvin - issued August 31, 1845, Bondsman:
James Calvin, m. by: Wm. Johns, J. P., September 3, 1845, MEIGS Co.

DOBBS, John Z. to Mary A. S. Toombs - m. by: Arch B. Duval April 1,
1834, SUMNER Co.

DOBBS, Lodaway to Pamelia Williams - issued November 18, 1834, Bondsman:
Samuel Williams, m. by: H. Hobson, J. P., WILSON Co.

DOBS, Henry to Hannah Ford - issued March 4, 1844, m. by:
C. L. Blanton, J. P., March 6, 1844, FRANKLIN Co.

DOBSON, Benjamin to Nancy Lannum - issued March 22, 1834, Bondsman:
John H. Flowers, RUTHERFORD Co.

DOBSON, Hugh to Eliza Alexander - December 23, 1815, WILLIAMSON Co.

DOBSON, Joseph C. to Mary N. Tweedy - issued September 10, 1822, m. by:
G. W. Oliver, J. P., September 10, 1822, RUTHERFORD Co.

DOBSON, G. P. to Mattie Gabbert - issued January 19, 1861, Bondsman:
Gus. Bate, Jos. H. Thompson, Clk., m. by: H. A. Graves, M. G.,
BEDFORD Co.

DOBSON, William to Margaret Greyham - issued August 19, 1836, m. by:
J. Hooker, M. G., August 21, 1836, WILSON Co.

DOBYNA, Dennis R. D. to Matilda Wadley - issued December 8, 1836,
Bondsman: William G. Parrish, m. by: James F. Fletcher, J. P.,
December 8, 1836, RUTHERFORD Co.

DOCKERY, Greenville to Sally Davis - issued November 4, 1824, Bondsman:
Hugh McConnel, m. by: J. C. Bunch, J. P., November 4, 1824,
GRAINGER Co.

DOCKEY (?), James to Elizabeth Barney (?) - issued December 23, 1811,
Bondsman: Pearson Barney, GRAINGER Co.

DOCKINGS, Ruben to Rhody Hankins - issued March 11, 1821, Bondsman:
Jonathan Baker, WILSON Co.

DOCKINGS, Willie to Fanny Goodall - issued March 14, 1821, Bondsman:
Benajah Cartwright, WILSON Co.

DOCKREY, Watson to Miss Martha Burton - issued January 31, 1850,
Bondsman: P. Priestly and S. M. Moody, m. January 31, 1850,
MONTGOMERY Co.

DODD, Joel to Margret Smith - issued March 17, 1850, m. by:
B. B. Knight, J. P., March 17, 1850, FRANKLIN Co.

DODD, John to Sarah Stonecypher - February 1, 1797, Security:
James Robinson, GREENE Co.

DODD, John to Sallie Leek - February 12, 1812, KNOX Co.

DODD, John to Mary Jane Clardy - issued February 2, 1847, Bondsman:
W. E. Suter, MONTGOMERY Co.

DODD, Marcus to Polly Wilson - issued December 22, 1806, Bondsman:
Laurence Owen, SUMNER Co.

DODD, Richard to Elizabeth Dodd - June 23, 1812, KNOX Co.

DODD, Robert C. to Sally C. Holt - m. by: Francis A. Jarratt, M. G.,
October 1, 1833, SUMNER Co.

DODD, Sam'l. to Zerinah Johnson - November 7, 1815, WILLIAMSON Co.

DODD, Willis to Polly Davis - issued July 15, 1823, Bondsman:
John Hill, m. by: John Haynie July 15, 1823, KNOX Co.

DODS, John A. to Margaret M. Thompson - issued March 7, 1828, Bondsman:
Joins B. Thompson, WILSON Co.

DODSON, Allen Morgan to Roda Churchman - issued February 11, 1818,
Bondsman: Elias Davis, m. by: John Hall, J. P., GRAINGER Co.

DODSON, Sam (?) to Elisha Dodson - May 19, 1808, Bondsman:
Greenham Dodson, MAURY Co.

DODSON, Bud to Judith Hollan - June 6, 1817, WILLIAMSON Co.

DODSON, David G. to Elizabeth Hudson - issued December 14, 1844, m. by:
Cyrus Murry, J. P., December 18, 1844, DICKSON Co.

DODSON, Elisha to Polley Midlock (Polly Medlock) - issued November 3,
1803, Bondsman: John Ogle, GRAINGER Co.

DODSON, Heram to Maryanne Grissom - issued July 26, 1854, VAN BUREN Co.

DODSON (Dotson), Hightower to Sally Dodson - July 4, 1807, WILLIAMSON Co.

DODSON, Isaac J. to Octave Bullard - issued April 29, 1834, Bondsman:
James M. Irwin, m. by: Coffield Mitchell, M. G., WILSON Co.

DODSON, J. A. to Mary A. E. Laird - issued September 20, 1848, Bondsman:
Thos. M. Boardman, MONTGOMERY Co.

DODSON, James to Roseanna McFadden - August 3, 1815, WILLIAMSON Co.

DODSON, James to Rachel Grantha - issued July 25, 1817, Bondsman:
James Robertson, m. by: Caleb Witt, M. G., July 29, 1817,
GRAINGER Co.

DODSON, John to Nancey Kenney - issued December 29, 1799, Bondsman:
John Ward, GRAINGER Co.

DODSON, John to Sarah Dodson - issued January 14, 1800, Bondsman:
Samuel Dodson, Witness: Sam'l Yancey, GRAINGER Co.

DODSON (x), John M. to Nancy M. Powers - October 3, 1849, Security:
Robert B. (x) Powers, GILES Co.

DODSON, Martha to Nicholas Roberts - GREENE Co.

DODSON, Martin to Polly Acuff - issued May 29, 1804, Bondsman:
Richard Acuff, GRAINGER Co.

DODSON, Monroe G. to Sarah E. Brewer - issued July 4, 1844, m. by:
    A. Nesbitt, J. P., July 4, 1844, DICKSON Co.

DODSON, Moses to Sarah Roberts - December 2, 1789, Security:
    John Roberts, GREENE Co.

DODSON, Newton to Nancy Sugg - issued November 9, 1846, DICKSON Co.

DODSON, Newton to Louisa J. Mason - issued September 23, 1850, m. by:
    R. C. Smith, J. P., September 25, 1850, FRANKLIN Co.

DODSON, Nimrod to Elizabeth Chisum - issued October 21, 1797, Bondsman:
    John Ward, GRAINGER Co.

DODSON, Ruben to Nancy McConico - October 14, 1805, WILLIAMSON Co.

DODSON, Sally to Amos Caldwell - MAURY Co.

DODSON, Samuel to Eliner Grison - issued March 14, 1808, Bondsman:
    Jesse Dodson, GRAINGER Co.

DODSON, Samuel to Betsey McDonnill - November 26, 1808, Bondsman:
    Alexander Black, MAURY Co.

DODSON, Samuel to Mary Williams - issued August 3, 1820, Bondsman:
    Samuel Dodson and William Moore, m. by: Goerge Elkin August 3,
    1820, GRAINGER Co.

DODSON, Samuel to Eliza A. Posey - issued September 25, 1857, m. by:
    Wm. R. Francis, J. P., September 25, 1857, FRANKLIN Co.

DODSON, Sarah to Jacob Kyle - GREENE Co.

DODSON, Solomon to Peggy Collins - issued February 15, 1802, Bondsman:
    David Collins, GRAINGER Co.

DODSON, Thomas to Jane Waddle - February 12, 1817, WILLIAMSON Co.

DODSON, William to Martha Holensworth - issued December 20, 1852, m. by:
    James Head, M. G., December 30, 1852, VAN BUREN Co.

DODSON, Wm. C. to Nancy E. Hudson - issued October 8, 1848, m. by:
    Wm. Hill, J. P., October 8, 1848, DICKSON Co.

DODSON, William H. to Martha P. Walker - November 18, 1826, WILLIAMSON Co.

DOGGET, Chatten to Polly Wells - December 11, 1807, WILLIAMSON Co.

DOHERTY, George to Nancy McDowell - April 1, 1799, Surety: John McDowell,
    BLOUNT Co.

DOHERTY, James B. to Sarah L. Alsup - issued July 23, 1834, m. by:
    W. R. D. Phipps, J. P., July 28, 1834, WILSON Co.

DOLAN, John J. to Elizabeth Reynolds - issued June 6, 1852, Bondsman:
    Hugh Fox, MONTGOMERY Co.

DOLBY, John to Elvira A. Farris - issued December 23, 1852, m. by:
    John S. Davis, M. G., December 26, 1852, FRANKLIN Co.

DOLBY, W. G. to Harriett C. Jones - issued January 5, 1863, Bondsman:
    James M. Keller, Jos. H. Thompson, Clk., BEDFORD Co.

DOLES, Ephriam to Ann Boatright - issued June 20, 1848, m. by:
    Thos. Stewart, J. P., June 20, 1848, STEWART Co.

DOLIN, John to Caroline Vickery - issued April 21, 1854, m. by:
    Robert Brown, J. P., April 23, 1854, COFFEE Co.

DOLLAR, D. C. to Catherine Dawson - issued February 17, 1854, m. by:
J. A. Walker, M. G., February 19, 1854, COFFEE Co.

DOLLINS, John A. to Elizabeth Jones - issued January 11, 1847,
FRANKLIN Co.

DOLLINS, Thomas F. to Virginia C. Lasater - issued October 18, 1848,
m. by: James Byrom, J. P., October 18, 1848, FRANKLIN Co.

DOLTON, Alford to Eliz Borders - issued May 31, 1842, m. by:
U. Young, J. P., ROBERTSON Co.

DOLTON, Robert to Mary A. Cook - issued June 29, 1844, DICKSON Co.

DOLWAY, William J. to Martha Roe - issued July 3, 1843, DAVIDSON Co.

DONAGHEE, James to Sarah Willoughby - March 18, 1797, Security:
Benjamin Willoughby, GREENE Co.

DONAGHEE, Thomas to Margaret Willoughby - April 2, 1797, Security:
Benjamin Willoughby, GREENE Co.

DONAHOO, Charles to Margaret Weir - January 8, 1802, Security:
Joseph Weir, BLOUNT Co.

DONAHUE, Alabama to M. S. Wallace - issued March 19, 1863, Bondsman:
J. A. Hodge, Jos. H. Thompson, Clk., BEDFORD Co.

DONAHUGH, Henry to Sarah Gill - issued May 22, 1826, Bondsman:
Samuel Jack, m. by: W. M. Lane, J. P., May 22, 1826, GRAINGER Co.

DONALD, James to Elizabeth Hendricks - September 9, 1796, BLOUNT Co.

DONALD, Matthew to Agnes Walker - December 9, 1802, Security:
John Cochron, BLOUNT Co.

DONALD, Matthew B. to Isabella D. Douglass - issued February 12, 1833,
KNOX Co.

DONALDSON, Andrew to Isabella Carmichael - October 4, 1794, Security:
Alex Thompson, GREENE Co.

DONALDSON, Buckley to Dida Mira Armstrong - February 2, 1811, WILLIAMSON Co.

DONALDSON, Elizabeth to Joseph Rodgers - GREENE Co.

DONALDSON, James M. to Dosha Ann Trigg - issued September 2, 1846,
m. by: C. A. Hunt, J. P., 1846, FRANKLIN Co.

DONALDSON, Lewis to Martha Damron - issued January 26, 1865, m. by:
D. J. Martin, J. P., January 2, 1865, FRANKLIN Co.

DONALDSON, R. S. to Missouri C. Eartherly - issued December 10, 1856,
m. by: John P. Wedington, J. P., December 11, 1856, FRANKLIN Co.

DONALDSON, Robt. S. to Cyntha T. Alspaugh - issued March 14, 1871,
m. by: G. W. Bowling, J. P., March 10, 1871, FRANKLIN Co.

DONALDSON, Silas to Elizabeth Ashley - issued December 19, 1849,
m. by: B. F. Wade, J. P., January 9, 1850, FRANKLIN Co.

DONALDSON, W. M. to N. S. Kilpatrick - issued April 22, 1859, m. by:
T. W. Bell, J. P., April 24, 1859, FRANKLIN Co.

DONALSON, Lewis G. to Nancy Rogers - issued November, 1822, m. by:
H. M. Cryer, J. P., November, 1822, SUMNER Co.

DON CARLOS, Achilles to Elizabeth Kidd - issued June 23, 1825, Bondsman:
Joseph Burnett, m. by: Robt. McBath June 23, 1825, KNOX Co.

DONE, Joseph to Caroline E. F. Fowler - issued April 20, 1840,
DICKSON Co.

DONELSON, Jr., A. J. to Sarah Melson - issued February 3, 1841,
DAVIDSON Co.

DONELSON, A. Y. to M. E. Parker - issued September 24, 1858, m. by:
W. L. Caskey, M. G., September 28, 1858, ROBERTSON Co.

DONELSON, Alexander to Patsey Smith - issued November 7, 1803, Bondsman:
John McElheney, GRAINGER Co.

DONELSON, Andrew J. to Cathrine Nelson - issued October 10, 1835,
Bondsman: Burton Yandell, m. by: John W. Bowen, M. G., October 13,
1835, RUTHERFORD Co.

DONELSON, Andrew J. to Elizabeth A. Randolph - issued November 9, 1841,
m. by: Robt. A. Lapsley November 10, 1841, DAVIDSON Co.

DONELSON, Barnett to Polly Andrews - August 8, 1808, WILLIAMSON Co.

DONELSON, Ebenezer to Elizabeth Davis - issued December 7, 1820,
Bondsman: Isham F. Davis, WILSON Co.

DONELSON, Humphry to Sally Kelly - issued February 17, 1808, Bondsman:
Obediah Woodwine, WILSON Co.

DONELSON, Joel to Sally Acuff - issued October 6, 1812, Bondsman:
William Glassop, GRAINGER Co.

DONELSON, John to Ceily Jourdon - issued October 14, 1811, Bondsman:
Thomas Whiteside, Witness: John F. Jack, J. P., GRAINGER Co.

DONELSON, Moses M. to Jane Zedacher - m. by: Jesse Gambling, J. P.,
March 5, 1835, SUMNER Co.

DONELSON, Robt. to Peggy Farris - December 24, 1806, WILLIAMSON Co.

DONELSON, Robt. to Peggy Feress - December 24, 1806, WILLIAMSON Co.

DONELSON, Robert to Elizabeth Rutherford - issued February 24, 1823,
m. by: Elijah Maddox, M. G., February 27, 1823, WILSON Co.

DONELSON, Savern to Mariah Stareky - issued January 5, 1837, m. by:
Burrell Perry, J. P., January 5, 1837, RUTHERFORD Co.

DONELSON, Wm. to Martha J. Anderson - issued July 23, 1845, m. by:
Robt. Lapsley July 23, 1845, DAVIDSON Co.

DONNEL, Elisha to Delpha E. Cato - issued January 9, 1847, m. December 13,
1847, STEWART Co.

DONNELL, Abnah to Elizabeth Donnell - issued January 13, 1836, Bondsman:
Stephen Comer, m. by: John Bone, J. P., January 14, 1836, WILSON Co.

DONNELL, Alfred E. to Adaline Donnell - issued January 13, 1835,
Bondsman: John Muirhead, m. by: B. Pyland, M. G., January 15,
1835, WILSON Co.

DONNELL, Calvin to Milly Hancock - issued October 19, 1833, m. by:
Levi P. Morrison October 26, 1833, WILSON Co.

DONNELL, Calvin to Martha Weatherspoon - issued September 7, 1836,
Bondsman: Levi Donnell, m. by: Jesse Alexander, V. D. M.,
September 8, 1836, RUTHERFORD Co.

DONNELL, Connell O. to Bridget O. Donnell - issued January 16, 1860,
m. by: T. B. Mathews, J. P., ROBERTSON Co.

DONNELL, Constantine O. to Deliah Suiter - m. by: J. F. Anderson, J. P., March 2, 1851, FRANKLIN Co.

DONNELL, Eden to Eliza Garmony - issued January 19, 1824, Bondsman: Lea Donnell, m. by: Jesse Alexander, V. D. M., January 29, 1824, WILSON Co.

DONNELL, Eli to Peggy Tague - issued September 30, 1809, Bondsman: Robert Donnell, WILSON Co.

DONNELL, Elusley A. to Mary McKee - issued December 8, 1835, Bondsman: Charles F. McKee, m. by: B. Pyland December 8, 1835, WILSON Co.

DONNELL, George to Armelia Shanks - issued May 14, 1810, Bondsman: Abel Williams, WILSON Co.

DONNELL, George to Elizabeth McMurry - issued June 11, 1827, Bondsman: F. G. Crutcher, WILSON Co.

DONNELL, James P. to Julet Waters - issued August 22, 1832, Bondsman: Calvin Donnell, m. by: Levi R. Morrison, V. D. M., August 23, 1832, WILSON Co.

DONNELL, Jesse to Sally Cropper - issued April 12, 1817, Bondsman: John Donnell, m. by: Sam'l Cannon, J. P., April 15, 1817, WILSON Co.

DONNELL, John to Elizabeth Davidson - issued January 27, 1810, Bondsman: Jesse Donnell, WILSON Co.

DONNELL, John W. to Agnes Julia Ann Wommack - issued September 1, 1836, m. by: Geo. Donnell, V. D. M., September 6, 1836, WILSON Co.

DONNELL, Josiah to Nancy P. Thompson - issued May 17, 1830, Bondsman: Thomas W. Brigson, m. by: Amzi Bradshaw May 18, 1830, WILSON Co.

DONNELL, Latimer to Susan ___ (?) - issued March 8, 1824, m. by: Richard Johnson March 8, 1824, SUMNER Co.

DONNELL, Levi to Cynthia Donnell - issued 1821, Bondsman: John F. Doak, WILSON Co.

DONNELL, Levi to Elizabeth Sherrill - issued October 26, 1836, Bondsman: James M. Weatherly, m. by: Jesse Alexander, V. D. M., October 27, 1836, RUTHERFORD Co.

DONNELL, Persis to Sally Hassell - issued January 22, 1824, Bondsman: Robert A. King, m. by: John R. Bain January 22, 1824, SUMNER Co.

DONNELL, R. W. to Lucy Ann Green - issued October 20, 1836, Bondsman: Robert T. Moore, SUMNER Co.

DONNELL, R. W. to Lucy Ann Green - m. by: Arch B. Duval October 20, 1836, SUMNER Co.

DONNELL, Robert to Cleopatra Hearn - issued December 2, 1830, Bondsman: Robert McKee, m. by: Obadiah Freeman, WILSON Co.

DONNELL, Robert to Mary I. Wallace - m. by: J. W. Hall October 9, 1833, SUMNER Co.

DONNELL, Robert to Jane F. McMinn - issued December 15, 1835, Bondsman: Howell Williams, m. by: B. Pyland December 17, 1835, WILSON Co.

DONNELL, Robert B. to Annis Lea - issued October 20, 1836, m. by: R. Comer, J. P., WILSON Co.

DONNELL, Robert S. to Anne B. McAdow - issued April 1, 1823, WILSON Co.

DONNELL, Samuel to Jane Andres - issued February 1, 1804, Bondsman: James Andres, RUTHERFORD Co.

DONNELL, Saml. H. to Mary Carter - issued November 19, 1835, Bondsman: Henry Major, m. by: Sion Bass, M. G., WILSON Co.

DONNELL, Samuel W. to Martha W. Hearn - issued June 1, 1831, Bondsman: Henry Major, m. by: Obadiah Freeman, M. G., June 2, 1831, WILSON Co.

DONNELL, Thomas B. to Isabella Jones - issued March 30, 1833, m. by: L. Moore, J. P., April 4, 1833, WILSON Co.

DONNELL, William to Mary Todd - issued August 20, 1827, Bondsman: Archibald Tennison, RUTHERFORD Co.

DONNELL, William H. to Susannah Benthol - issued June 11, 1830, Bondsman: David Standley, m. by: Wilson Hearn, M. G., June 17, 1830, WILSON Co.

DONNELL, William R. to Isabella Ann Foster - issued September 4, 1834, Bondsman: Thomas Pentecost, m. by: Levi R. Morrison, V. D. M., October 6, 1834, WILSON Co.

DONNEY, James P. to Hanah Shockley - issued May 19, 1851, m. by: W. B. Cumings, J. P., May 21, 1851, VAN BUREN Co.

DONOHO, Albert S. to Cynthia A. Wynne - issued October 24, 1829, Bondsman: C. Hart, m. by: H. Joyner October 24, 1829, SUMNER Co.

DONOHO, Anthony to Anna Coleman - issued July 1, 1816, Bondsman: James Stratton, m. by: Daniel Laitmer, J. P., July 1, 1816, SUMNER Co.

DONOHO, Isaac to Cretia Totwine - issued August 27, 1800, Bondsman: John Donoho, SUMNER Co.

DONOHO, James to Lotty Holmes - issued May 23, 1816, Bondsman: James McKain, SUMNER Co.

DONOHO, James to Nancy Johnson - m. by: Joseph Pitt March 17, 1835, SUMNER Co.

DONOHO, John to Sally Crews - issued November 27, 1819, Bondsman: Walter Donoho, SUMNER Co.

DONOHO, John to Betsey Dossitt - issued January 8, 1820, Bondsman: James Cartwright, SUMNER Co.

DONOHO, Noah to Polly Williams - issued August 8, 1826, Bondsman: Jacob Parks, m. by: Robert Guthrie, M. G., August 8, 1826, SUMNER Co.

DONOHO, Walter to Caty Haines - issued November 22, 1804, Bondsman: Willias Haines, SUMNER Co.

DONOHO, William to Jane C. Ready - issued July 14, 1835, Bondsman: R. D. Donoho, RUTHERFORD Co.

DOOLEY, George to Emily Jackson - issued August 11, 1830, Bondsman: Sam Golladay, WILSON Co.

DOOLEY, George R. to Nancy Y. Jackson - issued September 16, 1835, Bondsman: R. Barkley, m. by: Jas. C. Willeford, J. P., September 17, 1835, WILSON Co.

DOOLEY, Jacob to Susan Harris - June 23, 1813, WILLIAMSON Co.

DOOLEY, James to Nancy Woodward - issued June 5, 1813, m. by: Thos. Calhoon, V. D. M., WILSON Co.

DOOLEY, Michael to Eliza Williams - January 16, 1810, WILLIAMSON Co.

DOOLIN, Archibald to Malinda Haskew - issued April 8, 1831, Bondsman: Richard Marshall, m. by: Sam'l Love, M. G., April 9, 1831, KNOX Co.

DORA, John to Suckey Bunch - issued November 29, 1800, Bondsman:
Harmon Miller, GRAINGER Co.

DORAN, Alexander to Nancy Powell - issued June 21, 1824, Bondsman:
Thomas Powell, m. by: Jesse Alexander, V. D. M., June 24, 1824,
RUTHERFORD Co.

DORAN, James G. to Elizabeth Knox - issued December 24, 1818, Bondsman:
James McKnight, m. by: Jesse Alexander, V. D. M., December 31,
1818, RUTHERFORD Co.

DORAN, Joseph to Catharine C. Carmichael - issued October 15, 1828,
Bondsman: James McCampbell, m. by: Elijah M. Eagleton October 16,
1828, KNOX Co.

DORCH, John to Cynthia Walker - issued July 31, 1820, Bondsman:
Lewis Sutton, m. by: W. H. Race August 6, 1820, WILSON Co.

DORCH, John H. to Winny Todd - issued December 30, 1829, Bondsman:
P. H. Buckley, WILSON Co.

DORR, Henry to Eve Grimes - issued August 6, 1805, Bondsman:
Frederick Miller, SUMNER Co.

DORRIS, A. to A. E. Crawford - issued November 19, 1949, m. by:
Jas. Woodard, J. P., May 20, 1849, ROBERTSON Co.

DORRIS, Archer S. to Nancy Ellmore - issued March 1, 1843, m. by:
James Sprouse, J. P., March 2, 1843, ROBERTSON Co.

DORRIS, Cornelius to Lucy Aiken - issued July 4, 1851, m. by:
W. L. Baldry, Gospel Minister, July 8, 1851, ROBERTSON Co.

DORRIS, Eldnage W. to Louisa England - issued September 27, 1842,
m. by: James Sprouse, J. P., September 28, 1842, ROBERTSON Co.

DORRIS, Elias to Martha Rippy - issued July 19, 1830, Bondsman:
Abram Bradley, m. by: John Stone, M. G., July 19, 1830, SUMNER Co.

DORRIS, G. W. to Nancy Clayton - issued July 28, 1853, ROBERTSON Co.

DORRIS, Ira to Martha C. Elam - issued November 27, 1845, m. by:
Wm. D. Baldum, M. G., December 2, 1845, DAVIDSON Co.

DORRIS, Isaac C. to Pricilla Choat - issued July 15, m. by: J. R. Gunn,
J. P., July 16, 1854, ROBERTSON Co.

DORRIS, James to Anny Ivey - issued September 17, 1842, m. by:
W. C. Richmond, J. P., September 28, 1842, ROBERTSON Co.

DORRIS, James J. to Sarah Watson - issued December 12, 1853, m. by:
W. D. Baldwin, V. D. M., December 13, 1853, ROBERTSON Co.

DORRIS, James W. to Mary Powell - issued October 10, 1850, ROBERTSON Co.

DORRIS, Jesse to Polly Freeland - issued August 14, 1828, Bondsman:
Abraham Bordley, m. by: M. Hodges, J. P., August 14, 1828,
SUMNER Co.

DORRIS, John to Jane Dorris - issued February 9, 1816, Bondsman:
Isaac Dorris, m. February 9, 1816, SUMNER Co.

DORRIS, John to Jane Dorris - issued July 30, 1817, Bondsman:
Hugh Kirkpatrick, m. by: John McMurtry, J. P., July 30, 1817,
SUMNER Co.

DORRIS, John to Elizabeth Hinson - issued November 25, 1823, Bondsman:
Ezekiel C. Hodges, m. by: Robt. Norvell, M. G., November 25, 1823,
SUMNER Co.

DORRIS, John P. to E. Willson - issued January 7, 1850, m. by:
R. B. Dorris, ROBERTSON Co.

DORRIS, Josiah M. to Amanda Hampton - issued June 13, 1850, m. by:
D. G. Baird, J. P., ROBERTSON Co.

DORRIS, Levi A. to Mary Campbell - issued November 16, 1826, Bondsman:
Jehosephat Campbell, SUMNER Co.

DORRIS, Lewis to Mary Bush - m. by: Wm. Montgomery September 22, 1828,
SUMNER Co.

DORRIS, Marley to Susan Brumbelow - issued September 15, 1841, m. by:
Wm. D. Baldwin, M. G., ROBERTSON Co.

DORRIS, Meredith to Highly Robins - issued March 23, 1839, m. by:
James Sprouse, J. P., March 27, 1839, ROBERTSON Co.

DORRIS, Robert to Jinny Rippy - issued July 18, 1818, Bondsman:
William Dorris, m. by: Addison Foster, J. P., July 18, 1818,
SUMNER Co.

DORRIS, Robinson T. to Rebecca Beasley - issued August 2, 1839, m. by:
John G. Balarcy, M. G., August 8, 1839, ROBERTSON Co.

DORRIS, Roland A. to Jane Garret - issued March 26, 1832, Bondsman:
Absolom H. Dorris, m. by: Peter Ketring, J. P., March 26, 1832,
SUMNER Co.

DORRIS, Samuel to Susanna Pitt - issued March 13, 1811, Bondsman:
Wm. Dorris, SUMNER Co.

DORRIS, Stephen J. to Elizabeth Brumbelow - issued August 5, 1847,
m. by: Wm. D. Baldwin, M. G., ROBERTSON Co.

DORRIS, W. A. to Airy Phipps - issued July 28, 1855, m. by:
John Crafford, J. P., July 29, 1855, ROBERTSON Co.

DORRIS, W. L. to Martha Johnson - issued March 5, 1843, m. by:
J. L. Adams, J. P., ROBERTSON Co.

DORRIS, W. William to Lucy Ann Jones - issued May 16, 1859, m. by:
G. W. Featherston, M. G., May 19, 1859, ROBERTSON Co.

DORRIS, Wesley S. to Eliza Jane Freeland - issued April 22, 1856,
m. by: H. L. Covington, J. P., April 24, 1856, ROBERTSON Co.

DORRIS, Jr., William to Polly Rippey - issued July 16, 1812, Bondsman:
Robert Davis, Jr., SUMNER Co.

DORRIS, William to Nancy Right - issued December 21, 1821, Bondsman:
John Mitchell, m. by: John Gilbert, J. P., December 21, 1821,
SUMNER Co.

DORRIS, Wm. H. to Mary E. McMordie - issued January 23, 1849, Bondsman:
J. P. Morrison, MONTGOMERY Co.

DORRIS, William P. to Amanda Bagget - issued December 3, 1839, m. by:
Thos. Cook, J. P., December 10, 1839, ROBERTSON Co.

DORRIS, William R. to W. M. Blackburn - issued November 26, 1853, m. by:
J. C. Barbee, J. P., November 27, 1853, ROBERTSON Co.

DORSETT, Willis to Nancy Panky - issued July 20, 1811, Bondsman:
Adam Crump, SUMNER Co.

DORSEY, Charles to Eleanor Broyles - issued October 13, 1823, Bondsman:
John Howland, m. by: B. L. McFerrin, J. P., October 16, 1823,
RUTHERFORD Co.

DORTCH, Isaac to Martha Allen - issued April 25, 1827, Bondsman:
Abram Harpole, WILSON Co.

DORTCH, Nancy to John B. Bailey - Bondsman: J. E. Bailey, m. by:
J. B. Walker, M. G., MONTGOMERY Co.

DORTCH, Richard to Susan Hunt - issued September 16, 1823, Bondsman:
Thomas Scurlock, WILSON Co.

DOSE, T. J. to Susan E. Ellison - issued September 20, 1861, m. by:
T. O. Tarpley, J. P., September 22, 1861, ROBERTSON Co.

DOSE, Wm. to Nancy D. Elmore - issued January 1, 1850, m. by:
W. B. Kelly, M. G., January 2, 1850, ROBERTSON Co.

DOSEY, Doshea to William McNinch - October 7, 1796, Security:
John Newman, GREENE Co.

DOSHER, John to Rachel Fain - issued November 26, 1823, Bondsman:
Daniel Dosher, RUTHERFORD Co.

DOSIT, James to Elizabeth Donoho - issued August 14, 1810, Bondsman:
Isaac Forrest, SUMNER Co.

DOSS, A. to Juditha Broaderick - issued April 13, 1861, m. by:
Greenberry Kelly, M. G., April 14, 1861, ROBERTSON Co.

DOSS, Azariah to Rebecca Chapman - issued October 7, 1857, m. by:
G. B. Kellt, M. G., October 8, 1857, ROBERTSON Co.

DOSS, James to Nelly Graves - issued November 23, 1811, Bondsman:
John W. Byrns, SUMNER Co.

DOSS, James to Martha Bell - issued August 18, 1845, m. August 20,
1845, ROBERTSON Co.

DOSS, James M. to Mary Jane Harmon - May 30, m. by: J. Wm. Lee,
GILES Co.

DOSS, Joel R. to Caroline Jones - issued June 16, 1847, m. by:
Jas. W. Woodard, J. P., ROBERTSON Co.

DOSS, Joshua to Jemima Turner - issued February 1, 1832, Bondsman:
Benjamin Wilson, m. by: Jonathan Davis, J. P., February 1, 1832,
SUMNER Co.

DOSS, Samuel A. to Mary J. Farmer - issued January 22, 1846, m. by:
T. W. Felts June 23, 1846, ROBERTSON Co.

DOSS, W. W. to L. A. Murrah - issued October 20, 1857, m. by:
Jas. Woodard October 23, 1857, ROBERTSON Co.

DOSS, William R. to Mary Morris - issued November 13, 1840, m. by:
R. B. Mitchell November 15, 1840, ROBERTSON Co.

DOSSETT, George W. to Martha Nugent - issued June 28, 1858, FRANKLIN Co.

DOSSETT, Wm. to Nancy J. Gipson - issued July 6, 1854, m. by:
J. Campbell, M. G., July 9, 1854, FRANKLIN Co.

DOTEY, Agnes to Abraham Maines - July 1, 1793, Security:
Simeon Pennington, GREENE Co.

DOTEY, Susanna to Joseph Lane - GREENE Co.

DOTSON, Andrew to Eliza Conaway - issued March 24, 1873, FRANKLIN Co.

DOTSON, Cancess to John Hughey - MAURY Co.

DOTSON, Clabourn to Ellen Mallicoat - issued November 18, 1825,
    Bondsman: Saml. Dotson, GRAINGER Co.

DOTSON, Elish to Fanna Thompson - issued October 31, 1819, Bondsman:
    James Robertson, m. by: C. McAnally, J. P., November 4, 1819,
    GRAINGER Co.

DOTSON, Greenham to Marcy Brooks - January 9, 1806, MAURY Co.

DOTSON, Henderson to Lucinda A. Ashley - issued October 16, 1865,
    m. by: I. N. Martin, J. P., October 17, 1865, FRANKLIN Co.

DOTSON, J. M. to Hannah Karns - issued November 21, 1832, Bondsman:
    Jesse J. Parsley, m. by: J. Johnson, J. P., November 22, 1832,
    KNOX Co.

DOTSON, James to Mary Hommel - issued October 20, 1824, Bondsman:
    John Watkins, m. by: Wm. Coke, J. P., October 20, 1824, GRAINGER Co.

DOTSON, James C. to Mary F. Grimes - issued January 5, 1857, m. by:
    H. H. Orndorff, J. P., February 5, 1857, ROBERTSON Co.

DOTSON, John to Betsey Burk - issued March 8, 1805, Bondsman:
    Rilaw Burk, GRAINGER Co.

DOTSON, John to Martha Crownover - issued December 17, 1856, m. by:
    John Hendley, J. P., December 18, 1856, FRANKLIN Co.

DOTSON, John D. to Margret E. Leonard - issued October 24, 1867,
    m. by: W. W. Hawkins, M. G., October 24, 1867, FRANKLIN Co.

DOTSON, Jordon to Polly Etton - September 21, 1809, Bondsman:
    Elisha Dotson, MAURY Co.

DOTSON, Joseph to Maryan Moore - issued April 4, 1841, m. by:
    John Gillentine, J. P., April 6, 1841, VAN BUREN Co.

DOTSON, Rebekah to Thomas Mooney - GREENE Co.

DOTSON, Rodney to Rachiel Parker - issued January 20, 1843, m. by:
    Wiley Denson, J. P., January 20, 1843, FRANKLIN Co.

DOTSON, Rolly to Marth Johnson - issued January 4, 1822, Bondsman:
    Jaramiah Johnston, GRAINGER Co.

DOTSON, Rufus to Mary E. Dotson - issued November 28, 1871, m. by:
    E. A. Stevenson, M. G., December 12, 1871, FRANKLIN Co.

DOTSON, Jr., Samuel to Syntha Sellers - issued January 22, 1829,
    Bondsman: Ruben Dotson, GRAINGER Co.

DOTSON, Jr., Samuel to Nancy Hopson - issued December 17, 1833,
    Bondsman: Hugh W. Farmer, m. by: W. Williams, J. P., GRAINGER Co.

DOTSON, Solomon to Malinda Money - issued February 26, 1843, m. by:
    B. Sells, J. P., February 26, 1843, FRANKLIN Co.

DOTSON, Stephen to Nancy Parker - issued September 29, 1822, Bondsman:
    John Brown, m. by: William Lane, J. P., September 29, 1822,
    GRAINGER Co.

DOTSON, William to Matilda McAnally - issued January 14, 1828, Bondsman:
    William L. Cardwell, GRAINGER Co.

DOTSON, William to Elizabeth Hefley - issued July 9, 1828, Bondsman:
    Moses Harrison, m. by: James B. Taylor, J. P., July 10, 1828,
    WILSON Co.

DOTSON, William to Julia Ann Glaze - issued September 18, 1847, m. by:
    John Nugent September 19, 1847, FRANKLIN Co.

DOTSON, Z. R. to Julia D. M. M. Bratton - issued December 28, 1854,
m. by: R. C. Smith, J. P., December 10, 1854, FRANKLIN Co.

DOTSON, Zachariah R. to Agnes Comings - issued April 26, 1848, m. by:
Jas. R. Brown, M. G., April 27, 1848, FRANKLIN Co.

DOTY, Isaac to Nancy Flannery - April 25, 1798, Security: John Newman,
GREENE Co.

DOTY, Jas. to Sarah Hill - issued July 5, 1871, m. by: Stephen Kennedy,
M. G., July 5, 1871, FRANKLIN Co.

DOTY, Job P. to Sarah R. Ford - issued July 31, 1839, m. by:
W. Hand, J. P., August 4, 1839, DICKSON Co.

DOUGAN, Robert to Elizabeth Scoby - issued October 7, 1796, Bondsman:
Wilson Cage, SUMNER Co.

DOUGAN, Timothy to Briggett Dorrell - issued October 21, 1854, m. by:
Rev. John M. Jacquet October 24, 1854, FRANKLIN Co.

DOUGHERTY, M. L. to Maria P. Kinney - issued April 29, 1846, m. by:
Richard P. Miles, Bishop of Nashville, April 30, 1846, DAVIDSON Co.

DOUGHTON, Charles G. to Sarah W. Hodges - issued December 29, 1846,
Bondsman: W. C. Doughton, m. by: J. H. Batson, J. P., December 29,
1846, MONTGOMERY Co.

DOUGHTON, Malden to Martha Ann Warden - issued September 22, 1845,
Bondsman: James Bowe, m. by: J. B. Green, J. P., September 24,
1845, MONTGOMERY Co.

DOUGHTRY, Bryan to Lydia Dotson - issued June 3, 1839, m. by:
Isaiah Warren, J. P., June 12, 1839, ROBERTSON Co.

DOUGHTY, Benjamin to Polly Kemp - issued September 20, 1820, Bondsman:
James Kemp, m. by: P. Nance, J. P., KNOX Co.

DOUGHTY, Henry to Mary Axum - issued December 25, 1832, Bondsman:
William Stratton, SUMNER Co.

DOUGHTY, James to Elizabeth Brown - issued March 11, 1828, Bondsman:
John Alderson, m. by: Robert Norvell March 11, 1828, SUMNER Co.

DOUGHTY, Lorenza to Sarah Cooksey - issued August 3, 1831, Bondsman:
James A. Doughty, WILSON Co.

DOUGHTY, Reuben to Margaret R. Cocke - issued December 15, 1832,
Bondsman: Thos. Martin, KNOX Co.

DOUGHTY, William to Betsy Springs - issued September 8, 1829, Bondsman:
David Eckols, WILSON Co.

DOUGLAS, Alfred H. to Marilla Miles - issued December 15, 1845, m. by:
C. Rooker, L. E. Meth. Ch., December 18, 1845 (1846?), DICKSON Co.

DOUGLAS, Edward L. to Delia Douglas - issued January 26, 1827, m. by:
Thos. Calhoon, V. D. M., WILSON Co.

DOUGLAS, Elisha to Mary Martin - issued February 6, 1856, m. by:
H. Shackleford, J. P., February 6, 1856, COFFEE Co.

DOUGLAS, Eliza to William Dixon - GREENE Co.

DOUGLAS, Ennis to Matilda Corley - issued November 14, 1821, Bondsman:
James Browning, m. by: Richard Johnson, WILSON Co.

DOUGLAS, George to Polly White - issued December 28, 1826, Bondsman:
M. C. Abston, m. by: C. Cram December 28, 1826, SUMNER Co.

DOUGLAS, H. L. to Zuritha Allcorn - issued August 19, 1817, Bondsman: Harry Cage, WILSON Co.

DOUGLAS, H. L. to M. B. Hall - m. by: G. C. Pitts July 5, 1836, SUMNER Co.

DOUGLAS, Ila to Elizabeth Harris - issued January 5, 1824, Bondsman: F. G. Crutcher, m. by: William Algood January 8, 1824, WILSON Co.

DOUGLAS, Isaac C. to Eliza W. Baker - issued June 1, 1820, Bondsman: Wm. Trousdale, SUMNER Co.

DOUGLAS, John to Rachael West - issued February 13, 1827, Bondsman: Samuel West, m. by: James Kennon, M. G., February 13, 1827, GRAINGER Co.

DOUGLAS, Martin to Nancy Masey - issued August 3, 1820, Bondsman: John Springs, WILSON Co.

DOUGLAS, Martin to Margaret Warren - issued November 25, 1827, Bondsman: John Douglas, SUMNER Co.

DOUGLAS, Norval to Priscilla Cage - issued January 31, 1826, Bondsman: John F. Fulton, SUMNER Co.

DOUGLAS, Robert B. to Delia Mitchell - m. by: A. K. Duval December 14, 1835, SUMNER Co.

DOUGLAS, Rodham to Elizabeth Gillespie - issued January 6, 1819, m. by: H. Trott, J. P., January 6, 1819, RUTHERFORD Co.

DOUGLAS, Rodham to Sally Peason - issued June 23, 1827, Bondsman: William Webb, RUTHERFORD Co.

DOUGLAS, S. to Martha Ikard - issued December 30, 1870, FRANKLIN Co.

DOUGLAS, Thomas to Rebecca E. Birdwell - issued March 6, 1857, m. by: James W. Williams, M. G., March 6, 1857, COFFEE Co.

DOUGLAS, Thos. C. to F. A. Cantrell - m. by: J. W. Hall July 13, 1837, SUMNER Co.

DOUGLAS, William C. to Lucy Ann Sidwell - issued January 12, 1836, m. by: Arch B. Oneal, WILSON Co.

DOUGLAS, Willie J. to Eliza Watkins - issued June 13, 1820, Bondsman: Cullen Edwards, m. by: Edw. Douglas June 13, 1820, SUMNER Co.

DOUGLAS, Young M. to Bennetta E. Rawlings - m. by: J. W. Hall January 16, 1834, SUMNER Co.

DOUGLASS, Alexander to Rhoda Ruth - issued November 13, 1820, m. by: Sam. Sample November 14, 1820, KNOX Co.

DOUGLASS, Alfred M. to Cherry Ferrell - issued April 26, 1817, Bondsman: James Stratton, SUMNER Co.

DOUGLASS, Berryman to Susannah Bailes - issued October 19, 1808, Bondsman: Anthony Underwood, Witness: John F. Jack, J. P., GRAINGER Co.

DOUGLASS, Elmore to Eliza Fulton - issued October 22, 1818, Bondsman: A. Donnell, m. by: T. B. Craghead October 22, 1818, SUMNER Co.

DOUGLASS, Harry C. to Elizabeth Elliott - issued December 18, 1828, Bondsman: Edwd Stratton, m. by: F. E. Pitts December 18, 1828, SUMNER Co.

DOUGLASS, Harry L. to Priscilla Shelby - issued January 8, 1811, Bondsman: John H. Bowen, SUMNER Co.

DOUGLASS, J. S. to Elizabeth Morris - issued April 11, 1866, FRANKLIN Co.

DOUGLASS, James to Nancy Dodson - issued November 28, 1811, Bondsman: Abram Trigg, SUMNER Co.

DOUGLASS, James H. to Margaret Rodgers - issued March 8, 1838, Bondsman: Ramsey L. Mayson, m. by: John Beard, M. G., WILSON Co.

DOUGLASS, Jesse to Patsey Cunning - issued September 8, 1813, Bondsman: William Ring and Robert Payne, SUMNER Co.

DOUGLASS, Jno. to Margaret King - issued April 5, 1836, m. by: James H. Gass, M. G., April 7, 1836, KNOX Co.

DOUGLASS, John A. to D. D. Laughinhouse - issued December 13, 1854, m. by: Jno. G. Biddle, M. G., December 13, 1854, FRANKLIN Co.

DOUGLASS, Lishey to Alcy Rankins - issued March 27, 1840, m. by: Stephen Lytle, Test: Smith Criddle Me'th Preacher, March 27, 1840, DAVIDSON Co.

DOUGLASS, Reubin to Betsy Edwards - issued January 25, 1791, Bondsman: Edward Douglass, SUMNER Co.

DOUGLASS, Robert G. to Elizabeth Blythe - issued May 20, 1830, Bondsman: John P. Tyree, m. by: John R. Bain May 20, 1830, SUMNER Co.

DOUGLASS, Thomas to Betsy Bryan - issued February 10, 1816, m. by: John McCampbell, V. D. M., February 15, 1816, KNOX Co.

DOUGLASS, William to Elizabeth Martin - issued December 23, 1793, Bondsman: Thomas Douglass, Witness: Chas. McClung, C. K. C., KNOX Co.

DOUGLASS, William H. to Sally Edwards - issued January 21, 1810, Bondsman: John D. Gillespie, SUMNER Co.

DOUTHET, Stephen E. to Anne Brizendine - issued September 13, 1832, Bondsman: John P. Douthet, m. by: Robert Norvell September 13, 1832, SUMNER Co.

DOUTHETT, S. E. to M. B. Edwards - issued February 17, 1840, m. by: E. A. Williams, P. G., February 27, 1840, ROBERTSON Co.

DOVE, James to Polly Damewood - issued August 10, 1825, Bondsman: Nicholas Gibbs, m. by: Wm. Sawyers, J. P., Augsut 15, 1825, KNOX Co.

DOVE, William to Delia Clapp - issued November 5, 1827, Bondsman: Henry Carr, GRAINGER Co.

DOVER, J. D. to Jane Gentry - issued March 2, 1841, m. by: Banja. Rawls, G. M., March 3, 1841, ROBERTSON Co.

DOWD, John to Jean Powell - October 3, 1806, WILLIAMSON Co.

DOWDY, Allen to Martha Tucker - February 21, 1816, WILLIAMSON Co.

DOWDY, James G. to Martha Powers - issued April 10, 1848, Bondsman: Robert C. Powers, m. by: Allison Akin, M. G., April 12, 1848, MONTGOMERY Co.

DOWDY, Jesse W. to Mary Ann Powers - issued January 3, 1842, STEWART Co.

DOWDY, John C. to Lucinda Martin - issued July 28, 1849, Bondsman: Robert C. Powers, m. by: J. Moore, M. G., August 2, 1849, MONTGOMERY Co.

DOWDY, Micajah to Rebecca Tucker - November 20, 1810, WILLIAMSON Co.

DOWDY, Ureah G. to Mary Jane Washburn - issued March 6, 1847, STEWART Co.

DOWEL, David to Elizabeth Shook - issued August 13, 1813, Bondsman: Chas. B. Stubbins, SUMNER Co.

DOWELL, Coleby to Sally Elliott - November 14, 1815, KNOX Co.

DOWELL, David to Mary E. King - issued April 29, 1865, Bondsman: John Harrison, m. by: Samuel Baker, M. G., April 29, 1865, LAWRENCE Co.

DOWELL, Elisha to Elizabeth Barbee - issued February 5, 1827, Bondsman: Mathew Cartwright, WILSON Co.

DOWELL, James to Catherine Tomlinson - issued September 3, 1838, m. by: Jesse Edwards, Minister, September 3, 1838, STEWART Co.

DOWELL, John to Frances Stewart - issued March 19, 1836, Bondsman: Demcy Ashford, m. by: D. Ashford March 19, 1836, SUMNER Co.

DOWELL, John C. to Sally Mobley - issued December 26, 1846, m. by: William Ellis, J. P., December 26, 1846, STEWART Co.

DOWELL, John H. to Elizabeth S. Weatherhead - m. by: Jonathan Wiseman October 30, 1837, SUMNER Co.

DOWELL, Tandy to Elizabeth Childress - issued February 14, 1833, m. by: Elijah Johnson, J. P., February 17, 1833, KNOX Co.

DOWLAN, M. V. to E. R. H. Williams - issued September 6, 1852, m. by: Benj. Rawls, M. G., ROBERTSON Co.

DOWLEN, John G. to Rachel Carter - issued June 30, 1841, m. by: A. Justice, J. P., ROBERTSON Co.

DOWLER, Wm. to Susan McCaughen - issued March 1, 1830, Bondsman: M. M. Swan, m. by: Sam'l. Fleming, J. P., March 1, 1830, KNOX Co.

DOWLIN, James to Elizabeth Lacey - issued March 23, 1827, m. by: Mordecai Yarnell March 29, 1827, KNOX Co.

DOWNING, William D. V. to Nancy B. Campbell - issued October 12, 1842, m. by: T. J. Edgar October 13, 1842, DAVIDSON Co.

DOWNS, Ambrose to Eliza Lassiter - m. by: Stokley Vinson September 8, 1835, SUMNER Co.

DOWNS, Augustine to Polly Tilley - issued December 24, 1821, Bondsman: C. H. May, m. by: Thos. Anderson, J. P., December 24, 1821, SUMNER Co.

DOWNS, Ballard to Polly Joiner - issued July 18, 1827, Bondsman: Wm. Twopence, m. by: C. Crain July 18, 1827, SUMNER Co.

DOWNS, David to Clarissa McClain - issued October 13, 1847, m. by: B. Herndon, J. P., November 4, 1847, STEWART Co.

DOWNS, John to Clarissa Rutland - issued February 9, 1821, Bondsman: M. Anderson, SUMNER Co.

DOWNS, Thomas to Sally Soper - issued December 28, 1825, Bondsman: Samuel Works, m. by: Thos. Anderson, J. P., December 28, 1825, SUMNER Co.

DOWNS, Thomas W. to Mary A. Phelps - issued July 22, 1841, m. by: John Corbitt, J. P., July 22, 1841, DAVIDSON Co.

DOWNS, Tilley to Jane Robertson - issued December 23, 1823, Bondsman: Baley May, m. by: Thos. Anderson, J. P., December 23, 1823, SUMNER Co.

DOWNS, William to Elizabeth Soper - m. by: Elijah Boddie February 11, 1833, SUMNER Co.

DOWNS, William to Nancy Ferguson - issued May 6, 1834, Bondsman: John W. Spradling, m. by: Henry K. Winbourn May 6, 1834, SUMNER Co.

DOWNS, Jr., Wm. to Emeline Ralls - issued February 3, 1844, m. by: B. Herndon, J. P., February 22, 1844, STEWART Co.

DOWNS, William H. to Catharine Scruggs - issued May 12, 1841, m. by: J. B. Knowles May 12, 1841, DAVIDSON Co.

DOWNUM, James L. to Lucinda Vincent - issued March 17, 1847, m. by: J. W. Spearman, M. G., March 21, 1847, FRANKLIN Co.

DOWNUM, John R. to Mary F. Parks - issued December 8, 1846, m. by: John W. Spearman, M. G., December 22, 1846, FRANKLIN Co.

DOWNUM, Richard S. to Julia Ann Baggett - issued July 16, 1846, m. by: M. McQueen, J. P., July 16, 1846, FRANKLIN Co.

DOWNUM, Sidney to Lucinda Farris - issued December 23, 1858, m. by: J. T. Slatter, J. P., December 23, 1858, FRANKLIN Co.

DOWSON, James to Tomlin Seals - issued December 24, 1845, Bondsman: Sam'l McFall, MONTGOMERY Co.

DOXEY, Jeremiah to Hannah Wise - issued August 28, 1820, Bondsman: John L. Doxey, SUMNER Co.

DOXEY, John to Rebecca Daugherty - issued May 1, 1811, Bondsman: Stephen Doxey, SUMNER Co.

DOYAL, C. to E. Phepps - issued December 21, 1849, m. by: John Crafford, J. P., ROBERTSON Co.

DOYAL, William R. to Herriet Choat - issued April 25, 1849, m. by: John Crafford, J. P., April 29, 1849, ROBERTSON Co.

DOYALL (Doyle?), Isaac to Jane (?) Capshaw - December 24, 1813, KNOX Co.

DOYEL, James H. to Polly Ann Choat - issued December 30, 1850, m. by: John Crafford, J. P., January 3, 1851, ROBERTSON Co.

DOYLE, David to Sally Howser - issued May 3, 1823, Bondsman: Isaac Doyle, m. by: Robert McBath, J. P., May 5, 1823, KNOX Co.

DOYLE, Isaac to Peggy Campbell - issued December 14, 1826, Bondsman: Geo. M. White, KNOX Co.

DOYLE, James P. to Mahala Childress - issued August 29, 1833, m. by: Elijah Johnson, J. P., August 29, 1833, KNOX Co.

DOYLE, John to Eve Formwalt - issued November 12, 1824, Bondsman: Pryor Lea, m. by: Tho. H. Nelson November 12, 1824, KNOX Co.

DOYLE, John to Polly Thomas - issued December 16, 1834, Bondsman: Jno. Brown, KNOX Co.

DOYLE, Thomas to F. V. Williams - issued September 6, 1860, m. by: J. M. Speer, J. P., ROBERTSON Co.

DOYLE, William to Catharine Thomas - issued November 25, 1824, m. by: Geo. Atkin, M. G., November 25, 1824, KNOX Co.

DOYNE, James to Mary Woolsy - February 26, 1798, Security: Daniel Matthews and Stephen Woolsy, GREENE Co.

DOZIER, Cheatham to Virginia F. Starks - issued September 1, 1857, m. by: H. H. Orndorff, J. P., ROBERTSON Co.

DOZIER, Danul to Jude Maxey - issued August 25, 1813, KNOX Co.

DOZIER, David to Elizabeth Demoss - issued August 20, 1842, DAVIDSON Co.

DOZIER, Enoch T. to Louisa Ann Carney - issued August 15, 1846, m. by:
W. Crockett, J. P., September 6, 1846, DAVIDSON Co.

DOZIER, Enock to Judith Gupton - issued September 6, 1842, m. by:
T. W. Shearon, J. P., September 8, 1842, DAVIDSON Co.

DOZIER, Jasper N. to Nancy Fossett - issued July 28, DAVIDSON Co.

DOZIER, Peter to Rebeka Harris - issued August 22, 1821, m. by:
John Haynie, M. G., August 22, 1821, KNOX Co.

DOZIER, R. P. to Martha Holland - issued January 26, 1853, m. by:
John Gammon, M. G., January 27, 1853, ROBERTSON Co.

DOZIER, William N. to Sarah Ivans - issued October 14, 1840, m. by:
Wm. Shelton, J. P., November 15, 1840, DAVIDSON Co.

DRAIN, John to Sarah Henderson - issued December 5, 1824, Bondsman:
Hiram Henderson, Witness: Wm. Swan, KNOX Co.

DRAIN, John to Sallie Henderson - December 5, 1826 (?), KNOX Co.

DRAIN, Thomas H. to Malinda Summer - issued April 2, 1840, m. by:
Isaac Steele, ROBERTSON Co.

DRAKE, Albrittiam M. to Eliz. A. Hancock - issued October 20, 1841,
m. by: U. Young, J. P., December 26, 1841, ROBERTSON Co.

DRAKE, B. C. to Mary Jane Chandler - issued July 21, 1840, m. by:
David Abernathy, J. P., July 21, 1840, DAVIDSON Co.

DRAKE, Banj. F. to Julina Green - issued January 22, 1850, m. by:
Benjamin Rawls, M. G., ROBERTSON Co.

DRAKE, Carter to Hettey Gamble - issued March 13, 1854, m. by:
M. G. Brocket, M. G., March 14, 1854, VAN BUREN Co.

DRAKE, Charles to Clarisa James - issued October 20, 1804, Bondsman:
Jesse James, GRAINGER Co.

DRAKE, Elijah to Sarah Carter - issued December 12, 1842, VAN BUREN Co.

DRAKE, Elijah B. to Sarah M. Rowlstone - issued September 23, 1840,
Bondsman: James B. Rutland, m. by: Geo. Donnell, M. G., WILSON Co.

DRAKE, J. B. to A. F. Gooch - issued May 15, 1862, Bondsman:
J. W. Reavis, m. by: C. J. Herrin, J. J., May 18, 1862, LAWRENCE Co.

DRAKE, J. M. to Mary Wilson - issued February 11, 1861, m. by:
G. W. Trenary February 14, 1861, ROBERTSON Co.

DRAKE, Jacob to Polly Nolen - issued November 13, 1802, m. by:
John Love, Esq., KNOX Co.

DRAKE, James C. to Jane Ozment - issued December 6, 1832, Bondsman:
James Hancock, m. by: Levi Holloway, J. P., WILSON Co.

DRAKE, John to Fanny Damewood - issued August 27, 1835, Bondsman:
Wm. Rutherford, m. by: James Crippen, J. P., August 27, 1835,
KNOX Co.

DRAKE, John T. to Mary A. Newman - issued January 10, 1854, FRANKLIN Co.

DRAKE, R. N. to Elizabeth G. Ross - issued December 8, 1852, m. by:
J. M. Nolen, M. G., ROBERTSON Co.

DRAKE, William B. to Ann Robertson - issued August 14, 1828, Bondsman: Thomas K. Wynne, m. by: Ezekiel Cloyd, M. G., August 15, 1828, WILSON Co.

DRAKE, William P. to Margaret Herod - issued September 14, 1838, DAVIDSON Co.

DRANE, H. D. to Harriett Traughber - issued July 27, 1859, m. by: E. T. Hart August 2, 1859, ROBERTSON Co.

DRANE, T. J. to Nancy C. Gorham - issued April 25, 1861, m. by: E. Burr, J. P., ROBERTSON Co.

DRAPER, Daniel to Betsey Joyner - issued October 19, 1816, Bondsman: Thomas Shaw, m. by: John McMurtry, J. P., October 19, 1816, SUMNER Co.

DRAPER, Noah to Charity Arnold - issued October 26, 1848, m. by: Isaac Steel October 27, 1848, ROBERTSON Co.

DRAPER, Solomon to Isabella Hinds - issued September 6, 1827, m. by: Sam'l. Love, M. G., September 6, 1827, KNOX Co.

DRAUGHN, Wm. to Mary Murphy - issued November 30, 1848, m. by: T. B. Mathews, J. P., ROBERTSON Co.

DRAUGHON, G. W. to Piety Pittman - issued June 15, 1860, m. by: J. M. Speer, J. P., June 16, 1860, ROBERTSON Co.

DRAUGHON, Geo. E. to Tabitha Couts - issued November 8, 1842, m. by: W. Seal, J. P., ROBERTSON Co.

DRAUGHON, H. C. to Susan M. Ogg - issued September 5, 1857, m. by: Jeremiah Batts, J. P., September 6, 1857, ROBERTSON Co.

DRAUGHON, James to Avalina Frey - issued March 27, 1850, m. by: T. B. Mathews, J. P., ROBERTSON Co.

DRAUGHON, James W. to Nancy Huey - issued November 7, 1839, m. by: Geo. Childress, J. P., ROBERTSON Co.

DRAUGHON, Jesse B. to Miss B. A. Batts - issued April 10, 1860, m. by: J. W. Smith, J. P., April 16, 1860, ROBERTSON Co.

DRAUGHON, M. L. to S. H. Murphy - issued April 3, 1850, m. by: Tho. Farmer, J. P., ROBERTSON Co.

DRAUGHON, M. W. to P. B. Watson - issued May 5, 1852, m. by: Robert Draughon, J. P., ROBERTSON Co.

DRAUGHON, M. W. to Olive Peteway - issued May 12, 1855, m. by: Jas. Woodard May 13, 1855, ROBERTSON Co.

DRAUGHON, Mathew J. to Polly A. Solomon - issued December 5, 1850, m. by: Thos. B. Mathews, ROBERTSON Co.

DRAUGHON, Jr., Miles to Caroline Ann Clark - issued October 2, 1834, m. by: M. Powell, J. P., ROBERTSON Co.

DRAUGHON, Miles T. to Loretta Solomon - issued August 26, 1854, m. by: G. Benton, J. P., August 27, 1854, ROBERTSON Co.

DRAUGHON, Robert V. to Nancy Ann Cohea - issued September 29, 1855, m. by: Jesse B. White, J. P., September 30, 1855, ROBERTSON Co.

DRAUGHON, W. C. to E. H. Frey - issued August 28, 1851, m. by: T. B. Mathews, J. P., ROBERTSON Co.

DRAUGHON, William to Martha J. Ruffin - issued February 24, 1842, m. by: Robert Draughon, J. P., ROBERTSON Co.

DRAUGHON, Willie L. to C. L. Clark - issued June 11, 1854, m. by:
B. Rawls, M. G., ROBERTSON Co.

DRENNAN, David to Sarah Phillips - issued March 10, 1838, DAVIDSON Co.

DRENNAN, John to Mary Robinson - issued October 2, 1829, Bondsman:
William Arnold, m. by: Henry Ridley, J. P., October 10, 1829,
RUTHERFORD Co.

DRENNAN, John to Polly Bell - issued February 6, 1836, m. by:
G. A. Huddleston, J. P., February 25, 1836, WILSON Co.

DRENNAN, Joseph A. to Manerva C. Sanders - issued February 11, 1833,
Bondsman: Joseph Robertson, m. by: Thos. Sanders, J. P.,
February 11, 1833, RUTHERFORD Co.

DRENNEN, Thomas to Evaline Miles - Bondsman: John W. Huhueley, WILSON Co.

DRENNON, James to Fanny Daveult - issued June 21, 1809, Bondsman:
Mathias Devault, WILSON Co.

DRENNON, James to Cynthia Davis - issued September 12, 1834, Bondsman:
Thomas Partlow, m. by: John Beard, M. G., September 18, 1834,
WILSON Co.

DRENNON, James to Deletha Shelton - issued February 24, 1835, Bondsman:
Danl. N. Alsup, m. by: Joshua Woollen, M. G., February 24, 1835,
WILSON Co.

DRENNON, John to Rebecah A. Brown - issued July 31, 1830, Bondsman:
William Rice, WILSON Co.

DRENNON, Jonathan to Lucy G. Liggon - issued November 14, 1825,
Bondsman: Josiah Ligon, m. by: Jas. Drennon, J. P., November 18,
1825, WILSON Co.

DRENNON, Joseph to Lucinda Drennon - issued June 28, 1824, Bondsman:
James Drennon, m. by: James Drennon, J. P., WILSON Co.

DRENNON, William to Hetty Eddins - issued December 14, 1820, Bondsman:
Lewis Wright, WILSON Co.

DRENNON, William H. to ____(?) - issued May 3, 1832, Bondsman:
Albert Jones, WILSON Co.

DRESSER, Henry to Nancy Irvin - issued May 10, 1805, Bondsman:
Alexander Hamelton, GRAINGER Co.

DREW, James to Rebecca Brown - issued February 22, 1812, Bondsman:
Moses Brown, WILSON Co.

DREW, Jonathan to Jane Martin - issued September 1, 1821, m. by:
John Hoover, J. P., September 7, 1821, RUTHERFORD Co.

DRISKELL, Goerge to Elizabeth Campbell - issued December 24, 1818,
Bondsman: Jacob Campbell, RUTHERFORD Co.

DRISKELL, Warner E. to Mary E. Metcalf - issued November 13, 1852,
m. by: Henry Larkin November 14, 1852, FRANKLIN Co.

DRISKILL, G. W. to M. H. Driskill - issued August 26, 1849, m. by:
J. C. Bryan, J. P., August 26, 1849, MONTGOMERY Co.

DRIVER, Henry A. to Mahala Gipson - issued January 23, 1845, m. by:
D. D. Smith, J. P., January 26, 1845, FRANKLIN Co.

DRIVER, Joel to Louisa I. Winn - m. by: Richard Johnson December 27,
1833, SUMNER Co.

DRIVER, John to Mary Campbell - issued December 17, 1829, Bondsman:
Fisher Cloucess, m. by: Wilson Hearn, WILSON Co.

DRIVER, Jordan to Patsey Williams - issued March 24, 1834, Bondsman:
James Driver, m. by: Micajah Estes, M. G., March 31, 1834,
WILSON Co.

DRIVER, Jordan to Dicy Vaughan - issued February 12, 1840, m. by:
Jesse Graham, M. G., February 13, 1840, FRANKLIN Co.

DRIVER, William to Sarah Jane Park - issued January 12, 1838, m. by:
J. Thomas Wheat, M. G., Rc. of Cr. Ch., January 13, 1838,
DAVIDSON Co.

DRUMHELN, Nicholas L. to Eliza Hollis - issued April 7, 1827, Bondsman:
James M. Hollis, SUMNER Co.

DRUMING (?), Margaret to James Johnson - GREENE Co.

DRUMWRIGHT, George M. to Harriet Mustian - issued December 21, 1829,
Bondsman: Richard R. Rainey, RUTHERFORD Co.

DRURY, Daniel to Bridgett Epps - issued September 22, 1827, Bondsman:
Curry McGrier, RUTHERFORD Co.

DRURY, Richard C. to Martha L. McBride - February 1, 1813, WILLIAMSON Co.

DRYDEN, Nathaniel to Nancy Beggart - December 6, 1810, WILLIAMSON Co.

DUBOISE, Andrew to Mary E. Furman - issued March 27, 1845, FRANKLIN Co.

DUBOISE, James to Margaret Duboise - issued February 19, 1816, m. by:
Thomas Berry, J. P., February 20, 1816, RUTHERFORD Co.

DUBOSE, R. M. to Bessie Egleston - issued December 16, 1873, m. by:
W. P. DuBose December 18, 1873, FRANKLIN Co.

DUCKWORTH, E. L. to Ulis Elps - issued September 23, 1867, m. by:
J. Dean, M. G., September 26, 1867, FRANKLIN Co.

DUCKWORTH, J. W. to Gustin J. Huggins - issued December 5, 1870,
m. by: H. J. Byrom December 7, 1870, FRANKLIN Co.

DUCKWORTH, Samuel to Luvina Davenport - issued May 15, 1839, FRANKLIN Co.

DUCKWORTH, Wm. to Polly Hill - issued March 7, 1839, Bondsman:
Jno. Duckworth, m. by: Mark Renfrow, J. P., March 7, 1839, MEIGS Co.

DUDLEY, Francis N. B. to Nancy Myers - issued November 10, 1829, m. by:
Stephen Foster November, 1829, KNOX Co.

DUDLEY, Francis N. B. to Polly Murphy - issued December 16, 1836,
Bondsman: Wm. F. Edmonds, m. December 27, 1836, KNOX Co.

DUDLEY, John A. to Katherine Haydon - issued August 30, 1842, m. by:
U. Young, J. P., ROBERTSON Co.

DUDLEY, N. B. to Miss M. A. Ross - issued December 12, 1849, Bondsman:
R. McMordie, m. by: R. Ross, P. G., December 13, 1849, MONTGOMERY Co.

DUDLEY, Pullen A. to Lucyanah Graham - issued July 31, 1845, DICKSON Co.

DUDLEY, William to Jane Smith - issued January 23, 1840, Bondsman:
J. Organ, m. by: J. Organ, J. P., WILSON Co.

DUDLEY, Woodson to City Hearn - issued March 24, 1829, Bondsman:
Rolley Organ, WILSON Co.

DUE, Perry to Marg Smith - November 5, 1807, WILLIAMSON Co.

DUER, John A. to Mary A. Bigbee - issued August 20, 1840, m. by:
A. B. Young, J. P., ROBERTSON Co.

DUERSON, A. L. to Mary L. Leach - issued January 29, 1852, Bondsman:
Samuel Baker, m. by: Samuel Baker, M. G., January 29, 1852,
MONTGOMERY Co.

DUFF, Betsey to William Tombs - MAURY Co.

DUFF, Dennis to Nancy Jane Clark - issued November 28, 1842, m. by:
Charles Brooks, M. G., November 30, 1842, STEWART Co.

DUFF, Hugh A. to Sarah Brown - issued March 8, 1834, Bondsman:
William G. Eaton, GRAINGER Co.

DUFF, James to Elizabeth Easley - issued October 28, 1834, Bondsman:
Joshua Curl, m. by: Levi Satterfield, M. G., GRAINGER Co.

DUFF, Nathaniel L. to Eliza Jane Sullivan - issued January 12, 1846,
DICKSON Co.

DUFF, Thos. to Lela Boren - September 28, 1807, WILLIAMSON Co.

DUFFEE, Thomas to Nancy B. Glass - issued November 15, 1837, Bondsman:
Elijah Cason, m. by: James Bond, V. D. M., November 16, 1837,
WILSON Co.

DUFFEL, W. R. to Jane Ross - issued June 9, 1842, m. June 12, 1842,
STEWART Co.

DUFFEL, William R. to Nancy Hungerford - May 8, 1811, WILLIAMSON Co.

DUFFER, Ambrose to Mildred Flipping - m. by: John H. Robertson
November 9, 1837, SUMNER Co.

DUFFER, Auston to Sally Hunt - issued October 8, 1825, m. by: J. Davis,
J. P., October 8, 1825, SUMNER Co.

DUFFER, Edward to Emily T. McClary - m. by: Taylor G. Gilliam March 30,
1837, SUMNER Co.

DUFFER, Edward to Hiron Wilson - issued December 24, 1849, m. by:
J. C. Montgomery, J. P., December 25, 1849, FRANKLIN Co.

DUFFIL, Joseph A. to Mary A. Summers - issued February 7, 1846,
STEWART Co.

DUFFIELD, James to Katy Whurley - issued October 27, 1818, m. by:
John Bayless, J. P., October 29, 1818, KNOX Co.

DUFFIELD, S. L. to Marry Burns - issued July 22, 1865, Bondsman:
J. B. Clayton, LAWRENCE Co.

DUFFY, Francis to Pamelia Parker - issued November 10, 1824, Bondsman:
Charles Morgan, m. by: John Wiseman, M. G., November 10, 1824,
SUMNER Co.

DUGAN, Robert to Margaret Dunn - March 7, 1792, John Nelson, GREENE Co.

DUGER, Thomas M. to Martha Glenn - February 15, 1861, m. by:
James Kirkland, M. G., GILES Co.

DUGGAN, Henry to Ellen Winsett - issued June 25, 1863, Bondsman:
John Fagan, BEDFORD Co.

DUGGER, Allen to Susan Looney - issued July 28, 1830, Bondsman:
Flood Dugger, m. July 28, 1830, SUMNER Co.

DUGGER, Elvin to Amanda Jorey (Josey) - issued August 17, 1836,
Bondsman: John Morris, SUMNER Co.

DUGGER, Flood to Polly Bruce - issued August 29, 1810, Bondsman:
Jesse Skeen

DUGGER, James to Kesiah Smith - issued July 28, 1804, Bondsman:
Dred Dugger, SUMNER Co.

DUGGER, Jarroth to Polly McAdams - issued August 20, 1811, Bondsman:
Benjamin Taylor and Flood Dugger, SUMNER Co.

DUGGER, Leonard to Elizabeth Taylor - issued November 27, 1800,
Bondsman: Whitehead Joiner, SUMNER Co.

DUGGER, Luke to Isbel Gibs - issued April 26, 1800, Bondsman:
Isaac Lowell, SUMNER Co.

DUGGER, Shadrach S. to Martha Jane Lanere - July 18, 1850, m. by:
Joseph Brown, M. G., GILES Co.

DUGGER, Wesley to Charlotte Dugger - issued July 10, 1816, Bondsman:
Leonard Dugger, SUMNER Co.

DUGGER, Wilie to Cynthia Stanley - issued October 20, 1829, Bondsman:
Flood Dugger, SUMNER Co.

DUGGER, Wm. D. to Ann Q. Mitchell - issued January 7, 1845, m. by:
Wm. A. Whitsett January 9, 1845, DAVIDSON Co.

DUKE, Bennett C. to Martha Jones - issued July 24, 1838, m. by:
D. S. Ford, J. P., July 24, 1838, DICKSON Co.

DUKE, Green to Keziah Timmons - December 1, 1816, WILLIAMSON Co.

DUKE, Green W. to Rhoda Ann Simpkins - issued January 8, 1840, m. by:
J. B. McFerrin, M. G., January 9, 1840, DAVIDSON Co.

DUKE, James to Celia Garrett - issued May 12, 1836, Bondsman:
John Duke, SUMNER Co.

DUKE, John to Susannah Easely - issued July 14, 1803

DUKE, John to Elizabeth Bobo - issued January 23, 1838, m. by:
William L. Perry, J. P., ROBERTSON Co.

DUKE, Littleton C. to Milany Scott - issued October 6, 1830, Bondsman:
John H. Vowell, m. by: James Foster, J. P., October 7, 1830,
WILSON Co.

DUKE, Mathew to Sirena West - issued February 17, 1843, m. by:
James Yarbough, J. P., February 17, 1843, DAVIDSON Co.

DUKE, Richard to Hanna King - issued September 2, 1798, Bondsman:
James King, Witness: Sm'l Yancey, GRAINGER Co.

DUKE, Sion to Saly Bradshaw - issued December 12, 1823, Bondsman:
James Drake, m. by: Elijah Maddox, M. G., December 18, 1823,
WILSON Co.

DUKE, Thomas to Sally Boyd - issued August 5, 1820, Bondsman:
Eusebues Stone, m. by: Isaac Lindsey, E. M. E. C., August 5, 1820,
SUMNER Co.

DUKE, Wilkins E. to Louisa Yarrell - issued November 15, 1853, Bondsman:
Livingston Lindsay, m. by: John Ferguson, M. G., November 15, 1853,
MONTGOMERY Co.

DUKES, Jonathan to Holly Dobson - issued October 29, 1831, Bondsman:
James Edwards, m. by: Geo. Clark, J. P., October 31, 1831,
WILSON Co.

DUKES, Martin to Sarah E. Couburn - issued October 6, 1873, m. by:
J. L. Brown, M. G., October 8, 1873, FRANKLIN Co.

DUKEY, John to Nancy Page - January 19, 1807, WILLIAMSON Co.

DULANEY, Elizabeth to David Crowley (?) - GREENE Co.

DULASS, William to Caty Garrison - issued February 3, 1812, Bondsman:
Daniel Montgomery, SUMNER Co.

DULIN, H. H. to Martha A. Turman - issued May 30, 1860, m. by:
John T. Slatter, J. P., May 30, 1860, FRANKLIN Co.

DUNAHOO, Martin to Cynthia Dyer - issued February 19, 1834, Bondsman:
William Dunahoo, GRAINGER Co.

DUNAVANT, Joseph H. to Susannah Stuart - December 2, 1859, m. by:
William Peaton, J. P., GILES Co.

DUNAVANT, Pleasant to Mary Conoway - issued August 8, 1840, m. by:
John Corbitt, J. P., August 9, 1840, DAVIDSON Co.

DUNAWAY, Drury to Mary Hoover - issued December 13, 1841, m. by:
Chas. W. Moorman, J. P., January 17, 1842, DAVIDSON Co.

DUNAWAY, Elijah to Ann Todd - issued December 27, 1836, RUTHERFORD Co.

DUNAWAY, Harvey to Tresa Beatman - issued July 30, 1848, m. by:
O. L. V. Schmittou, J. P., July 30, 1848, DICKSON Co.

DUNBAR, William to Nancy Rowlett - issued July 30, 1847, m. by:
Wm. E. Clopton, M. G., August 1, 1847, STEWART Co.

DUNCAN, A. N. M. to Hannah M. Saddler - issued November 5, 1859,
m. by: G. W. Jackson, Mins., November 6, 1859, COFFEE Co.

DUNCAN, Abner to Rody Robertson - issued January 19, 1813, Bondsman:
Thomas Breeden, GRAINGER Co.

DUNCAN, Addison to Margaret Caruth - issued December 9, 1833, m. by:
F. N. Jarratt, M. G., December 10, 1833, WILSON Co.

DUNCAN, Alexnd to Issabella McKelvey - issued December 11, 1865, m. by:
W. G. Guinn, M. G., December 14, 1865, FRANKLIN Co.

DUNCAN, Andrew J. to Dicy Duncan - issued December 23, 1839, m. by:
B. B. Knight, J. P., December 23, 1839, FRANKLIN Co.

DUNCAN, B. K. to Edney Sharp - issued November 25, 1869, m. by:
Thos. E. Muse, M. G., November 25, 1869, FRANKLIN Co.

DUNCAN, Benj. to Harriet Nance - issued May 19, 1828, m. by:
Isaac Anderson, V. D. M., May 20, 1828, KNOX Co.

DUNCAN, D. H. to Mary L. Drew - issued October 30, 1859, m. by:
G. W. Jackson, Mins., October 31, 1859, COFFEE Co.

DUNCAN, Daniel H. to Margaret J. Coulder - issued June 10, 1852,
Bondsman: Henry Shannon, MONTGOMERY Co.

DUNCAN, David to Sally Lovelady - February 2, 1789, Security:
Marshall Lovelady and Thos. Brumley, GREENE Co.

DUNCAN, Edwin to Aley Cooper - issued April 16, 1828, Bondsman:
John Coe, WILSON Co.

DUNCAN, Elijah to Eliza Jane Martin - issued December 10, 1853, Bondsman:
Thomas Lee, m. by: B. Bayliss, J. P., December 12, 1853,
MONTGOMERY Co.

DUNCAN, Fleming W. to Lucy Greer - m. by: Elisha Oglesby June 25, 1837, SUMNER Co.

DUNCAN, Frank to Augusta Mantlo - August 21, 1852, m. by: David Herring, J. P., ROBERTSON Co.

DUNCAN, G. W. to ___(?) Corn - October 7, 1869, FRANKLIN Co.

DUNCAN, George A. to May Poe - July 9, 1838, Bondsman: Henry Ward, WILSON Co.

DUNCAN, Henry to ___(?) Sooter - January 11, 1848, STEWART Co.

DUNCAN, Hiram to Sally Key - Bondsman: Ricely Defrees April 15, 1820, SUMNER Co.

DUNCAN, J. A. to Virginia Rose - issued July 2, 1866, m. by: W. G. Guinn July 5, 1867, FRANKLIN Co.

DUNCAN, James A. to Mary J. Browning - August 1, 1850, m. by: Jas. Woodard, J. P., ROBERTSON Co.

DUNCAN, Jane to Mordecai Yarnel - GREENE Co.

DUNCAN, John to Lucinda Center - issued August 2, 1823, m. by: John Crenshaw, J. P., August 2, 1823, SUMNER Co.

DUNCAN, John to ___(?) J. Kilmer - April 12, 1863, m. by: Jacob H. Pennington, J. P., LAWRENCE Co.

DUNCAN, John H. to Levina Simmons - issued January 18, 1838, m. by: L. V. Griffin, E. C. C., January 18, 1838, FRANKLIN Co.

DUNCAN, John H. to Almira Bankston - issued March 20, 1843, m. by: J. B. Walker, M. G., March 20, 1843, DAVIDSON Co.

DUNCAN, John H. to Missouria Hart - issued December 22, 1866, m. by: J. L. Payne, M. G., December 23, 1866, FRANKLIN Co.

DUNCAN, Joseph to Peggy Davis - November 12, 1812, WILLIAMSON Co.

DUNCAN, M. D. to Caroline T. Chambers - issued April 6, 1837, Bondsman: F. A. Duncan, m. by: Elisha Oglesby April 6, 1837, SUMNER Co.

DUNCAN, O. H. B. to Virginia Sharp - issued April 8, 1843, m. by: J. P. Walker April 9, 1843, FRANKLIN Co.

DUNCAN, Sarah to John Smith - GREENE Co.

DUNCAN, Thomas to Martha Jane Kenedy - issued November 24, 1847, m. by: Allen Elliott, L. E., December 1, 1847, STEWART Co.

DUNCAN, William to Eliza Potts - issued February 12, 1828, m. by: Mills, J. P., February 12, 1828, SUMNER Co.

DUNCAN, William to D. Powell - issued January 7, 1854, m. by: David Herring, J. P., January 8, 1854, ROBERTSON Co.

DUNCAN, William A. to Louisa Hampton - issued August 27, 1860, m. by: Wm. W. Conn, M. G., August 30, 1860, COFFEE Co.

DUNCAN, William W. H. to Nancy Jane Ashley - issued August 18, 1856, m. by: J. A. Brantley, J. P., August 18, 1856, COFFEE Co.

DUNCOMB, Benjamin to Vita Foster - issued December 23, 1821, m. by: William Hankins, J. P., December 25, 1821, GRAINGER Co.

DUNCOMB, Benjamin to Visa Fortner - Bondsman: William Corum, GRAINGER Co.

DUNCOMB, Philip to Polly Crawford - issued October 25, 1821, Bondsman:
Benjamin Duncomb, m. by: Robert Gaines, J. P., October 25, 1821,
GRAINGER Co.

DUNEGAN, Benjn. B. to Elizabeth Adcock - issued May 15, 1846, DICKSON Co.

DUNHAM, Dan'l A. to Leurani Adkins - August 2, 1805, WILLIAMSON Co.

DUNHAM, Philip to Nancy Price - issued May 25, 1821, Bondsman:
Lewis Riggs, GRAINGER Co.

DUNHAM, Thomas to Sarah Jones - May 18, 1816, Witness: David Roane,
KNOX Co.

DUNKEN, Amos to Christinia Derryberry - August 6, 1807, WILLIAMSON Co.

DUNKIN, Joseph to Rebeccka Vandergriff - issued August 6, 1799,
Bondsman: Edward Carmack, Witness: Sm'l Yancey, GRAINGER Co.

DUNLAP, Adam to Margery Porter - January 31, 1797, BLOUNT Co.

DUNLAP, Anderson to Betsy McBride - issued January 10, 1824, Bondsman:
James Sumter, KNOX Co.

DUNLAP, James to Margaret Palmer - December 26, 1798, Surety:
Stephen Gra e, BLOUNT Co.

DUNLAP, James to Elizabeth Casteele - issued April 8, 1812, KNOX Co.

DUNLAP, James to Sarah A. Legg - issued August 21, 1837, Bondsman:
M. M. Swan, KNOX Co.

DUNLAP, John C. to Elizabeth R. Jarrett - issued September 27, 1833,
Bondsman: Jesse Adcock, RUTHERFORD Co.

DUNLAP, Moses to Mary Robertson (Robison) - issued August 8, 1798,
Bondsman: David Low, KNOX Co.

DUNLAP, Nathaniel to Polly Montgomery - issued March 11, 1820, m. by:
S. Montgomery March 14, 1820, KNOX Co.

DUNLAP, William to Ellen Thomas - August 14, 1806, WILLIAMSON Co.

DUNLAP, Wm. to Betsy Swagerty - issued September 17, 1819, m. by:
S. Montgomery September 22, 1819, KNOX Co.

DUNLAP, William to Patsy Yarnell - issued March 29, 1826, m. by:
Wm. Morris, J. P., March 30, 1826, KNOX Co.

DUNLAP, William Y. to Sarah E. Obarr - issued November 2, 1842,
STEWART Co.

DUNLOP, Hugh to Rebecca P. Talley - issued February 17, 1852, Bondsman:
M. E. Wilcox, m. by: H. Haddock February 18, 1852, MONTGOMERY Co.

DUNMORE, James to Delilah Gowen - issued September 21, 1820, Bondsman:
Shadrach Gowen, m. by: Geo. Clark, J. P., September 22, 1820,
WILSON Co.

DUNN, Abner to Polly ___ (?) - issued November 16, 1827, Bondsman:
Josiah Henson and Benj. Wilson SUMNER Co.

DUNN, Alfred to Sarah Ann Baker - issued July 11, 1840, m. by:
James Whitsitt, DAVIDSON Co.

DUNN, E. M. to Nancy M. Somers - issued March 4, 1840, Bondsman:
J. A. Somers, m. by: Silas Tarver, J. P., March 5, 1840, WILSON Co.

DUNN, George to Anny Smith - issued October 16, 1845, m. by:
B. F. Frazer, J. P., October, 1845, STEWART Co.

DUNN, Goerge to Angeline Robertson - issued December 23, 1847, m. by:
T. B. Matthews, J. P., ROBERTSON Co.

DUNN, Geo. J. G. to Edy Stow - issued November 29, 1834, m. by:
Michael Davis, J. P., November 30, 1834, KNOX Co.

DUNN, Henry to Elizabeth Farless - issued December 12, 1830, m. by:
M. Powell, J. P., ROBERTSON Co.

DUNN, Henry to Ann Moore - issued June 9, 1835, Bondsman:
Marcus Smotherman, RUTHERFORD Co.

DUNN, Hugh Torrence to Susannah Clark - issued July 13, 1805, Bondsman:
James Clark, SUMNER Co.

DUNN, J. R. to Emma E. Menees - issued December 1, 1856, m. by:
John A. Jones December 4, 1856, ROBERTSON Co.

DUNN, James to Margaret Winton - November 30, 1785, Security:
William Winton, GREENE Co.

DUNN, James to Margaret Seawell - m. by: Thomas Joyner July 12, 1834,
SUMNER Co.

DUNN, James F. to Nancy J. Menees - issued March 8, 1860, m. by:
F. R. Gooch, M. G., ROBERTSON Co.

DUNN, James S. to Sophia G. Couts - issued February 5, 1855, m. by:
F. C. Plaster February 7, 1855, ROBERTSON Co.

DUNN, James S. to Victoria A. Laprede - issued February 13, 1857,
m. by: F. C. Plaster, M. G., February 15, 1857, ROBERTSON Co.

DUNN, John to Mahala McClure - issued July 25, 1825, m. by:
W. B. A. Ramsey, J. P., July 28, 1825, KNOX Co.

DUNN, John to Sally Skinner - issued March 13, 1845, STEWART Co.

DUNN, John D. to Mary Jane Gilliam - issued June 12, 1828, m. by:
Jonathan Davis, J. P., June 12, 1828, SUMNER Co.

DUNN, John F. to Nancy W. Lester - issued April 17, 1833, m. by:
J. Lester, V. D. M., WILSON Co.

DUNN, John H. to Mary F. Gunn - issued October 21, 1852, m. by:
F. R. Gooch, M. G., ROBERTSON Co.

DUNN, John P. to Nancy Brown (Brandon?) - issued December 4, 1823,
Bondsman: Jacob Spear, RUTHERFORD Co.

DUNN, John R. to Jerana Catherine Bevins - issued June 29, 1833,
Bondsman: John G. Holloway, RUTHERFORD Co.

DUNN, Joseph B. to Poley Mahn - issued February 29, 1824, Bondsman:
Daniel Allsup, m. by: Jonathan Davis, J. P., February 29, 1824,
SUMNER Co.

DUNN, L. to M. L. Barnes - issued January 8, 1852, m. by:
Robert Draughon, J. P., ROBERTSON Co.

DUNN, Lowery to Rosina Taylor - issued June 28, 1847, m. by:
Allen Ellott, J. P., June 30, 1847, STEWART Co.

DUNN, M. to Margaret Foster - issued March 5, 1838, DICKSON Co.

DUNN, Margaret to Robert Dugan - GREENE Co.

DUNN, Mary to Abraham Hurst - GREENE Co.

DUNN, Millie to Jacob Bird - GREENE Co.

DUNN, Shedrack to Polly Pankey - issued May 30, 1805, Bondsman:
John Pankey, SUMNER Co.

DUNN, Thomas to Margaret Ferebee - issued January 4, 1841, m. by:
B. M. Barns, J. P., January 7, 1841, DAVIDSON Co.

DUNN, Timothy to Elizabeth Eress - issued November 7, 1797, Bondsman:
Hartin Dixon, GRAINGER Co.

DUNN, W. I. to Louisa Stolts - issued March 17, 1855, m. by:
J. Byrns, J. P., March 18, 1855, ROBERTSON Co.

DUNN, William to Elizabeth Brady - issued December 11, 1810, Bondsman:
John Dunn, WILSON Co.

DUNN, William to Sealy Jones - issued May 11, 1829, Bondsman:
William Chumley, WILSON Co.

DUNN, William to Sarah Cummings - issued January 5, 1835, m. by:
Wm. Lindsay, J. P., February 5, 1835, KNOX Co.

DUNN, Wm. to Sarah Cummings - issued January 5, 1836, Bondsman:
Geo. Cheata, KNOX Co.

DUNN, William to Margaret France - issued March 20, 1839, STEWART Co.

DUNN, William A. to Lucy Woodward - issued April 9, 1840, m. by:
Thos. Scott, J. P., April 16, 1840, DAVIDSON Co.

DUNN, William B. to Julia A. Cunningham - issued September 28, 1861,
m. by: John Charles, J. P., September 29, 1861, DAVIDSON Co.

DUNN, Wm. G. to Lydia Bales - issued May 23, 1835, Bondsman:
Geo. J. G. Dunn, KNOX Co.

DUNN, William D. to Ann Henry Neal - August 6, 1846, m. by:
Robt. Caldwell, V. D. M., GILES Co.

DUNN, William J. to Mary E. Lawrence - issued November 16, 1847, m. by:
R. W. Bell, J. P., November 18, 1847, ROBERTSON Co.

DUNN, Wilson to Martha M. Penticost - issued August 28, 1843, m. by:
J. T. Edgar August 31, 1843, DAVIDSON Co.

DUNNAGIN, Blount to Parthenia Dunnegan - m. by: L. Russell, J. P.,
March 11, 1841, DICKSON Co.

DUNNAWAY, Robert L. to Eveline Allen - issued November 17, 1840,
DICKSON Co.

DUNNAWAY, Williamson to Mary Burke - issued October 11, 1836, m. by:
Joshua Lester, V. D. M., WILSON Co.

DUNNEGAN, Joe. to Mary Harrison - issued August 30, 1832, Bondsman:
Jese Harrison, m. by: Peter Ketring, J. P., August 30, 1832,
SUMNER Co.

DUNNEGAN, Madison to Manerva Dodson - issued March 30, 1839, DICKSON Co.

DUNNEGAN, Mark to Jane Dunnegan - issued February 23, 1842, m. by:
G. W. Tatom, J. P., February 23, 1842, DICKSON Co.

DUNNEGAN, Stanford to Alcy Dunnegan - issued August 30, 1838, m. by:
L. Russell, J. P., August 30, 1838, DICKSON Co.

DUNNEGAN, Stanford to Caroline Floyd - issued March 3, 1843, m. by:
L. Russell, J. P., March 5, 1843, DICKSON Co.

DUNNEVIN, George to Anna Waldin - issued March 2, 1840, m. March 3,
1840, DICKSON Co.

DUNNING, James to Mary Hollis - issued March 14, 1836, Bondsman:
John Grainger, SUMNER Co.

DUNNING, Micajah to Tabitha Murphey - issued August 14, 1810, Bondsman:
Aaron Butler, SUMNER Co.

DUNNING, William to Anna Hamilton - issued August 7, 1818, Bondsman:
Lenord Brock, m. by: Martin Cleveland, J. P., August 7, 1818,
GRAINGER Co.

DUNNINGTON, Gustine to Priscilla Linn - June 15, 1811, KNOX Co.

DUNNIVANT, A. A. to Abegale Garrett - December 24, Security:
P. H. Dunivant, GILES Co.

DUNUM, Sarah to Richard Pickle - issued January 9, 1864, Bondsman:
Henry M. Liggett, Jos. H. Thompson, Clk., BEDFORD Co.

DUNWOODY, Esther to Alexander McCollum - GREENE Co.

DUPASS, William to Elisabeth Haston - issued May 24, 1849, m. by:
John Gillentine, J. P., May 24, 1849, VAN BUREN Co.

DURARD, Joseph to Nancy House - issued January 23, 1842, DAVIDSON Co.

DURARD, Lewis to Delana McCormack - issued February 26, 1845,
DAVIDSON Co.

DURHAM, Buckner S. to Susan Rippy - issued December 14, 1820, Bondsman:
John Durham, m. by: Addison Foster, J. P., December 14, 1820,
SUMNER Co.

DURHAM, Gatewood H. to Sarah Grissum - issued January 30, 1836,
Bondsman: Joseph Key, SUMNER Co.

DURHAM, George to Isabella Seat - issued October 23, 1842, m. by:
Benjamin Sharpe, J. P., October 23, 1842, DAVIDSON Co.

DURHAM, Henry to Jane Richardson - issued November 12, 1812, Bondsman:
Goldsberry Thurman, SUMNER Co.

DURHAM, Hiram to Levina Brooks - issued July 6, 1848, m. by:
Holden W. Nichols, J. P., July 13, 1848, STEWART Co.

DURHAM, James to Lydia Gillespie - issued July 14, 1820, Bondsman:
George McGuire, SUMNER Co.

DURHAM, James to Martha Brock - issued January 5, 1842, VAN BUREN Co.

DURHAM, James to Mary Jane Webb - issued July 18, 1845, m. by:
W. F. Luck, M. G., July 18, 1845, DAVIDSON Co.

DURHAM, John to Mary M. Watkins - issued August 12, 1839, Bondsman:
Robt. D. Reed, m. by: Wm. Barton, M. G., August 14, 1839, WILSON Co.

DURHAM, John Thomas to Lucinda Shaw - issued January 28, 1840, m. by:
Nathan Morris, J. P., February 4, 1840, ROBERTSON Co.

DURHAM, R. B. to Mary Senter - issued October 16, 1838, Bondsman:
William C. Durham, m. by: L. M. Woodson October 16, 1838, SUMNER Co.

DURHAM, Samuel to Sally Morris - issued September 7, 1811, Bondsman:
John Durham, SUMNER Co.

DURHAM, Samuel to Nancy M. Winters - issued November 6, 1854, m. by:
B. W. Bradley, J. P., November 9, 1854, ROBERTSON Co.

DURHAM, Sidney to Marey Deaton - issued September 19, 1855, m. by:
William Johnson, J. P., September 19, 1855, VAN BUREN Co.

DURHAM, Thomas to Elizabeth Johnson - issued April 30, 1816, m. by:
David Gordon April 30, 1816, RUTHERFORD Co.

DURHAM, William to Frances Marshall - issued July 15, 1808, SUMNER Co.

DURHAM, __(?) - issued January 4, 1851, m. by: B. B. Knight, J. P.,
January 5, 1851, FRANKLIN Co.

DURHAM, William to Pricilla Murphy - issued February 6, 1855, m. by:
B. W. Bradley, J. P., February 9, 1855, ROBERTSON Co.

DURHAM, William G. to Malinda Rippie - m. by: Rodney B. Durham
October 16, 1838, SUMNER Co.

DURHAM, William G. to Eliza York - issued June 4, 1852, VAN BUREN Co.

DURHAM, Willis F. to Armanda Deaton - issued March 26, 1853, m. by:
Harmon York, J. P., March 26, 1853, VAN BUREN Co.

DURHAM, Zachariah to Carline Winters - issued June 26, 1850, m. by:
B. W. Bradley, J. P., July 3, 1850, ROBERTSON Co.

DURIN, Elias to Lucy Burk - issued August 7, 1816, Bondsman:
Thos. Scurry, SUMNER Co.

DURIN, John to Nancy Jane Russell - issued November 16, 1848, m. by:
H. G. Townson, J. P., November 16, 1848, STEWART Co.

DURIN, Thomas to Polly Winn - issued August 24, 1812, Bondsman:
Josiah E. Giles, SUMNER Co.

DURNAL, Washington to Betsey Gibson - issued June 30, 1830, Bondsman:
Solomon Sholders, SUMNER Co.

DURNOLDS, James to Elizabeth Hendrick - September 9, 1796, Security:
Arch Leady (Lackey), BLOUNT Co.

DURRETT, E. L. to M. A. Clark - issued July 6, 1846, m. by:
Robert L. Tate, M. G., ROBERTSON Co.

DURRETT, E. L. to Medora Clark - issued December 29, 1854, m. by:
C. B. David, M. G., December 31, 1854, ROBERTSON Co.

DURRETT, Isaac to Sarah Coon - issued August 24, 1847, Bondsman:
Wm. Gaines, MONTGOMERY Co.

DURRETT, J. T. to E. J. Patton - issued August 3, 1842, ROBERTSON Co.

DURRETT, S. C. to Malinda Gingo (?) - issued October 29, 1851, m. by:
H. M. Pill, J. P., ROBERTSON Co.

DURRETT, Solomon to Mary C. Harding - issued October 3, 1865, Bondsman:
Wm. A. Smith, LAWRENCE Co.

DUTTON, Wiley to Eveline Rose - issued January 17, 1843, m. by:
Thos. Meadows, J. P., January 17, 1843, FRANKLIN Co.

DUTY, Hiram to Emaline Banks - issued February 21, 1824, m. by:
James Walton, J. P., February 21, 1824, SUMNER Co.

DUTY, John to Elizabeth C. Harval - issued March 16, 1824, Bondsman:
Wm. Turner, SUMNER Co.

DUTY, Thomas to Polly Tarkington - June 14, 1807, WILLIAMSON Co.

DUVAL, Alexander D. to Margaret Gwin - issued March 9, 1818, Bondsman:
George Blain, m. by: Wm. C. Stribbling, M. G., March 9, 1818,
SUMNER Co.

DUVALL, William R. to Louisa Shasteen - issued November 19, 1874,
m. by: R. P. Davis, M. G., November 19, 1874, FRANKLIN Co.

DUVAUGH, Paul to Martha Duran - issued June 26, 1844, m. by:
Allen Nesbitt, J. P., June 27, 1844, DICKSON Co.

DWPE, John to Martha Hearn - issued April 13, 1839, Bondsman:
Wm. Holbrook, m. by: Isaac Hunter, J. P., April 15, 1839, WILSON Co.

DWYER, Lewis to Elizabeth Warren - issued October 19, 1822, m. by:
John Bonner, p. P., November 4, 1822, WILSON Co.

DWYN, John to Rebecca Hearn - issued December 14, 1831, Bondsman:
Edward Hearn, m. by: Thos. P. Holman, J. P., December 22, 1831,
WILSON Co.

DYAL, David to Susan Jones - issued April 27, 1839, m. by:
Benjamin B. Knight, J. P., April 28, 1839, FRANKLIN Co.

DYAL, John to Hannah Guthrie - issued March 24, 1841, FRANKLIN Co.

DYCAS, F. E. to Mary F. Featherston - issued January 1, 1848, m. by:
R. W. Bell, J. P., January 2, 1848, ROBERTSON Co.

DYCHE, Michael to Rebcea Churchman - issued August 11, 1810, Bondsman:
Thomas Churchman, Witness: Sterling Cocke, J. P., GRAINGER Co.

DYCKE, Jr., Henry to Jane Delany - April 26, 1799, Security:
Henry Dycke, Sen., GREENE Co.

DYCUS, W. W. to Atalantus G. Duncan - issued April 30, 1849, Bondsman:
T. A. Dycus, m. by: J. G. Ward, M. G., May 1, 1849, MONTGOMERY Co.

DYE, Bonson W. to Rebecca S. Smith - issued February 24, 1852, Bondsman:
Jo. M. Dye, m. by: W. B. Walker, M. G., February 26, 1852,
MONTGOMERY Co.

DYE, Isreal to Elizabeth Anderson - issued March 8, 1830, Bondsman:
John Alderson, m. by: Robert Norvell March 8, 1830, SUMNER Co.

DYE, Joseph M. to Sally Ann Williams - issued January 27, 1854,
Bondsman: B. S. Green, m. by: John T. Hughes January 29, 1854,
MONTGOMERY Co.

DYE, Ross to Elizabeth Duncan - issued March 11, 1857, m. by:
M. A. Carden, J. P., March 11, 1857, COFFEE Co.

DYER, Abasuerus to Elizabeth Morgan - issued March 23, 1822, Bondsman:
John Piles, SUMNER Co.

DYER, Daniel to Elizabeth Cropper - issued August 8, 1821, Bondsman:
Jesse Donnell, WILSON Co.

DYER, George to Dorsey Wilson - issued August 28, 1824, Bondsman:
William Dyer, m. by: William Lane, J. P., August 28, 1824,
GRAINGER Co.

DYER, Ely to Sally Derman - issued October 7, 1820, Bondsman:
Mathew Rice, m. by: Isaac Lindsey October 7, 1820, SUMNER Co.

DYER, Goerge L. to Shelton Payne - issued February 21, 1850, Bondsman:
Peyton Wyatt, m. by: John Gold, J. P., MONTGOMERY Co.

DYER, Hazin to Lucretia Bryant - issued December 22, 1810, Bondsman:
William Gwin, SUMNER Co.

DYER, Isaac to Catherine Norris - issued May 18, 1835, Bondsman:
William Dennis, GRAINGER Co.

DYER, Isaac B. to Rachel Hall - issued July 6, 1818, Bondsman:
Thomas Dyer, m. by: John Hall, J. P., July 6, 1818, GRAINGER Co.

DYER, Isaiah to Frances P. Gambrill - issued July 6, 1829, Bondsman:
Dugald G. Ferguson, m. by: D. R. Gooch, J. P., July 9, 1829,
RUTHERFORD Co.

DYER, James to Elizabeth Garroth - issued October 11, 1802, Bondsman:
Frederick Moyers, GRAINGER Co.

DYER, James to Lucy Horn - issued December 6, 1820, Bondsman:
James Little, m. by: Wm. Johnson December 10, 1820, WILSON Co.

DYER, James to Milley Needham - issued December 6, 1821, Bondsman:
George Dyer, m. by: Martin Cleveland, J. P., December 6, 1821,
GRAINGER Co.

DYER, Jr., James to Stacy Elkins - issued February 5, 1828, Bondsman:
William T. Carden, m. by: N. Jarnagin, J. P., February 5, 1828,
GRAINGER Co.

DYER, James H. to Emaline Jordan - issued April 1, 1842, m. by:
John Russell, J. P., April 1, 1842, VAN BUREN Co.

DYER (or Dyke), Joel to Rachel Adkins - issued August 24, 1830,
Bondsman: Isaac Johnson, m. by: Wm. A. McCampbell, J. P.,
August 26, 1830, Witness: Wm. Swan, KNOX Co.

DYER, John to Polena Whitlock - issued March 28, 1833, Bondsman:
Lea Dyer, m. by: Henry Alsup, J. P., GRAINGER Co.

DYER, John to Susan Branson - issued September 19, 1835, Bondsman:
Benjamin Branson, GRAINGER Co.

DYER, Joseph to Nancey Metter (or Miller) - issued March 17, 1806,
Bondsman: Joseph Long, GRAINGER Co.

DYER, Josh to Susannah Smith - issued July 3, 1858, m. by:
J. Crawford July 4, 1858, FRANKLIN Co.

DYER, Joshua to Winny Dyer - issued June 21, 1815, Bondsman:
Joshua Washburn and Charlton Dyer, GRAINGER Co.

DYER, Owen to Elizabeth Condry - issued January 16, 1823, Bondsman:
John Sharp, m. by: Martin Cleveland, J. P., January 16, 1823,
GRAINGER Co.

DYER, Richard to Barbary Hise - April 23, 1787, Security:
Jacob Hise and Julius Wilhoit, GREENE Co.

DYER, Robert to Polly Sanford - August 30, 1816, WILLIAMSON Co.

DYER, Spilsby to Betsey Conley - issued January 23, 1808, Bondsman:
Robert Martin, GRAINGER Co.

DYER, Thomas to Celia Crabb - issued November 13, 1810, Bondsman:
Henry Shelby, SUMNER Co.

DYER, Thomas to Sarah Hammers - issued August 10, 1819, Bondsman:
James Malicoat, m. by: John Kidwell, J. P., August 10, 1819,
GRAINGER Co.

DYER, William to Anney Clifton - issued March 24, 1805, Bondsman:
Joel Dyer and Robert Henry, GRAINGER Co.

DYER, William to Polly McDaniel - issued January 1, 1827, m. by:
John Bayless, J. P., January 4, 1827, KNOX Co.

DYER, William A. to Margaret Brigman - issued March 11, 1833,
Bondsman: William Dyer, m. by: H. Alsup, J. P., GRAINGER Co.

DYER, William H. to Martha Ann Marshall - issued May 21, 1816, m. by:
Enid Jones, J. P., May 23, 1816, RUTHERFORD Co.

DYER, William H. to Rhoda Dennis - issued September 25, 1838, m. by:
John Wright, J. P., September 25, 1838, DAVIDSON Co.

DYER, Wilson to Rebecca Morgan - issued November 14, 1829, Bondsman:
William Dyer, GRAINGER Co.

DYER, James to Polly Harmon - issued September 7, 1814, Bondsman:
William Ball, GRAINGER Co.

DYRE, William to Mary Witcher - issued July 20, 1812, m. by:
William Hamilton, J. P., GRAINGER Co.

DYSART, Thos. J. to Francis A. E. Curtiss - issued December 23, 1861,
Bondsman: R. B. Blackwell, Jos. H. Thompson, Clk., m. by:
A. S. Riggs, M. G., December 24, 1861, BEDFORD Co.

DYSART, William to Catharine Petty - issued March 11, 1847, Bondsman:
J. W. Hempe, m. by: P. Priestly, J. P., March 11, 1847,
MONTGOMERY Co.

EADES, Isaac to Cynthia George - issued October 14, 1823, Bondsman:
John Sweet, m. by: H. Robinson, J. P., October, 1823, RUTHERFORD Co.

EADES, Samuel to Elizabeth Rainwater - issued December 30, 1847,
Bondsman: David Pierce, m. by: A. Vaughn, J. P., December 30,
1847, MONTGOMERY Co.

EADES, William to Sally Wells - issued January 21, 1822, m. by:
B. B. Dickens, J. P., January 24, 1822, RUTHERFORD Co.

EADS, J. B. to Drucilla Lake - issued May 9, 1853, Bondsman:
Robert Baxter, m. by: Charles Braly, J. P., May 9, 1853,
MONTGOMERY Co.

EAGAN, Barna B. to Deborah Whitson - issued July 23, 1831, Bondsman:
William Eagan, WILSON Co.

EAGAN, Barnaba to Sarah Cooper - issued December 19, 1829, Bondsman:
John R. Wright, WILSON Co.

EAGAN, Hugh H. to Sally Bandy - issued April 4, 1822, Bondsman:
Elisha Green, m. by: S. S. Turner, J. P., April 4, 1822, SUMNER Co.

EAGAN, Jesse to Narcisa Rieff - issued January 29, 1818, Bondsman:
Henry Howell, m. by: William Grey, J. P., WILSON Co.

EAGAN, John to Margaret Wray - issued May 16, 1812, Bondsman:
Luke Wray, WILSON Co.

EAGAN, Reese to Peggy Tipton - issued February 2, 1820, Bondsman:
Abraham Green, m. by: Joremiah Hendrick, J. P., February 3,
1820, WILSON Co.

EAGAN, Samuel to Nancy Johnson - issued July 1, 1835, Bondsman:
Joseph E. Johnson, m. by: John W. Bomer, M. G., WILSON Co.

EAGAN, Sam'l to Almyra Harris - issued July 30, 1835, Bondsman:
William Ames, WILSON Co.

EAGAN, William to Mary B. Cooper - issued May 25, 1833, m. by:
Thos. Burge, M. G., WILSON Co.

EAGAN, William W. to Melinda Tipton - issued August 5, 1833, m. by:
J. H. Davis, J. P., August 8, 1833, WILSON Co.

EAKER, M. H. to Mary Ellison - issued May 23, 1848, Bondsman:
Theodore Cobb, m. by: H. F. Beaumont, Local Eld. M. E. Church,
MONTGOMERY Co.

EAKIN, A. P. to Louise P. Wright - issued December 15, 1846, m. by:
J. T. Edgar December 15, 1846, DAVIDSON Co.

EAKIN, Pamela to Moses Smith - MAURY Co.

EAKIN, Samuel to Polly Walker - April 30, 1801, Security:
Humphrey Montgomery, BLOUNT Co.

EAKIN, William to Felicia Ann Grundy - issued July 5, 1842, m. by:
T. J. Edgar July 5, 1842, DAVIDSON Co.

EANES, Alexander to Mary Ann New - issued July 2, 1831, Bondsman:
Matt Martin, WILSON Co.

EARHART, John to Jane Hays - issued December 9, 1837, Bondsman:
H. Bernard, m. by: John Beard, M. G., December 10, 1837, WILSON Co.

EARHART, William L. to Ann Clay - issued April 2, 1840, m. by:
John B. McFerrin, M. G., April 2, 1840, DAVIDSON Co.

EARHEART, Joseph to Nancy Thompson - issued January 8, 1834, Bondsman:
James Rutland, m. by: Ezekiel Cloyd, M. G., January 9, 1834,
WILSON Co.

EARHEART, Mary to Charles Crowell - BEDFORD Co.

EARHEART, Wade H. to Rebecca J. Umphreys - issued September 21, 1841,
m. by: Jas. H. Cook, J. P., September 26, 1841, DAVIDSON Co.

EARL, Tabitha Cumie to P. J. Bailey - issued March 11, 1848, m. by:
E. M. Gunn, M. G., March 12, 1848, ROBERTSON Co.

EARLE, Ezeas W. to Rebecca W. Clark - issued September 25, 1817,
Bondsman: John W. Byrn, SUMNER Co.

EARLES, Balcaus to Maryann Sparkman - issued March 27, 1851, m. by:
W. B. Cummings, J. P., March 27, 1851, VAN BUREN Co.

EARLES, Birt to Frances Norton - issued July 16, 1859, m. by:
W. G. Pirtle, J. P., July 17, 1859, COFFEE Co.

EARLES, J. N. to Manirva D. Cass - issued May 24, 1858, m. by:
W. G. Pirtle, J. P., May 24, 1858, COFFEE Co.

EARLES, Mc. to Martha Ann Watts - issued March 1, 1856, m. by:
J. W. Williams, L. D., March 2, 1856, COFFEE Co.

EARLES, Nathan to Martha Jane Dodson - issued November 24, 1852, m. by:
James Head, M. G., November 28, 1852, VAN BUREN Co.

EARLES, Nathan D. to Rebecca Toliver - issued October 4, 1860, m. by:
W. G. Pirtle, J. P., October 4, 1860, COFFEE Co.

EARLES, Ocias to Elizabeth Jernigan - issued September 19, 1855, m. by:
J. H. Lawrence, J. P., September 23, 1855, COFFEE Co.

EARLEY, John to Amanda J. Howard - issued December 27, 1857, m. by:
E. B. Puckett, L. D. of M. E. Church So., December 27, 1857,
COFFEE Co.

EARLS, McGreger to Nancy J. Hastone - issued October 30, 1843, m. by:
Ozias Denton, M. G., November 2, 1843, VAN BUREN Co.

EARLS, T. J. to Vilia A. Cauff - issued February 10, 1861, m. by:
J. Campbell, M. G., February 11, 1861, FRANKLIN Co.

EARLY, Alexander to Leamy Moore - June 13, 1817, KNOX Co.

EARLY, Benjamin to Polly Lilburn - January 8, 1821, KNOX Co.

EARLY, Henry to Olive Reed - issued September 1, 1823, Bondsman: William Cobb, m. by: Peyton Smith September 18, 1823, RUTHERFORD Co.

EARLY, John to Sarah Kilby (Killy?) - December 10, 1808, Bondsman: John Kilby (Killy?), MAURY Co.

EARLY, Wm. to Betsy Burnett - issued January 14, 1825, Bondsman: John Campbell, Witness: Chas. McClugn, KNOX Co.

EARNDALE, R. A. to Ellen Seargent - issued January 5, 1859, FRANKLIN Co.

EARNEST, Anna to John Lotspeich - GREENE Co.

EARNEST, Anne to Stephen Brooks - GREENE Co.

EARNEST, Elizabeth to Joseph Evans - GREENE Co.

EARNEST, Felix to Sarah North - August 15, 1786, Security: Henry Earnest, GREENE Co.

EARNEST, Felix to Sally Oliphant - May 14, 1808, Security: James Oliphant, GREENE Co.

EARNEST, Jacob to Mary Warren - August 27, 1799, Security: Lawrence Earnest, GREENE Co.

EARNEST, Mary to George Wells - GREENE Co.

EARNEST, Sarah to Charles Warren - GREENE Co.

EARNHEART, H. O. to Nancy P. Stephens - issued February 17, 1862, Bondsman: W. D. Arnold, Jos. H. Thompson, Clk., m. by: L. T. Williams, J. P., BEDFORD Co.

EARP, George to Mary Starnes - issued June 15, 1854, m. by: J. H. Lawrence, J. P., June 15, 1854, COFFEE Co.

EARP, William A. to Mary Winfrey - issued March 3, 1859, m. by: John McGill, J. P., March 3, 1859, COFFEE Co.

EARTHMAN, Felix G. to Mary Ann Wilkerson - issued August 6, 1845, m. by: J. B. McFerrin, M. G., August 6, 1845, DAVIDSON Co.

EARTHMAN, Isaac to Catharine Garrett - issued December 4, 1810, Bondsman: Geo. Garrett, SUMNER Co.

EARWOOD, William to Eleanor Rankin - issued October 30, 1822, m. by: Jordan Willeford, J. P., October 31, 1822, RUTHERFORD Co.

EASKEW, James to Eliza Thornton - issued January 24, 1837, Bondsman: William Guill, m. by: Thomas Kirkpatrick, J. P., January 25, 1837, WILSON Co.

EASLEY, Drury to Cassander Farley - issued March 14, 1842, m. by: W. L. Payne, J. P., ROBERTSON Co.

EASLEY, Drury to Mary Jane Wells - issued September 1, 1846, Bondsman: Wm. Easley, m. by: Joseph E. Douglass, M. G., September 1, 1846, MONTGOMERY Co.

EASLEY, Francis P. to Sarah Doss - issued March 13, 1848, m. by: D. G. Baird, J. P., March 16, 1848, ROBERTSON Co.

EASLEY, Geo. W. to Mahala Miller - issued October 19, 1843, m. by: A. Justice, J. P., October 20, 1843, ROBERTSON Co.

EASLEY, John to Anny Worldrum - issued November 25, 1813, Bondsman: Isiah Trasey, SUMNER Co.

EASLEY, Joseph to Betsey Wethers - issued April 19, 1808, Bondsman:
Rhodam Allen, SUMNER Co.

EASLEY, Lemuel to Francis Staton - issued December 1, 1865, FRANKLIN Co.

EASLEY, Millington to Eliz. Ann Davis - issued June 6, 1842, m. by:
W. Seal, J. P., ROBERTSON Co.

EASLEY, Milton to Rachel Alsup - issued March 6, 1819, Bondsman:
John Henson and Josiah Henson, m. March 6, 1819, SUMNER Co.

EASLEY, Thos. to Prudy Lock - issued January 27, 1844, m. by:
B. Herndon, J. P., January 28, 1844, STEWART Co.

EASLEY, Wesley to Nancy Blachburn - issued February 28, 1846, m. by:
David Herring, J. P., ROBERTSON Co.

EASLEY, William to Elizabeth Curl - issued January 3, 1827, Bondsman:
Thomas Wier, m. by: Wm. Senter, Traveling Deacon, GRAINGER Co.

EASLEY, Worsham to Caty Countz - issued March 9, 1811, Bondsman:
David Noe, GRAINGER Co.

EASLEY, Worsham to Elizabeth Lathim - issued September 1, 1818,
Bondsman: Stephen Cocke, GRAINGER Co.

EASLICK, Thos. A. to Eliza Jones - issued November 15, 1859, m. by:
J. T. Slatter, J. P., November 15, 1859, FRANKLIN Co.

EASLY, Henry to Edy Caldwell - issued August 25, 1828, Bondsman:
James Butler, SUMNER Co.

EASLY, William to Levina Shaffitt - issued January 20, 1844, m. by:
Benj. Sells, J. P., January 20, 1844, FRANKLIN Co.

EASON, Ira E. to Dolly Vaughn - issued January 9, 1817, Bondsman:
James A. Hunter, WILSON Co.

EASON, James K. to Jane H. Fisher - issued September 7, 1831, Bondsman:
L. C. Shanklin, WILSON Co.

EASON, Mary A. to Jas. L. Black - BEDFORD Co.

EASON, Robert to Lydia Harriss - issued September 16, 1802, WILSON Co.

EASON, Samuel S. to Elizabeth J. Warren - issued September 20, 1837,
Bondsman: R. J. Evans, WILSON Co.

EASON, William to Eliza N. Corley - issued June 23, 1838, Bondsman:
David C. Wilson, m. by: Jas. Aston, J. P., June 26, 1838, WILSON Co.

EAST, Anderson to Sarah Johns - issued August 1, 1834, Bondsman:
John Lemar, RUTHERFORD Co.

EAST, Mathew to Jinsey W. Peak - issued June 4, 1811, Bondsman:
Aaron Sheron, WILSON Co.

EAST, Wm. A. to Elizabeth H. Searcy - issued May 5, 1846, m. by:
C. D. Elliott, M. G., May 5, 1846, DAVIDSON Co.

EASTAS, Willie to Nancy McReynolds - issued May 20, 1828, Bondsman:
James Wilson, SUMNER Co.

EASTERLY, Jacob to Mary Bible - January 26, 1798, Security:
Chirstopher Bible, GREENE Co.

EASTERLY, W. F. to N. E. Jones - issued June 3, 1871, m. by:
D. P. Armstrong, M. G., June 7, 1871, FRANKLIN Co.

EASTES, Jesse to Margaret Marsh - issued July 19, 1838, DICKSON Co.

EASTLAND, Thomas B. to Josephine M. Green - issued April 2, 1829, Bondsman: William T. Christy, RUTHERFORD Co.

EASTRIDGE, James to Lucy Boling - issued October 16, 1801, Bondsman: Joseph Boling, GRAINGER Co.

EASTUS, Henderson to Nancy Bond - issued January 8, 1835, Bondsman: William Mullins, m. by: Joseph B. Johns, J. P., January 8, 1835, RUTHERFORD Co.

EATHENRIDGE, Johnathan to Caty Lewis - April 5, 1810, WILLIAMSON Co.

EATHERLY, Alfred to Lucinda T. Harris - issued December 12, 1848, Bondsman: Robert E. Stewart, MONTGOMERY Co.

EATHERLY, Dickson L. to Susan A. Hall - issued May 5, 1846, m. by: Josiah Feriss, J. P., May 5, 1846, DAVIDSON Co.

EATHERLY, C. U. to C. M. Steward - issued July 28, 1845, Bondsman: Jonathan Etherly, MONTGOMERY Co.

EATHERLY, J. M. to Will L. Pitt - issued January 27, 1852, m. by: B. Randolph, J. P., ROBERTSON Co.

EATHERLY, Jonathan to Jenney Thompson - issued September 27, 1809, Bondsman: Warren Eatherly, WILSON Co.

EATHERLY, Robertson to Ameda Bone - issued March 24, 1829, Bondsman: Malcomb Smith, WILSON Co.

EATHERLY, Rufus to Louisa Donaldson - issued October 12, 1840, Bondsman: James Donaldson, WILSON Co.

EATHERLY, Thompson to Harriet Eatherly - issued March 18, 1837, Bondsman: Wm. Y. Eatherly, WILSON Co.

EATHERLY, William to Elizabeth Bernard - issued September 24, 1824, Bondsman: James Williams, m. by: David Foster, M. G., September 30, 1824, WILSON Co.

EATON, Alford to Mollie K. Carter - issued July 31, 1867, m. by: Wm. Green, M. G., August 1, 1867, FRANKLIN Co.

EATON, Campbell to Jane M. Paul - issued May 31, 1814, Bondsman: William Paul, KNOX Co.

EATON (Outon), Elisha to Dicey Majors - issued April 19, 1824, Bondsman: David Majors, GRAINGER Co.

EATON, Greenberry to Jensey McKinney - issued August 24, 1823, Bondsman: John Womach, m. by: John Green August 25, 1823, WILSON Co.

EATON, James to Lucy Johnson - issued November 11, 1833, Bondsman: John Meek, m. by: Jas. Kennon, M. G., November 13, GRAINGER Co.

EATON, John W. to Margaret Williams - issued December 5, 1833, Bondsman: Robert Masengill, m. by: Jas. Kennon, M. G., GRAINGER Co.

EATON, Joseph to Pricilla Cravs - issued October 16, 1811, m. by: John Cocke, J. P., GRAINGER Co.

EATON, Joseph to Precilla Craves - issued October 16, 1813, Bondsman: William Eaton, GRAINGER Co.

EATON, Joseph to Mary P. Underhill - issued April 5, 1826, m. by: John McMinn, J. P., April 30, 1826, WILSON Co.

EATON, Sarah C. to Robert C. Warren - BEDFORD Co.

EATON, William to Isabella Gillespie - July 22, 1815, KNOX Co.

EAVES, J. C. to Levina L. Rodes - issued September 18, 1860, m. by:
John J. Pittman, M. G., September 18, 1860, COFFEE Co.

EAVES, Thomas J. to Matilda J. Dearman - issued December 18, 1841,
Bondsman: Albert G. Locke, m. by: James Blevins, J. P., December 19,
1841, MEIGS Co.

EBLIN, Samuel to Martha Young - issued February 4, 1813, Bondsman:
Taply Young, Witness: W. Eblin and Chas. McClung, KNOX Co.

ECHOLS, Joel to Susannah Weir - issued October 13, 1810, Bondsman:
Jesse Cage, SUMNER Co.

ECHOLS, Joel to Nancy Compton - issued December 27, 1832, Bondsman:
Allison Sypert, m. by: H. Hobson, J. P., WILSON Co.

ECHOLS, John to Judith Compton - issued July 3, 1806, Bondsman:
William Allin, WILSON Co.

ECHOLS, John T. to Lurancey Clifton - issued February 19, 1835,
Bondsman: Mitchell Perry, WILSON Co.

ECHOLS, ___(?) - issued January 15, 1811, Bondsman: Markey Key, SUMNER Co.

ECHOLS, Richard A. to Abigail M. Brown - issued October 16, 1820,
Bondsman: Mathew Dew, m. by: John Jarratt October 17, 1820,
WILSON Co.

ECKLES, J. A. to G. P. Hockersmith - issued February 9, 1855, m. by:
Saml. D. Ogburn, M. G., February 11, 1855, ROBERTSON Co.

ECKOLS, David to Lytsy Bradshaw - issued August 8, 1823, Bondsman:
John Foster, WILSON Co.

ECKOLS, James to Elizabeth Ferrel - issued February 18, 1836, m. by:
Stephen McDonald, J. P., WILSON Co.

ECKOLS, Joseph to Margaret Coonrad - issued May 27, 1829, Bondsman:
John Smith, WILSON Co.

ECKOLS, Joseph to Margaret Coonrad - issued May 27, 1830, m. by:
James B. Taylor, J. P., WILSON Co.

EDAWRDS, M. W. to Artimissa Jones - issued November 17, 1857, m. by:
F. R. Gooch, M. G., ROBERTSON Co.

EDDLEMAN, John to Matilda Tucker - issued January 7, 1863, Bondsman:
Jesse Tucker, m. by: C. J. Herrin, J. P., January 8, 1863,
LAWRENCE Co.

EDDEY, Walter to Elizabeth Grimes - issued July 12, 1806, Bondsman:
Micheal Carter, WILSON Co.

EDDIE, Samuel D. to Calester Murphy - issued January 24, 1868, m. by:
John Chitwood, J. P., January 24, 1868, FRANKLIN Co.

EDDINES, James to Pothena Brown - issued August 29, 1827, Bondsman:
Samuel Creswell, m. by: James H. Davis, J. P., WILSON Co.

EDDINGS, Joseph to Parthena Henderson - issued January 18, 1817,
Bondsman: Benjamin Tucker, WILSON Co.

EDDINGS, Joseph to Miss Nancy Freeman - issued March 28, 1840, m. by:
Robert Green, J. P., ROBERTSON Co.

EDDINGS, Ozburn to Elizabeth Bone - issued December 16, 1828, Bondsman:
H. C. Hubbard, WILSON Co.

EDDINGS, William to Susan Samuel - issued October 24, 1850, m. by:
G. B. Mason, J. P., October 28, 1850, ROBERTSON Co.

EDDINGTON, Nicholas to Patience Wright - issued March 12, 1835, Bondsman:
Jas. H. Eddington, m. by: Richard Keyhill March 12, 1835, KNOX Co.

EDDINS, Henry to Milly Sparks - issued October 12, 1835, Bondsman:
(Little) Henry Eddins, m. by: John Bone, J. P., October 14, 1835,
WILSON Co.

EDDINS, William to Sarah Hooker - issued August 10, 1828, Bondsman:
Benj. T. Tucker, WILSON Co.

EDDLEMAN, Leonard to Charity Bowman - September 7, 1790, Security:
Jeremiah Laney, GREENE Co.

EDDS, John to Prudy Ann Peirce - issued March 27, 1845, Bondsman:
Philip Peirce, m. by: M. C. Atchley, Ord. M., March 27, 1845,
MEIGS Co.

EDDS, Wm. P. to Mira Knight - issued January 23, 1840, Bondsman:
Edward Brightwell, MEIGS Co.

EDDY, George to Lucy Taylor - issued May 4, 1830, Bondsman:
Wm. McDaniel, KNOX Co.

EDDY, Samuel to Susan C. Grayson - issued February 7, 1857, m. by:
Benjamin Gambill, J. P., January 8, 1857, ROBERTSON Co.

EDENS, Ezekiel to Mary Gammill - issued February 2, 1814, Bondsman:
John McCain, RUTHERFORD Co.

EDENS, Jobe to Patsey Douglass - issued September 28, 1836, Bondsman:
Samuel Edens, m. by: Sam'l. Laurence September 28, 1836, SUMNER Co.

EDGAR, Joseph R. to Jemima W. Yates - issued May 11, 1848, Bondsman:
A. Vaughn, m. by: Judson Hearn, J. P., May 13, 1846, MONTGOMERY Co.

EDGAR, Samuel C. to Amanda Tollison - issued August 24, 1832, Bondsman:
E. P. Lowe, m. by: Ennis Douglas August 26, 1832, WILSON Co.

EDGE, Elam to Mary Barbee - issued September 27, 1826, Bondsman:
Thomas Barbee, m. by: Jno. Rinas, M. G., WILSON Co.

EDINGTON, Holston to Polly Ann Ford - issued May 20, 1829, Bondsman:
Geo. C. Berry, m. by: Elijah Johnson, J. P., May 26, 1829,
Witness: Wm. Swan, KNOX Co.

EDINGTON, James H. to Fanny Johnston - issued August 5, 1824, Bondsman:
Kinzey Smith, m. by: Robt. McBath, J. P., August 5, 1824, Witness:
Wm. Swan, KNOX Co.

EDINGTON, John to Margat Smith - issued December 18, 1821, Bondsman:
Allen Smith, m. by: David Tate, J. P., December 19, 1821,
GRAINGER Co.

EDINGTON, John to Isabel Dunn - issued July 18, 1826, Bondsman:
Berry Burnett, m. by: David Nelson, J. P., July 19, 1826, Witness:
Wm. Swan, KNOX Co.

EDINGTON, Philip to Betsy Hall - issued February 12, 1814, m. by:
P. Nance, J. P., KNOX Co.

EDISON, Thomas C. to Nancy Powell - issued September 2, 1857, m. by:
A. Rose, J. P., September 3, 1857, ROBERTSON Co.

EDLIN, Oswald to Polly Shelton - February 11, 1812, WILLIAMSON Co.

EDMISTON, Covington to Margaret Fleming - December 21, 1816, WILLIAMSON Co.

EDMISTON, James to Agnes Alexander - October 7, 1797, BLOUNT Co.

EDMISTON, Mary to William Hankins - GREENE Co.

EDMONDSON, Benjamin to Minerva E. Orgain - issued May 13, 1851, Bondsman: A. P. Noblett, MONTGOMERY Co.

EDMONDSON, Isaac to Anne Wheeler - issued August 20, 1828, m. by: Wm. Morris, J. P., August 21, 1828, KNOX Co.

EDMONDSON, James to Frances Monday - issued December 26, 1828, m. by: Robt. Tindell, J. P., January 1, 1829, KNOX Co.

EDMONDSON, John to Sarah Grayson - August 13, 1816, KNOX Co.

EDMONDSON, John to Amanda S. Randolph - issued October 11, 1830, Bondsman: William H. Mitchell, RUTHERFORD Co.

EDMONDSON, John to Bridie H. Roberts - issued December 1, 1846, Bondsman: B. E. Orgain, m. by: J. Moore December 2, 1846, MONTGOMERY Co.

EDMONDSON, John B. to Polly Crawford - issued May 7, 1823, m. by: John McCampbell, V. D. M., May 8, 1823, KNOX Co.

EDMONDSON, Lewis to Polly Davis - issued July 26, 1825, Bondsman: James Edwards, m. by: Robt. Tindell, J. P., July 26, 1825, Witness: Wm. Swan, KNOX Co.

EDMONDSON, Sam'l. to Rebecka Hicks - issued December 21, 1821, m. by: Wm. Morris, J. P., December 23, 1821, KNOX Co.

EDMONDSON, Samuel to Rebecka White - issued February 7, 1827, m. by: Mordecai Yarnell, J. P., February 8, 1827, KNOX Co.

EDMONDSON, Sarah V. to Robert Erwin - issued December 13, 1862, Bondsman: K. L. Hamlin, Jos. H. Thompson, Clk., m. by: E. T. Haley, J. P., December 13, 1862, BEDFORD Co.

EDMONSON, Sterling to Rebecca Taylor - issued July 27, 1816, Bondsman: William Kendrick, Witness: A. Hutcheson, KNOX Co.

EDMONDSON, Thomas F. to Louisana McGee - issued November 29, 1854, Bondsman: John J. Sydrian, MONTGOMERY Co.

EDMONDSON, Upton to Martha A. Rice - issued September 14, 1853, Bondsman: Peyton M. Beasons, m. by: John F. Hughes, M. G., September 17, 1853, MONTGOMERY Co.

EDMONSON, William to Liley Holt - issued February 1, 1828, Bondsman: Jno. M. Havron and Francis Edmonson, KNOX Co.

EDMONDSON, William to C. V. Niblett - issued December 25, 1846, Bondsman: Jas. A. Mathis, m. by: Allison Akin, M. G., December 24, 1846, MONTGOMERY Co.

EDMONSON, A. E. to Susan F. Brown - issued December 8, 1868, m. by: J. S. Brown, M. G., December 8, 1868, FRANKLIN Co.

EDMONSON, Francis to Jane Grayson - issued February 1, 1828, m. by: Wm. Morris, J. P., February 3, 1828, KNOX Co.

EDMONSON, Wesley to Mollie Walker - issued October 8, 1869, m. by: Jas Campbell, M. G., October 8, 1869, FRANKLIN Co.

EDMUNDS, James A. to Tobitha M. Brackin - issued December 6, 1838, Bondsman: James Butler, m. December 6, 1838, SUMNER Co.

EDMUNDS, John to Lucinda Leach - issued December 31, 1846, DAVIDSON Co.

EDMUNDS, Samuel to Elisabeth Butler - issued December 18, 1832,
    Bondsman: Oscar Staley, m. by: Robert Norvell December 18, 1832,
    SUMNER Co.

EDNEY, Wm. to Elizabeth J. Kennedy - issued December 27, 1845, m. by:
    Wm. Cummins, J. P., December 28, 1845, DAVIDSON Co.

EDSON, Samuel to Nancy Dorris - issued February 8, 1820, Bondsman:
    Samuel Dorris, SUMNER Co.

EDMUNDSON, David to Sarah Kerr - November 29, 1798, Security:
    Samuel Robinson, GREENE Co.

EDMUNDSON, James to Elizabeth McGaughey - September 18, 1786, Security:
    Samuel Wilson, GREENE Co.

EDMUNDSON, Margaret to Carret Dillon - GREENE Co.

EDMUNDSON, Parnita to Cousil Hudspeth - January 21, 1810, Bondsman:
    James Birmingham, MAURY Co.

EDMUNDSON, Samuel to Elizabeth Johnson - September 25, 1791, Security:
    James Wilson, GREENE Co.

EDMUNDSON, Susannah to William Dillon - GREENE Co.

EDWARD, G. W. to Ann D. Norvell - issued September 8, 1858, m. by:
    W. B. Watterson, Mins., September 8, 1858, COFFEE Co.

EDWARD, James to Sally Jones - issued August 3, 1819, Bondsman:
    Petter Ragland, WILSON Co.

EDWARD, John to Nancy Vitito - issued July 11, 1817, Bondsman:
    Thomas Vitito, m. by: John Hall, J. P., September 24, 1817,
    GRAINGER Co.

EDWARD, John W. to Malvina Stark - issued January 18, 1845, m. by:
    Jas. Woodard, J. P., January 19, 1845, ROBERTSON Co.

EDWARD, S. Handy to Margaret F. Woods - issued December 7, 1843, m. by:
    R. A. Lapsley December 7, 1843, DAVIDSON Co.

EDWARD, Spencer to Sally Wilson - issued February 21, 1809, Bondsman:
    Bradford Howard, WILSON Co.

EDWARDS, Aaron to Elizabeth Hill - issued October 1, 1838, Bondsman:
    G. B. Edwards, WILSON Co.

EDWARDS, Abner to Sally Maxey - issued January 25, 1840, m. by:
    William Felts, M. G., ROBERTSON Co.

EDWARDS, Allison to Lavena Green - issued July 29, 1842, DAVIDSON Co.

EDWARDS, Andrew to Glathy Banks - issued November 24, 1857, FRANKLIN Co.

EDWARDS, Arthur M. to Nancy Harrell - issued August 19, 1829, Bondsman:
    Hubbard S. Wilkinson, m. by: Peyton Smith, RUTHERFORD Co.

EDWARDS, Augustus to Mary Robertson - issued February 21, 1824,
    Bondsman: Elisha Sanders, RUTHERFORD Co.

EDWARDS, B. W. to A. Moon - issued January 21, 1849, m. by:
    D. G. Baird, J. P., ROBERTSON Co.

EDWARDS, B. W. to Narcissa Edwards - issued March 9, 1855, m. by:
    G. R. Gunn, J. P., March 10, 1855, ROBERTSON Co.

EDWARDS, Balum to Rebecca Yates - issued February 8, 1840, m. by:
    P. B. Morris, J. P., February 8, 1840, DAVIDSON Co.

EDWARDS, Benjamin to Patsey Miers - issued November 16, 1817, Bondsman: John Bell, SUMNER Co.

EDWARDS, Betsey to Elijah Gosset (?) - MAURY Co.

EDWARDS, Bradford to Jenny Bond - issued August 29, 1814, Bondsman: Thos. Bond, WILSON Co.

EDWARDS, Bradford to Nancy Carraway - issued May 24, 1819, Bondsman: John Carraway, m. by: James Gray, J. P., June 3, 1819, WILSON Co.

EDWARDS, Brown to Sally Harrison - issued March 18, 1813, Bondsman: Richard Whalen, GRAINGER Co.

EDWARDS, Charles A. to Tabitha V. Ivie - issued December 1, 1834, Bondsman: Robert B. Warren, RUTHERFORD Co.

EDWARDS, Clayton T. to Pantha A. Stark - issued December 26, 1851, m. by: B. Randolph, J. P., ROBERTSON Co.

EDWARDS, Drew to Catherine Dorris - issued November 23, 1821, Bondsman: Thos. Edwards, SUMNER Co.

EDWARDS, Eaton to Merrim Bennett - issued May 29, 1832, Bondsman: Stokes Edwards, WILSON Co.

EDWARDS, Edward to Catharine Countryman - issued October 14, 1816, m. by: John L. Jetton October 17, 1816, RUTHERFORD Co.

EDWARDS, Edward to Nancy Clemons - issued December 19, 1815, Bondsman: Nicholas Edwards, m. by: Isaac Winston, J. P., December 28, 1815, WILSON Co.

EDWARDS, Edward to Solila Walker - issued March 23, 1849, Bondsman: Wm. E. Graham, m. by: R. P. Bowling, J. P., March 23, 1849, MONTGOMERY Co.

EDWARDS, Edward G. to Angelette Brewer - issued January 29, 1861, m. by: G. W. Featherston, M. G., January 30, 1861, ROBERTSON Co.

EDWARDS, Eli to Milly Hancock - issued June 17, 1817, Bondsman: Jonathan Doke, m. by: Edward Harris, J. P., June 19, 1817, WILSON Co.

EDWARDS, Elias to Nancy Mansfield - issued July 6, 1822, m. by: John Jarratt July 9, 1822, WILSON Co.

EDWARDS, George W. to Annie D. Norvell - issued September 8, 1859, m. by: W. B. Watterson, M. G., September 8, 1859, COFFEE Co.

EDWARDS, Green B. to Martha Howard - issued July 21, 1821, Bondsman: Benjamin Casilman, m. by: James Bond, V. D. M., July 23, 1821, WILSON Co.

EDWARDS, Henry to Nancy Edwards - issued November 13, 1835, Bondsman: William Fields, m. by: James Bond, V. D. M., November 16, 1835, WILSON Co.

EDWARDS, Henry to Jane Edwards - issued July 29, 1839, Bondsman: John A. Smart, m. by: Jas. Baird, J. P., July 30, 1839, WILSON Co.

EDWARDS, Hiram to Sally Bond - issued April 28, 1817, Bondsman: Bradford Edwards, m. by: Edward Willis, V. D. M., April 29, 1817, WILSON Co.

EDWARDS, Howard to Dize Bennett - issued February 19, 1816, Bondsman: Bradford Howard, m. by: Jacob Silivan February 20, 1816, WILSON Co.

EDWARDS, Hugh to Judy Hill - issued November 9, 1822, m. by: Elijah Maddox, M. G., November 12, 1822, WILSON Co.

EDWARDS, Isaac to ___(?) - issued May 1, 1847, Bondsman:
Asa W. Edwards, m. by: Wm. Dinwiddie, M. G., May 2, 1847,
MONTGOMERY Co.

EDWARDS, James to Patsey Cartwright - issued June 19, 1800, Bondsman:
William Hankins, SUMNER Co.

EDWARDS, James to Levy Henry - issued March 3, 1832, Bondsman:
J. H. Brittain, WILSON Co.

EDWARDS, James to Jemima Braves - issued August 2, 1838, m. by:
Edward Edwards, M. G., ROBERTSON Co.

EDWARDS, James A. to Sarah Clifton - issued September 5, 1866, FRANKLIN Co.

EDWARDS, James A. to Sarah Clifton - issued September 5, 1866, m. by:
R. P. Gannaway, M. G., September 31, 1866, FRANKLIN Co.

EDWARDS, Jesse to Elizabeth Smith - issued March 31, 1847, DICKSON Co.

EDWARDS, John to Sarah Cummins - issued July 21, 1804, Bondsman:
O. M. Benge, RUTHERFORD Co.

EDWARDS, John to Mary Richmond - issued January 25, 1819, Bondsman:
Bradford Howard, m. by: Benjamin Cassilman January 28, 1819,
WILSON Co.

EDWARDS, John to Mary C. Burch - February 4, 1822, m. by: Joshua Butcher
(1823?), GILES Co.

EDWARDS, John to Jane Edwards - issued June 25, 1835, Bondsman:
Henry Edwards, m. by: James Bond, V. D. M., WILSON Co.

EDWARDS, John to Marjah Annah Pentecost - issued October 25, 1846,
DICKSON Co.

EDWARDS, John J. to Nancy Ward - issued September 23, 1829, Bondsman:
John W. Richardson, RUTHERFORD Co.

EDWARDS, John K. to Elizabeth H. Billings - issued November 8, 1834,
Bondsman: James Hankins, WILSON Co.

EDWARDS, John L. to Euphrasha E. Lasater - issued October 3, 1850,
m. by: W. W. Fariss, M. G., October 3, 1850, FRANKLIN Co.

EDWARDS, John T. to Elizabeth McClure - issued December 31, 1840,
FRANKLIN Co.

EDWARDS, Jonathan to M. Lucas (Smith) - issued December 24, 1848,
m. by: John Forbes, J. P., ROBERTSON Co.

EDWARDS, Joseph J. to Sarah Frances Morgan - issued October 7, 1853,
m. by: Jo Lawrence, J. P., ROBERTSON Co.

EDWARDS, Justice to Elizabeth Hufner - issued October 27, 1838,
Bondsman: Wm. Waland, m. by: John Toff, J. P., October 28, 1838,
MEIGS Co.

EDWARDS, L. F. to M. W. Jackson - issued December 16, 1858, m. by:
W. S. Adams December 19, 1858, ROBERTSON Co.

EDWARDS, Lauson to Martha Hooper - issued April 10, 1845, m. by:
Joseph Willis, M. G., April 10, 1845, DAVIDSON Co.

EDWARDS, Levi to Delilah Smith - issued March 5, 1818, m. by:
Jacob Wright, J. P., March 5, 1818, RUTHERFORD Co.

EDWARDS, Lewis to Mary Chamberlain - issued January 29, 1807, Bondsman:
W. Hall, GRAINGER Co.

EDWARDS, Margaret to Isaic Wright - BEDFORD Co.

EDWARDS, Marvin to Polly Whitlaw - issued November 13, 1820, Bondsman:
    Joseph Stacy, WILSON Co.

EDWARDS, Mary to John Scott - GREENE Co.

EDWARDS, Mary Jane to Jessee W. Shockley - BEDFORD Co.

EDWARDS, Meredith L. to Eliza Newton - issued November 12, 1846,
    m. by: David Herring, J. P., ROBERTSON Co.

EDWARDS, Michael to Sarah Bennett - issued September 21, 1831, Bondsman:
    Crafford Edwards, m. by: S. A. Huddleston, J. P., September 22,
    1831, WILSON Co.

EDWARDS, Nicholas to Milly Powers - issued October 24, 1812, Bondsman:
    David Moses, m. by: Winston, J. P., October 25, 1812, WILSON Co.

EDWARDS, Oliver to Elizabeth Sherrod - issued November 22, 1843, m. by:
    W. W. Williams, J. P., ROBERTSON Co.

EDWARDS, Polly to Robert Logan - MAURY Co.

EDWARDS, Presley to Mary Sims - issued November 15, 1820, Bondsman:
    Thomas Edwards, m. by: John Atkinson, V. D. M., WILSON Co.

EDWARDS, Richard A. to Frances A. Mathis - issued September 16, 1833,
    Bondsman: R. H. White, RUTHERFORD Co.

EDWARDS, Robert B. to Ann Ewing - issued July 3, 1838, Bondsman:
    Robert Fakes, m. by: J. Hooker, M. G., July 5, 1838, WILSON Co.

EDWARDS, Robert H. to Minerva Robertson - issued January 24, 1829,
    Bondsman: John T. Lee, WILSON Co.

EDWARDS, Roderick to Anne D. Brumfield - issued September 24, 1823,
    Bondsman: William Wilson, RUTHERFORD Co.

EDWARDS, Ruthy to Isaac Mayes - MAURY Co.

EDWARDS, Seaborn to Sally Hodges - issued June 9, 1827, Bondsman:
    Ransom Hodges, SUMNER Co.

EDWARDS, Simon to Elizabeth Hail - issued March 6, 1808, Bondsman:
    Adonyah Edwards, SUMNER Co.

EDWARDS, Sterling to Mahala Pucket - issued December 24, 1827, Bondsman:
    James B. Guthrie, WILSON Co.

EDWARDS, Stokes to Sarah Lane - issued January 9, 1832, Bondsman:
    Eaton Edwards, WILSON Co.

EDWARDS, Theophilus to Martha Edwards - issued August 6, 1836, Bondsman:
    Joseph Maning, m. by: Sion Bass, M. G., WILSON Co.

EDWARDS, Thomas to Elizabeth Turner - issued February 7, 1792, Bondsman:
    Edward Williams, SUMNER Co.

EDWARDS, Thomas to Priscilla Edwards - issued May 4, 1810, Bondsman:
    William White, SUMNER Co.

EDWARDS, Thomas J. to Jane Dunlap - issued February 11, 1834, Bondsman:
    Thomas Edwards, m. by: A. S. Edwards, J. P., February 11, 1834,
    RUTHERFORD Co.

EDWARDS, W. A. to Amelia Huffman - issued September 27, 1836, Bondsman:
    Isaac W. Harris, m. by: Jas. Tompkins September 27, 1836, SUMNER Co.

EDWARDS, Warren to Polly Whitlaw - issued November 13, 1821, m. by:
Joshua Lester, V. D. M., November 15, 1821, WILSON Co.

EDWARDS, Welden to Rachel West - issued July 20, 1835, Bondsman:
William G. Cook, RUTHERFORD Co.

EDWARDS, Wiley to Malinda Canin - issued December 1, 1857, FRANKLIN Co.

EDWARDS, Wiley to Milley Gamble - issued October 27, 1843, m. by:
D. N. Brakefield, J. P., October 27, 1843, FRANKLIN Co.

EDWARDS, Jr., William to Peggy Hassel - issued September 13, 1806,
Bondsman: Richard Edwards, SUMNER Co.

EDWARDS, William to Sarah Williams - February 28, 1811, Bondsman:
Adanyah Edwards, MAURY Co.

EDWARDS, William to Mary Cantrell - issued October 31, 1821, Bondsman:
A. W. Reese, m. by: Hugh Kirkpatrick, M. G., October 31, 1821,
SUMNER Co.

EDWARDS, William to Judy Brazel - issued January 21, 1822, Bondsman:
Solomon Shoulders, SUMNER Co.

EDWARDS, William to Patsy Maning - issued September 8, 1828, Bondsman:
F. Brown, WILSON Co.

EDWARDS, William to Nancy D. Price - issued August 12, 1846, ROBERTSON Co.

EDWARDS, William to Melvina Crownover - m. by: M. Catchings, J. P.,
September 3, 1850, FRANKLIN Co.

EDWARDS, William A. to Nancy Caroline Eberly - Bondsman:
Theophilus Watkins, m. by: Joseph Sturdivant, J. P., February 3,
1846, MONTGOMERY Co.

EDWARDS, William A. to Sarah Banks - issued August 2, 1855, m. by:
John M. Brakefield, J. P., August 2, 1855, FRANKLIN Co.

EDWARDS, Wm. C. to Eliza A. Nelson - issued April 1, 1830, Bondsman:
Wm. T. Christy, m. by: Peyton Smith April 1, 1830, RUTHERFORD Co.

EDWARDS, William C. to Francis Durham - issued September 17, 1846,
m. by: W. B. Wagner, J. P., September 17, 1846, FRANKLIN Co.

EDWARDS, William H. to Manervia Ann Frey - issued December 22, 1854,
m. by: G. B. Mason, J. P., December 24, 1854, ROBERTSON Co.

EDYMAN, Kimblee to Polly Nicholas - issued October 10, 1797, Bondsman:
Isaiah Mid Kiff, GRAINGER Co.

EFFITOR, Archibald to Martha Lemon - issued October 6, 1796, Bondsman:
Peter Lemon, SUMNER Co.

EGGLESTON, John W. to Ann W. West - issued October 22, 1836, Bondsman:
Richmond Wood, m. by: John Landrum, J. P., October 24, 1836,
RUTHERFORD Co.

EGGLESTON, William C. to Elizabeth C. Hickman - issued October 28,
1857, m. by: D. B. Muse, J. P., October 29, 1857, FRANKLIN Co.

EGLETON, David to Elizabeth Hooks - June 2, 1797, BLOUNT Co.

EGMON, Bartholemew to Paulina Kelly - issued February 2, 1841, m. by:
Elisha House, M. G., ROBERTSON Co.

EGMON, Ibby (?) to Thomas Watson (?) - August 25, 1808, Bondsman:
William W. Thompson, MAURY Co.

EGNEW, Margaret to ___(?) - MAURY Co.

EHART, Christian to Mary Brady - issued May 26, 1810, Bondsman:
Matthew McClahahan, RUTHERFORD Co.

EIDSON, E. B. to Susan Browning - issued November 22, 1853, m. by:
John Crafford, J. P., ROBERTSON Co.

EIDSON, Isiaeh to Harriett Adams - issued October 4, 1843, m. by:
William L. Perry, J. P., ROBERTSON Co.

EIDSON, James E. to N. Randolph - issued July 10, 1858, m. by:
R. H. Harrison July 11, 1858, ROBERTSON Co.

EIDSON, Joseph to Peggy Dorris - issued February 9, 1821, Bondsman:
Samuel Edison, SUMNER Co.

EIDSON, Richard to Martha Crews - issued November 11, 1832, Bondsman:
Nathan Crews, SUMNER Co.

EIDSON, Thos. J. to Elizabeth Shy - issued May 7, 1860, m. by:
J. N. Thornhill, J. P., May 10, 1860, ROBERTSON Co.

EILY, Nicholas to Elizabeth Smelser - November 5, 1800, Security:
James McKeehen, GREENE Co.

ELAM, Archie S. to Sarah Cheek - issued July 25, 1832, Bondsman:
Wallace Honeycut, m. by: Dan'l Latimer, J. P., July 25, 1832,
SUMNER Co.

ELAM, Edward to Rebecca Wade - issued April 18, 1821, m. by:
Robt. Henderson April 18, 1821, RUTHERFORD Co.

ELAM, James A. to Catharine M. Lingow - issued November 3, 1841, m. by:
James Rowe, M. G., November 4, 1841, DAVIDSON Co.

ELAM, Joel to Mary Aikin - issued June 11, 1824, Bondsman:
Reuben Wright, RUTHERFORD Co.

ELAM, Josephus to Averrilla Turpin - issued February 8, 1832, Bondsman:
Joel Elam, m. by: Robt. Patton, J. P., February 8, 1832, SUMNER Co.

ELAM, Josiah to Elizabeth Catron - issued February 11, 1828, Bondsman:
A. H. Guthrie, SUMNER Co.

ELAM, Matthew to Mary W. Edmiston - April 10, 1817, WILLIAMSON Co.

ELAM, Matthew to Nancy Jackson - May 7, 1817, WILLIAMSON Co.

ELAM, Peter to Margaret King - m. by: Peter Ketring March 7, 1833,
SUMNER Co.

ELAM, William to Jemima Strange - issued February 2, 1830, Bondsman:
Samuel Winston, RUTHERFORD Co.

ELDER, A. W. to Susan J. Campbell - issued August 26, 1830, Bondsman:
Mat. M. Gaines, m. by: Tho. H. Nelson August 26, 1830, KNOX Co.

ELDER, Andrew to Elizabeth Snider - issued May 22, 1806, Bondsman:
Charles McEnelley, GRAINGER Co.

ELDER, Benjamin to Eliza A. Wade - issued February 7, 1827, Bondsman:
Charles Guyger, m. by: John Worthan Hall February 8, 1827,
RUTHERFORD Co.

ELDER, James to Polly Watwood - issued September 21, 1803, Bondsman:
James Suiter, SUMNER Co.

ELDER, James to Polly Wood - issued July 2, 1816, m. by: John Hoover,
J. P., July 15, 1816, RUTHERFORD Co.

ELDER, James to Jane Watson - issued March 26, 1829, Bondsman: David Myers, m. by: John Lane, RUTHERFORD Co.

ELDER, Joshua to Lydia Etter - issued January 29, 1824, Bondsman: Hezekiah House, m. by: Peyton Smith January 29, 1824, RUTHERFORD Co.

ELDER, Joshua to Miss M. M. Martin - issued November 27, 1849, Bondsman: F. A. Hammon, m. by: J. T. Hendrick November 27, 1849, MONTGOMERY Co.

ELDER, William to Tabitha Nance - issued December 18, 1828, m. by: John Lane, RUTHERFORD Co.

ELDER, Wm. B. to Mary Keenum - issued October 23, 1844, Bondsman: Wm. Elderd, m. by: Ezekial Ward October 24, 1844, MEIGS Co.

ELDRIDGE, Edwin H. to Elizabeth M. Haynes - issued October 26, 1854, Bondsman: W. H. Eldridge, m. by: J. C. Mickle, L. D. of M. E., October 27, 1854, MONTGOMERY Co.

ELDRIDGE, John to Sarah Gillaland - issued December 2, 1796, Bondsman: Jesse Aldridge, Witness: Andrew White, KNOX Co.

ELDRIDGE, Mary to William McBroom (?) - GREENE Co.

ELDRIDGE, Nathaniel to Rebecca Davis - issued May 12, 1798, Bondsman: William Davis, KNOX Co.

ELDRIDGE, Stephen to Milly Walker - issued December 18, 1823, Bondsman: Wm. Hazen, Witness: Wm. Swan, KNOX Co.

ELGIN, Samuel to Lucinda Jones - issued March 25, 1829, Bondsman: S. H. Laughlin, RUTHERFORD Co.

ELGIN, William B. to Elizabeth Ann Morris - issued November 1, 1833, Bondsman: John Smith, WILSON Co.

ELIESON, John C. to Polly Watts - issued August 29, 1836, Bondsman: Wm. O. Barnes, KNOX Co.

ELISTON, John to Ann Ridley - November 7, 1816, WILLIAMSON Co.

ELIM, Samuel to Elizabeth Jones - issued July 27, 1820, Bondsman: Daniel H. Slater and Ethelbert W. Sanders, m. by: Dan'l McAuloy, J. P., July 27, 1820, SUMNER Co.

ELIZER, James B. to Mary Garrett - issued September 14, 1829, Bondsman: Daniel Sample, m. by: N. Patton September 14, 1829, SUMNER Co.

ELKIN, David to Letty Gault - issued March 25, 1828, Bondsman: Jno. Caldwell, m. by: Jno. Bayless, J. P., March 26, 1828, KNOX Co.

ELKIN, Robt. to Nancy Colyar - issued January 1, 1857, m. by: W. W. Estill, M. G., FRANKLIN Co.

ELKINS, A. R. to M. E. Bennett - issued July 25, 1866, FRANKLIN Co.

ELKINS, Alsey to ___(?) - issued April 2, 1810, Bondsman: Mevell Elkins, WILSON Co.

ELKINS, Drury to Sarah Hill - issued July 29, 1837, Bondsman: Robert Hill, m. by: Wm. Dennis July 29, 1837, GRAINGER Co.

ELKINS, Sr., J. M. to Lucretia Tate - issued January 8, 1866, m. January 8, 1866, FRANKLIN Co.

ELKINS, James to Sytha Chesher - issued February 26, 1810, Bondsman: Thornton Chesher, GRAINGER Co.

ELKINS, James M. to Sallie Buckner - issued December 18, 1865, m. by: Asa D. Oakley, M. G., December 19, 1865, FRANKLIN Co.

ELKINS, Joseph to Patsy Whitecotton - issued October 7, 1817, m. by:
John Bayless, J. P., October 28, 1817, KNOX Co.

ELKINS, Merrel to Thankful Maddox - issued April 16, 1810, Bondsman:
Jacob Castleman, WILSON Co.

ELKINS, William to Mary Ann Davis - issued April 28, 1821, Bondsman:
Anthony Cardwell, GRAINGER Co.

ELKINS, Wm. to Sarah Larew - issued February 26, 1824, Bondsman:
Joel Kirkpatrick, m. by: John Bayless, J. P., February 26, 1824,
Witness: Wm. Swan, KNOX Co.

ELKS, Noah to Sary I. Clark - issued September 20, 1850, m. by:
Tho. West, Baptist Minister, September 24, 1850, ROBERTSON Co.

ELLEDGE, Hamilton to Nancy Holt - issued February 15, 1837, Bondsman:
Pharoa Price, m. by: Eli Hodges, J. P., February 15, 1837,
GRAINGER Co.

ELLEDGE, Isaac to Jane Morrow - issued September 15, 1837, KNOX Co.

ELLEDGE, John B. to Elizabeth Edwards - issued May 24, 1836, Bondsman:
Anderson Hopper, m. by: Eli Hodge, J. P., GRAINGER Co.

ELLESON, Andrew to Milly Swift - issued May 3, 1844, m. by:
James Sprouse, J. P., May 4, 1844, ROBERTSON Co.

ELLIMORE, Reuben to Julia Crawford - issued September 18, 1842, m. by:
Richd. Chowning, J. P., ROBERTSON Co.

ELLINGTON, John to Susan McDowell - issued January 8, 1856, m. by:
L. Burnum, J. P., January 8, 1856, COFFEE Co.

ELLIOT, Jr., David to Lutitia Davis - issued January 15, 1846, m. by:
R. W. Morrison, J. P., January 13, 1846, MONTGOMERY Co.

ELLIOT, James to Polly Carlock - issued January 16, 1806, Bondsman:
John Quesinberry, WILSON Co.

ELLIOT, Matthew to Ruth Underhill - issued February 26, 1802, Bondsman:
William Elliot, Witness: John Hall, GRAINGER Co.

ELLIOT, William to Dianna Stinnett (?) - issued July 19, 1806, m. by:
R. Houston, J. P., July 19, 1806, KNOX Co.

ELLIOTT, Alfred to Tennessee Smith - issued December 19, 1843, m. by:
Allen Nesbitt, J. P., December 19, 1843, DICKSON Co.

ELLIOTT, Alpheus to Mary Eliz. Barbee - issued October 28, 1839, m. by:
John Forbes, J. P., October 29, 1839, ROBERTSON Co.

ELLIOTT, B. T. to M. Rich - issued June 2, 1874, m. by: Wm. M. Sells,
J. P., June 7, 1874, FRANKLIN Co.

ELLIOTT, Barney to Rebecca Freeman - issued September 22, 1818,
Bondsman: Charles Lock, RUTHERFORD Co.

ELLIOTT, Benjamin to Elizabeth Gover - issued December 18, 1846,
m. by: Benjamin Sells, J. P., December 18, 1846, FRANKLIN Co.

ELLIOTT, David A. to Ann M. Adams - issued November 2, 1853, Bondsman:
A. J. Elliott, m. by: A. H. Berry, Minister, November 3, 1853,
MONTGOMERY Co.

ELLIOTT, Dawson E. to Mary R. Bradford - issued December 23, 1849,
m. by: F. B. Wade, J. P., December 23, 1849, FRANKLIN Co.

ELLIOTT, Dempsy to Levina Cage - issued January 2, 1831, Bondsman:
Y. N. Douglass, m. by: H. W. Hunt January 2, 1831, SUMNER Co.

ELLIOTT, F. M. to Sarah E. Frizzell - issued January 5, 1863, Bondsman: Sanders Elliott, Jos. H. Thompson, Clk., BEDFORD Co.

ELLIOTT, Francis M. to Fanny Sparks - issued July 28, 1873, m. by: Peyton Wilkerson, M. G., July 29, 1873, FRANKLIN Co.

ELLIOTT, Isaac to Feriby Williams - issued May 29, 1823, Bondsman: Wilson Parker, m. by: Wm. B. Carns, J. P., May 29, 1823, KNOX Co.

ELLIOTT, J. B. to M. C. Odear - issued December 2, 1871, m. by: C. C. Rose, J. P., December 3, 1871, FRANKLIN Co.

ELLIOTT, James to Elender Inman - issued September 10, 1812, Bondsman: John W. Byrn, SUMNER Co.

ELLIOTT, James H. to Martha C. Butts - issued December 14, 1852, m. by: D. Herring, J. P., ROBERTSON Co.

ELLIOTT, John to Mourning Drinkard - January 23, 1816, WILLIAMSON Co.

ELLIOTT, John to Polly Rose - issued December 1, 1825, Bondsman: Josiah Armstrong, m. by: Wm. Morris, J. P., December 1, 1825, KNOX Co.

ELLIOTT, John B. to Mary Kirby - issued December 5, 1856, m. by: James Seargent, J. P., December 5, 1856, FRANKLIN Co.

ELLIOTT, John R. to Frances A. Bobo - issued July 15, 1838, m. by: William L. Perry, J. P., ROBERTSON Co.

ELLIOTT, Joseph J. to Sarah Ann Toler - issued November 9, 1851, Bondsman: T. G. Driskoll, m. by: J. C. Bryan, J. P., November 9, 1851, MONTGOMERY Co.

ELLIOTT, Knacy H. to Martha W. Slack - issued May 6, 1834, Bondsman: Martin Clark, RUTHERFORD Co.

ELLIOTT, L. P. to Mary F. Bruce - issued March 21, 1867, m. by: J. B. Foster, J. P., March 21, 1867, FRANKLIN Co.

ELLIOTT, Lucy to Andrew Gowam - MAURY Co.

ELLIOTT, Peter P. to Susan J. Eddings - issued November 29, 1837, Bondsman: John A. Sneed, WILSON Co.

ELLIOTT, Richard J. to Mary E. Stanback - issued September 1, 1847, m. by: Benj. Sharpe, J. P., September 1, 1847, DAVIDSON Co.

ELLIOTT, Richard S. to Margaret Uselton - issued December 12, 1832, m. by: William Keele, M. G., December 20, 1832, RUTHERFORD Co.

ELLIOTT, Robert to Elizabeth Curry - issued September 18, 1824, Bondsman: Adam Elliot, m. by: John Beard, M. G., September 22, 1829, WILSON Co.

ELLIOTT, Robert to Ann Thorn - issued January 1, 1827, Bondsman: William Brady, RUTHERFORD Co.

ELLIOTT, S. M. to Nancy Frizzell - issued February 22, 1862, Bondsman: W. W. Tribble, Jos. H. Thompson, Clk., BEDFORD Co.

ELLIOTT, Samuel to Jane Manly - April 16, 1816, KNOX Co.

ELLIOTT, Saml. H. to Nancy Hyde - issued September 12, 1841, m. by: J. W. Hunt, J. P., ROBERTSON Co.

ELLIOTT, Simon to Candas Dean - issued May 26, 1820, m. by: John Clark, J. P., June 1, 1820, RUTHERFORD Co.

ELLIOTT, Stephen to Nancy Jane Porter - issued June 10, 1856, m. by:
A. B. Cummings, M. G., June 10, 1856, COFFEE Co.

ELLIOTT, Thomas to Margaret Miller - issued October 8, 1824, Bondsman:
William Johnston, RUTHERFORD Co.

ELLIOTT, Thomas to Jane Rushing - issued January 16, 1837, Bondsman:
Peter N. Elliott, RUTHERFORD Co.

ELLIOTT, Thomas L. to Ann Barber - issued December 22, 1847, m. by:
Benj. Sharpe, J. P., December 22, 1847, DAVIDSON Co.

ELLIOTT, William to Polly Elliott - February 6, 1811, WILLIAMSON Co.

ELLIOTT, Wm. to Lucinda R. Landrum - issued June 19, 1836, Bondsman:
Thos. M. Landrum, KNOX Co.

ELLIOTT, Wm. to Lucinda R. Landrum - issued June 19, 1836, m. by:
Jas. D. Murray, J. P., June 19, 1836, KNOX Co.

ELLIOTT, William to Huldah Holder - issued November 7, 1845, m. by:
Benjamin Sells, J. P., November 17, 1844, FRANKLIN Co.

ELLIOTT, Wm. F. to Irena Logan - issued October 17, 1844, m. by:
N. P., Modrall, M. G., October 17, 1844, FRANKLIN Co.

ELLIOTT, William H. to Virginia T. Naive - issued January 28, 1860,
m. by: M. W. Winters, J. P., February 9, 1860, ROBERTSON Co.

ELLIOTT, William John to Sophia Pierson - issued November 29, 1813,
Bondsman: William Boyd, KNOX Co.

ELLIS, Abraham to Prudence Lindsey - issued April 24, 1800, Bondsman:
Ezekiel Lindsey, SUMNER Co.

ELLIS, Absolom to Elender L. Jones - issued March 17, 1821, Bondsman:
Redding B. Jones, m. by: Brinkley Bridges, J. P., May 7, 1821,
WILSON Co.

ELLIS, B. F. to Faney P. Garrett - issued May 22, 1861, Bondsman:
C. P. Houston, Jr., Jos. H. Thompson, Clk., BEDFORD Co.

ELLIS, Edward J. to Caroline C. Dick - issued March 28, 1848, m. by:
R. Caldwell, J. P., April 6, 1848, STEWART Co.

ELLIS, Fletcher to Nancy Lightfoot - issued April 9, 1839, m. by:
M. F. Mitchell, J. P., April 9, 1839, STEWART Co.

ELLIS, George to Jane Perry - issued April 15, 1871, m. by: D. S. Long,
J. P., April 15, 1871, FRANKLIN Co.

ELLIS, George W. to Caroline Smith - issued August 24, 1859, m. by:
C. C. Chapman, J. P., August 24, 1859, COFFEE Co.

ELLIS, Hicks to Lucy Jones - issued September 25, 1827, Bondsman:
Micheal Jones, m. by: A. Provine October 25, 1827, WILSON Co.

ELLIS, Isaac to Polly Hudson - issued March 19, 1810, Bondsman:
John Hudson, SUMNER Co.

ELLIS, Isaac to Nancy Jennings - issued October 31, 1827, Bondsman:
Jesse B. White, m. by: James T. Tompkins November 2, 1827,
WILSON Co.

ELLIS, James to Nancy Wren - August 13, 1810, Bondsman: Micajah Brooks,
MAURY Co.

ELLIS, James to Susanah Cattron - issued September 4, 1813, Bondsman:
Everard Ellis, SUMNER Co.

415

ELLIS, James to Rebecca Belcher - issued January 3, 1818, Bondsman:
Martin Tally, WILSON Co.

ELLIS, James to Abba Proctor - issued April 27, 1848, m. by:
C. Grymes, J. P., April 27, 1848, DICKSON Co.

ELLIS, James R. to Jane B. McSpedden - issued October 6, 1835, Bondsman:
Robert Garrison, m. by: Robt. H. Ellis October 7, 1835, WILSON Co.

ELLIS, James T. to Susanna Wright - issued August 29, 1816, Bondsman:
Jacob Ellis, SUMNER Co.

ELLIS, Jehu to Phebe Nordyke - August 1, 1798, JEFFERSON Co.

ELLIS, John to Tamar Colson - December 4, 1800, Security:
Newhope Quaker Meeting, GREENE Co.

ELLIS, John to Sarah Clapp - issued September 14, 1816, m. by:
John Thompson, J. P., September 26, 1816, KNOX Co.

ELLIS, John to Mary Sandiford - issued January 18, 1817, Bondsman:
John Campbell, m. by: John Williamson, J. P., January 19, 1817,
WILSON Co.

ELLIS, John to Mary B. Adair - issued July 4, 1838, m. by:
Wm. S, Smith, M. G., FRANKLIN Co.

ELLIS, John A. to Martha Hearn - issued September 18, 1837, Bondsman:
William Ballenger, m. by: Markley S. Fare, M. G., January 1, 1838,
WILSON Co.

ELLIS, John A. to Martha J. Hall - issued December 4, 1871, FRANKLIN Co.

ELLIS, John B. to Juleitt E. A. Mathews - issued September 9, 1848,
m. by: A. Elliott, L. E., September 10, 1848, STEWART Co.

ELLIS, John E. to Harriett Hinson - issued March 31, 1840, m. by:
Willie Miller, J. P., March 31, 1840, DICKSON Co.

ELLIS, John J. to Sarah C. Irion - September 26, 1817, WILLIAMSON Co.

ELLIS, John W. to Cherry Parker - issued December 9, 1830, Bondsman:
John J. Ellis, m. by: Garrett, J. P., December 9, 1830, SUMNER Co.

ELLIS, John W. to Chelly Ann T. Sluder - issued April 30, 1839,
Bondsman: Wm. B. McLendon, WILSON Co.

ELLIS, Joseph to Francis L. Smith - issued December 15, 1855, m. by:
Lewis Anderson, J. P., December 18, 1855, FRANKLIN Co.

ELLIS, Jos. W. to Sally Winslow - March 5, 1808, WILLIAMSON Co.

ELLIS, Josiah to Ann Loyd - issued July 31, 1824, Bondsman: Hicks Ellis,
m. by: G. W. Banton, J. P., August 3, 1824, RUTHERFORD Co.

ELLIS, Levi to Cynthia Bradford - issued March 16, 1811, Bondsman:
Daniel Jones, SUMNER Co.

ELLIS, Lewis N. to Sally Jennings - issued September 4, 1827, Bondsman:
Bechman Bunch, m. by: J. C. Bunch, J. P., September 4, 1827,
GRAINGER Co.

ELLIS, Michael to Leona Moore - issued December 24, 1829, Bondsman:
Granville Moore, m. by: J. P. Hogan, J. P., December 24, 1829,
SUMNER Co.

ELLIS, Miles to Martha Hancock - issued December 27, 1838, Bondsman:
Pollas Lawrence, WILSON Co.

ELLIS, Nancy to Abraham Collett - GREENE Co.

ELLIS, Rachel to Aaron Hammer - GREENE Co.

ELLIS, Robert to Prudence Belcher - issued February 19, 1820, Bondsman: James Ellis, WILSON Co.

ELLIS, Shobal to Sarah Wright - November 7, 1796, Security: Abner Frazier, GREENE Co.

ELLIS, Simion to Delilas Smith - issued November 25, 1808, Bondsman: Abraham Ellis, SUMNER Co.

ELLIS, Smelling to Peggy Hudson - issued November 14, 1810, Bondsman: Benj. Hudson, SUMNER Co.

ELLIS, Susannah to Samuel Pickering - August 19, 1799, Security: Absalom Haworth, GREENE Co.

ELLIS, Thomas to Lydda Reese - July 23, 1793, Security: Jacob Humbard, GREENE Co.

ELLIS, Thomas to Jane Allen - February 8, 1815, WILLIAMSON Co.

ELLIS, Thomas to Malissa Tips - issued November 24, 1852, Bondsman: Benjamin Ferrill, m. by: T. H. Batson, J. P., November 25, 1852, MONTGOMERY Co.

ELLIS, Thomas B. to Susan M. Robinson - issued December 8, 1832, RUTHERFORD Co.

ELLIS, Thos. B. to Mary C. Mathis - issued December 6, 1843, m. by: James E. Nix, M. G., December 7, 1843, STEWART Co.

ELLIS, Thomas W. to Caroline Glanton - issued May 25, 1818, Bondsman: Richard Byrd, m. by: William Grey, J. P., May 23, 1818, WILSON Co.

ELLIS, Thomas W. to Sally Wright - issued September 10, 1821, Bondsman: John Blurton, m. by: William Gray, J. P., September 13, 1821, WILSON Co.

ELLIS, Thomas W. to Martha Cook - issued May 21, 1833, Bondsman: O. M. Rice, m. by: Thomas Babb, J. P., WILSON Co.

ELLIS, Travis to Mary Jane Hagan - issued November 9, 1847, m. by: Peter Fuqua November 10, 1847, DAVIDSON Co.

ELLIS, William to Hannah Beals - November 20, 1806, Security: Newhope Quaker Meeting, GREENE Co.

ELLIS, William to Pheby Lacy - issued November 16, 1817, Bondsman: John Cocke, m. by: Geo. Moody, J. P., GRAINGER Co.

ELLIS, Wm. to Ann Jane Finaly - issued April 16, 1838, m. by: Jesse Edwards, J. P., April 20, 1838, STEWART Co.

ELLIS, Wm. E. to Mary Ann Ellis - issued February 12, 1838, m. by: Thos. Jarragin, J. P., February 15, 1838, DICKSON Co.

ELLIS, William E. to Eliza Collishaw - issued August 23, 1853, Bondsman: John C. Read, MONTGOMERY Co.

ELLIS, William M. to George Ann West - issued April 11, 1842, m. by: Jesse Edward, M. G., April 12, 1841 (42), DICKSON Co.

ELLIS, Wm. R. to Hulda Hall - issued November 6, 1871, FRANKLIN Co.

ELLIS, William W. to Rhoda Curtis - issued June 27, 1829, Bondsman: Joseph P. Holt, RUTHERFORD Co.

ELLIS, Wm. W. to Susan Clark - issued August 16, 1847, m. by: R. B. C. Howell, M. G., August 16, 1847, DAVIDSON Co.

ELLIS, Wyatt H. to May Dixon - issued November 9, 1836, Bondsman:
L. D. Baker, RUTHERFORD Co.

ELLIS, Wyley to Sarah H. James - issued August 29, 1836, Bondsman:
C. G. Mitchell, m. by: John Lane, M. G., September, 1836,
RUTHERFORD Co.

ELLISON, Charles to Harriet Pepper - issued August 1, 1860, m. by:
Jas Cook, J. P., August 2, 1860, ROBERTSON Co.

ELLISON, Hugh H. to Nancy Becton - issued March 9, 1820, m. by:
Peyton Smith March 10, 1820, RUTHERFORD Co.

ELLISON, Jacob to Elizabeth Crenshaw - issued February 20, 1820,
Bondsman: Thos. Scurry, m. by: Thos. Anderson, J. P., February 20,
1820, SUMNER Co.

ELLISON, John to Eliza Brown - issued June 3, 1847, DICKSON Co.

ELLISON, John to Mary Gaines - issued November 22, 1847, m. by:
R. G. Cole, J. P., ROBERTSON Co.

ELLISON, John to Narcissa Morrow - issued July 31, 1861, Bondsman:
W. E. Carrell, m. by: Samuel McBride, J. P., July 31, 1861,
LAWRENCE Co.

ELLISON, Joseph to Sarah Ann Butler - issued April 14, 1857, m. by:
John Q. A. Farrar, J. P., April 16, 1857, COFFEE Co.

ELLISON, Sam'l to Ivorella Lankford - issued February, 1845, STEWART Co.

ELLISON, William B. to Ann Cannady - issued December 26, 1846, m. by:
Sam'l Kingston, M. G., December 27, 1846, DAVIDSON Co.

ELLISON, Z. J. to Mary Hendley - issued May 2, 1844, m. by: Wm. Lyons,
J. P., May 2, 1844, FRANKLIN Co.

ELLISTON, Alexander to Cinthia Hart - issued March 3, 1824, m. by:
John Wiseman, M. G., March 3, 1824, SUMNER Co.

ELLISTON, Joseph T. to Elizabeth Blackman - issued December 10, 1817,
Bondsman: A. B. Shelby, SUMNER Co.

ELLISS, Everard to Polly Calvin - issued September 17, 1806, Bondsman:
William Rainey, SUMNER Co.

ELLISS, John to Nancy Britton - issued August 11, 1804, Bondsman:
Wm. Garrett, SUMNER Co.

ELLY, Josiah to Jane Lawrence - issued June 2, 1821, Bondsman:
Oliver Oneal, m. by: John Gray June 7, 1821, WILSON Co.

ELMORE, G. C. to Sarah Thurman - issued December 20, 1860, ROBERTSON Co.

ELMORE, John to Elizabeth Jones - issued March 23, 1854, m. by:
James Sprouse, J. P., ROBERTSON Co.

ELMORE, William to Nancy J. Jones - issued August 10, 1858, m. by:
A. Rose, J. P., ROBERTSON Co.

ELOISS, Edmond to Pheby Farriss - December 28, 1808, Bondsman:
John Stephenson, MAURY Co.

ELROD, Adam A. to Margaret Work - issued January 20, 1836, Bondsman:
James Brown, RUTHERFORD Co.

ELROD, George to Thussey Peas - issued October 11, 1823, Bondsman:
John R. Rogers, m. by: John L. Jetton, J. P., October 14, 1823,
RUTHERFORD Co.

ELROD, Harmond to Jiney McKee - issued July 15, 1818, Bondsman: Ambrose McKee, RUTHERFORD Co.

ELROD, John to Mary Bishop - issued December 9, 1836, Bondsman: Joseph Trimble, RUTHERFORD Co.

ELROD, Montgomery to Mary E. Batey - issued December 19, 1833, Bondsman: Thos. W. Batey, RUTHERFORD Co.

ELSAY, Thomas to Elander A. Tillery - issued September 16, 1840, Bondsman: Lar. Runyon, m. by: D. L. Godsey, M. G., September 17, 1840, MEIGS Co.

ELSEY, John to Lucinda Morgan - issued July 18, 1801, Bondsman: Samuel Terrey, GRAINGER Co.

ELSEY, Joseph to Eliza Simpson - issued March 12, 1836, KNOX Co.

ELSEY, Joseph to Eliza Simpson - issued March 12, 1836, m. March 13, 1836, KNOX Co.

ELSY, Josiah to Martha W. Boothe - issued September 21, 1830, Bondsman: John S. Booth, WILSON Co.

ELTON, Barshaba to Solomon Patterson - MAURY Co.

ELUM, R. H. to Nancy C. Hinkle - issued December 15, 1858, m. by: T. J. Craig, J. P., December 16, 1858, ROBERTSON Co.

ELVIN, Sparkman to Parmelia Russell - issued August 1, 1860, m. by: P. Moore, M. G., August 2, 1860, VAN BUREN Co.

ELY, Quincy Adams to M. J. Douglas - issued February 28, 1854, m. by: James Anderson, J. P., ROBERTSON Co.

EMBERSON, C. W. to Jane E. Voss - issued December 12, 1861, Bondsman: A. J. M. White, LAWRENCE Co.

EMBERSON, Nancy to Jonathan Milburn - GREENE Co.

EMBREE, Elihu to Anne Williams - March 17, 1803, Security: Newhope Quaker Meeting, GREENE Co.

EMBREE, Lewis to Phebe Warwick - issued September 28, 1826, Bondsman: Jno. F. Pate, m. by: Daniel Graves, J. P., September, 1826, KNOX Co.

EMBREY, Clifton R. to Mary Ann Sharp - issued March 5, 1846, m. by: Henry Hunt, M. G., March 6, 1846, FRANKLIN Co.

EMBREY, John K. to Julia A. Darrell - issued January 24, 1843, FRANKLIN Co.

EMBREY, M. D. to Elizabeth Wells - issued August 16, 1869, FRANKLIN Co.

EMBREY, M. L. to Virginia E. Modena - issued May 2, 1860, m. by: Elex T. D. Jones May 3, 1860, FRANKLIN Co.

EMBREY, W. S. to M. L. Hines - issued December 10, 1870, FRANKLIN Co.

EMBREY, Wiley S. to Nancy Meredith - issued December 1, 1857, FRANKLIN Co.

EMBREY, Willis S. to Sarah Jane Stamps - issued December 22, 1847, m. by: Henry Hunt, M. G., December 23, 1847, FRANKLIN Co.

EMBRICK, John to Joanna Mattee - issued September 18, 1871, m. by: John Campbell, M. G., September 21, 1871, FRANKLIN Co.

EMERSON, F. W. to Sarah Susan Emerson - issued November 1, 1859, m. by: John J. Pittman, M. G., November 1, 1859, COFFEE Co.

EMERSON, H. W. to S. A. Hickman - issued May 2, 1861, Bondsman:
James M. Davis, m. by: J. P., Richardson, J. P., May 2, 1861,
LAWRENCE Co.

EMERSON, Thomas to Mary Seargent - issued December 19, 1839, m. by:
James Byrom, J. P., December 19, 1839, FRANKLIN Co.

EMERSON, Thomas M. to Sarah A. Koger - issued September 25, 1861,
m. by: E. A. Rutledge, J. P., September 25, 1861, COFFEE Co.

EMERY, John to Susannah Emery - issued August 3, 1824, Bondsman:
Ralph Jones, SUMNER Co.

EMERY, William to Nancy Scarborough - issued January 2, 1839, STEWART Co.

EMMERSON, B. H. to Elizabeth Meredith - issued November 10, 1840,
m. by: W. T. Wells, M. G., FRANKLIN Co.

EMMERY, Benjamin to Sarah Morris - issued December 30, 1815, Bondsman:
Moses Willis, m. by: Valentine Moulder, J. P., GRAINGER Co.

EMMERY, James to Mary Russell - issued May 17, 1847, Bondsman:
J. B. Little, m. by: W. L. Caskey, M. G., May 17, 1847, MONTGOMERY Co.

EMMERY, James to Amanda J. Spurrier - issued March 15, 1854, Bondsman:
David Tut, m. by: H. P. Carney, J. P., March 15, 1854, MONTGOMERY Co.

EMPSON, L. D. to N. A. Jernigan - issued April 15, 1859, ROBERTSON Co.

EMPSON, William to Betsey Morris - issued February 4, 1811, Bondsman:
Robert Parks, SUMNER Co.

EMPSON, William to Margaret Freeland - issued February 16, 1837,
Bondsman: William Empson, m. by: J. B. Brizendine February 16,
1837, SUMNER Co.

EMSON, William to Martha McKinny - issued April 10, 1846, m. by:
W. T. Weston, J. P., April 10, 1846, STEWART Co.

ENGLAND, Aaron to Nancy McCampbell - August 27, 1804, KNOX Co.

ENGLAND, Alfred to Bersheba Walker - issued November 11, 1820, Bondsman:
Reuben Walker, KNOX Co.

ENGLAND, C. M. to Mahaley E. Payne - issued July 31, 1855, m. by:
James Cook, J. P., ROBERTSON Co.

ENGLAND, Elijah to Elsey Scott - issued April 7, 1813, Bondsman:
John England, Witness: A. Hutcheson, KNOX Co.

ENGLAND, James to Elizabeth Roe - issued February 6, 1826, Bondsman:
Martin Johnson, m. by: David McAnally, J. P., February 6, 1826,
GRAINGER Co.

ENGLAND, James A. to Sarah J. Miller - issued November 30, 1843, m. by:
A. J. Steel, M. G., FRANKLIN Co.

ENGLAND, James E. to Nancy Willy - issued April 22, 1843, m. by:
A. Nesbitt, J. P., April 23, 1843, DICKSON Co.

ENGLAND, James M. to Elizabeth Jane Warren - issued July 22, 1859,
m. by: John Crawford, J. P., July 23, 1859, ROBERTSON Co.

ENGLAND, Jasper to Amanda Savage - issued August 30, 1857, m. by:
James Cook, J. P., ROBERTSON Co.

ENGLAND, John to Mary Scott - issued December 25, 1815, Bondsman:
D. B. Ayres, m. by: John Love, J. P., December 28, 1815, Witness:
A. Hutcheson, KNOX Co.

ENGLAND, John to Rebecka Edmondson - issued March 1, 1830, Bondsman:
Isaac Edmondson, m. by: Mordecai Yarnell, J. P., March 2, 1830,
Witness: Wm. Swan, KNOX Co.

ENGLAND, John F. to Susan I. Tucker - issued April 7, 1853, m. by:
James Sprouse, J. P., ROBERTSON Co.

ENGLAND, Memory to Malinda Hedge - issued June 5, 1841, m. by:
Joel Erranton, J. P., June 6, 1841, DICKSON• Co.

ENGLAND, Sinclair to Susan Kindred - issued December 24, 1838, Bondsman:
Edw. Kindred, WILSON Co.

ENGLAND, William to Seluda Fergerson - issued February 10, 1826,
Bondsman: James Irby, m. by: Brittain Drake, J. P., February 26,
1826, WILSON Co.

ENGLAND, William to Candis Travilion - issued August 11, 1828,
Bondsman: James Trovilion, WILSON Co.

ENGLAND, William to Mary Savage - issued January 8, 1842, m. by:
James Sprouse, J. P., January 9, 1842, ROBERTSON Co.

ENGLAND, William M. to Luvica Higgenbothum - issued January 9, 1841,
m. by: John Eubank, J. P., DICKSON Co.

ENGLEHARDT, George to Mary C. Anderson - issued April 23, 1861,
Bondsman: Louis Markel, Jos. H. Thompson, Clk. per James H. Neil,
Dep. Clk., BEDFORD Co.

ENGLER, William to S. A. Hunsacker - issued August 27, 1848, m. by:
James Woodard, ROBERTSON Co.

ENGLERT, John to Cynthia A. Gillaspie - issued October 3, 1871,
FRANKLIN Co.

ENGLISH, Agnes to James Johnson - GREENE Co.

ENGLISH, Alexander to Mary Hibbit Robinson - July 30, 1798, Security:
Andrew Hibbit, GREENE Co.

ENGLISH, Andrew to Mary Woolsey - February 3, 1790, Security:
Asahel Rawling, GREENE Co.

ENGLISH, Andrew to Agnes Robinson - March 31, 1790, Security:
Michael Rawling, GREENE Co.

ENGLISH, Charles G. to Martha E. Southall - issued October 24, 1843,
m. by: C. D. Elliott, M. G., October 24, 1843, DAVIDSON Co.

ENGLISH, Geo. W. to Mary Park - issued August 24, 1833, m. by:
Jacob Nutty, M. G., October 13, 1833, KNOX Co.

ENGLISH, Geo. W. to Mary Park - issued August 24, 1833, Bondsman:
Wm. Williams, KNOX Co.

ENGLISH, Jane to William Finley - GREENE Co.

ENGLISH, John T. to Sarah B. Lock - January 6, 1859, m. by:
Wm. Peaton, J. P., GILES Co.

ENGLISH, Matthew to Nancey Gordon - issued October 26, 1800, Bondsman:
Matthew English and Robert Gorden, Witness: Nelson Ore, GRAINGER Co.

ENGLISH, Rebecca to Philip Cole - GREENE Co.

ENGLISH, Rhoda to John Kincaid - GREENE Co.

ENNIS, J. to Eliz. Clinard - issued February 3, 1849, m. by: W. H. Bugg
March 11, 1849, ROBERTSON Co.

ENOCH, Alfred to Malissa Hancock - issued December 25, 1834, Bondsman: Geo. D. Cummings, WILSON Co.

ENOCH, Alfred to Malissa Hancock - issued December 25, 1834, Bondsman: Wilson Bloodworth, m. by: Obadiah Freeman, M. G., WILSON Co.

ENOCHS, Robert R. to Martha E. Smith - issued June 10, 1854, m. by: J. M. P. Hickerson, V. D. M., June 11, 1854, COFFEE Co.

EPLEY, Jesse M. to Matilda Toliver - issued January 24, 1859, m. by: Samuel Umbarger, J. P., January 24, 1859, COFFEE Co.

EPPERSON, Ananias to Elizabeth Davis - issued October 26, 1836, Bondsman: William Simpson, m. October 26, 1836, SUMNER Co.

EPPERSON, J. H. to Mary Ann Davis - issued July 9, 1845, m. by: W. D. F. Sawrie, M., June 29, 1845, DAVIDSON Co.

EPPERSON, John to Eliza Gregory - issued October 24, 1831, Bondsman: James H. Brittain, WILSON Co.

EPPERSON, Littleberry to Patsy Taner - September 27, 1810, WILLIAMSON Co.

EPPES, Thomas A. to Sarah A. Westerfield - issued October 18, 1837, m. by: G. S. White, M. G., October 19, 1837, KNOX Co.

EPPS, Ely to Rebecca Miller - issued December 26, 1822, Bondsman: Isaac Johnston, RUTHERFORD Co.

EPPS, F. B. to E. B. Persise - issued January 9, 1856, m. by: J. W. Cullum, M. G., ROBERTSON Co.

EPPS, Isham to Nancy E. Hendricks - issued December 24, 1849, m. by: J. Dean, M. G., December 25, 1849, FRANKLIN Co.

EPPS, Lafayette to Rebecca Allen - issued December 12, 1834, Bondsman: James McR. Frensley, RUTHERFORD Co.

EPPS, Larry to Elizabeth Craton - issued January 26, 1807, Bondsman: John Bradley, WILSON Co.

EPPS, William to Francis Easley - issued October 2, 1817, Bondsman: William E. Cocke, GRAINGER Co.

ERNWINE, John to Clacy Rector - issued December 24, 1802, Bondsman: Barton McFerson, GRAINGER Co.

ERSPY, Robert to Crury Cribbins - issued February 1, 1790, Bondsman: Thomas Mastin, SUMNER Co.

ERVIN, James to Polly Bates - issued March 30, 1808, Bondsman: Samuel Patterson, SUMNER Co.

ERVIN, William to Polly Hinds - issued December 6, 1826, Bondsman: Lazarus Johnston, m. by: J. Johnson, J. P., December 6, 1826, KNOX Co.

ERWIN, Alfred to Polly Ball - issued December 15, 1821, Bondsman: Abner Erwin, m. by: James Carr, J. P., December 15, 1821, SUMNER Co.

ERWIN, Anderson to Martha Ann Warren - issued January 2, 1847, m. by: James Sprouse, J. P., January 2, ROBERTSON Co.

ERWIN, Charles to Sarah Corder - issued January 22, 1820, m. by: E. MacGowan January 23, 1820, RUTHERFORD Co.

ERWIN, David to Polly Beard - November 2, 1809, Bondsman: Joseph Young, MAURY Co.

ERWIN, Elim A. to Elizabeth A. Duncan - issued December 7, 1816,
SUMNER Co.

ERWIN, George I. to Milley H. Duncan - issued December 26, 1826,
Bondsman: James Mills, m. by: P. C. Wills, J. P., December 26,
1826, SUMNER Co.

ERWIN, Hugh L. to Francis M. Lee - issued February 21, 1854, m. by:
Wm. R. Spindle, J. P., February 26, 1854, FRANKLIN Co.

ERWIN, James to Jane Kennedy - July 7, 1810, Bondsman: John Erwin,
MAURY Co.

ERWIN, James to Sarah Rodgers - issued September 24, 1827, Bondsman:
Joseph Rodgers, m. by: J. A. Swan, J. P., September 24, 1827,
Witness: Chas. McClung, KNOX Co.

ERWIN, James to Julia Frazier - August 12, 1846, m. by: C. D. Taylor,
GILES Co.

ERWIN, James G. to Marilla (Udrilla?) West - December 27, 1837,
Security: E. D. Jones, GILES Co.

ERWIN, James G. to Lucy Catharine (Pat(c?) - June 1, 1850, Security:
Nero H. Grove, GILES Co.

ERWIN, Leonidas to Zipporah Bonds - February 1, 1859, m. by:
Hardin Griggs, J. P., GILES Co.

ERWIN, Martha I. to Wilson Calhoun - BEDFORD Co.

ERWIN, Mathew to Irena Stephens - issued January 10, 1826, Bondsman:
Elim A. A. Erwin and Jas. Robb, m. by: John Wiseman, M. G.,
January 10, 1826, SUMNER Co.

ERWIN, Nathaniel to Betsy Miller - issued March 8, 1831, m. by:
Daniel Graves, J. P., March 9, 1831, KNOX Co.

ERWIN, Robert to Sarah V. Edmondson - issued December 13, 1862,
Bondsman: K. L. Hamlin, Jos. H. Thompson, Clk., m. by: E. T. Haley,
J. P., December 13, 1862, BEDFORD Co.

ERWIN, Robert W. to Jane E. Woods - December 12, 1843, m. by:
H. B. Warren, M. G., GILES Co.

ERWIN, Thos. to Fennetta S. Wiseman - issued December 16, 1863,
Bondsman: Solomon Womack, Jos. H. Thompson, Clk., BEDFORD Co.

ESCUE, Daniel to Malinda Rice - issued February 14, 1832, Bondsman:
Leonard C. Escue, m. by: Charles Watkins, J. P., February 14, 1832,
SUMNER Co.

ESCUE, Daniel to Henritta Donnell - issued February 9, 1837, Bondsman:
Samuel Gourly, m. by: Elisha Vaughn February 9, 1837, SUMNER Co.

ESCUE, James to Elizabeth Hondershall - issued March 3, 1830, Bondsman:
Wm. J. Lee, SUMNER Co.

ESCUE, John to Sarah Lumpkins - issued March 7, 1827, Bondsman:
Samuel Roberts, WILSON Co.

ESCUE, John to Elizabeth Smith - issued June 23, 1832, Bondsman:
James Escue, SUMNER Co.

ESCUE, Leonard to Polly Lee - issued June 4, 1817, Bondsman:
John Stewart, m. by: S. W. Blythe, J. P., June 4, 1817, SUMNER Co.

ESCUE, Robert C. to Eleanor Myers - issued July 21, 1838, Bondsman:
Thomas Williams, m. by: Micajah Estes, M. G., July 22, 1838,
WILSON Co.

ESCUE, William to Susan Warren - issued August 5, 1853, m. by:
David Henry, J. P., August 7, 1853, ROBERTSON Co.

ESKEN, Samuel to Nancy W. T. Watts - issued May 20, 1826, Bondsman:
James C. Shaver, SUMNER Co.

ESKEW, Alfred to Orenia Lane - issued February 14, 1832, m. by:
Wm. M. Swain, J. P., WILSON Co.

ESKEW, Andrew to Matilda Caroline McFarlin - issued April 29, 1839,
Bondsman: Alfred Eskew, WILSON Co.

ESKEW, John to Anny Stone - issued March 27, 1824, Bondsman:
James Charlton, SUMNER Co.

ESKEW, Russie to Margaret Brown - issued September 24, 1827, Bondsman:
Thomas Kirkpatrick, WILSON Co.

ESKEW, Willie to Minerva Hooser - issued July 7, 1840, Bondsman:
James Smart, m. by: Wm. Barton, M. G., July 8, 1840, WILSON Co.

ESKINS, Addison to Caroline Harrison - issued April 2, 1830, Bondsman:
John Barbee, WILSON Co.

ESKRIDGE, Richard to Maria Goodman - issued September 10, 1834,
Bondsman: G. W. Hill, WILSON Co.

ESLEY, Drewry to Mary Tracey - issued December 22, 1816, Bondsman:
Michael Tracey, m. by: Robert McClarey, J. P., December 22, 1816,
SUMNER Co.

ESLICK, Isaac B. to Jenney George - issued April 30, 1810, Bondsman:
Joseph Sharp, WILSON Co.

ESLICK, J. D. to Mrs. Editha Farris - issued October 11, 1870, FRANKLIN Co.

ESLICK, Thos. A. to Eliza Jones - issued November 15, 1859, FRANKLIN Co.

ESLIP (?), Samuel to Mary Lane - August 22, 1788, Security:
Corbin and Dutton Lane, GREENE Co.

ESON, Gideon to Sally Herring - issued February 6, 1816, Bondsman:
Drury Herring, SUMNER Co.

ESPEY, Alexander to Mirna Todd - issued April 6, 1837, Bondsman:
Miles Herrald, m. by: F. A. Witherspoon, J. P., April 9, 1837,
RUTHERFORD Co.

ESPEY, Charles to Elizabeth White - issued May 10, 1825, m. by:
B. B. Dickins, J. P., May 12, 1825, RUTHERFORD Co.

ESPEY, George to Mary Gillespie - issued September 22, 1820,
m. September 23, 1820, RUTHERFORD Co.

ESPEY, John to Catharine Wright - issued December 22, 1828, RUTHERFORD Co.

ESPEY, John to Mariah Cook - issued September 25, 1837, Bondsman:
Jefferson Earp, m. by: J. D. Gilman, J. P., September 25, 1837,
RUTHERFORD Co.

ESPEY, Robert to Lucinda Biles - issued July 31, 1823, Bondsman:
Willie Biles, m. by: Peyton Smith, M. G., July 31, 1823,
RUTHERFORD Co.

ESPEY, Robert to Amelia George - issued September 4, 1827, Bondsman:
Alexander Espey, RUTHERFORD Co.

ESPEY, William to Susanna Suiter - issued December 26, 1803, Bondsman:
Benjamin Suiter, SUMNER Co.

ESSEX, Thomas to Mildred Bledsoe - issued October 3, 1826, Bondsman: John F. Shabel, SUMNER Co.

ESSEX, Thomas W. to Nancy Malone - issued July 6, 1824, Bondsman: S. H. Lauderdale, SUMNER Co.

ESSLEY, Andrew to Cynthia Green - issued October 28, 1854, m. by: Samuel Umbarger, J. P., October 29, 1854, COFFEE Co.

ESSMAN, Margaret to Frederick Reeser - GREENE Co.

ESSMAN, Priscilla to John Brown - GREENE Co.

ESTAS, Rich'd. A. to Caroline Tatom - issued November 18, 1843, m. by: James W. Lloyd, J. P., November 19, 1843, DICKSON Co.

ESTES, Benjn. H. P., to Sarah Mosier - issued April 4, 1836, Bondsman: Josephus Walker, m. by: Levi Fisher, M. G., April 9, 1836, WILSON Co.

ESTES, Daniel J. to Christian Huckaby - issued August 22, 1861, Bondsman: George A. Selph, m. by: L. M. Sanford, J. P., August 22, 1861, LAWRENCE Co.

ESTES, David to Hannah Jackson - issued October 4, 1816, Bondsman: John Franklin, m. by: James McAdoo, J. P., WILSON Co.

ESTES, Duncan N. to Frances Atwood - issued September 18, 1837, Bondsman: A. J. Pendleton, WILSON Co.

ESTES, Edward to Nancy Lewis - issued August 19, 1815, Bondsman: Martin Franklin, WILSON Co.

ESTES, John to Synthia McDaniel - issued April 25, 1822, Bondsman: Burwell Reeves, WILSON Co.

ESTES, John to May Kidwell - issued July 16, 1823, Bondsman: William E. Cocke, GRAINGER Co.

ESTES, John to Martha Griffin - issued November 3, 1837, Bondsman: Robarts Howell, WILSON Co.

ESTES Mathew to Fanny Lassater - issued December 9, 1837, Bondsman: Henderson Estes, m. by: J. B. Lasater, J. P., December 10, 1837, WILSON Co.

ESTES, Peter to Polly Hicks - May 14, 1807, WILLIAMSON Co.

ESTES, Samuel to Martha M. Gee - December 12, 1811, WILLIAMSON Co.

ESTES, Samuel to Martha Estes - issued October 29, 1836, m. by: Levi Fisher November 3, 1836, WILSON Co.

ESTES, Searcy to Milly Payne - issued May 19, 1845, m. by: G. D. Fullmer, J. P., May 19, 1845, DAVIDSON Co.

ESTES, Thomas to Eliza Edkinson - issued December 31, Bondsman: Donnell Freeman, m. by: ___(?) Tompkins, WILSON Co.

ESTES, Wm. C. to Eliza Jane Matthews - issued September 8, 1842, DAVIDSON Co.

ESTILL, Francis T. to Cathrine H. Garner - issued February 12, 1846, m. by: N. P., Modrall, M. G., February 12, 1846, FRANKLIN Co.

ESTILL, Henry R. to E. E. Turney - issued March 2, 1848, m. by: Rev. A. J. Steel, FRANKLIN Co.

ESTILL, Isaac to Musadora Franklin - issued April 13, 1853, m. by: W. J. Fox, V. D. M., April 13, 1853, FRANKLIN Co.

ESTILL, James H. to Florinda Clements - issued February 12, 1851,
    m. by: Henry Hunt, M. G., February 13, 1851, FRANKLIN Co.

ESTILL, Jefferson to Francis Staples - issued January 17, 1843, m. by:
    N. P. Modrall, M. G., January 17, 1843, FRANKLIN Co.

ESTILL, William to Mary A. C. Perry - issued February 13, 1867,
    FRANKLIN Co.

ESTILL, William W. to Jane E. Brazelton - issued January 5, 1852,
    m. by: W. J. Fox, V. D. M., January 5, 1852, FRANKLIN Co.

ESTIS, W. to Betsy Perky - issued July 15, 1820, Bondsman: Hugh O. Taylor,
    m. by: John Harris, J. P., GRAINGER Co.

ESTIS, W. G. to Margaret Austin - issued August 6, 1848, m. by:
    A. V. Hicks, J. P., August 6, 1848, DICKSON Co.

ESTIS, William to Catharine Levington - issued January 15, 1827,
    Bondsman: Jacob Kline, m. by: Isaac Barton, M. G., January 15,
    1827, GRAINGER Co.

ETHERIDGE, James to Margaret McLain - issued August 24, 1842, DICKSON Co.

ETHERIDGE, Obadiah to Marsha Leake - issued July 4, 1856, m. by:
    R. H. Harrison, J. P., July 5, 1856, ROBERTSON Co.

ETHERIDGE, Stephen to Betsy Briant - issued September 7, 1819, Bondsman:
    Edward Briant, SUMNER Co.

ETHERIDGE, Wm. to Mary Underwood - issued April 13, 1847, DICKSON Co.

ETHERLY, T. H. to C. M. Stewart - issued July 28, 1845, m. by:
    J. C. Weakley, J. P., August 11, 1845, MONTGOMERY Co.

ETHRIDGE, Garrard to Polly Murnan - issued December 25, 1808, Bondsman:
    Benj. Dickerson, SUMNER Co.

ETHRIDGE, George to M. Power - issued December 18, 1858, m. by:
    W. D. Farris, J. P., December 20, 1858, FRANKLIN Co.

ETHRIDGE, Hardy H. to Susan Mayes - issued March 2, 1857, m. by:
    T. W. Bell, J. P., March 3, 1857, FRANKLIN Co.

ETHRIDGE, James to Martha McClure - issued August 29, 1864, m. by:
    N. T. Power, M. G., August 31, 1864, FRANKLIN Co.

ETHRIDGE, Jessee to Elizabeth Hill - issued August 24, 1853, m. by:
    G. W. Bowling, J. P., August 25, 1853, FRANKLIN Co.

ETHRDIGE, John to Eliza McKee - issued March 19, 1840, m. by:
    John R. Patrick, J. P., March 19, 1840, FRANKLIN Co.

ETHRIDGE, L. B. to Ella Damron - issued April 18, 1872, FRANKLIN Co.

ETHRIDGE, L. B. to Nancy Bradley - issued October 14, 1874, m. by:
    W. W. Hawkins, M. G., October 15, 1874, FRANKLIN Co.

ETHRIDGE, Mathew to Nancy Frances Justis - issued April 5, 1836,
    m. by: Joshua Lester, V. D. M., WILSON Co.

ETHRIDGE, Tilman to Polly McDaniel - issued January 19, 1837, Bondsman:
    A. H. Foster, WILSON Co.

ETHRIDGE, Tilman to Polly McDaniel - issued January 19, 1838, m. by:
    Wmson. Williams, M. G., January 20, 1838, WILSON Co.

ETTER, George to Eve Karnes (Carnes?) - March 31, 1812, KNOX Co.

ETTON, Polly to Jordon Dotson - MAURY Co.

EUBANK, E. to M. A. White - issued October 16, 1850, m. by:
    O. H, Morrow, Esq. Minister, ROBERTSON Co.

EUBANKS, Francis to Fanny Harland - issued August 17, 1830, Bondsman:
    David Standley, WILSON Co.

EUDALY, David to Lucy E. Blankenship - issued December 19, 1816,
    m. December 20, 1816, RUTHERFORD Co.

EURY, Francis to Peggy Espy - issued August 14, 1804, Bondsman:
    J. Yowell, SUMNER Co.

EVAN, Aaron to O. E. Pettie - issued February 5, 1859, m. by:
    Isaac Steel, ROBERTSON Co.

EVANS, Acy to Rebeccah Phipps - issued February 5, 1827, Bondsman:
    James Cheek, m. by: Thos. Brown, J. P., February 5, 1827,
    GRAINGER Co.

EVANS, Alvis to Lucy Ellmore - issued April 15, 1858, m. by:
    Benjamin Gambill, J. P., April 18, 1858, ROBERTSON Co.

EVANS, Ambrose to Louisa Magee - issued January 10, 1829, Bondsman:
    James Briant, m. by: Elishu Milliken, M. G., GRAINGER Co.

EVANS, Anderson to Mily Stuart - issued April 8, 1821, Bondsman:
    Alexander Stuart, WILSON Co.

EVANS, Anderson to Lucy Stuart - issued September 19, 1823, Bondsman:
    John Smith, m. by: John Drennon, WILSON Co.

EVANS, Andrew C. to Sally Yeadon (?) - issued April 9, 1812, Bondsman:
    William G. Yeadon, GRAINGER Co.

EVANS, Betsey to Thomas Mitchell - MAURY Co.

EVANS, Cornelius to Anna Harrell - issued August 7, 1816, Bondsman:
    Wm. H. Douglass and Jno Shelby, SUMNER Co.

EVANS, David to Margaret Blackburn - June 6, 1794, KNOX Co.

EVANS, David to Anney Claxton - issued March 27, 1800, Bondsman:
    David Evans and Isaiah Kidwell, Witness: Robert Yancey, GRAINGER Co.

EVANS, David to Jane Townsen - September 30, 1812, WILLIAMSON Co.

EVANS, David to Rachel Davis - issued December 13, 1831, Bondsman:
    Hugh Jones, GRAINGER Co.

EVANS, Elijah to Ruthey Holt - issued February 28, 1807, Bondsman:
    John Bunch, Jr., GRAINGER Co.

EVANS, Elizabeth to Jas. A. Sire - BEDFORD Co.

EVANS, Etheldred to Nancy Poarch - January 2, 1812, WILLIAMSON Co.

EVANS, Frances L. to Sarah Ann Hutcherson - issued March 17, 1853,
    m. by: R. W. Morrison, J. P., March 17, 1853, MONTGOMERY Co.

EVANS, George to Sally Morrison - issued June 7, 1796, Bondsman:
    Saml Rice, SUMNER Co.

EVANS, George to Matilda Lathum - issued January 18, 1820, Bondsman:
    William Evans, m. by: D. McAnally, J. P., January 21, 1820,
    GRAINGER Co.

EVANS, George A. to Thussey Higarty - issued November 17, 1818, Bondsman:
    Edward Burk, m. by: Wm. Steele, J. P., WILSON Co.

EVANS, Geor. M. to Lucinda Brazzell - issued April 30, 1845, m. by:
Jas. Thedford, J. P., May 1, 1845, DICKSON Co.

EVANS, Harris to Aurelia Lewis - 1815, KNOX Co.

EVANS, Henry to Sally Taylor - issued June 30, 1832, m. by:
Thos. Wilkerson June 5, 1832, KNOX Co.

EVANS, Henry to Mary Ann Dodson - July 7, 1851, Security:
Whitfield Dodson, GILES Co.

EVANS, Isaac to Mary Rutherford - issued August 6, 1824, Bondsman:
James Hutchison, m. by: Caleb Crane August 6, 1824, SUMNER Co.

EVANS, Isham to Susan Cates - August 21, 1813, WILLIAMSON Co.

EVANS, J. M. to Sarah C. Nevell - issued July 30, 1861, m. by:
J. L. Durrett, J. P., ROBERTSON Co.

EVANS, James to Mary A. Barr - m. by: Wm. Walton, J. P., December 2,
1834, SUMNER Co.

EVANS, James to Olly Tucker - issued October 4, 1856, m. by:
R. C. Smith, J. P., October 5, 1856, FRANKLIN Co.

EVANS, James C. to Nancy C. Byrom - issued November 13, 1855, m. by:
D. E. Muse November 15, 1855, FRANKLIN Co.

EVANS, James W. to Rhoda Willy - issued August 1, 1846, DICKSON Co.

EVANS, Jesse to Anne McConnico - October 14, 1809, WILLIAMSON Co.

EVANS, Jesse to Sarah Deshazor - issued August 17, 1821, Bondsman:
Cornelias Evans, SUMNER Co.

EVANS, Jesee to Nancy Counts - issued April 20, 1825, Bondsman:
Richard Williams, GRAINGER Co.

EVANS, John to Kezia Cotton - May 29, 1787, Security: Thomas Wallon,
GREENE Co.

EVANS, John to Lucy Lane - March 21, 1799, Security: William Love,
GREENE Co.

EVANS, John to Dokey McDowell - issued February 7, 1832, m. by:
Wm. P. Travis, J. P., February 9, 1832, RUTHERFORD Co.

EVANS, John to Martha Williams - issued August 20, 1836, Bondsman:
Thomas Williams, m. by: Wm. Vinson, J. P., September 1, 1836,
RUTHERFORD Co.

EVANS, John B. to Letticia B. Christian - issued January 6, 1844, m. by:
Tho. Palmer, J. P., January 6, 1844, DICKSON Co.

EVANS, John H. to Catharine Davis - issued July 14, 1821, Bondsman:
Gros Scruggs, m. by: Elijah Maddox July 19, 1821, WILSON Co.

EVANS, John R. to Nancy Ann Baker - issued November 12, 1842, m. by:
G. W. Charlton, J. P., November 17, 1842, DAVIDSON Co.

EVANS, Joseph to Elizabeth Earnest - May 10, 1785, Security:
James Houston, GREENE Co.

EVANS, Joseph to Hila Hoggett - issued August 10, 1819, m. by:
Sam'l Sample, J. P., August 12, 1819, KNOX Co.

EVANS, Joseph to Susannah Vann - issued October 2, 1829, Bondsman:
William B. Evans, RUTHERFORD Co.

EVANS, Lewis to Barthena Smith - issued March 25, 1822, Bondsman:
W. M. Smith, m. by: David Tate, J. P., March 25, 1822, GRAINGER Co.

EVANS, Lewis to Rachael Brazzell - issued January 4, 1839, DICKSON Co.

EVANS, Martha to Hugh Overton - BEDFORD Co.

EVANS, Martha to A. I. Barton - BEDFORD Co.

EVANS, Mary to Lewis Morgan - GREENE Co.

EVANS, Robert C. to Elizabeth Sherod - issued August 29, 1837, Bondsman:
Wm. McMillan, m. by: Wm. McMillan, J. P., August 31, 1837, KNOX Co.

EVANS, Samuel to Sarah Steel - issued March 17, 1819, m. by:
John McCampbell, J. P., March 18, 1819, KNOX Co.

EVANS, Samuel W. to Mariah Frith - issued October 11, 1853, Bondsman:
J. M. Raca, m. by: John Gold, J. P., October 11, 1853, MONTGOMERY Co.

EVANS, Stephen to Susannah Claxton - issued May 7, 1805, Bondsman:
Thos. Higgombothem, SUMNER Co.

EVANS, Susan to Mathew Lindsay - BEDFORD Co.

EVANS, Thomas W. to Mary E. Odom - issued December 30, 1840, m. by:
P. B. Morris, J. P., December 31, 1840, DAVIDSON Co.

EVANS, W. H, to Catherine Boyd - m. by: O. L. V. Schmitton, J. P.,
June 6, 1845, DICKSON Co.

EVANS, William to Kidey Freeman - issued March 26, 1810, Bondsman:
Hugh Elliott, SUMNER Co.

EVANS, William to Nancy Johnson - issued July 26, 1814, Bondsman:
Joseph Evans, KNOX Co.

EVANS, William to Elizabeth Cowan - March 18, 1815, WILLIAMSON Co.

EVANS, William to Mary Evans - issued March 30, 1819, m. by:
John McCampbell April 1, 1819, KNOX Co.

EVANS, Williams to Peggy Smith - issued April 14, 1830, Bondsman:
Abraham Green, m. by: Wm. Walton, J. P., April 14, 1830, SUMNER Co.

EVANS, William to Martha Nelms - issued July 1, 1839, m. by:
Geo. Childress, J. P., ROBERTSON Co.

EVANS, William to Ann Weaver - issued November 19, 1860, m. by:
Allen Tribble, Pastor, November 21, 1860, FRANKLIN Co.

EVANS, Wm. to Cordelia A. Marsh - issued August 16, 1861, Bondsman:
Joshn G. Bledsoe, Jos. H. Thompson, Clk. per N. F. Thompson,
Dep. Clk., m. by: J. M. H. Coleman, J. P., BEDFORD Co.

EVANS, William M. to Caroline Reagin - issued July 6, 1848, m. by:
W. A. Breeden, J. P., July 6, 1848, FRANKLIN Co.

EVANS, Wm. M. to Mary Ann Deaton - issued February 14, 1849, FRANKLIN Co.

EVANS, Wm. M. to Marinda Houston - issued November 10, 1852, m. by:
G. W. Bowling, J. P., November 10, 1852, FRANKLIN Co.

EVANS, Zachariah to Cynthia Sweat - issued March 6, 1820, Bondsman:
Alexander Stuart, m. by: Jno. Bonner, J. P., March 19, 1820,
WILSON Co.

EVERETT, Aquilla to Sarah Thompson - issued July 1, 1820, Bondsman:
Sam'l Ingram, m. by: Wm. A. McCampbell, J. P., July 1, 1820,
KNOX Co.

EVERETT, Byrd F. to Susanah Hayne (?) - issued March 1, 1828, m. by:
B. H. Merriman March 20, 1828, KNOX Co.

EVERETT, Joel D. to Nancy A. Smith - issued October 6, 1846, DICKSON Co.

EVERETT, John B. to Elizabeth R. Hunt - issued January 21, 1846, m. by:
J. T. Wheat, Rr. of Ct. Ch., January 21, 1846, DAVIDSON Co.

EVERETT, John C. to Pherriba Ayres - issued April 30, 1824, m. by:
Mordecai Yarnell, J. P., May 2, 1824, KNOX Co.

EVERETT, Ralph to Betsy Thompson - issued March 2, 1825, m. by:
S. S. McCampbell, J. P., March 4, 1825, KNOX Co.

EVERETT, Sylvinus to Mary Douglass - issued August 19, 1819, m. by:
Wm. A. Campbell August 19, 1819, KNOX Co.

EVERETT, Williard to Barbary Maxey - issued December 11, 1841, m. by:
John Forbes, J. P., December 19, 1841, ROBERTSON Co.

EVERETT, Wm. to Jane Belew - issued June 7, 1831, Bondsman:
Wm. M. Smith, KNOX Co.

EVERETT, Wm. C. to Polly Gillespie - issued September 30, 1817, m. by:
Amos T. Carden, J. P., October 2, 1817, KNOX Co.

EVERETTS, Theo. to Peggy Edmonson - December 6, 1812, KNOX Co.

EVINS, Daniel to Elizabeth Williams - issued November 19, 1834, Bondsman:
Hays B. Snell, m. by: J. K. Shapard November 29, 1834, RUTHERFORD Co.

EVINS, Isham to Susan Cates - August 21, 1813, WILLIAMSON Co.

EVINS, Joel to Sarah Fears - issued March 11 (or 12?), 1799, Bondsman:
Obediah Ginnins, Witness: John Word, GRAINGER Co.

EVINS, Robert to Emily Heughes - issued June 20, 1836, Bondsman:
E. R. M. Reynolds, m. by: Joseph Spradling June 20, 1836, SUMNER Co.

EWELL, Dabney to Dovey Davidson - issued June 7, 1821, m. by:
O. W. Crockett, J. P., June 8, 1821, RUTHERFORD Co.

EWELL, Jesse to Cynthia H. Robertson - issued January 27, 1834, Bondsman:
Isaac Robinson, RUTHERFORD Co.

EWEN, Henry C. to Betsey Hill - January 12, 1815, WILLIAMSON Co.

EWEN, John H. to Susan M. Goodwin - issued November 7, 1838, m. by:
T. Fanning, M. G., November 8, 1838, DAVIDSON Co.

EWING, Alexander C. to Cloe R. Sanders - issued May 17, 1825, Bondsman:
Wm. Hadley, m. by: Thos. Joyner May 17, 1825, SUMNER Co.

EWING, Andrew to Rowena J. Williams - issued September 9, 1841, m. by:
Robt. A. Lapsley September 9, 1841, DAVIDSON Co.

EWING, James to Mary Thompson - April 30, 1798, BLOUNT Co.

EWING, James to Nancy Smith - issued March 7, 1814, Bondsman:
A. G. Wasson, WILSON Co.

EWING, James to Malinda Beller - issued May 16, 1836, Bondsman:
J. H. Fisher, WILSON Co.

EWING, John to Mary Seabolt - issued May 11, 1830, Bondsman:
Anderson Hill, KNOX Co.

EWING, Samuel to Sarah Steel - March 17, 1819, KNOX Co.

EWING, William to Betty McNutt - November 9, 1796, Surety:
Alexander McCullock, BLOUNT Co.

EWING, William B. to Martha C. Graves - issued March 21, 1838, m. by:
A. L. P. Green, M. P., March 22, 1838, DAVIDSON Co.

EWING, William R. to Sally Byson - issued September 14, 1825, Bondsman:
Alexander Ewing, m. by: Thos. Joyner September 14, 1825, SUMNER Co.

EXUM, Arthur to Sarah Davidson - issued September 12, 1805, Bondsman:
Robert Bell, SUMNER Co.

EXUM, William to Eliza Allen - issued July 23, 1839, Bondsman:
L. Matherly, WILSON Co.

EXUM, William to Sarah E. Jackson - issued February 9, 1840, m. by:
Stephen McDonald, J. P., February 10, 1830, WILSON Co.

EYSOM, Richard to Pietta Gasaway - issued July 18, 1816, m. by:
James Whitsett July 18, 1816, RUTHERFORD Co.

EZEL, Absolam to Malinda Mathews - issued August 16, 1831, Bondsman:
James P. Wyatte, m. by: John Gold, J. P., August 16, 1851,
MONTGOMERY Co.

EZEL, Byrd to Sally Wade - issued September 13, 1827, m. by:
Wm. B. Carns, J. P., September 13, 1827, KNOX Co.

EZELL, A. V. to Julia A. Perkins - September 8, 1853, m. by:
William Levesque, M. G., GILES Co.

EZELL, Allen to Mary A. Holloway - issued September 2, 1865, Bondsman:
R. L. Bassham, m. by: Wm. McMasters, J. P., September 3, 1865,
LAWRENCE Co.

EZELL, Balaam to Keziah Tarkington - July 17, 1805, WILLIAMSON Co.

EZELL, Benjamin to Rhodiah Hampton - issued April 9, 1823, Bondsman:
William Lilley, m. by: Charles Watkins, J. P., April 9, 1823,
SUMNER Co.

EZELL, Charles to Mary Roberson - issued August 3, 1847, STEWART Co.

EZELL, Frederick to Polley Dodd - January 4, 1812, WILLIAMSON Co.

EZELL, Gillum to Phebe A. Green - issued October 9, 1841, m. by:
J. B. Gentry October 19, 1841, STEWART Co.

EZELL, Henry to Mary Elizabeth McCain - issued May 31, 1845, m. by:
Rev. Sam'l White June 2, 1845, STEWART Co.

EZELL, Jesse to Allie Seamans - issued July 2, 1816, Bondsman:
James Ezell, m. by: James Moore, J. P., July 2, 1816, GRAINGER Co.

EZELL, Marion P. to Mary E. Tarpley - December 16, 1858, m. by:
Jas. C. Stevenson, GILES Co.

EZELL, Sam'l D. to Mary Jane Barnes - issued January 12, 1843, m. by:
E. W. Smith, J. P., January 15, 1843, STEWART Co.

EZELL, Solomon to Mary Patterson - issued April 24, 1816, Bondsman:
James Ezell, m. by: James Moore, J. P., April 25, 1816, GRAINGER Co.

EZELL, Stephen to Mary Stills - issued May 22, 1847, m. by:
B. F. Fraser, J. P., 1847, STEWART Co.

EZELL, Thomas E. to Sarah E. Thompson - issued March 15, 1866, Bondsman:
Wm. H. Goad, m. by: Wm. McMasters, J. P., March 16, 1866,
LAWRENCE Co.

EZELL, Uberto D. to Isabella Marshall - issued February 10, 1829,
Bondsman: Benjamin Fisher, m. by: John Fletcher, J. P., February 11,
1829, RUTHERFORD Co.

EZELL, William to Elanor B. Mathis - issued March 5, 1849, Bondsman:
John J. Hester, m. by: John Gold, J. P., MONTGOMERY Co.

FADGETT, Elijah to Sally Underwood - issued November 8, 1831, m. by:
Russell Birdwell, M. G., November 9, 1831, KNOX Co.

FAGAN, Henry W. to Martha V. Barton - issued December 17, 1834,
Bondsman: Wm. A. McCombs, m. by: Jordan Willeford, J. P.,
December 17, 1834, RUTHERFORD Co.

FAGAN, Lucinda to Luther Gray - issued February 9, 1863, Bondsman:
J. W. Ellis, Jos. H. Thompson, Clk. per M. E. W. Dunaway, Dep.
Clk., BEDFORD Co.

FAGAN, Robert to Patsey Gibson - issued January 2, 1816, m. by:
Thomas Berry, J. P., January 17, 1816, RUTHERFORD Co.

FAGG, John F. to Sarah F. Petty - issued October 26, 1870, FRANKLIN Co.

FAGG, R. E. to Emma J. Bardy - issued November 28, 1870, m. by:
John Chitwood, J. P., November 30, 1870, FRANKLIN Co.

FAGG, Z. to Sarah J. Jones - issued March 21, 1871, m. by:
Asa D. Oakley, M. G., March 23, 1871, FRANKLIN Co.

FAGG, Zachariah to Mary Turner - m. by: Jonathan Davis, J. P.,
November 8, 1834, SUMNER Co.

FAIN, Isabella to Josiah Temple - GREENE Co.

FAIN, Jesse to Jenney Conaway - October 13, 1801, Security:
Jesse Conoway, BLOUNT Co.

FAIN, William J. to Darthula L. Bryant - issued September 26, 1855,
m. by: J. C. Hickman, M. G., September 26, 1855, VAN BUREN Co.

FAINTHAM, Martin to Charlotte Gardiner - July 1, 1816, WILLIAMSON Co.

FAIR, Poleman to Sally James - issued June 1, 1831, Bondsman:
E. E. Wallace, SUMNER Co.

FAIRCLOTH, Cordial to Sally Reynolds - October 29, 1816, WILLIAMSON Co.

FAIRCLOTH, Wm. to Martha Ann T. Seat - issued May 27, 1843, m. by:
Geo. W. Charlton, J. P., May 28, 1843, DAVIDSON Co.

FAIRFIELD, Saml. to Ellen Anderson - issued January 13, 1858, m. by:
A. Rose, J. P., ROBERTSON Co.

FAIRLESS, Lanty to Elizabeth Ralph - issued April 3, 1824, Bondsman:
Lewis Ralph, m. by: John McMurtry, J. P., April 3, 1824, SUMNER Co.

FAIRLESS, Robert to Arena Buchannon - issued December 29, 1829,
Bondsman: Robt. Fairless, m. by: Jas. Hogen, J. P., December 29,
1829, SUMNER Co.

FAIRLY, George to Jenny Pryor - issued February 14, 1794, Bondsman:
Wm. Pryor, SUMNER Co.

FAIRSTAIR, William to Nancy Wade - issued September 22, 1833, m. by:
G. H. Bussard, J. P., WILSON Co.

FAKES, Albert L. to Sarah B. Johnson - issued December 3, 1839,
Bondsman: Hugh Edwards, m. by: Melkijah L. Vaughn, M. G.,
December 5, 1839, WILSON Co.

FAKES, John to Mary Edwards - issued November 7, 1808, Bondsman:
Robert Edwards, WILSON Co.

FAKES, Robert to Susannah Alsup - issued July 3, 1837, Bondsman:
S. J. Alsup, WILSON Co.

FAKES, Robt. to Jemima Hogan - issued February 29, 1848, m. by:
John Wilson, J. P., February 29, 1848, STEWART Co.

FAKES, William to Elizabeth Moser - issued July 12, 1834, Bondsman:
Hugh Edwards, WILSON Co.

FALKENBERRY, Thomas J. to Martha S. Wright - issued September 6, 1834,
Bondsman: William Barton, RUTHERFORD Co.

FALKNER, Joseph to Martha Franks - July 21, 1800, BLOUNT Co.

FALKNER, William to Nancy Talent - issued April 3, 1815, Bondsman:
Robert Tunnell, Witness: A. Hutcheson, KNOX Co.

FALL, Alexander to Elizabeth Horton - issued October 20, 1842,
DAVIDSON Co.

FALL, John T. S. to Sarah W. Bradford - issued September 28, 1841,
m. by: T. Fanning September 28, 1841, DAVIDSON Co.

FALLER, Joseph to Elizabeth Old - issued June 5, 1845, DAVIDSON Co.

FAMBROUGH, Arland H. to Bertha A. Owens - issued September 9, 1853,
Bondsman: W. D. Hearn, m. by: John Perdue, J. P., September 11,
1853, MONTGOMERY Co.

FAMBROUGH, Jonathan to Sarah E. Miles - issued December 20, 1853,
Bondsman: John Perdue, m. by: John Perdue, J. P., December 20,
1853, MONTGOMERY Co.

FANE, William C. to Mary Ann Jackson - issued May 9, 1835, Bondsman:
Robert D. S. McMinn, WILSON Co.

FANE, William C. to Mary C. Smith - issued October 1, 1835, Bondsman:
G. W. Bond, m. by: John Bone, J. P., WILSON Co.

FANN, Barbara to John Mackey - GREENE Co.

FANN, Catherine to Obediah Mayboy (Mackey or McBee) - GREENE Co.

FANNING, W. C. to Francis Taylor - issued February 15, 1867,
m. February 15, 1867, FRANKLIN Co.

FANS, Austin R. to Louisa Simpkins - issued February 18, 1843, m. by:
David Abernathy February 23, 1843, DAVIDSON Co.

FARBANK, Wm. to Sarah Ramsey - issued January 26, 1839, Bondsman:
Hugh Tillery, m. by: Daniel Cate, J. P., January 27, 1839, MEIGS Co.

FARELL, Charles J. to Arabolla Zellers - issued January 16, 1853,
Bondsman: J. J. Wood, m. by: Jo Pollard, J. P., January 16, 1853,
MONTGOMERY Co.

FARES, Thomas H. to Nancy Gore - issued January 5, 1842, FRANKLIN Co.

FARGUS, Robert to Martha Childress - issued June 3, 1830, Bondsman:
Henry Haley, m. by: Henry Ridley, J. P., June 3, 1830, RUTHERFORD Co.

FARGUSON, Benj. to Fanny Coker - issued January 26, 1825, m. by:
Robt. McBath January 26, 1825, KNOX Co.

FARGUSON, William to Pheby Morgan - issued January 4, 1823, m. by:
Wm. B. Carns, J. P., January 4, 1823, KNOX Co.

FARIS, Alfred C. to Amanda Robertson - issued March 30, 1847, m. by:
J. B. McFerrin, M. G., March 31, 1847, DAVIDSON Co.

FARIS, F. B. to Martha Henley - issued July 11, 1838, m. by:
Wm. G. Quinn, M. G., July, 1838, FRANKLIN Co.

FARIS, G. W. to Mary J. Young - issued December 28, 1864, m. by:
J. Campbell, M. G., December 29, 1864, FRANKLIN Co.

FARIS, George W. to Eliza Ann Tucker - issued April 14, 1853, m. by:
G. W. Bowling, J. P., April 14, 1853, FRANKLIN Co.

FARIS, Geo. W. to Ann J. Upton - issued September 17, 1854, m. by:
John G. Biddle September 18, 1854, FRANKLIN Co.

FARIS, James to Margret Caroll - issued October 3, 1838, FRANKLIN Co.

FARIS, James S. to Lucy J. Faris - issued December 20, 1854, m. by:
Wiley Denson, J. P., December 21, 1854, FRANKLIN Co.

FARIS, John K. to Mary E. Austell - issued August 26, 1857, m. by:
J. L. Payne, Mins., Augsut 27, 1857, COFFEE Co.

FARIS, Reuben S. to Nancy Riddle - issued March 16, 1861, FRANKLIN Co.

FARIS, Richard to Salina Lester - issued February 14, 1855, m. by:
Thos. Finch, J. P., February 15, 1855, FRANKLIN Co.

FARISS, James to Peggy Whiteside - August 14, 1809, Bondsman:
Robert Whiteside, MAURY Co.

FARLESS, Martin to Mary Bench - issued November 31, 1843, Bondsman:
James H. Long, MEIGS Co.

FARLEY, John M. to Mary Skinner - Bondsman: F. A. Dycus, MONTGOMERY Co.

FARLEY, Robert T. to Zelica V. Gossett - issued April 30, 1853, m. by:
L. R. Dennis, M. G., May 3, 1853, ROBERTSON Co.

FARMER, Andrew to Susan Hague - issued September 19, 1838, Bondsman:
Henry Farmer, m. by: James Moore, J. P., September 20, 1838,
MEIGS Co.

FARMER, Aquilla to Mary T. Ford - issued May 24, 1845, Bondsman:
Samuel O. Wood, m. by: John Seabourn, J. P., May 25, 1845, MEIGS Co.

FARMER, Bailey W. to Catherine Hartwell - issued March 3, 1835, Bondsman:
Isaac L. Howse, m. by: John C. Parker March 3, 1835, RUTHERFORD Co.

FARMER, David to Nancy E. Edwards - issued July 14, 1863, Bondsman:
John Gist, m. by: C. B. Porter, M. G., July 17, 1863, LAWRENCE Co.

FARMER, George to Susan Langford - issued April 9, 1846, m. by:
Jesse L. Ellis, J. P., April 9, 1846, ROBERTSON Co.

FARMER, George W. to Julia F. Hayes - issued May 27, 1851, m. by:
Thomas Farmer, J. P., ROBERTSON Co.

FARMER, Gray to Elizabeth Hewett - issued December 7, 1846, Bondsman:
Rufus King, m. by: David Morrow December 8, 1846, MONTGOMERY Co.

FARMER, Henry L. to Mary E. Gooche - issued December 27, 1843, m. by:
R. W. Bell, J. P., ROBERTSON Co.

FARMER, Isaac to Elizabeth H. Mason - issued September 23, 1839, m. by:
Jeremiah Batts, J. P., September 26, 1839, ROBERTSON Co.

FARMER, J. H. to J. E. A. Izer - issued January 8, 1847, Bondsman:
Jacob Myres, m. by: Rev. D. C. Stephens, M. G., January 9, 1847,
MONTGOMERY Co.

FARMER, Jacob to Sarah Kirk - issued February 27, 1847, Bondsman:
Joel Heflin, MONTGOMERY Co.

FARMER, Jo. H. to Sarah C. Adams - issued November 17, 1858, m. by:
F. R. Gooch, M. G., ROBERTSON Co.

FARMER, John to Sarah Farmer - issued November 12, 1799, Bondsman:
Henry Farmer, Witness: A. White, KNOX Co.

FARMER, Joseph to Olive Fletcher - issued April 2, 1847, m. by:
R. W. Bell, J. P., ROBERTSON Co.

FARMER, Joseph M. to Fanton C. Mitchell - November 11, 1855, m. by:
Wm. Fry, J. P., GILES Co.

FARMER, Josiah to Nancy Long - issued August 10, 1850, m. by:
Lewis Adams, M. G., August 11, 1850, ROBERTSON Co.

FARMER, Lemuel to Rachel McMahon - February 13, 1822, WILLIAMSON Co.

FARMER, Nathaniel to S. C. Binkley - issued October 17, 1848, m. by:
J. W. Hunt, J. P., ROBERTSON Co.

FARMER, Robert A. to Mary Jane Putnam - issued September 25, 1856,
m. by: L. P. Whitten, M. G., September 25, 1856, COFFEE Co.

FARMER, Rufus E. to Lucy L. Vaughn - issued June 2, 1857, m. by:
F. C. Plaster June 5, 1857, ROBERTSON Co.

FARMER, Samuel M. to Rebecca J. Eskridge - issued November 14, 1843,
m. by: Wm. S. Smith, M. G., November 21, 1843, FRANKLIN Co.

FARMER, T. T. to Sarah Mumford - Bondsman: C. H. Smith, MONTGOMERY Co.

FARMER, Thomas to Nancy Ward - issued June 8, 1830, Bondsman:
E. C. Wilkinson, RUTHERFORD Co.

FARMER, Thonas H. to Catherine Martin - issued August 22, 1839, m. by:
John Sherrill, ROBERTSON Co.

FARMER, Thomas S. to Eleanor J. McCallon - issued January 24, 1842,
Bondsman: James Lillard, m. by: James M. Hoge, J. P., January 27,
1842, MEIGS Co.

FARMER, W. B. to Eliza S. Justice - issued December 27, 1855, m. by:
T. J. Craig, J. P., ROBERTSON Co.

FARMER, Welborn L. to Eliza Foster - issued October 19, 1844, m. by:
John Thomas Slatter, J. P., October 20, 1844, FRANKLIN Co.

FARMER, Wiley to Nancy Mosier - issued February 22, 1847, m. by:
Wm. Barton, M. G., February 24, 1847, DAVIDSON Co.

FARMER, William B. to Julia A. M. White - issued July 24, 1841, m. by:
H, Frey, J. P., July 25, 1841, ROBERTSON Co.

FARMER, Wm. B. to M. H. Stroud - issued December 24, 1870, m. by:
John T. Slatter, J. P., December 25, 1870, FRANKLIN Co.

FARMER, William H. to Elizabeth Couts - issued February 23, 1840,
m. by: D. R. Harris, M. G., February 24, 1840, ROBERTSON Co.

FARMER, Willie T. to Jane Dillard - issued December 7, 1855, m. by:
F. R. Gooch, M. G., ROBERTSON Co.

FARMON (?), Thomas to Betsy Swaddley - October 15, 1818 (?), KNOX Co.

FARNSWORTH, (illegible) - issued January 22, 1869, m. by:
J. P. Armstrong, J. P., FRANKLIN Co.

FARNSWORTH, George to Agnes Jamieson - 1791, Security: Henry Farnsworth, GREENE Co.

FARNSWORTH, Henry to Frances Allen - January 17, 1799, Security: John Farnsworth, GREENE Co.

FARNSWORTH, Jane to Alexander McCalpin - GREENE Co.

FARR, James to Polly King - issued March 13, 1793, Bondsman: Richard King, SUMNER Co.

FARR, William L. to Sarah Wilson - issued September 29, 1835, Bondsman: E. L. Farr, RUTHERFORD Co.

FARRAR, Abraham to Rebecca Moore - November 18, 1812, WILLIAMSON Co.

FARRAR, John to Elemor Word - issued August 27, 1861, Bondsman: I. Y. Norman, Jos. H. Thompson, Clk., m. by: John E. Frost, M. G., BEDFORD Co.

FARRAR, John L. to Santofe Bell - issued October 26, 1854, m. by: L. Burnum, J. P., October 29, 1854, COFFEE Co.

FARRAR, O. L. to Nancy Jane Stephens - issued December 28, 1854, m. by: J. J. Patton, M. G., December 28, 1854, COFFEE Co.

FARRELL, John to Barbara Jane Kirkman - issued October 15, 1838, m. by: Philip Lindsley October 15, 1838, DAVIDSON Co.

FARRELL, Smith to Mary McCowan (or McEwen) - September 9, 1800, Alexander Anderson, GREENE Co.

FARRIER, George to Sally Mooney - issued April 19, 1806, Bondsman: John Mooney, SUMNER Co.

FARRIER, John to Anne Thompson - issued October 1, 1796, Bondsman: Andrew Robinson, SUMNER Co.

FARRIER, Nathaniel to Agnes Patterson - issued March 4, 1796, Bondsman: Andrew Patterson, SUMNER Co.

FARRIS, Edward B. to Martha H. Dobson - issued November 12, 1850, m. by: F. D. Crittenden, R. M., November 13, 1850, FRANKLIN Co.

FARRIS, Fedrick (Frederick) G. to Mary Ann Miller - issued March 26, 1845, m. by: Wm. Burt, J. P., March 23, 1845, FRANKLIN Co.

FARRIS, G. S. to Sarah F. Custer - issued March 8, 1865, m. by: John T. Slatter, J. P., March 8, 1865, FRANKLIN Co.

FARRIS, Geo. W. to Mary E. King - issued November 28, 1838, Bondsman: J. B. Brackin, m. by: Freeman Senter November 28, 1838, SUMNER Co.

FARRIS, George W. to Margrett Barnes - issued March 18, 1842, m. by: I. T. Hines, J. P., March 20, 1842, FRANKLIN Co.

FARRIS, Geo. W. to C. A. Garner - issued May 1, 1845, m. by: B. C. L. Blanton, J. P., May 1, 1845, FRANKLIN Co.

FARRIS, H. L. to Eliza Jane Farris - issued February 15, 1866, m. by: J. Campbell, M. G., February 15, 1866, FRANKLIN Co.

FARRIS, Hezekiah to Sarah Cunningham - issued April 25, 1843, m. by: C. B. Farris, M. G., April 26, 1843, FRANKLIN Co.

FARRIS, John to Mary Seawell - issued August 15, 1822, RUTHERFORD Co.

FARRIS, John H. to Phebe Shasteen - issued September 15, 1865, m. by: A. Tribble, M. G., September 17, 1865, FRANKLIN Co.

FARRIS, John S. to Sarah L. Hines - issued November 29, 1839, m. by:
James Byrom, J. P., November 29, 1839, FRANKLIN Co.

FARRIS, John W. to Edith James - issued September 21, 1859, m. by:
J. T. Slatter, J. P., September 21, 1859, FRANKLIN Co.

FARRIS, Littleton to Margret E. Sims - issued July 30, 1856, FRANKLIN Co.

FARRIS, Mary J. to Giles W. Baker - BEDFORD Co.

FARRIS, Milton D. to Mary A. Sims - issued July 27, 1840, m. by:
Wm. G. Guinn July 30, 1840, FRANKLIN Co.

FARRIS, Richard C. to Mary E. Brown - issued January 30, 1854, m. by:
D. B. Muse, J. P., January 31, 1854, FRANKLIN Co.

FARRIS, Richard N. to Eliza Jane Blackwood - issued January 22, 1844,
m. by: William T. Wells, M. G., January 23, 1844, FRANKLIN Co.

FARRIS, Rubin to L. H. Norris (MB) - issued November 2, 1869,
m. November 3, 1869, FRANKLIN Co.

FARRIS, Samuel K. to Cathrine Smith - issued October 24, 1843, m. by:
J. Byrom, J. P., October 25, 1843, FRANKLIN Co.

FARRIS, T. B. to Fanny Phillips - issued December 4, 1868, FRANKLIN Co.

FARRIS, T. C. to M. J. Crawford - issued December 20, 1871, m. by:
J. M. Donaldson December 20, 1871, FRANKLIN Co.

FARRIS, T. W. to L. J. Wade - issued October 3, 1867, m. by:
Eld. Jas. A. Hudgins October 3, 1867, FRANKLIN Co.

FARRIS, Thomas D. to Eveline Farris - issued February 18, 1841,
FRANKLIN Co.

FARRIS, Wm. to Josephene McCullock - issued September 26, 1873, m. by:
D. S. Long, J. P., September 26, 1873, FRANKLIN Co.

FARRIS, William to Hannah Morris - issued June 29, 1874, m. by:
J. T. Merritt, J. P., June 29, 1874, FRANKLIN Co.

FARRIS, William D. to Mary Ward - issued January 8, 1833, m. by:
Thos. Sanders, J. P., January 10, 1833, RUTHERFORD Co.

FARRIS, Wm. D. to Ann Farris - issued March 30, 1843, m. by:
A. R. David, J. P., March 30, 1843, FRANKLIN Co.

FARRIS, William J. to Elizabeth Gamble - issued May 4, 1841, m. by:
John Nugent, J. P., May 4, 1841, FRANKLIN Co.

FARRIS, Wm. M. to Amanda M. Taylor - issued October 19, 1867, m. by:
G. W. Henderson, M. G., October 17, 1867, FRANKLIN Co.

FARRISS, Pheby to Samond Eloiss (?) - December 28, 1808, Bondsman:
John Stephenson, MAURY Co.

FARTHING, A. to W. A. Jones - issued November 20, 1851, m. by:
E. W. Gunn, M. G., ROBERTSON Co.

FARTHING, Coleman to Mariah Jones - issued January 2, 1843, m. by:
Robt. Green, J. P., ROBERTSON Co.

FARTHING, Ephraim to Polly Parsons - issued October 29, 1839, m. by:
Robert Green, J. P., ROBERTSON Co.

FARTHING, James to Sereno Adams - issued April 6, 1850, m. by:
G. B. Mason, J. P., April 7, 1850, ROBERTSON Co.

FARTHING, John B. to Martha Farthing - issued January 27, 1842, m. by:
Thomas Gunn, M. G., ROBERTSON Co.

FARTHING, Peter to Elizabeth Holland - issued January 9, 1847, m. by:
Robert ___(?), J. P., January 10, 1847, ROBERTSON Co.

FARTHING, Reuben to S. E. Ragsdale - issued March 6, 1845, m. by:
U. Young, J. P., ROBERTSON Co.

FARTHING, Reubin to Lucy A. Adams - issued March 2, 1853, m. by:
E. W. Gunn March 3, 1853, ROBERTSON Co.

FARTHING, Simon to Elizabeth Crane - issued February 16, 1845, m. by:
U. Young, J. P., ROBERTSON Co.

FARTHING, William to Rachel C. Parsons - issued July 15, 1833, m. by:
M. Powell, J. P., ROBERTSON Co.

FARVEAL, James to Sally Farveal - issued December 2, 1825, Bondsman:
William Cooper, WILSON Co.

FAUBION, Henry to Mary McKay - August 5, 1795, Security:
Samuel and Edom Kendricks, GREENE Co.

FAUGHT, Samuel to Nancy Doan (?) - January 6, 1810, WILLIAMSON Co.

FAULCONER, William to Catherine Winston - issued April 6, 1847, m. by:
Wile William, J. P., April 8, 1847, DAVIDSON Co.

FAULKENBURY, Jacob to Jane M. Fleming - issued September 26, 1827,
Bondsman: Hiram Tennison, RUTHERFORD Co.

FAULKNER, Edward P. to Rebecca New - issued June 4, 1830, WILSON Co.

FAULKNER, Robert P. to Mary A. Hunter - issued July 15, 1846, m. by:
A. G. Goodlett, M. G., July 16, 1846, DAVIDSON Co.

FAUST, John to Manerva Harper - issued December 5, 1863, Bondsman:
Thos. J. Wilburn, m. by: William McMasters, J. P., December 6,
1863, LAWRENCE Co.

FAVOR, John to Mary A. Morris - issued August 24, 1863, Bondsman:
A. J. McAdams, BEDFORD Co.

FAVOR, Martha S. to E. D. Wortham - BEDFORD Co.

FAVOUR, James to Anna Meban - issued November 2, 1804, Bondsman:
William Howell, RUTHERFORD Co.

FAWKE, Levi to Nancy White - issued December 29, 1806, Bondsman:
Littleberry White, SUMNER Co.

FAWNERTO, James W. to Margrett Short - issued February 5, 1847, m. by:
Jessee Graham, M. G., February 5, 1847, FRANKLIN Co.

FAXON, Leonard G. to Martha Atkinson - issued November 25, 1854,
Bondsman: W. Auchinlock, MONTGOMERY Co.

FAY (or Fry?), Nicholas to Gibby Moore - issued March 8, 1826, m. by:
Geo. Atkin, M. G., March 8, 1826, KNOX Co.

FEARS, Eben E. to Elizabeth Spence - issued June 17, 1833, Bondsman:
Samuel Spence, RUTHERFORD Co.

FEATHERSTON, Burrel to Sophia Hart - issued September 10, 1853, m. by:
James Woodard, J. P., September 11, 1853, ROBERTSON Co.

FEATHERSTON, Clement to Litha J. Kennerly - issued January 20, 1858,
FRANKLIN Co.

FEATHERSTON, David to Susan Crafford - issued January 13, 1854, m. by:
David Herring, J. P., ROBERTSON Co.

FEATHERSTON, Geo. W. to Patsy Redfern - issued March 29, 1842, m. by:
Benja. Gambill, J. P., ROBERTSON Co.

FEATHERSTON, H. D. to M. E. Davis - issued November 25, 1848, m. by:
Milton Ramey, M. G., November 26, 1848, ROBERTSON Co.

FEATHERSTON, Henry D. to Mary Draughon - issued April 7, 1846, m. by:
Thomas Farmer, J. P., ROBERTSON Co.

FEATHERSTON, John to Eliza J. Knight - February 17, 1859, m. by:
John M. Hewitt, J. P., GILES Co.

FEATHERSTON, Joshua W. to E. M. P. Jackson - issued February 27, 1844,
m. by; G. W. Sneed, M. G., ROBERTSON Co.

FEATHERSTONE, Calven to Elizabeth Putnam - issued September 11, 1862,
Bondsman: Brittain Spence, Jos. H. Thompson, Clk. per N. F. Thompson,
Dep. Clk., BEDFORD Co.

FEATHERSTONE (?), John to Eliza J. Knight - February 17, 1859, m. by:
John M. Hewitt, J. P., GILES Co.

FEATHERSTONE, Presley to Elizabeth Harris - issued December 20, 1834,
Bondsman: Robert Jarratt, RUTHERFORD Co.

FEEMSTER, John B. to Sarah E. Reeves - issued April 8, 1851, m. by:
C. L. Blanton, J. P., April 8, 1851, FRANKLIN Co.

FEIFER, John to Mary Sparkman - issued September 20, 1848, m. by:
F. E. Plumlee, J. P., September 22, 1848, VAN BUREN Co.

FEILDS, Edwin to Mary Ann Akin - issued October 20, 1842, m. by:
C. D. Elliott, M. G., October 20, 1842, DAVIDSON Co.

FELAND, W. L. to Eliza May - issued July 27, 1847, m. by: John Wilson,
J. P., July 27, 1847, STEWART Co.

FELIND, Sterling B. to Penniny Skinner - issued October 8, 1842,
STEWART Co.

FELKER, Wm. H. to Thirza Jane Anderson - December 25, 1852, m. by:
Harrison D. Hart, J. P., GILES Co.

FELLERS, Eve to Jacob Hise - GREENE Co.

FELLERS, Jacob to Catherine Yerrick - October 15, 1798, Security:
Youst Yerrick, GREENE Co.

FELTS, Amos G. to M. L. Coleman - issued December 16, 1848, m. by:
B. Rawls, ROBERTSON Co.

FELTS, Benjamin C. to Sarah R. Allen - issued December 29, 1852,
Bondsman: Archibald W. Howell, m. by: T. Ramey, J. P., December 29,
1852, MONTGOMERY Co.

FELTS, George M. to Mary Jane Mock - issued May 22, 1846, m. by:
J. D. Darrow June 7, 1846, DAVIDSON Co.

FELTS, Isam to Elizabeth Bennett - issued September 9, 1847, m. by:
W. Crockett September 12, 1847, DAVIDSON Co.

FELTS, John L. to Elizabeth Reed - issued March 3, 1854, m. by:
F. R. Gooch, M. G., March 9, 1854, ROBERTSON Co.

FELTS, Joseph to Frances J. Moor - issued November 2, 1846, m. by:
R. Moody, M. G., November 5, 1846, ROBERTSON Co.

FELTS, Joseph W. to S. A. R. Owen - issued December 30, 1850, m. by:
Thos. W. Felts January 1, 1851, ROBERTSON Co.

FELTS, L. F. to M. Harris - issued October 16, 1851, m. by:
A. B. Soyres, J. P., ROBERTSON Co.

FELTS, L. F. to S. L. Craig - issued November 21, 1857, m. by:
Geo. W. Martin, M. G., ROBERTSON Co.

FELTS, Richard B. to Margaret Murrah - issued March 5, 1846,
m. March 8, 1846, ROBERTSON Co.

FELTS, Robert to Susan Carter - issued October 3, 1846, m. by:
W. L. Baldry, M. G., October 7, 1846, ROBERTSON Co.

FELTS, Robert D. to Nancy M. Burnet - issued February 19, 1840, m. by:
J. W. Hunt, J. P., February 27, 1840, ROBERTSON Co.

FELTS, W. E. to M. J. Walker - issued December 6, 1848, m. by:
J. W. Hunt, J. P., December 7, 1848, ROBERTSON Co.

FELTS, W. I. to Louisa Herrington - issued August 24, 1855, m. by:
I. T. Craig, J. P., August 26, 1855, ROBERTSON Co.

FELTS, W. W. to S. A. McClain - issued June 13, 1848, m. by:
J. W. Hunt, J. P., June 15, 1848, ROBERTSON Co.

FELTS, William to Sarah Hastins - issued March 19, 1840, ROBERTSON Co.

FELTS, William E. to Huldy Holmes - issued November 5, 1855, m. by:
A. Rose, M. G., November 11, 1855, ROBERTSON Co.

FELTS, Wm. W. to S. A. McAllen - issued June 13, 1848, m. by:
J. W. Hunt, J. P., June 15, 1848, ROBERTSON Co.

FELTS, William W. to Martha J. Hunt - issued August 9, 1853, m. by:
Robert Williams, J. P., August 11, 1853, ROBERTSON Co.

FENIX, David O. to Mary Meador - m. by: Freeman Senter July 10, 1837,
SUMNER Co.

FENTRESS, David to Matilda C. McIver - issued January 17, 1833, m. by:
William Eagleton, V. D. M., January 17, 1833, RUTHERFORD Co.

FENTRESS, James B. to P. I . Herrington - issued October 8, 1857, m. by:
J. T. Craig, J. P., ROBERTSON Co.

FERGERSON, Betsey to Thomas McFall - MAURY Co.

FERGERSON, Stephen to Nancy Vandergriff - m. by: J. F. Anderson, J. P.,
March 2, 1851, FRANKLIN Co.

FERGESON, John to Patsey Harris - issued January 18, 1806, Bondsman:
Eli Harrell, WILSON Co.

FERGUSON, A. O. to Sarah A. Young - issued September 13, 1849, Bondsman:
G. F. Pendleton, MONTGOMERY Co.

FERGUSON, Andrew to Catherine Zachery - October 17, 1835 (?), KNOX Co.

FERGUSON, Calvin W. to Ellonnora H. Johnson - issued December 18, 1845,
m. by: J. B. McFerrin, M. G., December 18, 1845, DAVIDSON Co.

FERGUSON, Daniel S. to Mary T. Combs - September 15, 1853, m. by:
Adam S. Riggs, M. G., GILES Co.

FERGUSON, Edwin to Elvira S. Cantrell - issued January 14, 1846, m. by:
J. T. Edgar January 14, 1846, DAVIDSON Co.

FERGUSON, Greenberry to Polly Mabry - issued August 28, 1829, Bondsman:
William Mabry, SUMNER Co.

FERGUSON, Hugh to Martha Craig - November 19, 1796, BLOUNT Co.

FERGUSON, J. J. to Miss S. Keel - issued April 30, 1862, m. by:
John J. Pittman, M. G., April 3, 1862, COFFEE Co.

FERGUSON, James to Nancy Churchman - July 8, 1794 (?), KNOX Co.

FERGUSON, James to Elizabeth Wyatt - issued March 23, 1842, m. by:
Josiah Ferriss, J. P., March 23, 1842, DAVIDSON Co.

FERGUSON, Joel to Susannah Stockton - June 2, 1816, KNOX Co.

FERGUSON, John to Anny Bates - issued November 27, 1819, Bondsman:
John Bates, SUMNER Co.

FERGUSON, John to Any Bates - m. by: John L. Swaney, J. P., November 27,
1820, SUMNER Co.

FERGUSON, John W. to Martha W. Persise - issued January 9, 1853, m. by:
L. R. Dennis, ROBERTSON Co.

FERGUSON, Landus S. to Elizabeth Johnson - issued September 9, 1841,
m. by: W. E. Cartwright, J. P., September 9, 1841, DAVIDSON Co.

FERGUSON, Luke H. to Charlotte Grant - issued November 4, 1845,
Bondsman: Aqulla Grant, m. by: Drury C. Stephens, G. M.,
November 4, 1845, MONTGOMERY Co.

FERGUSON, Manda E. to W. H. Phillips - issued October 3, 1862, Bondsman:
L. M. Covington, Jos. H. Thompson, Clk. per M. E. W. Dunaway,
Dep. Clk., BEDFORD Co.

FERGUSON, Mint to Elizabeth Stansbury - issued October 25, 1817,
m. by: S. Montgomery November 6, 1817, KNOX Co.

FERGUSON, Nelson to Roxey Tyler - issued November 23, 1816, Bondsman:
J. W. Byrn, SUMNER Co.

FERGUSON, Robert to Patsy Stansberry - issued November 7, 1816, m. by:
S. Montgomery November 7, 1816, KNOX Co.

FERGUSON, Robert to Polly Farr - issued August 3, 1821, Bondsman:
Edward Jackson, m. by: J. Bonner, J. P., August 4, 1821, WILSON Co.

FERGUSON, Sam'l. to Lucy Hinds - issued October 7, 1837, m. by:
T. Sullins October 7, 1837, KNOX Co.

FERGUSON, Toliver to Catherine Minters - issued October 5, 1821, m. by:
Robert Miller, J. P., October 5, 1821, RUTHERFORD Co.

FERGUSON, William to Judah Woods - February 7, 1791, Security:
Robert Campbell and Bulfield Woods, GREENE Co.

FERGUSON, Wm. to Fanny Bowman - issued April 22, 1813, Bondsman:
Samuel Thomas, Witness: A. Hutcheson, KNOX Co.

FERGUSON, Wm. to Sally Harvey - issued October 20, 1830, m. by:
Martin B. Carter, J. P., October 21, 1830, KNOX Co.

FERGUSON, William D. to Margaret D. Neely - issued September 15, 1829,
Bondsman: F. B. Reod, m. by: John Wiseman, M. G., September 15,
1829, SUMNER Co.

FERGUSON, William T. to Mary E. Gish - issued August 5, 1856, m. by:
J. W. Cullum, M. G., ROBERTSON Co.

FERMAULT, John to Margaret Kerr - 1793 (?), KNOX Co.

441

FERMAULT, Thomas to Polly Matlock - May 28, 1798, KNOX Co.

FERNEYBOUGH, John to Frances Gilbert - issued July 16, 1812, Bondsman:
John Walters, SUMNER Co.

FERRELL, Benjamin to Polly M. Davis - issued November 18, 1810,
Bondsman: Benjamin Hobson, WILSON Co.

FERRELL, Birrom to Sally Clor - issued March 15, 1808, Bondsman:
James Douglas, SUMNER Co.

FERRELL, Birtis W. to Sally T. Hunt - issued November 3, 1825, Bondsman:
Burl Bender, m. November 3, 1825, SUMNER Co.

FERRELL, Clement to Salley Edwards - issued April 26, 1811, Bondsman:
John Fillingham, SUMNER Co.

FERRELL, Enoch to Nancy Nevill - issued February 5, 1799, Bondsman:
Goan Morgan, Witness: H. L. White, KNOX Co.

FERRELL, Hobson to Martha Parrish - issued December 10, 1822, m. by:
Daniel Moser December 12, 1822, WILSON Co.

FERRELL, James to Zina Jones - issued February 18, 1824, m. by:
William Keele February 22, 1824, RUTHERFORD Co.

FERRELL, James to Mary.Ann Duncan - issued October 4, 1858, m. by:
M. A. Carden, J. P., October 6, 1858, COFFEE Co.

FERRELL, John to Harriet Sanders - issued February 6, 1830, Bondsman:
Warner Beasley, m. by: D. Ashford, J. P., February 6, 1830,
SUMNER Co.

FERRELL, John to Maria Caster - issued October 15, 1830, Bondsman:
William Hannah, SUMNER Co.

FERRELL, Patrick to Margrett Jenkins - issued August 20, 1849, m. by:
J. C. Montgomery, J. P., August 20, 1849, FRANKLIN Co.

FERRELL, Robert R. to Mollie J. Heffington - issued September 13, 1859,
m. by: G. B. Messick, J. P., September 13, 1859, COFFEE Co.

FERRELL, Thomas to Betsy Shaw - issued January 27, 1806, Bondsman:
Joshua Smith, SUMNER Co.

FERRELL, Vincent B. to Rosebuda Cashin - issued May 8, 1843, FRANKLIN Co.

FERRELL, William to Elizabeth Wilson - issued August 22, 1823, Bondsman:
Ewing Wilson, m. by: John Provine, M. G., WILSON Co.

FERRIS, Charles to Susannah Mason - issued September 5, 1826, Bondsman:
John Mason, m. by: J. B. Lasiter, J. P., September 6, 1826,
WILSON Co.

FERRISS, John C. to Christina H. Clay - issued February 22, 1834,
Bondsman: Sam Clark, RUTHERFORD Co.

FERRISS, Wm. D. to Mary Ward - issued January 8, 1833, Bondsman:
E. W. Staton, RUTHERFORD Co.

FIELD, R. M. to Mary D. Smith - issued February 6, 1837, Bondsman:
Joseph Thompson, m. by: John Wiseman February 6, 1837, SUMNER Co.

FIELDING, Thomas W. to Elizabeth Hunter - January 23, 1812, WILLIAMSON Co.

FIELDING, Thos. W. to Mary Brandon - issued December 23, 1848, STEWART Co.

FIELDS, David to Rhody Ferrington - issued April 26, 1817, Bondsman:
Ivey Gibson, m. by: Sam'l Cannon, J. P., April 29, 1817, WILSON Co.

FIELDS, John to Elizabeth Taylor - issued October 7, 1816, Bondsman:
David Fields, m. by: Edward Harris October 8, 1816, WILSON Co.

FIELDS, John to Nancy Truett - issued February 24, 1834, Bondsman:
Reddin Fields, WILSON Co.

FIELDS, Nicholas to Elizabeth Moor - issued July 20, 1851, Bondsman:
J. Armstrong, m. by: P. H. Fraser, EB.C, July 27, 1851, MONTGOMERY Co.

FIELDS, Redding to Polly Ferrington - issued December 31, 1825,
Bondsman: David Fields, m. by: James Bond, V. D. M., January 3, .
1826, WILSON Co.

FIELDS, Richard to Polly Edwards - issued October 8, 1815, m. by:
Jacob Sullivan October 9, 1815, WILSON Co.

FIELDS, Richard to Polly Edwards - issued October 8, 1816, Bondsman:
Howard Edwards, WILSON Co.

FIELDS, Riley to Susan Wood - issued January 26, 1835, Bondsman:
Presley Stewart, RUTHERFORD Co.

FIELDS, William L. to Rebecca Justice - issued March 5, 1853, Bondsman:
Levi B. Darrow, m. by: G. Orgain, J. P., March 5, 1853,
MONTGOMERY Co.

FIFE, James to Samira H. Budleman - issued September 1, 1846, m. by:
Joseph Willis, P. G., September 1, 1846, DAVIDSON Co.

FIGUERS, M. to Lizzie Nash - issued February 11, 1848, Bondsman:
D. Brodie, MONTGOMERY Co.

FIGURES, Bartholomew to Caroline Matilda Davis - issued June 9, 1834,
Bondsman: William H. Crenshaw, WILSON Co.

FIGURES, Mathew to Eliza A. Thomas - issued July 27, 1820, Bondsman:
William Hadley, SUMNER Co.

FIKE, Henland (or Herlone?) to Jane Campbell - issued July 27, 1819,
m. by: Robt. Tunnell, J. P., July 29, 1819, KNOX Co.

FILLART, Samie to Elizabeth Watson - issued December 3, 1851, m. by:
B. A. Rose, M. G., ROBERTSON Co.

FILLINGAN, John to Prudence Valentine - issued April 29, 1812, Bondsman:
Stephen Puckett, SUMNER Co.

FILLOPS, David to Aney Frances - issued March 22, 1828, Bondsman:
David Fillops, m. by: Robert McKee, J. P., March 23, 1828, WILSON Co.

FILLOPS, Thomas to Cissey Jonston - issued February 12, 1828, Bondsman:
Benjamin Caleb, m. by: Joshua Lester, V. D. M., WILSON Co.

FILPOT, Wm. to Amanda Hendley - issued September 9, 1869, FRANKLIN Co.

FIN, William to Sealy Mayhew - issued August 23, 1825, Bondsman:
Benjamin Wilson, m. by: Samuel Davis, J. P., August 23, 1825,
SUMNER Co.

FINCH, Daniel to Nancy Wileman - issued November 24, 1845, FRANKLIN Co.

FINCH, George to Polina Arbuckle - issued September 12, 1833, Bondsman:
Thos. Cook, m. by: Jas. S. Jetton, J. P., September 12, 1833,
RUTHERFORD Co.

FINCH, Goerge to Martha Ann Wilson - issued July 3, 1854, m. by:
W. B. M. Williams, Min., June 28, 1854, COFFEE Co.

FINCH, Jarrott to Elizabeth Hill - issued November 17, 1818, Bondsman:
Thomas Broughton, m. by: John Fulton, J. P., November 19, 1818,
RUTHERFORD Co.

FINCH, John to Sarah Cook - issued August 24, 1833, Bondsman:
Jarrott Finch, RUTHERFORD Co.

FINCH, John W. to Rebecca J. Wileman - issued February 16, 1857,
FRANKLIN Co.

FINCH, Thomas to Ann Eliza Moffitt - issued December 16, 1846, m. by:
N. P. Modrall, M. G., December 17, 1846, FRANKLIN Co.

FINCH, THos. H. to Amelia A. Hill - issued February 8, 1854, m. by:
A. D. Trimble, M. G., February 8, 1854, FRANKLIN Co.

FINCH, William H. to Sarah Smith - issued May 24, 1855, m. by:
E. A. Rutledge, J. P., May 24, 1855, COFFEE Co.

FINDLAY, L. D. H. to Harriett E. Wyatt - issued May 14, 1844, m. by:
W. Ellis, J. P., May 14, 1844, STEWART Co.

FINDLEY, Isaac to Elinder Fowler - issued August 26, 1820, m. by:
Wm. Deloach, J. P., August 30, 1820, RUTHERFORD Co.

FINDLEY, John to Patsy Pean - issued December 8, 1821, Bondsman:
John Findley, KNOX Co.

FINDLEY, John to Sally M. Watson - issued March 29, 1828, m. by:
Eli King, J. P., April 10, 1828, KNOX Co.

FINDLY, James M. to Elizabeth Luton - issued January 26, 1843, m. by:
Peter Lynch, J. P., January 26, 1843, STEWART Co.

FINE, Peter to Elizabeth Alexander - issued November 25, 1816, KNOX Co.

FINIX, John to Polly Sloane - issued March 15, 1808, Bondsman:
Richard Ball, SUMNER Co.

FINK, George to Nancy Smith - December 24, 1832, KNOX Co.

FINLAY, James M. to Mary Holland - issued June 13, 1843, m. by:
Greenberry Kelly June 15, 1843, ROBERTSON Co.

FINLEY, D. G. to S. B. Montgomery - issued August 13, 1862, Bondsman:
John W. March, Joseph H. Thompson, Clk. per N. F. Thompson,
Dep. Clk., BEDFORD Co.

FINLEY, David to Serena C. Ford - issued December 14, 1858, m. by:
G. Fletcher, J. P., December 14, 1858, COFFEE Co.

FINLEY, Jesse L. to Amanda Yerger - issued October 3, 1832, Bondsman:
Richard H. Johnson, m. by: A. F. Drizkill, WILSON Co.

FINLEY, John to Margaret Kerr - issued November 13, 1793, Bondsman:
Jeremiah McCarter, Witness: Chas. McClung, C. K. C., KNOX Co.

FINLEY, Obadiah to Mary L. Johnson - issued February 22, 1811, Bondsman:
Joel Echols, SUMNER Co.

FINLEY, William to Jane English - December 24, 1798, Security:
Adonijah and James Penney, GREENE Co.

FINLEY, William to Margaret Benine - issued July 25, 1845, m. by:
Henry Crawley, J. P., July 25, 1845, VAN BUREN Co.

FINLEY, Wm. M. to Elizabeth West - issued January 13, 1845, DICKSON Co.

FINLEY, Wm. W. to Ann L. Dortch - issued April 3, 1849, Bondsman:
W. B. Dortch, MONTGOMERY Co.

FINN, John A. to M. B. Duval - issued January 25, 1845, m. by:
Y. Schenlet January 27, 1845, ROBERTSON Co.

FINN, Shadrick to Rebecca Henderson - issued October 31, 1808, Bondsman:
Thos. Keife and Porter Allen, SUMNER Co.

FINNEY, A. J. to Mary A. Tankersley - issued December 24, 1853, m. by:
Rev. James Watson, M. G., December 25, 1853, FRANKLIN Co.

FINNEY, A. J. to Sarah W. S. Rich - issued February 20, 1869, m. by:
T. F. Moseley, J. P., February 22, 1869, FRANKLIN Co.

FINNEY, Andrew to Nancy Phillips - issued January 15, 1815, Bondsman:
Armstrong Herd, WILSON Co.

FINNEY, Andrew to Mary Ann Goley - issued September 20, 1834, Bondsman:
R. Blair, RUTHERFORD Co.

FINNEY, John to Eliza Orear - issued April 2, 1847, m.. by:
John Nugent, J. P., April 18, 1847, FRANKLIN Co.

FINNEY, John M. to Drusilla Jane Covey - issued April 29, 1857, m. by:
L. W. Marbury, J. P., April 30, 1857, COFFEE Co.

FINNEY, Lewis to Mary Newman - issued January 7, 1860, m. by:
Wm. G. Guinn June 8, 1860, FRANKLIN Co.

FINNEY, Nelson to Martha Dyal - issued January 15, 1839, m. by:
B. B. Knight, J. P., January 17, 1839, FRANKLIN Co.

FINNEY, Thomas J. to Mary A. Slatter - issued November 8, 1841, m. by:
R. B. C. Howell, M. G., November 11, 1841, DAVIDSON Co.

FINNEY, W. T. to Ellen Morris - issued November 23, 1866, FRANKLIN Co.

FINNEY, William to Ruth Penn - issued July 22, 1823, Bondsman:
Amos S. Wallis, m. by: G. W. Banton, J. P., July 24, 1823,
RUTHERFORD Co.

FINNEY, William to Elizabeth Boyd - issued March 21, 1861, m. by:
J. W. Anderson, J. P., March 21, 1861, FRANKLIN Co.

FINNEY, Wm. R. to Sarah Runnels - issued August 14, 1851, m. by:
John F. Morris, J. P., August 14, 1851, FRANKLIN Co.

FISHER, Archibald to Elizabeth Sharp - issued December 11, 1797,
Bondsman: John Steele, Witness: Chas. McClung, Clk., KNOX Co.

FISHER, Benjamin to Peggy Crawford - issued November 17, 1811, Bondsman:
Anderson Fisher, WILSON Co.

FISHER, Cephas to Rachel Stanfield - August 24, 1803, GREENE Co.

FISHER, Daniel to Betsey Boyd - issued October 18, 1811, KNOX Co.

FISHER, Daniel to Penelope A. Williams - issued September 14, 1841,
m. by: Jno. Thos. Wheat September 14, 1841, DAVIDSON Co.

FISHER, David to Mary Flood - issued November 2, 1853, m. by:
J. C. Barbee, J. P., November 3, 1853, ROBERTSON Co.

FISHER, Edward to Martha Ann Hartwell - issued December 8, 1823,
Bondsman: Joseph H. Worthan, m. by: Peyton Smith December 9, 1823,
RUTHERFORD Co.

FISHER, Enisley (?) to Sarah McNutt - issued February 25, 1836, Bondsman:
W. M. Bounds, m. by: B. McNutt, J. P., February 25, 1836, Witness:
Geo. M. White, KNOX Co.

FISHER, George to Eliza Cable - July 22, 1836, KNOX Co.

FISHER, Geo. F. to Margaret E. Griffin - issued December 19, 1846, m. December 22, 1846, ROBERTSON Co.

FISHER, Hannah to Jacob Clearwater - GREENE Co.

FISHER, Hillery to Elizabeth Flood - issued November 18, 1849, m. by: B. Randolph, J. P., ROBERTSON Co.

FISHER, James to Elsunda Doss - issued January 7, 1851, m. by: B. Randolph January 9, 1851, ROBERTSON Co.

FISHER, James to Arnette Willis - issued July 21, 1860, m. by: T. O. Tarpley, J. P., July 23, 1860, ROBERTSON Co.

FISHER, Jeremiah to Sally Drennon - issued February 25, 1822, Bondsman: Green B. Lannom, m. by: Jas. Browning, D. D., March 13, 1822, WILSON Co.

FISHER, John to Jean Palmer - July 25, 1800, Security: James Craig, BLOUNT Co.

FISHER, John to Mary Pritchett - June 24, 1809, Bondsman: Samuel Radford, MAURY Co.

FISHER, John to Elizabeth Killingsworth - issued July 2, 1818, m. by: Edm'd Jones, D. M. C., RUTHERFORD Co.

FISHER, John to Martha Still - issued April 14, 1847, m. by: John Rain, M. G., April 14, 1847, DAVIDSON Co.

FISHER, John L. to Susan J. King - issued February 8, 1840, m. by: John Wright, J. P., February 8, 1840, DAVIDSON Co.

FISHER, Joseph B. to Priscilla A. Guilleford - issued July 28, 1843, m. by: John Barnett, M. G., July 30, 1843, DAVIDSON Co.

FISHER, Levi to Martha E. S. Guthrie - issued May 2, 1836, m. by: Thomas Smith, M. G., May 3, 1836, WILSON Co.

FISHER, M. L. to E. J. Babb - issued November 6, 1860, m. by: J. M. Copeland, J. P., November 8, 1860, ROBERTSON Co.

FISHER, Mary to Jesse Walker - GREENE Co.

FISHER, P. M. to Elizabeth Bourne - issued June 5, 1845, m. by: James Woodard, J. P., ROBERTSON Co.

FISHER, Richd. to Louisa Whitehead - issued May 1, 1840, m. by: George Childress, J. P., ROBERTSON Co.

FISHER, Samuel to Lavina Williams - isused December 22, 1841, m. by: John Beazley, J. P., December 22, 1841, DAVIDSON Co.

FISHER, Thomas to Mary J. Davis - issued September 24, 1862, Bondsman: M. C. Davis, m. by: R. L. McLaren, J. P., September 28, 1862, LAWRENCE Co.

FISHER, William to Faithy Hix - issued May 17, 1791, Bondsman: Robert Looney, SUMNER Co.

FISHER, William to Jenney Fisher - issued April 13, 1816, Bondsman: Benjamin Fisher, m. by: Jos. T. Williams, J. P., April 25, 1816, WILSON Co.

FISER, A. W. to M. A. E. Duke - issued November 23, 1853, m. by: J. B. Walton November 27, 1853, ROBERTSON Co.

FISER, James to B. Bartlett - issued December 29, 1847, m. by: T. B. Matthews, J. P., December 30, 1847, ROBERTSON Co.

FISER, Joseph H. to Sarah B. Davis - issued July 4, 1840, m. by:
Geo. Childress, J. P., July 5, 1840, ROBERTSON Co.

FISER, L. T. to Martha Stoltz - issued June 24, 1852, m. by:
J. Batts, J. P., June 27, 1852, ROBERTSON Co.

FISER, Lemuel to Julia Ann Dean - issued August 8, 1840, m. by:
Robt. Green, J. P., August 9, 1840, ROBERTSON Co.

FISER, Solomon to Matilda Crockett - issued October 10, 1839, m. by:
Benjamin Rawls, G. M., ROBERTSON Co.

FISER, Sollomon to Zelicha Hutcherson - issued December 31, 1846,
m. by: R. B. Rose, J. P., ROBERTSON Co.

FISK, John to Peggy Duffel - July 19, 1813, WILLIAMSON Co.

FISKE, James E. to Elizabeth Fooshee - issued October 7, 1845, Bondsman:
Thomas P. Davis, m. by: John Huff, Esq., October 9, 1845, MEIGS Co.

FITCH, James to Edy Tally - issued January 13, 1846, Bondsman:
Isaac Fitch, MEIGS Co.

FITCH, Victor to Rebeca L. Davis - issued April 24, 1839, STEWART Co.

FITE, Henry to Mary Grandstaff - issued October 7, 1823, Bondsman:
John Grandstaff, m. by: Cantrell Bethell, M. G., October 9, 1823,
WILSON Co.

FITTS, Sanford to Tabitha Hughes - issued November 4, 1817, Bondsman:
Thomas Scurry, m. by: Washington Ballard, V. D. M., November 4,
1817, SUMNER Co.

FITTS, Sanford to Frances F. Higgason - issued April 24, 1829, Bondsman:
William Harper, m. by: John Banks, J. P., April 24, 1829, SUMNER Co.

FITZGERALD, Geo. W. to Betsy Proctor - issued April 29, 1836, Bondsman:
Jno. Fitsgerald, m. by: M. L. Mynatt, J. P., May 5, 1836, Witness:
Geo. M. White, KNOX Co.

FITZGERALD, John to Sarah Ballard - February 14, 1797, Security:
Christopher Bullard, GREENE Co.

FITZGERALD, John to Nancy Hanks - October 2, 1809, Bondsman:
Thomas Hanks, MAURY Co.

FITZGERALD, John to Mary Hill - issued August 4, 1851, m. by:
J. C. Montgomery August 4, 1851, FRANKLIN Co.

FITZGERALD, Michael to Jane T. Swain - issued February 23, 1857, m. by:
James Seargent, J. P., February 23, 1857, FRANKLIN Co.

FITZGERRELD, John to Fanny Hanks - August 7, 1807, WILLIAMSON Co.

FITZGIBBONS, Thomas to Sarah C. Mederis - issued June 8, 1872, m. by:
E. H. Bennett, M. G., June 8, 1872, FRANKLIN Co.

FITZHUGH, B. S. to Julia Ann Carper - issued October 19, 1846, m. by:
Wm. A. Whitsett, M. G., October 20, 1846, DAVIDSON Co.

FITZHUGH, James M. to Nancy Amanda Whitemore - issued August 24, 1842,
m. by: T. W. Haynes, M. G., August 25, 1842, DAVIDSON Co.

FITZPATRICK, J. B. to Mag Marks - issued November 20, 1867, m. by:
M. H. Bone, M. G., November 20, 1867, FRANKLIN Co.

FITZPATRICK, James T. to Sarah J. Greer - issued October 11, 1865,
m. by: James Seargent, J. P., October 12, 1865, FRANKLIN Co.

FITZPATRICK, John to Lucy Freeman - July 15, 1812, WILLIAMSON Co.

FITZPATRICK, John W. to Mary M. Gambol - issued October 23, 1867,
    FRANKLIN Co.

FITZPATRICK, Morgan to Rebekah Evans - December 20, 1806, WILLIAMSON Co.

FITZPATRICK, Morgan to Fanny Evans - December 30, 1806, WILLIAMSON Co.

FLANAGIN, James to Nancy Flanagin - issued December 24, 1836, Bondsman:
    Lewis Dies, m. by: B. T. Mabry, M. G., December 25, 1836, WILSON Co.

FLANAGIN, Marcus to Susan Flanagin - issued December 24, 1836, m. by:
    B. T. Mabry December 25, 1836, WILSON Co.

FLANNERY, Nancy to Isaac Doty - GREENE Co.

FLANNERY, Thomas to Nancy Thedford - issued December 13, 1847, m. by:
    Samuel Tate, J. P., December 13, 1847, DICKSON Co.

F(L)AUGHT, Madison to Sarah Ann Coats - August 30, 1860, Security:
    John A. Coats, GILES Co.

FLEEMAN, F. M. to G. P. McCalister - issued June 5, 1862, Bondsman:
    James W. Fleeman, m. by: J. P. Richardson, M. G., June 8, 1862,
    LAWRENCE Co.

FLEET, William to Sally Edwards - issued December 28, 1838, m. by:
    Jas. Daniel, J. P., December 28, 1838, DICKSON Co.

FLEETWOOD, Hardy to Harriett Pagitt - issued May 16, 1824, m. by:
    J. L. Swaney, J. P., May 16, 1824, SUMNER Co.

FLEMING, Beverly to Polly Aspy - issued November 15, 1813, Bondsman:
    Joseph Moss, SUMNER Co.

FLEMING, David to Lydia Shelton - issued September 1, 1812, Bondsman:
    Sam'l Fleming, m. by: Jno. Love, Esq., September 1, 1812, KNOX Co.

FLEMING, Ferguson to Frances J. McCombs - issued January 25, 1842,
    DAVIDSON Co.

FLEMING, James to Polly Ross - issued September 20, 1813, Bondsman:
    Isiah Lauderdale, SUMNER Co.

FLEMING, James to Elizabeth Rasco - issued August 12, 1824, Bondsman:
    Bird Estham, m. by: J. B. Wynns, M. G., August 12, 1824, SUMNER Co.

FLEMING, John to Eleanor Fleming - issued December 27, 1825, m. by:
    Jas. S. Jetton, J. P., December 27, 1825, RUTHERFORD Co.

FLEMING, John to America Parrish - issued January 22, 1835, Bondsman:
    James Blanton, m. by: German Baker January 22, 1835, RUTHERFORD Co.

FLEMING, John H. to Jane Hardin - issued August 17, 1829, Bondsman:
    Robert Marley, m. by: Wm. Morris, J. P., August 17, 1829, KNOX Co.

FLEMING, Joseph J. to Frances Gillam - issued December 11, 1840,
    DAVIDSON Co.

FLEMING, Josiah to Jane B. Sharp - December 2, 1828, WILLIAMSON Co.

FLEMING, Mary (?) to (illegible) - May 26, 1808, Bondsman:
    David Frierson, MAURY Co.

FLEMING, Robert to Nancy Mitchell - issued June 16, 1806, Bondsman:
    John Mitchell, SUMNER Co.

FLEMMING, Pressley to Margaret Robertson - issued July 7, 1825, Bondsman:
    Jno. Craighead, m. by: W. B. A. Ramsey, J. P., July 7, 1825, KNOX Co.

FLEMING, Monroe to Elizabeth Guthrey - issued August 10, 1844, m. by:
James A. Haston, J. P., August 15, 1844, VAN BUREN Co.

FLEMING, Robert to Polly Barr - issued November 13, 1818, Bondsman:
Thos. Scurry, SUMNER Co.

FLEMING, Robert to Mary Gourley - issued February 16, 1821, Bondsman:
Wm. Jackson, SUMNER Co.

FLEMING, Robert F. G. to Jane Mailer - issued December 5, 1827, m. by:
Wm. Morris, J. P., December 6, 1827, KNOX Co.

FLEMING, S. L. to Nancy Grissom - issued November 9, 1858, m. by:
John Gillentine, J. P., December 2, 1858, VAN BUREN Co.

FLEMING, Samuel to Peggy Taylor - issued December 2, 1799, Bondsman:
John Love, Witness: Chas. McClung, KNOX Co.

FLEMING, Samuel to Jane Thompson - July 24, 1819, WILLIAMSON Co.

FLEMING, Thomas W. to Catherine Walland - December 27, 1837 (?), KNOX Co.

FLEMING, Washington L. (or S.) to Ruth Brown - April 21, 1826 (?),
KNOX Co.

FLEMING, Washington S. to Ruth Brown - issued April 21, 1827, Bondsman:
Wm. B. Carns, m. by: Wm. B. Carns, J. P., April 22, 1827, KNOX Co.

FLEMING, William to Micky Thompson - July 15, 1815, WILLIAMSON Co.

FLEMING, Wm. F. to Susan Roads - issued September 18, 1843, DAVIDSON Co.

FLEMMING, Ezekiel to Elvira McGaha - m. by: L. M. Woodson December 12,
1838, SUMNER Co.

FLEMMING, G. P. to Martha D. Harp - issued July 3, 1858, m. by:
G. Fletcher, J. P., July 4, 1858, COFFEE Co.

FLEMMING, Henry B. to Mary E. Harris - issued November 14, 1870,
m. by: Jas. Wagner, M. G., FRANKLIN Co.

FLEMMING, Richard L. to Eleanor Rankin - issued May 16, 1814,
RUTHERFORD Co.

FLEMMING, Thomas F. to Charlotte Parrish - issued September 20, 1831,
m. by: L. E. Jones September 20, 1831, RUTHERFORD Co.

FLENAKIN, John to Sally Cottrell - issued July 1, 1813, KNOX Co.

FLENNIKEN, Jno. to Sally Cottrell - issued July 1, 1823, Bondsman:
J. W. Flenniken, Witness: A. Hutcheson, KNOX Co.

FLENNIKEN, Samuel to Elizabeth Howell - issued February 15, 1826,
Bondsman: Jeremiah King, KNOX Co.

FLETCHER, Dean A. to Martha A. McGee - issued December 26, 1854, m. by:
John G. Biddle October 27, 1854, FRANKLIN Co.

FLETCHER, Drew S. to Mary Ann Wall - issued March 10, 1846, Bondsman:
James D. Barnes, m. by: John Mallory March 10, 1846, MONTGOMERY Co.

FLETCHER, George L. to Amanda Thomas - issued February 19, 1846, m. by:
L. C. Bryan, P. G., February 19, 1846, DAVIDSON Co.

FLETCHER, Granderson to Sarah A. J. Pritchett - issued October 12,
1837, Bondsman: William C. Duffy, m. by: G. T. Henderson,
E. M. E. C., October 12, 1837, RUTHERFORD Co.

FLETCHER, Henderson to Emeline Benton - issued __(?) 3, 1842, m. by:
Thos. E. T. McMurray, J. P., ROBERTSON Co.

449

FLETCHER, J. C. to M. C. Bowers - issued September 16, 1867, FRANKLIN Co.

FLETCHER, J. J. W. H. to E. C. P. Horn - issued December 10, 1850,
    Bondsman: J. P. Nolen, m. by: John Mallery, M. G., December 12,
    1850, MONTGOMERY Co.

FLETCHER, James to Ellen Oran - issued September 25, 1860, m. by:
    W. F. Pride, J. P., ROBERTSON Co.

FLETCHER, James F. to Jane M. Sims - issued October 26, 1824, Bondsman:
    M. H. Fletcher, m. by: Benj. Johnson, J. P., October 26, 1824,
    RUTHERFORD Co.

FLETCHER, James P. to Bertha Ann Street - issued April 22, 1860,
    m. by: E. L. Jones, L. D., May 2, 1860, COFFEE Co.

FLETCHER, Jeptha to Nancy Ann Brown - issued January 3, 1861, m. by:
    M. A. Carden, J. P., January 9, 1861, COFFEE Co.

FLETCHER, Jermon M. to Mary Ann Hooper - issued January 8, 1842,
    m. by: R. B. C. Howell, M. G., January 8, 1842, DAVIDSON Co.

FLETCHER, John to Elizabeth Yandell - issued September 17, 1820,
    Bondsman: Fredk. E. Becton, Jr., RUTHERFORD Co.

FLETCHER, John to Mary D. Gleaves - issued March 28, 1834, Bondsman:
    Richard Ledbetter, m. by: Burrell Perry, J. P., March 31, 1834,
    RUTHERFORD Co.

FLETCHER, John D. to Catherine Featherston - issued December 19, 1823,
    Bondsman: Montfort H. Fletcher, RUTHERFORD Co.

FLETCHER, John G. to Adeline Powell - issued September 30, 1847,
    m. by: James T. Morris, J. P., September 30, 1847, STEWART Co.

FLETCHER, John H. to Melvina Frazier - issued February 27, 1858,
    m. by: R. W. Casey, J. P., February 28, 1858, COFFEE Co.

FLETCHER, John L. to Mary A. Higginbotham - issued November 21, 1854,
    FRANKLIN Co.

FLETCHER, John W. to Tabitha Jinkins - issued August 20, 1822, m. by:
    Sol. Beesley, J. P., August, 1822, RUTHERFORD Co.

FLETCHER, Leonard M. to Amanda C. Butler - issued July 8, 1858, m. by:
    H. Shackleford, J. P., July 8, 1858, COFFEE Co.

FLETCHER, Leroy to Marina T. Ayres - issued March 25, 1840, m. by:
    J. W. Ferguson, J. P., ROBERTSON Co.

FLETCHER, Montford H. to Susan C. Smith - issued December 18, 1824,
    Bondsman: F. E. Becton, RUTHERFORD Co.

FLETCHER, Rize to Abigal Myers - issued February 22, 1861, m. by:
    J. R. Holmes, J. P., February 24, 1861, COFFEE Co.

FLETCHER, Robert to Louisanna Fletcher - issued August 12, 1848, m. by:
    B. C. Brandon, J. P., August 17, 1848, STEWART Co.

FLETCHER, William to Frances J. Dates - issued January 10, 1848,
    m. by: David Henry, J. P., ROBERTSON Co.

FLETCHER, William to Carina Hall - issued March 22, 1860, m. by:
    Jo Hardaway, J. P., ROBERTSON Co.

FLETCHER, William C. to Nancy G. MacGowen - issued January 22, 1835,
    Bondsman: Stephen D. Watkins, m. by: John Jones, Eld. M. C.,
    January 22, 1835, RUTHERFORD Co.

FLETCHER, Wm. D. to Adelphia A. Tanner - issued August 6, 1852, m. by:
Thos. Finch, J. P., August 8, 1852, FRANKLIN Co.

FLETCHER, William E. to Elizabeth Ann Coleman - issued November 3,
1847, Bondsman: Dudley Breedlove, m. by: Lemuel Cherry, J. P.,
November 3, 1847, MONTGOMERY Co.

FLINN, Hezekiah to Elizabeth Cassa - issued July 25, 1797, Bondsman:
William Pruett, Witness: H. L. White, KNOX Co.

FLINTOFF, Thomas to Elizabeth W. Compton - issued March 26, 1845,
m. by: J. T. Wheat, Rr. of Ct. Ch., April 1, 1845, DAVIDSON Co.

FLIPPEN, Henry G. to Polly Lawrence - issued June 1, 1837, Bondsman:
Joseph S. Barbee, m. by: M. J. Cartwright, J. P., WILSON Co.

FLIPPEN, Joseph to Olly Morton - December 1, 1852, m. by: Bill Booth,
J. P., GILES Co.

FLIPPIN, Grant A. to Anna Taylor - issued January 15, 1834, Bondsman:
James B. Taylor, m. by: Wilson Hearn, M. G., WILSON Co.

FLOOD, Daniel to Patsy Widner - issued November 28, 1828, m. by:
E. R. Davis, J. P., December 2, 1828, KNOX Co.

FLOOD, David to L. A. Fisher - issued January 6, 1849, m. by:
B. Randolph, J. P., ROBERTSON Co.

FLOOD, John to Mary A. Stark - issued December 30, 1842, m. by:
James Woodard, J. P., January 1, 1843, ROBERTSON Co.

FLOOD, John to Pricilla Chapman - issued November 2, 1846, m. by:
James Woodard, ROBERTSON Co.

FLOOD, Joseph W. to Miss Elizabeth Boren - issued April 8, 1840,
m. by: Robert Green, J. P., ROBERTSON Co.

FLORIDA, James P. to Mary Upchurch - issued May 8, 1832, Bondsman:
Samuel Allison, WILSON Co.

FLOURNOY, Wm. to Elizabeth M. Armstrong - issued November 9, 1846,
m. by: C. D. Elliott, M. G., November 10, 1846, DAVIDSON Co.

FLOURS, P. J. L. to Mary Corbin - issued July 7, 1844, m. by:
D. G. Baird, J. P., ROBERTSON Co.

FLOWERS, Green to Mary Sypert - issued February 26, 1817, Bondsman:
James T. Coats, WILSON Co.

FLOWERS, John to Rachel Deloach - issued January 27, 1816, Bondsman:
Benjamin Morris, m. by: Abner Stevenson, J. P., February 7, 1816,
WILSON Co.

FLOWERS, Joseph E. to Angeline Davis - issued January 27, 1848,
Bondsman: Lin H. Johnson, Jr., m. by: Joseph G. Ward January 27,
1848, MONTGOMERY Co.

FLOWERS, Joshua to Eliza M. A. Daly - issued September 18, 1845, m. by:
R. P. Miles, Bishop of Nashville, September 18, 1845, DAVIDSON Co.

FLOWERS, Joseph (?) to Cinthia Lannom - issued October 20, 1832,
m. by: Thos. Sanders, J. P., October 22, 1832, RUTHERFORD Co.

FLOWERS, Larry to Mazana Green - issued March 27, 1833, Bondsman:
William Flowers, m. by: Thos. Sanders, J. P., March 27, 1833,
RUTHERFORD Co.

FLOWERS, Mary A. to Joseph Hester - BEDFORD Co.

FLOWERS, Ruffin S. to Mary C. Bell - issued July 26, 1851, m. by:
D. G. Baird, J. P., ROBERTSON Co.

FLOWERS, T. I. to Martha Ann Johnson - m. by: Luke P. Allen May 5,
1838, SUMNER Co.

FLOWERS, Thomas to Nancy Krunk - issued November 25, 1813, m. by:
Peter Nance, J. P., KNOX Co.

FLOYD, A. B. to Eliza Lindsey - issued March 20, 1872, m. by:
C. C. Rose, J. P., March 21, 1872, FRANKLIN Co.

FLOYD, B. B. to S. C. Helton - issued February 3, 1862, Bondsman:
B. A. Howell, m. by: Wenston McAnally February 4, 1862, LAWRENCE Co.

FLOYD, George W. to Elizabeth T. Reagor - issued January 30, 1861,
Bondsman: Thos. W. Buchanan, Jos. H. Thompson, Clk, BEDFORD Co.

FLOYD, J. K. to Mary J. Gowen - issued October 10, 1863, Bondsman:
W. P. Gowen, Jos. H. Thompson, Clk. per M. E. W. Dunaway,
Dep. Clk., BEDFORD Co.

FLOYD, James S. to Martha M. Shofner - issued December 31, 1861,
Bondsman: Wm. J. Shofner, Jos. H. Thompson, Clk. per N. F. Thompson,
Dep. Clk., m. by: W. Jenkins, V. D. M., BEDFORD Co.

FLOYD, Jesse to Betsy Williams - issued September 17, 1818, m. by:
S. Montgomery September 18, 1818, KNOX Co.

FLOYD, John to Betsey Logan - May 10, 1806, WILLIAMSON Co.

FLOYD, Jno. to Mary Smith - April 13, 1809, WILLIAMSON Co.

FLOYD, John to Sally Hunt - issued December 10, 1833, m. by:
Wm. Lawrence, J. P., December 13, 1833, WILSON Co.

FLOYD, John R. to Lucenda Cook - issued August 8, 1860, m. by:
W. B. M. Williams, Mins. M. E. Church So., August 9, 1860, COFFEE Co.

FLOYD, Raney to Christian Baughman - June 25, 1813, WILLIAMSON Co.

FLOYD, Samuel to Eleanor Jane Nobles - issued October 11, 1855, m. by:
J. A. Williams, L. P., October 11, 1855, COFFEE Co.

FLOYD, William to Sally Morfet - February 11, 1811, WILLIAMSON Co.

FLOYD, Williamson R. to Mariah Oliver - issued May 24, 1856, m. by:
John Chitwood, J. P., May 25, 1856, FRANKLIN Co.

FLY, Elisah to Elizabeth Crutcher - November 30, 1816, WILLIAMSON Co.

FLY, J. W. to E. A. Baker - issued September 28, 1866, FRANKLIN Co.

FLY, John to Lydia Newton - June 18, 1811, Bondsman: James Birmingham,
MAURY Co.

FLY, Penelope to Jonathon Bullock - MAURY Co.

FLY, William to Mary Mitchell - November 10, 1809, Bondsman:
John Mitchell, MAURY Co.

FLY, William D. to Augusta Edwards - issued February 26, 1835, Bondsman:
John Heriford, m. by: William Eagleton, V. D. M., February 26,
1835, RUTHERFORD Co.

FLYNN, George to Sally Haynes - issued March 26, 1796, Bondsman:
Jacob Thomas, SUMNER Co.

FLYNT (Flint), Abijah to Polly Gideon - September 20, 1808, MAURY Co.

FOGG, Godfrey M. to Ellen M. Stephenson - issued December 17, 1839, m. by: Robt. A. Lapsley December 17, 1839, DAVIDSON Co.

FOGG, William to Sarah L. Morris - December 18, 1855, m. by: Rev. A. J. Gilmore, GILES Co.

FOGG, William B. to Martha Sublett - issued July 27, 1843, m. by: James Sharp, J. P., July 30, 1843, FRANKLIN Co.

FOGLEMAN, Catharine to Barclay Martin - BEDFORD Co.

FOGORTY (Forgorty), Edward to Margret J. Malone - issued July 5, 1858, m. by: Jas. A. England, J. P., July 5, 1858, FRANKLIN Co.

FOLLIS (Hollis?), Patsy to John Parchment - MAURY Co.

FOLLIS, William to Nancy Mayes - October 18, 1810, Bondsman: George Hay, MAURY Co.

FOLLIS, William R. to Eliza Myres - November 14, 1849, m. by: W. C. Moore, GILES Co.

FOLTZ, Reuben M. to Catherine C. Geary - issued January 28, 1846, m. by: J. T. Edgar January 28, 1846, DAVIDSON Co.

FOLWELL, G. E. to Florence M. Granes - issued August 1, 1865, m. by: M. B. Clement, M. G., August 2, 1865, FRANKLIN Co.

FONTAIN, George to Susan Lasater - issued November 24, 1865, FRANKLIN Co.

FONVILLE, John to Mary H. Green - issued December 31, 1829, Bondsman: Wm. L. Laurie, m. by: Wm. Walton, J. P., December 31, 1829, SUMNER Co.

FOOTE, Henry Stuart to Mrs. Rachel D. Smiley - m. June 14, 1859 in Nashville

FOOTE, Richard N. to Eliza M. Denton - issued January 11, 1844, ROBERTSON Co.

FOOTE, Wm. N. to M. B. Walton - issued February 7, 1850, m. by: B. Raldolph, J. P., February 10, 1850, ROBERTSON Co.

FOOTE, Wm. N. to Martha B. Walton - issued February 7, 1850, m. by: B. Randolph, J. P., February 10, 1850, ROBERTSON Co.

FORBES, Daniel to Elizabeth Horn - issued October 11, 1807, Bondsman: John McDaniel, WILSON Co.

FORBES, F. M. to S. E. McBride - issued December 3, 1870, m. by: John Nugent, J. P., December 4, 1870, FRANKLIN Co.

FORBES, Joseph J. to Martha Gent - issued February 7, 1854, m. by: B. F. Binkley, G. M., February 9, 1854, ROBERTSON Co.

FORBES, William A. to Mary E. Garland - issued December 26, 1853, Bondsman: Wm. A. Quarles, m. by: Jas. Ridley, M. G., December 29, 1853, MONTGOMERY Co.

FORBS, William to Judith McDowell - issued February 22, 1836, Bondsman: James Cooke, RUTHERFORD Co.

FORBUS, Arthur to Rachel Carruth - issued June 9, 1815, Bondsman: Alexander Carruth, WILSON Co.

FORBUS, Thomas W. to Nancy Clifton - issued April 5, 1824, Bondsman: Hugh Wiley, WILSON Co.

FORD, Andrew Jackson to Rachel Smith - issued August 24, 1854, MONTGOMERY Co.

FORD, Andrew Jackson to Rachel Smith - issued August 24, 1854, Bondsman: Ely Green Dupree, m. by: A. M. Johnson, J. P., August 24, 1854, MONTGOMERY Co.

FORD, Benjamin to Rachel Steel - October 20, 1818, KNOX Co.

FORD, Charles to Joby Grizzle - issued June 13, 1825, Bondsman: James Jones, m. by: B. McNutt, J. P., June 13, 1825, Witness: Wm. Swan, KNOX Co.

FORD, Edward to Sarah Whittle - issued October 16, 1826, Bondsman: Robert Barton, RUTHERFORD Co.

FORD, Miss Eliza Jane to Richard W. Ellis, Esq. - m. by: Rev. A. M. Stone December 19, 1846 in McMinnville

FORD, Eli J. to Julia Nicks - issued July 19, 1848, m. by: N. G. Morris, J. P., July 20, 1848, STEWART Co.

FORD, Frederic T. C. to Elizabeth Pearce - issued October 16, 1841, Bondsman: James Atkinson, MEIGS Co.

FORD, Frederick to Rhoda Maxey - issued February 24, 1831, Bondsman: Hiram Harris, m. by: Edward R. Davis, J. P., February 27, 1831, Witness: Wm. Swan, KNOX Co.

FORD, George W. to Mary O'Neal - issued December 11, 1853, Bondsman: George W. Bradbury, m. by: Stephen Cocke, J. P., December 11, 1853, MONTGOMERY Co.

FORD, Jacob to Elizabeth Needham - issued July 12, 1820, m. by: S. Montgomery July 13, 1820, KNOX Co.

FORD, James to Catherine Sessle - issued May 8, 1848, m. by: William Morris, J. P., May 8, 1848, STEWART Co.

FORD, James M. to Martha D. Beard - issued September 2, 1839, m. by: Alexander C. Chisholm, M. G., September 5, 1839, DAVIDSON Co.

FORD, James S. to Lucy Milam - issued September 20, 1842, STEWART Co.

FORD, James V. C. (?) to Susan Haines - issued January 14, 1831, Bondsman: Jno. King, m. by: Elijah Johnson, J. P., January 16, 1831, KNOX Co.

FORD, John to Love Northcut - issued October 10, 1821, m. by: Jordan Willeford, J. P., October 10, 1821, RUTHERFORD Co.

FORD, John W. to Elizabeth Rolin - issued July 23, 1818, Bondsman: Wm. C. Dew, SUMNER Co.

FORD, Joseph A. to Mary A. Hudgins - issued December 15, 1858, m. by: John H. Holt, M. G., December 15, 1858, FRANKLIN Co.

FORD, Joshua to Barbara Kittle - m. by: S. W. Blythe March 4, 1818, SUMNER Co.

FORD, M. B. to L. B. Cooksey - issued May 28, 1860, m. by: W. W. Pepper, Judge of 10th Circuit of Tennessee, ROBERTSON Co.

FORD, Nicholas J. to Mary A. Sharp - issued August 21, 1842, m. by: John Roleman, J. P., August 21, 1842, FRANKLIN Co.

FORD, Pascal to Harriet Cawthon - issued December 28, 1837, Bondsman: Thos. Ford, WILSON Co.

FORD, Paterick to Mary Scruder - issued April 5, 1858, m. by: R. H. Harrison, J. P., April 6, 1858, ROBERTSON Co.

FORD, R. L. to Lucy Beall - issued September 24, 1861, m. by:
Jo Hardaway, J. P., ROBERTSON Co.

FORD, Simeon to Margaret Sanders - issued January 10, 1824, m. by:
Jordan Willeford, J. P., January 21, 1824, RUTHERFORD Co.

FORD, Solomon to Ann Moody - issued January 22, 1830, Bondsman:
James Gilliam, RUTHERFORD Co.

FORD, William to Margaret Terwater - January 16, 1837, KNOX Co.

FORD, Wm. B. to Agnes Butler - issued March 10, 1841, Bondsman:
Mark Rentfrow, m. by: Mark Renfrow March 10, 1841, MEIGS Co.

FORD, William M. to Mary G. Stewart - issued December 2, 1874,
FRANKLIN Co.

FORD, William P. to Martha A. Anderson - issued July 2, 1856, m. by:
L. Burnum, J. P., July 2, 1856, COFFEE Co.

FORD, William R. to Sarah Childers - issued December 8, 1848, Bondsman:
James A. Swatwell, m. by: J. C. Bryant, J. P., December 18, 1848,
MONTGOMERY Co.

FORD, Willie M. to Charlotte C. Summers - issued March 9, 1848, m. by:
W. C. Jones, J. P., March 9, 1848, STEWART Co.

FORDE, George to Emeline Love - issued October 4, 1839, ROBERTSON Co.

FORE, William B. to Angeline E. A. Fuqua - issued December 26, 1843,
m. by: B. Henrdon, J. P., December 27, 1843, STEWART Co.

FOREHAN, Thos. to Elizabeth Grimes - September 11, 1809, WILLIAMSON Co.

FOREHAND, Berry Green to Matilda McDaniel - issued April 14, 1838,
m. by: William Roach, DAVIDSON Co.

FOREHAND, Richard to Nancy F. Moss - issued December 9, 1843, DAVIDSON Co.

FOREMAN, Jessee C. to Amelia Decherd - issued February 21, 1857, m. by:
John G. Biddle February 25, 1857, FRANKLIN Co.

FOREMAN, William to Eliza N. Porter - issued March 7, 1857, m. by:
J. M. Copeland March 8, 1857, ROBERTSON Co.

FORESTER, Edmund to Susan Forester - issued December 29, 1831, Bondsman:
John Wilson, m. by: Thos. R. Anderson, J. P., December 29, 1831,
SUMNER Co.

FORESTER, John to Rebecca T. Fowler - issued October 24, 1832, Bondsman:
Isaac Robertson, m. by: L. M. Woodson October 24, 1832, SUMNER Co.

FORESTER, John B. to Elizabeth Hall - issued June 17, 1830, Bondsman:
Jno. Brown, WILSON Co.

FORGORTY (Fogorty), Edward to Margret J. Malone - issued July 3, 1858,
m. by: Jas. A. England, J. P., July 5, 1858, FRANKLIN Co.

FERGUSON, Stephen to Anne Pickle - issued April 5, 1819, m. by:
Sam'l Sample, J. P., April 6, 1819, KNOX Co.

FORGUSON, Willie C. to Catharine Keith - issued October 30, 1826, m. by:
Sam'l Fleming, J. P., October 30, 1826, KNOX Co.

FORMAN, John to Jane Swadley (or Fannon) - July 27, 1819 (?), KNOX Co.

FORMWALT, Adam to Mary McAffrey - May 11, 1837, KNOX Co.

FORMWALT, John H. to Nancy Council - issued January 29, 1818, m. by:
T. H. Nelson January 29, 1818, KNOX Co.

FORREST, Elisha to Sally Vincent - issued January 2, 1821, m. by:
Jacob Payne, J. P., January 9, 1821, RUTHERFORD Co.

FORREST, Isaac to Nancy May - issued July 6, 1811, Bondsman:
Elisha Green, SUMNER Co.

FORREST, Reuben to Katy May - issued October 2, 1812, Bondsman:
Thomas Keefe, SUMNER Co.

FORREST, Richard to Polly Bishop - issued December 7, 1797, Bondsman:
Stephen Bishop, Witness: H. L. White, KNOX Co.

FORRESTER, Hardy to Martha Crumply - issued October 11, 1832, Bondsman:
Phillip Brown, SUMNER Co.

FORRESTER, Jacob to Polly McMurtry - issued July 17, 1817, Bondsman:
John W. Byrn, m. by: Wm. Montgomery, J. P., July 17, 1817, SUMNER Co.

FORRISTER, Martin to Mary McNew - November 4, 1795, Security:
James Magee and William McNew, GREENE Co.

FORSHAY, John to Agnes Weston - December 11, 1794, Security:
Isaac Armitage, GREENE Co.

FORSHER, Sidney to Mary Ann Vaughan - issued November 22, 1840,
Bondsman: John Cummings, m. by: M. T. Cartwright, J. P.,
November 27, 1840, WILSON Co.

FORSTER, Isaiah to Sarah Johnson - January 5, 1797, Security:
Thomas Richardson, GREENE Co.

FORSYTHE, J. to Sarah Cain - issued July 24, 1851, Bondsman:
James Field, m. by: R. H. Weakley July 24, 1850, MONTGOMERY Co.

FORSYTHE, John to Eliza Fane - issued February 21, 1842, m. by:
W. Hand, J. P., February 25, 1842, DICKSON Co.

FORT, David J. to Mary B. Farmer - issued February 1, 1847, m. by:
William L. Perry, M. G., February 4, 1847, ROBERTSON Co.

FORT, Elisha P. to Martha Ann Gardner - issued December 20, 1835,
m. by: William L. Perry, J. P., ROBERTSON Co.

FORT, J. T. to E. L. Fort - issued May 31, 1860, m. by: F. C. Plaster,
M. G., June 2, 1860, ROBERTSON Co.

FORT, Jackson to Sarah Head - issued January 7, 1860, m. by:
W. M. Winters April 15, 1860, ROBERTSON Co.

FORT, Joseph H. to Jack Ann Fort - issued November 3, 1849, Bondsman:
Chas. G. Royster, m. by: R. W. Nixon November, 1849, MONTGOMERY Co.

FORT, Joseph W. to Susan M. Whitfield - issued January 7, 1842, m. by:
R. B. Mitchell, J. P., ROBERTSON Co.

FORT, Josiah W. to Eliza P. Dancy - issued October 1, 1853, Bondsman:
J. W. Bourne, m. by: F. G. Plasler, M. G., MONTGOMERY Co.

FORT, Sugg to Virginia C. Sugg - issued November 21, 1857, m. by:
F. C. Plaster December 1, 1857, ROBERTSON Co.

FORT, Wm. W. to Mary A. Ligon - issued August 30, 1847, Bondsman:
W. W. Warfield, m. by: James E. Douglass, MONTGOMERY Co.

FORTENBERRY, James to Cinthia Prawley - issued September 5, 1821, m. by:
Cullin Curlee, J. P., September 5, 1821, RUTHERFORD Co.

FORTNER, Andrew J. to Virginia Sony - issued December 27, 1853, Bondsman:
G. M. Trice, m. by: R. W. Nixon, M. G., December 28, 1853,
MONTGOMERY Co.

FORTNER, David to Sarah White - issued March 27, 1834, Bondsman:
Nicholas Gibbs, m. by: James Crippen, J. P., March 31, 1834,
KNOX Co.

FORTNER, David to Melinda Barnes - August 27, 1836, KNOX Co.

FORTNER, Ezekiel to Sarah Balinger - issued February 21, 1833, m. by:
Wm. Sawyers, J. P., February 21, 1833, KNOX Co.

FORTNER, George to Polly Lewis - March 12, 1818 (?), KNOX Co.

FORTNER, John to Elizabeth Rutherford - issued April 21, 1836, Bondsman:
Wm. McDowel, KNOX Co.

FORTNER, Moses E. to Martha Grow - issued December 24, 1849, m. by:
D. G. Baird, J. P., ROBERTSON Co.

FORTNER, William to Caroline Hancock - issued February 28, 1832,
m. by: Wm. Sawyers, J. P., March, 1832, KNOX Co.

FOSSETT, William to Elizabeth Rogers - issued December 30, 1845, m. by:
Benj. Sharpe, J. P., December 30, 1845, DAVIDSON Co.

FOSTER, A. to M. J. Allison - issued February 15, 1864, m. by:
D. J. Martin, M. G., February 16, 1864, FRANKLIN Co.

FOSTER, A. M. B. to Julia Ann Sims - issued August 14, 1848, m. by:
Wm. Guinn August 15, 1848, FRANKLIN Co.

FOSTER, Albert to Lucinda Major - issued August 12, 1828, Bondsman:
Saml. Donnell, WILSON Co.

FOSTER, Albert to N. J. Russoe - issued January 6, 1868, m. by:
W. B. Watterson, M. G., January 7, 1868, FRANKLIN Co.

FOSTER, Alexander to Martha Doak - issued April 4, 1820, Bondsman:
James Foster, m. by: James Foster, J. P., April 6, 1820, WILSON Co.

FOSTER, Alexander to Patsey Plumbley - issued November 29, 1799,
Bondsman: Isaac Plumbley, Witness: A. White, KNOX Co.

FOSTER, Alfred H. to Nancy Hallum - issued July 24, 1838, DAVIDSON Co.

FOSTER, Allen F. to Lina Mitchell - issued May 19, 1855, m. by:
J. E. McKinder, M. G., May 20, 1855, VAN BUREN Co.

FOSTER, David to Anny Beard - issued June 29, 1806, Bondsman:
David Beard, Sr., SUMNER Co.

FOSTER, Elensley D. to Martha Ann Doak - issued November 30, 1831,
Bondsman: Samuel Stone, m. by: Geo. Donnell, M. G., December 1,
1831, WILSON Co.

FOSTER, Elijah to Polly Taylor - issued July 9, 1819, Bondsman:
Littleberry Belcher, m. by: Jas. Cross, J. P., July 10, 1819,
WILSON Co.

FOSTER, Frederick to Sally Broadway - issued September 7, 1813,
Bondsman: John Broadway, WILSON Co.

FOSTER, George to Phoebe Todd - issued October 20, 1834, Bondsman:
Wm. Johnson, m. October 30, 1834, RUTHERFORD Co.

FOSTER, Guinn to Sarah Reeves - issued December 21, 1830, Bondsman:
Michael Comer, RUTHERFORD Co.

FOSTER, Henry W. to Martha Bland - issued February 4, 1845, DAVIDSON Co.

FOSTER, Hugh L. to Virginia E. Thacher - issued November 24, 1846,
Bondsman: Henry C. Leavell, MONTGOMERY Co.

FOSTER, I. W. to Mary A. Avritt - issued May 25, 1848, Bondsman:
A. W. Austin, m. by: Wm. Shelton, M. G., May 24, 1848, MONTGOMERY Co.

FOSTER, Isaac to Mary Gibbs - issued March 16, 1822, Bondsman:
John Foster, m. by: John Bayless, J. P., March 21, 1822, KNOX Co.

FOSTER, J. H. to M. J. Hannah - issued February 29, 1868, m. by:
Thos. F. Moseley, M. G., March 1, 1868, FRANKLIN Co.

FOSTER, James to Catey Yandell - issued January 3, 1820, Bondsman:
Joseph Spradling, SUMNER Co.

FOSTER, James to Elenor Harris - issued June 3, 1830, Bondsman:
William Bohanon, SUMNER Co.

FOSTER, James B. to Susan J. Thurman - issued May 6, 1840, m. by:
A. J. Steel, M. G., FRANKLIN Co.

FOSTER, James J. to Mildred Johnson - issued October 25, 1823, Bondsman:
John D. Fletcher, RUTHERFORD Co.

FOSTER, Jane D. D. to Robert Lambert - BEDFORD Co.

FOSTER, John to Elizabeth Rogers - issued September 21, 1813, Bondsman:
John Doak, WILSON Co.

FOSTER, John to Patsy Fuller - issued December 31, 1823, m. by:
Jacob Payne, J. P., January 1, 1824, RUTHERFORD Co.

FOSTER, John to Mary Wright - issued January 2, 1836, Bondsman:
Henry Childress, RUTHERFORD Co.

FOSTER, John to Elizabeth Allen - issued February 27, 1836, Bondsman:
Reuben Allen, m. by: Wm. Vinson, J. P., February 28, 1836,
RUTHERFORD Co.

FOSTER, John B. to Susan Gwin - m. by: G. V. Henderson, E. M. E. C.,
October 14, 1834, SUMNER Co.

FOSTER, John H. to Maranda Martin - issued September 17, 1827, Bondsman:
A. W. Wormington, m. September 17, 1827, SUMNER Co.

FOSTER, John L. to Elizabeth Cox - issued December 23, 1820, Bondsman:
John Cox, m. by: John Green December 28, 1820, WILSON Co.

FOSTER, John W. to Nancy McMurry - issued July 13, 1835, m. by:
P. Y. Davis, M. G., December 13, 1836, WILSON Co.

FOSTER, Joseph H. to Mary F. Davis - issued December 14, 1838, Bondsman:
J. B. Moss, m. by: E. James T. Tompkins December 18, 1838, WILSON Co.

FOSTER, Mary to John Sterns - GREENE Co.

FOSTER, Raneelear to Matilda Robertson - issued January 26, 1837,
Bondsman: R. D. Hankins, m. by: Geo. Donnell, V. D. M., WILSON Co.

FOSTER, Nancy to James A. Morgan - BEDFORD Co.

FOSTER, Robert to Margaret Rea - issued June 26, 1827, Bondsman:
David Foster, WILSON Co.

FOSTER, Robert to Margaret Reay - issued June 26, 1827, m. by:
Francis Johnston, M. G., June 28, 1827, WILSON Co.

FOSTER, Rufus C. to Nancy C. Lucas - issued February 11, 1856,
FRANKLIN Co.

FOSTER, S. B. to Susan A. Allen - issued March 23, 1863, Bondsman:
Asa Elkins, Jos. H. Thompson, Clk., BEDFORD Co.

FOSTER, Stephen to Ann A. Davis - issued June 30, 1831, Bondsman:
Wm. Swan, m. by: John McCampbell, V. D. M., June 30, 1831, KNOX Co.

FOSTER, Thaddeus to Anzie Logan - issued July 4, 1865, m. by:
A. J. Baird, M. G., July 5, 1865, FRANKLIN Co.

FOSTER, Thomas to Tempy Jones - issued January 17, 1839, m. by:
James F. Green, J. P., January 17, 1839, FRANKLIN Co.

FOSTER, Thomas to Harriet Williams - issued November 8, 1843, m. by:
W. L. Baldry, Gospel Minister, November 9, 1843, ROBERTSON Co.

FOSTER, Thos. to H. E. Alspaugh - issued February 10, 1868, m. by:
G. W. Bowling, J. P., February 11, 1868, FRANKLIN Co.

FOSTER, Thos. to Ann Foster - issued September 24, 1870, m. by:
G. W. Bowling, J. P., September 24, 1870, FRANKLIN Co.

FOSTER, W. C. N. to Sarrah Jane Campbell - issued January 16, 1861,
m. by: G. D. Messick, J. P., January 13, 1861, COFFEE Co.

FOSTER, W. L. to Susan L. Cheatham - issued October 28, 1841, m. by:
D. R. Harris, G. M., ROBERTSON Co.

FOSTER, William to Sally Staggs - issued July 4, 1822, m. by:
John Fulton, J. P., July 5, 1822, RUTHERFORD Co.

FOSTER, William to Rebecca W. Rains - issued January 3, 1825, m. by:
Cary James January 6, 1825, RUTHERFORD Co.

FOSTER, William to Elizabeth Turner - issued June 8, 1833, Bondsman:
James Braden, WILSON Co.

FOSTER, William to Nancy Nichols - issued August 15, 1855, FRANKLIN Co.

FOSTER, William to Malena Ann Ward - February 10, 1859, m. by:
Stephen Od..., J. P., GILES Co.

FOSTER, Wm. C. to Julia A. T. Nowlin - issued February 6, 1865,
Bondsman: J. D. Davidson, m. by: A. Vernon, M. G., February 8,
1865, LAWRENCE Co.

FOTTRELL, A. to Amanda Holley - issued November 30, 1846, m. by:
G. D. Fullmer, J. P., November 30, 1846, DAVIDSON Co.

FOUST, Abram to Lydia Hashbarger - issued December 12, 1832, m. by:
George Graves, J. P., December 16, 1832, KNOX Co.

FOUST, Daniel to Martha Wills - issued March 22, 1827, m. by:
Geo. Graves, J. P., March 22, 1827, KNOX Co.

FOUST, Daniel to Polly Foust - issued February 10, 1829, m. by:
Wm. Sawyers, J. P., February 12, 1829, KNOX Co.

FOUST, David to Hanna Clapp - issued July 29, 1824, m. by:
Wm. Sawyers, J. P., July 29, 1824, KNOX Co.

FOUST, George W. to Sarah E. Fondrin - issued September 27, 1865,
Bondsman: Thomas Fondrin, m. by: A. P., Freeman, J. P.,
September 28, 1865, LAWRENCE Co.

FOUST, Henry to Carry Hashbarger - issued February 29, 1836, Bondsman:
P. H. Skaggs, KNOX Co.

FOUST, Jacob to Amanda Pate - issued March 6, 1824, m. by: Wm. Sawyers,
J. P., March 9, 1824, KNOX Co.

FOUST, John to Polly Sertain - issued May 29, 1797, Bondsman:
Christopher Foust, Witness: H. L. White, KNOX Co.

FOUST, John to Maria Pate - issued July 22, 1824, m. by: Wm. Sawyers, J. P., July 24, 1824, KNOX Co.

FOUST, John to Elizabeth Cord - issued November 30, 1826, Bondsman: Jacob Foust, Witness: Wm. Swan, KNOX Co.

FOUST, John to Polly Humphreys - issued September 9, 1828, m. by: Wm. Sawyers, J. P., September 11, 1828, KNOX Co.

FOUST, John to Judy Shinberry - issued August 31, 1836, m. by: G. S. White, M. G., September 1, 1836, KNOX Co.

FOUST, John H. to Louisa Violett - issued August 20, 1839, Bondsman: Peter A. Cartwright, m. by: M. T. Cartwright, J. P., August 21, 1839, WILSON Co.

FOUST, John M. to S. P. Holcomb - issued February 1, 1865, Bondsman: J. W. Foust, m. by: J. P. Richardson, M. G., February 1, 1865, LAWRENCE Co.

FOUST, Lewis to Elizabeth L. Wills - issued August 29, 1827, Bondsman: John Foust, KNOX Co.

FOUST, Philip to Catharine Foust - issued February 23, 1825, m. by: Wm. Sawyers, J. P., February 24, 1825, KNOX Co.

FOUST, Thomas to Eliza B. Hutchison - issued September 21, 1850, Bondsman: Andrew Powers, MONTGOMERY Co.

FOUT (?), Daniel D. to Dorcas M. King - issued October 7, 1823, m. by: Tho. H. Nelson October 7, 1823, KNOX Co.

FOUTCH, Herrod to Susan Williams - issued November 6, 1839, Bondsman: Benjamin Cluck, WILSON Co.

FOUTCH, Thomas to Caroline Reed - issued July 18, 1835, Bondsman: Kellar Mathis, m. by: Nace Overall, M. G., July 19, 1835, RUTHERFORD Co.

FOVELLE, Robert to Eliza P. Gilton - issued February 12, 1866, Bondsman: Joseph L. Bassham, LAWRENCE Co.

FOWLER, Abijah to Eleanor Watkins - February 12, 1787, Security: Elisha Baker, GREENE Co.

FOWLER, Benjamine to Marguritt Williams - issued June 11, 1827, Bondsman: Richard Harrison, m. by: Robert Patton June 11, 1827, SUMNER Co.

FOWLER, Edward to Martha Venable - February 22, 1808, WILLIAMSON Co.

FOWLER, Frances E. to Jane Robinson - issued October 18, 1838, DICKSON Co.

FOWLER, J. Smith to Maria Louise Embry - issued November 12, 1846, m. by: W. H. Wharton November 12, 1846, DAVIDSON Co.

FOWLER, Jefferson to Eliza Vanhook - issued December 7, 1845, m. by: Cyrus Murry, J. P., December 7, 1845, DICKSON Co.

FOWLER, John to Patsey Foster - May 13, 1817, WILLIAMSON Co.

FOWLER, Josiah to Nelly Jenning - issued February 5, 1846, m. by: Wm. Bell, J. P., February 5, 1846, STEWART Co.

FOWLER, Rezin to Hester Craft - issued November 17, 1829, Bondsman: Nathan Findly, RUTHERFORD Co.

FOWLER, Richard to Victoria Van hook - issued February 4, 1842, m. by: W. Hand, J. P., February 1, 1842, DICKSON Co.

FOWLER, S. H. to Louisianna Exom - issued September 29, 1829, Bondsman: C. Sheeke, SUMNER Co.

FOWLER, Thomas C. A. to Frances Norris - issued November 27, 1823, Bondsman: William Loftin, m. by: John Fletcher, J. P., November 27, 1823, RUTHERFORD Co.

FOWLER, Thomas J. to Tempy Simmons - issued September 18, 1838, DAVIDSON Co.

FOWLER, Thos. N. to Mary Ann Owens - issued August 5, 1872, FRANKLIN Co.

FOWLER, Thornton to Emily Stroud - issued June 21, 1845, m. by: M. Ussery, J. P., June 22, 1845, DAVIDSON Co.

FOWLER, Walter to Mary Willerford - issued June 6, 1829, Bondsman: John Fowler, m. by: Meredith Hodges, J. P., June 6, 1829, SUMNER Co.

FOWLER, William T. to Lucy Bank - issued July 4, 1845, m. by: P. Lynch, J. P., July 4, 1845, STEWART Co.

FOWLKES, James C. to Nancy Wright - issued March 28, 1846, m. by: John Beard, M. G., April 1, 1846, DAVIDSON Co.

FOWLKES, Jeptha to Mariah J. Ward - issued January 23, 1846, m. by: J. T. Wheat, M. G., January 23, 1846, DAVIDSON Co.

FOWLKES, John G. to Jean Wood - December 26, 1805, WILLIAMSON Co.

FOWLKES, Thompson to Priscilla Hyde - November 15, 1806, WILLIAMSON Co.

FOX, Andrew to Narcissa Genett - issued February 4, 1846, Bondsman: James Fox, m. by: William Johns, J. P., February 14, 1846, MEIGS Co.

FOX, Anne to David Shaw - GREENE Co.

FOX, Enoch to Peggy Dale - issued January 9, 1797, Bondsman: Alexander Dale, Witness: Hu. Law. White, KNOX Co.

FOX, Elizabeth to Philip Howell - GREENE Co.

FOX, Enoch D. to Mary A. Cooper - issued October 13, 1853, m. by: Rev. James Watson, M. G., October 17, 1853, FRANKLIN Co.

FOX, George to Rebecca Roberson - issued December 23, 1845, m. by: John Roleman December 23, 1845, FRANKLIN Co.

FOX, Gideon to Unis Bennett - issued December 25, 1823, Bondsman: Solomon Warren, WILSON Co.

FOX, Isah L. to M. E. Sisk - issued August 16, 1851, Bondsman: M. M. Green, m. by: A. Baggett, J. P., August 14, 1851, MONTGOMERY Co.

FOX, Jacob to Elizabeth Broyles - January 4, 1806, Security: Andrew Fox and Philip Nowel, GREENE Co.

FOX, James to Milberry Sills - issued February 14, 1843, STEWART Co.

FOX, James to Elizabeth Ramsey - issued February 19, 1846, Bondsman: Thomas Leuty, m. by: William Johns, J. P., February 19, 1846, MEIGS Co.

FOX, James N. to Prudence Felkner - December 1, 1802, Security: James Felkner, BLOUNT Co.

FOX, John to Margaret Carter - issued June 20, 1827, Bondsman: Bartlett Anderson, RUTHERFORD Co.

FOX, John to Martha M. Aaron - issued October 15, 1863, Bondsman:
W. F. Harrison, Jos. H. Thompson, Clk. per M. E. W. Dunaway,
Dep. Clk., BEDFORD Co.

FOX, John W. to Hannah Smith - issued October 9, 1851, m. by:
Lemuel Brandon October 14, 1851, FRANKLIN Co.

FOX, Joseph to Nancy Hannah Church - February 27, 1811, Bondsman:
Thomas Church, MAURY Co.

FOX, Joseph to Tabitha Pointer - issued February 11, 1835, Bondsman:
Henry Pruett, RUTHERFORD Co.

FOX, Mary to Simeon Broyles - GREENE Co.

FOX, Matthias to Jemimah Broyles - issued October 9, 1827, Bondsman:
Green Holland, RUTHERFORD Co.

FOX, Pervires to Narcissa Bennett - issued July 21, 1821, Bondsman:
James Baird, WILSON Co.

FOX, W. W. to Mary J. E. Drake - Bondsman: P. B. Stephens, m. by:
S. S. Mallory, M. G., September 30, 1851, MONTGOMERY Co.

FOX, Wm. B. to Sarah A. Hamleton - issued September 23, 1846, m. by:
W. C. Jones, J. P., STEWART Co.

FOXALL, Thomas to Mary Cryer - issued March 6, 1823, m. by:
George Elliott, J. P., March 6, 1823, SUMNER Co.

FRAIDLEY (Fraidy), Henry G. to Matilda Lynch (Linch) - issued May 23,
1863, Bondsman: J. B. Linch, BEDFORD Co.

FRAIL, Robt. S. to Mary A. Temple - issued May 19, 1862, Bondsman:
W. L. Thompson, Jos. H. Thompson, Clk., BEDFORD Co.

FRAIL, Solomon to Nancy Duren - issued October 24, 1809, Bondsman:
George Duren, SUMNER Co.

FRAILEY, Daniel to Milley Miller - issued February 22, 1808, Bondsman:
Henry Marrick, SUMNER Co.

FRAINHAM, William to Nancy Norwell - issued October 29, 1821, Bondsman:
Jesse Morris, SUMNER Co.

FRAIZER, Rebecca to Spencer Ballard - GREENE Co.

FRAKER, Geo. to Eliza Graybill - issued July 22, 1836, m. by:
John Mynatt, J. P., July 24, 1836, KNOX Co.

FRAKER, Michael to Winnifred Gillum - issued August 26, 1830, Bondsman:
John Murphy, m. by: Isaac Lewis August 26, 1830, KNOX Co.

FRALEY, Daniel to Polly Dillon - issued March 25, 1828, Bondsman:
Jonathan Davis, SUMNER Co.

FRAME, Benjamin to Martha E. Mann - issued September 7, 1848, m. by:
Wm. S. Smith, M. G., September 7, 1848, FRANKLIN Co.

FRAME, James M. to Susan D. Tripp - issued April 6, 1856, FRANKLIN Co.

FRAME, John W. to Heneretta D. Lee - issued March 22, 1854, m. by:
James C. Handley, J. P., March 22, 1854, FRANKLIN Co.

FRAME, Joseph to Elizabeth J. Roseborough - issued February 23, 1852,
m. by: Wiley Denson, J. P., February 23, 1852, FRANKLIN Co.

FRAME, Rebekah to Samuel Henderson - GREENE Co.

FRAME, William L. to Martha Franklin - issued January 31, 1844, m. by: Wm. H. Jordan February 1, 1844, FRANKLIN Co.

FRAME, William S. to Elizabeth Smith - issued October 26, 1850, FRANKLIN Co.

FRANCES, Epaphroditus to Nancy Coopper - issued February 21, 1825, Bondsman: James S. Leech, m. by: John McMinn, J. P., February 24, 1825, WILSON Co.

FRANCIS, Andrew to Katherine Searcy - issued September 3, 1833, m. by: Wilson Hearn September 4, 1833, WILSON Co.

FRANCIS, George W. to Margret E. Suddarth - issued July 29, 1851, m. by: Rev. A. J. Steel, FRANKLIN Co.

FRANCIS, Hugh to Catharine Buchanan - issued April 12, 1838, m. by: W. A. Scott, M. G., April 12, 1838, FRANKLIN Co.

FRANCIS, J. P. to Ellen Elliott - issued August 3, 1868, FRANKLIN Co.

FRANCIS, John B. to Mary Gross - issued June 30, 1842, m. by: A. J. Steel, M. G., June 30, 1842, FRANKLIN Co.

FRANCIS, Kirby to Elizabeth Ganius - issued March 28, 1861, m. by: Francis Barnes, J. P., ROBERTSON Co.

FRANCIS, Moses B. to Sarah Dickson - March 1, 1811, WILLIAMSON Co.

FRANCIS, Nathaniel T. to Mary E. Malone - issued September 6, 1849, m. by: James B. Foster, J. P., September 6, 1849, FRANKLIN Co.

FRANCIS, Stephen M. to Rosanna Gross - issued April 8, 1841, FRANKLIN Co.

FRANCIS, W. R. to Margret McIlheran (McIlherson) - issued February 12, 1840, FRANKLIN Co.

FRANCIS, William to Rebecca Miller - October 19, 1801, Security: James Danforth, BLOUNT Co.

FRANCIS, William A. to Caroline Jones - issued September 15, 1846, m. by: James Bledsoe, J. P., September 15, 1846, FRANKLIN Co.

FRANKLAND, Esom (Eason) to Rebecca Major - July 17, 1797, Surety: Samuel Major, BLOUNT Co.

FRANKLAND, John to Polly Erwin - August 20, 1797, Surety: Wm. E. Erwin, BLOUNT Co.

FRANKLIN, Absalom to Margaret Gullet - May 15, 1787, Security: Reese Gullet, GREENE Co.

FRANKLIN, Albert C. to Henrietta E. Watkins - issued March 30, 1836, Bondsman: William McElurath, SUMNER Co.

FRANKLIN, Anderson to Mariah Hodges - issued June 7, 1830, Bondsman: Elias Strange, SUMNER Co.

FRANKLIN, Anderson to J. B. Sisk - issued December 8, 1873, m. by: G. W. Bowling, J. P., December 9, 1873, FRANKLIN Co.

FRANKLIN, Benjamin to Louisa Talley - issued December 29, 1851, FRANKLIN Co.

FRANKLIN, Benj. W. to Martha E. Young - issued July 2, 1852, m. by: J. W. Spearman July 4, 1852, FRANKLIN Co.

FRANKLIN, Charles to L. Buster - issued August 17, 1839, Bondsman: James Shell, m. by: Prior Neil, J. P., August 18, 1839, MEIGS Co.

FRANKLIN, Coleman to Elizabeth L. Eskridge - issued November 11, 1845, m. by: W. S. Smith, M. G., FRANKLIN Co.

FRANKLIN, David A. to Elizabeth A. Young - issued November 8, 1849, m. by: J. J. Travis, J. P., November 9, 1849, FRANKLIN Co.

FRANKLIN, George to Jenney Shaw - September 1, 1802, Security: Josiah Payne, BLOUNT Co.

FRANKLIN, Geo. W. to Margaret Jane McCormick - issued February 18, 1840, m. by: P. M. Morris, J. P., February 18, 1840, DAVIDSON Co.

FRANKLIN, Isaac to Adelicia Hayes - issued July 1, 1839, m. by: J. T. Edgar July 2, 1839, DAVIDSON Co.

FRANKLIN, Isom to Lury Forester - February 3, 1802, Security: John McDowel, BLOUNT Co.

FRANKLIN, J. to Amanda Harrison - issued February 22, 1850, m. by: T. B. Mathews February 24, 1850, ROBERTSON Co.

FRANKLIN, Jr., James to Prudy McKain - issued February 19, 1803, Bondsman: James McKain, SUMNER Co.

FRANKLIN, James to Mariah Cage - m. by: J. W. Hall October 14, 1838, SUMNER Co.

FRANKLIN, James E. to Nancy Carr - issued October 28, 1847, Bondsman: W. B. Carney, m. by: W. B. Carney, J. P., October 28, 1847, MONTGOMERY Co.

FRANKLIN, James W. to Susan Dorsey - issued April 19, 1848, m. by: J. J. Travis, J. P., April 21, 1848, FRANKLIN Co.

FRANKLIN, Jeremiah to Amanda Hamson - issued February 22, 1850, m. by: T. B. Mathews, J. P., February 24, 1850, ROBERTSON Co.

FRANKLIN, John to Anna Luster - issued April 19, 1837, m. by: M. L. Mynatt, J. P., April 23, 1837, KNOX Co.

FRANKLIN, John B. to Mary A. Syler - m. by: I. N. Martin, J. P., March 15, 1860, FRANKLIN Co.

FRANKLIN, John J. to Sophia Cage - issued December 16, 1829, Bondsman: Josiah R. Franklin, SUMNER Co.

FRANKLIN, John W. to Mary Yancey - m. by: Richard Johnson October 17, 1828, SUMNER Co.

FRANKLIN, Joshua to Malinda Hill - issued November 23, 1846, m. by: M. W. Watson, J. P., November 24, 1846, FRANKLIN Co.

FRANKLIN, Moses C. to Nancy C. Silvertooth - issued October 20, 1851, m. by: Wiley Denson, J. P., October 23, 1851, FRANKLIN Co.

FRANKLIN, Samuel to Olivia Rudder - issued July 21, 1836, Bondsman: Sims Crawford, m. by: J. D. Bennett, J. P., July 21, 1836, KNOX Co.

FRANKLIN, Smith C. to Elizabeth Cage - issued May 23, 1831, Bondsman: D. L. Cage, SUMNER Co.

FRANKLIN, Thos. to Eliza Mulvaney - issued December 11, 1824, m. by: James McMillan, J. P., December 15, 1824, KNOX Co.

FRANKLIN, William to Sallie McMillan - March 11, 1811, KNOX Co.

FRANKLIN, William to Evaline Douglass - issued October 6, 1821, Bondsman: Wm. Edwards, m. by: Edward Douglass October 6, 1821, SUMNER Co.

FRANKLIN, William C. to Martha Strambler - issued November 19, 1841,
m. by: C. B. Farris, L. E., November 19, 1841, FRANKLIN Co.

FRANKLING, Martin to Nelly Watson - issued March 21, 1812, Bondsman:
Bethleham Estes, WILSON Co.

FRANKS, Green to Sarah J. Hughes - issued October 10, 1865, Bondsman:
Thomas J. Wilbourn, LAWRENCE Co.

FRANKS, Joseph to Nancy Christy - issued April 25, 1846, m. by:
John Nugent, J. P., April 26, 1846, FRANKLIN Co.

FRANTHAM, Martin to Rachel Holliday - January 4, 1812, WILLIAMSON Co.

FRASER, Andrew to Milley Barnes - issued May 18, 1842, m. by:
B. Herndon, J. P., May 29, 1842, STEWART Co.

FRASER, Daniel J. to Sallie A. Polk - issued February 16, 1857, m. by:
J. B. Walton February 17, 1857, ROBERTSON Co.

FRASER, Donald to Julia Jane Anthony - issued July 29, 1818, Bondsman:
J. Moore and Jas. Robb, m. by: Wm. Hume, D. D., July 29, 1818,
SUMNER Co.

FRASER, Isaac to Mary I. Fraser - issued December 15, 1854, m. by:
William L. Baldry, G. M., December 21, 1854, ROBERTSON Co.

FRASER, John Wesley to Mary Brigham - issued April 6, 1842, m. by:
Rev. Jas. T. Morris April 7, 1842, STEWART Co.

FRASIER, Howell to Sally Wall - issued December 19, 1843,
m. December 21, 1843, ROBERTSON Co.

FRAZER, George E. to Elizabeth Ann Cage - issued January 27, 1834,
Bondsman: Robt. Hallum, WILSON Co.

FRAZER, James to Hannah Shelby - issued November 17, 1818, Bondsman:
Jno. L. Wynne, m. by: Thos. Calhoon, V. D. M., November 16, 1818,
WILSON Co.

FRAZER, Joel to Mary Gilbert - issued June 15, 1825, Bondsman:
Alexander Rutledge, m. by: Dnl. Moser June 16, 1825, WILSON Co.

FRAZER, Thomas to Mahala Dickens - issued October 17, 1831, Bondsman:
Sam'l Dickens, WILSON Co.

FRAZER, William to Jenny Hambleton - issued January 31, 1789, Bondsman:
James Frazer, SUMNER Co.

FRAZIER, Ann to John Bowers - GREENE Co.

FRAZIER, Bariah to Ann Rees - October 4, 1797, Security:
Newhope Quaker Meeting, GREENE Co.

FRAZIER (?), Travis, Celia to Gideon Johnson - July 16, 1811, Bondsman:
Francis McBrae, MAURY Co.

FRAZIER, Eli to Rhoda A. Minnix - issued October 26, 1840, FRANKLIN Co.

FRAZIER, James H. to Margaret Hester Ann Teasley - issued December 21,
1846, Bondsman: G. Orgain, MONTGOMERY Co.

FRAZIER, John H. to Mary Carden - issued February 13, 1858, m. by:
J. W. Hazelwood, M. G., February 14, 1858, COFFEE Co.

FRAZIER, Leonard to Susan Maxey - issued January 31, 1846, m. by:
W. W. Williams, J. P., February 3, 1846, ROBERTSON Co.

FRAZIER, Samuel to Mary Parke - January 22, 1798, Adonijah Morgan,
GREENE Co.

FRAZIER, Samuel to Tinsey Craighead - issued February 7, 1832, Bondsman:
Wm. G. Frazier, m. by: Sam'l. Love, M. G., February 8, 1832,
KNOX Co.

FRAZIER, Samuel to Elizabeth Denson - issued January 21, 1846, m. by:
W. Denson, J. P., January 22, 1846, FRANKLIN Co.

FRAZIER, Samuel W. to Lydia Julian - issued March 6, 1835, Bondsman:
Rob't. B. Reynolds, m. by: Sam'l. Love, M. G., March, 1835, KNOX Co.

FRAZIER, Thomas to Polly Gillim - issued August 13, 1805, Bondsman:
Julian Frazier, Witness: W. Park, KNOX Co.

FRAZIER, William to Sarah Pickle - issued September 14, 1815, KNOX Co.

FRAZIER, Wm. C. to Melinda Golliher - issued July 4, 1832, m. by:
Abner W. Lansden, V. D. M., July 12, 1832, KNOX Co.

FRAZIERS, James to Mary J. Oliver - issued July 17, 1851, Bondsman:
A. Whiliss, m. by: James T. Garnett, J. P., July 5, 1851,
MONTGOMERY Co.

FRAZOR, Alexander to Elizabeth Harper - issued April 8, 1808, Bondsman:
William Harper, SUMNER Co.

FRAZOR, George to Polly Bates - issued November 27, 1820, m. by:
Wm. Montgomery, J. P., November 27, 1820, SUMNER Co.

FRAZOR, George to Polly Kisor - issued November 27, 1821, Bondsman:
James Jackson, SUMNER Co.

FRAZOR, James to Ann Shaws - m. by: B. S. Rutherford November 21, 1837,
SUMNER Co.

FRAZOR, Thomas to Ibby Kirkpatrick - issued September 4, 1820, Bondsman:
James Frazor, m. by: Hugh Kirkpatrick, M. G., September 4, 1820,
SUMNER Co.

FREAS, Joel to Missouri Hughes - issued February 2, 1838, m. by:
J. T. Edgar February 3, 1838, DAVIDSON Co.

FRECH, Jacob to Rebecca Langston - issued January 3, 1852, Bondsman:
W. C. Barksdale, m. by: J. T. Hendrick January 4, 1852, MONTGOMERY Co.

FRECH, Peter to Emily F. Langston - issued December 14, 1847, Bondsman:
Joseph Coleman, m. by: R. T. Gupton, J. P., December 16, 1847,
MONTGOMERY Co.

FREDERICK, Hezekiah to Ezelly Hobson - issued May 17, 1809, Bondsman:
John Spence, RUTHERFORD Co.

FREDERICK, John to S. A. Frederick - issued June 14, 1846, m. by:
Robert Draughon, J. P., ROBERTSON Co.

FREE, William to Sarah Morgan - issued August 26, 1847, STEWART Co.

FREELAND, Isaac to Nancy Ann Gra___ (?) - issued October 31, 1836,
Bondsman: Elijah Stalcup, SUMNER Co.

FREELAND, John to Catherine McKee - issued February 18, 1806, Bondsman:
William McKee, SUMNER Co.

FREELAND, W. L. to Martha May - issued December 21, 1844, STEWART Co.

FREELLS, Thomas to Polly Mattocks - issued May 23, 1798, Bondsman:
George Hallmark, Witness: Joseph Greer, KNOX Co.

FREEMAN, Alph to Eliza A. Vaughn - issued July 14, 1855, m. by:
L. W. Marbury, J. P., July 16, 1855, COFFEE Co.

FREEMAN, Anderson to Delila Yearnel - issued December 22, 1813,
Bondsman: Cater Freeman, m. by: Ranson Gwyn, J. P., December 23,
1813, WILSON Co.

FREEMAN, Asberry to Elizabeth Vandike - issued January 23, 1822, m. by:
Lent Brown, M. G. G. C., January 24, 1822, RUTHERFORD Co.

FREEMAN, B. B. to Lucy Dunn - issued February 21, 1861, m. by:
H. W. Carroll, J. P., February 22, 1861, COFFEE Co.

FREEMAN, Buena Vesta to W. J. Brown - issued November 13, 1863,
Bondsman: W. J. Miller, BEDFORD Co.

FREEMAN, Cader to Patsey Parker - issued January 24, 1821, m. by:
H. Robinson, J. P., January 25, 1821, RUTHERFORD Co.

FREEMAN, Cama to Charity Baber - issued February 5, 1818, Bondsman:
David Redditt, SUMNER Co.

FREEMAN, Daniel to Polly Ann Cunningham - issued November 13, 1827,
Bondsman: Jefferson Hamilton, m. by: John Bonner, J. P., WILSON Co.

FREEMAN, Daniel M. to Margaret Hayley - issued July 28, 1836, Bondsman:
John W. Yardley, m. by: James Kelton, J. P., July 28, 1836,
RUTHERFORD Co.

FREEMAN, Daniel M. to Elizabeth Abernathy - April 15, 1862, m. by:
R. G. Kimbrough, M. G., GILES Co.

FREEMAN, Darrell to Elizabeth E. Estes - issued January 27, 1830,
Bondsman: Joseph Freeman, WILSON Co.

FREEMAN, Edward to Charlott Everrett - issued August 26, 1826, Bondsman:
Brinkley Bridges, WILSON Co.

FREEMAN, George W. to Amanda C. Parker - issued March 6, 1861, Bondsman:
A. M. Gillespie, m. by: A. M. Gillespie, M. G., March 7, 1861,
LAWRENCE Co.

FREEMAN, Green to Priscilla Bowman - issued January 1, 1817, m. by:
H, Robinson, J. P., January 2, 1817, RUTHERFORD Co.

FREEMAN, H. F. to Harriett Williams - issued May 13, 1861, Bondsman:
Balie Freeman, Jos. H. Thompson, Clk. per N. F. Thompson,
Dep. Clk., m. by: John S. Brown, J. P., BEDFORD Co.

FREEMAN, Isham to Rebeccah McElyea - issued February 14, 1814, Bondsman:
John McElyea, WILSON Co.

FREEMAN, J. B. to Margaret O'Brien - issued April 1, 1840, m. by:
W. B. Carpenter April 2, 1840, DAVIDSON Co.

FREEMAN, James Y. to Nancy C. Miller - issued April 19, 1858, m. by:
Geo. W. Martin, M. G., ROBERTSON Co.

FREEMAN, Joel E. to Louisa M. Wilson - July 2, 1846, m. by:
A. M. Pickens, M. G., GILES Co.

FREEMAN, John to Elizabeth Gable - issued August 23, 1819, Bondsman:
John Stroud, RUTHERFORD Co.

FREEMAN, Joseph to Maria Dew - issued November 30, 1833, m. by:
Geo. Donnell, M. G., December 1, 1833, WILSON Co.

FREEMAN, Joseph I. to Elizabeth Vilott - issued May 21, 1851, m. by:
Jas. Woodard, ROBERTSON Co.

FREEMAN, Joshua to Peggy Counsel - issued May 27, 1812, KNOX Co.

FREEMAN, Littleberry to Elizabeth Young - issued January 26, 1820,
Bondsman: Isaiah Paschal, WILSON Co.

FREEMAN, Littleberry to Elizabeth Young - issued January 26, 1830,
m. by: J. T. Williams, J. P., January 27, 1830, WILSON Co.

FREEMAN, Martha I. to Rezin S. Brown - BEDFORD Co.

FREEMAN, Mathew to C. S. Appleton - issued September 1, 1848, m. by:
Jas. Woodard, ROBERTSON Co.

FREEMAN, Matthew to Anne King - issued July 18, 1831, m. by:
Henry Ridley, J. P., July 22, 1831, RUTHERFORD Co.

FREEMAN, Obediah to Elizabeth Hancock - issued February 12, 1824,
Bondsman: Joseph Freeman, m. by: John Rice February 18, 1824,
WILSON Co.

FREEMAN, Reubin B. to Nancy D. E. Swinebroad - March 30, 1858, m. by:
James C. Elliott, M. G., GILES Co.

FREEMAN, Saunders to Patsey Brown - September 26, 1812, WILLIAMSON Co.

FREEMAN, Squire to Clarissa Chism - issued July 20, 1824, Bondsman:
William Freeman, m. by: John Knight, J. P., August 5, 1824,
RUTHERFORD Co.

FREEMAN, Richard to Sally Haynes - issued June 6, 1793, Bondsman:
Sion Perry, SUMNER Co.

FREEMAN, Richard to Nelly Yates - issued March 10, 1794, Bondsman:
Rich. King, SUMNER Co.

FREEMAN, Silas to Sally Cooke - issued February 17, 1819, Bondsman:
William Babb, m. by: John Jarratt, WILSON Co.

FREEMAN, Smith to Martha R. Butler - issued December 25, 1843, m. by:
R. B. C. Howell December 26, 1843, DAVIDSON Co.

FREEMAN, W. G. to Allice Orear - issued November 19, 1870, m. by:
M. H. Bone, M. G., November 20, 1871, FRANKLIN Co.

FREEMAN, W. J. to Elizabeth J. Davidson - issued November 7, 1862,
Bondsman: John W. Moore, Jos. H. Thompson, Clk. per N. F. Thompson,
Dep. Clk., BEDFORD Co.

FREES, Jacob W. to Margaret McBell - issued January 24, 1842, m. by:
S. G. Burney, M. G., January 24, 1842, DAVIDSON Co.

FREESE, Ann to Nathaniel Stanfield - GREENE Co.

FRELAND, Samuel S. to Emily I. Barham - issued May 25, 1855, m. by:
W. R. Saddler, J. P., May 27, 1855, ROBERTSON Co.

FRENCH, Benjamin to Patsey Boiles - m. by: John Barr, J. P., September 9,
1819, SUMNER Co.

FRENCH, Berry A. to Mary Annah Wilson - issued March 14, 1848, m. by:
Jordan Moore, M. G., March 15, 1848, STEWART Co.

FRENCH, George to Betsy Howser - issued July 31, 1818, m. by:
Jeremiah King, M. G., August 4, 1818, KNOX Co.

FRENCH, John W. to Nancy McKinny - issued September 7, 1844, m. by:
William A. Martin, J. P., September 7, 1844, STEWART Co.

FRENCH, Jr., Peter to Malinda Ellison - issued December 19, 1827, KNOX Co.

FRENCH, Wm. to Mary Barnes - issued September 12, 1848, m. by:
James Chambers, J. P., September 12, 1848, STEWART Co.

FRENCH, Wm. B. to Issabella L. White - issued February 2, 1843, m. by:
   T. J. Edgar February 2, 1843, DAVIDSON Co.

FRENSLEY, George W. to Elizabeth Newburn - issued August 25, 1847,
   m. by: John Corbitt, J. P., August 26, 1847, DAVIDSON Co.

FRENSLEY, James M. R. to Jane Nance - issued February 16, 1835, Bondsman:
   Charles A. Frensley, RUTHERFORD Co.

FRENSLEY, Matthew P. to Mary Baldridge - issued January 30, 1836,
   Bondsman: Allen Nance, m. by: W. P. Booker, J. P., February 10,
   1836, RUTHERFORD Co.

FREY, Adam H. to Dorothy Quin - issued June 12, 1832, m. by:
   M. Powell, J. P., ROBERTSON Co.

FREY, And. J. to Julia A. Bernard - issued February 13, 1852, m. by:
   P. H. Fraser, B. E., February 15, 1852, ROBERTSON Co.

FREY, Geo. W. to Sarah B. Beadwell - issued November 15, 1849, m. by:
   B. Rawls November 16, 1849, ROBERTSON Co.

FREY, J. N. to Mary Morris - issued September 26, 1859, m. by:
   G. B. Mason, J. P., September 27, 1859, ROBERTSON Co.

FREY, James P. to Amelia Simmons - issued June 10, 1861, m. by:
   J. M. Copeland, J. P., ROBERTSON Co.

FREY, John M. to Mary H. Bradley - issued July 2, 1855, m. by:
   Robert Williams, J. P., July 4, 1855, ROBERTSON Co.

FREY, John N. to Lucinda Dean - issued January 31, 1843, m. by:
   D. G. Baird, J. P., ROBERTSON Co.

FREY, M. V. to Lucy S. Rust - issued October 21, 1859, m. by:
   G. B. Mason, J. P., October 23, 1859, ROBERTSON Co.

FREY, Martin to Urcilla Dowlen - issued November 21, 1855, m. by:
   Robt. Williams, J. P., November 22, 1855, ROBERTSON Co.

FREY, Simeon to Mary J. J. Deen - issued July 5, 1849, m. by:
   Robert Draughon, J. P., ROBERTSON Co.

FREY, Thomas to Jane Farthing - issued December 14, 1841, m. by:
   Wm. T. Baldry, G. M., December 20, 1841, ROBERTSON Co.

FREY, W. L. to Lucy J. Fountain - issued January 9, 1851, ROBERTSON Co.

FRIAR, John to Jobetha Avery - November 11, 1799, BLOUNT Co.

FRIDDLE, Emaline to J. L. Russell - BEDFORD Co.

FRIDDLE, Jessee to Nancy Snoddy - issued January 19, 1861, Bondsman:
   I. Y. Norman, Jos. H. Thompson, Clk., m. by: T. P. Wells, M. G.,
   BEDFORD Co.

FRIEND, Efford to Louisa F. Decherd - issued September 11, 1854, m. by:
   Sam'l M. Cowan, V. D. M., September 12, 1854, FRANKLIN Co.

FRIERSON, Elizabeth M. to Elias James Armstrong - MAURY Co.

FRIERSON, George to Mada Adams Moore - December 21, 1808, WILLIAMSON Co.

FRIERSON, Margaret G. to Binoni (Benoni) Dickey - MAURY Co.

FRIERSON, Thomas J. to Ann Blakely - November 6, 1810, Bondsman:
   Moses G. Frierson, MAURY Co.

FRIES, Michael to Jean Hannah - December 20, 1800, Security:
   John Doan and John McPharman, GREENE Co.

FRISTO, Markham to Catharine Grove - issued January 16, 1813, Bondsman:
   Isaac Campbell, Witness: A. Hutcheson, KNOX Co.

FRISTOE, Robert to Susan Grove - issued November 8, 1811, KNOX Co.

FRITS, Isaac to Franky Fortner - April 11, 1836, KNOX Co.

FRIZZELL, David to Sarah McKee - issued January 22, 1863, Bondsman:
   K. Daughtry, Jos. H. Thompson, Clk., BEDFORD Co.

FRIZZELL, Hugh to Frances Harris - issued December 12, 1835, Bondsman:
   John Fletcher, RUTHERFORD Co.

FRIZZELL, James H. to Sarah J. Farmer - issued May 30, 1860, m. by:
   Jas. H. Mallory, J. P., May 31, 1860, ROBERTSON Co.

FRIZZELL, Mary E. to David C. Taylor - issued December 25, 1862,
   Bondsman: J. P. Hooser, Jos. H. Thompson, Clk., BEDFORD Co.

FRIZZELL, Nancy to S. M. Elliott - BEDFORD Co.

FRIZZELL, Sarah E. to F. M. Elliott - BEDFORD Co.

FRIZZELL, William J. to Mary Deer - issued February 27, 1836, Bondsman:
   Reuben Curry, RUTHERFORD Co.

FRIZZELLE, Brice to Jane Alexander - issued September 10, 1833, Bondsman:
   Allen Frizzell, RUTHERFORD Co.

FRIZZELLE, Isaac to Susan Arnold - issued January 5, 1816, m. by:
   J. Burns January 11, 1836, RUTHERFORD Co.

FRIZZLE, Robert to Nancy McCloud - issued March 27, 1842, m. by:
   Thos. W. Felts, Minister, ROBERTSON Co.

FROQUEHAR, Wm. to Jenett Meclesal - issued January 2, 1849, m. by:
   J. T. Hendrickson, M. G., January 2, 1849, MONTGOMERY Co.

FROST, Eli to Katherine Varvel - issued April 19, 1828, m. April 19,
   1828, SUMNER Co.

FROST, Joel to Susannah Tindell - issued December 9, 1822, m. by:
   John Bayless, J. P., December 10, 1822, KNOX Co.

FROST, John to Sarah Burt - issued January 17, 1851, m. by:
   John Roleman, J. P., January 19, 1851, FRANKLIN Co.

FROST, Jonas to Nancy Hall - issued November 13, 1809, KNOX Co.

FROST, Sam to Nancy Childress - December 29, 1818, KNOX Co.

FROST, Thomas to Martha Naville - issued October 18, 1799, Bondsman:
   Israel Standifer, Witness: Andw. White, KNOX Co.

FROST, Thomas to Sally D. Lucas - issued April 23, 1826, Bondsman:
   Jno. D. Sanders, m. by: Mordecai Yarnell, J. P., April 23, 1826,
   Witness: Wm. Swan, KNOX Co.

FROST, Thomas to Matilda Wygal - issued September 25, 1831, Bondsman:
   James Alderson, SUMNER Co.

FRUDLE, James to Susan Boyles - issued November 27, 1827, Bondsman:
   John Bell, SUMNER Co.

FRUSHOUR, Catherine to Joseph Winter - GREENE Co.

FRY, Basil to Jane Mansker - issued March 8, 1791, Bondsman:
   John Dawson, SUMNER Co.

FRY, James to Polly Walker - September 13, 1815, WILLIAMSON Co.

FRY, John to Elizabeth Atkins - issued June 30, 1866, m. by:
John Nugent, J. P., July 4, 1866, FRANKLIN Co.

FRY, Martin to Thussey C. Crockett - issued December 10, 1842,
DAVIDSON Co.

FRY, Martin P. to Nancy Neely - issued August 2, 1847, m. by:
Wm. Randle August 5, 1847, DAVIDSON Co.

FRY, Newel C. to Lucinda Harrison - issued November 10, 1835, Bondsman:
Jno. R. Orr, m. by: James Crippen, J. P., November 10, 1835,
KNOX Co.

FRY, Nicholas to Cibby Moore - issued March 8, 1821, Bondsman:
Michael Beattie, Witness: Wm. Swan, KNOX Co.

FRY, Rhodes to Betsy Doyle - issued April 17, 1822, Bondsman:
Frederich Ault, m. by: Rob't. Lindsay, J. P., April 17, 1822,
KNOX Co.

FRY, V. W. to Martha Ann Morris - issued February 11, 1854, m. by:
J. B. Walton, ROBERTSON Co.

FRYER, Alfred to Nancy McAfee - issued February 9, 1839, m. by:
D. Ralston, J. P., February 12, 1839, DAVIDSON Co.

FRYER, Samuel to Juby Ann Jones - issued October 16, 1838, m. by:
D. Ralston, J. P., October 18, 1838, DAVIDSON Co.

FRYER, Saml. D. to Mary Binkley - issued May 7, 1856, m. by:
J. S. Hollis, J. P., May 8, 1856, ROBERTSON Co.

FRYOR, Isaac to Nancy Goodner - issued July 3, 1818, Bondsman:
Garrett Fryor, m. by: B. L. McFerrin, J. P., July 5, 1818,
RUTHERFORD Co.

FRYOR, James to Betsy Hill - issued December 17, 1816, m. by:
T. H. Nelson December 17, 1816, KNOX Co.

FRYOR, John to Lenora McAfee - issued September 22, 1846, m. by:
Jonas Shivers, J. P., September 25, 1846, DAVIDSON Co.

FUDGE, Jacob to Elizabeth Bloodworth - issued July 25, 1842, m. by:
S. B. Davidson, J. P., July 31, 1842, DAVIDSON Co.

FUDGE, John to Polly Parr - issued August 29, 1838, m. by:
Wm. Shelton, J. P., August 2, 1838, DAVIDSON Co.

FUDGE, John B. to Pamelia Barnes - issued April 5, 1824, Bondsman:
Washington Barrington, m. by: Solomon Beesley, J. P., April 15,
1824, RUTHERFORD Co.

FUDGE, Simpson to Sethe Abbott - issued August 11, 1841, m. by:
John McRobertson August 12, 1841, DAVIDSON Co.

FUGERSON, James L. to Elizabeth Mabry - issued December 7, 1831,
Bondsman: Wm. Mabry, SUMNER Co.

FUGETT, William to Eby Develing - November 29, 1815, WILLIAMSON Co.

FUKERSON, Thos. E. to Siscia B. Hunley - issued September 29, 1852,
Bondsman: Philip M. Fulkerson, m. by: R. P. Bowling, J. P.,
September 29, 1852, MONTGOMERY Co.

FULCHER, Edward to Nancy Burchett - issued January 1, 1845, DAVIDSON Co.

FULCHER, Valentine to Mary McCarty - issued February 8, 1838, m. by:
W. A. Scott, M. G., February 8, 1838, FRANKLIN Co.

FULCHER, William to Susan Lassater - issued September 9, 1841, m. by:
Wm. D. Baldwin, M. G., September 14, 1841, DAVIDSON Co.

FULCHER, Wm. W. to Unity W. Fulcher - issued October 30, 1848, Bondsman:
Tavner W. Wisdom, m. by: Robert Williams, M. G., November 2, 1848,
MONTGOMERY Co.

FULDEN, Samuel to Mary Gooden - issued September 30, 1839, STEWART Co.

FULFER, Joseph to Amanda Durin - issued October 14, 1840, DICKSON Co.

FULGHUM, B. F. to Caroline Ferebee - issued August 25, 1840, m. by:
Joseph Kellam, J. P., August 26, 1840, DAVIDSON Co.

FULGHUM, Theophelus to Polly Williamson - January 2, 1810, WILLIAMSON Co.

FULGHUM, Thomas W. to Martha Woodward - issued December 5, 1840, m. by:
Bill Barns, J. P., December 9, 1840, DAVIDSON Co.

FULGHUM, W. W. to Martha A. M. McQuary - issued September 22, 1840,
DAVIDSON Co.

FULGUM, William to Matilda King - m. by: John Graves November 14, 1838,
SUMNER Co.

FULK, Andrew to Jane Caplinger - issued July 30, 1831, Bondsman:
Henry Bundy, WILSON Co.

FULKES, Gabriel to Jincy Hyde - May 23, 1806, WILLIAMSON Co.

FULKS, Burwell to Patsey Locke - issued February 1, 1806, Bondsman:
Thos. White, SUMNER Co.

FULKS, John D. to Mary Rawlings - issued September 8, 1824, Bondsman:
Joel Fulks, m. by: John Clark, J. P., September 9, 1824, RUTHERFORD Co.

FULLBRIGHT, Alfred to Mary Clemons - issued December 1, 1842, m. by:
John Ogden, M. G., December 1, 1842, DAVIDSON Co.

FULLER, Allen to Nancy Harris - issued October 28, 1817, Bondsman:
Duke H. Harris, m. by: John W. Payton, J. P., November 13, 1817,
WILSON Co.

FULLER, Benjamin to Hannah Gum - issued December 9, 1815, Bondsman:
Travis Marable, RUTHERFORD Co.

FULLER, Caid to Sarah Garrett - October 23, 1849, Security:
John (x) Fuller, GILES Co.

FULLER, Isham to Sarah Caplinger - issued June 8, 1836, m. by:
Solomon Caplinger, J. P., WILSON Co.

FULLER, James to Elizabeth Dement - issued October 30, 1833, Bondsman:
Isaac Parker, RUTHERFORD Co.

FULLER, Jesse to Martha Caplinger - issued September 9, 1835, Bondsman:
Samuel Hooker, m. by: Solomon Caplinger, J. P., WILSON Co.

FULLER, John to Fanny J. Martin - issued May 21, 1862, Bondsman:
John Koonce, Security: Jos. H. Thompson, Clk. per James H. Neil,
Dep. Clk., BEDFORD Co.

FULLER, John M. to Lucretia Redden - issued January 31, 1861, m. by:
W. J. Jackson, Mins., February 3, 1861, COFFEE Co.

FULLER, Miles to Charity Seals - issued July 26, 1818, Bondsman:
James Moore, m. by: Robert Branch, J. P., July 29, 1818, WILSON Co.

FULLER, Miles to Nancy Clifton - issued September 12, 1821, Bondsman:
Anderson Loyd, m. by: John W. Payton, J. P., September 13, 1821,
WILSON Co.

FULLER, Mitchell to Mary Cross - issued May 2, 1864, Bondsman:
H. C. Ferguson, BEDFORD Co.

FULLER, W. N. M. to Mary Keeling - issued December 17, 1857, m. by:
James M. Buckaloo, J. P., December 17, 1857, COFFEE Co.

FULLER, Willie to Sarah Brown - issued October 8, 1862, Bondsman:
Ferdinan Joyce, m. by: P. L. Simms, J. P., October 9, 1862,
LAWRENCE Co.

FULLERTON, Robert to Priscilla Clifton - issued August 20, 1828,
Bondsman: David Berry, WILSON Co.

FULLINGTON, Geo. to Eliz. Butler - issued August 7, 1838, Bondsman:
Jno. Nelson, MEIGS Co.

FULLINGTON, George to Elizabeth Butler - issued August 7, 1838, m. by:
J. Baker, J. P., August 8, 1838, MEIGS Co.

FULLMORE, A. J. to Sarah L. Damron - issued March 14, 1853, m. by:
A. B. Cummings, M. G., March 24, 1853, FRANKLIN Co.

FULLMORE, H. C. to Nancy C. Smith - issued January 30, 1865, m. by:
B. Pennington, M. G., February 1, 1865, FRANKLIN Co.

FULTON, Hugh to Elizabeth Nichols - issued February 27, 1833, m. by:
Eli King, J. P., February 28, 1833, KNOX Co.

FULTON, Thos. (?) to Polly Wills - January 25, 1821 (?), KNOX Co.

FULTON, Wm. to Peggy Samples - issued August 2, 1819, m. by:
Alex, McMillan, J. P., August 2, 1819, KNOX Co.

FUQUA, Charles D. to Elizabeth Shaw - issued March 26, 1845, m. by:
B. Herndon, J. P., March 30, 1845, STEWART Co.

FUQUA, Jesse H. to Mantha A. Whitworth - issued September 22, 1845,
DAVIDSON Co.

FUQUA, John to Elizabeth A. Cowan - issued November 5, 1857, FRANKLIN Co.

FUQUA, John W. to Nancy E. Parker - issued January 31, 1857, m. by:
J. T. Craig, J. P., February 1, 1857, ROBERTSON Co.

FUQUA, Joseph to Susan Binkley - issued October 14, 1852, m. by:
B. Rawls, M. G., ROBERTSON Co.

FUQUA, Theadore to Margaret Lowe - issued October 11, 1848, m. by:
Thos. H, Stewart, J. P., October 22, 1848, STEWART Co.

FUQUA, Thomas to Nancy H. McLaughlin - issued November 1, 1841, m. by:
John Beard, M. G., November 4, 1841, DAVIDSON Co.

FUQUA, Thomas J. to Susan E. Randal - issued January 15, 1845, m. by:
Samuel D. Bawldwin January 15, 1845, MONTGOMERY Co.

FUQUA, Saml. to Malinda Clinard - issued November 17, 1841, m. by:
Benj. Rawls, G. M., November 18, 1841, ROBERTSON Co.

FUQUA, Washington L. to Nancy Mary Hobbs - issued September 15, 1848,
Bondsman: H. W. Lee, MONTGOMERY Co.

FUQUA, William to Mary A. Clinard - issued September 29, 1860, m. by:
W. C. Rawls, J. P., September 30, 1860, ROBERTSON Co.

FUQUAY, John C. to Rebecca Cook - issued March 9, 1842, DAVIDSON Co.

FUQUAY, William B. to Judith Ford - issued August 24, 1831, m. by:
Jordan Willeford, J. P., August 28, 1831, RUTHERFORD Co.

FURBANKS, M. to Miss Peggy - issued July 16, 1839, Bondsman:
Wm. Deatherage, m. by: B. F. McKenzie, J. P., July 18, 1839, MEIGS Co.

FURGARSON, Robert to Nancy Organ - issued January 9, 1824, Bondsman:
John Coe, m. by: Wilson Hearn, M. G., January 14, 1824, WILSON Co.

FURGASON, James to Mary Cheesman - July 8, 1794, KNOX Co.

FURGASON, Joel J. to Ruth Stovall - issued March 1, 1824, Bondsman:
Obadiah Furgason, RUTHERFORD Co.

FURGASON, Lemuel to Mary J. Magbee - issued March 25, 1867, m. by:
W. M. Prince, J. P., March 31, 1867, FRANKLIN Co.

FURGERSON, Frankie to James J. Wells (Neeley?) - January 14, 1811,
Bondsman: Henry Davis, MAURY Co.

FURGERSON, Jacob to Mary Furgerson - issued December 28, 1824, Bondsman:
Lemuel Furgerson, m. by: Wm. H. White, M. G., December 29, 1824,
WILSON Co.

FURGERSON, John to Sarah E. Malone - issued August 17, 1865, m. by:
Simpson West, J. P., August 17, 1865, FRANKLIN Co.

FURGERSON, Thomas to Rebecah Furgerson - issued January 16, 1827,
Bondsman: L. Ferguson, m. by: Wm. H. White, M. G., WILSON Co.

FURGERSON, W. T. to Mary Meacham - issued May 31, 1851, Bondsman:
R. T. McDaniel, MONTGOMERY Co.

FURGISON, Jasper R. to George Ann Ellis - issued April 7, 1845, DICKSON Co.

FURGUSON, John to Barbary Harpole - issued October 24, 1821, Bondsman:
Sion Duke, m. by: Edward Willis, WILSON Co.

FURGUSON, John D. to Nancy M. Merriweather - issued March 1, 1848,
Bondsman: C. H. Smith, m. by: R. F. Furguson, M. G., March 2,
1848, MONTGOMERY Co.

FURGUSON, Moses to Malinda Goff - issued July 19, 1832, Bondsman:
Daniel Gossadge, m. by: H. K. Winbourn, M. G., July 19, 1832,
SUMNER Co.

FURMAN, William B. to Polly H. Beckly - issued March 6, 1843, m. by:
Lemuel Brandon March 12, 1843, FRANKLIN Co.

FUSSELL, A. H. to Manerva Dunnegan - issued September 20, 1846, DICKSON Co.

FUSSELL, John W. to Mary Hammond - issued January 14, 1847, DICKSON Co.

FUSTEN, Joel to Ranny Hollingsworth - issued August 6, 1827, Bondsman:
Isaac Hollingsworth, WILSON Co.

FUSTON, James to Elizabeth Adams - issued February 3, 1820, Bondsman:
John Adams, m. by: Abner W. Bone, J. P., February 6, 1820, WILSON Co.

FUSTON, Jonathan to Rebecca Stanly - issued July 15, 1818, Bondsman:
Joseph Fuston, m. by: J. McMinn, M. G., July 20, 1818, WILSON Co.

FUSTON, Levy to Patsey Adams - issued June 24, 1823, Bondsman:
Sam'l Little, WILSON Co.

FUTERELL, Etheldred to __(?) Martin - issued September 19, 1837,
Bondsman: Wm. Lindsay, KNOX Co.

FUTRELL, Delmas to Mary Ann Rincut - issued March 26, 1838, m. by:
W. J. Jones, J. P., March 30, 1838, STEWART Co.

FUTRIL, Etheldred to Sarah Nichodemus - issued September 19, 1837, m. by:
Wm. Lindsay, J. P., September 19, 1837, KNOX Co.

FUTRILL, Elisha to Mary Brandon - issued April 10, 1845, m. by:
B. Herndon, J. P., April 17, 1845, STEWART Co.

FUTRILL, O'Bryan to Herse Ann Caroline Brigham - issued November 8,
1847, m. by: B. Herndon, J. P., November 11, 1847, STEWART Co.

FYKE, Jas. to A. Chilton - issued October 20, 1845, m. by:
Jas. L. Adams, J. P., ROBERTSON Co.

FYKE, Jeremiah to Beady Lellan - issued January 25, 1841, m. by:
Robt. Green, J. P., January 28, 1840, ROBERTSON Co.

FYKE, John P. to Elizabeth Solomon - issued January 21, 1846, m. by:
Robt. Draughon, J. P., ROBERTSON Co.

FYKE, Joshua to Louisa Lipscomb - issued January 25, 1847, m. by:
Robert Green, J. P., January 26, 1847, ROBERTSON Co.

FYKE, Mathew V. to Sally A. Mathews - issued February 28, 1842, m. by:
Robt. Green, J. P., ROBERTSON Co.